REPAIR MANUAL

HONDA ACCORD/ PRELUDE 1984-91

All U.S. and Canadian models of Accord and Prelude

Senior Vice President	Ronald A. Hoxter
Publisher and Editor-In-Chief	Kerry A. Freeman, S.A.E.
Executive Editors	Dean F. Morgantini, S.A.E., W. Calvin Settle, Jr., S.A.E.
Managing Editor	Nick D'Andrea
Special Products Manager	Ken Grabowski, A.S.E., S.A.E.
Senior Editors	Jacques Gordon, Michael L. Grady, Debra McCall, Kevin M. G. Maher, Richard J. Rivele, S.A.E., Richard T. Smith, Jim Taylor, Ron Webb
Project Managers	Martin J. Gunther, Will Kessler, A.S.E., Richard Schwartz
Production Manager	Andrea Steiger
Product Systems Manager	Robert Maxey
Director of Manufacturing	Mike D'Imperio

CHILTONBOOK COMPANY

CONTENTS

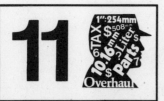

SAFETY NOTICE

Proper service and repair procedures are vital to the safe, reliable operation of all motor vehicles, as well as the safety of those performing repairs. This book outlines procedures for servicing and repairing vehicles using safe effective methods. The procedures contain many NOTES, CAUTIONS and WARNINGS which should be followed along with standard safety procedures to eliminate the possibility of personal injury or improper service which could damage the vehicle or compromise its safety.

It is important to note that repair procedures and techniques, tools and parts for servicing motor vehicles, as well as the skill and experience of the individual performing the work vary widely. It is not possible to anticipate all of the conceivable ways or conditions under which vehicles may be serviced, or to provide cautions as to all of the possible hazards that may result. Standard and accepted safety precautions and equipment should be used during cutting, grinding, chiseling, prying, or any other process that can cause material removal or projectiles.

Some procedures require the use of tools specially designed for a specific purpose. Before substituting another tool or procedure, you must be completely satisfied that neither your personal safety, nor the performance of the vehicle will be endangered.

Although the information in this guide is based on industry sources and is as complete as possible at the time of publication, the possibility exists that the manufacturer made later changes which could not be included here. While striving for total accuracy, Chilton Book Company cannot assume responsibilty for any errors, changes, or omissions that may occur in the compilation of this data.

PART NUMBERS

Part numbers listed in the reference are not recommendations by Chilton for any product by brand name. They are references that can be used with interchange manuals and aftermarket supplier catalogs to locate each brand supplier's discrete part number.

SPECIAL TOOLS

Special tools are recommended by the vehicle manufacturer to perform their specific job. Use has been kept to a minimum, but where absolutely necessary, they are referred to in the text by the part number of the tool manufacturer. These tools can be purchased, under the appropriate part number, from your Honda dealer or regional distributor. Before substituting any tool for the one recommended, read the SAFETY NOTICE at the top of this page.

ACKNOWLEDGEMENTS

Chilton Book Company expresses appreciation to Honda Motor Co. for their generous assistance

Copyright© 1992 by Chilton Book Company
All Rights Reserved
Published in Radnor, Pennsylvania 19089 by Chilton Book Company

Manufactured in the United States of America
    67890   0987

Chilton's Repair Manual: Honda Accord/Prelude 1984-91
ISBN 0–8019–8301–0 pbk.
Library of Congress Catalog Card No. 90–058848

General Information and Maintenance

1

HOW TO USE THIS BOOK

Chilton's Repair Manual for 1984–91 Accord and Prelude is intended to teach you about the inner workings of your car and save you money on its upkeep.

The first two chapters will be the most used, since they contain maintenance and tune-up information and procedures. Studies have shown that a properly tuned and maintained vehicle can get at least 10% better gas mileage (which translates into lower operating costs) and periodic maintenance will catch minor problems before they turn into major repair bills. The other chapters deal with the more complex systems of your Honda.

Operating systems from engine through brakes are covered to the extent that the average do-it-yourselfer becomes mechanically involved. This book will not explain such things as rebuilding the differential for the simple reason that the expertise required and the investment in special tools make this task impractical and uneconomical. It will give you the detailed instructions to help you change your own brake pads and shoes, tune the engine, replace spark plugs and filters, and do many more jobs that will save you money, give you personal satisfaction and help you avoid expensive problems.

A secondary purpose of this book is a reference guide for owners who want to understand their Honda and/or their mechanics better. In this case, no tools at all are required. Knowing just what a particular job requires in parts and labor time will allow you to evaluate whether you're getting a fair price quote and help decipher itemized bills from a repair shop.

Before attempting any repairs or service on your car, read through the entire procedure outlined in the appropriate chapter. This will give you the overall view of what tools and supplies will be required. There is nothing more frustrating than having to walk to the bus stop on Monday morning because you were short one gasket on Sunday afternoon. So read ahead and plan ahead. Each operation should be approached logically and all procedures thoroughly understood before attempting any work. Some special tools that may be required can often be rented from local automotive jobbers or places specializing in renting tools and equipment. Check the yellow pages of your phone book.

All chapters contain adjustments, maintenance, removal and installation procedures, and overhaul procedures. When overhaul is not considered practical, we tell you how to remove the failed part and then how to install the new or rebuilt replacement. In this way, you at least save the labor costs. Backyard overhaul of some components (such as the alternator or water pump) is not practical, but the removal and installation procedure is often simple and well within the capabilities of the average vehicle owner.

Many procedures in this book require you to "label and disconnect..." a group of lines, hoses or wires. Don't be lulled into thinking you can remember where everything goes — you won't. If you hook up vacuum or fuel lines incorrectly, the car will run poorly, if at all. If you hook up electrical wiring incorrectly, you may instantly learn a very expensive lesson.

You don't need to know the official or engineering name for each hose or line. A piece of masking tape on the hose and a piece on its fitting will allow you assign your own label such as the letter A or a short name. As long as you remember your own code, the lines can be reconnected by matching similar letters or names. Do remember that tape will dissolve in gasoline or other fluids; if a component is to be washed or cleaned, use another method of identification. A permanent felt-tipped marker can be very handy for marking metal parts. Remove any tape or paper labels after assembly.

It's necessary to mention the difference between maintenance and repair. Maintenance includes routine inspections, adjustments, and replacement of parts which show signs of normal wear. Maintenance compensates for wear or deterioration. Repair implies that something has broken or is not working. Need for repair is often caused by lack of maintenance. Example: Draining and refilling the automatic transmission fluid is maintenance recommended by the manufacturer at specific mileage intervals. Failure to do this will ruin the transmission, requiring very expensive repairs. While no maintenance program can prevent items from breaking or wearing out, a general rule can be stated: MAINTENANCE IS CHEAPER THAN REPAIR.

Hondas have a well-earned reputation for reliability and long service. They are, however, maintenance sensitive. A poorly maintained car will not operate to your satisfaction. Invest the time, effort and dollars in maintaining the car at the proper intervals, regardless of what you think it "needs". The minimal investment in maintenance will be paid back over years of continued operation.

Some basic mechanic's rules should be learned. One, whenever the left side of the car is mentioned, it means the driver's side of the car regardless of how you view the car. Conversely, the right side of the car means the passenger's side of the car. Second, most screws and bolts are removed by turning counterclockwise and tightened by turning clockwise.

Safety is the most important rule. Constantly be aware of the dangers involved in working on a vehicle and take the proper precautions. Think ahead, work slowly, and anticipate problems before they occur. Use jackstands when working under a raised vehicle. Don't smoke or allow an exposed flame to come near the battery or any parts of the fuel system. If you are using a kerosene heater during the winter, always turn it off or put it well away from the car when charging the battery or performing any item that could release liquid gasoline or gasoline vapors.

Use the proper tool and use it correctly. Bruised knuckles and skinned fingers aren't a mechanic's standard equipment. See the part of this chapter **Servicing Your Vehicle Safely**, and the **SAFETY NOTICE** on the acknowledgment page before attempting any service procedures. Pay attention to the instructions provided.

There are 3 common mistakes in mechanical work:

1. Incorrect order of assembly, disassembly or adjustment. When taking something apart or putting it together, doing things in the wrong order usually costs extra time — however, it CAN break something. Read the entire procedure before beginning disassembly. Do everything in the order in which the instructions say you should do it, even if you can't immediately see a reason for it. When you're taking apart something that is very intricate (for example a carburetor), you might want to draw a picture of how it looks when assembled at one point in order to make sure you get everything back in its proper position. We will supply exploded views whenever possible, but sometimes the job requires more attention to detail than an illustration provides. When making adjustments (especially tune-up adjustments), do them in order. One adjustment often affects another and you cannot expect satisfactory results unless each adjustment is made only when it cannot be changed by any other.

2. Overtightening (or undertightening) nuts and bolts. While it is more common for overtorquing to cause damage, undertorquing can cause a fastener to vibrate loose and cause serious damage, especially when dealing with aluminum parts. Pay attention to torque specifications and use a torque wrench in assembly. If a torque figure is not available, remember that if you are using the right tool to do the job, you will probably not have to strain yourself to get a fastener tight enough. The pitch of most threads is so slight that the tension you put on the wrench will be multiplied many times in actual force on what you are tightening.

An example of the importance of torque can be seen in the case of spark plug installation, especially when installing the plug into an aluminum cylinder head. Too little torque can fail to crush the gasket, causing leakage of combustion gases and consequent overheating of the plug and engine parts. Too much torque can damage the threads or distort the plug, which changes the spark gap at the electrode. Since more and more manufacturers are using aluminum in their engine and chassis parts to save weight, a torque wrench should be in any serious do-it-yourselfer's tool box.

There are many commercial chemical products available for ensuring that fasteners won't come loose, even if they are not torqued just right (a very common brand is Loctite®). If you're worried about getting something together tight enough to hold, but loose enough to avoid mechanical damage during assembly, one of these products might offer substantial insurance. Read the label on the package and make sure the product is compatible with the materials, fluids, etc. involved before choosing one.

3. Crossthreading. This occurs when a part such as a bolt is screwed into a nut or casting at the wrong angle and forced, causing the threads to become damaged. Crossthreading is more likely to occur if access is difficult. It helps to clean and lubricate fasteners, and to start threading with the part to be installed going straight in, using your fingers. If you encounter resistance, unscrew the part and start over again at a different angle until it can be inserted and turned several times without much effort.

Keep in mind that many parts, especially spark plugs, use tapered threads so that gentle turning will automatically bring the part you're threading to the proper angle if you don't force it or resist a change in angle. Don't put a wrench on the part until it's been turned in a couple of times by hand. If you suddenly encounter resistance and the part has not seated fully, don't force it. Pull it back out and make sure it's clean and threading properly.

Always take your time and be patient; once you have some experience, working on your Honda will become an enjoyable hobby.

TOOLS AND EQUIPMENT

Naturally, without the proper tools and equipment it is impossible to properly service your vehicle. It would be impossible to catalog each tool that you would need to perform every operation in this book. It would also be unwise for the amateur to rush out and buy an expensive set of tools on the theory that he may need one or more of them at sometime.

The best approach is to proceed slowly, gathering together a good quality set of those tools that are used most frequently. Don't be misled by the low cost of bargain tools. It is far better to spend a little more for better quality. Forged wrenches, 6- or 12-point sockets and fine-toothed ratchets are by far preferable to their less expensive counterparts. As any good mechanic can tell you, there are few worse experiences than trying to work on a vehicle with bad tools. Your monetary savings will be far outweighed by frustration and mangled knuckles.

Certain tools, plus a basic ability to handle tools, are required to get started. A basic mechanics' tool set, a torque wrench, a Torx® bits set. Torx® bits are hex lobular drivers which fit both inside and outside on special Torx® head fasteners used in various places on some vehicles.

Begin accumulating those tools that are used most frequently; those associated with routine maintenance and tune-up.

In addition to the normal assortment of screwdrivers and pliers, you should have the following tools for routine maintenance jobs. Virtually every fastener on your Accord or Prelude is metric, although dealer and aftermarket equipment may use SAE (US) hardware.

1. SAE and Metric wrenches, sockets and combination (open end/box end) wrenches in sizes from ⅛ in. (3mm) to ¾ in. (19mm), and a spark plug socket ($^{13}/_{16}$ in. or ⅝ in.). If possible, buy various length socket drive extensions. One good thing in this department is that the metric sockets available in the U.S. will all fit the ratchet handles and extensions you may already have (¼ in., ⅜ in., and ½ in. drive).

Many retail stores run periodic sales on starter sets of wrenches. Although a starter set may not contain every piece you want or need, once the basic set is purchased, specific items may be purchased individually.

2. Jackstands for supporting the vehicle.
3. Oil filter wrench.
4. Oil filler spout or funnel.
5. Small oil can and can(s) of spray grease.
6. Hydrometer for checking the battery.
7. A low flat pan for draining oil.
8. Lots of rags for wiping up the inevitable mess.

In addition to the above items there are several others that are not absolutely necessary, but handy to have around. These include oil-dry or cat litter for absorbing spilled fluid, a transmission fluid funnel and the usual supply of lubricants, antifreeze and fluids, although these can be purchased as needed. This is a basic list for routine maintenance, but only your personal needs and desires can accurately determine your list of necessary tools.

After performing a few projects on the car, you'll be amazed at the other tools and non-tools on your workbench. Some useful household items to have around are: a large turkey baster or siphon, empty coffee cans and ice trays (storing parts), ball of twine, electrical tape for wiring, small rolls of colored tape for tagging lines or hoses, markers and pens, a note pad, golf tees (for plugging vacuum lines), metal coat hangers or a roll of mechanics's wire (holding things out of the way), whisk broom, dental pick or similar long, pointed probe, a strong magnet, and a small mirror (for seeing into recesses and under manifolds).

The second list of tools is for tune-ups. While the tools involved here are slightly more sophisticated, they need not be outrageously expensive. There are several inexpensive tach/dwell meters on the market that are every bit as good for the average mechanic as a $300.00 professional model. Just be sure that it goes to at least

1200–1500 rpm on the tach scale and that it works on 4-, 6- and 8-cylinder engines — if you're going to spend the money, get one that will work on anything. A basic list of tune-up equipment could include:

1. Tach-dwell meter
2. Spark plug wrench
3. Timing light (a DC light that works from the battery is best, although an AC light that plugs into 110V house current will suffice at some sacrifice in brightness). Almost all the timing lights available now come with inductive pickups — make sure your's does. This neat little time-saver allows the probe to be clipped over the spark plug wire rather than having to disconnect a spark plug wire. Work smarter, not harder.
4. Wire spark plug gauge/adjusting tools
5. Set of feeler blades and/or spark plug gap adjusting tool.

In addition to these basic tools, there are several other tools and gauges you may find useful. These include:

1. A compression gauge. The screw-in type is slower to use, but eliminates the possibility of a faulty reading due to escaping pressure. The press-in type is quicker but may be less accurate. Additionally, the press-type may not be usable on certain engines with deeply recessed spark plug holes.
2. A manifold vacuum gauge.
3. A test light.
4. An induction meter. This is used for determining whether or not there is current in a wire. These are handy for use if a wire is broken somewhere in a wiring harness.
5. In this age of electronics, almost any diagnosis will require either a voltmeter or an ohmmeter. Happily, these tools are often combined into a volt-ohmmeter or VOM. The analog or sweep-needle type is adequate for most diagnostic work. If any work is to be done on solid-equipment or circuits, a high-impedance digital volt-ohmmeter (DVOM) is required. Small analog meters can be found for well under $50.00, although a larger one is easier to read and may have more scales and functions. DVOM's are more costly, but can be used in much wider applications.

As a final note, you will probably find a torque wrench necessary for all but the most basic work. The beam type models are perfectly adequate, although the newer click (breakaway) type are more precise and you don't have to crane your neck to see a torque reading in awkward situations. The breakaway torque wrenches are more expensive and should be recalibrated periodically.

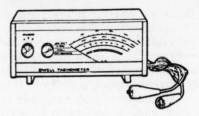

A good dwell-tach is always useful. Vehicles with solid-state ignition don't require the dwell meter

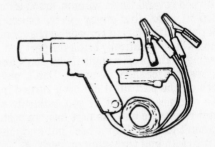

Don't cut corners on the purchase of a timing light; it should have a rugged case and well-insulated cables

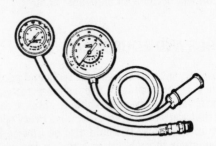

A compression gauge and a vacuum gauge are both essential for any diagnosis of engine operating problems

A good torque wrench will be fairly expensive. Once purchased, treat it with care. It's accuracy can be altered by dropping it, prying with it or subjecting it to other workshop torture. Keep it out of the way until needed. Don't use the torque wrench for non-torquing applications; use a regular ratchet.

Torque specification for each fastener will be given in the procedure in any case that a specific torque value is required. If no torque specifications are given, use the following values as a guide, based upon fastener size:

Bolts marked 6T
  6mm bolt/nut — 5–7 ft. lbs.; 4–5 Nm
  8mm bolt/nut — 12–17 ft. lbs.; 9–13 Nm
  10mm bolt/nut — 23–34 ft. lbs.; 17–25 Nm
  12mm bolt/nut — 41–59 ft. lbs.; 30–44 Nm
  14mm bolt/nut — 56–76 ft. lbs.; 41–56 Nm

Bolts marked 8T

  6mm bolt/nut — 6–9 ft. lbs.; 4–7 Nm
  8mm bolt/nut — 13–20 ft. lbs.; 10–15 Nm
  10mm bolt/nut — 27–40 ft. lbs.; 20–30 Nm
  12mm bolt/nut — 46–69 ft. lbs.; 34–51 Nm
  14mm bolt/nut — 75–101 ft. lbs.; 55–75 Nm

Special Tools

NOTE: *Special tools are occasionally necessary to perform a specific job or are recommended to make a job easier. Their use has been kept to a minimum. When a special tool is indicated, it will be referred to by manufacture's part number. Where possible, an illustration of the tool will be provided so that an equivalent tool may be used.*

Normally, the use of special factory tools is avoided for repair procedures, since these are not readily available for the do-it-yourselfer. When it is possible to perform the job with more commonly available tools, it will be pointed out, but occasionally, a special tool was designed to perform a specific function and should be used. Before substituting another tool, you should be convinced that neither your safety nor the performance of the vehicle will be compromised.

As you read the repair procedures, also look at the illustrations. You may be able to figure out that factory special tool 0000–XYZ is nothing more than a simple bearing puller. Assuming that you can find one of the correct size and installation type, you may use an equivalent tool of another manufacture. Note the key word equivalent — it means equal in every function. Use of an incorrect tool may cause severe damage or injury.

Some special tools are available commercially from major tool manufacturers. Others must be purchased through your Honda dealer; most factory tools are assigned a part number and may be ordered through normal parts channels.

SERVICING YOUR VEHICLE SAFELY

It is virtually impossible to anticipate all of the hazards involved with automotive maintenance and service but care and common sense will prevent most accidents.

The rules of safety for mechanics range from "don't smoke around gasoline," to "use the proper tool for the job." The trick to avoiding injuries is to develop safe work habits and take every possible precaution.

Do's

• Do keep a class B-C (dry powder) fire extinguisher within arm's reach and know how to use it. Keep a first aid kit in the work area.

• Do wear safety glasses, goggles or a full face shield when cutting, drilling, grinding or prying. If you wear glasses for the sake of vision, then they should be made of hardened glass that can serve also as safety glasses, or wear safety goggles over your regular glasses.

• Do shield your eyes whenever you work around the battery. Batteries contain sulfuric acid. In case of contact with the eyes or skin, flush the area with water or a mixture of water and baking soda and get medical attention immediately.

• Do work neatly. A few minutes spent clearing a workbench or setting up a small table for tools is well worth the effort. Make yourself put tools back on the table when not in use; doing so means you won't have to grope around on the floor for that wrench you need right now. Protect your car while working on it with fender covers. If you don't wish to buy a fender cover, an old blanket makes a usable substitute.

• Do follow manufacturer's directions whenever working with potentially hazardous materials. Both brake fluid and antifreeze are poisonous if taken internally. Housepets and small animals are attracted to the odor and taste of engine coolant (antifreeze). It is a highly poisonous mixture of chemicals; special care must be taken to protect open containers and spillage. If a housepet drinks any amount of coolant, it is a "drop everything" emergency — seek immediate veterinary care.

• Do use safety stands for any under-car service. Jacks are for raising vehicles; safety stands are for making sure the vehicle stays raised until you want it to come down. Whenever the vehicle is raised, block the wheels re-

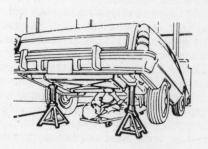

Always use jackstands to support any vehicle

maining on the ground and set the parking brake. Remember that all Hondas covered in this book are front wheel drive; leaving the vehicle in gear or Park won't help if the front end is elevated.

• Do disconnect the negative battery cable when working on the electrical system.

• Do follow manufacturer's directions whenever working with potentially hazardous materials. Both brake fluid and antifreeze are poisonous if taken internally. Never use a soda can or similar container to store drained fluids or bleed brakes; sooner or later somebody will grab it for a drink. Sounds silly, but really happens.

• Do properly maintain your tools. Loose hammerheads, mushroomed punches and chisels, frayed or poorly grounded electrical cords, excessively worn screwdrivers, spread wrenches (open end), cracked sockets, slipping ratchets, or faulty droplight sockets can cause accidents.

• Do use the proper size and type of tool for the job being done.

• Do, when possible, pull on a wrench handle rather than push on it, and adjust your stance to prevent a fall.

• Do be sure that adjustable wrenches are tightly adjusted on the nut or bolt and pulled so that the face is on the side of the fixed jaw.

• Do select a wrench or socket that fits the nut or bolt. The wrench or socket should sit straight, not cocked. Even though certain metric and SAE sizes are close, they are not the same.

• Do strike squarely with a hammer. Avoid glancing blows.

• Do set the parking brake and block the wheels if the work requires that the engine be running.

Don'ts

• Don't run an engine in a garage or anywhere else without proper ventilation — EVER! Carbon monoxide is odorless and colorless. Your senses cannot detect its presence. Early symptoms of monoxide poisoning include headache, irritability, improper vision (blurred or hard to focus) and/or drowsiness. When you notice any of these symptoms in yourself or your helpers, stop working immediately and get to fresh, outside air. Ventilate the work area thoroughly before returning to the car. Always use power vents, windows, fans or open the garage doors.

• Don't work around moving parts while wearing a necktie or other loose clothing. Short sleeves are much safer than long, loose sleeves. Hard-toed shoes with neoprene soles protect your toes and give a better grip on slippery surfaces. Jewelry such as watches, fancy belt buckles, beads, or body adornment of any kind is not safe while working around a vehicle. Long hair should be hidden under a hat or cap.

• Don't use pockets for toolboxes. A fall or bump can drive a screwdriver deep into your body. Even a wiping cloth hanging from the back pocket can wrap around a spinning shaft or fan.

• Don't smoke when working around gasoline, cleaning solvent or other flammable material.

• Don't smoke when working around the battery. When the battery is being charged, it gives off explosive hydrogen gas.

• Don't use gasoline to wash your hands. There are excellent soaps and hand cleaners available. Gasoline may contain lead, and lead can enter the body through a cut, accumulating in the body until you are very ill. Gasoline also removes all the natural oils from the skin so that bone dry hands will suck up oil and grease.

• Do not open any refrigerant lines or hoses while the air conditioning system is still charged. The refrigerant, R-12, becomes extremely cold and when exposed to the air, will instantly freeze any surface it comes in contact with, including your eyes. Although the refrigerant is normally non-toxic, R-12 becomes a deadly poisonous gas in the presence of an open flame. One good whiff of the vapors from burning refrigerant can be fatal.

NOTE: *R-12 refrigerant is a chlorofluorocarbon (CFC) which, when released into the atmosphere, can contribute to the depletion of the ozone layer in the upper atmosphere. Ozone filters out harmful radiation from the sun. An approved R-12 Recovery/Recycling machine meeting SAE standards must be used when discharging the system. Have the air conditioning system discharged and recharged at a qualified service facility.*

MODEL INDENTIFICATION

This repair manual for Hondas covers the various model changes from 1984 through 1991. While the model names Accord and Prelude are familiar to almost everyone, several families exist within each model. The vehicles encompass carbureted and fuel injected engines as well as hatchback, coupe, sedan and wagon body styles. Trim and equipment levels further divide the families into subgroups such as DX, LX, Si, LXi, EX and Si4WS.

The Accord and Prelude have endured through several generations or body styles; 4 for the Accord, and three for the Prelude.

- Accord 1st generation: 1976–81
- Accord 2nd generation: 1982–85
- Accord 3rd generation: 1986–89
- Accord 4th generation: 1990–91
- Prelude 1st generation: 1979–82
- Prelude 2nd generation: 1983–87
- Prelude 3rd generation: 1988–91

SERIAL NUMBER IDENTIFICATION

Vehicle Identification Number (VIN)

All 1984–91 Honda vehicles have the VIN stamped on a plate mounted to the left side of the instrument panel. The plate is visible by looking through the windshield from the outside. The number is also stamped into the firewall at the rear of the engine compartment. Additionally, the Vehicle Identification number

Vehicle Identification Number

Vehicle Identification Number

Transmission Number
(Manual)

Transmission Number
(Automatic)

Engine Number

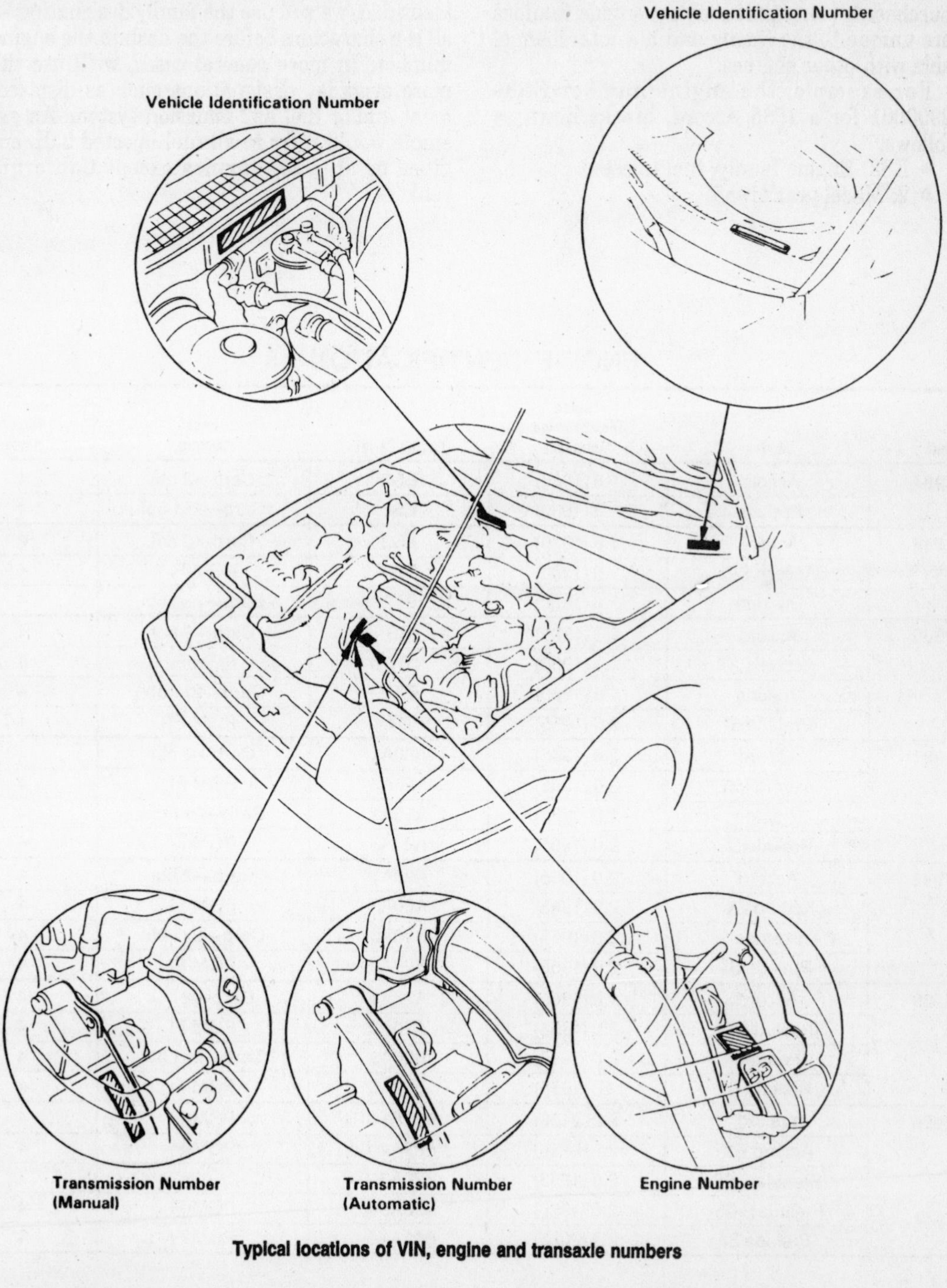

Typical locations of VIN, engine and transaxle numbers

appears on the FMVSS label, attached to the left door jamb.

Engine Number

The engine serial number is stamped into the right front side of the engine block. This number identifies the engine family, application and build sequence of the engine. The engine number should be used any time engine parts are purchased; many parts within engine families are unique to the family and not interchangeable with other engines.

For example, the engine number ES3–2900001 for a 1985 Accord, breaks down as follows:

- ES3: Engine family, fuel injected
- 2: Model year (1985)

- 9: Emission group, 49 state and high-altitude
- 00001: Serial number or production number

Meanings of numbers change from model to model and year to year. It isn't necessary to know what each digit means as long as the complete number is available when buying parts. From 1987 on, engines use a 5 character family designation, such as B21A1 or A20A3.

In this book, when specific engines must be identified, we will use the family designation — all the characters before the dash in the engine number. In more general cases, we'll use the more everyday designations such as displacement and/or fuel and emission system. An example would refer to all fuel injected 2.0L engines or all 1.8L engines except California vehicles.

ENGINE IDENTIFICATION

Year	Model	Engine Displacement Liters (cc)	Engine Series	Fuel System	No. of Cylinders
1984	Accord	1.8 (1830)	ES2	Carb—3 bbl	4
	Prelude	1.8 (1830)	ES1	Carb—2x1 bbl	4
1985	Accord	1.8 (1830)	ES2	Carb—3 bbl	4
	Accord SEi	1.8 (1830)	ES3	PGM-FI	4
	Prelude	1.8 (1830)	ET2	Carb—2x1 bbl	4
1986	Accord	2.0 (1955)	BS	Carb—2 bbl	4
	Accord LXi	2.0 (1955)	BT	PGM-FI	4
	Prelude	1.8 (1830)	ET2	Carb—2x1 bbl	4
	Prelude Si	2.0 (1955)	BT	PGM-FI	4
1987	Accord	2.0 (1955)	A20A1	Carb—2 bbl	4
	Accord LXi	2.0 (1955)	A20A3	PGM-FI	4
	Prelude	1.8 (1830)	A18A1	Carb—2x1 bbl	4
	Prelude Si	2.0 (1955)	A20A3	PGM-FI	4
1988	Accord	2.0 (1955)	A20A1	Carb—2 bbl	4
	Accord LXi	2.0 (1955)	A20A3	PGM-FI	4
	Prelude	2.0 (1955)	B20A3	Carb—2x1 bbl	4
	Prelude Si	2.0 (1955)	B20A5	PGM-FI	4
1989	Accord	2.0 (1955)	A20A1	Carb—2 bbl	4
	Accord LXi	2.0 (1955)	A20A3	PGM-FI	4
	Prelude	2.0 (1955)	B20A3	Carb—2x1 bbl	4
	Prelude Si	2.0 (1955)	B20A5	PGM-FI	4
1990	Accord	2.2 (2156)	F22A1 ①	PGM-FI	4
	Accord EX	2.2 (2156)	F22A4 ②	PGM-FI	4
	Prelude 2.0S	2.0 (1958)	B20A3 ④	Carb—2x1 bbl	4
	Prelude 2.0Si	2.0 (1958)	B20A5 ⑤	PGM-FI	4
	Prelude Si	2.1 (2056)	B21A1 ⑥	PGM-FI	4

ENGINE IDENTIFICATION

Year	Model	Engine Displacement Liters (cc)	Engine Series	Fuel System	No. of Cylinders
1991	Accord	2.2 (2156)	F22A1 ①	PGM-FI	4
	Accord EX	2.2 (2156)	F22A4 ②	PGM-FI	4
	Accord SE	2.2 (2156)	F22A6 ③	PGM-FI	4
	Prelude 2.0Si	2.0 (1958)	B20A5 ⑤	PGM-FI	4
	Prelude Si	2.1 (2056)	B21A1 ⑥	PGM-FI	4

① Single-pipe exhaust manifold
② Double-pipe exhaust manifold
③ Dual intake manifold and double-pipe exhaust manifold
④ 2.0L, SOHC, Carbureted
⑤ 2.0L, DOHC, Fuel injected
⑥ 2.1L, DOHC, Fuel injected

Transaxle Serial Number

The transaxle serial number is located on the top of the transaxle/clutch case. As with the engine numbers, this number uniquely identifies the unit and its application. Besides the obvious difference of 4- and 5-speed manual transmissions and 3 or 4 speed automatics, the transmissions differ internally with regard to gear and final drive ratios as well as the presence of electronic controls.

ROUTINE MAINTENANCE

Air Cleaner

REMOVAL AND INSTALLATION

The air cleaner element, housed above or to one side of the carburetor or throttle body, must be replaced every 30,000 miles or 24 months, whichever occurs first. This is a maximum interval; the filter should be checked periodically and replaced when dirty or obstructed. The air filter element is one of the cheapest forms of insurance for the engine. Never operate the engine with the filter element removed or the filter housing lid removed.

When buying replacement parts in the aftermarket, compare the replacement unit to the old one. Check that the diameter and height are identical. Cheap, poorly made filters will not seal properly, allowing dust and road grit into the engine.

1. To remove, release the wing nut(s), bolts and/or spring clips from the air cleaner cover; on some models, it may be necessary to also remove a standard nut. Some Preludes use a canister type filter; the lid is retained with bolts.

2. Remove the air cleaner cover and the air cleaner element. For 1990–1991 Preludes, also remove the small blow-by filter at the top of the

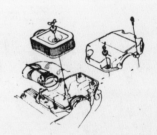

Air filter assemblies, 1985 Accord (above) and Accord SEI

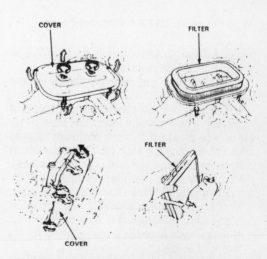

Air filter assemblies, 1986 Accord (above) and Accord LXI

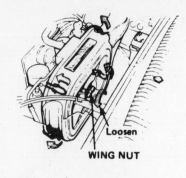

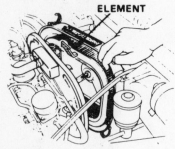

Air filter assembly, 1985 Prelude

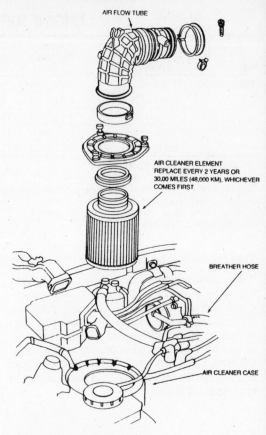

Air filter assembly, DOHC Prelude

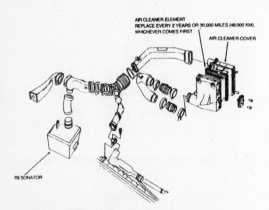

Air filter assembly, 1986-87 fuel injected Prelude

housing. 1984–86 Accords use a similar filter on the side of the air cleaner.

3. Using a clean rag, clean out the air cleaner housing.

4. Install a new air cleaner element, and, if necessary, a new blow-by filter. The blow-by filter may be reused if it is not obviously clogged with dirt or dripping with oil. Make absolutely certain the air filter element is properly seated; the lid will mate to the filter, sealing the housing and forcing all intake air through the filter.

NOTE: *Air cleaner elements are not interchangeable, although they may appear to be. Make sure you have the proper element for the year and model.*

5. Fit the lid or cover onto the housing. Many round housings have arrows stamped into the metal; align the arrows before attempting to install the lid. Correct alignment insures a tight seal.

Fuel Filter

All vehicles use a disposable type fuel filter which cannot be disassembled for cleaning. On 1984–91 models, the filter must be replaced at 60,000 miles or 48 months, whichever occurs first. Again, earlier replacement is indicated whenever restricted fuel flow is suspected. The filter cannot be inspected or tested.

Honda also recommends that all rubber fuel hoses be replaced at the 60,000 mile interval. This compensates for the aging and deterioration of the rubber over time.

CAUTION: *Fuel injected systems operate at high fuel pressures and maintain the pressure in the lines when the engine is OFF. The pressure must be safely released before any work is performed on fuel lines or fuel system components. Failure to relieve the fuel pressure may result in fire, personal injury and/or property damage.*

Carbureted vehicles may also hold some residual pressure in the tank and lines. Always remove the filler cap before performing any work on the fuel lines or fuel system components.

Always release pressure slowly and contain spillage. Observe no smoking/no open flame precautions. Have a Class B-C (dry powder) fire extinguisher within arm's reach at all times.

RELIEVING FUEL PRESSURE

Fuel Injected Vehicles

1. Disconnect the negative battery cable.
2. Remove the fuel filler cap.
3. The fuel hose at the top of the fuel filter is held by a large bolt (banjo bolt). On top of this bolt is a smaller bolt; this is the service bolt. Use an open end wrench to hold the banjo bolt and fit a closed (box end) 6mm wrench to the service bolt.
4. Place a cloth over the service bolt. Slowly loosen the service bolt one full turn. Fuel will escape the system into the cloth, releasing the system pressure. The cloth is now a flammable item; treat it carefully and dispose of it properly.
5. Although the system pressure is now much below normal, always wrap fuel line connections in a cloth before disconnecting them; some pressure differential may remain in the system.

REMOVAL AND INSTALLATION

Carbureted Engines

These vehicles use 2 replaceable fuel filters. A small one is in the fuel line under the hood; a larger one is located at the rear, just inboard of the left rear wheel.

Whenever the filter(s) are replaced, take great care to avoid the entry of dirt into the lines. Also, pay attention to the correct installation position. It is possible — and quite embarrassing — to install the filter backwards.

FRONT

1. Depress the tang and unclip the filter.
2. Loosen the fuel line clamps and slide them back.
3. Using a twisting motion, remove the fuel lines from the filter.
4. To install, use a new fuel filter and reverse the removal procedures. Start the engine and check for leaks.

REAR

1. Raise and safely support the rear of the vehicle. Remove the left rear wheel.
2. Push the fuel filter retaining tab and release it from the holder.
3. Using two fuel line clamps, clamp off both

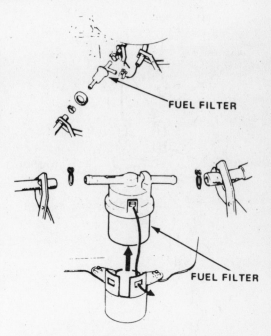

Front and rear fuel filters, carbureted Accords. 1985 shown, all others similar

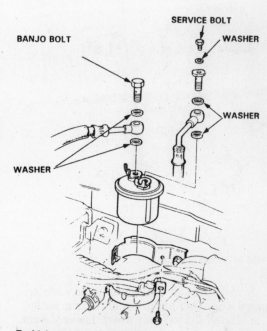

Fuel Injected Prelude fuel filter

fuel lines. Take care not to crush the lines; just clamp them shut.
4. Loosen the fuel line clamps and slide them back.
5. Using a twisting motion, pull the fuel lines from the fuel filter; remove the filter.
6. To install, use a new filter and reverse the removal procedures.

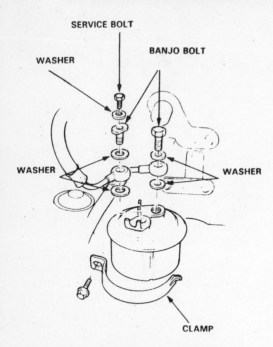

Fuel filter for fuel injected Accord through 1989

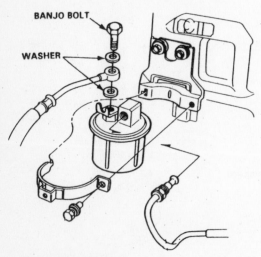

1990-91 Accord fuel filter

7. Make certain the retaining tabs are engaged when the filter is installed in the holder.

8. Install the left rear wheel. Lower the car to the ground.

9. Start the engine and check for leaks.

Fuel Injected Engines

The canister fuel filter is located in the engine compartment. When buying the new filter, also buy new washers for the banjo bolts and the service bolt. Failure to replace these washers invites high-pressure fuel leaks. Replacing the washers is required, not recommended.

1. Disconnect the negative battery terminal.

2. The fuel system is under pressure. Release pressure slowly and contain spillage. Observe no smoking/no open flame precautions. Have a Class B-C (dry powder) fire extinguisher within arm's reach at all times.

3. Remove the banjo bolts and washers from the fuel filter. For 1990 and 1991 Accord, disconnect the 1 banjo bolt and loosen the flare fitting for the fuel line. Use of a brake line or flare wrench is recommended for disconnecting and attaching this fitting.

4. Remove the fuel filter clamp bolt and the filter.

5. Install the new filter and secure the mounting bolts.

6. The upper and lower washers on each banjo bolt and the washer on the service bolt MUST be replaced whenever the bolts are loosened. Install the washers and banjo bolts. Tighten the banjo bolts to 22 Nm (16 ft. lbs.). For 1990–91 Accord, tighten the flare fitting to 38 Nm (27 ft. lbs.).

7. Tighten the service bolt to 9 Nm (12 ft. lbs.).

8. Start the engine and check for leaks. The engine may crank longer than normal until full fuel pressure is developed.

PCV Valve

The engine is equipped with a Positive Crankcase Ventilation (PCV) system in which blow-by gas is returned to the combustion chamber through the intake manifold and/or the air cleaner. Some of the normal combustion gasses get by the piston rings and pressurize the lower part of the engine. If not vented, these gasses will eventually force their way through gaskets at the top or bottom of the engine, causing improper running and/or fluid leaks.

The PCV system captures these gasses and routes them back into the engine where they can be reburned. Located in the valve cover, the PCV valve controls the flow into the engine. If the valve sticks closed, excess pressure can build in the engine. If it sticks open, too much gas may be admitted to the engine, causing a rich mixture, black exhaust smoke and generally poor driveability.

The function of the PCV valve should be checked every 30,000 miles or whenever an emission-related problem is being diagnosed. As long as the valve is functioning properly, it does not need replacement.

REMOVAL AND INSTALLATION

To remove the valve, disconnect the hose and pull the valve from the grommet. Install the

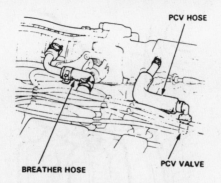

PCV HOSE

BREATHER HOSE PCV VALVE

1989 Prelude PCV valve location. All are similar.

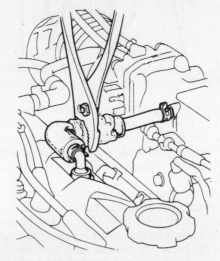

Gently pinching the hose should cause the valve to click. If it does, it's OK

new valve and connect the hose. Attempting to clean the valve is not recommended; always replace it.

Install the new valve firmly into the grommet. Connect and secure the hose.

For further information on servicing Honda emission control components, please refer to Chapter 4.

Evaporative Canister

The charcoal canister is part of the Evaporative Emission Control System. This system prevents the escape of raw gasoline vapors from the fuel tank and carburetor. The activated charcoal element within the canister acts as a storage device for the fuel vapors at times when the engine operating conditions do not allow efficient burning of the vapors.

The only required service for the canister is inspection periodically. If the charcoal element is saturated, (possibly from engine flooding) the entire canister will require replacement.

The canister is a coffee can-sized object locat-ed in the engine compartment. Label the hoses leading to the canister before disconnecting them. Remove the old canister from its mounting bracket and discard it. Install the new canister and connect the hoses as before.

SERVICING

The canister does not require periodic replacement. The entire system requires a careful operational check with a vacuum gauge at 60,000 miles, however. See Chapter 4 for testing procedures.

Battery

Loose, dirty, or corroded battery terminals are a frequent cause of "no-start" conditions. Approximately every 3 months, inspect the battery terminals. If necessary, remove the battery terminals and clean them, giving them a light coating of petroleum jelly when finished. This will help to retard corrosion.

WARNING: *Never disconnect the battery with the engine running or with the ignition turned ON. Severe and expensive damage to the on-board computers will result. With the ignition OFF and the key removed for safety, always disconnect the negative (−) cable first and connect it last.*

NOTE: *When the battery is disconnected, various solid state accessories on the car may lose their memory. Be prepared to re-program the radio and reset the clock.*

Check the battery cables for signs of wear or chafing and replace any cable or terminal that looks marginal. Battery terminals can be easily cleaned; inexpensive cleaning tools are an excellent investment that will pay for themselves many times over. They can usually be purchased from any well-equipped auto store or parts department. The accumulated white powder and corrosion can be cleaned from the top of the battery with an old toothbrush and a solution of baking soda and water.

Unless you have a low-maintenance battery, check the electrolyte (fluid) level frequently. Be sure that the vent holes in each cell cap are not blocked by grease or dirt. The vent holes allow hydrogen gas, formed by the chemical reaction in the battery, to escape safely.

Check the battery electrolyte level at least once a month, more often in hot weather or during periods of extended operation. The level should be maintained between the upper and lower levels marked on the battery case, or to the split ring within the well in each cell. If the electrolyte level is low, distilled water should be added until the proper level is reached. Tap water is to be avoided if possible; the minerals it contains can shorten battery life by reacting

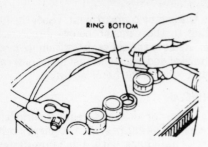

Fill the cells only to the bottom of the ring

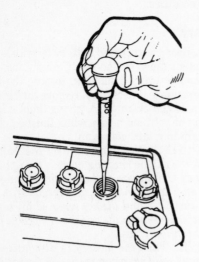

Check the specific gravity once per year

An inexpensive battery terminal tool will clean cables and posts

with the metal plates inside the battery. Each cell is completely separate from the others, so each cell must be filled individually. It's a good idea to add the distilled water with a squeeze bulb to avoid having electrolyte (sulphuric acid) splash out.

NOTE: *Cars that are regularly driven at highway speeds over moderate to long distances may require battery service more frequently. Constant charging of the battery will cause some water to evaporate.*

At least once a year check the specific gravity of the battery electrolyte. The tool to do this, a battery hydrometer, is available at almost every parts outlet or retail auto store. The test result should be between 1.22 and 1.28 in.Hg at room temperature. A reading of 1.00 in.Hg or slightly above indicates nothing but water within the battery. The electrical process has stopped and it's time for a new battery. You cannot successfully add acid to a used battery. If water is added in freezing weather, the vehicle should be driven several miles to allow the water to mix with the electrolyte and prevent freezing.

If the battery becomes corroded, or if electrolyte should splash out during additions of water, a mixture of baking soda and water will

neutralize the acid. This should be washed off with cold water after making sure that the cell caps are tight. Battery fluid is particularly nasty to painted surfaces; work carefully to avoid spillage on fenders and other painted bodywork.

If a charging is required while the battery is in the car, disconnect the battery cables, negative (ground) cable first. If you have removed the battery from the vehicle for charging, make sure the battery is not sitting on bare earth or concrete while being charged. A block of wood or a small stack of newspapers will prevent the battery from losing internal heat while charging.

When replacing a battery, it is important that the replacement have an output rating equal to or when greater than original equipment. Do not confuse physical size with electrical capacity. A stronger battery (capable of delivering more power) need not be much larger that the original. A physically larger battery may not fit in the battery holder and may actually deliver less power than the original. The size and capacity of the battery is indicated by a two-digit code on the battery label or case. Use this code when replacing the battery to insure equal performance.

CAUTION: *Keep flame or sparks away from the battery; it gives off explosive hydrogen gas. Battery electrolyte contains sulphuric acid. If you should splash any on your skin or in your eyes, flush the affected area with plenty of clear water. If it lands in your eyes, get medical help immediately.*

Many Accords and Preludes come with a low maintenance battery. While this may be billed as maintenance free by some, every battery

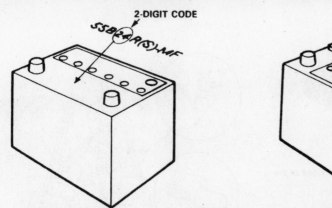
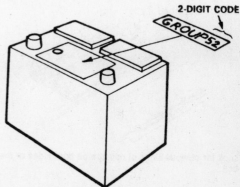

Examples of battery group codes. Use these to insure equal size and capacity when replacing the battery

should have the terminals checked for tightness and cleanliness periodically.

The fluid level may be viewed through the side of the case; the plastic is translucent and will show the fluid level. The case has UPPER and LOWER level lines embossed in the plastic; the fluid must be between the lines.

If the fluid is low, the cell cover may be removed. On some batteries, gently pry up the large caps to remove the group of 3 cell covers; on others, removing the label or plastic seal will expose the individual cell caps which must be unscrewed with a wide coin or screwdriver. Fill the cell(s) only to the UPPER level and replace the caps and covers.

CHILTON TIP: *Both new and replacement batteries a warranted for a period of years. If you think you may have a claim under warranty, be very careful when removing labels or other seals from the battery case. These may contain numbers required for the warranty claim. Additionally, if the claim is to made through a Honda dealer, there is a very exact test procedure which must be performed at the dealership to confirm that the battery has failed. The test may take up to 3 hours, depending on the specific procedures.*

Some of the low maintenance batteries contain an eye or built-in hydrometer. Looking straight down into the eye provides a rough visual indication of the battery status. If the eye shows green, the battery contains some charge; do not assume the battery is fully charged because the eye is green. When the battery is discharged, the eye turns black. A battery may need recharging even if the eye is green; a battery with the eye black must be recharged.

CAUTION: *If the eye appears yellowish or a cloudy yellow-white, do not attempt to recharge the battery, since it may explode. Replace it with a new one, turning the old one in for credit or recycling.*

Belts

INSPECTION

On Accord and Prelude models, inspect the drive belt(s) every at least every 30,000 miles or 24 months. Determine the belt tension at a point halfway between the pulleys by pressing on the belt with moderate thumb pressure. The belt should deflect about ¼ in. (6mm) over a 7–10 in. (178mm) span or ½ in. (13mm) over a 13–16 in. (330–406mm) span. If the deflection is found to be too much or too little, perform the tension adjustments.

NOTE: *When adjusting the belt, do not attempt the tightest possible adjustment by levering the component until the belt is rigid. The extreme tension of the belt will cause premature wear on the driven component. A belt adjusted to the correct amount of deflection will be loose enough to drive the component without noisy operation.*

CHECKING AND ADJUSTING TENSION

Before adjusting, inspect the belt to see that it is not cracked or worn. Be sure that its surfaces are free of grease and oil. A glazed belt will be perfectly smooth and shiny from slippage; a belt in good condition will have a slight texture of fabric visible on the faces. Cracks will generally start at the inner edge of the belt and run outward. Replace the belt at the first sign of cracking or if the glazing is severe.

1. Push down on the belt halfway between pulleys with moderate force. The belt should deflect approximately ½ in. (13mm). Deflection should be slightly less with a new belt as tension is lost rapidly for the first ½ hour or so of operation.

2. If the belt tension requires adjustment on 1984 Accord, loosen the adjusting link bolt and move the alternator outward. On all other models, loosen the top mounting bolt, then turn the adjusting nut outboard of the alternator. This

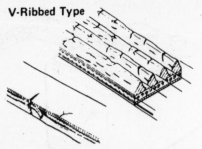

V-Ribbed Type

Look for obvious signs of damage on both sides of the belt

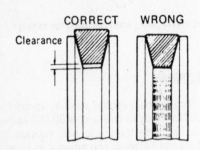

CORRECT   WRONG

Clearance

The new belt must fit the pulley correctly

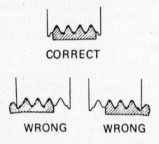

CORRECT

WRONG   WRONG

Make sure ribbed belts fit correctly on all pulleys

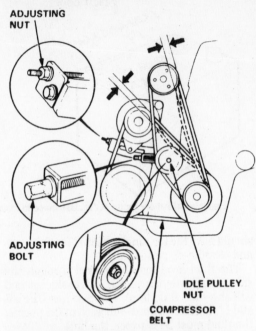

ADJUSTING NUT

ADJUSTING BOLT

IDLE PULLEY NUT

COMPRESSOR BELT

Examples of adjusting nuts and bolts. 1989 Prelude shown, others similar although location may vary

will reposition the alternator without prying.

3. When the belt tension is correct tighten the upper mounting bolt to about 16 ft. lbs. Recheck the tension, correcting the adjustment if necessary.

4. If the air conditioning compressor belt needs adjustment, tighten it by turning the threaded adjuster bolt. Depending on the model, this may act either on the compressor or on the idler pulley.

NOTE: *Do not apply pressure to the casing or body of the component.*

REMOVAL AND INSTALLATION

When buying replacement belts, remember that the fit is critical according to the length of the belt ("diameter"), the width of the belt, the depth of the belt and the angle or profile of the V shape. The belt shape should exactly match the shape of the pulley; belts that are not an ex-

act match can cause noise, slippage and premature failure.

If a belt must be replaced, first loosen the adjuster if one is present. The driven unit may also need to be loosened or moved towards the engine to allow removal of the belt. After removing the old belt, check the pulleys for dirt or built-up material which could affect belt contact. Carefully install the new belt, remembering that it is new and unused — it may appear to be just a little too small to fit over the pulley flanges.

Fit the belt over the largest pulley (usually the crankshaft pulley at the bottom center of the engine) first, then work on the smaller one(s). Gentle pressure in the direction of rotation is helpful. some belts run around a third or idler pulley, which acts as an additional pivot. Depending on which belt(s) you are replacing, it may be necessary to loosen or remove other interfering belts to get at the one you want.

After the new belt is installed, draw tension on it by moving the driven unit away from the engine and tighten the mounting bolts. This is sometimes a three- or four-handed job; an assistant can be helpful. Make sure that any bolts that were loosened get re-tightened. Turn the belt adjuster until the belt is at the correct tension.

A new belt can be expected to stretch a bit after installation. Be prepared to check, and if necessary, readjust the belt(s) within the first 100 miles of use.

HOW TO SPOT BAD HOSES

Both the upper and lower radiator hoses are called upon to perform difficult jobs in an inhospitable environment. They are subject to nearly 18 psi at under hood temperatures often over 280°F., and must circulate nearly 7500 gallons of coolant an hour—3 good reasons to have good hoses.

Swollen hose

A good test for any hose is to feel it for soft or spongy spots. Frequently these will appear as swollen areas of the hose. The most likely cause is oil soaking. This hose could burst at any time, when hot or under pressure.

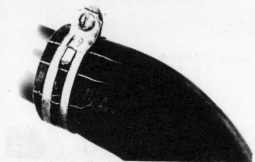

Cracked hose

Cracked hoses can usually be seen but feel the hoses to be sure they have not hardened; a prime cause of cracking. This hose has cracked down to the reinforcing cords and could split at any of the cracks.

Frayed hose end (due to weak clamp)

Weakened clamps frequently are the cause of hose and cooling system failure. The connection between the pipe and hose has deteriorated enough to allow coolant to escape when the engine is hot.

Debris in cooling system

Debris, rust and scale in the cooling system can cause the inside of a hose to weaken. This can usually be felt on the outside of the hose as soft or thinner areas.

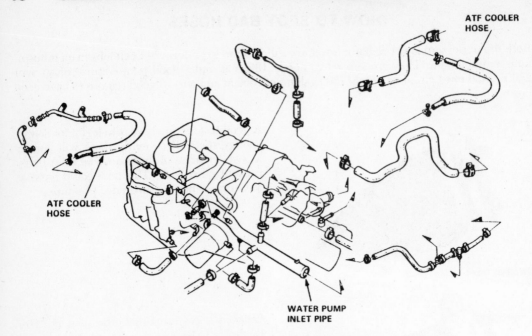

ATF COOLER HOSE

ATF COOLER HOSE

ATF COOLER HOSE

WATER PUMP INLET PIPE

Coolant hose locations, fuel injected 1989 Prelude

Hoses

CAUTION: *Always disconnect the negative battery cable, or fan motor wiring harness connector before replacing any radiator/heater hose. Under certain circumstances, the fan may come on even though the ignition is OFF!*

Inspect the condition of the radiator and heater hoses periodically. Early spring and at the beginning of the fall or winter, when you are performing other maintenance, are good times. Make sure the engine and cooling system are cold. Visually inspect for cracking, rotting or collapsed hoses, replace as necessary. Run your hand along the length of the hose. If a weak or swollen spot is noted when squeezing the hose wall, replace the hose.

Don't overlook the smaller hoses conducting coolant around the outside of the engine block, carburetor or throttle body. Honda recommends that all hoses be thoroughly inspected every 30,000 miles or 36 months.

REMOVAL AND INSTALLATION

Replacing hoses requires draining the cooling system. This potentially messy job involves working under the car and handling antifreeze, a slippery, smelly, stain-making chemical. Have a large drain pan or bucket available along with healthy supply of rags. Be prepared to deal with fluid spills immediately. See the previous list of Do's and Don'ts for other hints.

CAUTION: *When draining the coolant, keep*

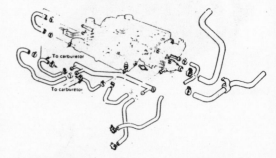

To carburetor

To carburetor

Coolant hose locations, carbureted 1986 Prelude

in mind that cats and dogs are attracted by the ethylene glycol antifreeze, and are quite likely to drink any that is left in an uncovered container or in puddles on the ground. This will prove fatal in sufficient quantity. Always drain the coolant into a sealable container. Coolant should be reused unless it is contaminated or several years old.

1. Drain the cooling system. This is always done with the engine cold. Attempting to drain hot coolant is very foolish; you can be badly scalded. Honda engines and radiators may be drained by opening the drain cock at the base of the radiator. If the coolant is drained in this fashion, remember to close the draincock before adding coolant again.

An alternative method is:

a. Remove the radiator cap.

b. Position the drain pan under the point where the lower radiator hose hooks to

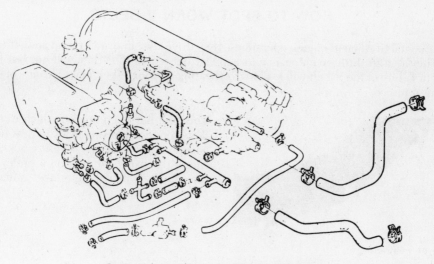

Coolant hose locations, fuel injected 1986 Accord

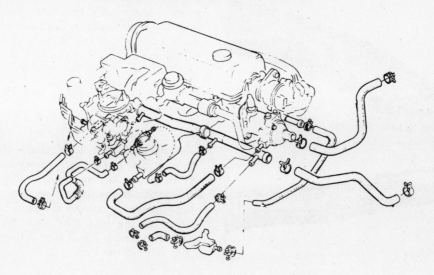

Coolant hose locations, carbureted 1986 Accord

the radiator. Loosen the clamp on the hose and slide it back so it's out of the way.

c. Gently break the grip of the hose on its fitting by twisting or prying with a suitable tool. Do not exert too much force or you will damage the radiator fitting. As the hose loosens, you can expect a gush of fluid to come out — be ready.

d. Remove the hose end from the radiator and direct the hose into the drain pan. You now have fluid running from both the hose and the radiator. When the system stops draining, proceed with replacement of the damaged hose.

2. Loosen the hose clamps on the damaged hose with a screwdriver and slide the clamps either off the hose altogether or in toward center.

3. Break the grip of the hose at both ends by prying it free with a suitable tool or by twisting it with your hand.

4. Remove the hose.

5. Install a new hose. A small amount of soapy water or window cleaner on the inside of the hose end will ease installation.

NOTE: *Radiator hoses should be routed with no kinks and, when installed, should be in the same position as the original. If other than specified hose is used, make sure it does not rub against either the engine or any other component while the engine is running, as this may wear a hole in the hose. Contact points may be insulated with a piece of sponge or foam; plastic wire ties are particularly handy for this job.*

HOW TO SPOT WORN V-BELTS

V-Belts are vital to efficient engine operation—they drive the fan, water pump and other accessories. They require little maintenance (occasional tightening) but they will not last forever. Slipping or failure of the V-belt will lead to overheating. If your V-belt looks like any of these, it should be replaced.

This belt has deep cracks, which cause it to flex. Too much flexing leads to heat build-up and premature failure. These cracks can be caused by using the belt on a pulley that is too small. Notched belts are available for small diameter pulleys.

Cracking or weathering

Oil and grease on a belt can cause the belt's rubber compounds to soften and separate from the reinforcing cords that hold the belt together. The belt will first slip, then finally fail altogether.

Softening (grease and oil)

Glazing is caused by a belt that is slipping. A slipping belt can cause a run-down battery, erratic power steering, overheating or poor accessory performance. The more the belt slips, the more glazing will be built up on the surface of the belt. The more the belt is glazed, the more it will slip. If the glazing is light, tighten the belt.

Glazing

The cover of this belt is worn off and is peeling away. The reinforcing cords will begin to wear and the belt will shortly break. When the belt cover wears in spots or has a rough jagged appearance, check the pulley grooves for roughness.

Worn cover

This belt is on the verge of breaking and leaving you stranded. The layers of the belt are separating and the reinforcing cords are exposed. It's just a matter of time before it breaks completely.

Separation

6. Slide the hose clamps back into position and re-tighten. When tightening the clamps, tighten them enough to seal in the coolant but not so much that the clamp cuts into the hose or causes it internal damage. If a clamp shows signs of any damage (bent, too loose, hard to tighten, etc.) now is the time to replace it. A good rule of thumb is that a new hose is always worth new clamps.

7. Reinstall the lower radiator hose and secure its clamp.

8. Fill the system with coolant. Honda strongly recommends that the coolant mixture be a 50/50 mix of antifreeze and water. This mixture gives best combination of anti-freeze and anti-boil characteristics for year-round driving.

NOTE: *Cold weather anti-freezing protection is best at the 50/50 mixture. If the mixture contains 40% water or less, engine cooling is impaired. Do not use additional rust inhibitors or other such products. The cooling system may be damaged by incompatible fluids.*

9. When adding coolant to the radiator and or the coolant reservoir (jug), take great care to prevent spillage onto the fuse and relay panel under the hood. Should spillage occur, wipe it off immediately.

10. Replace and tighten the radiator cap. Start the engine and check visually for leaks. Allow the engine to warm up fully and continue to check your work for signs of leakage. A very small leak may not be noticed until the system develops internal pressure. Leaks at hose ends are generally clamp related and can be cured by snugging the clamp. Larger leaks may require removing the hose again. To do this, YOU MUST WAIT UNTIL THE ENGINE HAS COOLED DOWN, GENERALLY A PERIOD OF HOURS. NEVER UNCAP A HOT RADIATOR! After all leaks are cured, check the coolant level in the radiator (with the engine cold) and top up as necessary.

Air Conditioning System

OPERATION

Refrigerant Cycle

Once the air conditioning system is fully charged and free of leaks, it is ready to operate on demand. When turned on, the compressor discharges high temperature and high pressure refrigerant. This refrigerant gas contains heat transferred from inside the car plus the heat developed by the compressor on the discharge stroke.

This gaseous refrigerant flows into the condenser. Because of the airflow through the condenser (either from the motion of the car or the action of the fans), heat is removed from the gas. Now cooled, the gas condenses into a liquid and flows into the receiver/dryer. The receiver/drier stores the liquid refrigerant and absorbs small amounts of moisture which may be present.

Flowing from the receiver, the liquid refrigerant passes through an expansion valve which changes it into a low temperature, low pressure mixture of gas and liquid. This cold and foggy refrigerant flows to the evaporator.

Once in the evaporator, (inside the cabin of the vehicle) the refrigerant is exposed to the warmer air being moved by the blower fan. The refrigerant changes to a gas within the evaporator and absorbs heat from the air being circulated by the fan. After being fully vaporized within the evaporator, the heated refrigerant gas is drawn out of the evaporator to the compressor where the cycle continues.

The efficiency of any air conditioning system is controlled not only by the system itself but by outside factors such as air temperature, humidity, forward speed of the car and amount of sunlight entering the car.

NOTE: *This book contains simple testing and charging procedures for your car's air conditioning system. More comprehensive testing, diagnosis and service procedures may be found in CHILTON'S GUIDE TO AIR CONDITIONING SERVICE AND REPAIR, book number 7580, available at your local retailer.*

SAFETY

There are two particular hazards associated with air conditioning systems and they both relate to the refrigerant gas. The refrigerant (generic designation: R-12, trade name: Freon, a registered trademark of the DuPont Co.) becomes an extremely cold substance. When exposed to air, it will instantly freeze any surface it comes in contact with, including your eyes. The other hazard involves fire. Although normally non-toxic, refrigerant gas becomes highly poisonous in the presence of an open flame. One good whiff of the vapor formed by burning refrigerant can be fatal. Keep all forms of fire (including cigarettes) well clear of the air conditioning system.

NOTE: *R-12 refrigerant is a chlorofluorocarbon (CFC) which, when released into the atmosphere, can contribute to the depletion of the ozone layer in the upper atmosphere. Ozone filters out harmful radiation from the sun. An approved R-12 Recovery/Recycling machine meeting SAE standards must be used when discharging the system. Have the air conditioning system discharged and recharged at an equipped facility.*

SYSTEM CHECKS

A lot of A/C problems can be avoided by simply running the air conditioner at least once a week, regardless of the season. Let the system run for at least 10 minutes a week (even in the winter), and you'll keep the internal parts lubricated as well as preventing the hoses from hardening. Note that the air conditioning can be switched on while the heater is in use. The cooled air is then immediately reheated for in-car comfort; the occupants don't suffer while the A/C system is exercised.

Oil Leaks

Refrigerant leaks show up as oily areas on the components because the compressor oil is transported around the entire system with the refrigerant. Look for oily spots on all the hoses and lines, and especially on the hose and tubing connections. If there are oily deposits, the system may have a leak. A small area of oil on the front of the compressor is normal and no cause for alarm.

Checking the Compressor Belt

The compressor drive belt (air conditioner belt) must be checked periodically for tension and condition. A loose or slipping belt can cause poor cooling or damage to components.

Keep the Condenser Clear

The condenser is mounted in front of the radiator (and is often mistaken for the radiator when viewed from the front of the vehicle). It serves to remove heat from the air conditioning system and cool the refrigerant. Proper air flow through the condenser is critical to the operation of the system. Periodically, inspect the front of the condenser for bent fins or foreign material (dirt, bugs, paper, etc.) If any cooling fins are bent, straighten them carefully with a blunt, soft tool such as a thin piece of wood. You can remove solid debris with a stiff bristle brush (never a wire brush) or the water pressure from a hose.

Checking the Refrigerant Level

The easiest way to check the air conditioning is to turn it on; if cold air is supplied, the system is probably in good order. A properly charged system which is used frequently is not likely to need maintenance. It is not uncommon to find cars several years old running on the original charge in the system. If working properly, the system does not require periodic recharging.

If a problem is suspected, the first order of business when checking the refrigerant is to

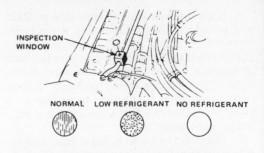

The view through the sight glass gives a rough estimate of the system charge. The glass may appear blank if the system is momentarily off, but cold air will be present at the vents. If the compressor is running, no bubbles should be seen. If the glass is milky or cloudy, have the receiver/dryer checked professionally.

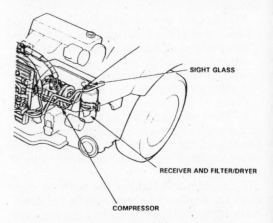

Example of sight glass mounted in the receiver/drier

find the sight glass. It is usually located in the head of the receiver/drier at the left front corner of the engine compartment. Due to the recessed locations of some receive/driers, the glass may be located in its own block, anywhere in the liquid line running to the evaporator. It should be visible by looking at the air conditioning lines running across the engine compartment near the radiator.

Once you've found it, wipe off the small glass window and proceed as follows:

1. With the engine running and the air conditioner switched on inside the vehicle, look for the flow of refrigerant through the sight glass. If the system is working properly, you'll see a continuous flow of clear refrigerant in the sight glass, with perhaps an occasional bubble if the system is operating at high temperatures.

2. Cycle the air conditioner on and off to make sure what you are seeing is refrigerant. Since the fluid is clear, it is possible to mistake a completely discharged system for one that is fully charged. Turn the system off and watch the sight glass; if there is refrigerant in the system, you'll see bubbles during the OFF cycle. If

you see no bubbles when the system is running and cold air is flowing from the air vents inside, the system is OK.

NOTE: *The air conditioning system may turn itself off automatically to prevent the evaporator from freezing. If this happens while you're looking at the sight glass, don't mistake it for a failure. Wait a short while and the system will re-engage.*

3. If you observe bubbles in the sight glass while the system is operating, the system is low on refrigerant. The only reason for this is a leak somewhere; have it checked by a professional. Running the air conditioning with an insufficient charge may damage the compressor.

4. Oil streaks in the sight glass are an indication of trouble. Most of the time, oil will appear as a series of streaks although it may also be a solid stream. In either case, it means reduced cooling and possibly compressor replacement.

Windshield Wipers
REFILL REPLACEMENT

For maximum effectiveness and longest element life, the windshield and wiper blades should be kept clean. Dirt, tree sap, road tar and etc. will cause streaking, smearing and blade deterioration, if left on the glass. It is advisable to wash the windshield carefully with a commercial glass cleaner at least once a month. Wipe off the rubber blades with the wet rag, afterwards.

If the blades are found to be cracked, broken or torn, they should be replaced immediately. Replacement intervals will vary with usage, although ozone deterioration usually limits blade life to about 6 months. If the wiper pattern is smeared, streaked or if the blade chatters across the glass, the elements should be replaced. It is easiest and most sensible to replace the elements in pairs. If the proper source can be found, it is only necessary to replace the rubber blades or inserts; replacing the metal blade holder is not necessary.

1. To replace the blade elements, raise the wiper arm assembly all the way off the glass. It will stay in the upright position. If needed, pivot the blade assembly until it is easier to work on. Removing the blade holder or arm is generally not necessary.

2. Identify the end of the blade with the double tabs; the narrow part between the bulges will be clipped into two holder or fingers at the base of the metal blade holder.

3. Support the wiper assembly with one hand (to avoid bending it) and pull the rubber insert out of the holder with the other hand. The only real force needed is to release the tabs

from the metal fingers. Carefully extract the rubber blade.

NOTE: *Later models use two small metal bars or ribs which fit into the edge of the rubber blade to stiffen it. Do NOT lose or discard these ribs; they do not come with new blades. If the stiffeners are bent or deformed, they may be straightened with gentle pressure.*

4. If stiffening ribs were removed from the old insert, install them into the new insert. They must be correctly placed and completely within the slot before installation.

5. Slide the new insert into the blade holder, making sure that the blade (and ribs) tracks correctly through each set of fingers.

6. After passing the blade through the last holder, align the locking tabs with the first set of fingers. Pop the lock tab through the fingers with a short, sharp tug. A bit of push from the bottom of the blade is also helpful.

7. Check the blade carefully for any part that did not correctly seat in the holders, particularly at the lock tabs. Metal ribs must be fully concealed and inside the holders as well. If anything doesn't look proper, remove the blade and start over.

8. Wash the windshield thoroughly with a quality glass cleaner. Many wiper related problems start on the glass, not on the wiper blade.

9. Pivot the wiper blade into the proper position and lower the arm to the glass.

Tires and Wheels

Common sense and good driving habits will afford maximum tire life. Fast starts, sudden stops and hard cornering are hard on tires and will shorten their useful life span. Make sure that you don't overload the car or run with incorrect ppressure in the tires. Both of these practices increase tread wear.

Inspect your tires frequently. Be especially careful to watch for bubbles in the tread or sidewall, deep cuts or under-inflation. Remove any tires with bubbles in the sidewall. If cuts are so deep that they penetrate to the cords, discard the tire. Any cut in the sidewall of a radial tire renders it unsafe. Also look for uneven tread wear patterns that indicate the front end is out of alignment or that the tires are out of balance.

TIRE ROTATION

Tires must be rotated periodically to equalize wear patterns that vary with a tire's position on the vehicle. Tires will also wear in an uneven way as the front steering/suspension system wears to the point where the alignment should be reset.

Rotating the tires will ensure maximum life for the tires as a set, as you will not have to discard a tire early due to wear on only part of the tread. This is particularly important with a front-wheel drive vehicle. Since the front tires handle all of the traction and turning as well as most of the stopping forces, they will wear noticeably faster than the rears. Regular rotation is required to equalize wear.

The usual rule to follow with radials is to make sure that they always roll in the same direction. This means that a tire used on the left side of the vehicle must not be switched to the right side and vice-versa. If a tire or tires is removed from a running position on the vehicle for a time for use as a spare or because of seasonal use of snow tires, make sure to clearly mark the wheel as to the side of the vehicle it was used on and to observe the mark when reinstalling the tire(s). Some styled or "mag" wheels have the designation on the wheel as well.

NOTE: *The compact or space-saver spare is strictly for emergency use. It must never be included in the tire rotation or placed on the car for everyday use.*

TIRE DESIGN

For maximum satisfaction, tires should be used in sets of four. Mixing of different types (radial, bias-belted, fiberglass belted) should be avoided. All Honda Accords and Preludes come equipped with quality radial tires. Radials should always be selected for replacements.

When radial tires are used, tire sizes and wheel diameters should be selected to maintain ground clearance and tire load capacity equivalent to the original specified tire. Radial tires should always be used in sets of four.

CAUTION: *Radial tires should never be used on only the front axle.*

When selecting tires, pay attention to the original size as marked on the tire. Tires used on Honda products use an industry size code sometimes referred to as P-Metric. This allows the exact identification of the tire specifications, regardless of the manufacturer. If selecting a different tire size or brand, remember to check the installed tire for any sign of interference with the body or suspension while the car is stopping, turning sharply or heavily loaded.

SNOW TIRES

Good radial tires coupled with front wheel drive give Honda products a big advantage in slippery weather, but in snow a street radial tire does not have sufficient tread to provide traction and control. The small grooves of a street tire quickly pack with snow and the tire behaves like a billiard ball on marble floor. The more open, chunky tread of a snow tire will self-

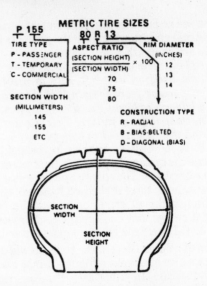

Common (P-Metric) tire coding. A performance code such as H or V may appear before the R; the designation, M + S, may appear at the end to designate a snow or all-season tire

clean as the tire turns, providing much better grip on snowy surfaces.

Snow tires used on Honda vehicles must be of radial construction. To satisfy municipalities requiring snow tires during weather emergencies, most snow tires carry either an M + S designation after the tire size stamped on the sidewall or the designation, All Season. In general, no change in tire size is necessary when buying snow tires. Since Accords and Preludes are all front wheel drive vehicles, the first two snow tires go on the front wheels.

Honda strongly recommends the use of 4 snow tires on their vehicles for reasons of stability. If snow tires are fitted only to the front, the rear end of the car may become very unstable under braking or turning on slippery surfaces. This instability can lead to unpleasant endings if the driver can't counteract the slide in time. Preludes with 4-wheel steering REQUIRE 4 snow tires.

Note that snow tires, whether 2 or 4, will affect vehicle handling in all non-snow situations. The stiffer, heavier snow tires will noticeably change the turning and braking characteristics of the car. Once the snow tires are installed, you must re-learn the behavior of the car and drive accordingly.

CHILTON TIP: *Consider buying extra wheels on which to mount the snow tires. Once done, the "snow wheels" can be installed and removed as needed. This eliminates the potential damage to tires from seasonal removal and installation. Even if your car has styled wheels, see if inexpensive steel wheels are available. Although the look of the car will change, the expensive wheels will be protected from salt, curb hits and pothole damage.*

TIRE STORAGE

Store the tires at proper inflation pressure if they are mounted on wheels. All tires should be kept in a cool, dry place. If they are stored in the garage or basement, do not let them stand on a concrete floor; set them on strips of wood, a mat or a large stack of newspaper. Keeping them away from direct moisture is of paramount importance. Tires should not be stored upright, but in a flat position.

TIRE INFLATION AND TREAD DEPTH

The importance of proper tire inflation cannot be overemphasized. A tire employs air as part of its structure. It is designed around the supporting strength of the air at a specified pressure. For this reason, improper inflation drastically reduces the tires's ability to perform as intended. A tire will lose some sir in day-to-day use; having to add a few pounds of air periodically is not necessarily a sign of a leaking tire.

Two items should be a permanent fixture in every glove compartment: an accurate tire pressure gauge and a tread depth gauge. Check the tire pressure (including the spare) regularly with a pocket type gauge. Too often, the gauge on the end of the air hose at your corner garage is not accurate because it suffers too much abuse. Always check tire pressure when the tires are cold, as pressure increases with temperature. If you must move the car to check the tire inflation, do not drive more than a mile before checking. A cold tire is one that has not been driven for more than three hours.

A plate located on the rear edge of the left door or on the left door post will show the proper pressure for the tires. Never counteract excessive pressure build-up by bleeding off air pressure (letting some air out). This will cause the tire to run hotter and wear quicker.

CAUTION: *Never exceed the maximum tire pressure embossed on the tire! This is the pressure to be used when the tire is at maximum loading, but is rarely the correct pressure for everyday driving. Consult the owner's manual or the tire pressure sticker on the door for the correct tire pressure.*

Once you've maintained the correct tire pressures for several weeks, you'll be familiar with the car's braking and handling personality. Slight adjustments in tire pressures can fine-tune these characteristics, but never change the cold pressure specification by more than 2

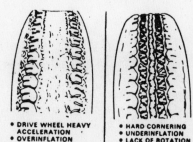

* DRIVE WHEEL HEAVY ACCELERATION
* OVERINFLATION

* HARD CORNERING
* UNDERINFLATION
* LACK OF ROTATION

Examples of inflation-related tire wear patterns. As little as 4 psi under specification can induce premature wear

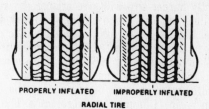

PROPERLY INFLATED   IMPROPERLY INFLATED

RADIAL TIRE

Radial tires have a characteristic sidewall bulge; don't try to measure tire pressure by looking at the tire. Use a quality air gauge

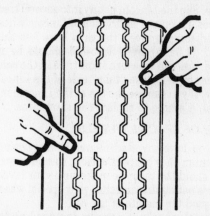

Tread wear indicators will appear when the tire is worn out

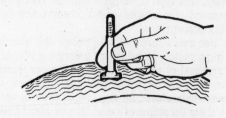

Accurate tread depth indicators are inexpensive and handy

A penny works as well as anything for a quick check of tread depth; when the top of Lincoln's head is visible, it's time for a new tire

psi. A slightly softer tire pressure will give a softer ride but also yield lower fuel mileage. A slightly harder tire will give crisper dry road handling but can cause skidding on wet surfaces. Unless you're fully attuned to the car, stick to the recommended inflation pressures.

All tires made since 1968 have built-in tread wear indicator bars that show up as ½ in. (13mm) wide smooth bands across the tire when 1/16 in. (1.5mm) of tread remains. The appearance of tread wear indicators means that the tires should be replaced. In fact, many states have laws prohibiting the use of tires with less than 1/16 in. (1.5mm) tread.

You can check your own tread depth with an inexpensive gauge or by using a Lincoln head penny. Slip the Lincoln penny into several tread grooves. If you can see the top of Lincoln's head in 2 adjacent grooves, the tires have less than 1/16 in. (1.5mm) tread left and should be replaced. You can measure snow tires in the same manner by using the "tails" side of the Lincoln penny. If you can see the top of the Lincoln memorial, it's time to replace the snow tires.

CARE OF SPECIAL WHEELS

If you have invested money in magnesium, aluminum alloy or sport wheels, special precautions should be taken to make sure your investment is not wasted and that your special wheels look good for the life of the car.

Special wheels are easily damaged and/or scratched. Occasionally check the rims for cracking, impact damage or air leaks. If any of these are found, replace the wheel, In order to prevent this type of damage and the costly replacement of a special wheel, observe the following precautions:
- Use extra care not to damage the wheels during removal, installation, balancing, etc. After removal of the wheels from the car, place them on a mat or other protective surface. If they are to be stored for any length of time, support them on strips of wood. Never store tires and wheels upright — the tread may develop flat spots.

- when driving, watch for hazards; it doesn't take much to crack a wheel.
- When washing, use a mild soap or dish detergent. Avoid cleansers with abrasives or the use of hard brushes. There are many cleaners and polishes for special wheels. Use them.
- If possible, remove the wheels during the winter. Salt and sand used for snow removal can severely damage the finish of a wheel.
- Make certain the recommended lug nut torque is never exceeded or the wheel may crack. Never use snow chains on special wheels; severe scratching will occur.

FLUIDS AND LUBRICANTS

Engine Oil and Fuel Recommendations

ENGINE OIL

Refined Oil

The SAE (Society of Automotive Engineers) grade number indicates the vis cosity of the engine oil; its resistance to flow at a given temperature. The lower the SAE grade number, the lighter the oil. For example, the mono-grade oils begin with SAE 5 weight, which is a thin, light oil, and continue in viscosity up to SAE 80 or 90 weight, which are heavy gear lubricants. These oils are also known as "straight weight", meaning they are of a single viscosity, and do not vary with engine temperature.

Multi-viscosity oils offer the important advantage of being adaptable to temperature extremes. These oils have designations such as 10W-40, 20W-50, etc. The "10W-40" means that in winter (the "W" in the designation) the oil acts like a thin, 10 weight oil, allowing the engine to spin easily when cold and offering rapid lubrication. Once the engine has warmed up, however, the oil acts like a straight 40 weight, maintaining good lubrication and protection for the engine's internal components. A 20W-50 oil would therefore be slightly heavier than and not as ideal in cold weather as the 10W-40, but would offer better protection at higher rpm and temperatures because when warm it acts like a 50 weight oil. Whichever oil viscosity you choose when changing the oil, make sure you are anticipating the temperatures your engine will be operating in until the oil is changed again. Refer to the oil viscosity chart for oil recommendations according to temperature.

NOTE: *Honda does not recommend the use of any oil additive or supplement in the en-*

gine. *A normal engine does not need them; if the engine is worn or damaged, it's usually too late for any benefit.*

The API (American Petroleum Institute) designation indicates the classification of engine oil used under certain given operating conditions. Only oils designated for use "Service SG" should be used. Oils of the SG type perform a variety of functions inside the engine in addition to the basic function as a lubricant. An SG-rated oil may be substituted for SF or SE oils in older vehicles. A new vehicle requiring SG oil may be damaged by using oil with a lesser rating. API labels may also carry other letter ratings such as CD or CC; these oils are acceptable for use as long as the designation SG is also present.

Through a balanced system of metallic detergents and polymeric dispersants, the oil prevents the formation of high and low temperature deposits and also keeps sludge and particles of dirt in suspension. Acids, particularly sulfuric acid, as well as other by-products of combustion, are neutralized. Both the SAE grade number and the API designation can be found on top of the oil can. For recommended oil viscosities, refer to the chart.

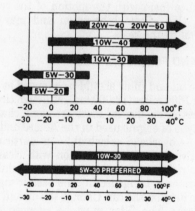

Engine oil viscosity chart. 1984-87 above, 1988-91 below

Synthetic Oil

There are many excellent synthetic oils currently available that can provide better gas mileage, longer service life, and in some cases better engine protection. These benefits do not come without a few hitches, however. The main drawback is the price of synthetic oils, which is three or four times the price per quart of conventional oil.

Synthetic oil is not for every car and every type of driving, so you should consider your engine's condition and your driving situation.

Also, check your vehicle's warranty conditions regarding the use of synthetic oils.

Both brand new engines and older, high mileage engines are the wrong candidates for synthetic oil. The synthetic oils are so slippery that they can prevent the proper break-in of new engines; most oil manufacturers recommend that you wait until the engine is properly broken in (3,000 miles) before using synthetic oil. Older engines with wear have a different problem with synthetics: they "use" (consume during operation) more oil as they age. Slippery synthetic oils get past these worn parts easily. If your engine is "using" conventional oil, it will use synthetics much faster. Also, if your car is leaking oil past old seals you'll have a much greater leak problem with synthetics.

Consider your type of driving. If most of your accumulated mileage is high speed, highway type driving, the more expensive synthetic oils may be a benefit. Extended highway driving gives the engine a chance to warm up, accumulating less acids in the oil and putting less stress on the engine over the long run. Cars with synthetic oils may show increased fuel economy in highway driving, due to less internal friction.

If synthetic oil is used, it should still be replaced at regular intervals as stated in the maintenance schedule. While the oil itself will last much longer than regular oil, pollutants such as soot, water and unburned fuel still accumulate within the oil. These are the damaging elements within a engine and must be drained regularly to prevent damage

Vehicles used under harder circumstances, such as stop-and-go, city type driving, short trips, or extended idling, should be serviced more frequently. For the engines in these cars, the much greater cost of synthetic oils may not be worth the investment. Internal wear increases much quicker, causing greater oil consumption and leakage.

NOTE: *The mixing of conventional and synthetic oils is not recommended. If using synthetic oil, it might be wise to carry two or three quarts with you no matter where you drive, as not all service stations carry this type of lubricant.*

Non-detergent or straight mineral oils must never be used.

FUEL

It is important to use fuel of the proper octane rating in your Honda. Octane rating is based on the quantity of anti-knock compounds added to the fuel and it determines the speed at which the gas will burn. The lower the octane rating, the faster it burns. The higher the octane, the slower the fuel will burn and a greater percentage of compounds in the fuel prevent spark ping (knock), detonation and pre-ignition (dieseling).

As the temperature of the engine increases, the air/fuel mixture exhibits a tendency to ignite before the spark plug is fired. If fuel of an octane rating too low for the engine is used, this will allow combustion to occur before the piston has completed its compression stroke, thereby creating a very high pressure very rapidly.

Fuel of the proper octane rating will slow the combustion process sufficiently to allow the spark plug enough time to ignite the mixture completely and smoothly. The use of super-premium fuel is no substitution for a properly tuned and maintained engine. Chances are that if your engine exhibits any signs of spark ping, detonation or pre-ignition when using regular fuel, the ignition timing should be checked against specifications or the cylinder head should be removed for decarbonizing.

All Accords and Preludes covered by this book are equipped with catalytic converters and must use UNLEADED GASOLINE only. Use of leaded fuel shortens the life of spark plugs, exhaust systems and EGR valves and can damage the catalytic converter. The engines are designed to operate quite efficiently using unleaded gasoline with a minimum rating of 91 octane. Use of unleaded gas with octane ratings lower than 91 can cause persistent spark knock which could lead to engine damage.

Some light spark knock may be noticed when accelerating or driving up hills, particularly with a carbureted engine. The slight knocking may be considered normal (with 91 octane) because the maximum fuel economy is obtained under conditions of minimal knock. Gasoline with an octane rating higher than 91 may be used, but it is not necessary for proper operation of a properly tuned engine.

NOTE: *Your engine's fuel requirement can change with time, mainly due to carbon buildup, which changes the compression ratio. If your engine pings, knocks or runs on, switch first to a different BRAND of fuel, not a higher grade. Each refiner incorporates certain chemicals into the fuel; some engines show a definite preference for one brand or another.*

Engine

OIL LEVEL CHECK

Checking the oil level is one of the simplest and most important checks. It should be done FREQUENTLY because low oil level can lead to engine overheating and eventual starvation of the oil pump. This can mean inadequate lubrication and **immediate, severe** engine dam-

age. Because oil consumption patterns of an engine can change quickly and unexpectedly due to leakage or internal causes, check the oil every time you stop for fuel.

NOTE: *The best time to check the oil is with the engine stone cold. If the engine has been running, allow it to rest for a few minutes until the oil accumulates in the sump, before checking the oil level.*

1. Raise the hood, pull the oil dipstick from the engine and wipe it clean.

2. Insert the dipstick into the engine until it is fully seated, then, remove it and check the reading.

NOTE: *The oil level on all Hondas should register within the crosshatch design on the dipstick or between the two lines or dots, depending on the type of stick.*

3. Oil is added through the capped opening of the rocker arm cover. Do not add oil if the level is significantly above the lower mark on the dipstick. If the level is near or below the lower line, ADD oil but do not overfill. The length covered by the area on the dipstick is roughly equivalent to one quart of oil.

4. If oil has been added, replace the dipstick and recheck the level. It is important to avoid overfilling the crankcase. Doing so will cause the oil to foam with the motion of the crankshaft; this affects lubrication and may also force oil by the seals.

OIL AND FILTER CHANGE

The oil and filter should be changed at least every 7500 miles (12,000 km), although circumstances often dictate more frequent changes. The type of engine used in the Accord and Prelude — overhead camshaft — is particularly sensitive to proper lubrication with clean oil. Don't risk an expensive repair or diminished performance by neglecting the easiest maintenance item on the car. Change the oil and filter regularly. The filter must be changed every time the oil is changed.

CAUTION: *Used engine oil may cause skin cancer if repeatedly left in contact with the skin for prolonged periods. Although this is unlikely unless you handle oil on a daily basis, it is wise to thoroughly wash your hands with soap and water immediately after handling used engine oil.*

● Avoid prolonged skin contract with used engine oil.

● Remove oil from skin by washing thoroughly with soap and water or waterless hand cleaner. Do not use gasoline, thinners or other solvents.

● Avoid prolonged skin contact with oil-soaked clothing.

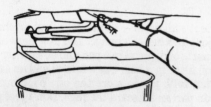

Keep inward pressure on the drain plug while unscrewing it; this will help prevent hot oil running down your hand

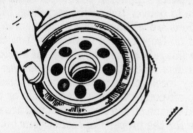

Lubricate the gasket on the new filter with clean engine oil. A dry gasket may not make a good seal and will allow the filter to leak

Install the new oil filter by hand, then snug with the wrench

Add oil through the capped opening in the valve cover

The oil drain plug is located on the bottom, rear of the oil pan (bottom of the engine, underneath the car). The oil plug has a washer on it to seal it to the oil pan. The washer should always be replaced when the oil is drained. Purchase a new washer at the same time you get the filter; if the store tells you they don't have the washer or the washer isn't required, take you business elsewhere.

The oil filter is located on the side of the en-

gine, between the block and the firewall. When purchasing an oil filter, spend the extra dollar or two for a quality part. It must be a Honda filter or its equivalent; not all aftermarket filters meet this specification.

NOTE: *The oil filter cannot be reached or changed without working from below. The car must be elevated, safely supported and the filter removed by reaching up between the block and firewall. Additionally, the space available makes removing the filter with a standard band wrench very difficult. Use of a cap or filter-end wrench is recommended; the tool is inexpensive and available in automotive retail stores.*

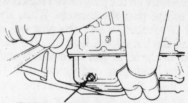

ENGINE OIL DRAIN BOLT

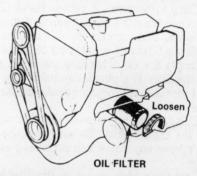

Loosen

OIL FILTER

While the oil drain bolt is very easy to reach, the oil filter can be very difficult because of its location

The mileage figures given are the Honda recommended intervals assuming normal driving and conditions. Normal driving requires that the vehicle be driven far enough to warm up the oil; usually this is about 10 miles or so. If your everyday use is shorter than this (one way), your use qualifies as severe duty.

Severe duty also includes dusty, polluted or off-road conditions, as well as stop-and-go short haul uses. Regularly towing a trailer also puts the car in this category, as does constant operation with a near capacity load. Change the oil and filter at ½ the normal interval. Half of 7500 equals 3750 miles; round it off to the easily remembered 3500 mile interval. For some owners, that may be once a month; for others, it may be six months.

Always drain the oil after the engine has been running long enough to bring it to normal operating temperature. Hot oil will flow easier and more contaminants will be removed along with the oil than if it were drained cold. To change the oil and filter:

1. Run the engine until it reaches normal operating temperature, then shut it off.

2. Jack up the front of the car and support it on safety stands.

3. Slide a drain pan of at least 6 quarts capacity under the oil pan.

CAUTION: *The oil and the engine components will be hot. Take precautions to avoid burns.*

4. Loosen the drain plug with a wrench. Turn the plug out by hand. By keeping an inward pressure on the plug as you unscrew it, oil won't escape past the threads. When the last thread is released, whisk the plug out of the way and the hot oil will flow into the pan.

5. Allow the oil to drain completely and then install the drain plug and tighten it to 45 Nm (33 ft. lbs.). Don't overtighten the plug, or you'll be buying a new pan or a replacement plug for stripped threads.

6. Using a filter wrench, remove the oil filter. Keep in mind that it's holding almost a quart of dirty, hot oil. Make certain the old gasket comes off with the filter and is not stuck to the block.

7. Empty the old filter into the drain pan. Place the filter in a plastic sandwich bag; dispose of the filter at a recycling center or your local gas station.

8. Using a clean rag, wipe off the filter adapter on the engine block. Be sure that the rag doesn't leave any lint which could clog an oil passage.

9. Coat the rubber gasket on the filter with fresh oil. Spin it onto the engine by hand; when the gasket touches the adapter surface give it another ½–¾ turn. No more, or you'll squash the gasket and it will leak.

10. Double check the drain plug; is it in place and snug? Refill the engine with the correct amount of fresh oil. See the "Capacities" chart.

11. Double check everything: Filler cap on? Dipstick in place? Oil drain pan and tools out from under the car? Lower the car to the ground.

12. Check the oil level on the dipstick. It is normal for the level to be a bit above the full mark. Start the engine without using the accelerator and allow it to idle for a few minutes.

CAUTION: *Do not run the engine above idle speed until it has developed oil pressure, indicated when the oil light goes out.*

13. Shut off the engine, allow the oil to drain for a minute, and check the oil level. Check around the filter and drain plug for any leaks, and correct as necessary.

WASTE OIL

So it's all done — either your first oil change or just another oil change. You now have about 5 quarts of dirty oil in a pan and one rather nasty oil filter in a bag. Use a funnel and an empty gallon milk jug to store the oil. Wipe out the drain pan and discard the rags. Don't just pour the oil onto the ground; sooner or later it will show up in somebody's drinking water.

Inquire by phone or in person at your gas station, parts supplier or municipal office about a place to deliver the oil for recycling. Most gas stations are willing to accept small amounts of used oil from regular customers. You can further this relationship by giving the station your business when buying the oil and/or filter. Many local governments have established oil drop-off points within the township or county. Used engine oil is a toxic waste; you are responsible for the proper disposal of your oil.

Manual Transaxles
FLUID RECOMMENDATIONS

All manual transaxles use engine oil — not gear oil — as a lubricant. The oil should meet the same standards as the oil used in the engine, i.e., SG preferred, SE or SF acceptable on 1984–89 vehicles.

Consult the viscosity charts for correct oil selection based on anticipated temperature. The transaxle oil must be changed every 30,000 miles or 3 years, whichever comes first. The level should be inspected once a year routinely or more frequently if leakage is noticed.

LEVEL CHECK

There's no dipstick on the manual transaxle. Fluid must be checked by removing the oil filler bolt on the side of the transaxle. The bolt is located by the right axle at approximately 9 o'clock when viewed over the right fender.

The vehicle must be level. If you're agile enough, the bolt may be removed with the car on the ground by working from the top. Some prefer to check the level from below. If this is the case, not only must the car be elevated and safely supported, it must be elevated and level, meaning installation of 4 jackstands. Just lifting the front yields an improper reading.

Once level, remove the bolt. The fluid level should be just to the bottom of the hole and may be felt with a finger. In the unlikely event that the fluid is low, oil should be added through the inspection hole. Adding oil is tricky since it must be conducted into a horizontal opening. Creative use of funnels and tubing is encouraged. When the oil is up to the correct level, reinstall the bolt and tighten it to 45 Nm

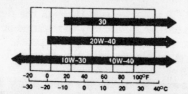

Manual transaxle oil viscosity chart, 1984-91 Accord and Prelude

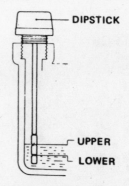

Do not screw in the dipstick to check fluid level

(33 ft. lbs.). Do not overtighten the nut; the penalty is a very expensive transmission case.

DRAIN AND REFILL

The oil drain plug for the manual transaxle is located by and below the right axle. The drain bolt is easily recognized by the round head with a square recess; it does not look like all the other bolts in the transaxle case. Like the engine oil drain bolt, this one also has a washer on it which must be replaced at each change.

1. The car should be at operating temperature before beginning. If possible, drive several miles to warm the transaxle oil before draining.

2. With the engine OFF, raise and support the front of the vehicle. Agility and long arms may allow the job to be done with the car on the ground but it's much easier with the car raised and safely supported.

3. Place a fluid catch pan under the transaxle.

4. Remove the lower drain plug by using a ratchet in the square recess; don't embarrass yourself by trying to grab a round bolt with a pair of pliers. Drain the fluid. Loosening or removing the upper (inspection) bolt will make draining easier.

5. Using a new washer, install the bottom plug and tighten it to 40 Nm (29 ft. lbs.).

6. Refill the transaxle through the inspection hole until the oil just runs out the hole. Reinstall the bolt and tighten it just finger tight.

7. Lower the car to the ground and check that it sits level. Remove the filler bolt and double check the level, topping up if necessary. Reinstall the bolt, tightening it to 45 Nm (33 ft. lbs.)

Automatic Transaxles

FLUID RECOMMENDATIONS

All Honda automatics use Dexron®II automatic transmission fluid (ATF). Only Dexron®II is available today. It replaces straight Dexron® fluid which is the actual recommendation for older models and can be mixed with it.

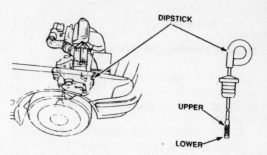

The push-in dipstick must be fully seated to read the fluid level accurately

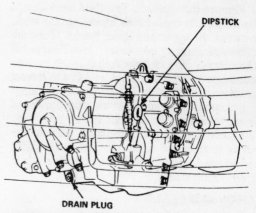

Dipstick and drain plug locations, 1984-89 Accord and all Prelude

LEVEL CHECK

The transaxle fluid should be checked about once a month and replaced after the first 30,000 miles or 2 years, then every 24,000 miles thereafter. The vehicle should be driven several miles to allow the oil to be fully warmed before checking. Before checking the fluid level, make certain the car is parked level with the engine off.

The dipstick is located on the right front of the transaxle housing, near or beneath the battery. The dipstick is either a threaded fit (un-

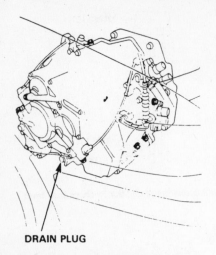

DRAIN PLUG

Drain Plug locations, 1990-91 Accord

screw it) or a small dipstick similar to the engine oil dipstick (pull it out). To check the fluid level, remove the dipstick, wipe it clean and reinsert it.

NOTE: *The threaded dipstick must NOT be rethreaded into the case to check the fluid level. The first part of the threads should just sit on the case. Rethreading the dipstick will yield a false reading.*

Remove the dipstick. The fluid level should be within the cross-hatch marks on the stick, between the upper and lower marks. If the addition of fluid is necessary, add Dexron®II through the dipstick hole. Add only the amount necessary to bring the fluid level to the correct point on the dipstick. Overfilling can damage the transaxle. The space between the upper and lower marks on the dipstick is less than 1 qt. When reinstalling the dipstick, thread the screw-in type and tighten it just finger tight; never use a wrench. Make certain the push-in type is fully seated.

DRAIN AND REFILL

1. The car should be at operating temperature before beginning. If possible, drive several miles to warm the transaxle oil before draining.

2. With the engine OFF, raise and support the front of the vehicle. Agility and long arms may allow the job to be done with the car on the ground but it's much easier with the car raised and safely supported.

3. Place a fluid catch pan under the transaxle.

4. Remove the lower drain plug by using a ratchet in the square recess; don't embarrass yourself by trying to grab a round bolt with a pair of pliers. Drain the fluid.

5. Using a new washer, install the bottom plug and tighten it to 40 Nm (29 ft. lbs.).

6. Refill the transaxle through the dipstick hole. A narrow funnel may be required on later models with the pull-out type dipstick. Check the level frequently with the dipstick. Do not overfill.

7. Lower the car to the ground and check that it sits level. Remove the dipstick and double check the level, topping up if necessary. Reinstall the dipstick securely.

Cooling System

FLUID RECOMMENDATIONS

Use a quality, ethylene-glycol based engine coolant specifically recommended for use with vehicles utilizing aluminum engine parts that are in contact with the coolant. Note that some coolants, although labeled for use in such vehicles, actually may fail to provide effective corrosion protection; if necessary, consult a your dealer or professional mechanic. Honda's engine warranty does not cover engine damage caused by the use of improper coolant.

It is best to buy a top quality product that is known to work effectively under such conditions. Always add coolant mixed with the proper amount of clean water. Never add either water or coolant alone. Mix the coolant at a 50/50 ratio in the amount needed. Consult the chart on the antifreeze container and utilize the proportions recommended for the lowest expected temperatures in your area.

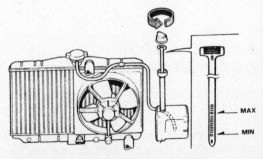

Fill the expansion tank to the MAX line

Some coolant tanks have their own dipsticks

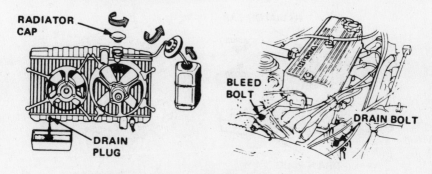

Coolant system drain and fill components — 1985-88 Prelude

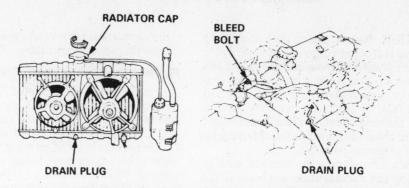

Coolant system drain and fill components — 1986-89 Accord

LEVEL CHECK

CAUTION: *Keep hands and clothing away from the radiator fans. On some vehicles, the fans may start automatically up to 15 minutes after the engine is shut OFF!*

WARNING: *Housepets and small animals are attracted to the odor and taste of engine coolant (antifreeze). It is a highly poisonous mixture of chemicals; special care must be taken to protect open containers and spillage.*

The coolant level should be checked with the engine at normal operating temperature. To check the coolant level, simply see if the coolant is up to the **FULL** line on the expansion tank. On newer cars, with the expansion tank buried in the front fender well, lift the lid of the tank and remove the plastic dipstick. Wipe it off and check the coolant level as you would check oil. The radiator cap should be removed only for the purpose of cleaning or draining the system.

Add coolant to the expansion tank if the level is low, being sure to mix it with clean water. Never add cold water or coolant to a hot engine as damage to both the cooling system and the engine could result. If any coolant mixture should spill or splash onto painted surfaces, rinse it off immediately with plenty of clean water. The coolant will damage the paint.

CAUTION: *The cooling system is under pressure when hot. Removing the radiator cap when the engine is warm or overheated will cause coolant to spill or spray out, possibly causing serious burns! The system should be allowed to cool for a period of hours before attempting removal of the radiator cap or hoses.*

DRAIN AND REFILL

The radiator coolant should be changed at 36 months or 45,000 miles whichever comes first; thereafter, replace every 24 months or 30,000 miles. Perform this maintenance only on a cold engine; overnight cold is best to avoid scalds.

1. Remove the radiator cap. Just turn it, don't press down on it.

2. Slide a fluid catch pan under the radiator. Loosen the draincock at the base of the radiator and drain the radiator. Honda engines are equipped with a drain bolt in the block as well, but these can be difficult to get to. The drain is either under the exhaust manifold or above the oil filter; in either case, getting it loose almost always requires working from under the engine.

An alternate method is to disconnect the lower radiator hose from the radiator.

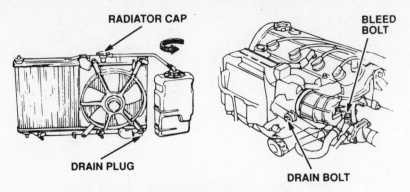

Coolant system drain and fill components — 1990-91 Accord

CAUTION: *When draining the coolant, keep in mind that cat and dogs are attracted by the ethylene glycol antifreeze, and are quite likely to drink any that is left in an uncovered container or in puddles on the ground. This will prove fatal in sufficient quantity. Always drain the coolant into a sealable container. Coolant should be reused unless it is contaminated or several years old.*

3. Drain the coolant in the reservoir tank by unclipping and disconnecting the hose. If the tank is buried in the fender well, use a mechanical siphon or suction tool such as a turkey baster to draw out the fluid.

4. Mix a solution of 50% ethylene glycol (designed for use in aluminum engines) and 50% clean water. Use a stronger solution, as specified on the antifreeze container if the climate in your area demands it. Tighten the drain bolt(s) and double check them. Reinstall the lower radiator hose if it was disconnected.

5. Loosen the cooling system bleed bolt on the top of the thermostat housing. Fill the radiator with the coolant mixture. When coolant flows out of the bleed port in a steady stream without air bubbles, close the bolt and refill the radiator with coolant up to the base of the neck.

6. To purge any air trapped in other parts of the cooling system, leave the radiator cap off and set the heater control to **Hot**. Start the engine and allow it to reach normal operating temperature; this means that the temperature gauge is in the normal range and the radiator fan has cycled on at least twice.

7. When the engine reaches normal operating temperatures, top off the radiator and keep checking until the level stabilizes; refill the coolant reservoir to the **Full** mark and make sure that the radiator cap is properly tightened.

NOTE: *Fresh antifreeze has a cleansing effect in the passages. If the coolant has not been changed on schedule, the new coolant may dislodge sludge within the system. If the*

discoloration is extreme, the system may need to be drained a second time.

FLUSHING AND CLEANING THE SYSTEM

1. Refer to the "Thermostat, Removal and Installation" procedures in Chapter 3 and remove the thermostat from the engine.

2. Using a water hose, force fresh water into the thermostat housing opening, allowing the water to back-flush into the engine, heater and radiator. Flush the system until the water flowing from the radiator hose is clear.

3. After cleaning, reverse the removal procedures. Refill the cooling system with fresh coolant.

Brake Master Cylinder
FLUID RECOMMENDATIONS

Use only DOT 3 or DOT 4 specification brake fluid from a tightly sealed container. If you are unsure of the condition of the fluid (whether or not it has been tightly sealed), use new fluid rather than taking a chance of introducing moisture into the system. It is critically important that the fluid meet the specification so the heat generated by modern disc brakes will not cause it to boil and reduce braking performance. Fluid must be moisture-free for the same reason.

LEVEL CHECK

The brake master cylinder fluid level should be checked every few weeks for indication of leaks or low fluid level. A sudden drop in fluid level may indicate a fluid leak in the system. The reservoir is located at the left rear of the engine compartment at the firewall. The reservoir is made of translucent plastic; the fluid level may be checked from the outside.

NOTE: *The normal wear of the brake pads and shoes will cause a gradual drop in the fluid level. The fluid is not missing; it is just*

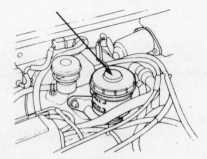

Typical brake master cylinder reservoir

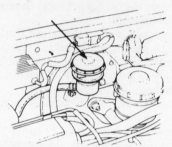

Clutch fluid reservoir for 1991 Prelude; all are similar

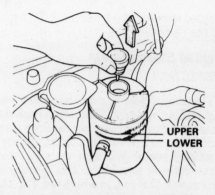

UPPER
LOWER

This power steering reservoir is on the right side; earlier models place it in the equivalent location on the left

relocated within the system. If the fluid has been dropping gradually, check the front brakes before refilling the fluid. If the system is refilled before new brakes are installed, the reservoir will overflow.

On all Hondas there is a MAX and MIN line on the brake fluid reservoir. The brake fluid should always be maintained at the MAX line, but not above it. The reservoir cap has an arrow on it which must always point to the front of the car when installed. When adding brake fluid, the following precautions should be observed:

1. Use only recommended brake fluid: DOT 3 or DOT 4; SAE J 1703b HD type.

2. Never reuse brake fluid and never use fluid that is dirty, cloudy or has air bubbles.

3. Store brake fluid in a clean dry place in the original container. Cap tightly and do not puncture a breather hole in the container.

4. Carefully remove any dirt from around the master cylinder reservoir cap before opening.

5. Take special care not to spill the fluid. The painted surface of the vehicle will be damaged by brake fluid.

CLUTCH FLUID

Manual transmissions in 1990–91 Accords and 1988–91 Preludes use a hydraulic clutch actuation system. When the clutch pedal is pushed to the floor, fluid is compressed and the clutch is activated. Other vehicles use a cable-actuated clutch.

The clutch fluid reservoir is located in the same area as the brake master cylinder reservoir. The clutch reservoir may not be as easily seen as it is smaller and sometimes lower on the firewall. The system uses brake fluid and is checked and filled in the same fashion as the brake fluid reservoir. Always wipe off the cover of the reservoir before removing it. The clutch reservoir may require periodic topping off to compensate for clutch wear.

Power Steering Pump
FLUID RECOMMENDATIONS

Only genuine Honda power steering fluid may be used when adding fluid. Honda states that ATF or fluids manufactured for use in other brands of vehicles are not compatible with the Honda power steering system. The use of any other fluid will cause the seals to swell and create leaks. Honda's proprietary fluid is not generally available in retail outlets; purchase a can of fluid at your dealer and keep it stored until needed.

LEVEL CHECK

The fluid in the power steering reservoir should be checked every few weeks for indications of leaks or low fluid level. The fluid is not routinely changed. If necessary to drain the fluid during repairs, the fluid may be reused if not contaminated by system failure or a dirty container.

The power steering fluid reservoir is located at either the left or right front of the engine compartment, just behind the headlight area. Check the fluid with the engine cold and the vehicle parked on a level spot. View the level through the side of the reservoir. The level should be between the upper and lower marks. Fluid need not be added right away unless it has dropped almost to the lower mark. Do not over-fill the reservoir.

Manual Steering gear

INSPECTION

The manual steering used on Hondas is of the rack and pinion design. This unit is packed with grease and therefore does not require a periodic fluid level check. However, inspect the box and associated rubber boot-type seals for obvious grease leaks or torn boots. This is easily done whenever the car is elevated for other maintenance.

Chassis Greasing

All the suspension fittings on the Hondas covered by this guide are permanently lubricated. However, at the time when the steering box is inspected for grease leakage, inspect the suspension and steering joints for grease leakage and/or torn rubber boots and make repairs as necessary.

Body Lubrication

Lubricate all locks and hinges with multipurpose grease every 6000 miles or 6 months. Make this easy maintenance part of every oil change. Pay particular attention to the hinges and latches which don't get a lot of use — they are the ones that will bind with age.

Rear Wheel Bearings

To check the wheel bearings for basic problems, jack up each wheel to clear the ground. Hold the wheel and shake it to check the bearings for any play. Also rotate the wheel to check for any roughness. If any play is felt or there is noticeable roughness, the bearing may have to be replaced.

NOTE: *Over tightening the spindle nuts will cause excessive bearing friction and will result in rough wheel rotation and eventual bearing failure. Therefore, follow the procedures given in Chapter 8 exactly, using the proper procedures and tools.*

CLEANING AND REPACKING

Only the 1984–85 Accord and 1984–87 Prelude use rear wheel bearings which can be serviced. All other rear bearings — and all front wheel bearings — are sealed. The sealed bearings are considered life-of-the-car components and are replaced only in the event of mechanical failure. Replacing the pressed-in bearings is discussed in Chapter 7.

CAUTION: *Servicing the wheel bearings exposes the brake shoes or pads. Brake pads and shoes contain asbestos, which has been* determined to be a cancer causing agent. Never clean the brake surfaces with compressed air. Avoid inhaling any dust from brake surfaces. When cleaning brakes, use commercially available brake cleaning fluids. Avoid getting any grease on the brake surfaces.

Prelude (1984-87)

NOTE: *A torque wrench is REQUIRED for this procedure.*

1. Slightly loosen the rear wheel lug nuts. Raise and support the rear of the vehicle.
2. Release the parking brake. Remove the rear wheel assembly.
3. If equipped, remove the caliper shield. Disconnect the parking brake cable from the caliper. Remove the caliper-to-bracket bolts and suspend the caliper on a wire; do not disconnect the brake hose.
4. Remove the caliper bracket mounting bolts and the bracket.
5. Remove the grease cap, the cotter pin, the castle nut, the spindle nut, the thrust washer and the outer bearing. Pull the rear disc assembly from the spindle.
6. Using a hammer and a drift punch, drive the outer bearing race from the hub of the disc.

NOTE: *When removing the bearing races, use a criss-cross pattern to avoid cocking the race in the hub bore.*

7. Turn the hub over and drive the inner bearing race and grease seal from the hub; discard the grease seal.
8. Using solvent, clean the bearings, races and the hub. Allow the components to air dry; never use compressed air to dry the bearing.
9. Using a bearing driver tool of the correct size, such as Honda tool 07749–0010000 and driver attachment tool 07946–6920100 or their equivalents, drive the bearing races evenly into the hub until they seat against the shoulders.
10. Using Multipurpose grease, pack the wheel hub and the wheel bearings. The bearings must be completely and thoroughly packed. Lightly coat the lips of the grease seal. Install the inner bearing into the hub.
11. Using a mallet, tap a new grease seal (using a criss-cross method) into the rear of the hub until it is flush with it.
12. To install the hub, fit the outer bearing into the disc. Holding the bearing loosely in place with a thumb, reinstall the disc and bearings onto the hub.
13. Assemble and install the bearing washer and the spindle nut. Tighten the spindle nut just finger tight.
14. Using the torque wrench, adjust the spindle nut as follows:
    a. Tighten the spindle nut to 25 Nm (18 ft.

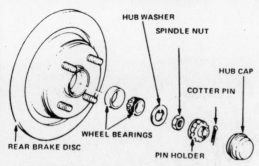

1984-87 Prelude rear wheel bearing components

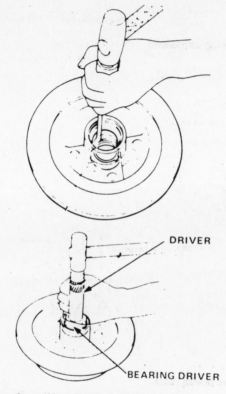

Removing and installing Prelude bearing races

lbs.). Rotate the brake disc two or three rotations. Retighten the spindle nut. Continue this rotating and tightening process until the spindle nut stays at 25 Nm (18 ft. lbs.) after the disc is rotated.

b. Loosen the spindle nut just to 0. The nut should just break free, but not be turned more than needed.

c. Tighten the nut to 5.5 Nm (4 ft. lbs.)

d. Install the castle nut and align a slot with the hole in the spindle.

NOTE: *If the cotter pin holes do not align, try removing the castle nut and reinstalling it after a slight rotation. If the holes still don't*

align, tighten the spindle nut slightly until they do.*

e. Using a new cotter pin, install it through the holes in the castle nut and axle.

15. To complete the installation, fill the grease cap with multi-purpose grease and install it on the disc. Make certain it is firmly and evenly seated.

16. Install the caliper bracket mounting bolts and the bracket. Tighten the caliper bracket mounting bolts to 38 Nm (28 ft. lbs).

17. Install the caliper and brake pads. Tighten the caliper-to-bracket bolts to 23 Nm (17 ft. lbs.).

18. Reconnect the parking brake cable to the caliper.

19. Install the caliper shield if it was removed.

20. Install the wheel and tighten the lug nuts evenly.

1984–87 Accord

NOTE: *A torque wrench is REQUIRED for this procedure.*

1. Slightly loosen the rear wheel lug nuts. Raise and support the rear of the vehicle.

2. Release the parking brake. Remove the rear wheel assembly.

3. Remove the grease cap, the cotter pin, the castle nut, the spindle nut, the thrust washer and the outer bearing. Pull the rear drum assembly from the spindle.

4. Remove the inner grease seal, then remove the inner bearing.

5. Using a hammer and a drift punch, drive the outer bearing race from the drum.

NOTE: *When removing the bearing races, use a criss-cross pattern to avoid cocking the race in the hub bore.*

7. Turn the drum over and drive the inner bearing race and from the hub; discard the grease seal.

8. Using solvent, clean the bearings, races and the inner or hub area of the drum. Allow the components to air dry; never use compressed air to dry the bearing.

9. Using a bearing driver tool of the correct size, such as Honda tool 07749–0010000 and driver attachment tool 07947–67101000 or their equivalents, drive the bearing races evenly into the hub until they seat against the shoulders.

10. Using Multipurpose grease, pack the wheel hub and the wheel bearings. The bearings must be completely and thoroughly packed. Lightly coat the lips of the grease seal. Install the inner bearing into the hub.

11. Using a mallet, tap a new grease seal (using a criss-cross method) into the rear of the hub until it is flush with it.

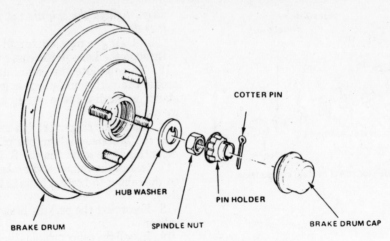

1984-85 Accord rear wheel bearing components

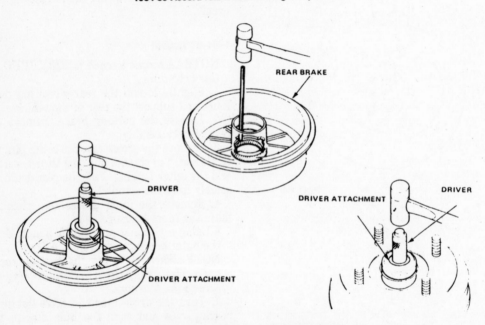

Removing and Installing Accord bearing races

12. To install the hub, fit the outer bearing into the drum. Holding the bearing loosely in place with a thumb, reinstall the drum and bearings onto the hub.

13. Assemble and install the bearing washer and the spindle nut. Tighten the spindle nut just finger tight.

14. Using the torque wrench, adjust the spindle nut as follows:

a. Tighten the spindle nut to 25 Nm (18 ft. lbs.). Rotate the brake drum two or three rotations.

b. Loosen the spindle nut just to 0. The nut should just break free, but not be turned more than needed.

c. Tighten the nut to 5.5 Nm (4 ft. lbs.)

d. Install the castle nut and align a slot with the hole in the spindle.

NOTE: *If the cotter pin holes do not align, try removing the castle nut and reinstalling it after a slight rotation. If the holes still don't align, tighten the spindle nut slightly until they do.*

e. Using a new cotter pin, install it through the holes in the castle nut and axle.

13. To complete the installation, fill the grease cap with multi-purpose grease and install it on the disc. Make certain it is firmly and evenly seated.

14. Install the wheel. Hand tighten the lug nuts.

15. Lower the car to the ground and tighten the lug nuts evenly.

TRAILER TOWING

General Recommendations

Honda does not recommend that 1984–88 vehicles tow any type of trailer. Your car was primarily designed to carry passengers and cargo. Towing a trailer will place additional loads on your vehicle's engine, drive train, steering, braking and other systems.

1989–91 Accords and Preludes may tow trailers subject to the following rules. All rules must be met for safe towing:

• Do not tow a trailer during the 600 mile break-in period.

• The weight of the trailer and its cargo cannot exceed 1000 lbs. (450 kg).

• The Gross Vehicle Weight must not exceed the Gross Vehicle Weight Rating (GVWR) shown on the certification label inside the left door. The gross weight of the vehicle is the grand total of vehicle, passengers, luggage and loaded trailer.

• The maximum trailer tongue load or weight is 100 lbs. (45 kg). If a smaller trailer is being used, tongue weight should be approximately 10% of trailer weight. This is usually achieved by loading the trailer with about 60% of the weight forward of the trailer axle.

• the total weight supported by each axle must not exceed the gross Axle Weight Rating shown on the certification label. This requires that the load – passengers, cargo and trailer – be evenly distributed within the car.

• Electric trailer brakes are recommended for all but the smallest trailers. Never tap the car's hydraulic brake system for trailer brakes. Consult a reputable recreational vehicle dealer for information on electric brake controllers.

• All trailers must be secured to the tow vehicle by safety chains as well as the hitch.

Local laws may require specific equipment such as fender mounted mirrors. Check your state or provincial laws.

Trailer Hitches

The hitch should be appropriate for the type of trailer being towed. The most common is the familiar ball hitch although receiver hitches are sometimes found on Honda vehicles. Honda does not provide hitches at the time of purchase; they must be purchased and installed separately. The hitch mounts must be securely attached to the body of the car. Never use a

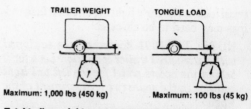

Maximum: 1,000 lbs (450 kg)   Maximum: 100 lbs (45 kg)

Total trailer weight must not exceed 1000 lbs.; tongue weight must not exceed 100 lbs.

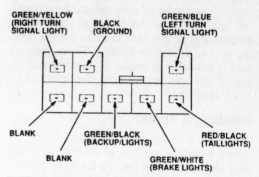

Trailer connector, 1991 Accord Wagon

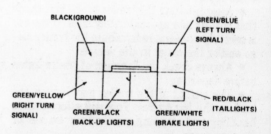

Trailer connector, 1991 Accord and Accord Coupe

hitch attached only to the bumper and never use a hitch designed for temporary use.

When you've determined the hitch that you'll need, follow the manufacturer's installation instructions exactly, especially when it comes to fastener torques. The hitch will subjected to a lot of stress and good hitches come with hardened bolts. Never substitute an inferior bolt for a hardened bolt.

Trailer Lighting

Trailer lighting ranges from primitive to sophisticated depending on the unit. The smallest trailers still require stop and turn lighting; a modern camping trailer may have side markers, reverse lights and separate turn signals.

The trailer wiring connections must be made by a competent automotive electrician. A poor or incorrect job can damage the lighting system or render it inoperative. Remember that when properly connected, the trailer lamps add electrical load to the car's lighting circuits; fuse ratings may need to be checked.

NOTE: *The 1991 Accord comes equipped with a pre-wired trailer connector. Look for it behind the access panel for the left tail light bulbs or in the spare tire compartment of the Wagon.*

All Accords and Preludes use separate-function turn signals; the amber lamps operate separately from the red stop and tail lamps. Most trailers use combined stop, tail and turn signals (all red, one bulb). An electrical converter or adapter will be required to make the car lighting control the trailer lighting. These units are readily available at trailer or camping outlets. Install the unit according to the manufacturer's instructions.

Handling A Trailer

Towing a trailer with ease and safety requires a certain amount of experience. It's a good idea to learn the feel of a trailer by practicing turning, stopping and backing in an open area such as an empty parking lot. Observe these rules:

- After hitching the trailer to the car, check that the car sits approximately level. If the car is severely nose-up, redistribute the trailer cargo and/or the cargo in the vehicle.
- Always check the function of trailer lights before departing.
- The weight of the trailer may lighten the load on the front tires. This will affect vehicle handling and stopping, particularly on wet or slippery roads.
- Allow for much greater stopping distances when towing.
- Drive smoothly. Jerky starts and hard stops increase wear and may cause handling problems.
- Avoid any sudden or sharp maneuvers. Allow for wider turning radius.
- Crosswinds and turbulence from larger vehicles will cause your car and trailer to become unstable. Be prepared.
- Maintain vehicle and trailer tire pressures at the proper inflation at all times.

- Any problems or changes in vehicle feel while towing will be magnified greatly in foul weather. Slow down.
- Passing requires considerable time and distance due to the length and weight of the trailer. Plan ahead.
- Backing up accurately with a trailer must be learned. Practice with the trailer in a remote area before the skill is needed.
- Use the mirrors frequently to check oncoming traffic as well as status of the trailer.
- If the trailer begins to sway, DON'T make any sudden changes in speed. Depending on traffic, very gradual acceleration or deceleration will bring the trailer into line. A sudden change may cause the trailer to jackknife.

PUSHING AND TOWING

If an Accord or Prelude must be towed, use of a flat-bed or rollback is the first choice. This type of truck transports the car completely off the ground so the risk of damage is greatly reduced. If this is not available, a wheel-lift truck which can lift the car by the front tires (not the axles) is recommended. The classic tow truck with boom and winch can be used, but great care must be taken to prevent damage to drive axles and front body panels.

If your Honda's rear wheels are operable, you can tow your vehicle with the rear wheels on the ground. Due to its front wheel drive, the Honda is a relatively easy vehicle to tow with the front wheels up. Before doing so, you should release the parking brake.

If the rear axle is defective, the vehicle must then be transported on a flat bed. Towing the vehicle with the front wheels on the ground may cause damage to the driveline and/or transmissions. A vehicle with an automatic transmission must NEVER be towed with the front wheels on the ground.

JUMP STARTING A DEAD BATTERY

The chemical reaction in a battery produces explosive hydrogen gas. This is the safe way to jump start a dead battery, reducing the chances of an accidental spark that could cause an explosion.

Jump Starting Precautions

1. Be sure both batteries are of the same voltage.
2. Be sure both batteries are of the same polarity (have the same grounded terminal).
3. Be sure the vehicles are not touching.
4. Be sure the vent cap holes are not obstructed.
5. Do not smoke or allow sparks around the battery.
6. In cold weather, check for frozen electrolyte in the battery. Do not jump start a frozen battery.
7. Do not allow electrolyte on your skin or clothing.
8. Be sure the electrolyte is not frozen.

CAUTION: *Make certain that the ignition key, in the vehicle with the dead battery, is in the OFF position. Connecting cables to vehicles with on-board computers will result in computer destruction if the key is not in the OFF position.*

Jump Starting Procedure

1. Determine voltages of the two batteries; they must be the same.
2. Bring the starting vehicle close (they must not touch) so that the batteries can be reached easily.
3. Turn off all accessories and both engines. Put both cars in Neutral or Park and set the handbrake.
4. Cover the cell caps with a rag—do not cover terminals.
5. If the terminals on the run-down battery are heavily corroded, clean them.
6. Identify the positive and negative posts on both batteries and connect the cables in the order shown.
7. Start the engine of the starting vehicle and run it at fast idle. Try to start the car with the dead battery. Crank it for no more than 10 seconds at a time and let it cool off for 20 seconds in between tries.
8. If it doesn't start in 3 tries, there is something else wrong.
9. Disconnect the cables in the reverse order.
10. Replace the cell covers and dispose of the rags.

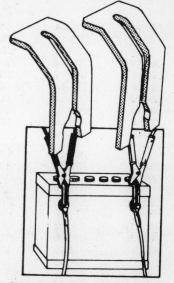

Side terminal batteries occasionally pose a problem when connecting jumper cables. There frequently isn't enough room to clamp the cables without touching sheet metal. Side terminal adaptors are available to alleviate this problem and should be removed after use.

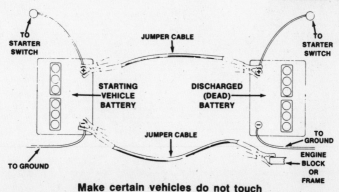

Make certain vehicles do not touch

This hook-up for negative ground cars only

Tire Size Comparison Chart

"Letter" sizes			Inch Sizes	Metric-inch Sizes		
"60 Series"	"70 Series"	"78 Series"	1965–77	"60 Series"	"70 Series"	"80 Series"
		Y78-12	5.50-12, 5.60-12	165/60-12	165/70-12	155-12
			6.00-12			
		W78-13	5.20-13	165/60-13	145/70-13	135-13
		Y78-13	5.60-13	175/60-13	155/70-13	145-13
			6.15-13	185/60-13	165/70-13	155-13, P155/80-13
A60-13	A70-13	A78-13	6.40-13	195/60-13	175/70-13	165-13
B60-13	B70-13	B78-13	6.70-13	205/60-13	185/70-13	175-13
			6.90-13			
C60-13	C70-13	C78-13	7.00-13	215/60-13	195/70-13	185-13
D60-13	D70-13	D78-13	7.25-13			
E60-13	E70-13	E78-13	7.75-13			195-13
			5.20-14	165/60-14	145/70-14	135-14
			5.60-14	175/60-14	155/70-14	145-14
			5.90-14			
A60-14	A70-14	A78-14	6.15-14	185/60-14	165/70-14	155-14
	B70-14	B78-14	6.45-14	195/60-14	175/70-14	165-14
	C70-14	C78-14	6.95-14	205/60-14	185/70-14	175-14
D60-14	D70-14	D78-14				
E60-14	E70-14	E78-14	7.35-14	215/60-14	195/70-14	185-14
F60-14	F70-14	F78-14, F83-14	7.75-14	225/60-14	200/70-14	195-14
G60-14	G70-14	G77-14, G78-14	8.25-14	235/60-14	205/70-14	205-14
H60-14	H70-14	H78-14	8.55-14	245/60-14	215/70-14	215-14
J60-14	J70-14	J78-14	8.85-14	255/60-14	225/70-14	225-14
L60-14	L70-14		9.15-14	265/60-14	235/70-14	
	A70-15	A78-15	5.60-15	185/60-15	165/70-15	155-15
B60-15	B70-15	B78-15	6.35-15	195/60-15	175/70-15	165-15
C60-15	C70-15	C78-15	6.85-15	205/60-15	185/70-15	175-15
	D70-15	D78-15				
E60-15	E70-15	E78-15	7.35-15	215/60-15	195/70-15	185-15
F60-15	F70-15	F78-15	7.75-15	225/60-15	205/70-15	195-15
G60-15	G70-15	G78-15	8.15-15/8.25-15	235/60-15	215/70-15	205-15
H60-15	H70-15	H78-15	8.45-15/8.55-15	245/60-15	225/70-15	215-15
J60-15	J70-15	J78-15	8.85-15/8.90-15	255/60-15	235/70-15	225-15
	K70-15		9.00-15	265/60-15	245/70-15	230-15
L60-15	L70-15	L78-15, L84-15	9.15-15			235-15
	M70-15	M78-15				255-15
		N78-15				

Note: Every size tire is not listed and many size comparisons are approximate, based on load ratings. Wider tires than those supplied new with the vehicle, should always be checked for clearance.

JACKING

Your Honda comes equipped with a scissor jack. This jack is fine for changing a flat tire or other operations not requiring you to go beneath the vehicle. There are four lifting points where this jack may be used: one behind each front wheel well and one in front of each rear wheel well in reinforced sheet metal brackets beneath the rocker panels.

A more convenient way of jacking is the use of a garage or floor jack. You may use the floor jack beneath any of the four scissors jacking points or you can raise the entire front of the vehicle using the front crossmember. On some models, the rear of the vehicle may be jacked beneath the center of the rear axle beam.

Never place the jack under the radiator, engine or transmission components. Severe and expensive damage will result when the jack is raised. Additionally, never jack under the floorpan or bodywork; the metal will deform.

The following safety points cannot be overemphasized:

- Always block the opposite wheel or wheels to keep the vehicle from rolling off the jack.
- When raising the front of the vehicle, firmly apply the parking brake.
- Always use jack stands to support the vehicle when you are working underneath. Place the stands beneath the scissors jacking brackets. Before climbing underneath, rock the vehicle a bit to make sure it is firmly supported.

Jacking points for all Accords and Preludes are located at reinforced points in the left and right rocker panels

CAPACITIES

Year	Model	Engine Displacement (cc)	Engine Crankcase With Filter	Transmission (pts.) 5-Spd	Transmission (pts.) Auto. ①	Fuel Tank (gal.)	Cooling System (qts.)
1984	Accord	1829	3.7	5.0	6.0	15.8	6.4
	Prelude	1829	3.7	5.0	5.8	15.9	6.3②
1985	Accord	1829	3.7	5.0	6.0	15.8	6.4
	Prelude	1829	3.7	5.0	5.8	15.9	6.3②
1986	Accord	1955	3.7	5.0	5.2	15.9	5.2③
	Prelude	1829 1955	3.7	5.0	5.8	15.9	6.3②
1987	Accord	1955	3.7	5.0	5.2	15.9	5.2③
	Prelude	1829 1955	3.7	5.0	5.8	15.9	6.3②
1988	Accord	1955	3.7	5.0	6.0	15.9	5.8
	Prelude	1955	4.1	4.0	6.0	15.9	8.2
1989	Accord	1955	3.7	5.0	5.0	15.9	5.2③
	Prelude	1955	4.0	4.0	12.5	15.9	4.7④⑤
	Prelude Si	1955	4.0	4.0	12.5	15.9	5.4⑤⑥
1990	Accord	2156	4.0	4.0	5.0	17.0	7.0⑧
	Prelude	1958	4.0	4.5	6.0	15.9	5.6⑦
	Prelude Si	2056	4.0	4.5	6.0	15.9	6.4
1991	Accord	2156	4.0	4.0	5.0	17.0	7.0⑧
	Prelude	1958	4.0	4.5	6.0	15.9	5.6⑦
	Prelude Si	2056	4.0	4.5	6.0	15.9	6.4

① Does not include torque converter.
② Auto. Trans.: 7.1
③ Auto. Trans.: 5.8
④ Auto. Trans.: 5.4
⑤ Plus ¾ qt. for reserve tank
⑥ Auto. Trans.: 5.7
⑦ Auto. Trans.: 6.5
⑧ Auto. Trans.: 7.5

MAINTENANCE INTERVALS

Intervals are maximum allowable. Cars in severe duty use (such as cold weather, stop-and-go, short trip, constant towing, or heavy loads) require more frequent service and oil changes. Severe conditions require oil changes at 3500 miles or 3 month intervals.

Perform maintenance by mileage or time, whichever occurs first.

		Accord		Prelude		Notes
		1000 Miles	Years	1000 Miles	Years	
Replace engine oil & filter*		7.5	1/2	7.5	1/2	*3500 miles or 3 mos. in severe duty
Replace transmission oil	Manual	30	2	30	2	
	Automatic	15-45-75	1-3-5	15-45-75	1-3-5	
Replace engine coolant		45*	3	45*	3	*Then every 2 years or 30,000 miles
Replace air filter element		15*	1	30	2	*1990–91 Accord 30,000 miles or 2 yr.
Replace fuel filter(s)		60	5	60	5	
Replace spark plugs		30	2	30	2	
Replace distributor cap & rotor		30*	2	30*	2	* —Inspect— Replace if worn
Replace brake fluid		30	2	30	2	
Inspect front & rear brake linings		7.5	1/2	7.5	1/2	
Check wheel alignment		15	1	15*	1	*Front & rear alignment on 4ws
Clean & repack rear wheel bearings* (Perform every 30,000 miles or 2 years in areas of snow, sand, dust or salt water)		60	4	60	4	*84–85 Accord and 84–87 Prelude only
Check & adjust belt tension		30	2	30	2	
Inspect & adjust valve clearance		15	1	15	1	
Check & adjust clutch		7.5	1/2	7.5	1/2	
Check & adjust parking brake		15	1	15	1	

Engine Performance and Tune-Up

2

GASOLINE ENGINE TUNE-UP SPECIFICATIONS

Year	Model	Engine Displacement cu. in. (cc)	Spark Plugs Gap (in.)	Ignition Timing (deg.) MT	Ignition Timing (deg.) AT	Fuel Pump (psi)	Idle Speed (rpm) MT	Idle Speed (rpm) AT	Valve Clearance In.	Valve Clearance Ex.
1984	Accord	111.6 (1829)	0.042	22B	18B	2.5	700–800	650–750	0.005–0.007	0.010–0.012
	Prelude	111.6 (1829)	0.042	20B	12B	2.5	750–850	750–850	0.005–0.007	0.010–0.012
1985	Accord	111.6 (1829)	0.042	22B ①	18B	2.5	700–800	650–750	0.005–0.007	0.010–0.012
	Accord SE-i	111.6 (1829)	0.042	18B	18B	35	700–800	700–800	0.005–0.007	0.010–0.012
	Prelude	111.6 (1829)	0.042	20B	12B	2.5	750–850	750–850	0.005–0.007	0.010–0.012
1986	Accord	119.3 (1955)	0.042	24B ②	15B	3.0	700–800	650–750	0.005–0.009	0.010–0.012
	Accord LX-i	119.3 (1955)	0.042	15B	15B	35	700–800	700–800	0.005–0.007	0.010–0.012
	Prelude	111.6 (1829)	0.042	20B	12B	2.5	750–850	750–850	0.005–0.007	0.010–0.012
	Prelude Si	119.3 (1955)	0.042	15B	15B	35	700–800	700–800	0.005–0.007	0.010–0.012
1987	Accord	119.3 (1955)	0.042	24B ②	15B	3.0	700–800	650–750	0.005–0.007	0.010–0.012
	Accord LX-i	119.3 (1955)	0.042	15B	15B	35	700–800	700–800	0.005–0.007	0.010–0.012
	Prelude	111.6 (1829)	0.042	20B	12B	2.5	750–850	750–850	0.005–0.007	0.010–0.012
	Prelude Si	119.3 (1955)	0.042	15B	15B	35	700–800	700–800	0.005–0.007	0.010–0.012
1988	Accord DX/LX	119.3 (1955)	0.042	24B ②	15B	3.0	800–850	700–800	0.005–0.007	0.010–0.012
	Accord LX-i	119.3 (1955)	0.042	15B	15B	35	750–800	750–800	0.005–0.007	0.010–0.012
	Prelude	119.3 (1955)	0.042	20B	12B	2.5	800–850	750–800	0.005–0.007	0.010–0.012
	Prelude Si	119.3 (1955)	0.042	15B	15B	35	750–800	750–800	0.003–0.005	0.006–0.008

GASOLINE ENGINE TUNE-UP SPECIFICATIONS

Year	Model	Engine Displacement cu. in. (cc)	Spark Plugs Gap (in.)	Ignition Timing (deg.) MT	AT	Fuel Pump (psi)	Idle Speed (rpm) MT	AT	Valve Clearance In.	Ex.
1989	Accord DX/LX	119.0 (1955)	0.042	24B ②	15B	2.6–3.3	750–850	680–790	0.005–0.007	0.010–0.012
	Accord LX-i	119.0 (1955)	0.042	15B	15B	33–39	700–800	700–800	0.005–0.007	0.010–0.012
	Prelude	119.0 (1955)	0.042	20B ③	15B ④	1.3–2.1	750–850	700–800	0.005–0.007	0.010–0.012
	Prelude Si	119.0 (1955)	0.042	15B	15B	36	700–800	700–800	0.003–0.005	0.006–0.008
1990	Accord DX/LX	132.0 (2156)	0.042	15B	15B	36	650–750	650–750	0.0094–0.011	0.011–0.012
	Accord EX	132.0 (2156)	0.042	15B	15B	36	650–750	650–750	0.0094–0.011	0.0110–0.0126
	Prelude S	119.0 (1955)	0.042	20B ③	15B ④	1.3–2.1	750–850	700–800	0.005–0.007	0.010–0.012
	Prelude Si	119.0 (1955)	0.042	15B	15B	36	700–800	700–800	0.003–0.005	0.006–0.008
	Prelude Si	125.0 (2056)	0.042	15B	15B	36	700–800	700–800	0.003–0.005	0.006–0.008
1991	Accord DX/LX	132.0 (2156)	0.042	15B	15B	36	700–800	700–800	0.0094–0.011	0.011–0.012
	Accord EX	132.0 (2156)	0.042	15B	15B	36	700–800	700–800	0.0094–0.011	0.011–0.012
	Accord SE	132.0 (2156)	0.042	15B	15B	36	700–800	700–800	0.0094–0.011	0.011–0.012
	Prelude Si	119.0 (1958)	0.042	15B	15B	36	700–800	700–800	0.003–0.005	0.006–0.008
	Prelude Si	125.0 (2056)	0.042	15B	15B	36	700–800	700–800	0.003–0.005	0.006–0.008

① Calif. models: 18B
② Calif. models: 20B
③ Calif. models: 15B
④ Calif. models: 10B

TUNE UP PROCEDURES

In order to extract the best performance and economy from your engine it is essential that it be properly tuned at regular intervals. Although computerized engine controls and more durable components have reduced ignition maintenance, a regular tune-up will keep your Honda's engine running smoothly and will prevent the annoying minor breakdowns and poor performance associated with an untuned engine.

Federal law now requires that manufacturers certify that their vehicle's spark plugs will meet emission rules for 30,000 miles (48,300 km). The maintenance schedules reflect this, showing a mandatory replacement at this mileage. This is a minimum specification; for many vehicles, 30,000 miles (48,300 km) is too long.

Plan on at least checking spark plugs and other ignition components at least once per year. Check them anytime a deterioration of engine performance is noted. Replaceable tune-up components are relatively inexpensive compared to the inconveniences of a poorly running vehicle or one that will not start.

This inspection interval should be halved if the car is operated under severe conditions, such as trailer towing, prolonged idling, continual stop and start driving, or if starting or running problems are noticed. It is assumed that the routine maintenance described in Chapter 1 has been kept up, as this will have a profound effect on the results of a tune-up. All of the applicable steps of a tune-up should be followed in order, as the result is a cumulative one.

If the specifications on the tune-up or emission label in the engine compartment of your

Honda disagree with the "Tune-Up Specifications" chart in this chapter, the figures on the sticker must be used. The sticker often reflects changes made during the production run.

Spark Plugs

Spark plugs ignite the air and fuel mixture in the cylinder as the piston reaches the top of the compression stroke. The controlled explosion that results forces the piston down, turning the crankshaft and the rest of the drive train.

The average life of a spark plug is dependent on a number of factors: the mechanical condition of the engine, the type of fuel, the driving conditions and the driver. Although the standard factory plugs will last a considerable period of time, extended life may be gained in some engines by using platinum-tipped plugs. You must decide if the benefits outweigh the extra cost.

When you remove the spark plugs, check their condition. They are a good indicator of the condition of the engine. A small deposit of light tan or gray material (or rusty red with unleaded fuel) on a spark plug that has been used for any period of time is to be considered normal. Any other color, or abnormal amounts of deposit, indicates that there is something amiss in the engine.

The gap between the center electrode and the side or ground electrode can be expected to increase very slightly under normal conditions.

When a spark plug is functioning normally or, more accurately, when the plug is installed in an engine that is functioning properly, the plugs can be taken out, cleaned, regapped, and reinstalled in the engine without doing the engine any harm. This is acceptable as an improvement or emergency measure, but new plugs are always recommended.

When, and if, a plug fouls and begins to misfire, you will have to investigate, correct the cause of the fouling, and either clean or replace the plug. Replacement is always recommended if possible.

Spark plugs suitable for use in your engine are offered in different heat ranges. The amount of heat which the plug absorbs is determined by the length of the lower insulator. The longer the insulator the hotter the plug will operate; the shorter the insulator, the cooler it will operate. A spark plug that absorbs little heat and remains too cool will accumulate deposits of lead, oil, and carbon, because it is not hot enough to burn them off. This leads to fouling and consequent misfiring.

A spark plug that absorbs too much heat will have no deposits, but the electrodes will burn

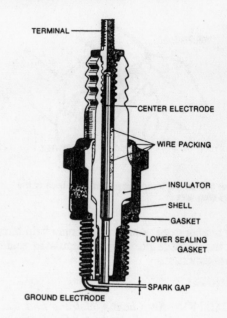

TERMINAL

CENTER ELECTRODE

WIRE PACKING

INSULATOR

SHELL

GASKET

LOWER SEALING GASKET

SPARK GAP

GROUND ELECTRODE

Cross section of a spark plug

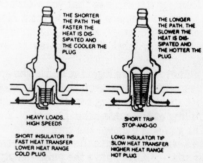

THE SHORTER THE PATH THE FASTER THE HEAT IS DISSIPATED AND THE COOLER THE PLUG

THE LONGER THE PATH. THE SLOWER THE HEAT IS DISSIPATED AND THE HOTTER THE PLUG

HEAVY LOADS. HIGH SPEEDS

SHORT INSULATOR TIP FAST HEAT TRANSFER LOWER HEAT RANGE COLD PLUG

SHORT TRIP STOP-AND-GO

LONG INSULATOR TIP SLOW HEAT TRANSFER HIGHER HEAT RANGE HOT PLUG

Correct spark plug heat range depends on your type of driving

away quickly and, in some cases, preignition may result. Preignition occurs when the spark plug tips get so hot that they ignite the air/fuel mixture before the actual spark fires. This premature ignition will usually cause a pinging sound under conditions of low speed and heavy load. In severe cases, the heat may become high enough to start the air/fuel mixture burning throughout the combustion chamber rather than just to the front of the plug. In this case, the resultant explosion will be strong enough to damage pistons, rings, and valves.

In most cases the factory recommended heat range is correct; it is chosen to perform well under a wide range of operating conditions. However, if most of your driving is long distance, high speed travel, you may want to install a spark plug one step colder than standard. If most of your driving is of the short trip variety, when the engine may not always reach operat-

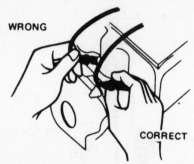

Never pull on the wire; always grasp the boot of the spark plug wire

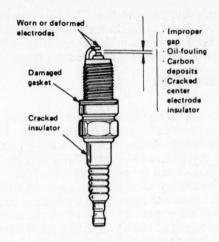

Inspect the plugs carefully for damage or fouling

ing temperature, a hotter plug may help burn off the deposits normally accumulated under those conditions.

REMOVAL

CAUTION: *Keep hands, clothing and tools away from the radiator fan(s). On certain vehicles, the fans may start automatically up to 15 minutes after the engine is switched off.*

1. Number the wires so that you won't cross them when you replace them. On most Honda engines the wire length is just long enough to reach the plug; label them anyway to avoid errors.

2. Remove the wire from the end of the spark plug by grasping the wire on the rubber boot. If the boot sticks to the plug, remove it by twisting and pulling at the same time. Do not pull wire itself or you will damage the core.

Engines with two camshafts (Dual Overhead Camshafts — DOHC) have the plugs deeply recessed between the cams. The wires have long, solid tubes running through the tunnels to the plugs; use great care in removing the wires and tubes.

3. Use a spark plug socket to loosen all of the plugs about two turns. Depending on location of the plug, a short extension on the wrench can be very handy. Make certain to keep the line of the wrench exactly on the line of the plug; if the wrench is cocked to one side, the plug may break off. Breaking a plug will spoil your afternoon — and most of the next day as well.

NOTE: *The cylinder head is cast from aluminum alloy. Remove the spark plugs when the engine is cold, if possible, to prevent damage to the threads.*

If removal of the plugs is difficult, apply a few drops of penetrating oil or silicone spray to the area around the base of the plug, and allow it some time to work.

4. If compressed air is available, apply it to the area around the spark plug holes. Otherwise, use a rag or a brush to clean the area. Be

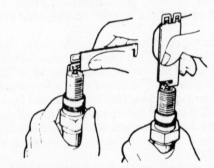

The correct tool will both measure the electrode gap and adjust it

careful not to allow any foreign material to drop into the spark plug holes.

5. Remove the plugs by unscrewing them the rest of the way from the engine. If the plug can be reached by hand, remove the plug manually. On DOHC engines, the plug must be unscrewed and lifted out with the plug wrench.

INSPECTION

Check the plugs for deposits and wear. Refer to the color insert for spark plug analysis. If they are not going to be replaced, clean the plugs thoroughly. This may be done with very fine sandpaper or a small flat file. Do not use a wire brush. Remember that any kind of deposit will decrease the efficiency of the plug. Plugs can be cleaned on a spark plug cleaning machine, which can sometimes be found in service stations. If the plugs are cleaned, the electrodes must be filed flat. Use an ignition points file, not an emery board or the like, which will leave deposits. The electrodes must be filed perfectly flat with sharp edges; rounded edges reduce the spark plug voltage by as much as 50%.

Check spark plug gap before installation. The

ground electrode (the L-shaped one connected to the body of the plug) must be parallel to the center electrode and the specified-size wire gauge must fit in the gap with slight resistance. Correct gap for all Accords and Preludes covered by this book is 1.0–1.1mm. (0.039–0.043 in.).

NOTE: *NEVER adjust the gap on a platinum-tipped spark plug.*

Always check the gap on new plugs, too; any given plug may require different gaps for use in different engines. Do not use a flat feeler gauge when measuring the gap; the reading will be inaccurate. Wire-type plug gapping tools usually have a bending tool attached. Use that to adjust the side electrode until the proper distance is

These marks indicate use of a new design spark plug. Do not substitute conventional plugs in these engines

obtained. Absolutely never bend the center electrode. Also, be careful not to bend the side electrode too far or too often; it may weaken and break off within the engine, requiring removal of the cylinder head to retrieve it.

INSTALLATION

NOTE: *1990–91 Accords and Preludes use a new type of plug with an extended tip and shorter terminal. When replacing these plugs, make certain the identical type of spark plug is used. Vehicles using this type of plug have small reminder emblems sealed onto the air cleaner cover.*

1. Lubricate the threads of the spark plugs with a drop of oil or anti-seize compound. Install the plugs by hand and tighten them just finger tight. Never attempt to perform the initial installation with a wrench; take care not to cross-thread them. For DOHC engines, detach the ratchet driver; use your hand to turn the socket and extension very gently until the plug threads seat and the plug turns in.

2. Tighten the spark plugs with the socket. Do not apply the same amount of force you would use for a bolt; just snug them in. If a torque wrench is available, tighten to 18 Nm (13 ft. lbs.).

3. Install the wires on their respective plugs. Make sure the wires are firmly connected. You will be able to feel them click into place. Additionally, make certain each wire is replaced into any clip or holder on its path. These wiring clips

keep the spark plug wires from creating electrical interference in each other and also keep the engine looking neat.

Spark Plug Wires
CHECKING AND REPLACEMENT

At every tune-up, visually inspect the spark plug cables for burns, cuts, or breaks in the insulation. Refer to the color insert for spark plug analysis. Check the boots and the nipples on the distributor cap and coil. Replace any damaged wiring. Always replace spark plug wiring in sets, with a coil wire as well. Length is important; get the correct set for your vehicle.

Every 36,000 miles (58,000 km) or so, the resistance of the wires should be checked with an ohmmeter. Wires with excessive resistance will cause misfiring, and may make the engine difficult to start in damp weather. Generally, the useful life of the cables is 36,000-50,000 miles (58,000–80,000 km).

To check resistance, remove the wire from the plug and the distributor cap. Look at each contact inside the wire for any sign of cracking or burning. A small amount of discoloration is normal but there should be no heavy burn marks. Connect one lead of an ohmmeter to each end of the cable. Replace any wire which shows a resistance over 25,000Ω (25 kΩ).

Test the high tension lead from the coil in the same fashion. If resistance is more than 25,000Ω, replace the cable. It should be remembered that resistance is also a function of length; the longer the cable, the greater the resistance. Thus, if the cables on your car are longer than the factory originals, resistance will be higher, quite possibly outside these limits. Honda recommends the 25 kΩ limit be observed in all cases.

When installing new cables, replace them one at a time to avoid mixups. Start by replacing the longest one first. Install the boot firmly over the spark plug. Route the wire over the same path as the original. Insert the nipple firmly into the tower on the cap or the coil. Make certain each cable is replaced in any holding or retaining clips along the route.

FIRING ORDER

NOTE: *To avoid confusion, remove and tag the wires one at a time, for replacement.*

The firing order is the order in which spark is sent to each cylinder. The spark must arrive at the correct time in the combustion cycle or damage may result. For this reason, connecting the correct plug to the correct distributor ter-

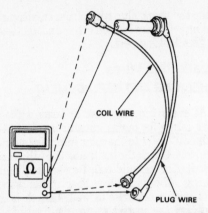

Testing plug and coil wire resistance. DOHC plug wire shown, SOHC similar without extension

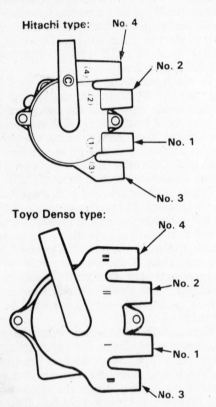

Different types of distributor caps are used on 1984–89 Accord and Prelude

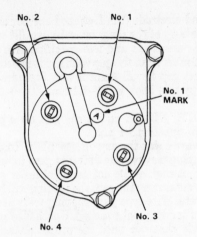

1990–91 Accord distributor cap. Note the mark showing cylinder No. 1

and mounting points; know which one you have or take an old one with you when buying tune-up parts.

An additional aid to correct installation is that most Honda distributor caps are marked either with cylinder numbers or at least a single mark for cylinder No. 1. All distributors rotate in a clockwise direction when viewed from the top or cap side.

ELECTRONIC IGNITION

The electronic ignition system on your Honda requires special handling. Unlike conventional ignition systems, it is very sensitive to abrupt changes in voltage or voltage applied in the wrong direction. Observe the precautions listed below to prevent expensive system damage.

1. Always disconnect the battery cables before doing repair work on the electronic ignition system.

2. Always double check the markings on the battery and the routing of the cables before making connections, especially if the battery has been removed and might have been reinstalled in the opposite position. Hooking the battery connections up backwards will cause current to flow through the electronic ignition system in an improper way and immediately damage it.

3. Do not allow the wires connected to the pulse generator to touch other ignition wiring connections.

4. Abnormal voltage pulses may damage the system. Be sure to either disconnect the battery or switch the ignition OFF before doing any work on the vehicle that is of an electrical nature.

minal is critical. To avoid confusion, always re-place the spark plug wires one at a time.

Cylinder No.1 is the cylinder closest to the timing belt or pulley end of the engine. All Accord and Prelude engines fire in the order 1-3-4-2. Accords and Preludes use distributors from two different manufacturers, Hitachi and Toyo Denso (also called Denso). While the firing order and plug wire placement is the same for both, the caps have differently shaped bases

5. Connect any electrical tachometer to the negative (−) terminal of the ignition coil — not to any other connection.

6. Always double check any connection involving the ignition system before reconnecting the battery and putting the system into operation.

7. When cranking the engine for compression testing or similar purposes, disconnect the coil wire at the distributor.

ADJUSTMENTS

The following adjustment is for the reluctor gap on the 1984–89 Accord and 1984–90 carbureted Prelude.

1. Remove the distributor cap and the rotor.
2. Turn the crankshaft to align the reluctor points with the stator ends.
3. Using a non-metallic feeler gauge, check the reluctor-to-stator air gaps; they must be equal.
4. To adjust, loosen the stator-to-distributor screws, adjust the stator-to-reluctor air gaps and tighten the screws.
5. Recheck the air gaps.

PARTS REPLACEMENT

Distributor Cap and Rotor

The distributor cap is held by screws to the case. With the ignition **OFF**, loosen or remove the screws and remove the cap. Inspect the inside of the cap for cracking, burning or heavy wear on the wire terminals. Replace the cap if there is any sign of anything abnormal. Slight wear on the terminals is normal.

Remove the ignition rotor by lifting it straight off the shaft. Fuel injected 1989-91 Preludes use a set screw to hold the rotor to the shaft; loosen or remove (but don't lose) the screw before attempting to remove the rotor. Inspect the rotor for any sign of wear; dressing or refiling the rotor is not recommended except in emergency circumstances.

Before installing, align the rotor and shaft; both have a flat side to insure correct placement. Press the rotor onto the shaft. Install and tighten the Prelude set screw if it was removed. Install the cap and any seal or gasket carefully onto the distributor; tighten the screws just snug.

Reluctor

1. Disconnect the negative battery terminal.
2. Remove the distributor cap and rotor.
3. Use two small-to-medium flat tools to pry the reluctor smoothly and evenly from the shaft. Protect the case of the distributor with rags or cloth. Use great care not to damage the stator or other components.

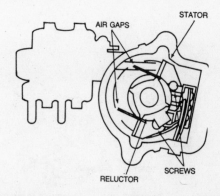

Inspect the air gap with a non-magnetic or non-metallic feeler gauge

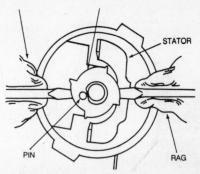

Use care when removing the reluctor

4. Position the reluctor with the manufacturer's number facing up. Install the reluctor by pushing it firmly onto the distributor shaft.

5. Install the roll pin with the slot of the pin facing away from the distributor shaft.

Pickup Coil

1. Remove the distributor cap, rotor and reluctor.
2. Disconnect the electrical connector from the pickup coil.
3. Remove the retaining screws holding the pickup coil; remove the coil assembly.
4. Install in reverse order. Adjust the air gap as necessary.

Igniter

Externally mounted igniters are removed in straightforward fashion. Always perform the work with the ignition **OFF**. Toyo Denso igniters mounted on the side of the distributor require the removal of two bolts and the harness clip. The igniter plugs directly to the distributor case. Before installation, coat the igniter pins with silicone grease.

Internally mounted igniters, such as on the Hitachi distributors, require the removal of the cap, rotor and reluctor. The igniter may be re-

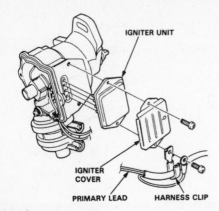

Removing the external igniter

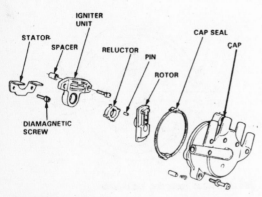

Hitachi igniter removal

moved by removing the retaining screws. Note the position of the retaining screws; one is diamagnetic and must be reinstalled in the original location.

IGNITION TIMING

Ignition timing is the measurement, in degrees of crankshaft rotation, at the instant the spark plugs in the cylinders fire, in relation to the location of the piston.

It takes a fraction of a second for the spark from the plug to completely ignite the mixture in the cylinder. Because of this, the spark plug must fire before the piston reaches TDC so the mixture is completely ignited as the piston passes TDC. This measurement is given in degrees of crankshaft rotation before the piston reaches top dead center (BTDC). If the ignition timing setting is 6° BTDC, this means that the spark plug must fire at a time when the piston for that cylinder is 6° BTDC of its compression stroke. However, this only holds true while the engine is at idle.

The mechanical distributor has two means of advancing the ignition timing. One is centrifu-

gal advance and is actuated by weights in the distributor. The other is vacuum advance and is controlled in that large circular housing on the side of the distributor. Fully electronic systems use the engine control unit (ECU) to control the trigger signal to the coil. The computer can provide much more accurate spark control than mechanical units.

In addition, some Honda distributors have a vacuum retard mechanism which is contained in the same housing on the side of the distributor as the vacuum advance. Models having two hoses going to the distributor vacuum housing have both vacuum advance and retard. The function of this mechanism is to regulate the timing of the ignition spark under certain engine conditions. This causes more complete burning of the air/fuel mixture in the cylinder and consequently lowers exhaust emissions.

If ignition timing is set too far advanced (BTDC), the ignition and burning of the air/fuel mixture in the cylinder will try to oppose the motion of the piston in the cylinder while it is still traveling upward. This causes engine ping, a sound similar to marbles in a coffee can. If the ignition timing is too far retarded (after, or ATDC), the piston will have already started down on the power stroke when the air/fuel mixture ignites. This will cause the piston to be forced down with much less power. This will result in rough engine performance and poor gas mileage.

CHECKING AND ADJUSTING

On 1984-91 models, check the timing and adjust (if necessary) every 60,000 miles (96,500 km).

1984–89 Accord
1984–87 Prelude
1988 Prelude (Carbureted)

The timing marks are located on the flywheel (manual transaxle) or torque converter drive plate (automatic transaxle), with a pointer on the rear of the cylinder block. All are visible from the front right side of the engine compartment after removing a special rubber access plug in the timing mark window. In all cases, the timing is checked with the engine warmed to operating temperature and at idle.

1. Stop the engine and install a tachometer to the engine. The positive lead connects to the distributor side terminal of the ignition coil and the negative lead to a good ground, such as an engine bolt.

2. Following the manufacturer's instructions, install a timing light to the engine. The positive and negative leads connect to their cor-

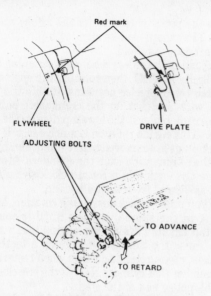

Examples of timing marks and distributor adjustment

responding battery terminals and the spark plug lead to No. 1 spark plug wire.

3. Make sure that all wires are clear of the cooling fan and hot exhaust manifolds.

4. Set the parking brake and block the front wheels. Start the engine. Check that the idle speed is set to specifications with the transaxle in Neutral (manual transaxle) or Drive (automatic transaxle).

5. If the distributor is equipped with a vacuum advance mechanism, label and disconnect the hose(s), plug it (them) and reinstall on the vacuum advance.

NOTE: *At any engine speed other than specified, the distributor advance or retard mechanisms will actuate, leading to an erroneous timing adjustment.*

6. Point the timing light at the timing marks. The flywheel or drive plate may have more than one mark on it. If more than one mark is present, the red mark must be used to set the timing. The white line or mark indicates TDC or 0°. When the engine is idling the red mark must align with the pointer. Some timing marks are indicated by 3 lines; the center one must be aligned with the pointer.

7. If necessary to adjust the timing, loosen the distributor hold down bolt(s) and/or nut and slowly rotate the distributor in the required direction while observing the timing marks.

CAUTION: *Do NOT grasp the top of the distributor cap while the engine is running, as you might get a nasty shock. Instead, grab the distributor housing to rotate.*

NOTE: *Some models are equipped with two bolts, others are equipped with a bolt and a*

nut, which may be loosened to adjust ignition timing. If there is a smaller bolt on the underside of the distributor swivel mounting plate, it should not be loosened, unless you cannot obtain a satisfactory adjustment using the upper bolt. Its purpose is to provide an extra range of adjustment, such as in cases where the distributor was removed and then installed one tooth off.

8. To complete the adjustment operation, tighten the hold down bolt, taking care not to disturb the adjustment. If equipped with a vacuum advance mechanism, unplug and reinstall the hose(s).

9. Switch the engine **OFF**. Reinstall the rubber plug in the timing window and remove the test equipment.

1988 Prelude SI
1989–91 Prelude
1990–91 Accord

NOTE: *The timing on these cars is controlled by the engine computer. It should not be necessary to routinely reset the timing during other maintenance work.*

1. Remove the rubber cap from the timing window at the back of the engine.

2. Start the engine and allow it to warm up. The engine is fully warmed when the cooling fans come on at least once. Shut the engine **OFF**.

3. Remove the cap from the service check connector. On Preludes, the cap is yellow and the connector is located just behind the ignition coil. On Accords, the connector is blue. The Accord connector is located behind the right front kick panel, under the dashboard. Use a jumper wire to connect the two terminals of the service connector.

4. Following the manufacturers instructions, install a timing light to the engine. The positive and negative leads connect to their corresponding battery terminals and the spark plug lead to No. 1 spark plug wire.

5. Make sure that all wires are clear of the cooling fan and hot exhaust manifolds.

6. Set the parking brake and block the front wheels. Start the engine. Check that the idle speed is set to specifications with the transaxle in Neutral (manual transaxle) or Drive (automatic transaxle).

NOTE: *At any engine speed other than specified, the distributor advance or retard mechanisms will actuate, leading to an erroneous timing adjustment.*

7. Point the timing light at the timing marks. The flywheel or drive plate may have more than one mark on it. If more than one mark is present, the red mark must be used to

set the timing. The white line or mark indicates TDC or 0°. When the engine is idling the red mark must align with the pointer. Some timing marks are indicated by 3 lines; the center one must be aligned with the pointer.

8. If necessary to adjust the timing, loosen the distributor hold down bolt(s) and/or nut and slowly rotate the distributor in the required direction while observing the timing marks.

NOTE: *Some models are equipped with two bolts, others are equipped with a bolt and a nut, which may be loosened to adjust ignition timing. If there is a smaller bolt on the underside of the distributor swivel mounting plate, it should not be loosened, unless you cannot obtain a satisfactory adjustment using the upper bolt. Its purpose is to provide an extra range of adjustment, such as in cases where the distributor was removed and then installed one tooth off.*

CAUTION: *Do NOT grasp the top of the distributor cap while the engine is running, as you might get a nasty shock. Instead, grab the distributor housing to rotate.*

9. To complete the adjustment operation, tighten the hold down bolt, taking care not to disturb the adjustment.

10. Switch the engine **OFF**. Reinstall the rubber plug in the timing window and remove the test equipment.

VALVE LASH

As part of every major tune-up or service interval, the valve clearance should be checked and adjusted if necessary. For all Accords and Preludes Covered by this book, the specification is every 15,000 miles (24,000 km) or 12 months.

NOTE: *While all valve adjustments must be as accurate as possible, it is better to have the valve adjustment slightly loose than slightly tight, as burnt valves may result from overly tight adjustments.*

ADJUSTMENT

Valve lash must always be adjusted with the engine cold. The head temperature must be below 100°F (38°C). Generally, this means allowing the engine to cool for at least 3 hours after driving. Overnight cold is best. If the valve adjustment is being done as part of a routine maintenance or mileage service regimen, do this work first, before the engine is warmed up to check timing or idle

Valve location — intake, exhaust and auxiliary (if used) — will vary with the type of engine. As a guide, the intake valves always are aligned with the ports or runners of the intake manifold. The exhaust valves align with the tubes of the exhaust manifold.

Adjusting the valves requires positioning No. 1 cylinder at TDC, then rotating the engine to certain other precise positions. Rotate the engine with a socket on the crankshaft pulley. (The crank pulley is the lowest pulley on the engine.) This engine rotation is much easier if the spark plugs are removed before hand, eliminating the compression from the cylinders. Always rotate the engine in a counterclockwise direction as viewed from the pulley end.

If you miss a mark during the rotation, keep going in the same direction until it comes around again. Turning the engine backwards may cause the timing belt to jump a tooth or slacken, risking engine damage when restarted. Remember that cylinder No. 1 is the one closest to the pulley end of the engine.

The engine is at TDC No. 1 if ALL of the following are true:

● The TDC mark on the flywheel or flexplate is aligned with the pointer in the timing inspection window at the rear of the engine. The TDC mark is generally white; it is never red.

● The distributor rotor is pointing at cap terminal or plug wire No. 1. Mark the cap with wire numbers, then lift the cap and look.

● The alignment marks on the camshaft pulley are located and aligned as indicated in the individual procedure.

● The rocker arms for at least one of the valves on cylinder No. 1 is loose; the points or lobes of the cam are not putting pressure on the rocker arm(s).

1984–1985 Accord
1986–1989 Accord
1984–1987 Prelude
1988–1990 SOHC Prelude

All engines in these vehicles use a Single Overhead Camshaft (SOHC). One cam operates the 12 or 16 valves. The engines in 1984-85 Accord use 2 intake valves, 1 exhaust and 1 auxiliary valve per cylinder. The auxiliary valves are located on the exhaust side and are smaller than the other valves. The other vehicles use the same arrangement without the auxiliary valve.

Valve clearances for the valves are:
● Intake: 0.12–0.17mm (0.005–0.007 in.)
● Exhaust: 0.25–0.30mm (0.010–0.012 in.)
● Auxiliary: 0.12–0.17mm (0.005–0.007 in.)

1. With the ignition **OFF**, remove the valve cover.

2. Set the engine to TDC No. 1 cylinder. The **UP** mark on the camshaft pulley should be at

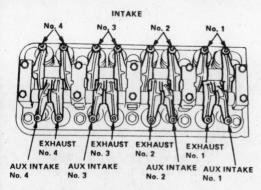

Valve placement – 1984–85 Accord

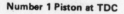

Number 1 Piston at TDC

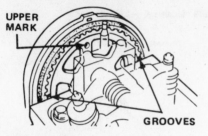

Position the engine at TDC for No. 1 piston – all SOHC engines 1984–89

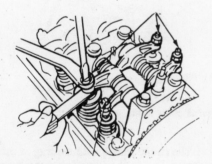

Adjusting the valve clearance

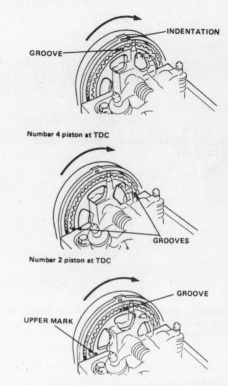

Number 4 piston at TDC

Number 2 piston at TDC

Markers for correct positioning of pistons 3, 4 and 2

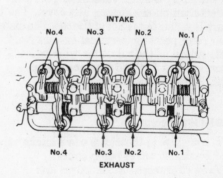

Valve placement – 1986–89 Accord and SOHC Prelude

the top of the pulley. The two grooves on the back (valve) side of the pulley should both be visible and aligned with the surface of the cylinder head. The distributor rotor points to No. 1 terminal or wire.

3. Check the clearance on all the valves for cylinder No. 1 with a flat feeler gauge inserted between the tip of the valve and the contact surface of the rocker. The gauge should pass the gap with slight drag.

4. If the gauge passes with no drag or cannot be inserted, loosen the adjusting screw locknut.

5. Turn the adjusting screw to obtain the proper clearance. Hold the adjusting screw in position and tighten the locknut. Correct locknut torque is:

Intake and Exhaust, 20 Nm (14 ft. lbs.); Auxiliary, 14 Nm (10 ft. lbs.). After the locknut is tightened, recheck the clearance and readjust as necessary.

6. Rotate the crankshaft 180°; the camshaft will turn 90°. One of the grooves in the pulley is now vertical and aligned with the indented mark on the timing belt cover. The UP mark is not visible and the distributor rotor points to terminal or wire No. 3.

7. Adjust all the valves for cylinder No. 3, repeating Steps 3, 4 and 5 as necessary.

8. Rotate the crankshaft 180°. Both grooves on the cam pulley are visible and aligned with the head surfaces. The distributor rotor points to terminal or wire No. 4.

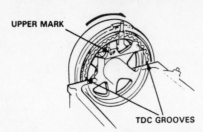

Cam pulley alignment marks – 1986–89 Accord; SOHC Prelude similar

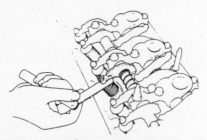

Checking the valve clearance with a feeler gauge. The proper size feeler should just pass the gap with minimal drag

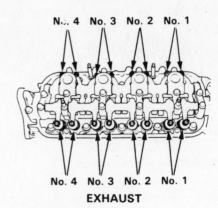

Valve placement – 1990–91 Accord

Number 1 piston at TDC

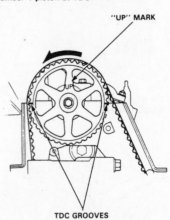

Camshaft pulley marks – 1990–91 Accord

9. Adjust all the valves for cylinder No. 4, repeating Steps 3, 4 and 5 as necessary.

10. Rotate the crankshaft 180°. One groove on the pulley is again vertical, aligned with the indentation on the timing belt cover. The UP mark is visible but is not at the top. The distributor rotor points to terminal or wire No. 2.

11. Adjust all the valves for cylinder No. 2, repeating Steps 3, 4 and 5 as necessary.

12. Reinstall the valve cover.

1990–1991 Accord

The engines in these cars use 2 intake valves and 2 exhaust valves per cylinder.

Valve clearances for the valves are:
- Intake: 0.24–0.28mm (0.009–0.011 in.) with 0.26mm (0.10 in.) preferred
- Exhaust: 0.28–0.32mm (0.011–0.013 in.) with 0.30mm (0.012 in.) preferred.

1. With the ignition **OFF**, remove the valve cover.

2. Set the engine to TDC No. 1 cylinder. The **UP** mark on the camshaft pulley should be at the top of the pulley. The two grooves on the side of the pulley should both be visible and aligned with the surface of the cylinder head. The distributor rotor points to No. 1 terminal or wire.

3. Check the clearance on all the valves for cylinder No. 1 with a flat feeler gauge inserted between the tip of the valve and the contact surface of the rocker. The gauge should pass the gap with slight drag.

4. If the gauge passes with no drag or cannot be inserted, loosen the adjusting screw locknut.

5. Turn the adjusting screw to obtain the proper clearance. Hold the adjusting screw in position and tighten the locknut. Correct locknut torque is:

Intake and Exhaust, 20 Nm (14 ft. lbs.). After the locknut is tightened, recheck the clearance and readjust as necessary.

6. Rotate the crankshaft 180°; the camshaft will turn 90°. One of the grooves in the pulley is now vertical and aligned with the indented mark on the timing belt cover. The **UP** mark is now at the exhaust side and the distributor rotor points to terminal or wire No. 3.

7. Adjust all the valves for cylinder No. 3, repeating Steps 3, 4 and 5 as necessary.

8. Rotate the crankshaft 180°. Both grooves on the cam pulley are visible and aligned with the head surfaces. The distributor rotor points

to terminal or wire No. 4. The **UP** mark is upside down or at the bottom of the cam pulley.

9. Adjust all the valves for cylinder No. 4, repeating Steps 3, 4 and 5 as necessary.

10. Rotate the crankshaft 180°. One groove on the pulley is again vertical, aligned with the indentation on the timing belt cover. The **UP** mark is at the intake side. The distributor rotor points to terminal or wire No. 2.

11. Adjust all the valves for cylinder No. 2, repeating Steps 3, 4 and 5 as necessary.

12. Reinstall the valve cover.

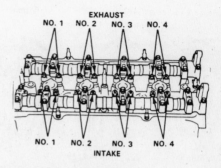

Valve placement — DOHC Prelude

1988–91 DOHC Prelude

These engines employ Dual Overhead Camshafts (DOHC) and use 4 valve per cylinder, 2 intake and 2 exhaust. The intake valves are operated by one cam and the exhaust valves by the other. Valve adjustment on these engines is similar to other engines. Each camshaft pulley has **UP** marks and grooves; when the engine is rotated during the adjustment, the marks must be aligned both with the cylinder head and with each other.

The dual cam engines use rocker arms mounted under the camshaft; for this reason, checking the clearance with straight feeler gauges may be difficult. Use a curved set if at all possible. Valve clearances are:

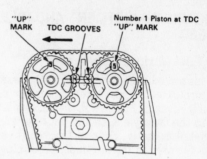

Positioning the motor at TDC for No.1 cylinder — DOHC Prelude

- Intake: 0.08–0.12mm (0.003–0.005 in.)
- Exhaust: 0.16–0.20mm (0.006–0.008 in.)

1. With the ignition **OFF**, remove the valve cover.

2. Set the No. 1 piston at top dead center (TDC). The **UP** marks on the pulleys should be at the top, and the TDC grooves on the edge or side of the pulley should align with the cylinder head surface. The distributor rotor should be pointing towards the No. 1 spark plug wire.

3. Check the clearance on all the valves for cylinder No. 1 with a feeler gauge. The gauge should pass the gap with slight drag.

4. If the gauge passes with no drag or cannot be inserted, loosen the adjusting screw locknut.

5. Turn the adjusting screw to obtain the proper clearance. Hold the adjusting screw in position and tighten the locknut. Correct locknut torque is:
Intake and Exhaust, 27 Nm (20 ft. lbs.). After the locknut is tightened, recheck the clearance and readjust as necessary.

6. Rotate the crankshaft 180° counterclockwise (the cam pulley will turn 90°). The **UP** marks should be at the exhaust side. The distributor rotor should point to the number three spark plug wire. At this point the valves on No. 3 cylinder can be adjusted. Repeat Steps 3, 4 and 5 as needed.

7. Rotate the crankshaft 180° counterclock-

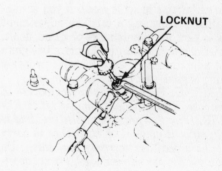

Adjusting DOHC Prelude valves

wise to bring the No. 4 piston up to TDC. Both **UP** marks should be at the bottom and the distributor rotor should point to the number four spark plug wire. the grooves on the pulley align with the cylinder head surface and with each other. Adjust the valves for cylinder No. 4 by repeating Steps 3, 4 and 5 as necessary.

8. Rotate the crankshaft 180° counterclockwise to bring the No. 2 cylinder up to TDC. The **UP** marks should be at the intake side. The distributor rotor should point at the number two spark plug wire. Adjust all the valves for cylinder No. 2, repeating Steps 3, 4, and 5 as needed.

9. Once all the valves have been adjusted and rechecked, reinstall the valve cover on the engine. Reinstall the distributor cap. Start the engine and check for oil leaks.

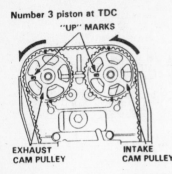

Number 3 piston at TDC

"UP" MARKS

EXHAUST CAM PULLEY

INTAKE CAM PULLEY

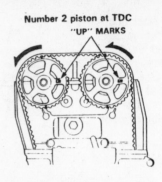

Number 2 piston at TDC

"UP" MARKS

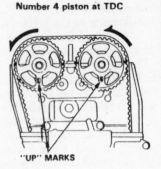

Number 4 piston at TDC

"UP" MARKS

Marker positions for aligning pistons 3, 4 and 2 — DOHC Prelude

MIXTURE ADJUSTMENT AND IDLE SPEED

Air/Fuel Mixture Adjustment

This procedure is used to adjust the base idle on carbureted engines after carburetor disassembly or repair. In general, the mixture is preset at the factory and should not be altered or adjusted casually. Federal law requires the manufacturer to insert tamper-proof plugs or other devices to keep the uninformed out of the carburetor. These procedures require a fair amount of disassembly, including the removal of the carburetor in some cases. If you are anticipating performing a mixture adjustment solely as part of a maintenance program, don't. The risk of creating more problems outweighs a slight adjustment on an otherwise properly running engine.

WARNING: *The use of the correct tools — in this case, a propane enrichment kit is REQUIRED for this procedure. Also required is a significant amount of experience to carry out the procedures correctly and safely. Do not begin the procedure if the kit is not available. Make certain the propane bottle is sufficiently full before beginning the work.*

The mixture may also be determined through the use of an exhaust gas analyzer or emissions tester. This is a piece of equipment that is meant for the professional.

Fuel injected vehicles do not allow the manual adjustment of the air/fuel mixture. The engine control unit or ECU is in charge of that and controls the function of the fuel injectors according to the electric signals sent to it by a host of sensors and monitors. If a fuel injected engine suffers an emission related problem, the sensors and computer-controlled output components must be tested and repaired.

Keihin 2-bbl Carburetor
1984-85 Accord
1986-89 Accord with Manual Transmission

1. Place the vehicle in the Park or Neutral

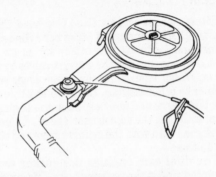

Remove the hose from the intake air diaphragm

position, apply the emergency brake and block the drive wheels. Start the engine and warm it up to normal operating temperature. The cooling fan(s) should come on at least once.

2. Remove the vacuum hose from the intake air control diaphragm and clamp the hose end.

3. Connect a suitable tachometer to the engine using the manufacturers instructions.

4. Check the idle speed with all the accessories turned off. Adjust the idle speed by turning the throttle stop screw, if necessary.

5. Disconnect the air cleaner intake tube from the air duct on the radiator bulkhead.

6. Insert the hose from the propane kit into the intake tube approximately 4 inches.

CAUTION: *Propane is a flammable gas. Observe no smoking/no open flame precautions.*

Have a Class B-C (dry powder) fire extinguisher within arm's reach at all times.

7. With the engine idling, depress the push button on top of the propane device then slowly open the propane control valve to obtain the maximum engine speed. The engine speed should increase as the percentage of propane injected goes up.

NOTE: *Open the propane control valve slowly; a sudden burst of propane may cause the engine to stall.*

8. The engine idle speed should increase as follows:

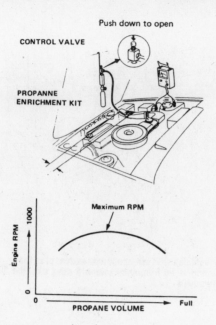

Maximum RPM

Engine RPM

PROPANE VOLUME — Full

Injecting propane into the air stream should cause the idle to increase, then decrease. Adjust the flow to hold the maximum idle

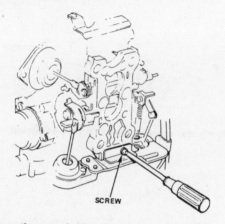

Remove the screw holding the throttle control bracket — 1984 Accord shown

- 1984-85 Accord with manual transmission 100 ± 25 rpm.
- 1984-85 Accord with automatic transmission 50 ± 20 rpm.
- 1986 Accord with manual transmission 35 ± 20 rpm.
- 1987-89 Accord with manual transmission 50 ± 20 rpm.

9. If the engine speed increases according to specifications, remove the propane kit, all test equipment and reconnect all disconnected vacuum hoses. If the engine speed fails to increase as specified, continue with the following Steps. Switch the ignition **OFF**.

10. Disconnect the vacuum hose to the fast

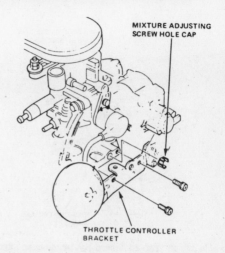

The hole cap can be removed after the bracket is removed from 1984–85 Accord

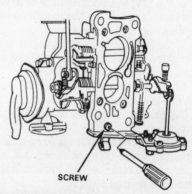

Removing the screw holding the throttle control bracket — 1987 Accord shown

idle unloader. Pull the throttle cable out of the bracket.

11. Remove the carburetor nuts, washers and bolts securing the steel tubing vacuum manifold. Lift the carburetor clear of the studs, then tilt it backward to obtain the access to the throttle controller bracket screws.

12. Remove the throttle controller bracket. Remove the mixture adjusting screw hole cap from the throttle controller bracket and then reinstall the bracket. With the plug removed, the adjusting screw can now be reached from the outside of the carburetor body with the carburetor in place.

13. Reinstall the carburetor, reconnect the vacuum hose to the fast idle unloader. Reinstall the air cleaner.

14. Start the engine and let it warm up again to normal operating temperature.

15. Remove the vacuum hose from the intake air control diaphragm and clamp the hose end. Reinstall the propane enrichment kit and recheck the maximum propane enrichment rpm.

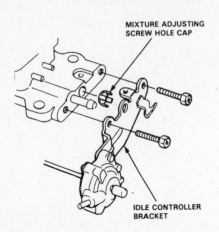

The hole cap on 1986–89 Accord can be removed after the bracket is removed

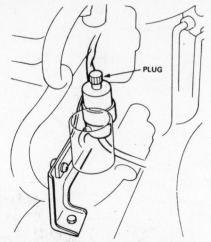

For vehicles with automatic transaxles, plug the opening in the frequency solenoid valve after the filter is removed

16. If the propane enriched speed is too low, the mixture is rich. Turn the mixture screw a ¼ turn clockwise and recheck.

17. If the propane enriched speed is too high, the mixture is lean. Turn the mixture screw a ¼ turn counterclockwise and recheck.

18. Close the propane control valve and recheck the idle speed. Be sure to run the engine at 2500 rpm for 10 seconds to stabilize the idle condition.

19. If the engine speed is set to specifications, remove the propane enrichment kit, all test equipment and reconnect all vacuum hoses and the air cleaner intake tube.

20. If the engine speed is not set to specifications, recheck the engine speed and if necessary adjust by turning the throttle stop screw, then repeat Steps 14-19.

21. Adjust the idle speed, if necessary by turning the idle control screw.

22. If equipped with air conditioning, make a second check with the air conditioning engaged. Adjust the speed if necessary by turning the adjusting screw on the idle boost diaphragm.

NOTE: *Some 1984 Accord models may develop a stalling problem at idle. The probable cause of this stalling is a sticking slow mixture cut-off solenoid. If this is the case the solenoid should be removed and replaced with the updated type of solenoid. Additionally, various cold starting and driveability problems on these cars were cured through the addition of assorted "cold-start" kits from Honda. Consult your dealer's service department for details.*

Keihin 2-bbl Carburetor
1986-89 Accord with Automatic Transmission

1. Place the vehicle in Park or Neutral, apply the emergency brake and block the drive

Throttle stop screw for mechanical idle adjustment

Idle control screw location for 1986–89 automatic Accords

wheels. Start the engine and warm it up to normal operating temperature. The cooling fan(s) should come on at least once.

2. Remove vacuum hose from the intake air control diaphragm and clamp the hose end.

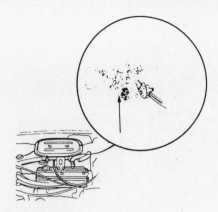

Adjusting screw A

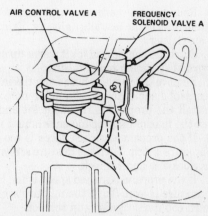

AIR CONTROL VALVE A   FREQUENCY SOLENOID VALVE A

Disconnect the hose form the frequency solenoid valve A; connect it to the control valve

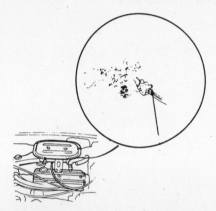

Use adjusting screw B to adjust the idle with A/C on

3. Connect a suitable tachometer to the engine using the manufacturer's instructions.

4. Remove air filter from frequency solenoid valve **C** and plug opening in solenoid valve.

5. With no engine load, lower idle speed as much as possible by turning the throttle stop screw.

6. Adjust idle speed by turning idle control screw to 600 ± 50 rpm (630 ± 50 on 1987-89 models).

7. With headlights on, rear defroster on, and heater blower to maximum, adjust idle speed by turning adjusting screw **A**. Idle should be 600 ± 50 rpm on 1986 models and 700 ± 50 on 1987-89 models.

8. If equipped with air conditioning, adjust idle speed by turning adjusting screw **B** to 700 ± 50 rpm with air conditioning on.

9. With no engine load, remove the inside vacuum hose from the idle boost throttle controller and plug hose.

10. Adjust idle speed by turning throttle stop screw to 700 ± 50 rpm (650 ± 50 rpm at high altitude).

11. Disconnect the hose from frequency solenoid valve **A** and connect to air control valve **A**.

12. Disconnect the air cleaner intake tube from the air duct on the radiator bulkhead.

13. Insert the hose from the propane kit into the intake tube approximately 4 inches.

CAUTION: *Propane is a flammable gas. Observe no smoking/no open flame precautions. Have a Class B-C (dry powder) fire extinguisher within arm's reach at all times.*

14. With the engine idling, depress the push button on top of the propane device then slowly open the propane control valve to obtain the maximum engine speed. The engine speed should increase as the percentage of propane injected goes up.

NOTE: *Open the propane control valve slowly; a sudden burst of propane may cause the engine to stall.*

15. The engine idle speed should increase 135 ± 35 rpm.

16. If the engine speed increases according to specifications, remove the propane kit, all test equipment and reconnect all disconnected vacuum hoses. If the engine speed fails to increase as specified, continue with the following Steps. Switch the ignition **OFF**.

17. Disconnect the vacuum hose to the fast idle unloader. Pull the throttle cable out of the bracket.

18. Remove the carburetor nuts, washers and bolts securing the steel tubing vacuum manifold. Lift the carburetor clear of the studs, then tilt it backward to obtain the access to the throttle controller bracket screws.

19. Remove the throttle controller bracket. Remove the mixture adjusting screw hole cap from the throttle controller bracket and then reinstall the bracket. With the plug removed, the adjusting screw can now be reached from the outside of the carburetor body with the carburetor in place.

20. Reinstall the carburetor, reconnect the vacuum hose to the fast idle unloader. Reinstall the air cleaner.

21. Start the engine and let it warm up again to normal operating temperature.

22. Remove the vacuum hose from the intake air control diaphragm and clamp the hose end. Reinstall the propane enrichment kit and recheck the maximum propane enrichment rpm.

23. If the propane enriched speed is too low, the mixture is rich. Turn the mixture screw a ¼ turn clockwise and recheck.

24. If the propane enriched speed is too high, the mixture is lean. Turn the mixture screw a ¼ turn counterclockwise and recheck.

25. Close the propane control valve and recheck the idle speed. Be sure to run the engine at 2500 rpm for 10 seconds to stabilize the idle condition.

26. If the engine speed is set to specifications, remove the propane enrichment kit, all test equipment and reconnect all vacuum hoses and the air cleaner intake tube.

27. If the engine speed is not set to specifications, recheck the engine speed and, if necessary, adjust by turning the throttle stop screw, then repeat the adjusting Steps.

28. Stop the engine. Close the propane control valve, remove all plugs, and reconnect all the hoses.

29. Restart the engine and recheck idle speed. NOTE: *Raise the engine speed to 2500 rpm 2 or 3 times in 10 seconds, and then check idle speed. Idle speed should be 700 ± 50 rpm on 1986 models and 730 ± 50 on 1987-89 models.*

30. Recheck the idle speed with headlights, heater blower and rear window defroster on. Idle speed should be 700 ± 50 rpm.

31. Recheck the idle speed with automatic transmission lever in gear. Idle speed should be 700 ± 50 rpm.

32. Recheck the idle speed with air conditioning on and with the shift lever in PARK or NEUTRAL position. Idle speed should be 750 ± 50 rpm.

33. Recheck idle speed with air conditioning on and in gear. Idle should be 750 ± 50 rpm.

34. If idle speed does not reach specified idle speeds in Steps 30 through 33, inspect the idle control system.

Keihin Dual Sidedraft Carburetors
1984-90 Prelude

NOTE: *Check that the carburetors are synchronized properly before making idle speed and mixture inspection. It will also be necessary to remove the ECU fuse from the fuse box*

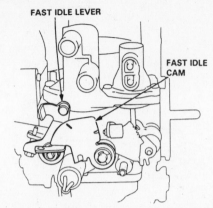

FAST IDLE LEVER

FAST IDLE CAM

The Prelude fast idle cam must not be engaged during propane enrichment testing

THROTTLE STOP SCREW

Prelude throttle stop screw

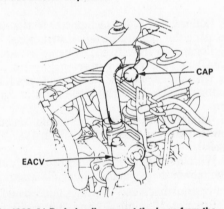

CAP

EACV

On 1988–91 Prelude, disconnect the hose from the hose manifold and plug the end

for at least 10 seconds to reset the control unit after this procedure is complete.

1. Start engine and warm up to normal operating temperature. The cooling fans should come on at least once.

2. Remove the vacuum hose from intake air control diaphragm and clamp or plug the hose end.

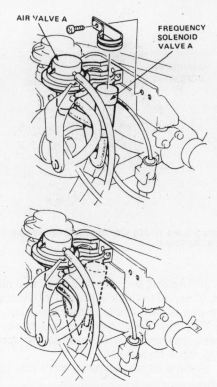

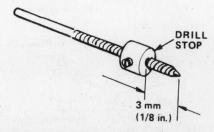

On Preludes through 1987, the plug must be drilled before removal. A drill stop is required to prevent damage to the adjusting screw

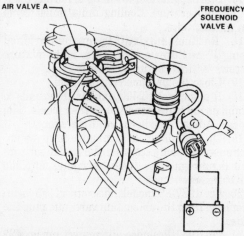

On 1984–86 automatic transaxle vehicles, disconnect the hoses and connect the lower hose to air control valve A

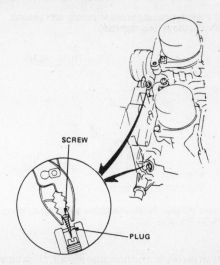

Once drilled, remove the plug

Automatic 1987 Preludes require the EACV to be jumpered to 12 volts when disconnected

NOTE: *All wires and hoses should be labeled at the time of removal. The amount of time saved during reassembly makes the extra effort well worthwhile.*

3. Connect a tachometer. Check that the fast idle lever is not seated against the fast idle cam.

NOTE: *If the fast idle lever is seated against the fast idle cam, it may be necessary to replace the left carburetor.*

4. Check the idle speed with all accessories turned off. Idle speed should be 800 ± 50 rpm (750 ± 50 rpm on automatic transmission in gear). Adjust the idle speed, if necessary, by turning the throttle stop screw.

NOTE: *If the idle speed is excessively high, check the throttle control.*

5. On 1987 automatic transmission cars only, disconnect the wiring connector from frequency solenoid valve A and use jumper wires to connect the valve to 12 volts. On all other vehicles, disconnect the two prong connector from the EACV, disconnect the hose from the vacuum hose manifold and cap the hose end.

6. Disconnect the vacuum tubes and connect lower hose to air control valve A. Disconnect the vacuum hose from the air conditioning idle boost throttle controller. Disconnect the air cleaner intake tube from the air intake duct.

7. Insert propane enrichment hose into the opening of intake tube about 4 inches.

CAUTION: *Propane is a flammable gas. Observe no smoking/no open flame precautions. Have a Class B-C (dry powder) fire extinguisher within arm's reach at all times.*

8. With the engine idling, depress the push

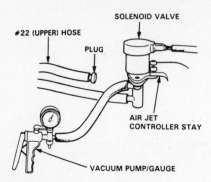

1987 Preludes require propane testing with vacuum applied to the air leak solenoid

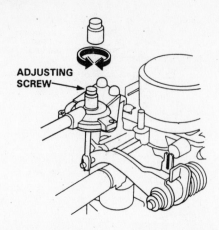

Adjusting screw for idle with air conditioning engaged — 1988–90 Prelude

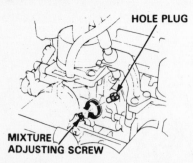

Remove the plug for access to the adjusting screw on 1988–90 Preludes

button on top of the propane device, then slowly open propane control valve to obtain maximum engine speed. Engine speed should increase as percentage of propane injected goes up.

NOTE: *Open the propane control valve slowly. A sudden burst of propane may stall the engine.*

9. Propane enrichment maximum rpm:

• 1984-86 manual transmission — 45 ± 25 rpm.

• 1984-86 automatic transmission — 110 ± 25 rpm (in D3 or D4).

• 1987 manual transmission — 65 ± 20 rpm.

• 1987 automatic transmission — 130 ± 25 rpm (in D3 or D4).

• 1988-90 manual transmission — 170 ± 20 rpm.

• 1988-90 automatic transmission — 50 ± 10 rpm.

10. If the engine speed change is proper, the procedure is complete. Disconnect the test equipment and reassemble the disconnected lines and hoses. If engine speed does not increase per specification, the mixture must be adjusted. On Preludes through 1987, remove the carburetors and use Steps 11–13, below. On later cars, the plugs may be removed without removing the carburetors; proceed with Step 15.

11. Place a drill stop on a drill bit so that only ⅛ in. (3mm) of the bit is exposed. Drill through the center of each mixture screw hole plug.

NOTE: *If drilled deeper than this measurement, damage to mixture adjusting screw may result from the bit.*

12. Screw a 5mm sheet metal screw into hole plugs.

13. Grab the screw head with a pair of pliers and remove the hole plugs. With the plugs

14. Reinstall the carburetors.

15. Start engine and warm up to normal operating temperature. Cooling fan(s) must come on at least once.

16. Recheck maximum propane enriched rpm. If mixture is rich, turn both mixture screws ¼ turn counterclockwise.

17. Close the propane control valve.

18. Run engine at 2500 rpm for 10 seconds to stabilize mixture conditions, then check idle speed. Adjust the idle speed, if necessary.

19. On 1984-86 models, remove propane enrichment kit and reconnect the intake air control diaphragm hose. Install new plugs into idle mixture screw holes.

20. On 1987-89 models, disconnect #5 vacuum hose from the air suction valve and plug the hose.

21. On 1987 Preludes, disconnect upper #22 vacuum hose from the air leak solenoid valve at air jet controller support and plug the end of hose. Connect a vacuum gauge to the solenoid valve.

22. With the engine idling, depress the push button on top of the propane device, then slowly open the propane control valve and check vacuum. Vacuum should be available.

23. If no vacuum is present, inspect the air leak solenoid valve.

24. Inspect thermovalve **C**.

25. Remove the propane enrichment kit and reconnect connector.

NOTE: *Some 1984-85 Prelude models may experience hesitation on acceleration before the engine has reached normal operating temperature. This can be corrected by installing a cold driveability kit from the manufacturer. This kit holds full vacuum advance to the distributor when the engine is cold.*

26. 1988-90 vehicles equipped with air conditioning should have the idle checked with the A/C running at the end of the procedure. If adjustment is necessary, remove the small cap from the adjusting screw and make external adjustments.

Idle Speed

ADJUSTMENT

Minor adjustments of warm idle speed may be needed as a result of an ignition tune-up or other maintenance procedures. In general, engine idle speed adjustment does not change by itself; if the idle is too low or a stalling problem is present, search out the real cause instead of hiding it with a higher idle speed.

Carbureted Engines

On carbureted engines, the idle should be checked with the engine at normal operating temperature and the fast idle system fully disengaged. Either connect a tachometer to the vehicle or use the one on the dashboard; the on-board one is at least as accurate as an external one.

Adjustments are made at the throttle stop screw on the carburetor. This is a mechanical adjustment which simply opens or closes the throttle plate a small amount, thus altering the idle speed. On Accords, the throttle stop has a knurled plastic knob to make adjustment easier. The knob, however, is located on the firewall side of the carburetor and may be difficult to reach. The spring on the adjuster also makes the knob a bit stiff to turn.

Preludes, with their dual carb arrangement use a vertically placed screw acting on the throttle linkage. The screw is located between the two carburetors on the linkage.

WARNING: *Particularly on Preludes, but on Accord also, be very certain that you have found the proper screw before making adjustments. Any linkage screw sealed with a dot of paint, usually yellow, is NOT to be altered. These adjusters are factory set; in some cases, they are not resettable in the field.*

Fuel Injected Engines

1985 ACCORD SEI

1. Start the engine and warm up to normal

Accord throttle adjusting screw. 1986–89 shown, 1984–85 similar

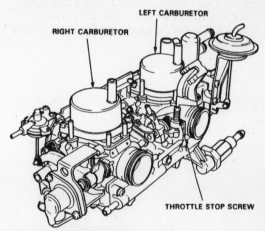

Prelude throttle stop screw

operating temperature; cooling fan must come on at least once.

2. Connect a suitable tachometer using the manufacturer's instructions.

3. Check idle speed with all accessories **OFF**.

NOTE: *To prevent the idle control system from operating, pinch off vacuum hose #27.*

4. Idle speed should be 750 ± 50 rpm (in neutral). Adjust idle speed, if necessary, by turning idle adjusting screw.

5. Check idle controller boosted speed with air conditioning on. Idle speed should be 800 ± 50 rpm (in neutral).

6. Adjust idle speed, if necessary, by turning adjusting screw **B**.

1986-91 ACCORD AND PRELUDE

1. Start engine and warm up to normal operating temperature; cooling fan will come on twice.

2. Connect tachometer.

3. On 1986-87 Accords and 1984-87 Preludes, disconnect the upper vacuum hose to the idle control solenoid valve (between valve and

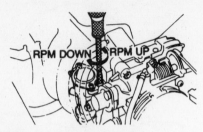

Idle adjustment screw, 1985 Accord SEI

intake manifold) from the intake manifold. Cap end of hose and intake manifold.

4. On 1988-91 vehicles, disconnect the 2-pin EACV connector.

5. With all accessories off, check idle speed. Idle speed should be 750 ± 50 rpm (in neutral). Adjust idle speed, if necessary, by turning idle adjusting screw.

6. Turn the ignition switch **OFF**.

7. Reconnect the connector, then remove either the **CLOCK** or **BACK UP** fuse in the underhood fuse box for at least 10 seconds; this resets the ECU.

8. Check idle speed with heater fan switch at HI and air conditioning on. Idle speed should be 750 ± 50 rpm (in neutral). Adjust idle speed, if necessary, by turning adjusting bolt on air conditioning idle boost valve.

9. After adjustment, connect idle control solenoid valve vacuum hose.

10. On automatic transmission model, after adjusting idle speed, check that it remains within specified limit when shifted in gear. Idle speed should be 750 ± 50 rpm.

11. Check the idle speed with all accessories **ON** and air conditioning off. Idle should remain at 750 ± 50 rpm.

Engine and Engine Overhaul

3

ENGINE ELECTRICAL

Ignition Coil

TESTING

NOTE: *All test resistance values are given for a coil temperature of 70°F (21°C). Resistance will vary with temperature. Use common sense and good judgment when interpreting readings.*

1984–85
ACCORD AND 1984–86 PRELUDE

1. Label and disconnect the wiring from the coil. The small external primary winding terminals are marked + and − on the coil case. The large coil terminal (from which the wire runs to the distributor) is the secondary winding terminal.
2. With the ignition OFF, measure the resistance across the primary terminals. Resistance should be 1.06–1.24Ω.
3. Measure the resistance between the secondary terminal and the primary positive terminal; resistance should be 7400–11,000Ω.
4. If the coil circuit resistances are outside the test specifications, the coil must be replaced.

1986–89 Accord and 1987–91 Prelude

1. These vehicles use a 4-pin primary wiring configuration. With the ignition OFF, disconnect the primary and secondary wiring connectors from the coil.
2. Measure resistance between terminals A and D; the resistance on the primary side should be: 1986–89 Accord and 1987–89 Prelude, 1.2–1.5Ω; 1990–91 Prelude, 0.3–0.4Ω.
3. Measure the resistance between terminal A and the secondary terminal. Resistance should be: 1986–89 Accord and 87 Prelude,

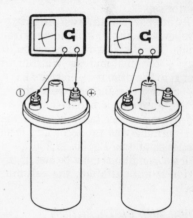

Testing the coil — 1984–85 Accord and 1984–86 Prelude

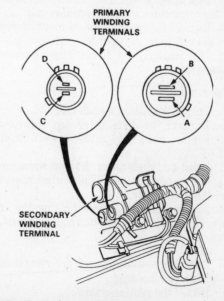

Coil testing 1986–89 Accord and 1987–91 Prelude

11,074–11,526Ω; 1988–91 Prelude, 9040–13,560Ω.

4. Check the resistance between terminals B and D; it should be approximately 2100–2300Ω for all vehicles.

5. Test at terminals A and C. Continuity must be present.

NOTE:Terminal C is not used on fuel-injected 1988–91 Preludes. No test is possible on these vehicles.

6. All test conditions must be met; if any test condition is not satisfied the coil must be replaced.

1990–91 Accord

1. The ignition coil is contained within the distributor. With the ignition OFF, remove the distributor cap.

2. Remove the screws holding the black/yellow wire and white/blue wires from the terminals. The Blk/Yl wire is connected to the primary + terminal and the Wht/Blu wire is connected to the primary − terminal.

3. Measure resistance between the terminals. Resistance should be 0.6–0.8Ω.

4. Measure the resistance between the primary + terminal and the secondary terminal. Resistance should be 12,800–19,200Ω.

5. All test conditions must be met; if any test condition is not satisfied, the coil must be replaced.

REMOVAL AND INSTALLATION

1984–89 Accord
1984–91 Prelude

1. Turn the ignition switch OFF.

2. Disconnect the primary and the secondary wiring connectors from the ignition coil.

3. Remove the ignition coil-to-mount screws and the coil from the vehicle.

4. To install, reverse the removal procedures.

1990–91 Accord

1. Turn the ignition switch OFF.

2. Remove the distributor cap, rotor, cap seal. Remove the shield or leak cover from the coil.

3. Label and disconnect the two wires running to the coil terminals. These wires must be reinstalled correctly.

4. remove the two screws holding the coil unit. Slide the coil out of the distributor housing.

To install

5. Carefully position the coil and slide it into the distributor housing.

6. Install the retaining screws.

7. Connect the wires to the terminals. The

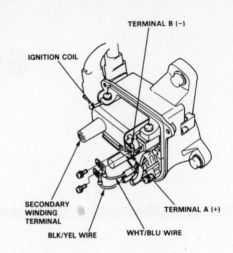

Ignition coil testing, 1990–91 Accord

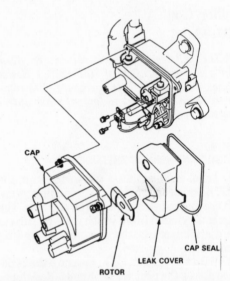

Make certain the distributor seal and coil cover is in place at reassembly

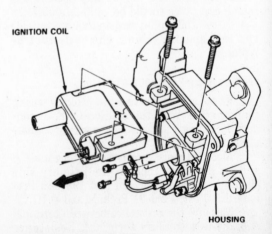

Coil removal, 1990–91 Accord

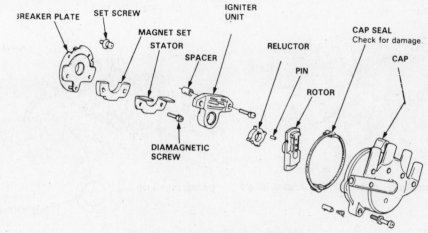

The igniter is inside the Hitachi distributor

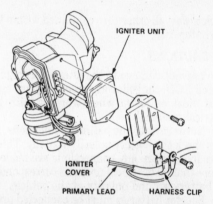

External igniters are used on Toyo Denso distributors

black/yellow wire should connect to terminal A, the + terminal. The white/blue wire connects to the B or − terminal.

8. Install the leak cover and cap seal. Make certain these seals align properly with their mounts.

9. Install the rotor and cap.

Igniter

Externally mounted igniters are removed in straightforward fashion. Always perform the work with the ignition OFF. Toyo Denso igniters mounted on the side of the distributor require the removal of two bolts and the harness clip. The igniter plugs directly to the distributor case. Before installation, coat the igniter pins with silicone grease.

Internally mounted igniters, such as on the Hitachi distributors, require the removal of the cap, rotor and reluctor. The igniter may be removed by removing the retaining screws. Note the position of the retaining screws; one is diamagnetic and must be reinstalled in the original location.

Distributor

The distributor is the device responsible for sending the spark to the correct plug. It is essentially a rotating switch, turning the current on and off to each terminal. For the vehicles covered in this book, all distributors are driven directly by a camshaft and are mounted at the end of the head. Except for the 1990–91 Accords, all distributors employ some combination of mechanical and vacuum advance system. These systems cause the spark timing to change in proportion to the speed of the engine. Some engines also employ vacuum retard. The 1990–91 Accord system is fully electronic, with all timing control handled by the Program Fuel Injection computer. No mechanical or vacuum advance is used.

A visual inspection of the distributor will reveal its type of advance; if only one vacuum hose is present, running to a round diaphragm housing on the side of the distributor, the system uses vacuum advance only. Two hoses indicate an advance and retard system.

REMOVAL AND INSTALLATION

1. Using masking tape, remove the spark plug wires from the cap and number them for installation as they are removed. Factory distributor caps will have a mark indicating cylinder No. 1.

2. Label and disconnect the vacuum hoses, the primary wire and the high tension wire. Some early models require disconnection of these wires at the coil. Label and disconnect any external wiring connectors at the distributor.

3. Remove the hold-down bolt(s) and remove the distributor from the head.

4. Recover the O-ring from the distributor shaft; discard the ring.

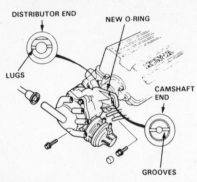

Distributor Installation, carbureted 1987 Accord. All are similar

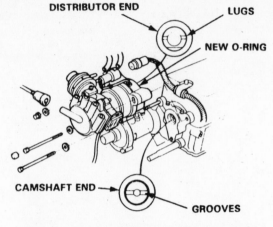

Example of distributor used on fuel injected engines

To install

5. Using a new O-ring, install it on the distributor shaft. Coat it lightly with a thin coat of clean oil.

6. The drive lugs in the end of the distributor shaft are slightly offset to match the offset in the end of the camshaft. Position the distributor shaft for an approximate match, then fit the distributor in place.

NOTE: *The distributor will only engage the cam in the correct matching position. This enlightened design allows the distributor to be installed correctly regardless of engine position, even if the engine was turned with the distributor out.*

7. Make certain the drive lugs are correctly engaged and the O-ring is in place. Install the retaining bolts centered in the mounts and just snug enough to hold the distributor in place.

8. Reconnect the external wiring and install the spark plug wires. Double check their placement.

9. Start the engine and set the timing. Tighten the distributor bolts.

Alternator

The alternator converts the mechanical energy which is supplied by the drive belt into electrical energy by electromagnetic induction. When the ignition switch is turned **ON**, current flows from the battery, through the charging system light, to the voltage regulator and finally to the alternator.

All present day Hondas use a nominal 12 volt alternator. (Exact output should be higher, generally 13.5–15.1 volts.) Amperage ratings may vary according to year, model and accessories. All use either a transistorized, non-adjustable voltage regulator or control the alternator output through the engine computer (ECU) used for the fuel injection. 1984–87 Preludes use an external regulator mounted on the right

shock tower; all others are contained within the alternator case.

PRECAUTIONS

To prevent damage to the alternator, regulator and ECU, the following precautionary measures must be taken when working with the electrical system.

1. Never reverse the battery connections. Always check the battery polarity visually. This is to be done before any connections are made to ensure that all of the connections correspond to the battery ground polarity of the vehicle.

2. Booster batteries must be connected properly. Make sure the positive cable of the booster battery is connected to the positive terminal of the battery which is getting the boost.

3. Disconnect the battery cables before using a fast charger; the charger has a tendency to force current through the diodes in the opposite direction. This causes damage.

4. Never use a fast charger as a booster for starting the car.

5. Never disconnect the alternator or regulator connectors while the engine is running.

6. Do not ground the alternator output terminal.

7. Do not operate the alternator on an open circuit with the field energized.

8. Do not attempt to polarize the alternator.

9. Disconnect the battery cables and remove the alternator before using an electric arc welder on the vehicle.

10. Protect the alternator from excessive moisture. If the engine is to be steam cleaned, cover or remove the alternator.

REMOVAL AND INSTALLATION

The alternator is generally mounted low on the engine on the firewall side. This makes access very awkward. The work must be done both over-the-fender and from below, depending on your agility and reach. Whenever the work is to be performed from below, the vehicle must be safely supported on jackstands. If only the front is supported, the parking brake must be applied and the rear wheels firmly blocked. Once elevated, the gravel or splash shield must be removed from under the engine.

1984–85 Accord

1. With the ignition OFF, disconnect the negative battery cable.
2. Disconnect the alternator wire harness connector and remove the terminal nut.
3. Remove the alternator adjusting bolt; loosen the nut on the mount bolt.
4. Swing the alternator towards the engine; remove the belt.
5. Remove the bolts holding the alternator bracket to the engine and remove the alternator with the bracket.

To install:

6. Install the alternator and bracket. Once in position with the bolts finger tight, install the belt. Tighten the mounting bracket bolts and the alternator mount (pivot) bolt to 45 Nm (33 ft. lbs).
7. Install the adjusting bolt, adjust the belt and tighten the nut to 22 Nm (16 ft. lbs).
8. Install the wire harness connector and secure the terminal nut.
9. Reconnect the negative battery cable.
10. If the vehicle was elevated, reinstall the splash shield. Lower the vehicle to the ground.

1986–1989 Accord

1. Disconnect the negative battery cable.
2. Elevate and safely support the vehicle.
3. Remove the splash shield from under the vehicle.
4. Disconnect the left driveshaft from the steering knuckle. Refer to Chapter 7 for procedure.
5. Disconnect the multi-pin connector from the back of the alternator. Remove the clip from the harness bracket.
6. Remove the terminal nut and disconnect the white wire from the B terminal.
7. Remove the alternator pivot or upper bolt and nut, then remove the belt from the alternator pulley.
8. Support the alternator; remove the through-bolt and remove the alternator.
9. The alternator mount or bracket may be removed if desired.

To install:

10. Fit the alternator into its mount; install the through-bolt finger-tight. Fit the belt onto the pulley.

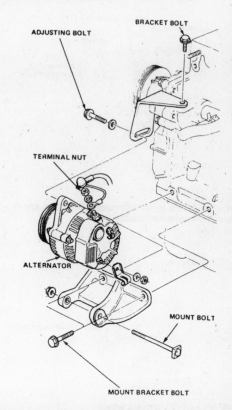

Alternator removal, 1984–85 Accord

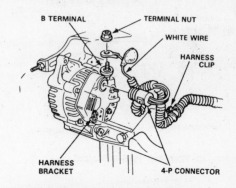

Don't forget the wiring clip and bracket when disconnecting 1986–89 Accord alternators

11. Install the upper alternator bolt. Make certain it goes through the eye of the adjusting bolt.
12. Adjust the belt tension. Tighten the nut on the through-bolt to 45 Nm (33 ft. lbs.) and tighten the upper bolt to 24 Nm (17 ft. lbs).
13. Install the white wire on the B terminal and tighten the nut.
14. Install the multi-pin harness to the alternator and secure the harness clip(s).
15. Reinstall the left driveshaft to the steering knuckle.

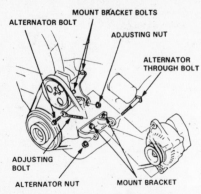

Make certain the upper bolt goes through the eye of the adjuster when reinstalling

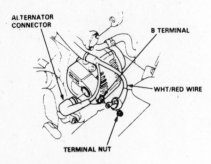

1990–91 Accord alternator wiring

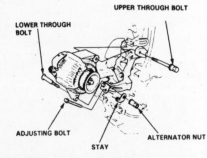

Removing the alternator, 1990–91 Accord

16. Install the splash shield. Lower the car to the ground.

17. Connect the negative battery cable.

1990–91 Accord

1. With the ignition OFF, disconnect the negative battery cable.

2. Remove the power steering pump. Refer to Chapter 8 for complete procedure.

3. Remove the cruise control actuator but do not disconnect the actuator cable; simply move the unit out of the way with the cable attached.

4. Disconnect the multi-pin electrical connector.

5. Remove the terminal nut and remove the wire from the B terminal.

6. Loosen the adjusting bolt; remove the alternator nut.

7. Remove the belt from the alternator pulley.

8. Remove the adjusting bolt, the lower through-bolt and the small support stay.

9. Support the alternator. Remove the upper through-bolt and remove the alternator.

10. If desired, remove the alternator mounting brackets.

To install:

11. If the alternator brackets were removed, reinstall them. Coat the bolts with a thread sealer or liquid thread lock. Install the bracket bolts and tighten them to 50 Nm (36 ft. lbs).

12. Fit the alternator into place. Install the upper through-bolt and tighten it to 45 Nm (33 ft. lbs).

13. Install the small stay, the lower through-bolt and the adjusting bolt. Make certain the adjusting bolt is properly installed.

14. Install the belt. Install the alternator nut. Adjust the belt tension. Tighten the alternator nut to 26 Nm (19 ft. lbs).

15. Connect the wire to the B terminal and tighten the nut.

16. Install the multi-pin connector to the alternator.

17. Install the cruise control actuator.

18. Install the power steering pump.

19. Connect the negative battery cable.

1984–87 Prelude

1. Disconnect the negative battery cable.

2. Remove the air cleaner assembly.

3. On carbureted engines, disconnect the engine wiring harness. The connector uses locking tabs on the top and bottom; lift both tabs at the same time before pulling the connector loose.

4. On fuel injected engines, disconnect the connector from the alternator and remove the clip at the harness bracket.

5. Remove the terminal nut; remove the wiring.

6. On carbureted engines, remove the alternator adjusting bolt and nut, then remove the belt from the pulley.

7. On fuel injected engines, remove the alternator bolt and nut and remove the belt from the pulley.

8. Remove the alternator through-bolt (lower bolt) and remove the alternator.

9. The mounting brackets may be removed if desired.

To install:

10. Install the mounting brackets if they were removed. Tighten the bolts to 45 Nm (33 ft. lbs.)

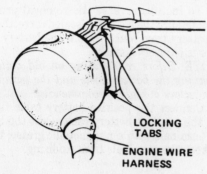

Alternator connector on carbureted engine

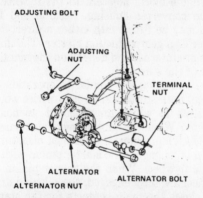

Alternator mounting and components, carbureted
Prelude through 1987

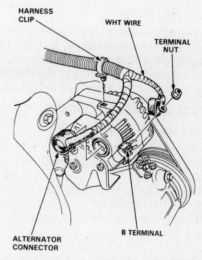

1988–91 Prelude alternator wiring connections

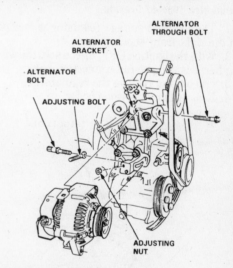

Alternator mounting and components, 1988–91 Prelude

11. Fit the alternator into position and install the through-bolt.

12. Install the belt. Install the adjusting or upper alternator bolt. Make certain the adjuster is correctly positioned.

13. Adjust the belt. Tighten the lower alternator nut or bolt to 45 Nm (33 ft. lbs). Tighten the upper alternator or adjusting nut to 24 Nm (17 ft. lbs).

14. Install the wiring on the terminal stud and tighten the terminal nut.

15. Connect the wiring harness connector to the alternator.

16. Install the air cleaner housing.

17. Connect the negative battery cable.

1988–91 Prelude

1. Disconnect the negative battery cable.

2. Remove the alternator connector from the alternator; remove the wire harness clip from the bracket.

3. Remove the terminal nut; remove the wiring from the terminal.

4. Loosen the through-bolt and the adjusting nut.

5. Remove the alternator bolt, then remove the belt.

6. Remove the through-bolt and remove the alternator.

To install:

7. Install the alternator in position and fit the through-bolt.

8. Install the belt on the pulley, then install the alternator bolt. Make certain the alternator bolt engages the adjuster.

9. Adjust the belt. Tighten the through-bolt to 45 Nm (33 ft. lbs.) and the alternator bolt to 25 Nm (18 ft. lbs).

10. Install the wiring on the B terminal and secure the nut.

11. Secure the wiring harness connector to the alternator.

12. Connect the negative battery cable.

Voltage Regulator

The regulator controls the output of the alternator. If the regulator did not limit the voltage output of the alternator, the excessive output could damage components of the electrical system, as well as the alternator or battery.

REMOVAL AND INSTALLATION

All Accord and 1988–91 Prelude

1. Remove the alternator.
2. Remove the brush holder (see previous procedure).
3. Remove the bolts holding the regulator and remove the regulator.
4. Reinstall the regulator and install the retaining screws.
5. Install the brush holder.
6. Reassemble and reinstall the alternator.

Carbureted 1984–87 Prelude

1. The external voltage regulator is located on the right front shock tower.
2. With the ignition OFF, disconnect the wiring harness and ground connection bolt.
3. Unbolt and remove the regulator.
4. Reassemble in reverse order.

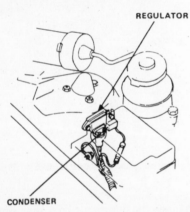

Carbureted Preludes use an external voltage regulator

Battery

Please refer to Chapter 1 for battery maintenance and care.

REMOVAL AND INSTALLATION

The battery is located in the engine compartment on all models.
1. Make sure the ignition switch is turned OFF.
2. Disconnect the negative battery cable first, then the positive cable from the battery.
3. Remove the battery hold down clamp nuts, the clamp and the battery from the vehicle.

4. To install, reverse the removal procedures; be sure the battery is seated correctly on the battery tray. Make certain the battery retainer is securely fastened.

NOTE: *Before re-installing an old battery, cleaning the battery posts and the terminal connectors is highly recommended.*

5. Connect the positive battery cable first, then the negative battery cable. Coat the battery terminals with a non-metallic grease; this will keep the terminals from oxidizing.

Starter

The starter is located on the firewall side of the engine block, adjacent to the flywheel or torque converter housing. Accords and Preludes may be fitted with either a direct-drive starter or a gear reduction starter. The differences are internal and depend on the manufacturer of the starter.

The two units are similar in operation and service. Both starters are 4-pole, series wound, DC units to which an outboard solenoid is mounted. When the ignition switch is turned to the START position, the solenoid armature is drawn in, engaging the starter pinion with the engine flywheel. When the starter pinion and flywheel are fully engaged, the solenoid armature closes the main contacts for the starter, causing the starter to crank the engine.

When the engine starts, the increased speed of the flywheel causes the gear to overrun the starter clutch and rotor. The gear continues in full mesh until the ignition is released from the START to the ON position, interrupting the starter current. A spring then returns the gear to its neutral position.

REMOVAL AND INSTALLATION

1. Disconnect both battery terminals, negative first.
2. Disconnect the starter cable from the starter motor; label and disconnect the wiring to the starter solenoid. Certain engine/transmission combinations have an engine harness secured in a clip on the starter. Remove the harness from the clip and position it out of the way.
3. Remove the starter motor by loosening the attaching bolts.
4. To install, reverse the removal procedures. Tighten the starter-to-engine bolts to 45 Nm (32 ft. lbs).
5. Connect the wiring to the starter securely.
6. Connect the battery cables, positive cable first.

ALTERNATOR SPECIFICATIONS

Year	Model	Alternator Output (amps)	Regulated Volts @ 75°F
1984	Accord	65A @ 5.500	14V @ 1000
	Prelude	60A @ 3.500	14V @ 820
1985	Accord	65A @ 5.500	14V @ 1000
	Prelude	60A @ 3.500	14V @ 820
1986	Accord	65A @ 5.500	14V @ 1000
	Prelude—Carb.	60A @ 3.500	14V @ 820
	Prelude—F. Inj.	65A @ 5.500	14V @ 1000
1987	Accord	65A @ 5.500	14V @ 1000
	Prelude—Carb.	60A @ 3.500	14V @ 820
	Prelude—F. Inj.	65A @ 5.500	14V @ 1000
1988	Accord	65A @ 5.500	14V @ 1000
	Prelude	70A @ 3.500	13.5V @ 1000
1989	Accord	65A @ 5.500	14V @ 1000
	Prelude	70A @ 3.500	13.5V @ 1000
1990	Accord	80A @ 3.500	13.5V @ 1000
	Prelude	70A @ 3.500	13.5V @ 1000
1991	Accord	80A @ 3.500	13.5V @ 1000
	Prelude	70A @ 3.500	13.5V @ 1000

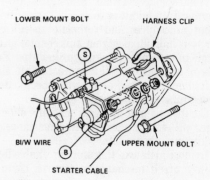

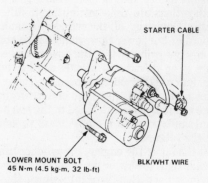

Starter replacement — 1988-91 Prelude

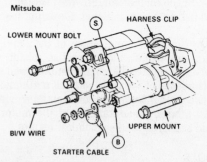

Starter replacement — 1986-89 Accord

ENGINE MECHANICAL
Description

The piston engine is a metal block containing a series of round chambers or cylinders. These chambers may be arranged in line or in a V;

hence, the description of an engine as an "inline 4 or 6" or a V6 or V8. The engines used in the Honda Accord and Prelude are water cooled, overhead cam, transversely mounted, inline four cylinder powerplants. The upper part of the engine block is usually an iron or aluminum-alloy casting. The casting forms outer walls around the cylinders with hollow areas in between, through which coolant circulates. The lower block provides a number of rigid mounting points for the crankshaft and its bearings. The lower block is referred to as the crankcase.

The crankshaft is a long, steel shaft mounted at the bottom of the engine and free to turn in its mounts. The mounting points (generally four to seven) and the bearings for the crankshaft are called main bearings. The crankshaft is the shaft which is made to turn through the function of the engine; this motion is then passed into the transmission/transaxle and on to the drive wheels.

Attached to the crankshaft are the connecting rods which run up to the pistons within the cylinders. As the air/fuel mixture explodes within the tightly sealed cylinder, the piston is forced downward. This motion is transferred through the connecting rod to the crankshaft and the shaft turns. As one piston finishes its power stroke, its next upward journey forces the burnt gasses out of the cylinder through the now-open exhaust valve. By the top of the stroke, the exhaust valve has closed and the intake valve has begun to open, allowing the fresh air/fuel charge to be sucked into the cylinder by the downward stroke of the piston. The intake valve closes, the piston once again comes back up and compresses the charge in the closed cylinder. At the top (approximately) of this stroke the spark plug fires, the charge explodes and another power stroke takes place. If you count the piston motions between power strokes, you'll see why automotive engines are called four-stroke or four-cycle engines.

While one cylinder is performing this cycle, all the others are also contributing in different timing. Obviously, all the cylinders cannot fire at once or the power flow would not be steady. As any one cylinder is on its power stroke, another is on its exhaust stroke, another on intake and another on compression. These constant power pulses keep the crank turning; a large round flywheel attached to the end of the crankshaft provides a stable mass to smooth out the rotation.

At the top of the engine, the cylinder head(s) provide tight covers for the cylinders. They contain machined chambers into which the fuel charge is forced as the piston reaches the top of its travel. These combustion chambers contain at least one intake and one exhaust valve which are opened and closed through the action of the camshaft. The spark plugs are screwed into the cylinder head so that the tips of the plugs protrude into the chamber.

Since the timing of the valve action (opening and closing) is critical to the combustion process, the camshaft is driven by a belt or chain. The valves are operated either by pushrods (called overhead valves—the valves are above the cam) or by the direct action of the cam pushing on the valves (overhead cam). All Accord and Prelude engines use overhead cam (OHC) engines. Some vehicles use two cams; thus the designation Dual Overhead Cam (DOHC).

Lubricating oil is stored in a pan or sump at the bottom of the engine. It is force fed to all the parts of the engine by the oil pump which may be driven by either the crank or the camshaft. The oil lubricates the entire engine by travelling through passages in the block and head. Additionally, the circulation of the oil provides 25–40% of the engine cooling.

If all this seems very complicated, keep in mind that the sole purpose of any motor—gas, diesel, electric, solar—is to turn a shaft. The motion of the shaft is then harnessed to perform a task such as pumping water, moving the vehicle, etc. Due to the constantly changing operating conditions found in a motor vehicle, accomplishing this shaft-turning in an automotive engine requires many supporting systems such as fuel delivery, exhaust handling, lubrication, cooling, starting, etc. Operation of these systems involve principles of mechanics, vacuum, electronics, etc. Being able to identify a problem by what system is involved will allow you to begin accurate diagnosis of the symptoms and causes.

Engine Overhaul Tips

Most engine overhaul procedures are fairly standard. In addition to specific parts replacement procedures and complete specifications for your individual engine, this chapter also is a guide to accepted rebuilding procedures. Examples of standard rebuilding practice are shown and should be used along with specific details concerning your particular engine.

Competent and accurate machine shop services will ensure maximum performance, reliability and engine life.

In most instances it is more profitable for the do-it-yourself mechanic to remove, clean and inspect the component, buy the necessary parts and deliver these to a shop for actual machine work.

On the other hand, much of the rebuilding work (crankshaft, block, bearings, piston rods, and other replaceable components) is well within the scope of the do-it-yourself mechanic. Patience, proper tools, and common sense coupled with a basic understanding of the motor can yield satisfying and economical results.

TOOLS

The tools required for an engine overhaul or parts replacement will depend on the depth of your involvement. With a few exceptions, they will be the tools found in a mechanic's tool kit (see Chapter 1). More in-depth work will require any or all of the following:

• A dial indicator (reading in thousandths of an inch or metric equivalent) mounted on a universal base. The base may or may not come with a new unit.

- Micrometers and telescope gauges
- Jaw and screw-type pullers
- Gasket scrapers; the best are wood or plastic
- Valve spring compressor
- Ring groove cleaner
- Piston ring expander and compressor
- Ridge reamer
- Cylinder hone or glaze breaker
- Plastigage®
- Engine stand. This single tool may be the most expensive piece of equipment in your garage but is well worth the cost. The engine can be bolted to it and then rotated into any position for work on the upper or lower end.
- Engine hoist or crane. Generally not worth the high cost of purchase unless you plan to remove engines on a regular basis, these units can be rented from many supply houses. Engine hoists are superior to overhead chain lifts because the castered lift can be repositioned instead of moving the vehicle.

The use of most of these tools is illustrated in this chapter. Many can be rented for a one-time use from a local parts jobber or tool supply house specializing in automotive work.

Occasionally, the use of special tools is called for. See the information on Special Tools and Safety Notice in the front of this book before substituting another tool.

INSPECTION TECHNIQUES

Procedures and specifications are given in this chapter for inspecting, cleaning and assessing the wear limits of most major components. Other procedures such as MagnaFlux® and Zyglo® can be used to locate material flaws and stress cracks. MagnaFlux® is a magnetic process applicable only to ferrous (iron and steel) materials. The Zyglo® process coats the material with a fluorescent dye penetrant and can be used on any material. Checks for suspected surface cracks can be more readily made using spot check dye. The dye is sprayed onto the suspected area, wiped off and the area sprayed with a developer. Cracks will show up brightly.

OVERHAUL TIPS

Aluminum has become extremely popular for use in engines, due to its low weight. Observe the following precautions when handling aluminum parts:

- Never hot tank aluminum parts (the caustic hot tank solution will eat the aluminum.)
- Remove all aluminum parts (identification tag, etc.) from engine parts prior to the tanking.
- Always coat threads lightly with engine oil or anti-seize compounds before installation to prevent seizure.
- Never overtighten bolts or spark plugs especially in aluminum threads.

Stripped threads in any component can be repaired using any of several commercial repair kits (Heli-Coil®, Microdot®, Keenserts®, etc).

When assembling the engine, any parts that will be in frictional contact must be pre-lubed to provide lubrication at initial start-up. Any product specifically formulated for this purpose can be used, but engine oil is not recommended as a pre-lube.

When semi-permanent (locked, but removable) installation of bolts or nuts is desired, threads should be cleaned and coated with Loctite® or other similar, commercial non-hardening sealant.

GENERAL ENGINE SPECIFICATIONS

Year	Model	Engine Displacement cu. in. (cc)	Fuel System Type	Net Horsepower @ rpm	Net Torque @ rpm (ft. lbs.)	Bore × Stroke (in.)	Compression Ratio	Oil Pressure @ rpm
1984	Accord	111.6 (1829)	3 bbl	86 @ 5800	99 @ 3500	3.15 × 3.58	9.0:1	50 @ 2000
	Prelude	111.6 (1829)	Dual Sidedraft	100 @ 5500	104 @ 4000	3.15 × 3.58	9.1:1	60 @ 1500
1985	Accord	111.6 (1829)	2 bbl	86 @ 5800	99 @ 3500	3.15 × 3.58	9.0:1	50 @ 2000
	Accord SE-i	111.6 (1829)	EFI	101 @ 5800	108 @ 2500	3.15 × 3.58	8.8:1	50 @ 2000
	Prelude	111.6 (1829)	Dual Sidedraft	100 @ 5500 ①	104 @ 4000	3.15 × 3.58	9.1:1	55 @ 2000
1986	Accord	119.3 (1955)	2 bbl	98 @ 5500	110 @ 3500	3.25 × 3.58	9.1:1	55 @ 2000
	Accord LX-i	119.3 (1955)	EFI	110 @ 5500	114 @ 4500	3.25 × 3.58	8.8:1	55 @ 2000
	Prelude	111.6 (1829)	Dual Sidedraft	100 @ 5500	107 @ 4000	3.15 × 3.58	9.1:1	50 @ 2000
	Prelude Si	119.3 (1955)	EFI	110 @ 5500	114 @ 4500	3.25 × 3.58	8.8:1	50 @ 2000

GENERAL ENGINE SPECIFICATIONS

Year	Model	Engine Displacement cu. in. (cc)	Fuel System Type	Net Horsepower @ rpm	Net Torque @ rpm (ft. lbs.)	Bore × Stroke (in.)	Compression Ratio	Oil Pressure @ rpm
1987	Accord	119.3 (1955)	2 bbl	98 @ 5500	109 @ 3500	3.25 × 3.58	9.1:1	55 @ 2000
	Accord LX-i	119.3 (1955)	EFI	110 @ 5500	114 @ 4500	3.25 × 3.58	8.8:1	55 @ 2000
	Prelude	111.6 (1829)	Dual Sidedraft	100 @ 5500	107 @ 4000	3.15 × 3.58	9.1:1	50 @ 2000
	Prelude Si	119.3 (1955)	EFI	110 @ 5500	114 @ 4500	3.25 × 3.58	8.8:1	50 @ 2000
1988	Accord DX/LX	119.0 (1955)	2 bbl	98 @ 5500	109 @ 3500	3.25 × 3.58	9.1:1	55 @ 2000
	Accord LX-i	119.0 (1955)	MP-PFI	110 @ 5500	114 @ 4500	3.25 × 3.58	9.3:1	55 @ 2000
	Prelude	119.0 (1955)	Dual Sidedraft	100 @ 5500	107 @ 4000	3.19 × 3.74	9.1:1	50 @ 2000
	Prelude Si	119.0 (1955)	EFI	110 @ 5500	114 @ 4500	3.18 × 3.74	9.0:1	50 @ 2000
1989	Accord DX/LX	119.0 (1955)	2 bbl	98 @ 5500	109 @ 3500	3.26 × 3.58	9.1:1	55–65 @ 3000
	Accord LX-i/SE-i	119.0 (1955)	MP-PFI	120 @ 5800	122 @ 4000	3.26 × 3.58	9.3:1	55–65 @ 3000
	Prelude	119.0 (1955)	Dual Sidedraft	①	111 @ 4800	3.19 × 3.74	9.1:1	75–87 @ 3000
	Prelude Si	110.3 (1955)	MP-PFI	135 @ 6200	127 @ 4500	3.19 × 3.74	9.0:1	75–87 @ 3000
1990	Accord DX/LX	132.0 (2156)	MP-FI	125 @ 5200	137 @ 4000	3.35 × 3.74	8.8:1	50 @ 3000
	Accord EX	132.0 (2156)	MP-FI	130 @ 5200	142 @ 4000	3.35 × 3.74	8.8:1	50 @ 3000
	Prelude S	119.0 (1955)	Dual Sidedraft	①	111 @ 4000	3.19 × 3.74	9.1:1	50 @ 3000
	Prelude Si	119.0 (1955)	MP-FI	135 @ 6200	127 @ 4000	3.19 × 3.74	9.0:1	50 @ 3000
	Prelude Si	125.0 (2056)	MP-FI	140 @ 5800	135 @ 5000	3.27 × 3.74	9.4:1	50 @ 3000
1991–92	Accord DX/LX	132.0 (2156)	MP-FI	125 @ 5200	137 @ 4000	3.35 × 3.74	8.8:1	50 @ 3000
	Accord EX	132.0 (2156)	MP-FI	130 @ 5200	142 @ 4000	3.35 × 3.74	8.8:1	50 @ 3000
	Accord SE	132.0 (2156)	MP-FI	140 @ 5600	142 @ 4500	3.35 × 3.74	8.8:1	50 @ 3000
	Prelude Si	119.0 (1955)	MP-FI	135 @ 6200	127 @ 4000	3.19 × 3.74	9.1:1	50 @ 3000
	Prelude Si	125.0 (2056)	MP-FI	140 @ 5800	135 @ 5000	3.27 × 3.74	9.4:1	50 @ 3000

MP-FI—Multipoint Fuel Injected
MP-PFI—Multipoint Port Fuel Injected
① Manual transaxle—104 @ 5800
   Automatic transaxle—105 @ 5800

VALVE SPECIFICATIONS

Year	Engine Displacement cu. in. (cc)	Seat Angle (deg.)	Face Angle (deg.)	Spring Test Pressure (lbs.)	Spring Installed Height (in.)	Stem-to-Guide Clearance (in.) Intake	Stem-to-Guide Clearance (in.) Exhaust	Stem Diameter (in.) Intake	Stem Diameter (in.) Exhaust
1984	111.6 (1829)	45	45	NA	①	0.0010–0.0020	0.002–0.004	0.2591–0.2594	0.2732–0.2736
1985	111.6 (1829)	45	45	NA	①	0.0010–0.0020	0.002–0.004	0.2591–0.2594	0.2732–0.2736
1986	111.6 (1829) 119.3 (1955)	45	45	NA	②	0.0010–0.0020	0.002–0.004	0.2591–0.2594	0.2732–0.2736
1987	111.6 (1829) 119.3 (1955)	45	45	NA	②	0.0010–0.0020	0.002–0.004	0.2591–0.2594	0.2732–0.2736
1988	119.0 (1955) Accord Prelude	45	45	NA	③	0.0010–0.0020	0.002–0.004	0.2591–0.2594	0.2732–0.2736
	119.0 (1955) Prelude Si	45	45	NA	1.683	0.0010–0.0020	0.002–0.003	0.2591–0.2594	0.2579–0.2583

VALVE SPECIFICATIONS

Year	Engine Displacement cu. in. (cc)	Seat Angle (deg.)	Face Angle (deg.)	Spring Test Pressure (lbs.)	Spring Installed Height (in.)	Stem-to-Guide Clearance (in.)		Stem Diameter (in.)	
						Intake	Exhaust	Intake	Exhaust
1989	119.0 (1955) Accord Prelude	45	45	NA	③	0.0010– 0.0020	0.000– 0.004	0.2591– 0.2594	0.2732– 0.2736
	119.0 (1955) Prelude Si	45	45	NA	1.683	0.0010– 0.0020	0.002– 0.003	0.2591– 0.2594	0.2579– 0.2583
1990	132.0 (2156)	45	45	NA	NA	0.0009– 0.0019	0.002– 0.003	0.2157– 0.2161	0.2146– 0.2150
	119.0 (1955)	45	45	NA	NA	0.0010– 0.0020	④	0.2591– 0.2594	⑤
	125.0 (2056)	45	45	NA	NA	0.0010– 0.0020	0.002– 0.003	0.2591– 0.2594	0.2579– 0.2583
1991–92	132.0 (2156)	45	45	NA	NA	0.0009– 0.0019	0.002– 0.003	0.2157– 0.2161	0.2146– 0.2150
	119.0 (1955)	45	45	NA	NA	0.0010– 0.0020	④	0.2591– 0.2594	⑤
	125.0 (2056)	45	45	NA	NA	0.0010– 0.0020	0.002– 0.003	0.2591– 0.2594	0.2579– 0.2583

① 1829 cc & 1955 cc
Intake: 1.660
Exh. Inner: 1.460
Exh. Outer: 1.670
Aux: 0.984 (carbureted)

② Intake: 1.913
Exhaust: 1.876
③ Intake: 1.913
Exhaust: 1.876

④ Prelude 2.0S: 0.002–0.004
Prelude 2.0Si: 0.002–0.003
⑤ Prelude 2.0S: 0.2732–0.2736
Prelude 2.0Si: 0.2579–0.2583

CAMSHAFT SPECIFICATIONS

All measurements given in inches.

Year	Model	Lobe Height	Bearing Clearance	Camshaft End Play	Max. Run-Out
1984	Accord	Manual: Aux in: 1.446 in A: 1.492 in B: 1.497 exh: 1.487 Automatic: Aux in: 1.446 in A: 1.484 in B: 1.502 exh: 1.487	Journals 1, 3, 5: 0.002–0.006 Journals 2 & 4: 0.002–0.004	0.002–0.006	0.001
	Prelude	Manual: in A: 1.530 in B: 1.512 exh: 1.532 Automatic: in A: 1.522 in B: 1.505 exh: 1.513	Journals 1, 3, 5: 0.002–0.004 Journals 2 & 4: 0.005–0.007	0.002–0.006	0.001
1985	Accord	All Fuel Injected: in A: 1.5297 in B: 1.5200 exh: 1.5274 Carbureted Manual: Aux in: 1.446 in A: 1.492 in B: 1.497 exh: 1.487 Carbureted Automatic: Aux in: 1.446 in A: 1.484 in B: 1.502 exh: 1.487	Journals 1, 3, 5: 0.002–0.004 Journals 2 & 4: 0.005–0.007	0.002–0.006	0.001

CAMSHAFT SPECIFICATIONS

All measurements given in inches.

Year	Model	Lobe Height	Bearing Clearance	Camshaft End Play	Max. Run-Out
1985	Prelude	Manual: in A: 1.530 in B: 1.512 exh: 1.532 Automatic: in A: 1.522 in B: 1.505 exh: 1.503	Journals 1, 3, 5: 0.002–0.004 Journals 2 & 4: 0.005–0.007	0.002–0.006	0.001
1986	Accord	Fuel Injected: in A: 1.5296 in B: 1.5198 exh: 1.5274 Carbureted Manual: in: 1.5148 exh: 1.5218 Carbureted Automatic: in: 1.5174 exh: 1.5200	Journals 1, 3, 5: 0.002–0.004 Journals 2 & 4: 0.005–0.007	0.002–0.006	0.001
	Prelude	Fuel Injected: in A: 1.5296 in B: 1.5198 exh: 1.5274 Carbureted Manual: in A: 1.530 in B: 1.512 exh: 1.532 Carbureted Automatic: in A: 1.522 in B: 1.505 exh: 1.513	Journals 1, 3, 5: 0.002–0.004 Journals 2 & 4: 0.005–0.007	0.002–0.006	0.001
1987	Accord	Fuel Injected: in A: 1.5296 in B: 1.5198 exh: 1.5274 Carbureted Manual: in: 1.5148 exh: 1.5218 Carbureted Automatic: in: 1.5174 exh: 1.5200	Journals 1, 3, 5: 0.002–0.004 Journals 2 & 4: 0.005–0.007	0.002–0.006	0.001
	Prelude	Fuel Injected: in A: 1.5296 in B: 1.5198 exh: 1.5274 Carbureted Manual: in A: 1.530 in B: 1.512 exh: 1.532 Carbureted Automatic: in A: 1.522 in B: 1.505 exh: 1.513	Journals 1, 3, 5: 0.002–0.004 Journals 2 & 4: 0.005–0.007	0.002–0.006	0.001
1988	Accord	Fuel Injected: in A: 1.5296 in B: 1.5198 exh: 1.5274 Carbureted Manual: in: 1.5148 exh: 1.5218 Carbureted Automatic: in: 1.5174 exh: 1.5200	Journals 1, 3, 5: 0.002–0.004 Journals 2 & 4: 0.005–0.007	0.002–0.006	0.001
	Prelude	Fuel Injected: in: 1.3274 exh: 1.3359 Carbureted: in A: 1.5198 in B: 1.5298 exh: 1.5274	Fuel Inj: 0.002–0.040 Carbureted: Journals 1, 3, 5: 0.002–0.004 Journals 2 & 4: 0.005–0.007	0.002–0.006	0.006

CAMSHAFT SPECIFICATIONS

All measurements given in inches.

Year	Model	Lobe Height	Bearing Clearance	Camshaft End Play	Max. Run-Out
1989	Accord	Fuel Injected: in A: 1.5296 in B: 1.5198 exh: 1.5274 Carbureted Manual: in: 1.5148 exh: 1.5218 Carbureted Automatic: in: 1.5174 exh: 1.5200	Journals 1, 3, 5: 0.002–0.004 Journals 2 & 4: 0.005–0.007	0.002–0.006	0.001
	Prelude	Fuel Injected: in: 1.3072 exh: 1.3200 Carbureted: in A: 1.5198 in B: 1.5298 exh: 1.5274	Fuel Inj: 0.002–0.004 Carbureted: Journals 1, 3, 5: 0.002–0.004 Journals 2 & 4: 0.005–0.007	0.002–0.006	0.006
1990	Accord	in: 1.5167 exh: 1.5266	0.002–0.0035	0.002–0.006	0.0006
	Prelude	DOHC: in: 1.3072 exh, B20A: 1.3200 exh, B21A: 1.3300 SOHC: in A: 1.5198 in B: 1.5298 exh: 1.5274	DOHC: Journals 1, 2, 3, 4, 6: 0.002–0.004 Journal 5: 0.004–0.006 SOHC: Journals 1, 3, 5: 0.002–0.004 Journals 2 & 4: 0.005–0.007	0.002–0.006	0.0006
1991	Accord	Single intake manifold: in: 1.5167 exh: 1.5266 Dual intake manifold: in: 1.5252 exh: 1.5343	0.002–0.004	0.002–0.006	0.0006
	Prelude	in: 1.3072 exh, B20A: 1.3200 exh, B21A: 1.3300	Journals 1, 2, 3, 4, 6: 0.002–0.004 Journal 5: 0.004–0.006	0.002–0.006	0.0006

CRANKSHAFT AND CONNECTING ROD SPECIFICATIONS

All measurements are given in inches.

Year	Engine Displacement cu. in. (cc)	Crankshaft				Connecting Rod		
		Main Brg. Journal Dia.	Main Brg. Oil Clearance	Shaft End-play	Thrust on No.	Journal Diameter	Oil Clearance	Side Clearance
1984	111.6 (1829)	1.9673–1.9683	0.0010–0.0022	0.004–0.014	3	1.7707–1.7717	0.0006–0.0015	0.006–0.012
1985	111.6 (1829)	1.9673–1.9683	0.0010–0.0022	0.004–0.014	3	1.7707–1.7717	0.0006–0.0015	0.006–0.012
1986	111.6 (1829)	1.9673–1.9683	0.0010–0.0022 ①	0.004–0.014	3	1.7707–1.7717	0.0008–0.0015	0.006–0.012
1987	111.6 (1829) 119.3 (1955)	1.9673–1.9683 ②	0.0010–0.0022 ①	0.004–0.014	3	1.7707–1.7717	0.0006–0.0015	0.006–0.012

CRANKSHAFT AND CONNECTING ROD SPECIFICATIONS
All measurements are given in inches.

Year	Engine Displacement cu. in. (cc)	Crankshaft				Connecting Rod		
		Main Brg. Journal Dia.	Main Brg. Oil Clearance	Shaft End-play	Thrust on No.	Journal Diameter	Oil Clearance	Side Clearance
1988	119.0 (1955) Accord	②	0.0010–0.0022 ①	0.004–0.014	3	1.7707–1.7717	0.0008–0.0015	0.006–0.012
	119.0 (1955) Prelude	2.1644–2.1654	0.0010–0.0017 ③	0.004–0.014	3	1.7707–1.7717 ④	0.0010–0.0017	0.006–0.012
1989	119.0 (1955) Accord	②	0.0010–0.0022 ①	0.004–0.014	3	1.7707–1.7717	0.0008–0.0015	0.006–0.012
	119.0 (1955) Prelude	2.1644–2.1654	0.0010–0.0017 ③	0.004–0.014	3	1.7707–1.7717 ④	0.0010–0.0017 ⑤	0.006–0.012
	119.0 (1955) Prelude Si	2.1644–2.1654	0.0010–0.0017 ③	0.004–0.014	3	1.8888–1.8900 ④	0.0010–0.0017	0.006–0.012
1990	132.0 (2156)	⑥	⑧	0.004–0.014	4	1.7710–1.7717	0.0008–0.0017	0.006–0.012
	119.0 (1955)	2.1644–2.1654 ⑩	⑦	0.004–0.014	3	1.7707–1.7717	⑨	0.006–0.012
	125.0 (2056)	2.1644–2.1654 ⑩	⑦	0.004–0.014	3	1.8888–1.8900	0.0010–0.0017	0.006–0.012
1991–92	132.0 (2156)	⑥	⑧	0.004–0.014	4	1.7710–1.7717	0.0008–0.0017	0.006–0.012
	119.0 (1955)	2.1644–2.1654 ⑩	⑦	0.004–0.014	3	1.7707–1.7717	⑨	0.006–0.012
	125.0 (2056)	2.1644–2.1654 ⑩	⑦	0.004–0.014	3	1.8888–1.8900	0.0010–0.0017	0.006–0.012

① No. 3—0.0013–0.0024
② Accord:
  No. 1—1.9676–1.9685
  No. 3—1.9671–1.9680
  No. 2, 4, 5: 1.9673–1.9683
③ No. 3—0.0012–0.0019
④ Prelude Si—1.8888–1.8900
⑤ Prelude with fuel injection—0.0010–0.0017
⑥ No. 1, 2—1.9676–1.9685
  No. 3—1.9674–1.9683
  No. 4, 5—1.9655–1.9688
⑦ No. 1, 5—0.0007–0.0014
  No. 2, 4—0.0010–0.0017
  No. 3—0.0012–0.0019
⑧ No. 1, 2—0.0009–0.0018
  No. 3—0.0014–0.0017
  No. 4, 5—0.0005–0.0015
⑨ Prelude 2.0S—0.0008–0.0015
  Prelude 2.0Si—0.0010–0.0017
⑩ No. 3—2.1642–2.1651

PISTON AND RING SPECIFICATIONS
All measurements are given in inches.

Year	Engine Displacement cu. in. (cc)	Piston Clearance	Ring Gap			Ring Side Clearance		
			Top Compression	Bottom Compression	Oil Control	Top Compression	Bottom Compression	Oil Control
1984	111.6 (1829)	0.0008–0.0016	0.008–0.014	0.008–0.014	0.008–0.035	0.0008–0.0018	0.0008–0.0018	Snug
1985	111.6 (1829)	0.0008–0.0016	0.008–0.014	0.008–0.014	0.008–0.035	0.0008–0.0018	0.0008–0.0018	Snug

PISTON AND RING SPECIFICATIONS

All measurements are given in inches.

| Year | Engine Displacement cu. in. (cc) | Piston Clearance | Ring Gap | | | Ring Side Clearance | | |
			Top Compression	Bottom Compression	Oil Control	Top Compression	Bottom Compression	Oil Control
1986	111.6 (1829)	0.0008–0.0016	0.008–0.014	0.008–0.014	0.008–0.035	0.0008–0.0018	0.0008–0.0018	Snug
	119.3 (1955)	0.0008–0.0016	0.008–0.014	0.010–0.015	0.008–0.020	0.0012–0.0022	0.0012–0.0022	Snug
1987	111.6 (1829)	0.0008–0.0016	0.008–0.014	0.008–0.014	0.008–0.035	0.0008–0.0018	0.0008–0.0018	Snug
	119.3 (1955)	0.0008–0.0016	0.008–0.014	0.010–0.014	0.008–0.020	0.0012–0.0024	0.0012–0.0024	Snug
1988	119.0 (1955)	0.0008–0.0016	0.008–0.014	0.016–0.022	0.008–0.028 ①	0.0012–0.0024 ②	0.0012–0.0024 ②	Snug
1989	119.0 (1955)	0.0008–0.0016	0.008–0.014	0.016–0.022 ③	0.008–0.028 ①	0.0012–0.0024 ②	0.0012–0.0024	Snug
1990	132.0 (2156)	0.0008–0.0016	0.008–0.014	0.016–0.022	0.007–0.027	0.0014–0.0024	0.0011–0.0022	Snug
	119.0 (1955)	0.0008–0.0016	0.008–0.014	0.016–0.022	0.008–0.020	0.0012–0.0022	0.0012–0.0022	Snug
	125.0 (2056)	0.0004–0.0013	0.010–0.014	0.018–0.022	0.008–0.020	0.0014–0.0026	0.0012–0.0024	Snug
1991–92	132.0 (2156)	0.0008–0.0016	0.008–0.014	0.016–0.022	0.007–0.027	0.0014–0.0024	0.0011–0.0022	Snug
	119.0 (1955)	0.0008–0.0016	0.008–0.014	0.016–0.022	0.008–0.020	0.0012–0.0022	0.0012–0.0022	Snug
	125.0 (2056)	0.0004–0.0013	0.010–0.014	0.018–0.022	0.008–0.020	0.0014–0.0026	0.0012–0.0024	Snug

① Prelude equipped with carburetor—0.008–0.020
② Prelude—0.0012–0.0022
③ Prelude—0.016–0.022

TORQUE SPECIFICATIONS

All readings in ft. lbs.

| Year | Engine Displacement cu. in. (cc) | Cylinder Head Bolts ① | Main Bearing Bolts | Rod Bearing Bolts | Crankshaft Pulley Bolts | Flywheel Bolts | Manifold | | Spark Plugs | Lug Nuts |
							Intake	Exhaust		
1984	111.6 (1829)	49	48②	23	83	76①	16	22	13	80
1985	111.6 (1829)	49	48②	23	83	76①	16	22	13	80
1986	111.6 (1829) 119.3 (1955)	49	48②	23	83	76①	16	22	13	80
1987	111.6 (1829) 119.3 (1955)	49	48⑧	23	83	76①	16	22	13	80
1988	119.0 (1955)	49	49	23②	83	76①	20③	23④	13	80
1989	119.0 (1955)	49	49⑤	23	108⑤	76①	16	23⑥	13	80
1990	132.0 (2156)	78	52⑤	34	159⑤	76①	16	23	13	80
	119.0 (1955)	49⑤	49⑤	23⑦	108⑤	76①	16	23	13	80
	125.0 (2056)	49⑤	49⑤	34	108⑤	76①	16	22	13	80

TORQUE SPECIFICATIONS

All readings in ft. lbs.

Year	Engine Displacement cu. in. (cc)	Cylinder Head Bolts ①	Main Bearing Bolts	Rod Bearing Bolts	Crankshaft Pulley Bolts	Flywheel Bolts	Manifold		Spark Plugs	Lug Nuts
							Intake	Exhaust		
1991	132.0 (2156)	78	52⑤	34	159⑤	76①	16	23	13	80
	119.0 (1955)	49⑤	49⑤	23⑦	108⑤	76①	16	22	13	80
	125.0 (2056)	49⑤	49⑤	34	108⑤	76①	16	22	13	80

① Automatic Transaxle—54
② Fuel Injected Engine—33
③ Prelude—16
④ Prelude—26
⑤ Dip bolts in clean engine oil
⑥ Fuel Injected Prelude—26
⑦ Fuel Injected Engine—34
⑧ Fuel Injected Engine—49

Engine

REMOVAL AND INSTALLATION

CAUTION: *If any repair operation requires the removal of a component of the air conditioning system (on vehicles equipped), do not disconnect the refrigerant lines. If it is impossible to move the component out of the way with the lines attached, have the air conditioning system evacuated by a trained service professional. The air conditioning system contains refrigerant under pressure. This gas can be very dangerous.*

When draining the coolant, keep in mind that cats and dogs are attracted by the ethylene glycol antifreeze, and are quite likely to drink any that is left in an uncovered container or in puddles on the ground. This will prove fatal in sufficient quantity. Always drain the coolant into a sealable container. Coolant should be reused unless it is contaminated or several years old.

The EPA warns that prolonged contact with used engine oil may cause a number of skin disorders, including cancer! You should make every effort to minimize your exposure to used engine oil. Protective gloves should be worn when changing the oil. Wash your hands and any other exposed skin areas as soon as possible after exposure to used engine oil. Soap and water, or waterless hand cleaner should be used.

1984–85 Accord: 1.8L Engine
1984–87 Prelude: 1.8L or 2.0L Engines

NOTE: *All wires and hoses should be labeled at the time of removal. The amount of time saved during reassembly makes the extra effort well worthwhile.*

1. Apply the parking brake and place blocks behind the rear wheels. Raise and support the front of the vehicle on jackstands.

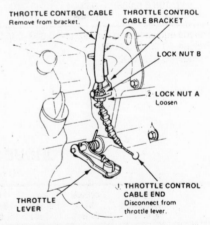

Shift cable mounting

Disconnecting the throttle control cable. Don't loosen lock nut B

2. Disconnect the negative battery cable, then the positive battery cable. Remove the battery and the battery tray from the engine compartment.

3. Double check the security of the jackstands and supports under the car.

4. Remove the splash guard under the en-

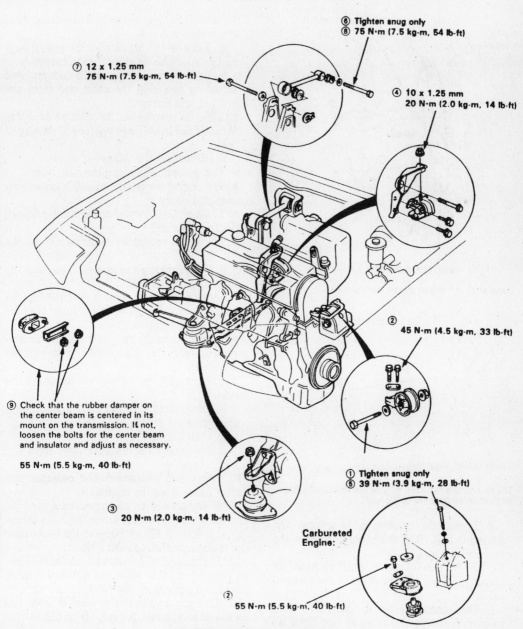

⑥ Tighten snug only
⑧ 75 N·m (7.5 kg-m, 54 lb-ft)

⑦ 12 x 1.25 mm
75 N·m (7.5 kg-m, 54 lb-ft)

④ 10 x 1.25 mm
20 N·m (2.0 kg-m, 14 lb-ft)

② 45 N·m (4.5 kg-m, 33 lb-ft)

⑨ Check that the rubber damper on the center beam is centered in its mount on the transmission. If not, loosen the bolts for the center beam and insulator and adjust as necessary.

55 N·m (5.5 kg-m, 40 lb-ft)

① Tighten snug only
⑤ 39 N·m (3.9 kg-m, 28 lb-ft)

③ 20 N·m (2.0 kg-m, 14 lb-ft)

Carbureted Engine:

② 55 N·m (5.5 kg-m, 40 lb-ft)

Disconnect the engine mount bolts...

gine. Using a felt tip marker, mark the hood hinge outline on the hood; remove the hood bolts and the hood.

NOTE: *For Prelude, remove the caps on the headlight motor manual control knobs. Raise the headlights to the UP position. Remove the 5 screws holding the grille and remove the grille.*

5. Drain the engine oil.

NOTE: *When replacing the drain plug be sure to use a new washer.*

6. Remove the radiator cap. Open the radia-

tor drain petcock and drain the coolant from the radiator.

7. Remove the transaxle filler plug; remove the drain plug and drain the transaxle.

8. If equipped with a carburetor, perform the following procedures:

a. Label and remove the coil wires and the engine secondary ground cable located on the valve cover.

b. Remove the air cleaner cover and filter.

c. Remove the air intake ducts, the air cleaner nuts/bolts, the air control valve and the air cleaner.

ENGINE MOUNT TOWER

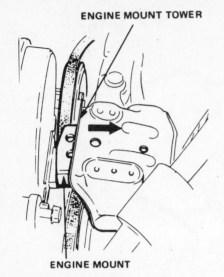

ENGINE MOUNT

...and push the engine mount into the tower

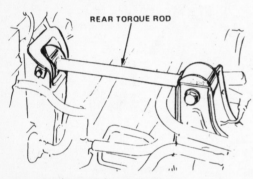

REAR TORQUE ROD

The rear torque rod need only be disconnected at the engine; swing it up out of the way

d. Loosen the throttle cable locknut and adjusting nut. Slip the cable end from the carburetor linkage.

NOTE: *Be careful not to bend or kink the throttle cable. Always replace a damaged cable.*

e. Disconnect the No. 1 control box connector. Remove the control box from its bracket; support it with stiff wire and allow it hang next to the engine.

f. Disconnect the fuel line from the fuel filter and the solenoid vacuum hose from the charcoal canister.

g. For California or High Altitude models, remove the air jet controller.

9. If equipped with fuel injection, perform the following procedures:

a. Remove the air intake duct. Disconnect the cruise control vacuum hose from the air intake duct and remove the resonator tube.

b. Remove the secondary ground cable from the top of the engine.

c. Disconnect the air box connecting tube.

Unscrew the tube clamp bolt and disconnect the emission tubes.

d. Remove the air cleaner mounting nuts and remove the air cleaner case assembly.

e. Loosen the throttle cable locknut and adjusting nut. Slip the cable end from the bracket and linkage.

NOTE: *Be careful not to bend or kink the throttle cable. Always replace a damaged cable.*

f. Disconnect the following wires:

• The ground cable from the fuse box.

• The engine compartment sub harness connector and clamp.

• The high tension wire and ignition primary leaks from the coil.

• The radio condenser connector from the coil.

g. To relieve the fuel pressure, perform the following procedures:

• Using a shop rag, place it over the fuel filter to absorb any gasoline which may be sprayed on the engine.

• Slowly loosen the service bolt approximately one full turn; this will relieve any pressure in the system.

• Using a new sealing washer, retighten the service bolt.

h. Disconnect the fuel return hose from the pressure regulator. Remove the banjo nut, then the fuel hose.

i. Disconnect the vacuum hose from the brake booster.

10. Label and disconnect the radiator and heater hoses from the engine.

11. If equipped with an automatic transaxle, disconnect the oil cooler hoses from the transaxle and drain the fluid. Support the hoses near the radiator without kinking them.

12. If equipped with a manual transaxle, loosen the clutch cable adjusting nut and remove the clutch cable from the release arm.

13. Disconnect the battery cable from the transaxle and the starter cable from the starter motor terminal.

14. Disconnect both electrical harness connectors from the engine.

15. Remove the speedometer cable clip. Pull the cable from the holder.

NOTE: *DO NOT remove the holder as the speedometer gear may drop into the transaxle. This is not good.*

16. If equipped with power steering perform the following procedures:

a. Remove the speed sensor-to-transaxle bolt and the sensor complete with the hoses.

NOTE: *Do not disconnect the hoses from the speed sensor; simply move the sensor out of the way with the hoses attached.*

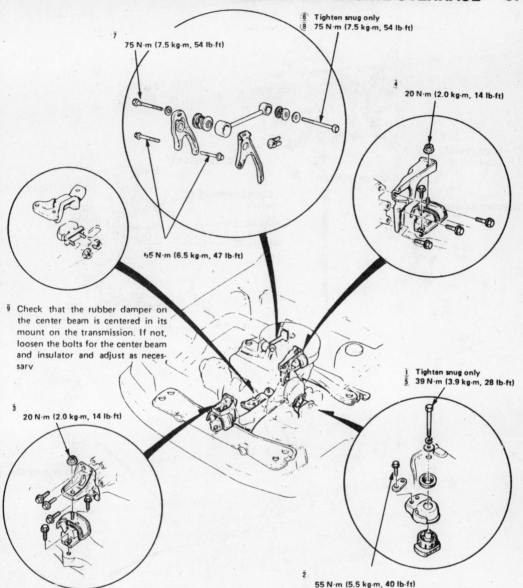

6 Tighten snug only
8 75 N·m (7.5 kg·m, 54 lb·ft)

7 75 N·m (7.5 kg·m, 54 lb·ft)

4 20 N·m (2.0 kg·m, 14 lb·ft)

5 55 N·m (6.5 kg·m, 47 lb·ft)

9 Check that the rubber damper on the center beam is centered in its mount on the transmission. If not, loosen the bolts for the center beam and insulator and adjust as necessary

1 Tighten snug only
5 39 N·m (3.9 kg·m, 28 lb·ft)

3 20 N·m (2.0 kg·m, 14 lb·ft)

2 55 N·m (5.5 kg·m, 40 lb·ft)

Accord engine mounts tightening order and torque

b. Remove the power steering pump adjusting bolt, mounting bolt and the V-belt.

c. Without disconnecting the hoses, pull the pump away from its mounting bracket and position it out of the way. Support it with stiff wire—do NOT allow it to hang by the hoses.

d. Remove the power steering hose bracket from the cylinder head.

17. Remove the center beam beneath the engine. Loosen the radius rod nuts to aid in the later removal of the halfshafts.

18. If equipped with air conditioning, perform the following procedures:

a. Remove the compressor clutch lead wire.

b. Loosen the belt adjusting bolt and the drive belt.

NOTE: *DO NOT loosen or disconnect the air conditioner hoses. The air conditioner compressor can be moved without discharging the air conditioner system.*

c. Remove the compressor mounting bolts and lift the compressor out of the bracket, with the hoses attached. Support it on the front bulkhead with a piece of strong wire. Never hang the compressor by its hoses.

19. If equipped with a manual transaxle, remove the shift rod yoke attaching bolt and disconnect the shift lever torque rod from the clutch housing.

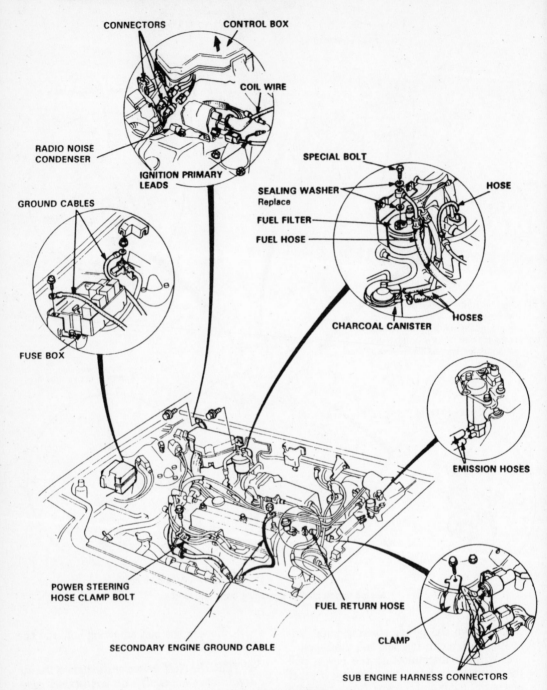

CONNECTORS

CONTROL BOX

COIL WIRE

RADIO NOISE
CONDENSER

IGNITION PRIMARY
LEADS

SPECIAL BOLT

SEALING WASHER
Replace

HOSE

GROUND CABLES

FUEL FILTER

FUEL HOSE

FUSE BOX

CHARCOAL CANISTER

HOSES

EMISSION HOSES

POWER STEERING
HOSE CLAMP BOLT

FUEL RETURN HOSE

CLAMP

SECONDARY ENGINE GROUND CABLE

SUB ENGINE HARNESS CONNECTORS

Prelude component details

20. If equipped with an automatic transaxle, perform the following procedures:

a. Remove the center console.

b. Place the shift lever in Reverse. Remove the lock pin from the end of the shift cable.

c. Remove the shift cable mounting bolts and the shift cable holder.

d. Remove the throttle cable from the throttle lever. Loosen the lower locknut and remove the cable from the bracket.

NOTE: *DO NOT loosen the upper locknut as it will change the transaxle shift points.*

21. Disconnect the right and left lower ball joints and the tie rod ends.

22. To remove the halfshafts, perform the following procedures:

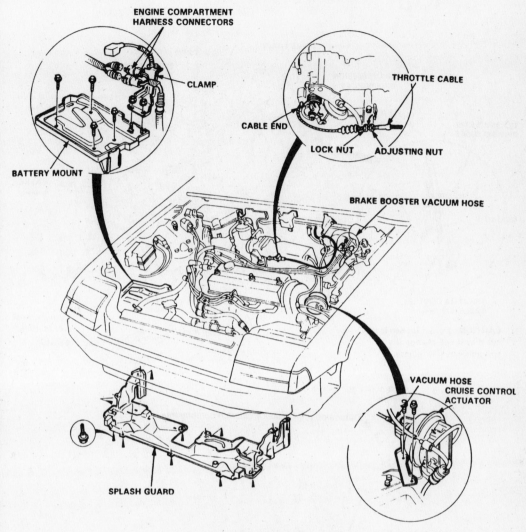

Prelude engine compartment details

a. Remove the jackstands and lower the vehicle. Using a 32mm socket, loosen the spindle nuts. Again raise and support the vehicle on jackstands.

b. Remove the front wheel and the spindle nut.

c. Remove the ball joint bolt and separate the ball joint from the front hub.

d. Disconnect the tie rods from the steering knuckles.

e. Remove the sway bar bolts.

f. Pull the front hub outward and off the halfshafts.

g. Using a small pry bar, pry out the inboard CV-joint approximately ½ inch to release the spring clip from the differential. Pull the halfshaft from the transaxle case.

NOTE: *When installing the halfshaft, insert the shaft until the spring clip clicks into the*

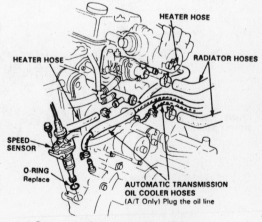

● Remove speed sensor complete with hoses.

Prelude hoses and speed sensor

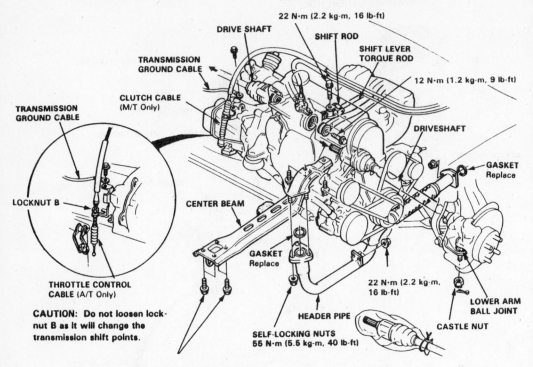

SHIFT ROD YOKE ATTACHMENT BOLT
22 N·m (2.2 kg·m, 16 lb-ft)

DRIVE SHAFT

SHIFT ROD

SHIFT LEVER
TORQUE ROD

12 N·m (1.2 kg·m, 9 lb-ft)

TRANSMISSION
GROUND CABLE

CLUTCH CABLE
(M/T Only)

DRIVESHAFT

TRANSMISSION
GROUND CABLE

GASKET
Replace

LOCKNUT B

CENTER BEAM

THROTTLE CONTROL
CABLE (A/T Only)

GASKET
Replace

22 N·m (2.2 kg·m, 16 lb-ft)

LOWER ARM
BALL JOINT

CASTLE NUT

HEADER PIPE

SELF-LOCKING NUTS
55 N·m (5.5 kg·m, 40 lb-ft)

CAUTION: Do not loosen locknut B as it will change the
transmission shift points.

50 N·m (5.0 kg·m, 36 lb·ft)
Replace

Prelude engine/transaxle external components

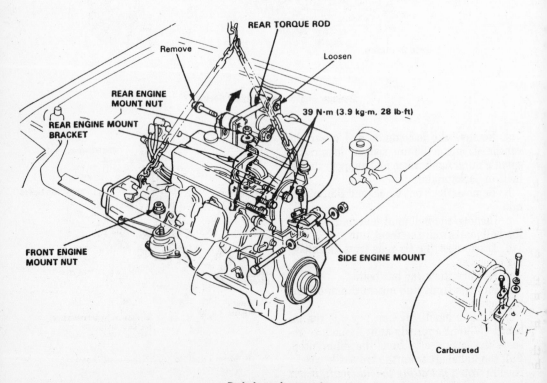

REAR TORQUE ROD

Remove

Loosen

REAR ENGINE
MOUNT NUT

39 N·m (3.9 kg·m, 28 lb-ft)

REAR ENGINE MOUNT
BRACKET

FRONT ENGINE
MOUNT NUT

SIDE ENGINE MOUNT

Carbureted

Prelude engine mounts

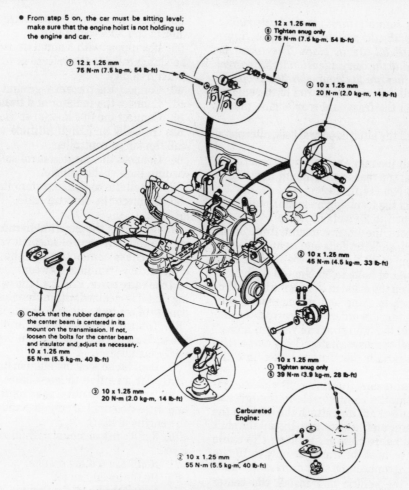

• From step 5 on, the car must be sitting level; make sure that the engine hoist is not holding up the engine and car.

⑦ 12 x 1.25 mm
75 N·m (7.5 kg-m, 54 lb-ft)

12 x 1.25 mm
⑥ Tighten snug only
⑧ 75 N·m (7.5 kg-m, 54 lb-ft)

④ 10 x 1.25 mm
20 N·m (2.0 kg-m, 14 lb-ft)

② 10 x 1.25 mm
45 N·m (4.5 kg-m, 33 lb-ft)

⑨ Check that the rubber damper on the center beam is centered in its mount on the transmission. If not, loosen the bolts for the center beam and insulator and adjust as necessary.
10 x 1.25 mm
55 N·m (5.5 kg-m, 40 lb-ft)

③ 10 x 1.25 mm
20 N·m (2.0 kg-m, 14 lb-ft)

10 x 1.25 mm
① Tighten snug only
⑤ 39 N·m (3.9 kg-m, 28 lb-ft)

Carbureted Engine:

② 10 x 1.25 mm
55 N·m (5.5 kg-m, 40 lb-ft)

Prelude engine mount tightening order and torque

groove. *Always use a new spring clip when installing halfshafts.*

23. On fuel injected models, disconnect the sub-engine harness connectors and clamp.

24. Remove the exhaust header pipe.

25. Attach a chain hoist to the engine and raise it slightly to remove the slack.

26. Disconnect the No. 2 control box connector, lift the control box off of its bracket and allow it hang next to the engine.

27. If equipped with air conditioning, remove the idle control solenoid valve.

28. If equipped with an air chamber (Calif. and High Altitude), remove it.

29. From under the air chamber, remove the three engine mount bolts. Push the engine mount into the engine mount tower.

30. Remove the front and rear engine mount nuts.

31. Loosen the alternator bolts and remove the drive belt. Disconnect the alternator wire harness and remove the alternator.

32. At the engine, remove the bolt from the rear torque rod; loosen the bolt in the frame mount, swing the rod up and out of the way.

33. Carefully raise the engine from the vehicle, checking that all wires and hoses have been removed from the engine/transaxle. Remove it from the vehicle.

34. Remove the transmission.

35. If manual transmission, remove the clutch cover (pressure plate) and clutch disc.

36. Mount the engine on an engine stand, making sure the mounting bolts are tight. If an engine stand is not available, support the engine in an upright position with blocks. Never leave an engine hanging from a lift or hoist.

To install:

37. The transaxle assembly should be installed to the engine before reinstallation. The engine should be completely assembled with oil pan, valve cover, etc. in place, even if they are to be remove later.

38. Lower the engine into the vehicle.

NOTE: *When installing the engine mounts and vibration dampers in the following steps, the bolts running through the large rubber bushings should only be set snug or finger tight until all are in place. They must be tightened to the correct tension in the correct order if they are to damp vibration properly.*

39. Install the rear torque rod to the engine.

40. Install the front and rear engine mount nuts.

41. Install the alternator brackets, alternator and belt.

42. Install the rear engine mount bracket.

43. install the rear engine mount nut. Tighten it to 20 Nm (14 ft. lbs.)

44. Install the front engine mount nut, tightening the bolt to 20 Nm (14 ft. lbs).

45. Retrieve the engine mount from inside the tower; install the bolts and tighten the solo bolt (on top) to 39 Nm (28 ft. lbs). Tighten the adjacent pair of bolts to 55 Nm (40 ft. lbs).

46. Slacken the chain in the engine hoist. Proceed to each bushing and motor mount bolt, tightening them in order to the correct torque.

47. Install the cruise control vacuum hoses.

48. Install the drive shafts. Use a new circlip and make certain the shaft is locked into the transaxle.

49. For automatic transmission vehicles, connect the throttle control cable to the bracket, tighten the locknut and attach the cable to the throttle lever on the transaxle. Install the shift cable and cable clamps; tighten the cable mounting bolts at the transaxle only to 10 Nm (7 ft. lbs). Reconnect the shift cable at the shifter inside the vehicle and install the center console.

50. For manual transmission vehicles, install the shift rod yoke and bolt; tighten it to 22 Nm (16 ft. lbs).

51. Connect the shift lever torque rod; tighten the bolt to 10 Nm (7 ft. lbs.).

52. Install the air conditioning compressor and belt.

53. Using new gaskets and self-locking bolts, connect the exhaust system to the engine. Tighten the nuts to 55 Nm (40 ft. lbs). Install and tighten the 2 bolts for the support bracket.

54. Tighten the radius rod nuts to 44 Nm (32 ft. lbs).

55. Install the center beam under the engine. Use new nuts and tighten them to 50 Nm (35 ft. lbs.)

56. Install the power steering pump and belt. Install the speed sensor, tightening the bolt only to 10 Nm (7 ft. lbs.)

57. Install the speedometer cable. Align the cable end with the slot in the holder. Install the locking clip so that the bent leg is in the groove. double check this installation by pulling gently on the cable; it should not come loose.

58. If equipped with automatic transaxle, connect the ATF cooler lines.

59. If equipped with manual transaxle, install the clutch cable to the release arm. Adjust the clutch free play.

60. Connect the transaxle ground cable.

61. Connect the radiator and heater hoses.

62. Connect the fuel hose(s) at the fuel filter.

63. On Calif. and High Altitude vehicles, install the air jet controller.

64. Connect the purge control solenoid valve vacuum hose at the canister.

65. Install the control box onto its bracket.

66. Connect the throttle cable. Tighten the locknut.

67. Reconnect the electrical harnesses including the coil, idle control solenoid valve, engine wire harness connector and the secondary ground cable running between the bodywork and the valve cover. Check all the wiring, insuring that it is retained within the clips and not in danger of contact with hot or moving parts.

68. Install the air cleaner and air intake tubes. Make certain the vacuum hoses are correctly installed.

69. Double check all installation items, paying particular attention to loose hoses or hanging wires, untightened nuts, poor routing of hoses and wires (too tight or rubbing) and tools left in the engine area.

70. Refill the transmission fluid to the proper level.

71. Refill the cooling system.

72. Refill the engine oil.

73. Install the hood. On Prelude, reinstall the grille and crank the headlamps to the DOWN position.

74. Connect the battery cables, positive first.

75. Disconnect the coil wire from the distributor. Insulate or protect the end of the cable so it does not arc to the engine or surrounding metal. Without touching the accelerator, turn the ignition switch to the START position and crank the engine for about 5–10 seconds; this will develop some oil pressure within the motor. Do not exceed 10 seconds cranking.

76. Switch the ignition OFF and reconnect the coil.

77. Start the engine, allowing it to idle. Check the hoses and lines carefully for any sign of leakage.

78. Bleed the air from the cooling system; check the timing and idle speed.

79. After the engine has warmed up fully and the fan(s) have come on at least once, recheck the engine for fluid leaks. Switch the engine OFF.

80. Adjust the belts, clutch and throttle cable as necessary.

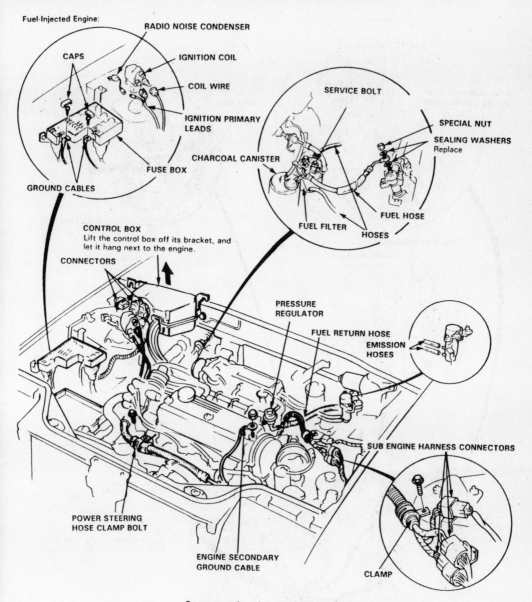

Component location, 1986–89 Accord

1986–89 Accord: 2.0L Engine

1. Elevate and safely support the vehicle on jackstands. Double check the security of the supports.

2. Disconnect the negative battery cable, then the positive cable.

3. Use a felt-tip marker to outline the hood hinges on the inside of the hood. Disconnect the washer fluid hose and remove the hood.

4. Remove the splash shield from below the engine. Drain the engine oil. Install a new washer on the drain plug, reinstall it and tighten it properly. This prevents embarrassment after the engine is reinstalled.

5. With the engine cold, drain the coolant into a container and save it for re-use.

6. Drain the transaxle. Reinstall the drain plug with a new washer and tighten properly.

7. Remove the air intake duct. Remove the retaining bolts holding the air filter housing and remove the housing assembly.

8. On fuel injected vehicles, relieve the fuel pressure using the correct procedure.

CAUTION: *The fuel system is under pressure. Release pressure slowly and contain spillage. Observe no smoking/no open flame precautions. Have a Class B-C (dry powder)*

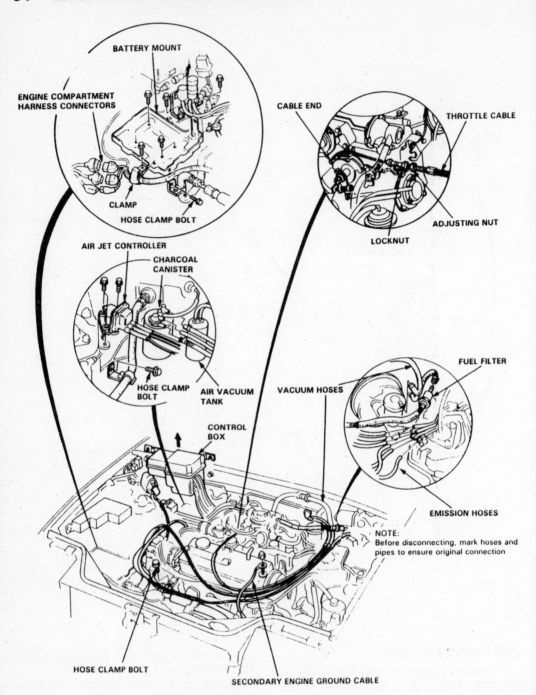

Component location and detail, 1986–89 Accord

fire extinguisher within arm's reach at all times.

9. All wires and hoses should be labeled at the time of removal. The amount of time saved during reassembly makes the extra effort well worthwhile. Whenever possible, disconnect a vacuum hose from a component on the firewall or fender, not at the engine. The engine will be removed with the lines and hoses attached.

10. On fuel injected vehicles, disconnect or remove the following items:

a. At the fusebox: ground cables (remove the plastic caps for access), condenser, coil wires and ignition leads.

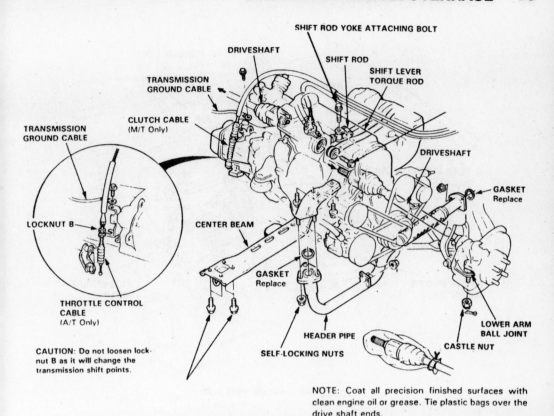

SHIFT ROD YOKE ATTACHING BOLT
DRIVESHAFT
SHIFT ROD
SHIFT LEVER
TORQUE ROD
TRANSMISSION
GROUND CABLE
CLUTCH CABLE
(M/T Only)
DRIVESHAFT
TRANSMISSION
GROUND CABLE
GASKET
Replace
LOCKNUT B
CENTER BEAM
GASKET
Replace
THROTTLE CONTROL
CABLE
(A/T Only)
HEADER PIPE
SELF-LOCKING NUTS
LOWER ARM
BALL JOINT
CASTLE NUT

CAUTION: Do not loosen lock-nut B as it will change the transmission shift points.

NOTE: Coat all precision finished surfaces with clean engine oil or grease. Tie plastic bags over the drive shaft ends.

External engine components — 1986–89 Accord

b. Hoses from the charcoal canister.

c. Fuel line and return line at the pressure regulator. Plug the hoses and ports to prevent fuel spillage or the entry of dirt.

d. Control box on right side firewall. Lift the box off its bracket, support it with wire and allow it to hang next to the engine. It will come out with the engine.

e. Electrical connectors near the control box.

f. Clamp bolt holding the power steering hose at the front of the engine.

g. Ground cable running from the valve cover to the radiator support.

h. Engine harness connectors at the left side of the engine.

i. Remove the battery and battery tray, then disconnect the harness connectors found below the tray. Remove the bracket holding the engine harness.

j. Disconnect the vacuum hose(s) from the cruise control actuator. Remove the two bolts holding the actuator and move the assembly well out of the way. Do not disconnect or kink the cable.

k. Disconnect the large vacuum hose running to the brake booster.

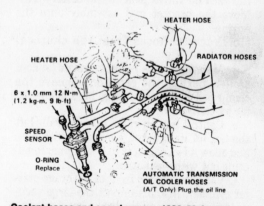

HEATER HOSE
HEATER HOSE
RADIATOR HOSES
6 x 1.0 mm 12 N·m
(1.2 kg-m, 9 lb-ft)
SPEED
SENSOR
O-RING
Replace
AUTOMATIC TRANSMISSION
OIL COOLER HOSES
(A/T Only) Plug the oil line

Coolant hoses and speed sensor, 1986–89 Accord

l. Disconnect the throttle cable by loosening the lock and adjusting nuts; slip the cable out of the bracket and linkage. Do NOT kink the cable; do not use pliers to remove the cable from the linkage.

11. On carbureted engines, disconnect or remove the following items:

a. The battery and battery tray. Disconnect the wiring harness connectors found below the tray. Remove the clips holding the engine side of the wiring harnesses

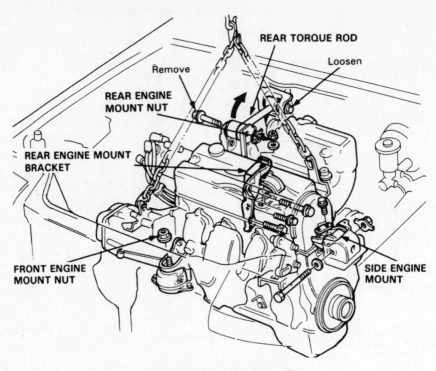

Accord engine mounts, 1986 — 89

b. Disconnect the retaining screws holding the vacuum valves next to the battery tray. Move the bracket and assembly onto the engine.

c. Vacuum hoses from the charcoal canister.

d. Mounting bolts holding the air jet controller, next to the canister. Remove the clamp bolt holding the large hose below the air jet controller.

e. Control box on right side firewall. Lift the box off its bracket, support it with wire and allow it to hang next to the engine. It will come out with the engine.

f. Vacuum hoses in front of the brake master cylinder. Also disconnect the large vacuum hose running to the brake booster.

g. Fuel line at the inline fuel filter near the firewall. Plug the lines to prevent fuel leakage or entry of dirt.

h. Ground cable running from the valve cover to the radiator support. Also remove the hose clamp bolt at the front right of the engine.

i. Disconnect the throttle cable by loosening the lock and adjusting nuts; slip the cable out of the bracket and linkage. Do NOT kink the cable; do not use pliers to remove the cable from the linkage.

12. On all vehicles, disconnect the heater and radiator hoses from the engine. Be prepared to contain spillage of the remaining coolant.

13. On automatic transaxles, disconnect the oil cooler lines from the transaxle case. Plug the lines immediately to eliminate oil spillage.

14. Remove the retaining bolt holding the speed sensor; remove the sensor from the transaxle case. Do not disconnect the hoses from the sensor.

15. For automatic transaxle vehicles:

a. Remove the center console.

b. Place the shift lever in R. Remove the lock pin from the end of the shift cable.

c. Remove the bolts holding the shift cable and remove the cable bracket. Separate the shift cable from the shifter.

d. At the transaxle, loosen the lower bolt (A) on the throttle control cable and disconnect the cable from the transaxle. Do NOT loosen or change the upper bolt (B); the shift points of the transaxle will be affected.

16. On manual transaxle vehicles, disconnect the clutch cable at the transaxle.

17. Disconnect the transaxle ground strap at the case.

18. Disconnect the shift rod yoke and shift lever torque rod at the transaxle.

19. Disconnect the exhaust pipe at the manifold. Discard the self-locking nuts—they are not reusable.

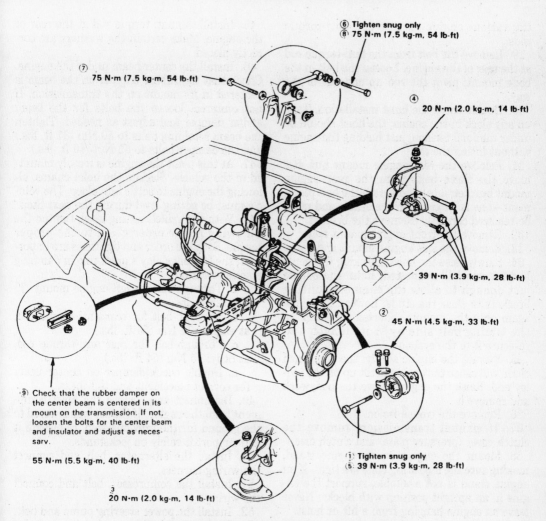

⑥ Tighten snug only
⑧ 75 N·m (7.5 kg-m, 54 lb-ft)

⑦
75 N·m (7.5 kg-m, 54 lb-ft)

④
20 N·m (2.0 kg-m, 14 lb-ft)

39 N·m (3.9 kg-m, 28 lb-ft)

②
45 N·m (4.5 kg-m, 33 lb-ft)

⑨ Check that the rubber damper on the center beam is centered in its mount on the transmission. If not, loosen the bolts for the center beam and insulator and adjust as necessary.

55 N·m (5.5 kg-m, 40 lb-ft)

① Tighten snug only
⑤ 39 N·m (3.9 kg-m, 28 lb-ft)

③
20 N·m (2.0 kg-m, 14 lb-ft)

Engine mount tightening order and torque — 1986–89 Accord

20. Disconnect the exhaust pipe at the joint just behind the flexible section and remove the pipe.

21. Remove the cotter pin and castle nut from the left and right lower ball joints. Carefully separate the joint using the correct tool.

22. Disconnect the driveshafts from the transaxle. Remove the circlip from the each shaft and discard them—they must be replaced at installation. Wrap the splined end of each shaft in a plastic bag and secure the wrapping. The machined splines must be protected from dirt and damage.

23. Remove the power steering pump adjusting bolt and remove the belt. Remove the pump from its mount and move it out of the way with the hoses attached. Support it out of the work area with stiff wire.

24. Disconnect the wiring to the air conditioning compressor. Loosen the mounting bolts and remove the belt. Remove the compressor from

its mounts and suspend it out of the work area with stiff wire. Do NOT disconnect or loosen any A/C hoses.

25. Disconnect the alternator wire harness connectors. Remove the belt after loosening the adjusting bolt. Remove the alternator from its mount.

26. Remove the center beam under the engine.

27. Install the engine hoisting equipment. Attach one chain to the eyehook on the left end of the engine, near the timing belt. Secure the other to the eyehook at the transaxle. Adjust the chain and hoist to remove the slack from all chains.

28. Carefully inspect the area surrounding the engine and transaxle, making sure that there are no hoses, vacuum lines or wiring running between the bodywork and engine/trans assembly. At this point, the only items connecting the engine/trans to the bodywork should be

the various engine mounts and anti-torque rods.

29. Remove the bolt from the anti-torque rod at the rear of the engine. Loosen the bolt in the body mount; pivot the rod up and out of the way.

30. Double check the hoist installation. Take up any slack in the chains; the hoist should be under minimal tension, just holding the engine without lifting the car.

31. Remove the rear engine mount nut. Remove the three bolts from the rear engine mount bracket; label or diagram the bolt placement—one is longer than the others and must be replaced correctly. Remove the bracket.

32. Remove the front engine mount bolt.

33. Remove the side engine mount and bolts.

34. Slowly raise the hoist, checking frequently for items still connected. Raise the engine just enough to allow the engine mounting brackets to clear the studs. Lower the engine again onto the mounts. Shorten the chain to the timing belt side by ½ its length and resecure it to the eyehook.

35. Elevate the engine slowly; the shortened chain will cause the engine to tilt up on the pulley end. Raise the engine above the bodywork and remove it.

36. Remove the transmission.

37. If manual transmission, remove the clutch cover (pressure plate) and clutch disc.

38. Mount the engine on an engine stand, making sure the mounting bolts are tight. If an engine stand is not available, support the engine in an upright position with blocks. Never leave an engine hanging from a lift or hoist.

To install:

39. Assemble the clutch disc and pressure plate to the flywheel for manual transaxle vehicles.

40. Install the transaxle.

41. Lift the engine into position and lower it into the car, aligning the mounts and bushings.
NOTE: *When installing the engine mounts and vibration dampers in the following steps, the bolts running through the large rubber bushings should only be set snug or finger tight until all are in place. They must be tightened to the correct tension in the correct order if they are to damp vibration properly.*

42. Install the through-bolt for the left engine mount. Install the two smaller bolts, tightening them to 45 Nm (33 ft. lbs.)

43. Install the nut on the front motor mount, tightening it to 20 Nm (14 ft. lbs).

44. Install the three bolts holding the rear engine mount bracket to the engine; tighten them to 39 Nm (28 ft. lbs). Tighten the nut to 20 Nm (14 ft. lbs).

45. Install the anti-torque rod at the rear of the engine. Make certain the washers are correctly placed.

46. Install the center beam under the engine. Check that the rubber damper on the beam is centered in its mount on the transmission. If not centered, loosen the bolts for the beam and/or damper and adjust as needed. Tighten the beam retaining bolts to 50 Nm (37 ft. lbs.) and the damper bolts to 55 Nm (40 ft. lbs.)

47. At this point the engine is loosely mounted in the vehicle. Slacken the hoist chains, allowing the engine to settle into place. The vehicle must be sitting level during the next Step.

48. With the vehicle sitting level, tighten the following in the order given to the proper torque. Both the order and tightness are important; the bushings play a great role in damping engine vibration.

   a. Through-bolt for left engine mount: 39 Nm (28 ft. lbs.)

   b. Through-bolt for rear anti-torque rod, at engine: 75 Nm (54 ft. lbs.)

   c. Through-bolt for rear anti-torque rod, at body: 75 Nm (54 ft. lbs.)

   d. Double check damper on center beam for correct placement and tightness.

49. Disconnect and remove the hoist equipment from the engine. If the car was lowered to the ground for the previous step, re-elevate it and support it safely on jackstands.

50. Install the alternator, belt and connect the wiring harness.

51. Install the compressor, belt and connect the wiring.

52. Install the power steering pump and belt.

53. Replace the circlip on each drive shaft. Install the shafts, making sure each clip is heard to click into place.

54. Reassemble the lower ball joints and install the nuts. Install a new cotter pin.

55. Using new nuts and gaskets, install the exhaust header pipe. Tighten the nuts at the manifold to 55 Nm (40 ft. lbs.)

56. Install the shift rod anti-torque rod, tightening the through-bolt to 12 Nm (9 ft. lbs).

57. On manual transmissions, attach the shift rod to the transmission and tighten the bolt to 22 Nm (16 ft. lbs).

58. Install the transaxle ground strap at the case.

59. Install the clutch cable, if so equipped.

60. For automatic transaxle vehicles, install or connect:

   a. The throttle control cable to the lever. Do not adjust or tighten the top bolt; tighten the lower locknut.

   b. Shifter and shifter cable inside the car. Install the lock pin onto the cable, secure the cable bracket or guide, and install the retaining bolts holding the cable assembly to the shifter housing. Reinstall the console.

61. Install the speed sensor assembly, tightening the bolt only to 12 Nm (9 ft. lbs).

62. Connect the automatic transaxle oil cooler lines if so equipped.

63. Connect the heater and radiator hoses.

64. For carbureted vehicles, install or connect:

 a. The throttle cable.

 b. Ground cable to the valve cover.

 c. Fuel line at the filter near the firewall.

 d. Vacuum hose to the brake booster.

 e. Emission vacuum hoses near the brake booster.

 f. Control box to its mounts on the firewall.

 g. Air jet controller if it was removed.

 h. Vacuum hoses to the charcoal canister.

 i. Vacuum valves next to the battery tray.

 j. Wiring connectors under the battery tray.

 k. Battery tray and battery.

65. On fuel injected engines, connect or install the following:

 a. Throttle cable.

 b. Brake booster vacuum hose.

 c. Cruise control actuator and vacuum hose.

 d. Harness connectors under the battery tray.

 e. Harness connectors at the left side of the engine.

 f. Ground cable to the valve cover and clamp bolt holding hose to the front of the engine.

 g. Harness connectors near the control box.

 h. Control box to its mount on the right firewall.

 i. Fuel lines at the pressure regulator.

 j. Vacuum hoses to the charcoal canister.

 k. Ground, ignition and coil wires at the right side of the engine compartment.

 l. Battery tray and battery.

66. Install the air cleaner housing. Install the intake ductwork.

67. Double check the drain plug on the transaxle, tightening it if needed. Fill the transaxle with correct amount of fluid.

68. Double check the draincock on the radiator. Refill the cooling system.

69. Double check the engine oil drain bolt. Install the correct amount of engine oil.

70. Double check all installation items, paying particular attention to loose hoses or hanging wires, untightened nuts, poor routing of hoses and wires (too tight or rubbing) and tools left in the engine area.

71. Install the hood.

72. Connect the battery cables, positive first.

73. Disconnect the coil wire from the distributor. Insulate or protect the end of the cable so it does not arc to the engine or surrounding metal. Without touching the accelerator, turn the ignition switch to the START position and crank the engine for about 5–10 seconds; this will develop some oil pressure within the motor. Do not exceed 10 seconds cranking.

74. Switch the ignition OFF and reconnect the coil.

75. Start the engine, allowing it to idle. Check the hoses and lines carefully for any sign of leakage.

76. Bleed the air from the cooling system; check the timing and idle speed.

77. After the engine has warmed up fully and the fan(s) have come on at least once, recheck the engine for fluid leaks. Switch the engine OFF.

78. Adjust the belts, clutch and throttle cable as necessary.

1990–91 Accord: 2.2L Engine

1. Disconnect the battery cables, negative first. Remove the battery and battery case.

2. Raise and safely support the vehicle. Double check the security and placement of the stands.

3. Place the hood in a vertical position and safely support it in place. Do not remove the hood.

4. Remove the engine splash shield. Drain the engine oil, coolant and transaxle fluid.

5. Remove the air intake duct and the air cleaner case.

6. Relieve the fuel system pressure using the correct procedure.

7. Remove the fuel feed hose from the fuel pipe and the return hose from the pressure control valve.

8. Disconnect the 2 connectors and remove the control box from the firewall.

NOTE: *Do not disconnect the vacuum hoses.*

9. Disconnect the vacuum hose from the charcoal canister and the charcoal canister hose from the throttle body.

10. Remove the ground cable from the transaxle.

11. Remove the throttle cable by loosening the locknut, then slip the cable end out of the throttle bracket and accelerator linkage.

NOTE: *Be careful not to bend the cable when removing. Do not use pliers to remove the cable from the linkage. Always replace a kinked cable with a new one.*

12. Disconnect the connector and the vacuum hose, then remove the cruise control actuator.

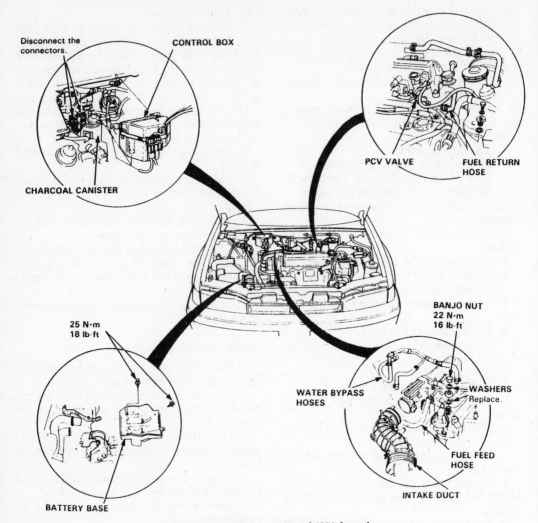

Component location — 1990 and 1991 Accord

13. Remove the brake booster vacuum hose and mount; remove the vacuum hose from the intake manifold.

14. Disconnect the 3 engine harness connectors from the main wire harness at the right side of the engine compartment. Remove the engine wire harness terminal and the starter cable terminal from the underhood relay box and clamps. Then remove the transaxle ground terminal.

15. Disconnect the 2 engine wire harness connectors from the main harness and the resistor at the left side of the engine compartment.

16. Remove the engine ground wire from the valve cover. Remove the power steering pump bracket.

17. Remove the mounting bolts and the power steering belt from the power steering pump, then, without disconnecting the hoses, pull the pump away from its mounting bracket. Support the pump out of the way.

18. Remove the mounting bolts and belt from the air conditioning compressor. Without disconnecting the hoses, pull the compressor away from it's mounting bracket. Support the compressor with stiff wire out of the way.

19. Disconnect the heater hoses. Disconnect the radiator hoses, automatic transaxle cooler hoses and the cooling fan connectors. Remove the radiator/cooling fan assembly.

20. Remove the speed sensor without disconnecting the hoses or connector.

21. Remove the center beam.

22. Remove the exhaust pipe nuts and bracket mounting bolts.

23. Remove the halfshafts as follows:

    a. Remove the front wheels.

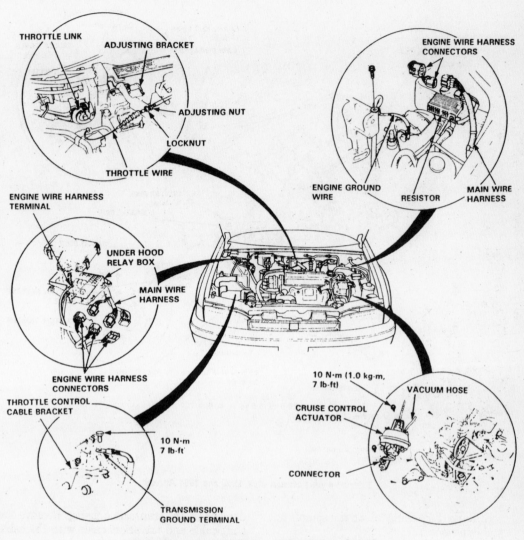

THROTTLE LINK

ADJUSTING BRACKET

ADJUSTING NUT

LOCKNUT

THROTTLE WIRE

ENGINE WIRE HARNESS CONNECTORS

ENGINE GROUND WIRE

RESISTOR

MAIN WIRE HARNESS

ENGINE WIRE HARNESS TERMINAL

UNDER HOOD RELAY BOX

MAIN WIRE HARNESS

ENGINE WIRE HARNESS CONNECTORS

THROTTLE CONTROL CABLE BRACKET

10 N·m
7 lb·ft

TRANSMISSION GROUND TERMINAL

10 N·m (1.0 kg·m, 7 lb·ft)

VACUUM HOSE

CRUISE CONTROL ACTUATOR

CONNECTOR

Component location and detail — 1990 and 1991 Accord

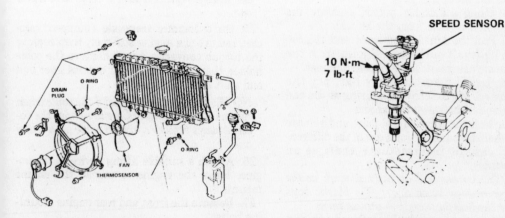

DRAIN PLUG

O RING

O RING

FAN

THERMOSENSOR

SPEED SENSOR

10 N·m
7 lb·ft

Removing the radiator and fan

1990–91 Accord speed sensor

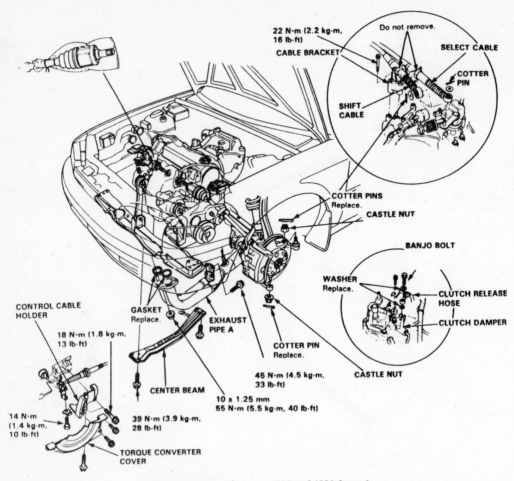

22 N·m (2.2 kg-m, 16 lb-ft)

CABLE BRACKET

Do not remove.

SELECT CABLE

COTTER PIN

SHIFT CABLE

COTTER PINS
Replace.

CASTLE NUT

BANJO BOLT

WASHER
Replace.

CLUTCH RELEASE HOSE

CLUTCH DAMPER

CASTLE NUT

COTTER PIN
Replace.

45 N·m (4.5 kg-m, 33 lb-ft)

10 x 1.25 mm
55 N·m (5.5 kg-m, 40 lb-ft)

CONTROL CABLE HOLDER

18 N·m (1.8 kg-m, 13 lb-ft)

GASKET
Replace.

EXHAUST PIPE A

CENTER BEAM

14 N·m (1.4 kg-m, 10 lb-ft)

39 N·m (3.9 kg-m, 28 lb-ft)

TORQUE CONVERTER COVER

External engine components, 1990 and 1991 Accord

b. Raise the locking tab on the spindle nut and remove it.

c. Remove the damper fork nut, damper pinch bolt and remove the damper fork.

d. Remove the cotter pin and castle nut from the lower ball joint.

e. Using a suitable puller, separate the lower control arm from the knuckle.

f. Pull the knuckle outward and remove the halfshaft outboard CV-joint from the knuckle using a suitable plastic hammer.

g. Using a suitable pry bar, pry the halfshaft out to force the set ring at the end of the halfshaft past the groove.

h. Pull the inboard CV-joint and remove the halfshaft and CV-joint out of the differential case or intermediate shaft as an assembly.

NOTE: *Do not pull on the halfshaft, as the CV-joint may come apart. Tie plastic bags over the halfshaft ends to protect them.*

24. On manual transaxle equipped vehicles, remove the clutch release hose from the clutch

damper on the transaxle housing. Remove the shift cable and the select cable with the cable bracket from the transaxle.

NOTE: *Be careful not to bend the cable when removing. Do not use pliers to remove the cable. Always replace a kinked cable with a new one.*

25. On automatic transaxle equipped vehicles, remove the engine stiffener, then remove the torque converter cover. Remove the cable holder, then remove the shift control lever bolt and shift control cable.

NOTE: *Be careful not to bend the cable when removing. Do not use pliers to remove the cable. Always replace a kinked cable with a new one.*

26. Attach a suitable lifting device to the engine. Raise the engine to unload the engine mounts.

27. Remove the front and rear engine mounting bolts.

28. Remove the engine side mount and

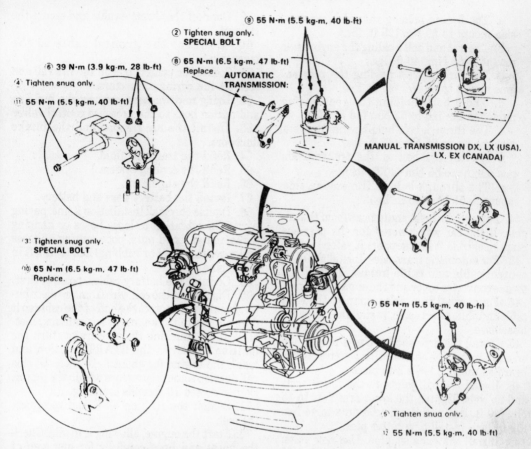

⑨ 55 N·m (5.5 kg-m, 40 lb-ft)

② Tighten snug only.
SPECIAL BOLT

⑥ 39 N·m (3.9 kg-m, 28 lb-ft)   ⑧ 65 N·m (6.5 kg-m, 47 lb-ft)
                                  Replace.
④ Tighten snug only.   **AUTOMATIC**
                                  TRANSMISSION:
⑪ 55 N·m (5.5 kg-m, 40 lb-ft)

MANUAL TRANSMISSION DX, LX (USA),
LX, EX (CANADA)

③ Tighten snug only.
SPECIAL BOLT

⑩ 65 N·m (6.5 kg-m, 47 lb-ft)
Replace.

⑦ 55 N·m (5.5 kg-m, 40 lb-ft)

⑤ Tighten snug only.

① 55 N·m (5.5 kg-m, 40 lb-ft)

Engine mount tightening order and torque — 1990–91 Accord

mounting bolt. Remove the side transaxle mount and mounting bolt.

29. Make sure the engine/transaxle assembly is completely free of vacuum hoses, fuel and coolant hoses and electrical wires.

30. Slowly raise the engine approximately 6 in. (152mm). Check again that all hoses and wires have been disconnected from the engine/transaxle assembly.

31. Raise the engine/transaxle assembly all the way and remove it from the vehicle.

32. Remove the transmission.

33. If manual transmission, remove the clutch cover (pressure plate) and clutch disc.

34. Mount the engine on an engine stand, making sure the mounting bolts are tight. If an engine stand is not available, support the engine in an upright position with blocks. Never leave an engine hanging from a lift or hoist.

To install:

35. Assemble the clutch disc and pressure plate to the flywheel for manual transaxle vehicles.

36. Install the transaxle.

37. Lift the engine into position and lower it into the car, aligning the mounts and bushings.

NOTE: *When installing the engine mounts and vibration dampers in the following steps, the bolts running through the large rubber bushings should only be set snug or finger tight until all are in place. They must be tightened to the correct tension in the correct order if they are to damp vibration properly.*

39. Install the side engine mount and mounting bolt. Install the through bolt.

40. Install the side transmission mount and bolt.

41. Install the front and rear engine mounting bolts.

42. At this point the engine is loosely mounted in the vehicle. Slacken the hoist chains, allowing the engine to settle into place. The vehicle must be sitting level during the next Step.

43. With the vehicle sitting level, tighten the following in the order given to the proper torque. Both the order and tightness are important; the bushings play a great role in damping engine vibration.

a. The 3 nuts holding the side transmission mount to 39 Nm (28 ft. lbs.)

b. The nut and bolt holding the engine side mount to 55 Nm (40 ft. lbs.)

c. The through-bolt holding the rear engine mount to 65 Nm (47 ft. lbs).

d. The 3 bolts holding the rear engine mount to the rail to 55 Nm (40 ft. lbs.)

e. The through-bolt holding the front engine mount to 65 Nm (47 ft. lbs).

f. The through-bolt at the transmission side mount to 55 Nm (40 ft. lbs).

g. The through-bolt at the engine side mount to 55 Nm (40 ft. lbs).

44. Remove the hoist equipment from the engine. If the car was lowered for the previous Step, re-elevate it and support it safely.

45. For automatic transaxles, install the shift control cable and cable holder. Install the torque converter cover and the engine stiffener.

46. For manual transaxles, connect the shift cable and shift select cable. Install the clutch release hose.

47. Install the driveshafts. Use a new circlip on each; install the shaft until a positive click is heard as the axle locks into place.

48. Install the ball joints to the lower arms and tie rods. Tighten the lower arm nuts to 55 Nm (40 ft. lbs.) and the tie rod nuts to 44 Nm (32 ft. lbs). Install new cotter pins.

49. Install the exhaust pipe. Use new nuts; tighten the pipe-to-manifold nuts to 55 Nm (40 ft. lbs.)

50. Install the center beam. Tighten the bolts to 39 Nm (28 ft. lbs.)

51. Install the speed sensor. Tighten the retaining bolt to 10 Nm (7 ft. lbs.)

52. Install the radiator; connect the coolant and transmission oil cooler lines. Connect the cooling fan connectors.

53. Connect the heater inlet and outlet hoses to the cylinder head and connecting pipe, respectively.

54. Install the A/C compressor and belt, tightening the mounting bolts to 22 Nm (16 ft. lbs.)

55. Install the power steering pump and belt. Tighten the bolt to 45 Nm (33 ft. lbs.) and the nut to 22 Nm (16 ft. lbs).

56. Connect the engine ground wire to the valve cover and the power steering pump bracket.

57. Connect the transmission ground strap. Connect the starter cable terminal and install the engine wire harness terminal. Connect the three connectors for the main wire harness at the right side of the engine compartment.

58. Connect the brake booster vacuum hose to the manifold and to the brake booster.

59. Connect the throttle cable and secure the locknut.

60. Connect the ground cable to the transaxle.

61. Install the control box on the firewall and connect the wiring connectors.

62. Using new washers, connect the fuel line and return hose to the pressure control valve.

63. Install the air cleaner and the intake ductwork.

64. Refill the transaxle fluid.

65. Refill the cooling system.

66. Refill the engine oil.

67. Install the battery base and battery.

68. Double check all installation items, paying particular attention to loose hoses or hanging wires, untightened nuts, poor routing of hoses and wires (too tight or rubbing) and tools left in the engine area.

69. Connect the battery cables, positive first.

70. Disconnect the coil wire from the distributor. Insulate or protect the end of the cable so it does not arc to the engine or surrounding metal. Without touching the accelerator, turn the ignition switch to the START position and crank the engine for about 5–10 seconds; this will develop some oil pressure within the motor. Do not exceed 10 seconds cranking.

71. Switch the ignition OFF and reconnect the coil.

72. Start the engine, allowing it to idle. Check the hoses and lines carefully for any sign of leakage.

73. Bleed the air from the cooling system; check the timing and idle speed.

74. After the engine has warmed up fully and the fan(s) have come on at least once, recheck the engine for fluid leaks. Switch the engine OFF.

75. Adjust the belts, clutch and throttle cable as necessary.

76. Install the front wheels. Lower the hood.

1988–91 Prelude: 2.0L and 2.1L Engines

1. Elevate and safely support the vehicle. Double check the placement and stability of the stands.

2. Disconnect the negative battery terminal, then the positive cable.

3. Disconnect the washer hose at the hood. Outline the hood hinges on the inner surface of the hood; remove the bolts and remove the hood.

4. Drain the engine oil. Replace the washer on the drain plug and reinstall the plug.

5. Drain the transaxle fluid. Reinstall the drain plug and tighten it.

6. Drain the coolant from the radiator and

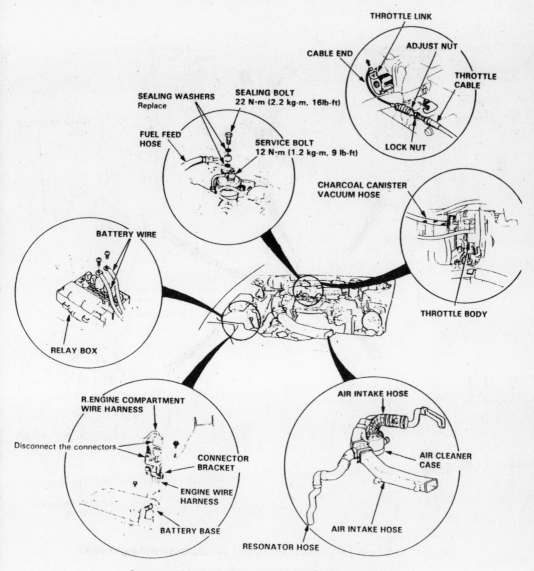

Component location and detail, 1988–91 fuel Injected Prelude

engine. Use a large container and save the coolant for reuse.

7. For carbureted vehicles:

a. Remove the battery and battery base.

b. Remove the air intake duct and air filter housing.

c. Disconnect the fuel hose at the fuel filter. Plug the line to prevent spillage.

d. Disconnect the brake booster vacuum hose at the one-way valve.

e. Remove the air jet controller but do not disconnect the vacuum hoses.

8. For fuel injected vehicles:

a. Remove the battery and base.

b. Remove the air intake hose, air cleaner and resonator assembly.

c. Disconnect the battery wires from the relay box.

d. Relieve the fuel pressure using the proper procedure.

e. Disconnect the fuel feed and fuel return hoses.

9. Disconnect the vacuum hose to the charcoal canister at the throttle valve.

10. Disconnect the throttle cable, either at the carburetor or throttle body.

11. On carbureted engines, disconnect the coil wire, condenser, and ignition primary wires.

12. Remove the distributor.

13. Disconnect the heater inlet and outlet hoses.

14. For automatic transaxles, disconnect and plug the oil cooler lines.

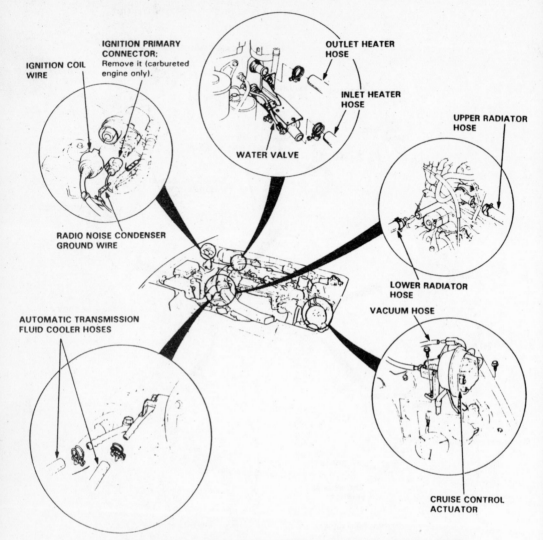

Component location and detail, 1988–91 fuel injected Prelude. Carbureted engine similar.

15. Disconnect the vacuum hose to the cruise control actuator; remove the actuator.

16. For fuel injected engines, disconnect the wire harness connectors at the right side of the engine compartment.

17. Disconnect the two harness connectors; remove the control box from its mount; remove the vacuum tank.

18. Disconnect the brake booster vacuum hose.

19. Loosen the power steering pump and the alternator; remove the belts.

20. Cover the alternator with a thick rag or cloth. Disconnect the power steering inlet hose. Fluid will flow out—protect the alternator. Remove the power steering pump.

21. Remove the alternator.

22. Remove the condenser fan shroud if equipped with air conditioning.

23. Remove the air conditioning compressor but do NOT disconnect any hoses from it. Move the compressor out of the work area and support it with stiff wire; do not let it hang by the hoses.

24. For manual transaxles, disconnect the shift and select cables from the transaxle and remove the cable bracket.

25. For automatic transaxles, disconnect the shift cable.

26. Disconnect the transmission ground wire.

27. Remove the left and right axles or halfshafts.

28. Remove the clutch slave cylinder but do not disconnect the hose.

29. Remove the speed sensor and speedometer cable. Take great care not to bend the cable. Do not use pliers to remove the cable.

30. Install the hoisting equipment. Attach the

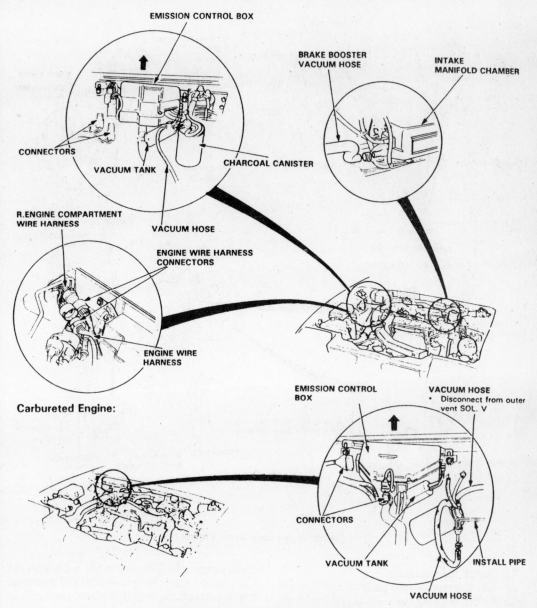

Component location and detail, 1988–91 Prelude

chains to the eyehooks at the pulley and transaxle ends of the engine. The chain to the pulley-end eyehook should be shorter than the other to tilt the pulley end up on removal. Take the slack out of the chains but do not put lift the engine.

31. Remove the rear engine mount bolt, then remove the mount bracket.

32. Remove the front engine mount bolt.

33. Remove the side engine mount bolts.

34. Remove the transmission mount bolt.

35. Lift the engine about 4–6 inches; inspect the area for any remaining wires, vacuum lines or hoses.

36. Tilt the engine, pulley end up, and remove the engine/transaxle from the vehicle.

37. Remove the transmission.

38. If manual transmission, remove the clutch cover (pressure plate) and clutch disc.

39. Mount the engine on an engine stand, making sure the mounting bolts are tight. If an engine stand is not available, support the engine in an upright position with blocks. Never leave an engine hanging from a lift or hoist.

To install:

40. Assemble the clutch disc and pressure plate to the flywheel for manual transaxle vehicles.

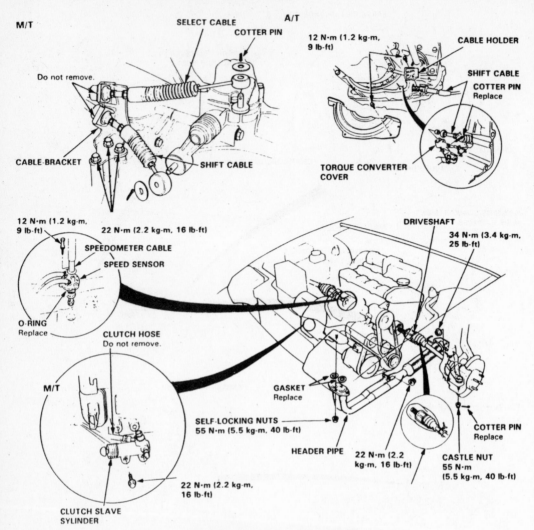

External engine components, Prelude

41. Install the transaxle.

42. Lift the engine into position and lower it into the car, aligning the mounts and bushings.

NOTE: *When installing the engine mounts and vibration dampers in the following steps, the bolts running through the large rubber bushings should only be set snug or finger tight until all are in place. They must be tightened to the correct tension in the correct order if they are to damp vibration properly.*

43. Install the transmission mount bolt.

44. Install the side engine mount bracket bolts. Install the through-bolt.

45. Install the front engine mount bolt.

46. Install the rear engine mount bolts.

47. At this point the engine is loosely mounted in the vehicle. Slacken the hoist chains, allowing the engine to settle into place.

48. With the vehicle sitting approximately level, tighten the following in the order given to the proper torque. Both the order and tightness are important; the bushings play a great role in damping engine vibration.

a. Rear engine mount bracket bolts to 75 Nm (54 ft. lbs).

b. Transmission bracket mount bolts to 39 Nm (28 ft. lbs).

c. Front engine mount through-bolt to 60 Nm (43 ft. lbs).

d. Engine side mount bolts to 40 Nm (29 ft. lbs).

e. Engine side mounting through-bolt to 75 Nm (54 ft. lbs).

f. Rear engine mount through bolt to 75 Nm (54 ft. lbs.)

49. Install the speed sensor and speedometer cable. Tighten the retaining bolt only to 12 Nm (9 ft. lbs).

50. Install the clutch slave cylinder.

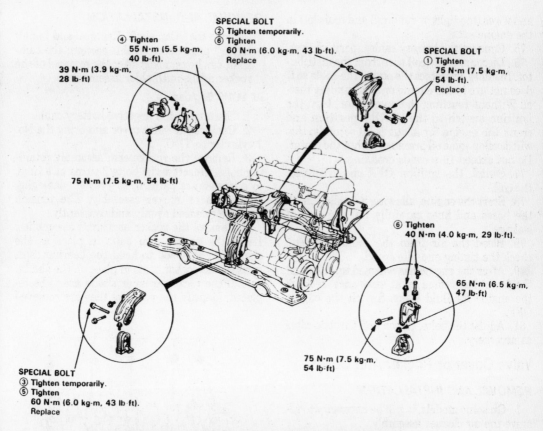

④ Tighten
55 N·m (5.5 kg-m, 40 lb-ft).

39 N·m (3.9 kg-m, 28 lb-ft)

SPECIAL BOLT
② Tighten temporarily.
⑥ Tighten
60 N·m (6.0 kg-m, 43 lb-ft).
Replace

SPECIAL BOLT
① Tighten
75 N·m (7.5 kg-m, 54 lb-ft).
Replace

75 N·m (7.5 kg·m, 54 lb-ft)

⑥ Tighten
40 N·m (4.0 kg-m, 29 lb-ft).

65 N·m (6.5 kg·m, 47 lb-ft)

75 N·m (7.5 kg·m, 54 lb-ft)

SPECIAL BOLT
③ Tighten temporarily.
⑤ Tighten
60 N·m (6.0 kg-m, 43 lb-ft).
Replace

Engine mount tightening order and torque — 1988–91 Prelude

51. Install the left and right axles. Use new circlips; make certain each axle is heard to click into place as the clip engages the groove.

52. Install the transaxle ground wire.

53. Connect the shift cable to the automatic transaxle or connect the shift and select cables to the manual transaxle. Secure the cable bracket.

54. Install the A/C compressor and belt. Tighten the mounting bolts to 25. Nm (18 ft. lbs).

55. Install the alternator, tightening the mounting bolts to 45 Nm (33 ft. lbs).

56. Install the power steering pump. Tighten the mounting bolts to 27 Nm (20 ft. lbs.) and connect the inlet hose.

57. Install the drive belts for the power steering pump and alternator.

58. Connect the brake booster hose.

59. Install the vacuum tank and control box back on the firewall. Connect the wiring connectors.

60. Reinstall the cruise control actuator and connect the vacuum hose.

61. Connect the automatic transaxle oil cooler lines if they were removed.

62. Connect the heater inlet and outlet hoses.

63. Connect the upper and lower radiator hoses.

64. Install the distributor. For carbureted engines, connect the ignition wiring, condenser and primary wires.

65. Connect the throttle cable.

66. For fuel injected engines, reconnect the fuel supply and return hoses. Use new washers on the banjo fitting. Tighten the banjo bolt to 22 Nm (16 ft. lbs)

67. For fuel injected engines, connect the battery wires to the relay box. Install the air cleaner assembly with the intake hose and resonator.

68. For carbureted engines, install the air jet controller; check that the vacuum lines are not crimped or twisted.

69. For carbureted engines, connect the fuel line at the filter. Install the air cleaner housing and air intake ducts.

70. Install the battery tray and battery.

71. Refill the engine coolant.

72. Refill the engine oil.

73. Refill the transaxle fluid.

74. Double check all installation items, paying particular attention to loose hoses or hanging wires, untightened nuts, poor routing of hoses

and wires (too tight or rubbing) and tools left in the engine area.

75. Connect the battery cables, positive first.

76. Disconnect the coil wire from the distributor. Insulate or protect the end of the cable so it does not arc to the engine or surrounding metal. Without touching the accelerator, turn the ignition switch to the START position and crank the engine for about 5–10 seconds; this will develop some oil pressure within the motor. Do not exceed 10 seconds cranking.

77. Switch the ignition OFF and reconnect the coil.

78. Start the engine, allowing it to idle. Check the hoses and lines carefully for any sign of leakage.

79. Bleed the air from the cooling system; check the timing and idle speed.

80. After the engine has warmed up fully and the fan(s) have come on at least once, recheck the engine for fluid leaks. Switch the engine OFF.

81. Adjust the belts, clutch and throttle cable as necessary.

Valve Cover or Rocker Arm Cover

REMOVAL AND INSTALLATION

1. On some models, it will be necessary to remove the air cleaner assembly.

2. Remove the ground cable, the spark plug wires (if necessary) and the throttle cable (if necessary) from the rocker arm cover.

3. If equipped, remove the PCV hose from the rocker arm cover.

4. Remove the rocker arm cover-to-cylinder head nuts, the washer/grommet assemblies and the rocker arm cover.

NOTE: *If the cover is difficult to remove, use a plastic mallet to bump it loose. Never use a metal object to strike the cover.*

5. Clean the gasket mounting surfaces and check the gasket for deformation.

To install:

6. Generally, the rubber gasket may be reused if in good condition. Fit it into the flange in the cover, making sure it is not twisted.

7. Install the cover and gasket onto the head. Install the insulators.

8. Install the ground wire, then install the nuts. Tighten the rocker arm cover-to-cylinder head nuts to 10 Nm (7 ft. lbs).

9. Reinstall the air cleaner, spark plug wires or other components removed for access.

Rocker Arms/Shafts

The rocker arms and shafts are an assembly; they must be removed from the engine as a unit.

REMOVAL AND INSTALLATION

Refer to the "Camshaft, Removal and Installation" procedures in this section; the camshaft can be removed after the removal of the rocker arm/shaft/holder assemblies.

All SOHC Engines

1. Disconnect the negative battery cable.

2. Remove the valve cover and bring the No. 1 cylinder to TDC.

3. Remove the rocker arm assembly retaining bolts. Unscrew the bolts 2 turns at a time, in a criss-cross pattern, to prevent damaging the valves or rocker assembly. The tension must be released evenly and constantly.

4. Remove the rocker arm/shaft assemblies. Leave the rocker arm bolts in place as the shafts are removed to keep the bearing caps, springs and rocker arms in place on the shafts.

5. If the rocker arms or shafts are to be replaced, identify the parts as they are removed

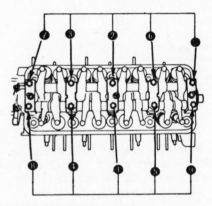

Rocker shaft cap bolt tightening sequence, all SOHC Prelude and 1984–89 Accord engines

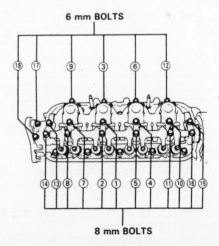

Rocker shaft cap bolt tightening sequence, all 1990–91 Accord

from the shafts to insure reinstallation in the original location.

To install:

6. Lubricate the camshaft journals and lobes.

7. Set the rocker arm assembly in place and loosely install the bolts. Tighten each bolt 2 turns at a time in the proper sequence to insure that the rockers do not bind on the valves. Tighten the 6mm bolts to 12 Nm (9 ft. lbs.) and the 8mm bolts to 22 Nm (16 ft. lbs).

8. Replace the valve cover and connect the negative battery cable.

DOHC Engine

1. Disconnect the negative battery cable.

2. Remove the valve cover and bring the No. 1 cylinder to TDC.

3. Remove the timing belt cover and the timing belt.

4. Remove the camshaft bearing caps and remove the camshafts.

5. Remove the rocker arms.

To install:

6. Make certain the keyways on the camshafts are facing up. Valve locknuts should be loosened and the adjusting screws backed off before installation.

7. Place the rocker arms on the pivot bolts and valve stems.

8. Install the camshafts and seals. The seals should be installed with the open or spring side facing inward.

9. Note that the cam retainers are marked I or E and consecutively numbered to indicate correct placement. Do not apply oil to the surfaces of the holders which mate with the seals. Apply a liquid gasket or sealer to the head mating surfaces for the No. 1 and No. 6 camshaft holders.

10. Install the camshaft holders.

11. Tighten the camshaft holders temporarily.

12. Use a seal driver of the correct size to install the camshaft oil seals.

13. Tighten the bolts two turns at a time, starting with the bolts on holder I3. Proceed in a widening spiral outward, turning each two turns. When all are done, return to I3 and repeat the procedure, bringing each bolt to the correct tension of 12 Nm (9 ft. lbs.)

14. Adjust the valve lash.

15. Reinstall the valve cover.

Thermostat

CAUTION: *When draining the coolant, keep in mind that cats and dogs are attracted by the ethylene glycol antifreeze, and are quite likely to drink any that is left in an uncovered*

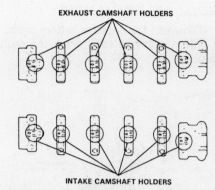

EXHAUST CAMSHAFT HOLDERS

INTAKE CAMSHAFT HOLDERS

The DOHC cam holders are labeled for correct installation

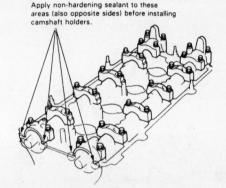

Apply non-hardening sealant to these areas (also opposite sides) before installing camshaft holders.

Apply non-hardening sealant to areas indicated

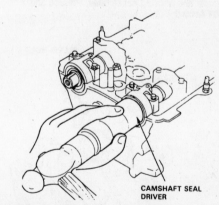

CAMSHAFT SEAL DRIVER

Carefully install the camshaft end seals

container or in puddles on the ground. This will prove fatal in sufficient quantity. Always drain the coolant into a sealable container. Coolant should be reused unless it is contaminated or several years old.

The thermostat housing is located on the cylinder head with the exception of 1990–91 Accord, where it is located at the end of the water pump inlet tube.

REMOVAL AND INSTALLATION

1. Disconnect the negative battery cable.
2. With the engine cold, drain the cooling system.

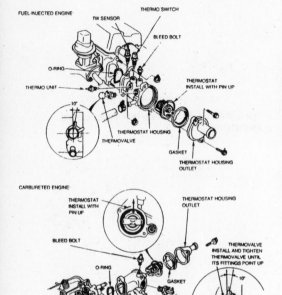

Thermostat and housing assemblies, Prelude and 1984–89 Accord

3. Disconnect the radiator hose from the thermostat housing outlet.
4. Remove the thermostat housing outlet and remove the thermostat.
5. Using a putty knife, clean the gasket mounting surfaces.

NOTE: *If the thermostat is equipped with a pin valve, be sure to install the thermostat with the pin facing upward.*

6. To install, use a new thermostat (if necessary), gasket, O-ring (if used), sealant (if necessary) and reverse the removal procedures. Always install the spring end of the thermostat facing the engine. Torque the thermostat cover-to-thermostat housing bolts to 12 Nm (9 ft. lbs) Bleed the cooling system.

Intake Manifold

REMOVAL AND INSTALLATION

CAUTION: *When draining the coolant, keep in mind that cats and dogs are attracted by the ethylene glycol antifreeze, and are quite likely to drink any that is left in an uncovered container or in puddles on the ground. This will prove fatal in sufficient quantity. Always drain the coolant into a sealable container. Coolant should be reused unless it is contaminated or several years old.*

Carbureted Models

1. Position a clean drain pan under the radiator, remove the drain plug and drain the cooling system.

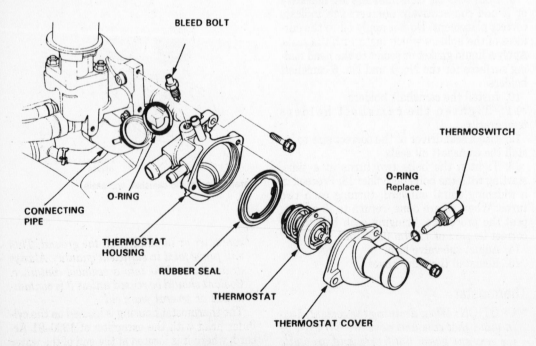

1990–91 Accord thermostat and housing

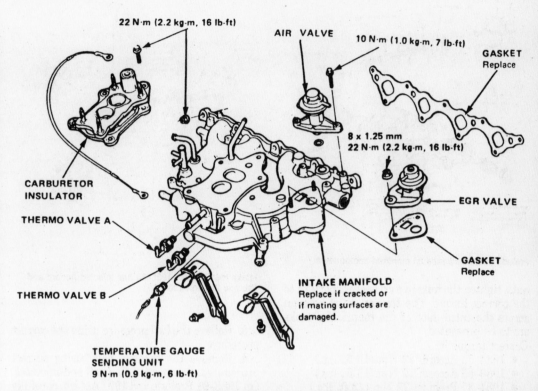

22 N·m (2.2 kg-m, 16 lb-ft)

AIR VALVE

10 N·m (1.0 kg-m, 7 lb-ft)

GASKET
Replace

CARBURETOR
INSULATOR

8 x 1.25 mm
22 N·m (2.2 kg-m, 16 lb-ft)

THERMO VALVE A

EGR VALVE

GASKET
Replace

THERMO VALVE B

INTAKE MANIFOLD
Replace if cracked or
if mating surfaces are
damaged.

TEMPERATURE GAUGE
SENDING UNIT
9 N·m (0.9 kg-m, 6 lb-ft)

Intake manifold for 1984–85 Accord

2. Remove the air cleaner and housing from the carburetor(s).

3. Remove the air valve, the EGR valve, the air suction valve and the air chamber (if equipped).

4. Label and disconnect any electrical connectors from the carburetor(s) and intake manifold.

5. Disconnect the fuel line(s) from the carburetor. Disconnect the throttle cable from the carburetor.

6. Remove the carburetor(s) from the intake manifold.

7. Remove the intake manifold-to-cylinder head nuts (using a crisscross pattern), beginning from the center and moving out to both ends, then remove the manifold.

8. Using a putty knife or piece of stiff plastic, clean the gasket mounting surfaces on the head. Do not use razor scrapers; the machined surfaces may be damaged, resulting in a leak.

9. If the intake manifold is to be replaced, transfer all the necessary components to the new manifold.

To install:

10. Use new gaskets and position the gasket and manifold on the head. Hand tighten the nuts snug. Starting with the inner or center

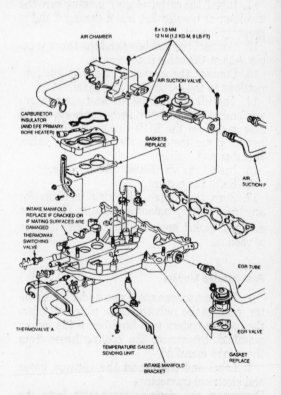

AIR CHAMBER

6 x 1.0 MM
12 N·m (1.2 KG-M, 9 LB-FT)

AIR SUCTION VALVE

CARBURETOR
INSULATOR
(AND EFE PRIMARY
BORE HEATER)

GASKETS
REPLACE

AIR
SUCTION P

INTAKE MANIFOLD
REPLACE IF CRACKED OR
IF MATING SURFACES ARE
DAMAGED

THERMOWAX
SWITCHING
VALVE

EGR TUBE

THERMOVALVE A

EGR VALVE

TEMPERATURE GAUGE
SENDING UNIT

GASKET
REPLACE

INTAKE MANIFOLD
BRACKET

Exploded view of intake manifold components, 1986–89
Accord

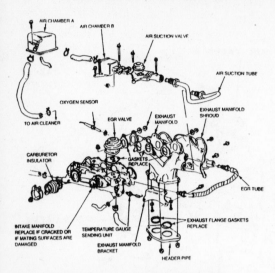

Prelude intake and exhaust manifold components

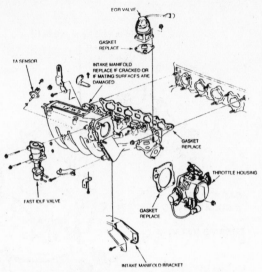

Intake manifold for 1986–88 fuel injected Accord and Prelude through 1987

nuts, tighten the nuts in a criss-cross pattern to the correct torque. The tension must be even across the entire face of the manifold if leaks are to be prevented.
Correct torque is:

- 1984–85 Accord: 22 Nm (16 ft. lbs.)
- 1986–89 Accord: 22 Nm (16 ft. lbs.)
- 1984–87 Prelude: 32 Nm (23 ft. lbs.)
- 1988–90 Prelude: 24 Nm (17 ft. lbs.)

11. Install the carburetor(s), making sure the insulator or base gasket is not damaged and is properly seated.

12. Connect the fuel lines and the throttle cable. Adjust the cable if necessary.

13. Connect the electrical and vacuum connections to the carburetor and manifold.

14. Install the emissions and air-control equipment removed for access. Always use a new gasket for the EGR valve; use care when handling and installing the air control valve, chamber and piping.

15. Install the air cleaner and housing.

16. Refill the coolant.

17. Start the engine, checking carefully for any leaks of fuel, coolant or vacuum. Check the manifold gasket area carefully for any leakage of vacuum.

Fuel Injected Models

1. Position a clean catch pan under the radiator, remove the radiator drain plug and drain the cooling system to a level below the intake manifold. Disconnect the cooling hoses from the intake manifold.

2. Label and disconnect the vacuum hoses and electrical connectors.
Disconnect the electrical connector from the EGR valve.

3. Relieve the fuel pressure using the correct procedure.

4. Remove the throttle body using correct procedures. Remove the fuel rail and injectors. On 1988–91 Prelude and 1991 Accord, carefully remove the bypass valve body from the intake manifold.

5. Remove the fast idle valve, the air bleed valve, the EGR valve and their related brackets.

6. Remove the intake manifold support bracket bolts and the bracket(s). While supporting the intake manifold, remove the intake manifold-to-cylinder head nuts; remove the manifold and the gasket from the cylinder head.

7. Using a putty knife or similar tool, clean the gasket mounting surfaces. Using a straight edge, check the surfaces for warpage; replace any warped parts.
NOTE: *If the cylinder head/manifold mating surface is warped, it must be machined or replaced.*

To install:

8. Using a new gasket, place the manifold into position and support it. Install the nuts snug on the studs.

9. Install the support bracket(s) below the manifold. Tighten the bolt holding the bracket to the manifold to 22 Nm (16 ft. lbs).

10. Starting with the inner or center nuts, tighten the nuts in a criss-cross pattern to the correct torque. The tension must be even across the entire face of the manifold if leaks are to be prevented. Correct torque is 22 Nm (16 ft. lbs.) for all fuel injected vehicles.

11. Install the air bleed valve, EGR valve and other components mounted directly on the

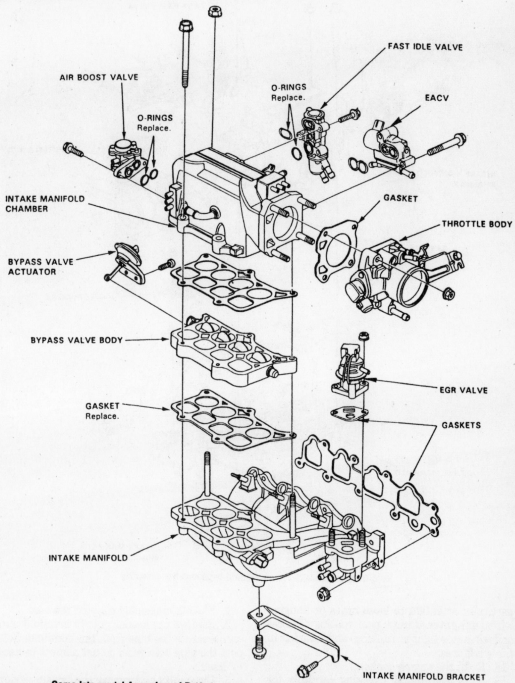

AIR BOOST VALVE

O-RINGS
Replace.

INTAKE MANIFOLD
CHAMBER

BYPASS VALVE
ACTUATOR

BYPASS VALVE BODY

GASKET
Replace.

INTAKE MANIFOLD

FAST IDLE VALVE

O-RINGS
Replace.

EACV

GASKET

THROTTLE BODY

EGR VALVE

GASKETS

INTAKE MANIFOLD BRACKET

Some late model Accords and Preludes use a bypass valve assembly in the intake system

manifold. Use a new gasket for each component.

12. If the bypass valve assembly was removed, install a new gasket and install the bypass valve assembly onto the manifold.

13. Install a new gasket and install the air plenum or manifold chamber if it was removed as a separate unit. Tighten the nuts and bolts hold-

ing the chamber to 22 Nm (16 ft. lbs.).

14. Install the throttle body and connect the throttle cable.

15. Connect the fuel lines. Always use new washers at the banjo fittings.

16. Connect the electrical and vacuum connectors.

17. Double check all installation items, paying

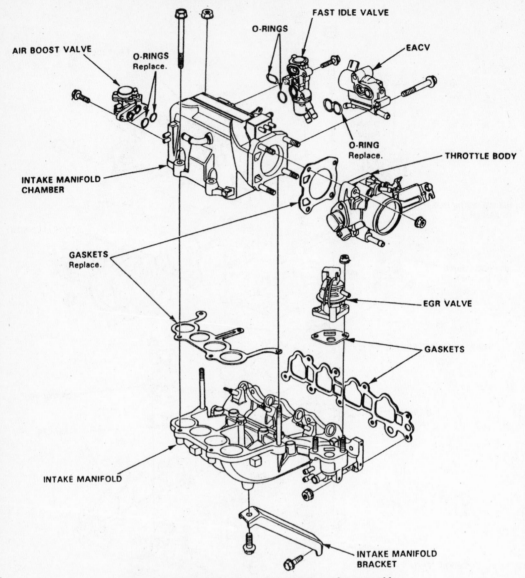

FAST IDLE VALVE

O-RINGS

AIR BOOST VALVE

EACV

O-RINGS
Replace.

O-RING
Replace.

THROTTLE BODY

INTAKE MANIFOLD
CHAMBER

EGR VALVE

GASKETS
Replace.

GASKETS

INTAKE MANIFOLD

INTAKE MANIFOLD
BRACKET

1990–91 Accord Intake system without bypass valve assembly

particular attention to loose hoses or hanging wires, untightened nuts, poor routing of hoses and wires (too tight or rubbing) and tools left in the work area.

18. Refill the engine coolant.

19. Start the engine, checking carefully for any leaks of fuel, coolant or vacuum. Check the manifold gasket areas carefully for any leakage of vacuum.

Exhaust Manifold
REMOVAL AND INSTALLATION
Carbureted Engines

WARNING: *Do not perform this operation on a warm or hot engine.*

1. Elevate and safely support the car.

2. Remove the header pipe to manifold nuts and separate the pipe from the manifold. Support the pipe with wire; do not allow it to hang by itself.

3. Disconnect and remove the oxygen sensor.

4. Remove the exhaust manifold shroud or heat shield.

5. Remove the exhaust manifold bracket bolts.

6. Using a criss-cross pattern (starting from the center), remove the exhaust manifold-to-cylinder head nuts, the manifold and the gaskets (discard them).

NOTE: *Breaking loose exhaust manifold bolts is one of the nastiest jobs around. They*

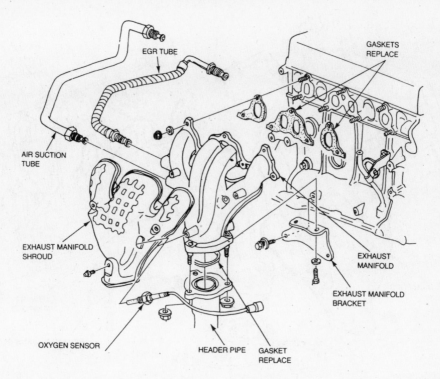

Carbureted exhaust manifold — Accord and Prelude. Certain models may differ slightly but all are similar.

are usually rusted solid; a generous application of penetrating oil several hours before beginning the job will make it easier.

7. Using a putty knife or similar tool, clean the gasket mounting surfaces. Inspect the mating faces with a straight-edge, checking that they are not warped.

To install:

8. Using a new gasket, place the manifold into position and support it. Install the nuts snug on the studs.

9. Install the support bracket(s) below the manifold. Tighten the bolt holding the bracket to the manifold to 28 Nm (20 ft. lbs).

10. Starting with the inner or center nuts, tighten the nuts in a criss-cross pattern to the correct torque. The tension must be even across the entire face of the manifold if leaks are to be prevented. Correct torque is 32 Nm (23 ft. lbs.) for all carbureted vehicles.

11. Install the heat shield or shroud.

12. Connect the exhaust pipe, using a new gasket and new nuts. Tighten the exhaust pipe-to-manifold nuts to 55 Nm (40 ft. lbs).

Fuel Injected Engines

WARNING: *Remove the exhaust manifold only when the engine is cold.*

1. Elevate and safely support the vehicle.

2. Remove the front grille for access. Disconnect the electrical connector from the oxygen sensor and remove the sensor from the exhaust manifold.

3. Remove and discard the header pipe-to-exhaust manifold nuts. Disconnect the header pipe and discard the gasket.

4. Remove the shroud-to-exhaust manifold bolt and the shroud. Remove the exhaust manifold bracket-to-engine bolts. Remove the exhaust manifold-to-cylinder head nuts/washers, the manifold and the gaskets (discard them).

5. Clean the gasket mounting surfaces. Using a straightedge, inspect for warping; replace any warped parts. If the cylinder head/manifold mating surface is warped, it must be machined.

To install:

6. Using new gasket(s), place the manifold into position and support it. Install the nuts snug on the studs.

7. Install the support bracket(s) below the manifold. Tighten the bolt holding the bracket to the manifold to 28 Nm (20 ft. lbs).

8. Starting with the inner or center nuts, tighten the nuts in a criss-cross pattern to the correct torque. The tension must be even across the entire face of the manifold if leaks are to be prevented. Correct torque is 32 Nm (23 ft. lbs.) for all fuel injected vehicles.

9. Install the heat shroud.

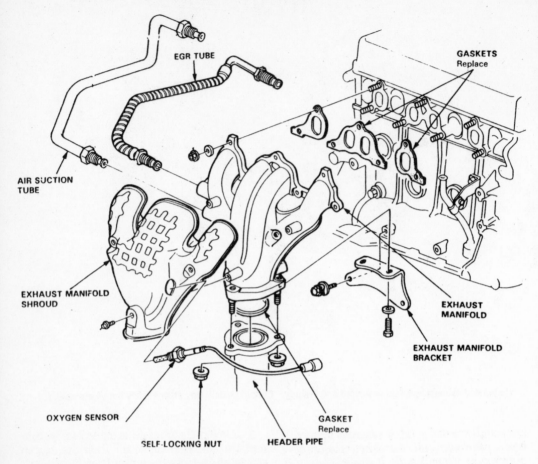

EGR TUBE

GASKETS
Replace

AIR SUCTION
TUBE

EXHAUST MANIFOLD
SHROUD

EXHAUST
MANIFOLD

EXHAUST MANIFOLD
BRACKET

OXYGEN SENSOR

SELF-LOCKING NUT

HEADER PIPE

GASKET
Replace

Exhaust manifold components, 1986–89 Accord

10. Connect the exhaust pipe to the manifold, using new nuts and a new gasket. Tighten the nuts to 55 Nm (40 ft. lbs.)

11. Install the oxygen sensor, tightening it to 45 Nm (33 ft. lbs). Connect the sensor wiring.

12. Install the EGR tube if it was removed; use a new gasket.

13. Install the grille.

Radiator and Electric Fans

Honda engines use water-cooling for engine heat dissipation. The coolant, circulated by the water pump, is heated as it flows through the passages in the engine. When the coolant flows through the radiator, it is cooled by airflow, either from the forward motion of the car or from the operation of the fan(s). The radiator fan system is triggered by a temperature sensor which energizes the fans if coolant temperature exceeds a certain level.

CAUTION: *Do NOT attempt to open the cooling system when the engine is hot; the system will be under pressure and scalding may occur. Wait until the radiator and hoses* are cool to the touch, generally a period of hours after the engine was operated.

REMOVAL AND INSTALLATION

The electric radiator fan(s) may be removed without removing the radiator. Disconnect the electrical connectors. Remove the mounting bolts holding the fan shroud and remove the shroud with the fan. Once removed, the fan blade may be unbolted from the shaft and the fan motor removed from the shroud.

To remove the radiator:

1. Position a clean drain pan under the radiator, open the drain plug, remove the radiator cap and drain the cooling system.

CAUTION: *When draining the coolant, keep in mind that cats and dogs are attracted by the ethylene glycol antifreeze, and are quite likely to drink any that is left in an uncovered container or in puddles on the ground. This will prove fatal in sufficient quantity. Always drain the coolant into a sealable container. Coolant should be reused unless it is contaminated or several years old.*

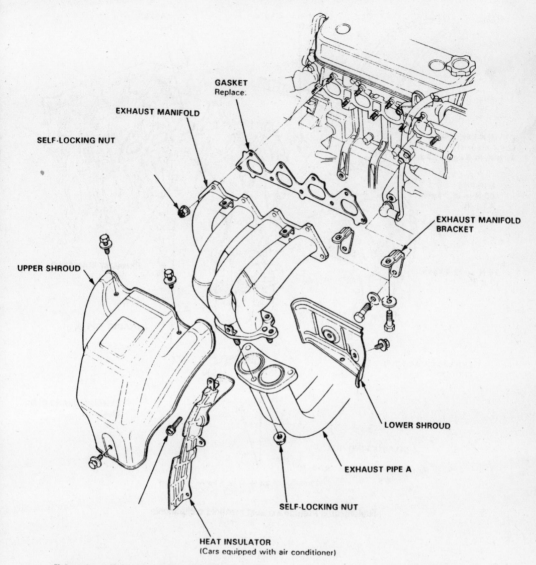

GASKET
Replace.

EXHAUST MANIFOLD

SELF-LOCKING NUT

EXHAUST MANIFOLD
BRACKET

UPPER SHROUD

LOWER SHROUD

EXHAUST PIPE A

SELF-LOCKING NUT

HEAT INSULATOR
(Cars equipped with air conditioner)

Exhaust manifold components for 1990–91 Accord. Dual exhaust header shown, single similar

2. Disconnect the electrical connectors from the thermo-switch and the cooling fan motor.

3. Disconnect the upper coolant hose at the upper radiator tank and the lower hose at the water pump connecting pipe. Disconnect the overflow hose from the coolant tank.

4. Remove the retaining bolts and remove the radiator with the fan attached. The fan can be easily unbolted from the back of the radiator. NOTE: *When removing the radiator, take care not to damage the core and fins.*

5. Take note of the rubber mounts or bushings; they must be replaced in their exact original positions. The radiator is used as a damper to smooth engine vibration.

6. Inspect the hoses for damage, leaks and/or deterioration; if necessary, replace them. If the radiator fins are clogged, wash off any insects or dirt with low pressure water. Fins may be straightened using a blunt, non-metallic tool such as an ice cream stick or similar.

7. When installing, fit the radiator into place, making certain the rubber bushings or grommets are in place at the bottom and/or sides of the mounts.

8. Install the retaining bolts, tightening them to 10 Nm (7 ft. lbs).

9. Connect the hoses to their ports; use new hose clamps.

10. Connect the electrical connectors for the fans.

11. Double check the draincock on the radiator, making sure it is closed. Refill the coolant.

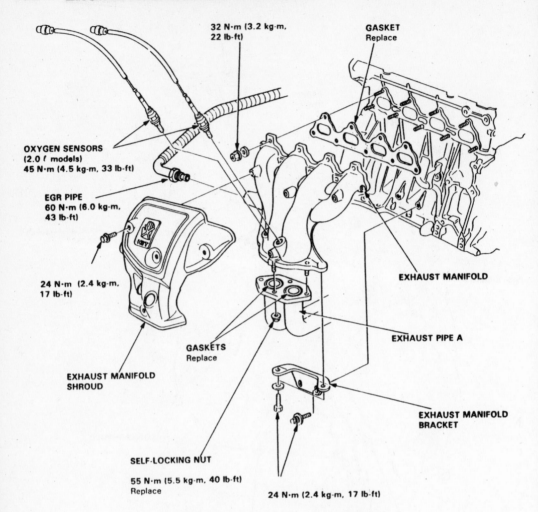

32 N·m (3.2 kg·m, 22 lb·ft)

GASKET
Replace

OXYGEN SENSORS
(2.0 ℓ models)
45 N·m (4.5 kg·m, 33 lb·ft)

EGR PIPE
60 N·m (6.0 kg·m, 43 lb·ft)

24 N·m (2.4 kg·m, 17 lb·ft)

EXHAUST MANIFOLD
SHROUD

GASKETS
Replace

EXHAUST MANIFOLD

EXHAUST PIPE A

EXHAUST MANIFOLD
BRACKET

SELF-LOCKING NUT

55 N·m (5.5 kg·m, 40 lb·ft)
Replace

24 N·m (2.4 kg·m, 17 lb·ft)

Fuel injected Prelude exhaust manifold components

Oil Cooler
REMOVAL AND INSTALLATION

CAUTION: *When draining the coolant, keep in mind that cats and dogs are attracted by the ethylene glycol antifreeze, and are quite likely to drink any that is left in an uncovered container or in puddles on the ground. This will prove fatal in sufficient quantity. Always drain the coolant into a sealable container. Coolant should be reused unless it is contaminated or several years old.*

Fuel injected Preludes from 1988 employ a water-cooling collar at the oil filter to absorb some heat from the oil stream; the system also appears on certain 1991 Accords. Coolant flows through the oil cooler and conducts the heat to the radiator. Under most conditions, the oil will be hotter than the coolant so the heat exchange cools the oil. This simple system eliminates the

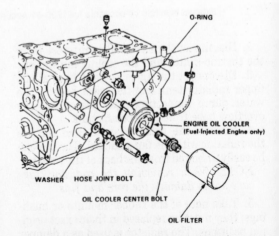

O-RING

ENGINE OIL COOLER
(Fuel-Injected Engine only)

WASHER   HOSE JOINT BOLT

OIL COOLER CENTER BOLT

OIL FILTER

Oil cooler for 1988–91 fuel injected Prelude. 1991 Accord location similar but coolant hose routing differs slightly

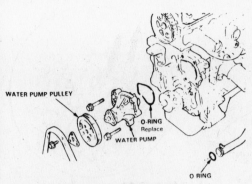

Water pump components, 1984–89 Accord.

need for additional radiator-type coolers at the front of the car.

1. With the engine cold, drain the coolant at least to a level below the oil filter. Drain the coolant into a clean container and save it for re-use. Cap the container and clean up spills immediately.

2. Disconnect the coolant lines running to the oil cooler.

3. Remove the oil filter. Although the engine is cold and most of the oil is in the sump, be prepared for some oil spillage; clean it up immediately.

NOTE: *Take great care not to allow coolant to drip into the oil system. If this occurs, the oil must be drained and refilled with fresh, unpolluted oil.*

4. Remove the oil cooler center bolt; this is the fitting onto which the oil filter is installed.

5. Remove the oil cooler and its O-ring.

To install:

6. Install a new O-ring on the cooler. Install the cooler, positioning it properly to align the hose ports. Install the center bolt and tighten it to 75 Nm (54 ft. lbs.)

7. Install the oil filter.

8. Connect the hoses to the cooler; use new hose clamps. Check that the hoses are properly routed and that there are no kinks or sharp bends.

9. Refill the coolant.

Water Pump

REMOVAL AND INSTALLATION

CAUTION: *When draining the coolant, keep in mind that cats and dogs are attracted by the ethylene glycol antifreeze, and are quite likely to drink any that is left in an uncovered container or in puddles on the ground. This will prove fatal in sufficient quantity. Always drain the coolant into a sealable container. Coolant should be reused unless it is contaminated or several years old.*

NOTE: *These operations require removal of many individual components. Some are more easily performed from either above or below, depending on arm's length and agility. Whenever you must elevate the car, it MUST be safely supported on jackstands. Never work under a car supported only by a jack.*

1984–89 Accord
1984–87 Prelude

1. Place a clean drain pan under the radiator, remove the drain plug (from the front side of the engine block and the drain the cooling system to a level below the water pump.

2. Loosen and remove the water pump drive belt.

3. Remove the pulley bolts and remove the pulley.

4. Remove the water pump retaining bolts and the pump together with the pulley and the O-ring.

5. Clean the mounting surfaces.

To install:

6. Use a new O-ring and install the pump to the block. Make certain the O-ring does not deform or move.

7. Install the retaining bolts, tightening them to 12 Nm (9 ft. lbs).

8. Install the pulley and pulley bolts; tighten the pulley bolts to 12 Nm (9 ft. lbs.)

9. Install the belt and adjust it to the proper tension; do not overtighten the belt.

10. Refill the engine coolant.

1990–91 Accord

WARNING: *This operation requires removal of the timing belt. Do not attempt to replace the water pump if you are not familiar with timing belt procedures.*

1. Disconnect the negative battery cable.

2. Turn the engine to align the timing marks and set cylinder No.1 to TDC. Once in this position, the engine must NOT be turned or disturbed.

3. Remove the splash shield from below the engine.

4. Drain the engine coolant. Use a clean container; cap or cover the container and wipe up spillage.

5. Disconnect the electrical connector at the cruise control actuator, then remove the actuator. Don't disconnect the cable; simply move the actuator out of the work area.

6. Remove the belt from the power steering pump. Remove the mounting bolts for the pump. Without disconnecting the hoses, move the pump out of the way.

7. Disconnect the alternator wiring and con-

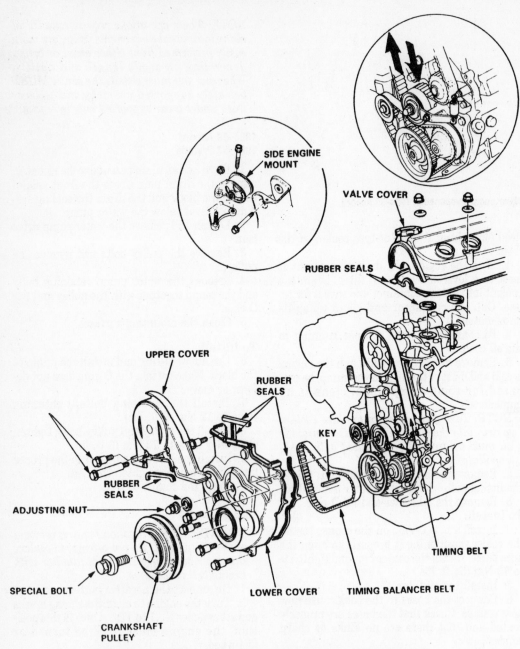

Replacing the 1990–91 Accord water pump requires removal of the timing belt

nectors; remove the engine wiring harness from the valve cover.

8. Loosen the adjusting and mounting bolts for the alternator and/or compressor. Remove the drive belt(s).

9. Remove the valve cover.

10. Remove the side engine mount support bracket, if so equipped.

11. Remove the upper timing belt cover.

12. Support the engine with a floor jack below the center of the center beam. Tension the jack

so that it is just supporting the beam but not lifting it.

13. Remove the through-bolt for the side engine mount and remove the mount.

14. Remove the dipstick and dipstick tube.

15. Remove the adjusting nut.

16. Remove the crankshaft pulley bolt and remove the crankshaft pulley.

NOTE: *This bolt is one of the tightest on the entire car. The pulley must be held in place while the bolt is loosened. One trick is to wrap an old drive belt around the pulley to hold it steady—don't try this with a belt that is to go back on the car; it will be stretched or damaged.*

17. Remove the two rear bolts from the center beam. Slowly lower the jack and the engine until clearance is gained to remove the lower timing belt cover.

18. Remove the lower timing belt cover.

19. There are two belts in this system; the one running to the camshaft pulley is the timing belt. The other, shorter one drives the balance shaft and is referred to as the balancer belt or timing balancer belt. Push the tensioner for the belts away from the belts to relieve the tension. Hold the tensioner, reinstall the adjusting nut and tighten it to hold the tensioner in place.

20. Carefully remove the balancer belt and timing belts. Do not crimp or bend the belts; protect them from contact with oil or coolant. Slide the belts off the pulleys.

21. Remove the bolts holding the water pump; pay attention to the location of the long bolt.

22. Remove the water pump and the O-ring.

To install:

23. Install a new O-ring and make certain it is properly seated. Install the water pump and retaining bolts. Tighten the retaining bolts to 12 Nm (9 ft. lbs)

24. Check the position of the engine. The timing pointer must be perfectly aligned with the white mark on the flywheel or flex-plate; the camshaft pulley must be aligned so that the word UP is at the top of the pulley and the marks on the edge of the pulley are aligned with the surfaces of the head. Additionally, the face of the front timing balancer pulley has a mark which must be aligned with the notch on the oil pump body. This pulley is the one at "10 o'clock" to the crank pulley when viewed from the pulley end.

25. Align the rear timing balancer pulley ("2 o'clock" from the crank pulley) using a 6 × 100 mm bolt or rod. Mark the bolt or rod at a point 74 mm (2.913 inches) from the end. Remove the bolt from the maintenance hole on the side of the block; insert the rod into the hole. Align the 74mm mark with the face of the hole. This pin will hold the shaft in place during installation.

26. Fit the timing belt over the pulleys and tensioners. Install the balancer belt. Once the belts are in place, double check that all the en-

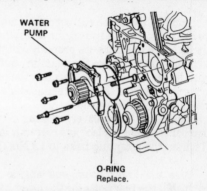

Detail of 1990 Accord water pump

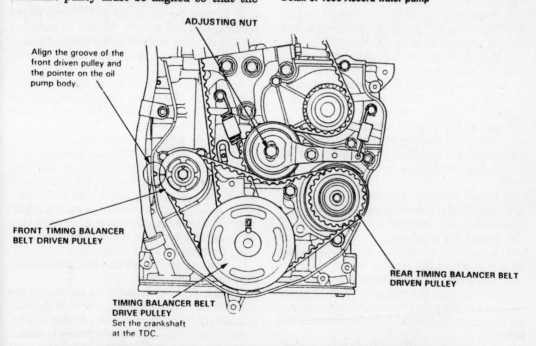

End view of Accord engine with belts installed. Note alignment marks for front balancer pulley

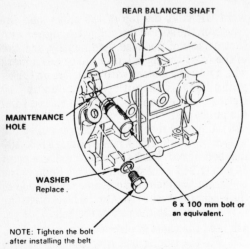

REAR BALANCER SHAFT

MAINTENANCE HOLE

WASHER
Replace .

6 x 100 mm bolt or
an equivalent.

NOTE: Tighten the bolt
after installing the belt

Remove the bolt for access to the maintenance hole

gine alignment items are still correct. If not, re-move the belts, realign the engine and reinstall the belts. Once the belts are properly installed, slowly loosen and remove the adjusting nut, al-lowing the tensioner to move against the belts. Remove the pin from the maintenance hole and reinstall the bolt and washer.

27. Install the lower cover, making certain the rubber seals are in place and correctly locat-ed. Tighten the retaining bolts to 12 Nm (9 ft. lbs).

28. Raise the lower beam and engine into place. Install the rear bolts for the lower beam, tightening them to 39 Nm (28 ft. lbs).

29. Install the key on the crankshaft and in-stall the crankshaft pulley. Apply oil to the bolt threads and tighten it to 230 Nm (153 ft. lbs).

30. Adjust the timing belt tension. Turn the crankshaft counterclockwise until the cam pul-ley has moved 3 teeth; this creates tension on the timing belt. Install the adjusting nut and tighten it to 45 Nm (33 ft. lbs).

31. Install the dipstick tube and dipstick.

32. Install the side engine mount. Tighten the mount bolt, nut and through-bolt to 55 Nm (40 ft. lbs). Remove the jack from under the center beam.

33. Install the upper belt cover.

34. Install the side engine mount support bracket if it was removed.

35. Install the valve cover.

36. Install the compressor and/or alternator drive belt; adjust the tension.

37. Route the wiring harness over the valve cover and connect the wiring to the alternator.

38. Install the power steering pump, tighten-ing the bolt to 45 Nm (33 ft. lbs.) and install the belt.

39. Reinstall the cruise control actuator. Con-

nect the vacuum hose and the electrical connector.

40. Double check all installation items, paying particular attention to loose hoses or hanging wires, untightened nuts, poor routing of hoses and wires (too tight or rubbing) and tools left in the engine area.

41. Refill the engine coolant.

42. Install the splash shield under the engine.

43. Connect the negative battery cable.

44. Start the engine, allowing it to idle. Check for any signs of leakage or any sound of the belts rubbing or binding.

1988–91 Prelude

WARNING: *This operation requires removal of the timing belt. Do not attempt to replace the water pump if you are not familiar with timing belt procedures.*

1. Disconnect the negative battery cable.

2. Turn the engine to align the timing marks and set cylinder No.1 to TDC. Once in this posi-tion, the engine must NOT be turned or disturbed.

3. Drain the engine coolant. Use a clean con-tainer and cap it when full. Wipe up spillage immediately.

4. Remove the engine support bolts and nuts, then remove the side mount rubber and bracket. Remove the cruise control actuator if so equipped; move the actuator out of the way without disconnecting or kinking the cable.

5. Remove the splash shield from below the engine.

6. Loosen the adjusting nut for the power steering belt and remove the belt. Remove the adjusting pulley and the power steering pump. Move the pump out of the way with the hoses attached.

7. Disconnect the wiring at the alternator. Remove the alternator through-bolt; remove the mounting and adjusting bolts and remove the alternator and belt.

8. On cars with air conditioning, remove the compressor mounting bolts. Remove the com-pressor and belt; do not disconnect the lines from the compressor. Position the compressor out of the way and support it with stiff wire.

9. On fuel injected vehicles, remove the igni-tion wires from the valve cover and remove the harness protector from the cylinder head.

10. Remove the valve cover.

11. Remove the crankshaft bolt and remove the crankshaft pulley.

NOTE: *This bolt is one of the tightest on the entire car. The pulley must be held in place while the bolt is loosened. One trick is to wrap an old drive belt around the pulley to hold it steady—don't try this with a belt that is to go*

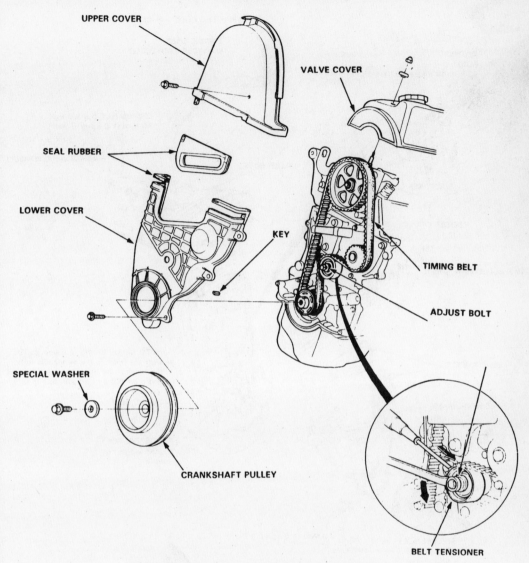

UPPER COVER

VALVE COVER

SEAL RUBBER

LOWER COVER

KEY

TIMING BELT

ADJUST BOLT

SPECIAL WASHER

CRANKSHAFT PULLEY

BELT TENSIONER

Timing belt components, carbureted Prelude — 1988–91

back on the car; it will be stretched or damaged.

11. Remove the timing belt covers.

12. Loosen, but do not remove, the adjusting bolt on the timing belt tensioner. Move the tensioner off the belt and retighten the bolt.

13. Use a piece of chalk or a marker to place an identifying arrow on the timing belt. The arrow can identify the direction of rotation or the outer edge of the belt. The belt must be reinstalled so it moves in the same direction. Carefully remove the belt from the pulleys without crimping it. Protect the belt from oil, coolant, etc.

14. **Remove the bolts holding the water pump; remove the pump and O-ring.**

To install:

15. Replace the O-ring and install the water pump. Make certain the O-ring does not deform or come out of place. Tighten the mounting bolts to 12 Nm (9 ft. lbs).

16. Double check the engine position; it must be at TDC for No. 1 cylinder. All of the following conditions must be met: The timing pointer is aligned with the white mark on the flywheel or flexplate, the UP mark on each camshaft pulley is at the top and the alignment marks on each cam pulley are aligned with the edges of the cylinder head.

NOTE: *On fuel injected engines, each of the camshafts may be held in the TDC position by inserting 5mm diameter punches into the*

10 N·m (1.0 kg-m, 7 lb-ft)

ENGINE WIRE
HARNESS PROTECTOR

ADJUST
BOLT
43 N·m (4.3 kg-m, 31 lb-ft)

CROWN NUT 6 x 1.0 mm
10 N·m (1.0 kg-m, 7 lb-ft)

VALVE COVER

WASHER and GROMMET

TENSIONER

MIDDLE COVER

10 N·m (1.0 kg-m, 7 lb-ft)

SEAL RUBBER

NOTE: To set the No. 1 piston at TDC,
align the holes in the camshafts with
the holes in the No. 1 camshaft holders
and drive 5.0 mm pin punches in to
the holes
TIMING BELT

LOWER COVER

KEY

ADJUSTING BOLT
Loosen but do not
remove.

CRANKSHAFT
PULLEY

SPECIAL BOLT
150 N·m (15.0 kg·m, 108 lb-ft)
Apply engine oil to
the bolt threads.

10 N·m (1.0 kg-m, 7 lb-ft)

Timing belt components, fuel injected Prelude — 1988– 91

alignment holes just behind each cam pulley. This makes installing the belt much easier.

17. Install the timing belt so that it rotates in the same direction as before. Remove the pins holding the cams if they were installed.

18. Loosen the adjuster and allow it to tension the belt. Tighten the adjuster bolt.

19. Reinstall the belt covers except the upper cover on single cam engines.

20. Reinstall the crankshaft pulley and key. Coat the threads of the bolt with light oil, but do not lubricate the face of the bolt which contacts the washer. On fuel injected engines, tighten the bolt to 150 Nm (108 ft. lbs.); on carbureted engines, tighten the bolt to 115 Nm (83 ft. lbs).

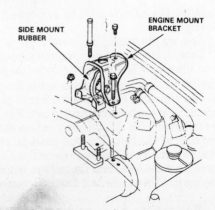

ENGINE MOUNT
BRACKET

SIDE MOUNT
RUBBER

Remove the Prelude engine mount with the through-bolt still in it

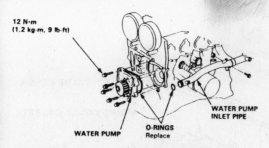

12 N·m
(1.2 kg·m, 9 lb-ft)

WATER PUMP
INLET PIPE

WATER PUMP

O-RINGS
Replace

Prelude water pump — DOHC shown, SOHC similar

NOTE: *This tightening is best accomplished with the wheels blocked, the parking brake applied and the transmission in gear (manual) or in PARK.*

21. Rotate the engine counterclockwise until the camshaft pulley has moved 3 teeth. Loosen the adjusting bolt, then retighten it to 43 Nm (31 ft. lbs).

22. Install the valve cover and upper belt cover on carbureted vehicles. On fuel injected vehicles, reinstall the ignition wires and the harness protector.

23. Reinstall the A/C compressor and belt. Tighten the mounting bolts to 25 Nm (18 ft. lbs). Adjust the belt tension.

24. Reinstall the alternator and belt. Tighten the through-bolt to 45 Nm (33 ft. lbs).

25. Install the power steering pump and belt, tightening the bolts to 27 Nm (20 ft. lbs).

26. Install the side engine mount and the cruise control actuator if it was removed. Tighten the engine mount bolts to 40 Nm (29 ft. lbs.) and the nuts to 65 Nm (47 ft. lbs).

27. Refill the engine coolant. bleed the cooling system.

28. Connect the negative battery cable.

29. Start the engine, allowing it to idle. Check the work area carefully for any sign of fluid leakage or any indication of the belt rubbing or slapping the covers.

30. Switch the engine OFF. Reinstall the splash shield.

Cylinder Head

REMOVAL AND INSTALLATION

CAUTION: *When draining the coolant, keep in mind that cats and dogs are attracted by the ethylene glycol antifreeze, and are quite likely to drink any that is left in an uncovered container or in puddles on the ground. This will prove fatal in sufficient quantity. Always drain the coolant into a sealable container. Coolant should be reused unless it is contaminated or several years old.*

The EPA warns that prolonged contact with used engine oil may cause a number of skin disorders, including cancer! You should make every effort to minimize your exposure to used engine oil. Protective gloves should be worn when changing the oil. Wash your hands and any other exposed skin areas as soon as possible after exposure to used engine oil. Soap and water, or waterless hand cleaner should be used.

1984–89 Accord and Prelude SOHC Engine

WARNING: *The cylinder head temperature must be below 100°F (38°C). before starting the work. Allow the car to cool several hours if recently driven.*

1. Disconnect the negative battery terminal from the battery.

2. Place a clean drain pan under the radiator, remove the drain plug and the radiator cap, then, drain the cooling system.

3. Remove the vacuum hose from the brake booster and the air intake ducts from the air cleaner case.

NOTE: *All wires and hoses should be labeled at the time of removal. The amount of time saved during reassembly makes the extra effort well worthwhile.*

4. If equipped with fuel injection, relieve the fuel pressure using the proper procedures. Disconnect the fuel return hose from the pressure regulator. Remove the banjo nut and the fuel hose; be sure to replace the washers.

5. Remove the ground cable from the valve cover.

6. Label and disconnect the hoses from the air cleaner.

7. On carburetor models, disconnect the wires from the thermosensor temperature gauge sending unit, idle cut-off solenoid valve, primary/main cut-off solenoid valve and the automatic choke.

8. Disconnect the throttle control cable and/or the accelerator cable from the carburetor or throttle body.

9. Label and disconnect all emission hoses from the carburetor(s).

10. Label and disconnect electrical connectors and hoses from the distributor; remove the distributor.

11. On fuel injected models, label and disconnect the following sub-harness connectors and couplers from the cylinder head and intake manifold:

- The four injector connectors
- The TA sensor connector
- The ground connector located near the fuel pipe
- The throttle sensor connector
- The TW sensor connector

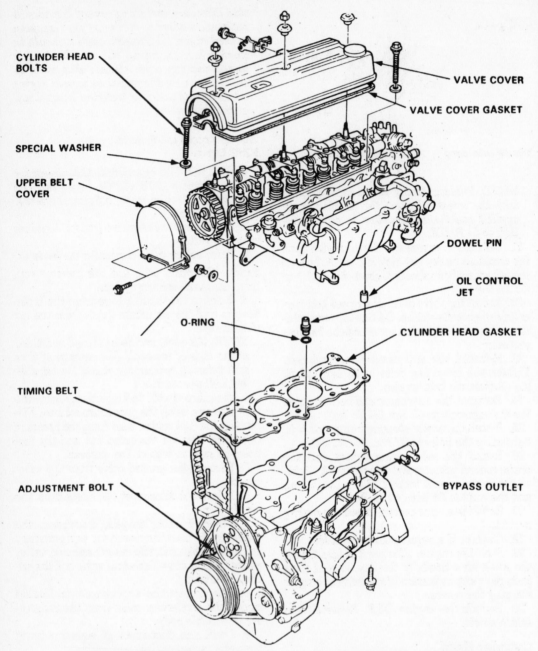

CYLINDER HEAD
BOLTS

SPECIAL WASHER

UPPER BELT
COVER

O-RING

TIMING BELT

ADJUSTMENT BOLT

VALVE COVER

VALVE COVER GASKET

DOWEL PIN

OIL CONTROL
JET

CYLINDER HEAD GASKET

BYPASS OUTLET

Cylinder head removal, 1984–87 Accord and Prelude. Fuel injected shown, carbureted similar.

● The crankshaft angle sensor coupler
● The EGR valve connector
● The 4-wire harness clamps
● The oxygen sensor connector
12. On carbureted models, disconnect the following items:
    a. Label and disconnect the No. 1 control box emission hoses from the tubing manifold.
    b. Disconnect the air jet controller hoses.
13. Remove the coolant hoses from the cylinder head.

14. If equipped with power steering, perform the following procedures:
    a. Remove the pump bracket from the cylinder head.
    b. Remove the hose clamp bolt from the cylinder head.
    c. Remove the power steering pump bracket from the cylinder head.
15. If equipped with air conditioning, disconnect the idle control solenoid hoses.
16. If equipped with cruise control, remove

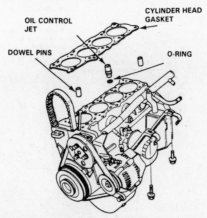

OIL CONTROL JET

CYLINDER HEAD GASKET

DOWEL PINS

O-RING

Detail of head gasket installation. The dowels and jet must be correctly installed.

the cruise control actuator. Do not disconnect the cable; simply move the actuator out of the way.

17. Remove the exhaust header pipe nuts, the header pipe bracket and pull the pipe away from the exhaust manifold.

18. Remove the air cleaner base mount bolts. Disconnect the intake manifold-to-breather chamber hose.

19. Remove the valve cover and the upper timing belt cover.

20. Loosen the tensioner adjusting bolt and remove the timing belt.

NOTE: *When removing the timing belt, DO NOT bend or crimp the belt.*

21. Remove the cylinder head bolts, in sequence, working from the ends toward the center. Loosen each bolt about ½ turn each time and make several passes to release the tension evenly. Failure to follow this procedure may cause the head to warp.

22. Remove the cylinder head from the engine. The head may resist coming loose due to bonding at the gasket. Loosen the head by tapping it gently with a plastic or rubber mallet. Lift the head straight up to remove it.

23. Remove the exhaust manifold from the cylinder head.

24. Remove the air cleaner base from the intake manifold; remove the carburetors.

25. Remove the intake manifold from the cylinder head.

26. Using a putty knife or similar blunt instrument, clean the gasket mounting surfaces. Inspect the parts for damage, replace them if necessary.

To install:

24. Assemble the manifolds and carburetor to the head. Use new gaskets for each manifold. Make certain the carburetor is correctly tightened.

25. Install a new head gasket on the engine deck, making certain the gasket is positioned correctly. The cylinder head dowel pins and the oil jet must be in place.

26. Install the head. Lower it straight down onto the block, aligning it correctly.

27. Apply clean engine oil to the bolt threads and the contact face of the bolt head. Install the head bolts finger tight. Install the bolts that secure the intake manifold to its bracket but do not tighten them yet.

28. Position the camshaft and pulley correctly; the UP mark must be at the top and the alignment marks on the edge of the pulley aligned with the edge of the head. Carbureted Preludes use a small round mark or dot on the pulley; this must be at the top.

29. Tighten the head bolts in two steps, following the pattern shown. The first pass should bring the bolts to about 30 Nm (22 ft. lbs); the second and final pass should bring the bolts to their final torque of 68 Nm (49 ft. lbs.)

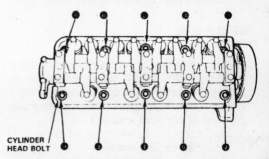

CYLINDER HEAD BOLT

Tighten the head bolts in this order in two passes.

30. Tighten the bolts for the intake manifold support bracket.

31. Install the timing belt. Release the tensioner against the belt.

32. Adjust the valve clearance. Install the valve cover and upper timing belt cover.

33. Connect the hose from the intake manifold to the breather.

34. Install the air cleaner base mounts.

35. Install the header pipe to its bracket; install new nuts.

36. Reinstall the cruise control actuator.

37. connect the idle control solenoid hoses.

38. Install the power steering pump and belt.

39. Connect the coolant hoses at the thermostat housing and intake manifold.

40. Connect the upper radiator hose, heater hoses and bypass inlet hose.

41. Connect the air jet controller hoses. Install the control box hoses to the vacuum manifold.

42. Connect the lines and hoses to the distributor.

43. Install the fuel lines and throttle control cable and/or the accelerator cable.

44. Connect the electrical lines to the carburetor and related components.

45. Install the air cleaner and cover. Connect the vacuum hoses.

46. On fuel injected engines, connect the harness and wiring connectors removed in Step 11.

47. Connect the charcoal canister lines.

48. Connect the fuel hoses to the fuel injected throttle body.

49. Connect the ignition wires, coil wire and radio noise condenser.

50. Install the engine ground cable to the valve cover. Connect the vacuum line to the brake booster.

51. Double check all installation items, paying particular attention to loose hoses or hanging wires, untightened nuts, poor routing of hoses and wires (too tight or rubbing) and tools left in the engine area.

52. Refill the cooling system.

53. Connect the negative battery cable.

1988–89 Prelude
DOHC Engine

NOTE: *The cylinder head temperature must be below 100°F (38°C); allow the engine to cool several hours if the car has been recently driven. Turn the flywheel so that number one piston is at top dead center.*

1. Disconnect the battery ground cable.

2. Drain the cooling system.

3. Remove the brake booster vacuum hose from the intake manifold.

4. Remove the engine ground cable from the valve cover. Disconnect the radio condenser connector and the ignition coil wire.

5. Remove the air cleaner assembly. Relieve the fuel pressure using the proper procedure.

6. Disconnect the fuel lines and fuel return line. Remove the air intake hose and the resonator hose. Disconnect the throttle cable at the throttle body.

7. For automatic transaxles, disconnect the throttle control cable at the throttle body.

8. Disconnect the charcoal canister hose at the throttle valve. Disconnect and tag all the wire harness connectors from the cylinder head. Remove the emission control box and vacuum tank, then disconnect the two connectors. Do not remove the emission hoses.

9. Disconnect the upper radiator hose. Remove the heater hoses from the cylinder head. Remove the water bypass hoses from the water pump inlet pipe.

10. Remove the power steering pump belt and the alternator belt. Also remove the air conditioning belt if so equipped.

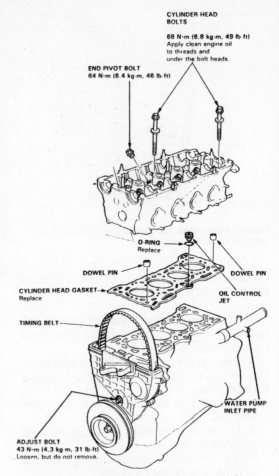

CYLINDER HEAD BOLTS

68 N·m (6.8 kg·m, 49 lb·ft)
Apply clean engine oil to threads and under the bolt heads.

END PIVOT BOLT
64 N·m (6.4 kg·m, 46 lb·ft)

O-RING
Replace

DOWEL PIN

DOWEL PIN

CYLINDER HEAD GASKET
Replace

OIL CONTROL JET

TIMING BELT

WATER PUMP INLET PIPE

ADJUST BOLT
43 N·m (4.3 kg·m, 31 lb·ft)
Loosen, but do not remove.

Prelude DOHC head and gasket. Note that the timing belt is not removed from the engine.

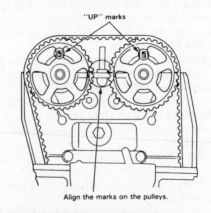

"UP" marks

Align the marks on the pulleys.

Both cam pulleys must be correctly aligned

11. Disconnect the inlet hose from the power steering pump and plug the hose immediately to prevent fluid leakage. Remove the power steering pump from the cylinder head. Remove the alternator.

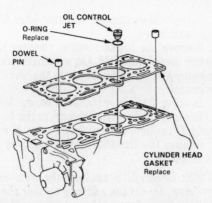

Detail of head gasket Installation for 1988–89 DOHC Prelude. The dowels and jet must be correctly Installed.

NOTE: *When the power steering hose is disconnected, the fluid will flow out. Cover the alternator with a shop towel to prevent any internal damage.*

12. Remove the intake manifold bracket. Remove the exhaust manifold bracket and then the header pipe.

13. Remove and tag the ignition wires and remove the distributor assembly. Be sure to scribe a line relating the position of the distributor assembly to the engine block for easy installation.

14. Remove the cylinder sensor. Remove the valve cover.

15. Remove the timing belt middle cover.

16. Loosen but do not remove the timing belt adjusting bolt; remove the timing belt from the camshaft pulleys.

NOTE: *Do not crimp or bend the timing belt.*

17. Remove the camshaft holders, camshafts and rocker arms. Remove the cylinder head bolts (take notice of the bolt holes occupied by the two longer bolts) and remove the cylinder head. The head may resist removal, even with the bolts out. Tap the edge of the head with a plastic or rubber mallet; lift the head straight up to remove it.

18. Remove the exhaust manifold shroud and EGR pipe, then remove the exhaust manifold from the cylinder head.

19. Remove the intake manifold from the cylinder head.

To install:

20. Assemble the intake and exhaust manifolds to the head. Use new gaskets.

21. Install a new head gasket on the engine deck, making certain the gasket is positioned correctly. The cylinder head dowel pins and the oil jet must be in place.

22. Install the head. Lower it straight down onto the block, aligning it correctly.

23. Apply clean engine oil to the bolt threads

and the contact face of the bolt head. Install the head bolts finger tight.

24. Tighten the head bolts in two steps, following the pattern shown. The first pass should bring the bolts to about 30 Nm (22 ft. lbs); the second and final pass should bring the bolts to their final torque of 68 Nm (49 ft. lbs.)

25. Install the cam, rockers and camshaft holders.

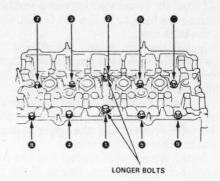

LONGER BOLTS

Tighten the head bolts In this order In two passes.

26. Double check the engine position; it must be at TDC for No. 1 cylinder. All of the following conditions must be met: The timing pointer is aligned with the white mark on the flywheel or flexplate, the UP mark on each camshaft pulley is at the top and the alignment marks on each cam pulley are aligned with the edges of the cylinder head.

NOTE: *Each of the camshafts may be held in the TDC position by inserting 5mm diameter punches into the alignment holes just behind each cam pulley. This makes installing the belt much easier.*

27. Install the timing belt so that it rotates in the same direction as before. Remove the pins holding the cams if they were installed.

28. Loosen the adjuster and allow it to tension the belt. Tighten the adjuster bolt.

29. Reinstall the belt covers.

30. Reinstall the crankshaft pulley and key. Coat the threads of the bolt with light oil, but do not lubricate the face of the bolt which contacts the washer. On fuel injected engines, tighten the bolt to 150 Nm (108 ft. lbs.); on carbureted engines, tighten the bolt to 115 Nm (83 ft. lbs).

NOTE: *This tightening is best accomplished with the wheels blocked, the parking brake applied and the transmission in gear (manual) or in PARK.*

31. Rotate the engine counterclockwise until the camshaft pulley has moved 3 teeth. Loosen the adjusting bolt, then retighten it to 43 Nm (31 ft. lbs.)

32. Install the valve cover and upper belt cover. Install the CYL sensor. Reinstall the ignition wires and the harness protector.

33. Install the distributor and the ignition wire.

34. Install the intake manifold support bracket.

35. Reinstall the alternator and belt. Tighten the through-bolt to 45 Nm (33 ft. lbs).

36. Install the power steering pump and belt, tightening the bolts to 27 Nm (20 ft. lbs). Connect the inlet hose.

37. Install the side engine mount and the cruise control actuator if it was removed. Tighten the engine mount bolts to 40 Nm (29 ft. lbs.) and the nuts to 65 Nm (47 ft. lbs).

38. Connect the bypass coolant hoses to the water pump inlet pipe. Connect the heater hose to the cylinder head and the upper radiator hose to the thermostat housing.

39. Install the emission control box and connect the wiring connectors. Double check the vacuum hoses to insure none came loose.

40. Connect the electrical harness and wiring connectors at and around the head.

41. connect the charcoal canister hose at the throttle valve.

42. Connect the throttle control cable and/or accelerator cable at the throttle body.

43. Install the air intake hose and resonator.

44. connect the fuel hose and fuel return line.

45. Install the air cleaner cover.

46. Connect the radio condenser and the coil wire. Connect the engine ground cable.

47. Connect the vacuum hose to the brake booster.

48. Refill the engine coolant. Bleed the cooling system.

49. Connect the negative battery cable.

50. Start the engine, allowing it to idle. Check the work area carefully for any sign of fluid leakage or any indication of the belt rubbing or slapping the covers.

1990–91 Accord

1. Disconnect the negative battery cable.

2. Bring the No. 1 cylinder to TDC by turning the crankshaft.

3. Drain the cooling system. Use a clean container; cap it when full and wipe up spillage immediately.

4. Relieve the fuel system pressure using the proper procedure.

5. Remove the fuel feed and return hose.

6. Remove the vacuum hose, breather hose and air intake duct.

7. Remove the water bypass hose from the cylinder head.

8. Remove the charcoal canister hose from the throttle body.

9. Remove the brake booster vacuum hose from the intake manifold. On automatic transaxle equipped vehicles, remove the vacuum hose mount.

10. Remove the cruise control vacuum hose.

11. Remove the throttle cable from the throttle body. On automatic transaxle equipped vehicles, remove the throttle control cable at the throttle body.

NOTE: *Be careful not to bend the cable when removing. Do not use pliers to remove the cable from the linkage. Always replace a kinked cable with a new one.*

12. Disconnect the 2 connectors from the distributor and the spark plug wires from the spark plugs. Mark the position of the distributor and remove it from the cylinder head.

13. Disconnect the 2 connectors from the emission control box and remove the box. Do not disconnect the emission hoses.

14. Remove the connector and the terminal from the alternator, then remove the engine wire harness from the valve cover.

15. Disconnect the engine wire harness connectors, then remove the harness clamps from the cylinder head and the intake manifold.

16. Remove the upper radiator hose and the heater inlet hose from the cylinder head, then remove the heater outlet pipe bracket bolt from the intake manifold.

17. Remove the thermostat assembly from the intake manifold.

18. Disconnect the connector and the vacuum line, then remove the cruise control actuator. Do not disconnect the cable; move the actuator out of the work area with the cable attached.

19. Remove the mounting bolts and drive belt from the power steering pump, then without disconnecting the hoses, pull the pump away from the mounting bracket. Support the pump out of the work area.

20. Raise and safely support the vehicle.

21. Remove the front wheels.

22. Remove the splash shield.

23. Remove the intake manifold bracket bolts.

24. Remove the exhaust manifold and the exhaust manifold heat insulator.

25. Remove the intake manifold.

26. Remove the valve cover and engine ground wire.

27. Remove the side engine mount bracket stay, then remove the timing belt upper cover.

28. Mark the rotation of the timing belt if it is to be used again. Loosen the timing belt adjusting bolt and then release the timing belt.

NOTE: *Push the tensioner to release tension*

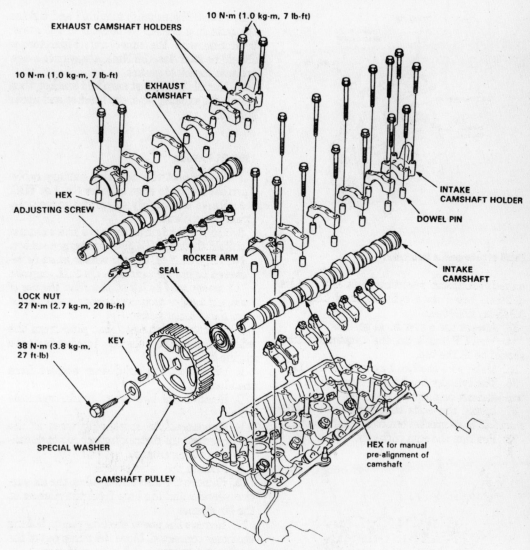

10 N·m (1.0 kg·m, 7 lb-ft)

EXHAUST CAMSHAFT HOLDERS

10 N·m (1.0 kg·m, 7 lb-ft)

EXHAUST CAMSHAFT

HEX
ADJUSTING SCREW

ROCKER ARM

SEAL

LOCK NUT
27 N·m (2.7 kg·m, 20 lb-ft)

38 N·m (3.8 kg·m, 27 ft-lb)   KEY

SPECIAL WASHER

CAMSHAFT PULLEY

INTAKE CAMSHAFT HOLDER

DOWEL PIN

INTAKE CAMSHAFT

HEX for manual pre-alignment of camshaft

1990–91 Accord head and related components

from the belt, then retighten the adjusting bolt.

29. Remove the timing belt from the camshaft pulley.

30. Remove the cylinder head bolts, then remove the cylinder head.

NOTE: *To prevent warpage, unscrew the bolts in sequence ⅓ turn at a time. Repeat the sequence until all bolts are loosened.*

To install:

31. Installation is the reverse of the removal procedure. Attention to the following steps will aid installation.

32. Make sure all cylinder head and block gasket surfaces are clean. Check the cylinder head for warpage. If warpage is less than 0.002 in. (0.05mm), cylinder head resurfacing is not re-

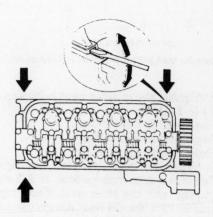

The head may be lifted to remove it.

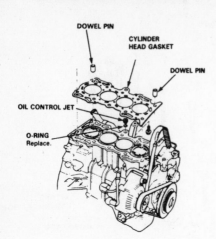

DOWEL PIN

CYLINDER
HEAD GASKET

DOWEL PIN

OIL CONTROL JET

O-RING
Replace.

Detail of head gasket installation

quired. Maximum resurface limit is 0.008 in. (0.2mm) based on a cylinder head height of 3.935 in. (99.95mm).

33. Always use a new head gasket.

34. The **UP** mark on the camshaft pulley should be at the top.

35. Make sure the No. 1 cylinder is at TDC.

36. The cylinder head dowel pins and oil control jet must be properly installed.

37. Install the bolts that secure the intake manifold to its bracket but do not tighten them.

38. Position the cam correctly.

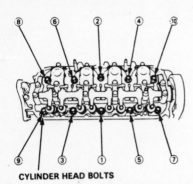

CYLINDER HEAD BOLTS

Tighten the head bolts in this order in three passes

39. Tighten the cylinder head bolts sequentially in 3 steps:

Step 1–29 ft. lbs. (40 Nm).
Step 2–51 ft. lbs. (70 Nm).
Step 3–78 ft. lbs. (108 Nm).

40. Install the intake manifold and tighten the nuts in a criss-cross pattern, in 2–3 steps, beginning with the inner nuts. Final torque should be 16 ft. lbs. (22 Nm). Always use a new intake manifold gasket.

41. Install the heat insulator to the cylinder head and the block.

42. Install the exhaust manifold and tighten the nuts in a criss-cross pattern in 2–3 steps, beginning with the inner nut. Final torque should be 23 ft. lbs. (32 Nm). Always use a new exhaust manifold gasket.

43. Install the exhaust manifold bracket, then install the exhaust pipe, the bracket and upper shroud.

1990–91 Prelude

1. Disconnect the negative battery cable. Turn the engine to align cylinder No. 1 at TDC.

2. Raise and safely support the vehicle. Drain the coolant.

3. On 2.0L engines, remove the exhaust manifold shroud, EGR pipe and oxygen sensor.

NOTE: *The 2.0L oxygen sensor must be removed before the next step. On 2.1L engines, the sensor may be left in place but the use of impact tools or hammers is not recommended on the exhaust system*

5. Disconnect the exhaust pipe from the manifold; disconnect the pipe bracket from the engine block.

6. Disconnect the air cleaner bracket from the block.

7. Remove the two lower intake manifold nuts.

8. Disconnect the spark plug wires at the plugs; remove the distributor but do not disconnect any wiring from it.

9. Remove the valve cover.

10. Remove the air suction valve, the air suction silencer and the hose from the silencer to the air cleaner.

11. Remove the power steering pump, leaving the hoses connected. Move the pump out of the work area and support it with stiff wire.

12. Remove the exhaust manifold.

13. Remove the three upper mounting bolts on the intake manifold. Separate the manifold from the head and push it back or away from the head.

14. Remove the thremostat housing as a unit without disconnecting any of the hoses.

15. Disconnect the heater hose from the head.

16. Remove the upper timing belt cover. Loosen–but do not remove–the adjusting bolt for the timing belt. Slide the timing belt off the cam pulleys. Do not crimp the belt or allow it to come in contact with engine fluids.

17. Remove the cylinder head bolts. Remove the cylinder head.

NOTE: *To prevent warpage, unscrew the bolts in sequence 1/3 turn at a time. Repeat the sequence until all bolts are loosened.*

To install:

18. Use a putty knife or similar blunt tool to

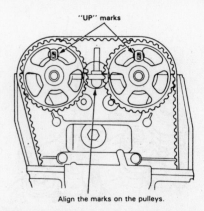

Align the marks on the pulleys.

The pulleys must be aligned before reinstalling the timing belt

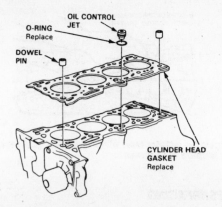

Detail of 1990–91 Prelude head and gasket Installation

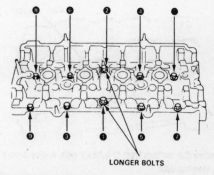

Tighten the head bolts In this order In two passes

remove all traces of gasket from the head and engine deck.

19. Place the new gasket on the engine, correctly positioned. Make certain the dowel pins and oil control jet are correctly placed.

20. Install the head. Apply a light coat of clean engine oil to the bolt threads and the contact face of the bolt head. Insert the bolts finger tight, making certain the two long bolts go in the center holes.

21. Tighten the cylinder head bolts in two steps, using the correct pattern. On the first pass, tighten the bolts to approximately 30 Nm (22 ft. lbs). On the second pass, bring each bolt to the final torque of 68 Nm (49 ft. lbs).

22. Double check the engine position; it must be set to TDC No. 1 cylinder. The timing pointer must align with the white mark on the flywheel. The camshaft pulley UP marks must be vertical and the alignment marks on the edges of the cam pulley must align with the lip of the cylinder head.

23. Carefully fit the timing belt onto the pulleys.

24. Tighten the adjusting bolt.

25. Rotate the engine counterclockwise until the cam pulley has moved 3 teeth.

26. Loosen the adjusting bolt; this tensions the timing belt. Retighten the adjusting bolt to 43 Nm (31 ft. lbs.)

27. Install the upper timing belt cover.

28. Install the thermostat housing.

29. Replace the gasket (always) and install the intake manifold. Begin at an inner or center bolt; make two or three complete passes in a criss-cross pattern when tightening the nuts. Final torque is 22 Nm (16 ft. lbs).

30. Using a new gasket, install the exhaust manifold. Begin at an inner or center bolt; make two or three complete passes in a criss-cross pattern when tightening the nuts. Final torque is 32 Nm (26 ft. lbs).

31. Install the power steering pump.

32. Install the air silencer, suction valve and hose.

31. Install the valve cover.

32. Install the distributor; connect the spark plug wires.

33. Install the air cleaner bracket to the engine block.

34. Connect the exhaust pipe to the manifold. Use new self-locking nuts and tighten them to 55 Nm (40 ft. lbs). Do not use an impact or air gun if the oxygen sensors are mounted in the pipe.

35. For 2.0L engines, install the oxygen sensors, the EGR pipe and the heat shield.

36. Refill the cooling system.

37. Connect the negative battery cable. Start the engine and allow it to idle. Check the work area carefully for any sign of fluid leakage.

CLEANING AND INSPECTION

1. Refer to Valve Removal and Installation in this chapter; remove the valve assemblies from the cylinder head.

2. Using a small wire power brush, clean the carbon from the combustion chambers and the valve ports.

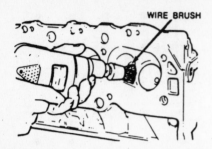

Remove the carbon from the head with a wire brush and electric drill

Use a dial indicator to measure the valve stem clearances

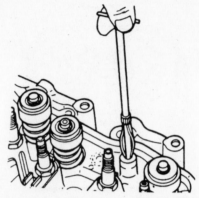

Use an expanding wire cleaner to clean the valve guides

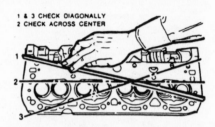

Inspect the cylinder head with a straight-edge. Check for warpage in all planes

3. Inspect the cylinder head for cracks in the exhaust ports, combustion chambers or external cracks in the water chamber.

4. Thoroughly clean the valve guides using a suitable wire bore brush.

NOTE: *Excessive valve stem-to-bore clearance will cause oil consumption and may cause valve breakage. Insufficient clearance will result in noisy operation of the valves.*

5. Measure the valve stem clearance as follows:

a. Mount a dial indicator on one side of the cylinder head rocker arm cover gasket rail.

b. Locate the indicator so movement of the valve stem from side-to-side (crosswise to the head) will cause a direct movement of the indicator stem. The indicator stem must contact the side of the valve stem just above the valve guide.

c. Prop the valve head about $^1/_{16}$ in. (1.6mm) off the valve seat.

d. Move the stem of the valve from side-to-side using light pressure to obtain a clearance reading. If the clearance exceeds specifications, it will be necessary to ream or replace the valve guides.

6. Inspect the rocker arm studs for wear or damage.

7. Install a dial micrometer into the valve guide and check the valve seat for concentricity.

RESURFACING

1. Using a straightedge, check the cylinder for warpage.

2. If the warpage exceeds 0.05mm (0.002 in.), the cylinder head must be replaced. Resurfacing can be performed but the total reduction in head thickness is 0.05mm or 0.002 inch. Since almost any warpage will exceed this, resurfacing is not generally recommended for Honda heads.

Valve Springs and Stem Seals

The valve springs provide the tension to close the valve after the camshaft action has opened it. Honda valve springs rarely fail except in cases of abuse or neglect. The springs must be removed for access to the valve stem seals.

The valve stem seals do just that, sealing the valve shaft or stem against the oil being circulated around the camshaft and rockers. Any oil running down the valve shaft enters the cylinder and is immediately burned. Additionally, leaking valve seals allow some gasses to escape from the cylinder, causing pressure-induced leaks at the valve cover gasket and cam seals.

Valve seals are the first place to look if your otherwise well-running engine begins to consume oil. Assuming all the simple items such as leaks are checked, deteriorated valve seals are a common culprit due to deterioration from heat and chemical exposure. They may be replaced without removing the head, although care must be used. Replacing the valve seals is a lot cheaper than replacing the piston rings, too.

REMOVAL AND INSTALLATION
On-Car Procedure

Several tools and items are required for this job. A source of compressed air and a spark plug air-hold fitting are required. The air fitting screws into the spark plug hole and allows compressed air to enter the cylinder. Additionally, an old rocker arm shaft is required to substitute for the one in use. Do not plan to use the present one; it may get bent or scratched.

A spring compressor suitable for use on an overhead cam motor with the head in place is required. These tools are commercially available but check the specific application for your engine; one tool does not fit all engines. Additionally, a small magnetic probe is required to manipulate the locking collets off and onto the valve shaft. The job is exacting, but not difficult.

1. With the engine cold and the ignition OFF, remove the valve cover.
2. Remove the rocker arm assembly and shaft(s). Don't loosen or remove the camshaft holder bolts.
3. Temporarily install an old rocker shaft to serve as support for the spring compressor. The shaft should be bare, i.e., without rockers, springs, etc. Don't be tempted to use the shaft from the valve train; it almost certainly will become damaged or bent, rendering it unusable.
4. Turn the crankshaft pulley to bring cylinders No. 1 and 4 to TDC.
5. Install the spring compressor tool on any valve for cylinder 1 or 4; do not compress the spring.
6. Fit the air hold device to the spark plug hole of the cylinder whose valve seal is to be changed and apply compressed air, pressurizing the cylinder.
WARNING: *The idea of the air hold is to keep the valve from falling into the cylinder when the spring and collet are removed. If any but minimal air leakage is heard when the tool is in use, recheck the piston position before continuing.*
7. Cover any oil passages in the head with a cloth. Compress the spring with the tool. Use the magnetic probe to remove the keepers or collets from the top of the valve stem. Keep a close watch on these small parts; they will vanish quickly if they escape your custody.
8. Release tension on the spring compressor and lift it clear of the valve. Remove the retain-er or upper washer and remove the valve spring(s). Keep the springs in their correct orientation; they must be reinstalled exactly as they were, not upside down.
9. Remove the valve seal, either with your fingers or with a valve seal removal tool.
10. Install the new valve seal on the shaft. All exhaust valves use seals with black springs and intake valves use seal with white springs. The seals are NOT interchangeable. Make certain the seal is firmly placed against the spring seat.
11. Install the valve spring(s). The painted end or the end with the closely spaced coils goes against the head or down. Install the retainer or upper washer.
12. Refit the compressor tool. Compress the spring and fit the keepers on the shaft. Make certain they are properly seated in the valve stem.
13. Once in place, remove the compressor tool and the rag over the oil passages.
14. Repeat Steps 6–13 for each additional valve or cylinder. Remember that if valves for cylinders 2 or 3 are to be worked on, the engine must be rotated to bring the those cylinders to TDC. It is recommended that all the seals be changed, rather than just one or two.
15. When all the seals are replaced, remove the compressor and shaft. Using only a small plastic or rubber mallet, tap the top of each valve two or three times. This is done to insure proper seating of the valve and valve keepers; if the keepers are not correctly installed this will cause them to fly out, spoiling your afternoon but saving your engine.
16. Reinstall the rocker arm and shaft assembly.
17. Install the valve cover.

Off-Car

With the head removed, both sides of the head are accessible. Use a valve spring compressor capable of holding the valve from both sides. These common tools look like a very large C-clamp and reach around the head to the face of the valve.

Compress the spring and remove the valve keepers. Don't lose them. Remove the spring retainer, spring(s) and valve seal. In most cases, each valve should be removed for inspection or replacement before reinstallation.

Once the valve is reinstalled, place the new seal on the shaft, making certain it is firm against the lower spring seat. Install the spring and retainer. Compress the spring and install the keepers. When all the valve seals are replaced, use a rubber or plastic mallet to tap the top of each valve two or three times. This seats the valve and keeper correctly.

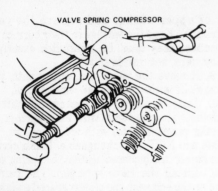

VALVE SPRING COMPRESSOR

Valve spring compressor for repairs with head removed

Valves and Springs

REMOVAL AND INSTALLATION

A valve spring compressor is needed to remove the valves and springs; these are available at most auto parts and auto tool shops. A small magnet is very helpful for removing the keepers and spring seats.

Set the head on its side on the bench. Install the spring compressor so that the fixed side of the tool is flat against the valve head in the combustion chamber, and the screw side is against the retainer. Slowly turn the screw in towards the head, compressing the spring. As the spring compresses, the keepers will be revealed; pick them off of the valve stem with the magnet as they are easily fumbled and lost. When the keepers are removed, back the compressor screw out and remove the retainers and springs. Remove the compressor and pull the valves out of the head from the other side. Remove the valve seals by hand and remove the spring seats with the magnet.

Since it is very important that each valve and its spring, retainer, spring seat and keepers is reassembled in its original location, you must keep these parts in order. The best way to do this to cut holes in a piece of heavy cardboard or wood. Label each hole with the cylinder number and either **IN** or **EX**, corresponding to the location of each valve, intake or exhaust, in the head. As you remove each valve, insert it into the holder, and assemble the seats, springs, keepers and retainers to the stem on the labeled side of the holder. This way each valve and its attendant parts are kept together, and can be put back into the head in their proper locations.

After lapping each valve into its seat (see Valve Lapping), oil each valve stem, and install each valve into the head in the reverse order of removal, so that all parts except the keepers are assembled on the stem. Always use new valve stem seals.

Install the spring compressor, compress the retainer and spring until the keeper groove on the valve stem is fully revealed. Coat the groove with a wipe of grease (to hold the keepers until the retainer is released) and install both keepers, wide end up. Slowly back the screw of the compressor out until the spring retainer covers the keepers. Remove the tool. Lightly tap the end of each valve stem with a rubber hammer to ensure proper fit of the retainers and keepers.

INSPECTION

Before the valves can be properly inspected, the stem, lower end of the stem and the entire valve face and head must be cleaned. An old valve works well for chipping carbon from the valve head, and a wire brush, gasket scraper or putty knife can be used for cleaning the valve face and the area between the face and lower stem. Do not scratch the valve face during cleaning. Clean the entire stem with a rag soaked in thinners to remove all varnish and gum.

Thorough inspection of the valves requires the use of a micrometer, and a dial indicator is needed to measure the inside diameter of the valve guides. If there instruments are not available to you, the valves and head can be taken to a reputable machine ship for inspection. Refer to the Specifications Charts for valve stem and stem-to-guide specifications.

If the above instruments are at your disposal, measure the diameter of each valve stem at the top, middle, and bottom of the stem. Measure in two dimensions (when viewed from the top of the stem). This is six measurements per valve; jot these measurements down in order for each valve.

Using the dial indicator, measure the inside diameter of the valve guides at their bottom, top and midpoint, again in two dimensions. Six measurements for each guide; jot these measurements down also.

Subtract the valve stem measurement from the valve guide inside measurement; if the clearances exceed that listed in the specifications chart under Stem-to-Guide Clearance, replace the valve(s). Stem-to-guide clearance can also be checked at a machine shop, where a dial indicator would be used.

Check the top of each valve stem for pitting, mushrooming and unusual wear due to improper rocker adjustment, etc. The stem tip can be ground flat if it is worn, but very little can be removed; if more than just a touch of grinding is needed to make the tip flat and square the valve must be replaced. If the valve stem tips are ground, make sure you fix the valve securely

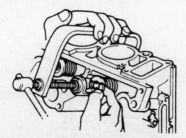

After compressing the valve springs, keep careful track of the small keepers; they are easily fumbled

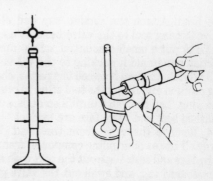

Use the micrometer to measure the valve stem at 6 locations

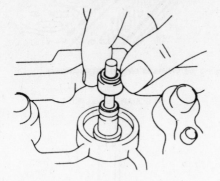

Always install new valve stem seals

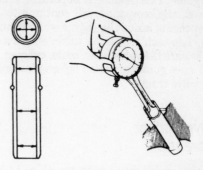

Use a dial gauge to check valve diameter at 6 locations

into a jig designed for this purpose, so the tip contacts the grinding wheel squarely at exactly 90°. Most machine shops that handle automotive work are equipped for this job.

REFACING

Valve refacing should only be handled by a reputable machine shop, as the experience and equipment needed to do the job are beyond that of the average owner/mechanic. During the course of a normal valve job, refacing is necessary when simply lapping the valves into their seats will not correct the seat and face wear. When the valves are reground (resurfaced), the valve seats must also be recut, again requiring special equipment and experience.

VALVE LAPPING

The valves must be lapped into their seats after resurfacing, to insure proper sealing. Even if the valves have not been refaced, they should be lapped into the head before reassembly. Lapping is nothing more than very fine metal polishing to get an accurate match between two contacting surfaces.

Set the cylinder head on the workbench, combustion chamber side up. Rest the head on wooden blocks on either end, so there are two or three inches between the tops of the valve guides and the bench.

1. Lightly lube the valve stem with clean en-

Carefully scrape carbon from the valve head.

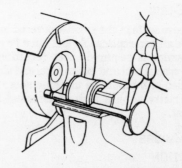

If the head is ground, it must be held at exactly 90°

gine oil. Coat the valve seat completely with valve grinding compound. Use just enough compound that the full width and circumference of the seat are covered.

2. Install the valve in its proper location in

the head. Attach the suction cup end of the valve lapping tool to the valve head. It usually helps to put a small amount of saliva into the suction cup to aid it sticking to the valve.

3. Rotate the tool between the palms, changing position and lifting the tool often to prevent grooving. Lap the valve until a smooth, evenly polished seat and valve face are evident.

4. Remove the valve from the head. Wipe away all traces of grinding compound from the valve face and seat. Wipe out the port with a solvent-soaked rag, and swab out the valve guide with a piece of solvent-soaked rag to make sure there are no traces of compounding grit inside the guide. This cleaning is important. If not removed, the compound will continue to grind components inside the engine while running.

5. Lap each remaining valve, one at a time. Make sure the valve faces, seats, cylinder ports and valve guides are clean before reassembling the valve train.

Lapping the valves is simple but necessary

Valve Springs
INSPECTION

Valve spring squareness, length and tension should be checked while the valve train is disassembled. Place each valve spring on a flat surface next to a steel square. Measure the length of the spring, and rotate it against the edge of the square to measure distortion. If spring length varies (by comparison) by more than 1.0mm or if distortion exceeds 1.0mm, replace the spring.

Spring tension must be checked on a spring tester. Springs used on most Honda engines should be within one pound of each other when tested at their specified installed heights.

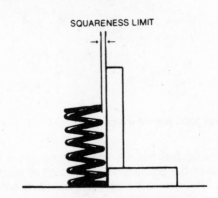

SQUARENESS LIMIT

Check each spring for height and squareness

Valve Seats

The valve seats in the engines covered in this guide are all non-replaceable and must be recut when service is required. Seat recutting requires a special tool and experience, and should be handled at a reputable machine shop. Seat concentricity should also be checked by a machinist.

Valve Guides
INSPECTION

Valve guides should be cleaned as outlined earlier, and checked when valve stem diameter and stem-to-guide clearance is checked. Generally, if the engine is using oil through the guides (assuming the valve seals are OK) and the valve stem diameter is within specification, it is the guides that are worn and need replacing.

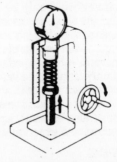

A special testing tool is needed to check spring compression

Valve guides which are not excessively worn or distorted may, in some cases, be knurled rather than replaced. Knurling is a process in which metal inside the valve guide bore is displaced and raised (forming a very fine cross-hatch or spiral pattern), thereby reducing clearance. Knurling also provides for excellent oil control. The possibility of knurling rather than replacing the guides should be discussed with a machinist.

REMOVAL AND INSTALLATION

Valve guide replacement on all Accord and Prelude requires heating the cylinder head to 300°F (149°C), then driving the guide out of the head with a hammer and drift of precise size. Unless you and your family don't mind baking an oily cylinder head in the oven (and probably smelling it in the house for months), take the head to a machine shop and have a machinist replace the guides.

Oil Pan

REMOVAL AND INSTALLATION

CAUTION: *The EPA warns that prolonged contact with used engine oil may cause a number of skin disorders, including cancer! You should make every effort to minimize your exposure to used engine oil. Protective gloves should be worn when changing the oil. Wash your hands and any other exposed skin areas as soon as possible after exposure to used engine oil. Soap and water, or waterless hand cleaner should be used.*

All Engines

1. Firmly apply the parking brake and block the rear wheels.
2. Raise and support the front of the vehicle on jackstands.
3. Position a clean drain pan under the engine, remove the drain plug and drain the engine oil.
4. If necessary, remove the center beam and the engine lower mount.
5. If equipped with flywheel dust shield, it may be necessary to remove it for access.
6. Remove the oil pan nuts and bolts (in a criss-cross pattern) and the oil pan; if necessary, use a mallet to tap the corners of the oil pan. Do NOT pry on the pan to get it loose.

To install:

7. Use a new gasket. Apply sealant at the inner corners of the pan, where it matches to the crank seals.
8. Install the pan. Tighten the nuts and bolts to 14 Nm (10 ft. lbs). Use an alternating or criss-cross pattern to tighten the nuts and bolts.
9. Install the flywheel dust cover, center beam and lower mount if they were removed.
10. Lower the vehicle to the ground. Install clean, fresh oil.
11. Start the engine, allowing it to idle. Check for leaks.

Oil Pump

REMOVAL AND INSTALLATION

CAUTION: *The EPA warns that prolonged contact with used engine oil may cause a number of skin disorders, including cancer! You should make every effort to minimize your exposure to used engine oil. Protective gloves should be worn when changing the oil. Wash your hands and any other exposed skin areas as soon as possible after exposure to used engine oil. Soap and water, or waterless hand cleaner should be used.*

1988–91 Prelude
1990–91 Accord

1. Drain the engine oil. Turn the crankshaft and align the white groove on the crankshaft pulley with the pointer on the timing belt cover (align the T mark on the flywheel with the pointer on the crankcase on the Prelude).
2. Remove the valve cover and upper timing belt cover.
3. Remove the power steering pump belt and the alternator belt, also the air conditioning belt if so equipped.
4. Remove the crankshaft pulley and the lower timing belt cover.
5. Remove the tensioner, timing belt and driven pulley. Be sure to mark the rotation of the timing belt if it is going to be reused. On '90–91 Accord, also remove the balancer belt.
   a. For 1990–91 Accord, remove the balancer drive gear case and the balancer driven gear.
6. Remove the oil pan, oil screen and remove the oil pump mount bolts. Remove the oil pump assembly.

To install:

7. Install the two dowel pins and new O-ring to the cylinder block.
8. Be sure that the mating surfaces are clean and dry. Apply a liquid gasket evenly in a narrow bead, centered on the mating surface.
9. To prevent leakage of oil, apply a suitable thread sealer to the inner threads of the bolt holes.

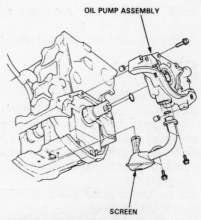

OIL PUMP ASSEMBLY

SCREEN

Shaft driven oil pump, 2.0L DOHC shown

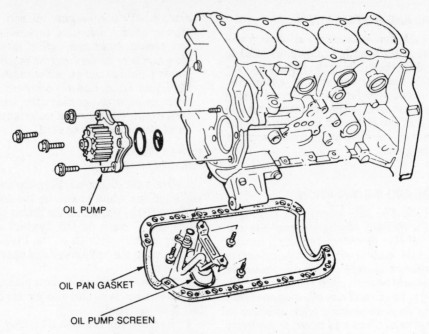

OIL PUMP

OIL PAN GASKET

OIL PUMP SCREEN

Belt driven oil pump used on earlier Accord and Prelude

10. Once the sealant is applied, do not wait longer than 20 minutes to install the parts; the sealant will become ineffective. After final assembly, wait at least 30 minutes before adding oil to the engine, giving the sealant time to set.

11. Install the oil screen and pan.

12. Install the balancer drive gear case and the driven gear if they were removed.

13. Install the drive pulley, timing belt balancer belt and tensioners.

14. Install the crankshaft pulley.

15. Install the lower timing belt cover.

16. Set the tension on the timing belt(s), using the correct procedure.

17. Install the drive belts for the alternator, power steering and A/C compressor; adjust the tension.

18. Install the valve cover and upper timing belt cover.

19. Refill the engine with clean, fresh oil.

1984–87 Prelude
1984–89 Accord

1. Remove the timing belt.

2. On 1984–85 Accord and 1984 Prelude, remove the oil pump drive pulley by unbolting it. Use caution; this nut has LEFT-HAND threads. On later models, the pulley is attached to the shaft by other means and comes off with the front pump cover.

3. Remove the oil pump retaining bolts and nut; remove the oil pump.

4. Clean the gasket mounting surfaces.

NOTE: *If removing the oil pump pick-up screen, follow the procedure to remove the oil pan.*

5. Remove the pump cover-to-pump housing bolts and the cover.

6. Inspect the pump for wear and/or damage; replace the parts, if necessary.

7. Reassemble the pump assembly and torque the pump cover-to-pump housing bolts to 5 ft. lbs.

8. To install, use a new O-rings and install the pump. Torque the oil pump mounting nut and bolts to 12 Nm (9 ft. lbs).

9. Install the oil pump drive pulley if it was removed. Remembering that the nut is left-hand threaded, apply thread sealant before the nut is installed. Tighten the nut to 30 Nm (22 ft. lbs).

10. Reinstall the timing belt and set the tension correctly.

11. Start the engine and check for leaks.

Timing Belt and Covers
REMOVAL AND INSTALLATION

1984–89 Accord
1984–87 Prelude

1. Rotate the crankshaft to align the flywheel pointer to Top Dead Center (TDC) of the No. 1 cylinder's compression stroke.

2. Remove the valve cover and upper timing belt cover bolts and the covers.

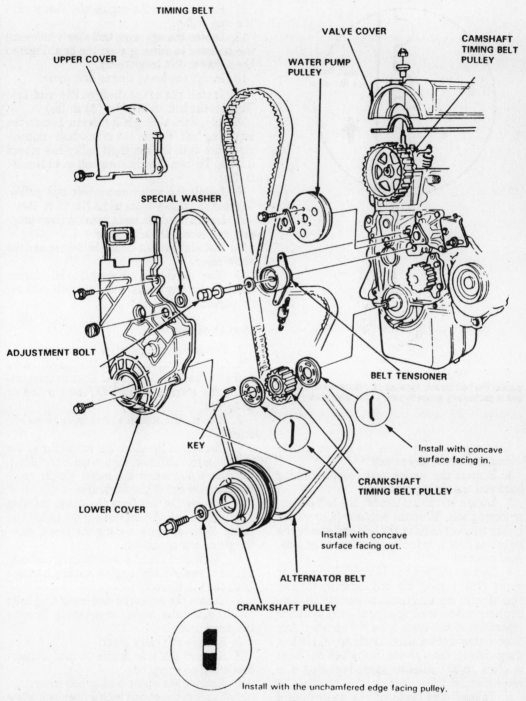

Timing belt components for 1984–89 Accord and 1984– 87 Prelude. Take care to return each bolt to its proper location; lengths vary greatly.

3. Loosen the alternator and remove the pulley belt(s).

4. On all vehicles with externally driven water pumps, remove the water pump pulley bolts, the belt and the pulley.

5. Remove the crankshaft pulley retaining bolt. Using a wheel puller or pulley extractor tool, remove the crankshaft pulley.

NOTE: *Expect this bolt to be very tight. Make certain the vehicle is securely supported before applying force to the bolt; the amount of*

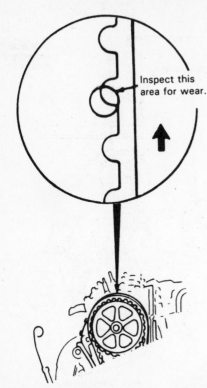

Inspect this area for wear.

Inspect the belt closely for wear or deterioration. The belt is particularly prone to wear in the area shown

force required may cause the car to become unstable on the jackstands.

6. Remove the timing gear cover retaining bolts and the timing gear cover.

7. Loosen but do not remove the belt adjuster locking bolt. Move the adjuster (against the spring tension) to relax the belt and secure the adjusting bolt to hold the adjuster in the loosened position.

8. Remove the belt by sliding it off the upper pulley first. Inspect the belt carefully for any sign of wear, cracking, loose or worn teeth (particularly on the trailing edge of each tooth) or separation of the teeth from the backing. Any fluid contamination, particularly oil, on the belt disqualifies it from re-use. If the belt has been in place 10,000 miles or more, replacing it is recommended.

9. Inspect the teeth of the pulleys and sprockets, making sure the faces are clean and square.

To install:

10. Double check the position of the engine. The timing pointer must be aligned with the white mark on the flywheel; the cam pulley must be set so the small dot or the word UP is vertical and the marks on the edges of the pulley are aligned with the surface of the head.

11. Fit the belt to the engine and slide it onto the cam pulley.

12. Loosen the adjusting bolt slowly, allowing the adjuster to move against the belt. Tighten the adjuster bolt temporarily.

13. Install the lower timing belt cover.

14. Install the crankshaft pulley and key. Tighten the bolt to 115 Nm (83 ft. lbs).

15. Adjust the timing belt tension. Loosen the adjusting bolt. Rotate the crankshaft counterclockwise until the camshaft pulley has moved 3 teeth. Tighten the adjusting bolt to 43 Nm (31 ft. lbs).

16. Install the water pump belt and pulley. Tighten the pulley bolts to 12 Nm (9 ft. lbs).

17. Install the drive belts, tension them properly and secure the alternator.

18. Install the upper timing belt cover and the valve cover.

19. Start the engine, allowing it to idle. Listen carefully for any indication of the belt rubbing or slapping the covers.

1990–91 Accord

1. Disconnect the negative battery cable.

2. Turn the engine to align the timing marks and set cylinder No.1 to TDC. Once in this position, the engine must NOT be turned or disturbed.

3. Remove the splash shield from below the engine.

4. Disconnect the electrical connector at the cruise control actuator, then remove the actuator. Don't disconnect the cable; simply move the actuator out of the work area.

5. Remove the belt from the power steering pump. Remove the mounting bolts for the pump. Without disconnecting the hoses, move the pump out of the way.

6. Disconnect the alternator wiring and connectors; remove the engine wiring harness from the valve cover.

7. Loosen the adjusting and mounting bolts for the alternator and/or compressor. Remove the drive belt(s).

8. Remove the valve cover.

9. Remove the side engine mount support bracket, if so equipped.

10. Remove the upper timing belt cover.

11. Support the engine with a floor jack below the center of the center beam. Tension the jack so that it is just supporting the beam but not lifting it.

12. Remove the through-bolt for the side engine mount and remove the mount.

13. Remove the dipstick and dipstick tube.

14. Remove the adjusting nut.

15. Remove the crankshaft pulley bolt and remove the crankshaft pulley.

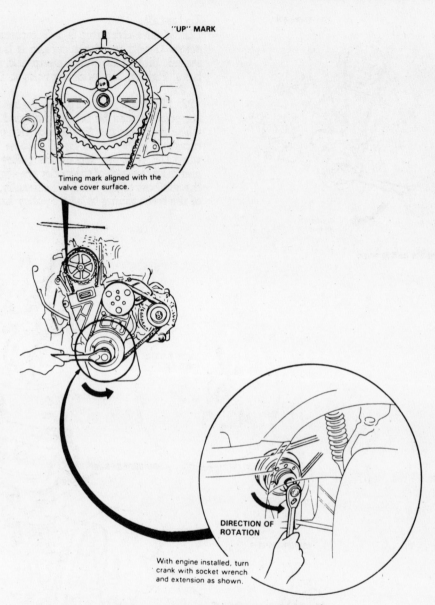

"UP" MARK

Timing mark aligned with the valve cover surface.

DIRECTION OF ROTATION

With engine installed, turn crank with socket wrench and extension as shown.

Align the cam pulley correctly before Installing the belt.

NOTE: *This bolt is one of the tightest on the entire car. The pulley must be held in place while the bolt is loosened. One trick is to wrap an old drive belt around the pulley to hold it steady—don't try this with a belt that is to go back on the car; it will be stretched or damaged.*

16. Remove the two rear bolts from the center beam. Slowly lower the jack and the engine until clearance is gained to remove the lower timing belt cover.

17. Remove the lower timing belt cover.

18. There are two belts in this system; the one running to the camshaft pulley is the timing belt. The other, shorter one drives the balance shaft and is referred to as the balancer belt or timing balancer belt. Push the tensioner for the belts away from the belts to relieve the tension. Hold the tensioner, reinstall the adjusting nut and tighten it to hold the tensioner in place.

19. Carefully remove the balancer belt and timing belts. Do not crimp or bend the belts; protect them from contact with oil or coolant. Slide the belts off the pulleys.

20. This is an excellent time to check or replace the water pump. Even if the timing belt is only being replaced as part of a good maintenance schedule, consider replacing the pump at the same time.

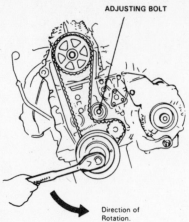

Adjusting the belt tension

To install:

21. If the water pump is to be replaced, install a new O-ring and make certain it is properly seated. Install the water pump and retaining bolts. Tighten the retaining bolts to 12 Nm (9 ft. lbs).

22. Check the position of the engine. The timing pointer must be perfectly aligned with the white mark on the flywheel or flex-plate; the camshaft pulley must be aligned so that the word UP is at the top of the pulley and the marks on the edge of the pulley are aligned with the surfaces of the head. Additionally, the face of the front timing balancer pulley has a mark

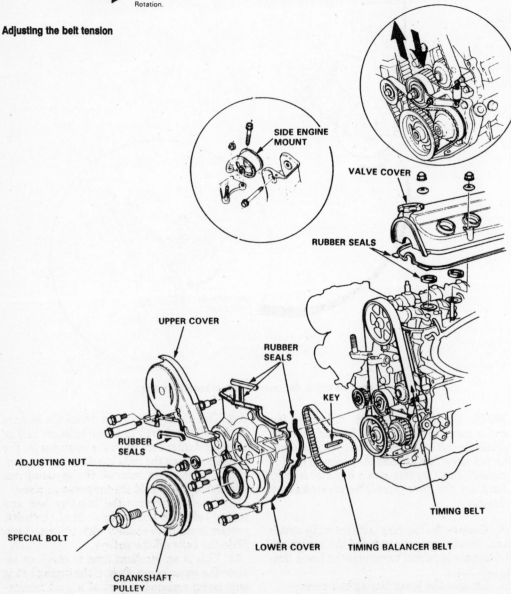

Replacing the 1990–91 Accord water pump requires removal of the timing belt

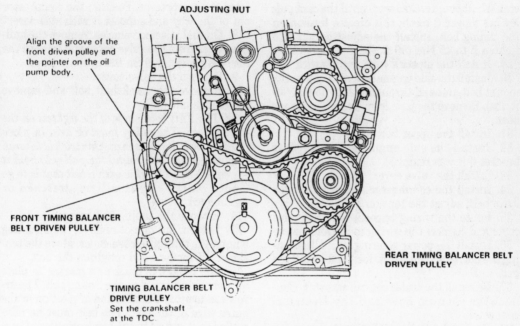

End view of Accord engine with belts installed. Note alignment marks for front balancer pulley

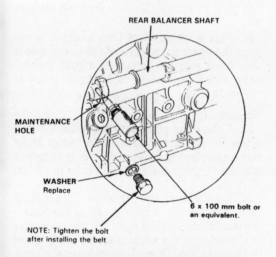

Remove the bolt for access to the maintenance hole

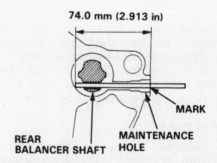

A pin of the proper thickness and length will hold the rear balance shaft in place

which must be aligned with the notch on the oil pump body. This pulley is the one at "10 o'clock" to the crank pulley when viewed from the pulley end.

23. Align the rear timing balancer pulley ("2 o'clock" from the crank pulley) using a 6 x 100 mm bolt or rod. Mark the bolt or rod at a point 74 mm (2.913 inches) from the end. Remove the bolt from the maintenance hole on the side of the block; insert the rod into the hole. Align the 74mm mark with the face of the hole. This pin will hold the shaft in place during installation.

24. Fit the timing belt over the pulleys and tensioners. Install the balancer belt. Once the

belts are in place, double check that all the engine alignment items are still correct. If not, remove the belts, realign the engine and reinstall the belts. Once the belts are properly installed, slowly loosen and remove the adjusting nut, allowing the tensioner to move against the belts. Remove the pin from the maintenance hole and reinstall the bolt and washer.

25. Install the lower cover, making certain the rubber seals are in place and correctly located. Tighten the retaining bolts to 12 Nm (9 ft. lbs).

26. Raise the lower beam and engine into place. Install the rear bolts for the lower beam, tightening them to 39 Nm (28 ft. lbs).

27. Install the key on the crankshaft and install the crankshaft pulley. Apply oil to the bolt threads and tighten it to 230 Nm (153 ft. lbs).

28. Adjust the timing belt tension. Turn the

crankshaft counterclockwise until the cam pulley has moved 3 teeth; this creates tension on the timing belt. Install the adjusting nut and tighten it to 45 Nm (33 ft. lbs).

29. Install the dipstick tube and dipstick.

30. Install the side engine mount. Tighten the mount bolt, nut and through-bolt to 55 Nm (40 ft. lbs). Remove the jack from under the center beam.

31. Install the upper belt cover.

32. Install the side engine mount support bracket if it was removed.

33. Install the valve cover.

34. Install the compressor and/or alternator drive belt; adjust the tension.

35. Route the wiring harness over the valve cover and connect the wiring to the alternator.

36. Install the power steering pump, tightening the bolt to 45 Nm (33 ft. lbs.) and install the belt.

37. Reinstall the cruise control actuator. Connect the vacuum hose and the electrical connector.

38. Double check all installation items, paying particular attention to loose hoses or hanging wires, untightened nuts, poor routing of hoses and wires (too tight or rubbing) and tools left in the engine area.

39. Install the splash shield under the engine.

40. Connect the negative battery cable.

41. Start the engine, allowing it to idle. Check for any signs of leakage or any sound of the belts rubbing or binding.

1988–91 Prelude

1. Disconnect the negative battery cable.

2. Turn the engine to align the timing marks and set cylinder No.1 to TDC. Once in this position, the engine must NOT be turned or disturbed.

3. Remove the engine support bolts and nuts, then remove the side mount rubber and bracket. Remove the cruise control actuator if so equipped; move the actuator out of the way without disconnecting or kinking the cable.

4. Remove the splash shield from below the engine.

5. Loosen the adjusting nut for the power steering belt and remove the belt. Remove the adjusting pulley and the power steering pump. Move the pump out of the way with the hoses attached.

6. Disconnect the wiring at the alternator. Remove the alternator through-bolt; remove the mounting and adjusting bolts and remove the alternator and belt.

7. On cars with air conditioning, remove the compressor mounting bolts. Remove the compressor and belt; do not disconnect the lines

from the compressor. Position the compressor out of the way and support it with stiff wire.

8. On fuel injected vehicles, remove the ignition wires from the valve cover and remove the harness protector from the cylinder head.

9. Remove the valve cover.

10. Remove the crankshaft bolt and remove the crankshaft pulley.

NOTE: *This bolt is one of the tightest on the entire car. The pulley must be held in place while the bolt is loosened. One trick is to wrap an old drive belt around the pulley to hold it steady—don't try this with a belt that is to go back on the car; it will be stretched or damaged.*

11. Remove the timing belt covers.

12. Loosen, but do not remove, the adjusting bolt on the timing belt tensioner. Move the tensioner off the belt and retighten the bolt.

13. Use a piece of chalk or a marker to place an identifying arrow on the timing belt. The arrow can identify the direction of rotation or the outer edge of the belt. The belt must be reinstalled so it moves in the same direction. Carefully remove the belt from the pulleys without crimping it. Protect the belt from oil, coolant, etc.

14. This is an excellent time to check or replace the water pump. Even if the timing belt is only being replaced as part of a good maintenance schedule, consider replacing the pump at the same time.

To install:

15. If the water pump is to be replaced, install a new O-ring and install the water pump. Make certain the O-ring does not deform or come out of place. Tighten the mounting bolts to 12 Nm (9 ft. lbs)

16. Double check the engine position; it must be at TDC for No. 1 cylinder. All of the following conditions must be met: The timing pointer is aligned with the white mark on the flywheel or flexplate, the UP mark on each camshaft pulley is at the top and the alignment marks on each cam pulley are aligned with the edges of the cylinder head.

NOTE: *On fuel injected engines, each of the camshafts may be held in the TDC position by inserting 5mm diameter punches into the alignment holes just behind each cam pulley. This makes installing the belt much easier.*

17. Install the timing belt so that it rotates in the same direction as before. Remove the pins holding the cams if they were installed.

18. Loosen the adjuster and allow it to tension the belt. Tighten the adjuster bolt.

19. Reinstall the belt covers except the upper cover on single cam engines.

20. Reinstall the crankshaft pulley and key.

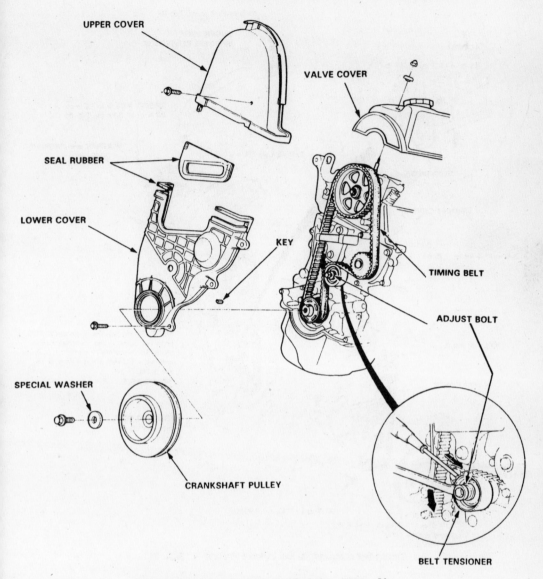

UPPER COVER

VALVE COVER

SEAL RUBBER

LOWER COVER

KEY

TIMING BELT

ADJUST BOLT

SPECIAL WASHER

CRANKSHAFT PULLEY

BELT TENSIONER

Timing belt components, carbureted Prelude — 1988– 91

Coat the threads of the bolt with light oil, but do not lubricate the face of the bolt which contacts the washer. On fuel injected engines, tighten the bolt to 150 Nm (108 ft. lbs.); on carbureted engines, tighten the bolt to 115 Nm (83 ft. lbs).

NOTE: *This tightening is best accomplished with the wheels blocked, the parking brake applied and the transaxle in gear (manual) or in PARK.*

21. Rotate the engine counterclockwise until the camshaft pulley has moved 3 teeth. Loosen the adjusting bolt, then retighten it to 43 Nm (31 ft. lbs).

22. Install the valve cover and upper belt cover on carbureted vehicles. On fuel injected vehi-

cles, reinstall the ignition wires and the harness protector.

23. Reinstall the A/C compressor and belt. Tighten the mounting bolts to 25 Nm (18 ft. lbs). Adjust the belt tension.

24. Reinstall the alternator and belt. Tighten the through-bolt to 45 Nm (33 ft. lbs).

25. Install the power steering pump and belt, tightening the bolts to 27 Nm (20 ft. lbs).

26. Install the side engine mount and the cruise control actuator if it was removed. Tighten the engine mount bolts to 40 Nm (29 ft. lbs.) and the nuts to 65 Nm (47 ft. lbs).

27. Connect the negative battery cable.

28. Start the engine, allowing it to idle. Check the work area carefully for any sign of fluid

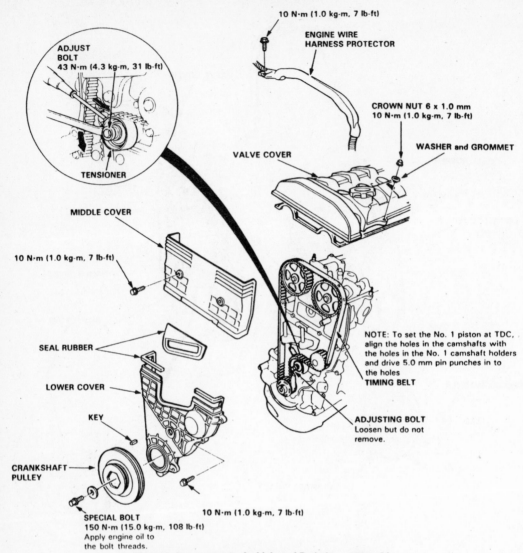

10 N·m (1.0 kg-m, 7 lb-ft)

ENGINE WIRE
HARNESS PROTECTOR

ADJUST
BOLT
43 N·m (4.3 kg-m, 31 lb-ft)

CROWN NUT 6 x 1.0 mm
10 N·m (1.0 kg-m, 7 lb-ft)

VALVE COVER

WASHER and GROMMET

TENSIONER

MIDDLE COVER

10 N·m (1.0 kg-m, 7 lb-ft)

NOTE: To set the No. 1 piston at TDC,
align the holes in the camshafts with
the holes in the No. 1 camshaft holders
and drive 5.0 mm pin punches in to
the holes
TIMING BELT

SEAL RUBBER

LOWER COVER

KEY

ADJUSTING BOLT
Loosen but do not
remove.

CRANKSHAFT
PULLEY

SPECIAL BOLT
150 N·m (15.0 kg-m, 108 lb-ft)
Apply engine oil to
the bolt threads.

10 N·m (1.0 kg-m, 7 lb-ft)

Timing belt components, fuel injected Prelude — 1988– 91

leakage or any indication of the belt rubbing or
slapping the covers.

29. Switch the engine OFF. Reinstall the
splash shield.

Camshaft Sprockets

REMOVAL AND INSTALLATION

NOTE: *Although the timing belt need not be
fully removed, it will need to be removed from
the camshaft pulley(s). Take great care to protect the belt from crimping, twisting or exposure to oil or coolant.*

1. Turn the crankshaft pulley until cylinder
No. 1 is at Top Dead Center of the compression
stroke. Confirm the position by checking that
the timing pointer is aligned with the white
mark on the flywheel.

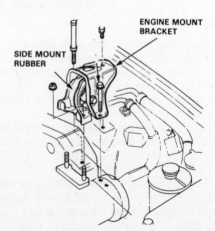

ENGINE MOUNT
BRACKET

SIDE MOUNT
RUBBER

Remove the Prelude engine mount with the through-
bolt still in it

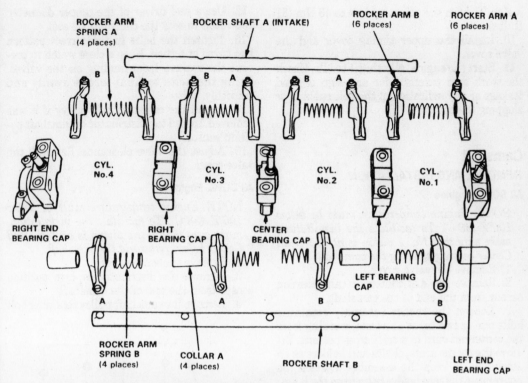

ROCKER ARM SPRING A (4 places)

ROCKER SHAFT A (INTAKE)

ROCKER ARM B (6 places)

ROCKER ARM A (6 places)

CYL. No.4

CYL. No.3

CYL. No.2

CYL. No.1

RIGHT END BEARING CAP

RIGHT BEARING CAP

CENTER BEARING CAP

LEFT BEARING CAP

ROCKER ARM SPRING B (4 places)

COLLAR A (4 places)

ROCKER SHAFT B

LEFT END BEARING CAP

Rocker arm components must be reassembled exactly. 1987 Accord shown.

2. Remove the valve cover. Remove the upper timing belt cover.

3. Loosen, but do not remove, the tensioner adjusting bolt and pivot bolt.

4. Slide the timing belt off the camshaft sprocket. The belt may remain standing within the covers.

5. To remove the camshaft sprocket, remove the center bolt and then remove the sprocket with a pulley remover or a brass hammer. The pulley is aligned to the shaft with a Woodruff-type key or guide; don't lose it.

To install:

6. Make certain the groove in the end of the camshaft is facing up. If necessary, the cam(s) may be turned at the faceted casting in the middle of the shaft; use an adjustable wrench or other tool with parallel jaws.

7. Install the key or guide, then install the pulley. Make certain the original washer is reinstalled with the retaining bolt. Tighten the retaining bolt to 38 Nm (27 ft. lbs).

8. Make certain the cam pulley(s) are aligned properly; the marks on the pulley edges must align with the surface of the head. Carefully slide the timing belt onto the pulley(s).

9. Rotate the crankshaft counterclockwise until the camshaft pulley has moved 3 teeth. This places tension on the timing belt by the ad-

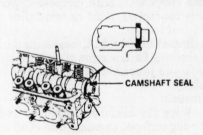

CAMSHAFT SEAL

Seal housing surface should be dry. Apply a light coat of oil to camshaft and inner lip of seal.

The camshaft seal must be fully seated before final assembly

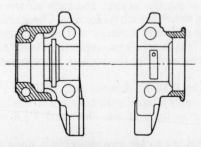

Apply liquid gasket sealant to the shaded areas. View is looking down on the head

juster. Tighten the adjusting bolt to 43 Nm (31 ft. lbs).

10. Install the upper timing cover and the valve cover.

11. Start the engine, allowing it to idle. Check the work area carefully for any sign of fluid leakage or any indication of the belt rubbing or slapping the covers.

Camshaft

REMOVAL AND INSTALLATION

All SOHC Engines

NOTE: *Engine temperature must be below 100°F (38°C). To facilitate the installation, make sure that No. 1 piston is at Top Dead Center before removing the camshaft.*

1. Remove the valve cover.

2. Remove the distributor or cam position sensor from the end of the camshaft.

3. Loosen the rocker assembly retaining bolts one or two turns at a time, working from the center outward in a criss-cross pattern. Remove the rocker arms, shafts and holders as an assembly. To keep the assembly together, do not remove the cam holder bolts from the holes.

NOTE: *If the assembly must be disassembled, use great care to catalog the position of each component. Each component, particularly the rockers, must be reinstalled in its original location.*

4. Inspect the camshaft, measuring the lobes and checking for any signs of wear or scoring. Check the journals as well as the lobes carefully.

To install:

5. Wipe the camshaft surfaces and the mounting surfaces, cleaning them of all oil and grit. Lubricate the cam journals and mounting surfaces with a thin coat of assembly grease.

6. Fit the camshaft to the head with the keyway on the sprocket end facing upward.

7. Install a new camshaft oil seal with the spring end facing inward or towards the valves.

8. Lightly lubricate the cam lobes with clean engine oil.

9. Loosen the locknut and back off the adjusting screw for each rocker arm. Check the integrity of rocker assembly if it was disassembled. If the camshaft was replaced, it is strongly recommended that the rockers be replaced as well.

10. On 1986–91 Accords and 1985–91 Preludes, apply a liquid gasket sealant to the head mating surfaces of the No.1 and No.6 cam holders.

11. Set the rocker arm assembly in place and install the bolts finger tight.

12. Use a seal driver of the proper diameter and reach to seat the camshaft oil seal.

13. Tighten the bolts in the correct pattern two turns at a time. Keep a close watch to prevent the rockers from binding on the valves. Bring the bolts to final torque evenly and smoothly.

14. Install the camshaft belt pulley if it was removed. Install the distributor or camshaft position sensor.

15. Adjust the valve clearance. Reinstall the valve cover.

All DOHC Engines

NOTE: *Engine temperature must be below 100°F. (38°C). To facilitate the installation, make sure that No. 1 piston is at Top Dead Center before removing the camshaft.*

1. Remove the valve cover.

2. Remove the distributor or cam position sensor from the end of the camshaft.

3. Remove the camshaft pulley retaining bolt

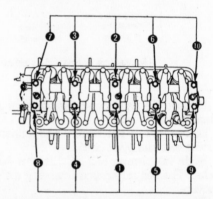

Rocker shaft cap bolt tightening sequence, all SOHC Prelude and 1984–89 Accord engines

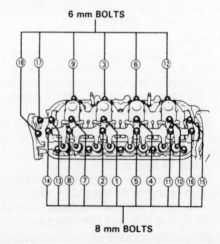

Rocker shaft cap bolt tightening sequence, all 1990–91 Accord

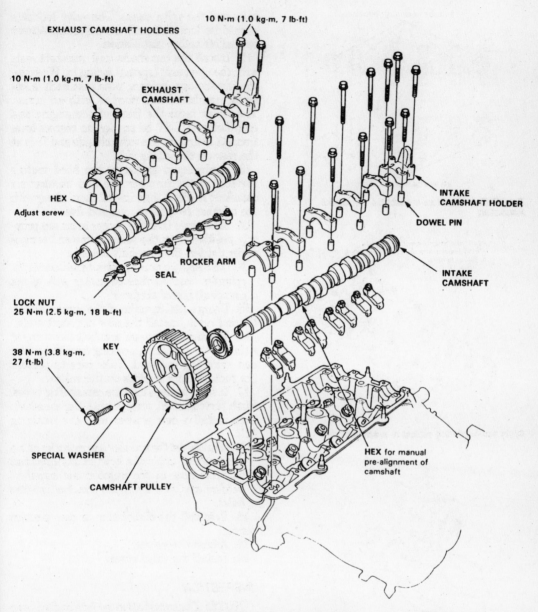

10 N·m (1.0 kg-m, 7 lb-ft)

EXHAUST CAMSHAFT HOLDERS

10 N·m (1.0 kg-m, 7 lb-ft)

EXHAUST CAMSHAFT

HEX

Adjust screw

ROCKER ARM

SEAL

LOCK NUT
25 N·m (2.5 kg-m, 18 lb-ft)

38 N·m (3.8 kg-m, 27 ft-lb)

KEY

SPECIAL WASHER

CAMSHAFT PULLEY

INTAKE CAMSHAFT HOLDER

DOWEL PIN

INTAKE CAMSHAFT

HEX for manual pre-alignment of camshaft

Dual camshaft and rocker components

and washer and remove the camshaft pulleys along with the woodruff keys, if so equipped.

4. Before removing the rocker arm assembly, check the camshaft end play as follows:

NOTE: *Do not rotate the camshaft during inspection. Loosen the rocker arm adjusting screws before starting.*

  a. Seat the camshaft by prying it toward the distributor end of the head.

  b. Set a dial indicator on the end of the camshaft. Zero the dial indicator against the end of the distributor drive, then pry the camshaft back and forth, and read the end play; do this to both camshafts.

  c. The standard camshaft end play for a new camshaft is 0.05–0.15mm.

  d. The standard service limit for the camshaft end play is 0.5mm.

5. Loosen the camshaft and rocker arm shaft holder bolts in a criss-cross pattern, beginning on the outside holder.

6. Remove the rocker arms, shafts, and holders as an assembly.

7. Lift out the camshafts.

8. Wipe the camshaft clean, then inspect the lift ramps. Replace the camshaft if the cam lobes are pitted, scored or excessively worn.

NOTE: *Be sure to Plastigage® the camshaft*

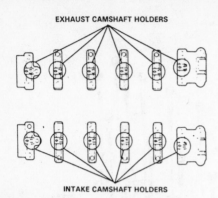

EXHAUST CAMSHAFT HOLDERS

INTAKE CAMSHAFT HOLDERS

The DOHC cam holders are labeled for correct installation

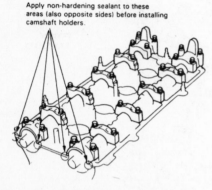

Apply non-hardening sealant to these areas (also opposite sides) before installing camshaft holders.

Apply non-hardening sealant to areas indicated

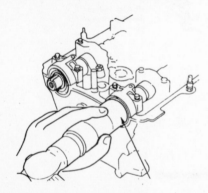

Carefully install the camshaft end seals

bearing journals. If the camshaft bearing radial clearance is out of tolerance and the camshaft has already been replaced, then the cylinder head must be replaced.

To install:

9. After cleaning the camshaft and journal surfaces, lubricate both surfaces with the assembly grease and install the camshaft.

10. Turn the camshaft until its keyway is facing up (number one cylinder at TDC).

11. Replace the rocker arms in their original positions. Place the rocker arms on the pivot bolts and the valve stems. The valve locknuts should be loosened and the adjusting screws backed off before installation.

12. Install the camshafts and camshaft seals with the open side (spring) facing in. When installing the cam holders, note that each is lettered, numbered and marked with an arrow. The arrow faces the front of the engine and each holder MUST be put in the correct location; E1 is first on the exhaust side and I6 is at the rear on the intake side.

13. Apply liquid gasket to the head mating surfaces of the number one and number six camshaft holders, then install them along with the number two, three, our and five.

14. Make sure that the rocker arms are properly positioned on the valve stems and temporarily tighten the camshaft holders.

NOTE: *Apply a non-hardening sealant to the cylinder head surface on either side of the camshaft(s) seal surfaces.*

15. Using a seal installer of the correct diameter and reach, install the new camshaft seals.

16. Tighten each rocker arm bolt two turns at a time in the sequence, working from the center and spiralling outward. Take care to prevent the rockers from binding on the valves.

17. Install the keys into the camshaft grooves. Push the camshaft pulleys onto the camshaft, then install a new washer with the retaining bolt.

NOTE: *To set the number one cylinder at top dead center, align the hole on the camshaft with the hole in the number one camshaft holders and fit 5.0mm pin punches into the holes.*

18. Reinstall the distributor or cam position sensor.

19. Adjust the valves.

20. Install the valve cover.

INSPECTION

NOTE: *The camshaft must be handled carefully; it will break if dropped or subjected to sharp impact.*

Degrease the camshaft using safety solvent. Clean all the oil grooves and passages. Visually inspect the cam lobes and bearing journals for excessive wear. If a lobe is questionable, check all lobes and journals with a micrometer. A worn cam may be your report card for poor maintenance intervals or infrequent oil and filter changes.

Measure the lobes from nose to base and again at 90°. The lift is determined by subtracting the second measurement from the first. If all exhaust lobes and all intake lobes are not identical (compare intake to intake and exhaust to exhaust), the camshaft must be replaced.

Measure the bearing journals and compare to the chart in this chapter. If a journal is worn, the cam must be replaced.

If the lobes and journals appear intact, place the front and rear cam journals in V-blocks and rest a dial indicator on the center journal. Rotate the camshaft to check for straightness, if deviation exceeds 0.025mm, replace the camshaft.

Pistons and Connecting Rods
REMOVAL

NOTE: *This procedure requires removal of the head and oil pan. It is much easier to perform this work with the engine removed from the vehicle and mounted on a stand.*

These procedures require certain hand tools which may not be in your tool box. A cylinder ridge reamer, a numbered punch set, piston ring expander, snapring pliers and piston installation tool (ring compressor) are all necessary for correct piston and rod repair. These tools are commonly available from retail tool suppliers; you may be able to rent them from larger automotive supply houses.

1. If the pistons and rods are being removed as part of a complete tear-down, follow the procedures described in Crankshaft and Main Bearings in this chapter. If you are removing the pistons and connecting rods without removing the crankshaft and main bearings, proceed from this point.

2. Remove the cylinder head, following the procedures given in this chapter.

3. Remove the oil pan.

4. The connecting rods are marked to indicate which surface faces front, but the bearing caps should be matchmarked before disassembly. Use a marking punch and a small hammer; install the number over the seam so that each piece will be reused in its original location. Note that the rods and bearing caps may already have numbers stamped on them; these are indicators of original bearing thickness, not of location or sequence.

5. Remove the connecting rod cap bolts, pull the caps off the rods and place them on a bench in order.

6. Inspect the upper portions of the cylinder (near the head) for a ridge formed by ring wear. If there is a ridge, it must be removed by first shifting the piston down in the cylinder and then covering the piston top completely with a clean rag. Use a ridge reamer to remove metal at the lip until the cylinder is smooth. If this is not done, the pistons may be damaged during removal. Remove the rag and all the metal chips; use a magnet if necessary.

7. Place pieces of vacuum or other rubber hose over the bolts to keep the ends from scoring the cylinder. Use a piece of wood or a hammer handle under the piston to tap it upward. If you're working under an engine that's still installed in the car with the crankshaft still in place, turn the crankshaft until the crankpin for each cylinder is in a convenient position. Be careful not to subject the piston and/or rod to heavy impact and do not allow the piston rod to damage the cylinder walls on the way out. The slightest nick in the metal can cause problems after reassembly.

8. Clean the pistons, rings, and rods in parts solvent with a bristle brush. Do not use a wire brush even to remove heavy carbon. The metal may be damaged. Use a piece of a broken piston ring to clean the lands (grooves) in the piston.

CAUTION: *War goggles and gloves during cleaning. Do not spatter solvent onto painted surfaces.*

CONNECTING ROD BEARING REPLACEMENT

Connecting rod bearings on all Honda engines consist of two halves or shells which are not interchangeable in the rod and cap. When the shells are in position, the ends extend slightly beyond the rod and cap surfaces so that when the bolts are tightened, the shells will be clamped tightly in place. This insures positive seating and prevents turning. A small tang holds the shells in place within the cap and rod housings.

NOTE: *The ends of the bearing shells must never be filed flush with the mating surface of the rod or cap.*

If a rod becomes noisy or is worn so that its clearance on the crankshaft is sloppy, a new bearing of the correct undersize must be selected and installed. There is no provision for adjustment. Under no circumstances should the rod end or cap be filed to compensate for wear, nor should shims of any type be used.

Inspect the rod bearings while the rods are out of the engine. If the shells are scored or show flaking they should be replaced. ANY scoring or ridge on the crankshaft means the crankshaft must be replaced. Because of the metallurgy in the crankshaft, welding and/or regrinding the crankshaft is not recommended. The bearing faces of the crank may not be restored to their original condition causing premature bearing wear and possible failure.

Replacement bearings are available in standard sizes, usually marked either on the bearing shell or possibly on the rod cap. Do not confuse the mark on the bearing cap with the cylinder number. It is quite possible that No. 3 piston rod contains a number 1 size bearing.

The rod cap may have a "1" marked on it. (You should have stamped a 3 or other identifying code on both halves of the rod before disassembly.)

Measuring the clearance between the connecting rod bearings and the crankshaft (oil clearance) is done with a plastic measuring material such as Plastigage® or similar product.

1. Remove the rod cap with the bearing shell. Completely clean the cap, bearing shells and the journal on the crankshaft. Blow any oil from the oil hole in the crank. The plastic measuring material is soluble in oil and will begin to dissolve if the area is not totally free of oil.

2. Place a piece of the measuring material lengthwise along the bottom center of the lower bearing shell. Install the cap and shell and tighten the bolts in three passes to the correct torque.

NOTE: *Do not turn the crankshaft with the measuring material installed.*

3. Remove the bearing cap with the shell. The flattened plastic material will be found sticking to either the bearing shell or the crank journal. DO NOT remove it yet.

4. Use the scale printed on the packaging for the measuring material to measure the flattened plastic at its widest point. The number within the scale which is closest to the width of the plastic indicates the bearing clearance in thousandths of an inch.

5. Check the specifications chart in this chapter for the proper clearance. If there is any measurement approaching the maximum acceptable value, replace the bearing.

6. When the correct bearing is determined, clean off the gauging material, oil the bearing thoroughly on its working face and install it in

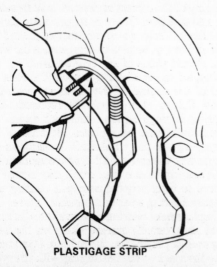

PLASTIGAGE STRIP

Use the scale printed on the package to measure the width of the measuring media.

the cap. Install the other half of the bearing into the rod end and attach the cap to the rod. Tighten the nuts evenly, in three passes to the proper value.

7. With the proper bearing installed and the nuts properly tightened, it should be possible to move the connecting rod back and forth a bit on the crankshaft. If the rod cannot be moved, either the bearing is too small or the rod is misaligned.

INSPECTION

1. measure the bore of the cylinder at three levels and in two dimensions (fore-and-aft and side-to-side). That's six measurements for each cylinder. By comparing the 3 vertical readings, the taper of the cylinder can be determined and by comparing the front-rear and left-right readings the out-of-round can be determined. The block should be measured: at the level of the top piston ring at the top of piston travel; in the center of the cylinder; and at the bottom. Compare your readings with the specifications in the chart.

2. If the cylinder bore is within specifications for taper and out-of-round and the wall is not scored or scuffed, it need not be bored. If not. It should be bored oversize as necessary to insure elimination of out-of-round and taper. Under these circumstances, the block should be taken to a machine shop for proper boring by a qualified machinist using specialized equipment.

NOTE: *If the cylinder is bored, oversize pistons and rings must be installed. Since all pistons must be the same size, all cylinders must be rebored if any one is out of specification.*

3. Even if the cylinders need not be bored, they should be fine-honed for proper break-in. A deglazing tool may be used in a power drill to remove the glossy finish on the cylinder walls. Use only the smooth stone type hone, not the beaded or bottle brush type.

4. The cylinder head top deck (gasket surface) should be inspected for warpage. Run a straightedge along all four edges of the block, across the center and diagonally. If you can pass a feeler gauge of 0.1mm (0.004 in.) under the straightedge, the top surface of the block should be machined or trued.

5. The rings should be removed from the pistons with a ring expander. Keep all rings in order and with the piston from which they were removed.The rings and piston ring grooves should be cleaned thoroughly with solvent and a brush as deposits will alter readings of ring wear.

6. Before any measurements are begun, visually examine the piston (a magnifying glass is

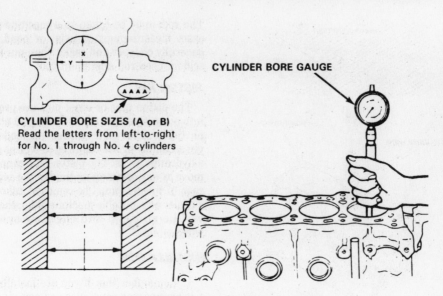

CYLINDER BORE SIZES (A or B)
Read the letters from left-to-right
for No. 1 through No. 4 cylinders

CYLINDER BORE GAUGE

Six measurements are required for each cylinder

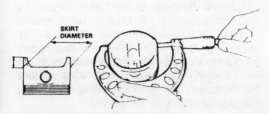

SKIRT DIAMETER

Measuring the piston skirt diameter

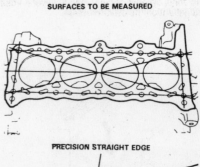

SURFACES TO BE MEASURED

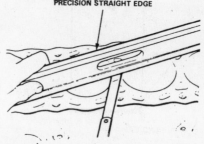

PRECISION STRAIGHT EDGE

Inspect the deck of the engine block for warpage

helpful) for any signs of cracks, particularly in the skirt area. Anything other than light surface scoring disqualifies the piston from further use. The metal will become unevenly heated and the piston may break apart during use. Very noisy; very expensive—don't risk it.

7. Piston diameter should be measured at the skirt, at right angles to the piston pin. Compare the measurement either with the specified piston diameter or subtract the diameter from the cylinder bore dimension to get clearance. If clearance is excessive, the piston should be replace. If a new piston still does not produce piston-to-wall clearance within specifications, select an oversize piston and have the cylinders bored accordingly.

8. Compression ring side clearance should be measured by using a ring expander to put cleaned rings back in their original positions on the pistons. Measure side clearance on one side by attempting to slide a feeler gauge of the thickness specified between the ring and the edge of the ring groove. If the gauge will not pass into the groove, the ring may be re-used although new rings are always recommended. If the gauge will pass, but a gauge of slightly greater thickness representing the wear limit

will not, the piston may be re-used, but new rings must be installed.

9. Ring end gap must be measured for all three rings in the cylinder by using a piston to (upside down) to press the ring squarely into the cylinder. The rings must be at least 15–20mm (0.6–0.8 in) from the bottom of the cylinder. Use a feeler gauge to measure the end gap and compare it with specifications. If the gap is too great, the ring should be checked with a gauge representing the wear limit.

If cylinder bore wear is very slight, you may use new rings to bring the end gap to specification

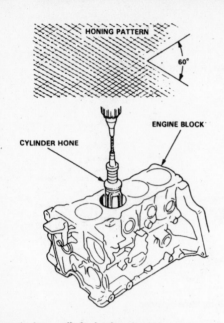

Properly done, cylinder honing should leave a cross-hatched pattern on the cylinder walls

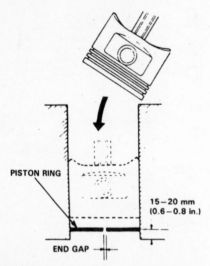

Install the rings near the bottom of the cylinder to measure end gap

The rods may be taken to a machine shop for exact measurement of twist or bend. This is generally cheaper and easier than purchasing a seldom-used rod alignment tool.

PISTON PIN

The piston pins or wrist pins are press fitted into place. Special tools including an adjustable pin driver, pilot collar, and spring loaded piston pin assembly jig are required as well as access to a hydraulic press. The piston pins cannot be remove by any common method in the average garage. If the pins must be removed, take them to a dealer or reputable machine shop; the charges will be minimal and the time saved well worthwhile.

INSTALLATION

1. Remember that if you are installing oversize pistons, you must also use new rings of the correct oversize.

2. Install the rings on the piston, lowest ring first. Generally, the side rails for the oil control ring can be installed by hand with care. The other rings require the use of the ring expander. There is a high risk of ring breakage or piston damage if the rings are installed without the expander. The correct spacing of the ring end gaps is critical to oil control. No two gaps should align; they should be evenly spaced around the piston with the gap in the oil ring expander facing the front of the piston (aligned with the mark on the top of the piston). Once the rings are installed, the pistons must be handled carefully and protected from dirt and impact.

3. Install the number two compression ring next and then the top compression ring using the ring expander. Note that these rings have the same thickness but different cross-sections or profiles; they must be installed in the proper locations. Make sure all markings face upward and that the gaps are all staggered. Gaps must also not be in line with either the piston pin or thrust faces of the piston.

4. All the pistons, rods, and caps must be reinstalled in the correct cylinder. Make certain that all labels and stamped numbers are present and legible. Double check the piston rings; make certain that the gaps do NOT line up but are evenly spaced around the piston at about 120° intervals. Double check the bearing insert at the bottom of the rod for proper mounting. Reinstall the protective pieces of rubber hose on the rod bolts.

5. Liberally coat the cylinder wall and the crankshaft journals with clean, fresh motor oil. Also apply oil to the bearing surfaces on the connecting rod and the cap.

without boring the cylinder. Measure the gap with the ring located near the minimum dimension at the bottom of the cylinder, not near the top where wear is greatest.

10. The connecting rods must be free from wear, cracking and bending. Visually examine the rod, particularly at its upper and lower ends. Look for any sign of metal stretching or wear. The piston pin should fit cleanly and tightly through the upper end, allowing no sideplay or wobble. The bottom end should also be an exact ½ circle with no deformity of shape. The bolts must be firmly mounted and parallel.

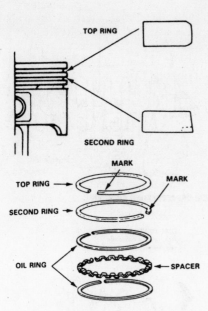

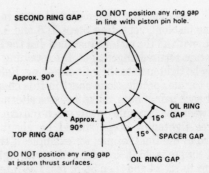

Align the ring gaps as shown

The rings must be installed in their correct locations

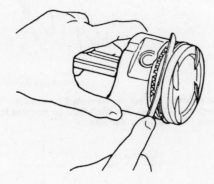

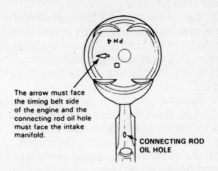

The arrow must face the timing belt side of the engine and the connecting rod oil hole must face the intake manifold.

CONNECTING ROD OIL HOLE

The arrow on each piston must point to the timing belt. If the rod was removed from the piston, it must be reinstalled with the oil hole in the proper location.

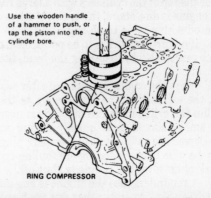

Use the wooden handle of a hammer to push, or tap the piston into the cylinder bore.

RING COMPRESSOR

Check the ring to land clearance after new rings are installed

With the rings compressed, use a wooden handle to push the piston into place.

6. Identify the FRONT mark on each piston and rod. Position the piston and rod assembly loosely in each cylinder with the marks facing the front or timing belt end of the engine. Make certain the number stamped on each piston corresponds to the number of the cylinder.

WARNING: *Failure to observe the "FRONT" marking and its correct placement can lead to sudden and catastrophic engine failure.*

7. Install the ring compressor around one piston and tighten it gently until the rings are compressed almost completely.

8. Gently press down on the piston top with a wooden hammer handle or similar soft faced tool; drive the piston into the cylinder bore. Once all three rings are in the bore, the piston will move with some ease.

WARNING: *If any resistance or binding is encountered during the installation, DO NOT apply force. Tighten or adjust the ring compressor and/or reposition the piston. Brute force will break the ring(s) or damage the piston.*

9. From underneath, pull the connecting rod into place on the crankshaft. Remove the rubber hoses from the bolts. Check the rod cap to confirm that the bearing is present and correctly mounted, then install the rod cap (observing the correct number and position and its nuts. Leaving the nuts finger-tight will make installation of the remaining pistons easier.

10. Assemble the remaining pistons in the same fashion , repeating Steps 7, 8 and 9.

11. with all the pistons installed and the bearing caps secured finger tight, the retaining nuts may be tightened to their final setting. Refer to the torque specifications chart in this chapter. For each pair of nuts, make 3 passes alternating between the two nuts on any given rod cap. The three tightening steps should be about one third of the final torque; for example, if the final torque is 36 ft. lbs. draw the nuts tight in steps to 12, 24 and then 36 ft. lbs. The intent is to draw each cap up to the crank straight and under even pressure.

12. Turn the crankshaft through several rotations, making sure everything moves smoothly and there is no binding. With the piston rods connected, the crank may be stiff to turn. Try to turn it in a smooth continuous motion so that any stiff spots may be felt.

13. Reinstall the oil pan. Even if the engine is to remain apart for other repairs, install the pan to protect the bottom end. Install all the pan bolts and tighten them to the correct tightness; this eliminates one easily overlooked item during future reassembly.

14. If the engine is to remain apart for other repairs, pack the cylinders with crumpled newspaper or clean rags to keep out dust and grit; cover the top of the cylinders with a large rag. If the engine is on a stand, the entire block can be covered with a large trash bag.

15. If no further work is to be performed, continue reassembly by installing the head, timing belt, etc.

16. When the engine is restarted after assembly, the exhaust will be very smoky as the oil within the cylinders burns off. This is normal; the smoke should clear quickly during warm up. Depending on the state of the spark plugs, it may be wise to check for any oil fouling on the spark plugs after the engine is shut off.

17. A reminder: once the engine is assembled and driveable, remember that you are breaking in an essentially new engine — follow the break-in driving regimen as you would for a new car.

Crankshaft and Main Bearings

REMOVAL AND INSTALLATION

Except 90–91 Accord

1. Remove the engine from the vehicle and place it on a work stand.

2. Remove the crankshaft pulley attaching bolts and washer.

3. Remove the front cover and the air conditioning idler pulley assembly, if so equipped. Remove the cover assembly.

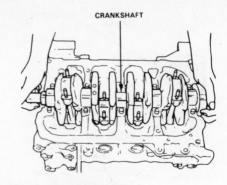

Handle the crankshaft carefully

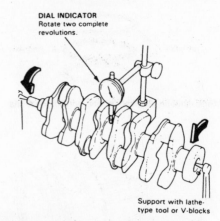

Once removed, inspect the crankshaft for run-out through two rotations. The shaft must be mounted to either a lathe holder or V-blocks

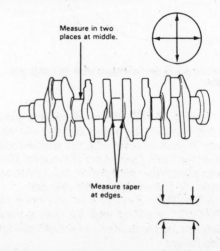

Checking the crankshaft journals for out-of-round and taper

4. Check the timing belt deflection. Remove the timing belt and sprockets.

5. Invert the engine on work stand. Remove the flywheel and the rear seal cover. Remove the oil pan and gasket. Remove the oil pump inlet and the oil pump assembly.

6. Insure all bearing caps (main and connecting rod) are marked so they can be installed in their original positions. Turn the crankshaft until the connecting rod from which the cap is to be removed is up. Remove the connecting rod cap. Push the connecting rod and piston assembly up in the cylinder. Repeat the procedure for the remaining connecting rod assemblies.

7. Remove the main bearing caps.

8. Carefully lift crankshaft out of the block so the upper thrust bearing surfaces are not damaged.

WARNING: *Handle the crankshaft with care to avoid damage, fracture or scratching of the finished surfaces.*

To install:

NOTE: *If the bearings are to be reused they should be identified to insure that they are installed in their original position.*

9. Remove the main bearing inserts from the block and bearing caps.

10. Remove the connecting rod bearing inserts from the connecting rods and caps.

11. Install a new rear oil seal in rear seal cover.

12. Apply a thin coat of grease to the rear crankshaft surface. Do not apply sealer to the area forward of oil sealer groove. Inspect all the machined surfaces on the crankshaft for nicks, scratches or scores which could cause premature bearing wear.

13. If the crankshaft main bearing journals have been refinished to a definite undersize, install the correct undersize bearings. Ensure the bearing inserts and bearing bores are clean. Foreign material under the inserts will distort the bearing and cause a failure.

14. Place the upper main bearing inserts in position in the bores with the tang fitted in the slot provided.

15. Install the lower main bearings inserts in the bearing caps.

16. Carefully lower the crankshaft into place.

17. Check the clearance of each main bearing. Select fit the bearings for proper clearance.

18. After the bearings have been fitted, apply a light coat of assembly grease to journals and bearings. Install all the bearing caps.

NOTE: *The main bearing caps must be installed in their original positions.*

19. Align the upper thrust bearing.

20. Check the crankshaft end play.

21. If the end play exceeds specification, replace the upper thrust bearing. If the end play is less than the specification, inspect the thrust bearing faces for damage, dirt or improper alignment. Install the thrust bearing and align the faces. Check the end play.

22. Install the new bearing inserts in the connecting rods and caps. Check the clearance of each bearing.

23. If the bearing clearances are to specification, apply a light coat of assembly grease to the journals and bearings.

24. Turn the crankshaft throw to the bottom of the stroke. Push the piston all the way down until the rod bearings seat on the crankshaft journal.

25. Install the connecting rod caps and tighten to the proper value.

26. After the piston and connecting rod assemblies have been installed, check the connecting rod crankshaft journals.

CRANKSHAFT AND BALANCER SHAFTS

1990–91 Accord

NOTE: *Steps are given for crankshaft removal with the pistons in place in the block.*

1. With the engine removed from the car and the flywheel removed from the engine, unbolt the rear or right side cover from the engine.

2. Remove the balancer drive case.

3. Insert a metal dowel or similar tool in the maintenance hole of the front balancer shaft to hold it in place. Unbolt the belt sprocket and remove it.

4. Remove the bolt from the maintenance hole for the rear balancer shaft. Align the bolt hole and the balancer shaft hole. Insert a 6 x 100mm dowel or bolt to engage and hold the shaft; remove the sprocket or drive gear.

5. Remove the oil screen and the oil pump. Remove the baffle plate.

6. Remove the bolts and the bearing cap bridge, then remove the bearing caps. Release the tension by turning each bolt about $\frac{1}{3}$ of a turn at a time, beginning at one corner, then moving to the diagonally opposite corner. Follow the sequence shown in the illustration.

7. Turn the crankshaft so that No.s 2 and 3 crankpins are at the bottom. Remove the rod caps and bearings, keeping them in order.

8. Lift the crankshaft out of the engine, being careful not to damage the journals.

9. Remove the bolts and the thrust metal, then remove the front and rear balancer shafts.

To install:

10. Insert the bearing halves into the block and piston rods.

11. Hold the crankshaft so that the journals for pistons No. 2 and 3 are straight down; lower the crankshaft into the block. Make certain the crank journals seat into piston rods 2 and 3.

12. Install the rod caps and nuts finger tight.

13. Rotate the crankshaft clockwise and seat the journals into connecting rods 1 and 4. Install the rod caps and nuts finger tight.

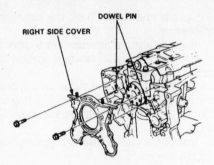

Removing the rear or right side cover

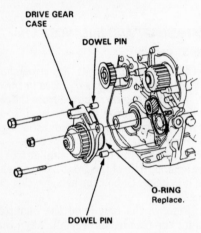

Balancer drive gear case

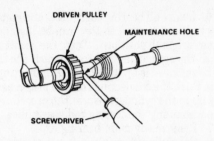

Pin the front balancer when removing or installing the pulley

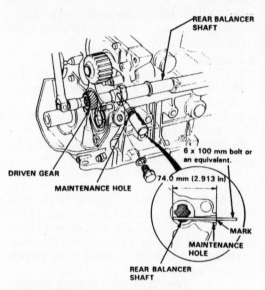

Access to the rear balancer is through the maintenance hole

14. Check the rod bearing clearance using compressible measuring media.

15. Coat the thrust washer and bolt threads with a light coat of clean oil. Install the thrust washers, main bearing caps and bearing cap bridge. Check the bearing clearance using compressible measuring media.

16. Tighten the bolts in two passes: On the first pass, in the correct sequence, bring each bolt to approximately 30 Nm (22 ft. lbs). On the second pass, in the correct sequence, bring each bolt to its final torque of 72 Nm (52 ft. lbs).

17. Insert the balancer shafts into the block, then install the thrust metal to the front balancer shaft and block. Tighten the retaining bolt to 12 Nm (9 ft. lbs.)

18. Make certain the mating surfaces of the right side cover and the block are absolutely clean and dry. Apply a liquid gasket sealant to the contact face of the cover, then install it on the block. Tighten the retaining bolts to 12 Nm (9 ft. lbs.)

19. Make certain the mating surfaces of the oil pump and engine block are absolutely clean and dry. Apply a liquid gasket sealant to the contact surface of the oil pump. Apply grease to the lips of the oil pump seal and the balancer

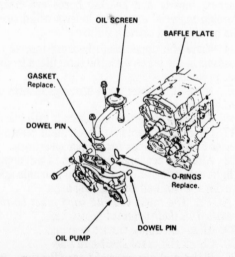

The oil pump, screen and baffle must be removed.

seal. Install the oil pump and tighten the bolts to 12 Nm (9 ft. lbs). Wipe the excess grease from the crank and balancer shafts; check that the oil seals did not distort during installation.

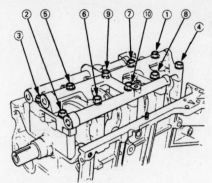

Loosen the bolts in this sequence

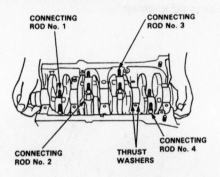

Placement of the crank and thrust washers

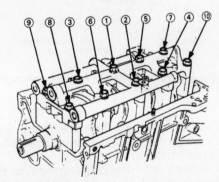

Tighten the bolts in this order

20. Install the baffle plate, then install the oil screen.

21. Apply molybdenum disulfide grease to the thrust surfaces of the balance gears before installation of the driven gear and the drive gear case.

22. Use the 6 x 100mm tool to hold the rear balancer shaft in place. Install the balancer pulley and gear. Tighten the bolt to 25 Nm (18 ft. lbs.)

23. Pin the front balancer shaft in place and install its pulley; tighten the bolt to 30 Nm (22 ft. lbs).

24. On the balancer gear case, align the

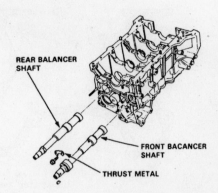

Installation of the balancer shafts and thrust metal

groove on the pulley edge to the pointer on the gear case.

25. Hold the rear balancer shaft in place and install the gear case. Tighten the nut and bolts to 25 Nm (18 ft. lbs).

CLEANING AND INSPECTION
BEARING OIL CLEARANCE

Remove the cap from the bearing to be checked. Using a clean, dry rag, thoroughly clean all oil from crankshaft journal and bearing insert.

NOTE: *Plastigage® and similar compressible measuring media is soluble in oil, therefore oil on the journal or bearing could result in erroneous readings.*

Place a piece of measuring media along the full width of the bearing insert, reinstall the cap, and tighten to specification. Remove the bearing cap, and determine the bearing clearance by comparing width of the compressed media to the scale on the packaging envelope. Refer to Fig. 264.

NOTE: *Do not rotate crankshaft with the measuring media installed. If the bearing insert and journal appear intact, and are within tolerances, no further main bearing service is required. If bearings or journals appear defective, the cause of failure should be determined before replacement.*

CRANKSHAFT ENDPLAY/CONNECTING
ROD SIDE PLAY

Place a small pry bar between a main bearing cap and crankshaft casting, taking care not to damage any journals. Pry backward and forward; measure the distance between the thrust bearing and crankshaft with a feeler gauge. Compare the reading with specifications. If too great a clearance is determined, a main bearing with a larger thrust surface or crank replacement may be required. Check with an automotive machine shop for their advice.

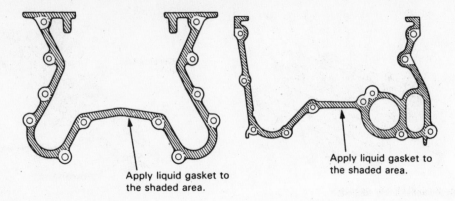

Apply liquid gasket to the shaded area.

Apply liquid gasket to the shaded area.

Apply sealant to the faces of the oil pump and side cover

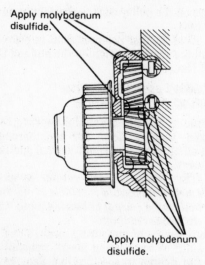

Apply molybdenum disulfide.

Apply molybdenum disulfide.

Apply moly grease to the thrust faces before the drive gear case is installed

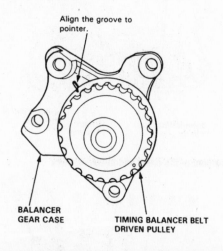

Align the groove to pointer.

BALANCER GEAR CASE

TIMING BALANCER BELT DRIVEN PULLEY

The groove must be aligned with the pointer before the gear case is installed

Connecting rod clearance between the rod and crankthrow casting can be checked with a feeler gauge. Pry the rod carefully on one side as far as possible and measure the distance on the other side of the rod.

Crankshaft Main Seals

REMOVAL AND INSTALLATION

1984–89 Accord
1984–87 Prelude

1. The front and rear main or crankshaft seals are held by the crankshaft endcaps; they are released and removed with the crankshaft. When reassembling, apply non-hardening sealant along the seams where the cap joins the block before installing the seals. The crank and caps should be in place, although the bolts for the crank endcaps should not be fully tightened until after the seals are installed.

2. Apply a light coat of grease to the sealing surfaces of both seals. Pack the back of each seal with grease to hold the spring in place during installation.

3. Using a seal driver of the correct diameter and reach, such as Honda tool 07947–SB00200 or its equivalent, install the pulley-end seal until the driver bottoms out against the snout of the crankshaft. The seal should be installed with the part number facing the outside.

4. Using a seal driver of the correct size and reach, such as Honda tool 07948–SB00101, install the rear or flywheel-end seal. Align the hole in the driver to fit over the pin on the crankshaft. Drive the seal in until the driver bottoms on the block.

5. Tighten the remaining crank bearing caps to specification.

1990–91 Accord
1988–91 Prelude

The rear oil seal on these engines is contained within a separate housing on the rear of the en-

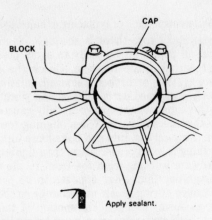

The crankshaft cap must be in place before seal installation

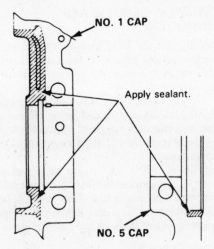

Apply sealant as shown

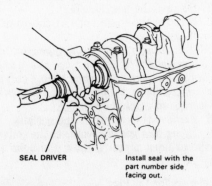

Installing the pulley-end seal

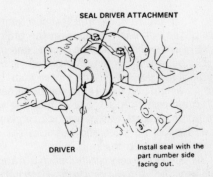

The seal driver for the rear seal must accommodate the flywheel pin on the crankshaft

Flywheel/Flex Plate

REMOVAL AND INSTALLATION

1. Remove the transaxle.
2. Remove the flywheel/flex plate attaching bolts and the flywheel.
3. The rear cover plate can be removed (manual transmission only).

To install:

All major rotating components including the flex plate/flywheel are individually balanced to zero. Engine assembly balancing is not required. Balance weights should NOT be installed on new flywheels.

1. Install the rear cover plate, if removed.
2. Position the flywheel on the crankshaft and install the attaching bolts. Tighten the attaching bolts to the correct torque using a cross-tightening sequence. For all manual transaxles, tighten the flywheel bolts to 105 Nm (76 ft. lbs). For all automatic transaxles, tighten the flexplate bolts to 75 Nm (54 ft. lbs).

EXHAUST SYSTEM

Safety Precautions

For a number of reasons, exhaust system work can be the most dangerous type of work you can do on your car. Always observe the following precautions:

• Support the car extra securely. Not only will you often be working directly under it, but you'll frequently be using a lot of force, say, heavy hammer blows, to dislodge rusted parts. This can cause a car that's improperly supported to shift and possibly fall.

• Wear goggles. Exhaust system parts are always rusty. Metal chips can be dislodged, even when you're only turning rusted bolts. Attempting to pry pipes apart with a metal tool makes the chips fly even more frequently.

• If you're using any source of heat, keep it a great distance from either the fuel tank or lines.

gine. When this housing or right side cover is removed, the seal may be easily removed. Coat the lip of the seal with a light coat of clean oil. Install the seal using a seal driver. Reinstall the right side cover; tighten the bolts to 12 Nm (9 ft. lbs).

Stop what you're doing and feel the temperature of the fuel-bearing pipes on the tank frequently. Even slight heat can expand and/or vaporize fuel, resulting in accumulated vapor, or even a liquid leak. • Watch where your hammer blows fall and make sure you hit squarely. You could easily tap a brake or fuel line when you hit an exhaust system part with a glancing blow. Inspect all lines and hoses in the area where you've been working.

CAUTION: *Be very careful when working on or near the catalytic converter. External temperatures can reach well over 500 degrees, causing severe burns. Removal or installation should be performed only on a cold exhaust system.*

• It is quite helpful to use solvents designed to loosen rusted bolts or flanges. Soaking rusted parts the night before you do the job can speed the work of freeing rusted parts considerably. Remember that these solvents are often flammable. Apply only to parts after they are cool!

The exhaust system of Accord and Prelude vehicles consists of several pieces. Thankfully, the pieces are attached by nuts and bolts rather than being press fit. Each bolted joint contains a gasket which must be replaced whenever repairs are made.

The first section of pipe connects the exhaust manifold to the catalytic converter. The catalytic converter is a sealed, non-serviceable unit which can be easily unbolted from the system and replaced if necessary.

The exhaust system is attached to the body by several welded hooks and flexible rubber hangers; these hangers absorb exhaust vibrations and isolate the system from the body of the car. The hangers MUST be in place and correctly mounted to avoid vibration and body-contact. A series of metal heat shields runs along the exhaust piping, protecting the underbody from excess heat. The heat shields must always be reinstalled when a pipe or component is replaced.

NOTE: *The heat shields can be a source of several irritating sounds including buzzes or rattles related to engine speed. Make certain the shields are tightly attached and free of gravel. If the car develops a sound rather like a 400 lb. cricket at certain engine speeds, check the heat shields for looseness or contact with the exhaust pipe.*

The system terminates in the muffler and tailpipe at the rear of the car. The entry pipe, muffler and tailpipe are one-piece and must be replaced as a unit. If anyone offers to cut the pipe and install just the muffler or just the lead-in pipe, take your business elsewhere.

When inspecting or replacing exhaust system parts, make sure there is adequate clearance from all points on the body to avoid possible overheating of the floorpan. Check the complete system for broken damaged, missing or poorly positioned parts. Rattles and vibrations in the exhaust system are usually caused by misalignment of parts. When aligning the system, leave all the nuts and bolts loose until everything is in its proper place, then tighten the hardware working from the front to the rear. Remember that what appears to be proper clearance during repair may change as the car moves down the road. The motion of the engine, body and suspension must be considered when replacing parts.

COMPONENT REMOVAL AND INSTALLATION

CAUTION: *Do NOT perform exhaust repairs with the engine or exhaust hot. Allow the system to cool completely before attempting any work.*

Exhaust systems are noted for sharp edges, flaking metal and rusted bolts. Gloves and eye protection are required. A healthy supply of penetrating oil and rags is highly recommended.

NOTE: *ALWAYS use a new gasket at each pipe joint whenever the joint is disassembled. Use new nuts and bolts to hold the joint properly. These two low-cost items will serve to prevent future leaks as the system ages.*

Catalytic Converter

1. Raise and safely support the car.
2. Remove the heat shield(s).
3. Remove the three bolts at the front and rear of the converter.

NOTE: *Always support the pipe running to the manifold, either by the normal clamps/hangers or by using string, stiff wire, etc. If left loose, the pipe can develop enough leverage to crack the manifold.*

5. Remove the converter and gaskets.
6. Using new gaskets, connect the converter to the exhaust pipes. Tighten the bolts to 35 Nm (25 ft. lbs).

Muffler and/or Tail Pipe

The muffler and tail pipe on all Hondas is one piece and should be replaced as a unit. The chromed tailpipe extension is a separate part and does not come with replacement units; if yours is still in good shape, remove it by loosening the set screw on the bottom of the extension. To remove the muffler and tailpipe:

1. Elevate and firmly support the rear of the vehicle.

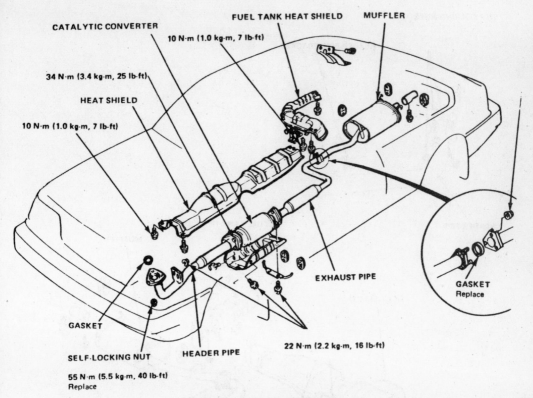

CATALYTIC CONVERTER

FUEL TANK HEAT SHIELD   MUFFLER

10 N·m (1.0 kg·m, 7 lb-ft)

34 N·m (3.4 kg·m, 25 lb-ft)

HEAT SHIELD

10 N·m (1.0 kg·m, 7 lb-ft)

EXHAUST PIPE

GASKET
Replace

GASKET

SELF-LOCKING NUT   HEADER PIPE

22 N·m (2.2 kg·m, 16 lb-ft)

55 N·m (5.5 kg·m, 40 lb-ft)
Replace

Exhaust system, 1984–85 Accord

2. Disconnect the nuts holding the muffler and/or tailpipe to the adjacent pipes.

3. Remove or disconnect the clamps and supports holding the pipe at either end. Leave the supports closest to the center in place until last.

4. Remove the last supports or hangers and lower the unit to the ground. At NO TIME should the muffler be allowed to hang partially supported; the leverage can break the next component in line.

NOTE: *If the muffler or tailpipe is being replaced due to rust or corrosion, adjacent pipes should be checked for the same condition. The pieces tend to age at about the same rate.*

5. Lift the new unit into place and loosely attach the hangers or supports to hold it in place. Allow some play to adjust the muffler.

6. Using new gaskets, connect each end to the adjoining pipe. Tighten the joint bolts and nuts to 25–35 Nm (18–26 ft. lbs).

7. Tighten the supports and hangers. Make certain the rubber hangers are securely attached to their mounts.

Complete System

If the entire exhaust system is to be replaced, it is much easier to remove the system as a unit than remove each individual piece. Disconnect the first pipe at the manifold joint and work towards the rear removing brackets and hangers as you go. Remove the rear muffler bracket and slide the entire exhaust system out from under the car.

The new system can then be bolted up on the workbench and easily checked for proper tightness and gasket integrity. When installing the new assembly, suspend it from the flexible hangers first, then attach the fixed (solid) brackets. Always use new self-locking bolts, particularly at the pipe to manifold joint. Tighten the pipe to manifold nuts to 55 Nm (40 ft. lbs). Check the clearance to the body and suspension and install the manifold joint bolts, tightening them correctly.

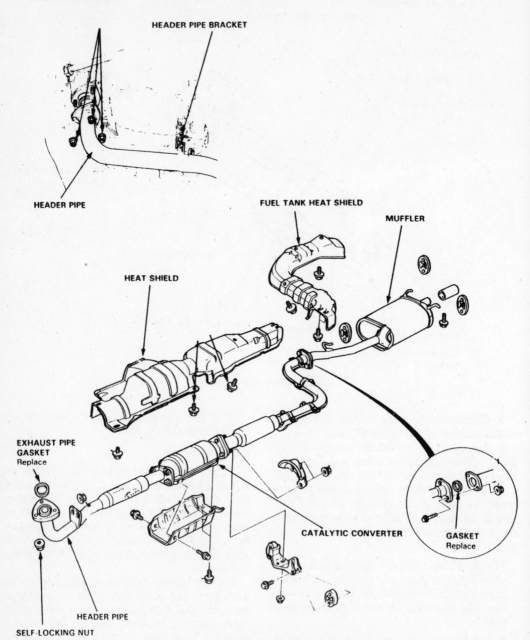

SELF-LOCKING NUTS

HEADER PIPE BRACKET

HEADER PIPE

FUEL TANK HEAT SHIELD

MUFFLER

HEAT SHIELD

EXHAUST PIPE
GASKET
Replace

CATALYTIC CONVERTER

GASKET
Replace

HEADER PIPE

SELF-LOCKING NUT

Exhaust system components, 1986–89 Accord

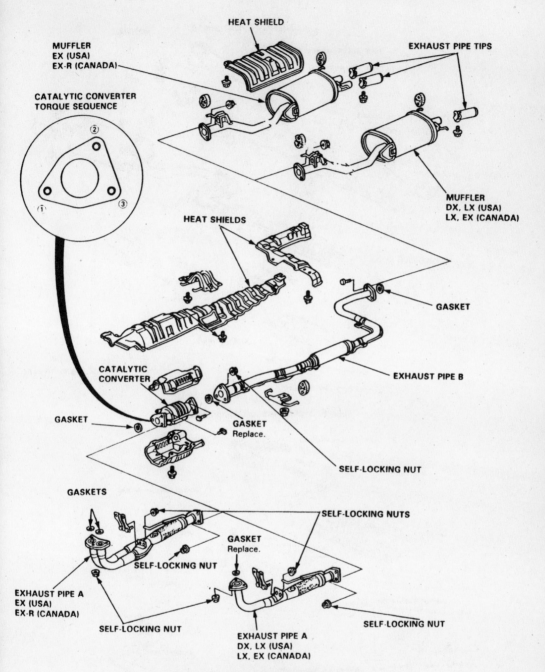

Exhaust system components, 1990–91 Accord

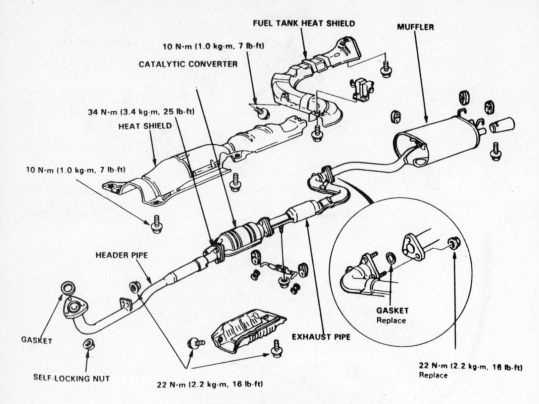

1984–87 Prelude exhaust components

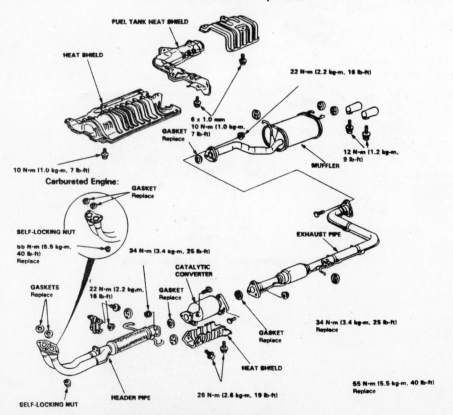

1988–91 Prelude exhaust components

EMISSION CONTROLS

There are three sources of automotive pollutants; crankcase fumes, exhaust gases, and gasoline evaporation. The pollutants formed from these substances fall into three categories: unburnt hydrocarbons (HC), carbon monoxide (C), and oxides of nitrogen (NOx). The equipment used to limit these pollutants is called emission control equipment and is required by national and state or provincial laws.

Due to varying state, federal, and provincial regulations, specific emission control equipment have been devised for each. The U.S. emission equipment is divided into two categories: California and 49 State (Federal). In this chapter, the terms "California", "Calif." or "Cal" applies only to vehicles originally built to be sold in California. California emissions equipment includes the Federal equipment as well as other items required by California's more stringent regulations. Models built to be sold in Canada also have specific emissions equipment, although in most years Federal and Canadian equipment is the same.

TERMS USED IN THIS CHAPTER

CO: Carbon Monoxide, a federally regulated exhaust emission
CVC: Constant Volume Control valve
EACV: Engine Air Control Valve
ECU: Electronic Control Unit
HC: Unburnt Hydrocarbon, a federally regulated exhaust or fuel system emission
MAP Sensor: Manifold Absolute Pressure sensor
PA Sensor: Atmospheric pressure sensor
TA Sensor: Intake air temperature sensor
TDC: Top Dead Center
TW Sensor: Engine coolant temperature sensor

SERVICE PRECAUTIONS

- Do not operate the fuel pump when the fuel lines are empty.
- Do not operate the fuel pump when removed from the fuel tank.
- Do not reuse fuel hose clamps.
- The washer(s) below any fuel system bolt (banjo fittings, service bolt, fuel filter, etc.) must be replaced whenever the bolt is loosened. Do not reuse the washers; a high-pressure fuel leak may result.
- Make sure all ECU harness connectors are fastened securely. A poor connection can cause an extremely high voltage surge and result in damage to integrated circuits.
- Keep ECU all parts and harnesses dry during service. Protect the ECU and all solid-state components from rough handling or extremes of temperature.
- Before attempting to remove any parts, turn the ignition switch **OFF** and disconnect the battery ground cable.
- Always use a 12 volt battery as a power source, never a booster or high-voltage charging unit.
- Do not disconnect the battery cables with the engine running.
- Do not disconnect any wiring connector with the engine running or the ignition **ON** unless specifically instructed to do so.
- On fuel injected models, do not depress the accelerator pedal when starting.
- Do not rev up the engine immediately after starting or just prior to shutdown.
- On fuel injected models, do not apply battery power directly to injectors.
- Whenever possible, use a flashlight instead of a drop light.
- Keep all open flame and smoking material out of the area.
- Use a shop cloth or similar to catch fuel when opening a fuel system.

• Relieve fuel system pressure before servicing.

• Always use eye or full-face protection when working around fuel lines, fittings or components.

• Always keep a dry chemical (class B-C) fire extinguisher near the area.

Positive Crankcase Ventilation (PCV) System

OPERATION

A closed, positive crankcase ventilation system is employed on all Honda vehicles. This system cycles incompletely burned fuel (which works its way past the piston rings) back into the intake manifold for reburning with the air/fuel mixture. The oil filler cap is sealed; the air is drawn from the top of the crankcase into the intake manifold through a valve with a variable orifice.

This valve (commonly known as the PCV valve) regulates the flow of air into the manifold according to the amount of manifold vacuum. When the throttle is open fairly wide, the PCV opens to maximize the flow. However, at idle speed, when manifold vacuum is at a maximum, the PCV valve reduces the flow in order to to unnecessarily affect the small volume of mixture passing into the engine.

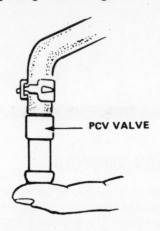

One way of checking the PCV; the other choice is to pinch the hose shut.

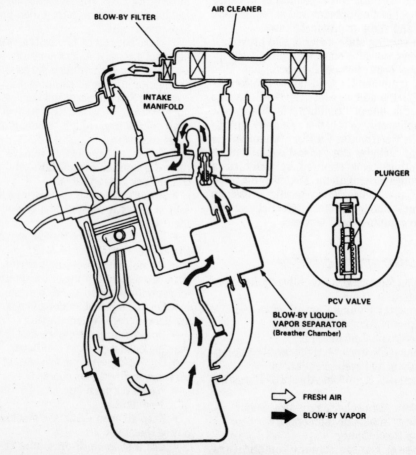

PCV system, 1986–89 Accord

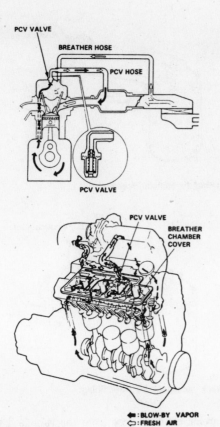

1988–91 PCV system

The recirculation system relies on the integrity of the engine seals. Any air leak around a valve cover, head gasket, oil pan, dipstick, oil filler cap air intake ducts or vacuum hoses can introduce excess air into the fuel/air mixture, causing rough running or reduced efficiency. Likewise, a plugged hose or passage can cause sludging, stalling and/or oil leaks.

SERVICE

The PCV valve is easily checked with the engine running at normal idle speed (warmed up). Gently pinch the hose shut and release it; the valve should be heard to click. Alternatively, remove the valve from the valve cover or vapor separator (breather chamber); place a finger over the end and release. The valve should be heard to click and vacuum should be felt.

If there is no vacuum, check for plugged hoses or ports. If these are open, the valve is faulty. With the engine OFF, remove the valve completely. Shake it end-to-end, listening for the rattle of the plunger inside the valve. If no rattle is heard, the plunger is jammed (probably with oil sludge) and the valve should be replaced. Never operate the engine without the PCV or with the hose blocked.

NOTE: *Don't blow directly into the valve; petroleum vapors and deposits within the valve are harmful*

Evaporative Emission Control System

OPERATION

This system prevents gasoline vapors from escaping into the atmosphere from the fuel tank and carburetor. Systems vary between vehicle families, based on year and equipment. Purge control — the admission of fresh air to the canister — may be accomplished either by mechanical means (temperature and vacuum operated controls) or electrically by the Engine Control Unit (ECU). Note that later vehicles, notably Preludes, use ECU control for the carburetors; the use of computers is not limited solely to fuel injected vehicles.

Fuel vapor is stored in the expansion chamber, in the fuel tank and in the vapor line. When the vapor pressure becomes higher than the set pressure of the one-way valve, the valve opens and allows vapor into the charcoal canister. While the engine is stopped or idling, the idle cut-off valve or purge control system is closed and the vapor is absorbed by the charcoal.

At partially opened throttle, the idle cut-off valve is opened by manifold vacuum. The vapor that was stored in the charcoal canister and in the vapor line is purged into the intake manifold. Any excessive pressure or vacuum which might build up in the fuel tank is relieved by the two-way valve in the filler cap or fuel line.

SERVICE

Carbureted 1984–85 Accord and Prelude

THERMOVALVE A

Engine Cold

NOTE: *The engine must be cold; coolant temperature must be below the thermosensor(s) set temperature. The thermosensor(s) must have continuity.*

1. Using a hand vacuum pump disconnect the upper hose (purge control diaphragm valve) from the evaporative canister and connect the hose to the gauge.

2. Start the engine and allow it to idle; there should be no vacuum.

3. If there is vacuum, replace thermosensor A on Accord or thermosensor B on Prelude and retest.

Engine Hot

1. The engine must be fully warmed up; the cooling fan(s) must cycle at least once. Using a hand vacuum pump, disconnect the upper hose (purge control diaphragm valve) from the evap-

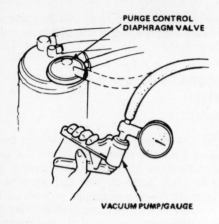

Connect the vacuum gauge to the purge control diaphragm valve

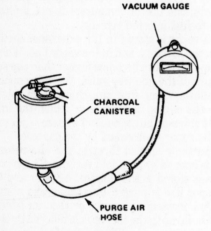

Use a vacuum gauge on the purge air hose

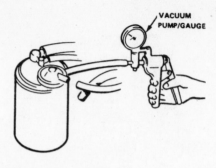

Testing the canister circuits

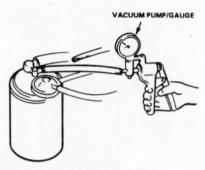

Check vacuum at the TANK fitting

orative canister and connect the hose to the gauge.

2. Start the engine and allow it to idle; there should be vacuum at idle.

3. If there is no vacuum, inspect thermovalve A on Accord or B on Prelude by pinching its hose to the air filter. If vacuum is now available to the canister, replace the thermovalve. If vacuum is still not available, inspect hose No. 19 to the intake manifold for leaks or blockage.

CHARCOAL CANISTER

NOTE: *This procedure is to be performed with the engine Hot.*

1. Using a tachometer, connect it to the engine. Start the engine and allow it to reach normal operating temperatures; the cooling fan should turn on at least once.

2. Remove the fuel filler cap.

3. Using a vacuum gauge, disconnect the charcoal canister hose from the vehicle frame and connect the gauge to it.

4. Raise the engine speed to 3,500 rpm; vacuum should appear on the gauge in 1 minute. If vacuum appears, go to Step 10.

5. If no vacuum appears, perform the following procedures:

a. Disconnect the vacuum gauge and reinstall the fuel filler cap.

b. Remove the charcoal canister and check for signs of damage or defects.

c. If necessary, replace the canister.

6. Stop the engine and disconnect the PCV hose from the charcoal canister.

7. Using a hand vacuum pump , install it to PURGE fitting on the canister. Hand pump the vacuum gauge to create vacuum. If the vacuum remains steady, proceed with the next step; if the vacuum drops, replace the canister and retest.

8. Reconnect the PCV hose and start the engine; the Purge side vacuum should drop to zero. If the vacuum does not drop to zero, replace the canister and retest.

9. If Purge-side vacuum does drop to zero, connect the vacuum pump to the canister PCV fitting and draw vacuum; vacuum should remain steady. If vacuum remains steady, disconnect the pump and recheck the operation of thermovalve A. If vacuum drops, replace the canister and retest.

10. Connect the vacuum pump to the TANK fitting on the canister and draw vacuum; no vacuum should be held. If there is no vacuum present, reinstall the fuel filler cap; the test is complete. If vacuum is held, replace the canister and retest

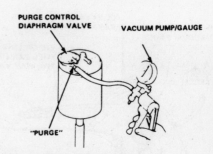

Checking vacuum at the PURGE port

Fuel Injected 1985 Accord

CHARCOAL CANISTER

1. Connect a tachometer to the engine. Start the engine and allow it to reach normal operating temperatures; the cooling fan should turn on at least once.

2. Remove the fuel filler cap.

3. Using a vacuum gauge, disconnect the charcoal canister hose from the vehicle frame and connect the gauge to it.

4. Raise the engine speed to 3,500 rpm; vacuum should appear on the gauge in 1 minute. If vacuum appears, go to Step 10.

5. If no vacuum appears, perform the following procedures:

   a. Disconnect the vacuum gauge and reinstall the fuel filler cap.

   b. Remove the charcoal canister and check for signs of damage or defects.

   c. If necessary, replace the canister.

6. connect the vacuum pump to the canister PURGE fitting and draw vacuum; vacuum should remain steady. If the vacuum drops, replace the canister and retest.

7. Using a 2nd vacuum pump, draw air from the canister PCV fitting. PURGE-side vacuum should drop to zero. If vacuum does not drop, replace the canister and retest.

8. Disconnect the vacuum pump from the PURGE port. Draw vacuum at the PCV port; steady vacuum should be held. If vacuum drops, replace the canister.

9. Connect the vacuum pump to the TANK port and draw vacuum. There should be no vacuum. If no vacuum is present, reinstall the filler cap; the test is complete. If vacuum is present, replace the canister and retest.

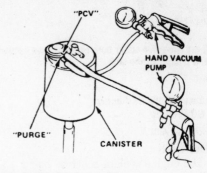

Use two pumps to test the PCV circuit

TWO WAY VALVE

1. Remove the fuel filler cap.

2. Elevate and safely support the vehicle.

3. Remove the vapor line from the liquid/vapor separator pipe at the side of the fuel tank. Connect a T-fitting for both a vacuum gauge and vacuum pump to the hose running into the tank.

4. Slowly draw a vacuum while watching the gauge. Vacuum should stabilize as the two-way valve opens at between 5 and 15 mmHg (0.2–

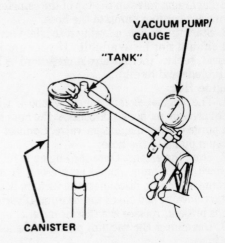

No vacuum should be present at the TANK port

0.6 in. Hg). If the valve opens too early or too late, replace the two-way valve and retest.

5. Move the vacuum pump hose from the vacuum to the pressure fitting on the pump and, if necessary, move the gauge hose to the pressure side.

6. Slowly pressurize the vapor line while watching the gauge. Pressure should stabilize between 25 and 55 mmHg (1.0–2.2 in Hg.). If this is true, the valve is OK. If the pressure stabilizes too early or too late, replace the valve.

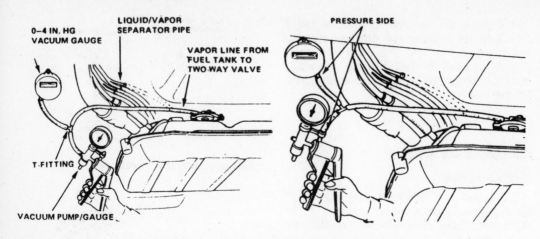

Check the two-valve under both pressure and vacuum. Note that the hose connection has been changed at the hand pump, not the tank

Carbureted 1986–89 Accord
1986–90 Prelude

THERMOVALVE A or B

Engine Cold

1. The engine coolant must be below 131°F (55°C) on Accord or 104°F (40°C) on Prelude. Disconnect the vacuum hose at the purge control diaphragm valve on the top of the canister. Connect a vacuum pump to the hose.
2. Start the engine, allowing it to idle. Vacuum should not be available. If vacuum is present, replace thermovalve A on Accord or B on Prelude and retest.

Engine Hot

1. The engine coolant must be above the thermosensor set point. Disconnect the hose at the purge control diaphragm valve. Connect a vacuum pump to the hose.
2. Start the engine. Once the engine is fully warmed up, vacuum should be present. If no vacuum is present, disconnect the vacuum hose at thermovalve and check for vacuum. If vacuum is present, replace the thermovalve.
3. Disconnect the vacuum pump; reconnect the hose.
4. Remove the fuel filler cap.
5. Remove the canister purge air hose from the frame and connect the hose to a vacuum gauge.
6. Raise the engine speed to 3500 rpm. Vacuum should appear on the gauge within 1 minute. If no vacuum is present, switch the engine OFF. Reinstall the filler cap. Remove the charcoal canister and inspect for physical damage, replacing it as necessary.
7. If vacuum was present in Step 6, switch the engine OFF. Disconnect the hose from the canister PCV fitting. Connect a vacuum pump to the PURGE fitting and draw vacuum. Vacu-

um should remain steady. If vacuum drops, replace the canister.
8. Restart the engine; connect the PCV hose to the fitting. Vacuum at the purge port should drop to 0. If it does not drop to 0, replace the canister.
9. If vacuum does drop to zero at the purge side, connect a vacuum pump to the canister PCV fitting and draw vacuum. Steady vacuum should be held. If not, replace the canister and retest.
10. Connect the vacuum pump to the TANK fitting on the canister and draw vacuum. No vacuum should be held; if vacuum is present, replace the canister.

CARBURETOR THERMOVALVE

Accord Only

1. Begin the test on a cold engine; the coolant must be below 86°F (30°C).
2. Disconnect the hose at the carburetor thermovalve; connect a hand vacuum pump to the valve. Draw a vacuum of 200 mmHg or 7.8 in Hg to the valve; the vacuum should remain steady. If the vacuum cannot be held, replace the thermovalve.
3. Reconnect the vacuum hose to the carburetor thermovalve. Start the engine, allowing it to warm up to normal operating temperature. Coolant temperature must be above 104°F (40°C).
4. Repeat Step 2. No vacuum should be held. If vacuum is held, replace the carburetor thermovalve.

Fuel Injected 1986–89 Accord
And 1986–91 Prelude

SYSTEM TEST

1. Begin the test on a cold engine. Coolant temperature must be below 131°F (55°C). In-

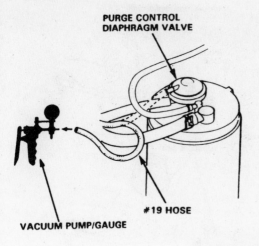

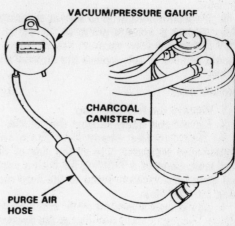

Connections for the Hot Engine test.

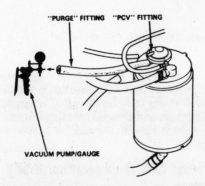

Make certain the vacuum pump is connected to the correct port when testing the PCV circuit

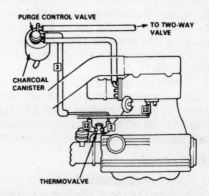

Canister vacuum schematic, fuel injected 1986–89 Accord

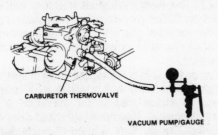

Test the carburetor thermovalve on both a cold and warm engine.

spect the vacuum lines for cracks, blockages and proper connections.

2. Disconnect No. 3 vacuum hose from the purge control diaphragm valve and connect a vacuum gauge to the hose.

3. Start the engine and allow it to idle. While the engine is cold, vacuum should not be available. If vacuum is present, replace the thermovalve and retest.

4. Allow the engine to warm up to normal operating temperature. Vacuum should become available as the engine coolant passes 131 degrees. If vacuum is not present when the engine is warm, replace the thermovalve.

5. Disconnect the vacuum gauge and reconnect the hose.

6. Remove the fuel filler cap.

7. Remove the canister purge air hose from the frame and connect the hose to a vacuum gauge.

8. Raise the engine speed to 3500 rpm. Vacuum should appear on the gauge within 1 minute. If no vacuum is present, switch the engine OFF. Reinstall the filler cap. Remove the charcoal canister and inspect for physical damage, replacing it as necessary.

9. If vacuum was present in Step 6, switch the engine OFF. Disconnect the hose from the canister PCV fitting. Connect a vacuum pump to the PURGE fitting and draw vacuum. Vacuum should remain steady. If vacuum drops, replace the canister.

10. Restart the engine; connect the PCV hose to the fitting. Vacuum at the purge port should

drop to 0. If it does not drop to 0, replace the canister.

11. If vacuum does drop to zero at the purge side, connect a vacuum pump to the canister PCV fitting and draw vacuum. Steady vacuum should be held. If not, replace the canister and retest.

TWO WAY VALVE

1. Remove the fuel filler cap.
2. Elevate and safely support the vehicle.
3. Remove the vapor line from the liquid/vapor separator pipe at the side of the fuel tank. Connect a T-fitting for both a vacuum gauge and vacuum pump to the hose running into the tank.
4. slowly draw a vacuum while watching the gauge. Vacuum should stabilize as the two-way valve opens at between 5 and 15 mmHg (0.2–0.6 in. Hg). If the valve opens too early or too late, replace the two-way valve and retest.
5. Move the vacuum pump hose from the vacuum to the pressure fitting on the pump and, if necessary, move the gauge hose to the pressure side.
6. Slowly pressurize the vapor line while watching the gauge. Pressure should stabilize between 25 and 55 mmHg (1.0–2.2 in Hg.). If this is true, the valve is OK. If the pressure stabilizes too early or too late, replace the valve.

1990–91 Accord

1. With the engine cold, disconnect the vacuum hose from the top of the purge control diaphragm and connect a vacuum gauge to it. The gauge on a hand vacuum pump can be used.
2. With the engine cold and at idle, the solenoid valve should be closed. The gauge should show no vacuum when the engine is first started. As the engine warms up, the solenoid valve will open to open the purge control valve.
3. If there is no vacuum by the time the radiator fan has run, check the purge cut-off solenoid and the wiring to it. The solenoid should have 12 volts at the black/yellow wire when the ignition switch is **ON**. The ECU completes the ground circuit.
4. Reconnect the vacuum line to the valve and connect the gauge to the bottom of the canister where fresh air is admitted. Run the engine at about 3500 rpm. If no vacuum appears when the solenoid valve is open, the canister may be broken. Test the 2-way valve and make sure the fuel filler cap is not leaking.
5. Stop the engine. To test the 2-way valve, remove the fuel filler cap, disconnect the fuel tank vent line, connect a hand vacuum pump to the line and draw a vacuum. It should momentarily stabilize at 0.2–0.6 in. Hg (5–15mm Hg) of vacuum.

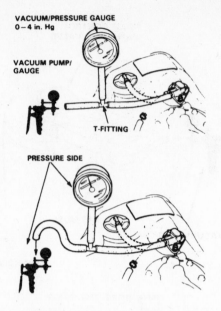

Two-way valve test for 1990–91 Accord

6. At the same line, apply low air pressure. The pressure should momentarily stabilize at 0.4–1.4 in. Hg (10–35mm Hg) of vacuum. Correct vacuum and pressure readings mean the 2-way valve is functioning and the tank is venting properly.

Exhaust Gas Recirculation (EGR) System

OPERATION

The EGR system is designed to control oxides of nitrogen (NOx) emissions by recirculating part of the exhaust gas into the intake manifold through the EGR valve mounted on the intake manifold.

On carbureted vehicles, the valve is operated by ported vacuum and provides EGR proportional to engine load by the operation of the control valve(s). The valves open and close very rapidly. The air flow volume through the air passages maintains a constant ratio, proportional to carburetor intake rate and engine load.

On fuel injected engines, the ECU contains memories for ideal EGR lift for all operating conditions. The EGR valve lift sensor detects the amount of lift in the valve and sends the information to the ECU. The ECU uses that and other electrical signals to determine the amount of time the EGR control solenoid should be energized. When energized, the control solenoid allows vacuum to flow to the EGR valve.

Both systems incorporate means of limiting

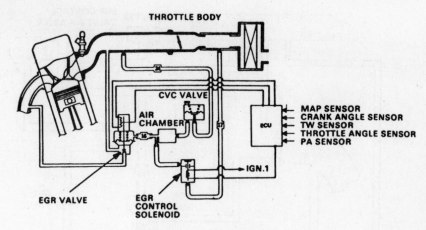

Fuel Injected EGR system.

EGR function when the engine is cold. Since combustion temperatures are lower, the engine emits comparitively low levels of NOx; EGR function is disabled to allow improved cold driveability.

Fuel Injected Vehicles

The EGR valve is not simply open or closed but is modulated by controlling the amount of engine vacuum to the valve diaphragm, up to a maximum of 8 in. Hg of vacuum. The ECU modulates the position of the control solenoid valve to control the EGR valve lift according to an internal program. Upstream of the control solenoid valve, the CVC provides a constant supply of vacuum so EGR control is precise under all manifold vacuum conditions. An air chamber inline between the CVC and control solenoid acts as an expansion chamber to dampen any vacuum pulses. The control solenoid valve, CVC and air chamber are in the control box on the firewall.

SERVICE

1. First check that all vacuum lines and electrical connections are in good condition. If the engine will not run at idle, disconnect the vacuum hose to the EGR valve and plug it. If the engine will now idle, the problem is in the EGR control system. Run the engine until the radiator fan runs. Disconnect the vacuum supply hose to the EGR valve and connect a hand vacuum pump with a gauge to the valve.

2. With the engine at idle, draw a vacuum on the EGR valve. The engine should stall and the valve should hold vacuum. If not, replace the EGR valve.

3. Connect the hand pump with vacuum gauge to the vacuum hose from the control solenoid valve and restart the engine; there should be no vacuum at idle.

4. If there is vacuum to the EGR valve at idle, check the wiring for the control solenoid. One wire should have 12 volts any time the engine is running. The ground wire goes to the ECU, which modulates the control solenoid opening by controlling the ground circuit. Turn the ignition switch **OFF** and use a DIGITAL ohmmeter to see if the wire between the ECU and control solenoid is shorted to ground. If the wiring is correct, the ECU is getting an incorrect input signal or the ECU is faulty.

5. The vacuum going to the control solenoid valve should be about 8 in. Hg at idle. Connect the pump with gauge to the hose coming from the air chamber. If the vacuum is not correct, read the vacuum at the CVC valve outlet. Full manifold vacuum should be available at the CVC inlet. If the air chamber or CVC valve leak or are not functioning properly, the units cannot be repaired.

6. To test the EGR valve lift sensor, turn the ignition **OFF** and disconnect the wiring to the EGR valve. Turn the ignition switch **ON** and check for 5 volts to the sensor at one of the connector terminals. Switch the ignition **OFF**, connect an ohmmeter across the center and either of the end terminals on the EGR valve lift sensor connector and operate the EGR valve with the vacuum pump. The resistance should change as the valve opens and closes.

Carbureted Vehicles

This system is controlled by a pair of vacuum operated control valves using a compound ported vacuum strategy. Ported vacuum upstream of the throttle opens valve A, which allows manifold vacuum to open valve B. As B opens, some of the ported vacuum is bled off to the carburetor venturi, causing A to begin closing and the EGR valve to open. Eventually a balance is reached that is dependent on mani-

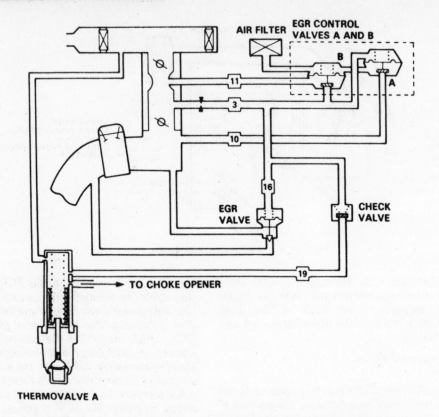

AIR FILTER

EGR CONTROL
VALVES A AND B

B

A

11

3

10

16

EGR
VALVE

CHECK
VALVE

19

→ TO CHOKE OPENER

THERMOVALVE A

Vacuum schematic for carbureted EGR system. 1987 Accord shown, others similar

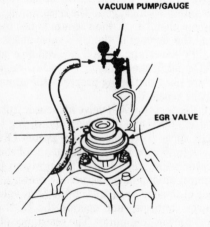

VACUUM PUMP/GAUGE

EGR VALVE

Testing the vacuum to the EGR valve

fold vacuum versus ported vacuum. This ties EGR valve opening to throttle valve opening and, therefore, to engine load. When the engine is cold or the vehicle is not moving, the purge cut-off solenoid valve for the evaporative emission control system turns off the vacuum to valve B, preventing the venturi vacuum from reaching the EGR valve. The system is far easier to test than to understand. Except for the cut-off solenoid valve, the system is entirely mechanical. Any malfunctions are due to vacuum hose leakage or misrouting or EGR control valve failure.

SERVICE

1. With the engine cold, connect a vacuum gauge to the EGR valve vacuum hose and run the engine at about 3000 rpm. There should be no vacuum. If there is, test the evaporative emission control system. Let the engine idle to warm up to operating temperature (radiator fan will run) and open the control box on the firewall.

2. Remove the top hose from the purge cut-off solenoid valve and cap the valve. Check the vacuum to the EGR valve hose under the following conditions:
- At idle, no vacuum.
- At 3000 rpm, 2–6 in. (51–152mm) Hg of vacuum.
- At 3000 rpm with venturi hose No. 11 blocked, less than 2 in. (51mm) Hg of vacuum.
- Rapid acceleration, 2–6 in. (51–150mm) Hg of vacuum.
- Deceleration, no vacuum.

3. To test the EGR valve, plug the vacuum hose and connect a hand vacuum pump to the valve. Draw a vacuum of about 6 in. (150mm)

Hg with the engine at idle. The engine should stall and the vacuum should remain steady, indicating the diaphragm is good. If the engine did not stall, either the valve is not opening or the passageway is blocked.

Oxygen Sensor
REMOVAL AND INSTALLATION

The sensor(s) may be removed by unscrewing the unit from the manifold or exhaust pipe. Make absolutely certain that the exhaust system is cold to avoid serious burns.

Disconnect the wiring connector near the sensor. Use a special oxygen sensor socket to remove and install the unit. These sockets have a slot in the side to prevent damage to the wiring; they are also sized to be an exact fit on the sensor. Keep the wrench straight so the sensor is not bent or broken.

To install the sensor, carefully coat the threads only with an anti-seize compound. Take great care to keep all compounds and petroleum products off the tip of the sensor; its operation will be impaired by pollutants. Install the sensor and tighten it to 45 Nm (33 ft. lbs.). Reconnect the sensor wiring.

Fault Codes

While all carbureted Accords after 1984 and 1984–87 Preludes use some form of feedback control, i.e., a small computer operating the air control solenoids in response to inputs from the oxygen and other sensors, none of the control units possess self-diagnostic capabilities. If a fault occurs in a circuit, careful diagnosis and testing methods must be used to find the culprit. A thorough understanding of the system is required.

Beginning with 1988 Preludes, the control unit or ECU includes the self-diagnostic abilities found on fuel injected vehicles. This function makes troubleshooting much easier because the computer is capable of telling you "where it hurts".

The engine control unit is programmed to monitor input and output signals; if it detects a signal out-of-range, either high or low, the CHECK ENGINE warning lamp on the dashboard is triggered ON. This advises the operator that a problem exists; additionally, the ECU assigns a fault code to the occurrence and stores the code in its memory. This code can be retrieved at a later time for diagnostic use.

NOTE: *The ECU is equipped with a back-up function. Should a signal fault occur, the ECU ignores the actual signal and substitutes a fixed value in its place. When the dash warning lamp is lit, the controller is using at least one fixed value and driveability may suffer.*

The fixed values are set for the most common driving conditions, i.e., warm engine, moderate throttle openings, etc. If the fixed value does not match the present condition, engine response will not be as expected.

Multiple codes can be stored. The ability to

The stored fault codes are displayed by the flashing of the LED

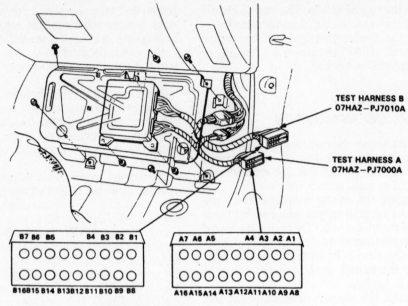

TERMINAL LOCATION

Test harness connection for 1988–89 Prelude

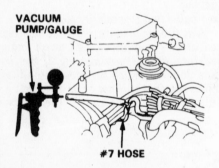

VACUUM
PUMP/GAUGE

#7 HOSE

Test harness connection for 1990 Prelude

narrow a problem to one or two circuits saves much diagnostic time. The most common error when using fault codes is to assume the indicated component has failed rather than checking the entire circuit. (Example: Code 1 — oxygen content — does not automatically mean the oxygen sensor has failed. Usually, it hasn't; the wire is loose at the connector.) The ECU watches electrical signals, so any electrical item may cause a fault to set. A loose connector, bad ground, loose component or even a blown fuse may cause the controller to note a change in the signal. When using diagnostic or fault codes always remember that the entire circuit including the component must be checked carefully. The single most common cause of faults are loose or corroded connections. The actual components rarely fail in normal circumstances.

READING CODES

The ECU is located on the front floor, about under the passenger's toes. Pull the carpet down; a large protective cover will be seen over the ECU. Pull down the inspection flap from under the dashboard. On the upper edge of the cover is a window or opening, allowing the Light Emitting Diode (LED) to be viewed. Turn the ignition ON but do not start the engine; the LED will begin to flash. By recording the number of flashes, the codes may be retrieved and read. Codes are transmitted by the number of flashes: 14 flashes, a pause and 5 flashes would indicate Code 14 and Code 5.

CLEARING CODES

Stored codes are removed from memory by removing power to the ECU. Disconnecting the power will also clear the memories used for other solid-state equipment such as the clock and radio. For this reason, always make note of the radio presets before clearing the system.

While disconnecting the battery will clear the memory, this is not the recommended procedure. The memory should be cleared by removing the appropriate fuse for at least 10 seconds. In all cases, the correct fuse is located in the underhood fuse and relay box. On Accord, remove the BACK-UP fuse; on Prelude, remove the CLOCK fuse.

CARBURETED FUEL SYSTEM

Electric Fuel Pumps

All Accords and Preludes covered by this book use an electric fuel pump located either near or inside the fuel tank. Accords through 1985 and Preludes through 1987 use an external fuel pump mounted under the car just forward of the left rear wheel. All other (later) vehicles use an electric fuel pump mounted inside the fuel tank. Note that on some vehicles, the fuel tank need not be removed to change the internal pump.

The fuel pump should be heard to run for just a few seconds when the ignition is turned ON without starting the engine. This builds pressure within the lines. In the event that a car with an external fuel pump is stranded, not starting, and the fuel pump is not heard, first check the applicable fuses. An emergency measure that sometimes works is to thump the fuel pump housing with a wooden hammer handle two or three times; occasionally the pump will come back to life. This is one of the few instances where a bit of controlled violence may get you home.

Fuel pumps mounted in the fuel tank are smaller, more efficient and quieter; they are also inaccessible in a hurry. Thankfully, they are protected from road hazards and rarely fail.

REMOVAL AND INSTALLATION

Externally Mounted Fuel Pumps

1. Remove the gas filler cap to relieve any excess pressure in the system.
2. Use a pair of suitable clamps to pinch shut the fuel lines to the pump.
3. Disconnect the negative battery cable.
4. Elevate the rear of the car and support it safely on properly placed stands. Remove the left rear wheel.
5. Label the fuel lines. Pinch the inlet and

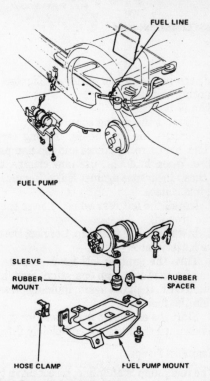

1985–85 Accord electric fuel pump

outlet fuel lines shut. Loosen the hose clamps. Slide the clamps back; twist or rotate the hoses while removing them.

6. Disconnect the positive lead wire and ground wire from the pump at their connectors.
7. Remove the fuel pump retaining bolts, taking care not to lose the spacers and bolt collars.
8. Remove the fuel pump and its protective cover as a unit.
9. The pump cannot be disassembled and must be replaced if defective.
10. Install the fuel pump and cover. Make certain the mounting collars and insulators, if

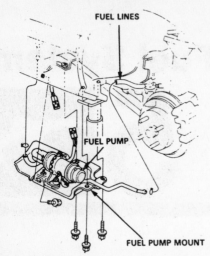

FUEL LINES

FUEL PUMP

FUEL PUMP MOUNT

Prelude external fuel pump

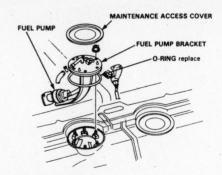

MAINTENANCE ACCESS COVER

FUEL PUMP

FUEL PUMP BRACKET

O-RING replace

Accord In-tank fuel pump

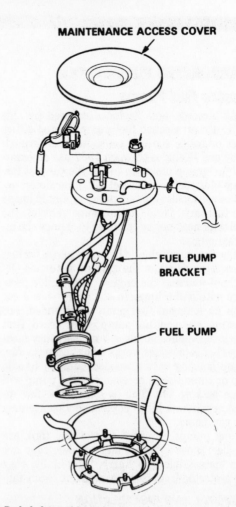

MAINTENANCE ACCESS COVER

FUEL PUMP BRACKET

FUEL PUMP

Prelude Internal fuel pump

used, are in the proper location. Tighten the mounting bolts to
10 Nm (7 ft. lbs.)

11. Connect the wiring connector.

12. Connect the fuel hoses, making certain the lines are correctly placed and the clamps are secure. When in doubt, use new clamps; they are cheap insurance against leaks. Remove the fuel line clamps.

13. Install the left rear wheel. Lower the car to the ground.

14. Install the fuel filler cap. Connect the negative battery cable.

15. Turn the ignition ON for 3 seconds, listening for the fuel pump operation. Switch the ignition OFF, then ON again, building pressure within the fuel lines.

16. Start the engine. It may crank for several seconds until the lines are completely filled.

In-Tank Fuel Pumps

The fuel pump is an inline, direct drive type. Fuel is drawn into the pump through a filter, flows around the armature through the one-way valve and is delivered to the engine compartment. A baffle is provided to prevent fuel pulsation. The fuel pump has a relief valve to prevent excessive pressure. It opens if there is a blockage in the discharge side. When the relief valve opens, fuel flows from the high pressure to the low pressure side. A check valve is provided to maintain fuel pressure in the line after the pump is stopped. This is to ease restarting.

The pump section is composed of a rotor, rollers and pump spacer. When the rotor turns, the rollers turn and travel along the inner surface of the pump spacer by centrifugal force. The volume of the cavity enclosed by these three

parts changes, drawing and pressurizing the fuel.

CAUTION: *Gasoline vapors are explosive. Remove components slowly and contain spillage. Observe no smoking/no open flame precautions. Have a Class B-C (dry powder) fire extinguisher within arm's reach at all times.*

1. Turn the ignition OFF; leave it OFF throughout the procedure.

2. Lift or reposition the carpet in the luggage area. Remove the left maintenance access cover in the floor.

3. Disconnect the electrical connector at the pump unit.

4. Label and disconnect the fuel lines.

5. Carefully remove the retaining nuts holding the pump. When all are removed, lift the pump up and out of the tank.

NOTE: *The pump sits on an angle and may require some manipulation to remove. If the pump still won't come out, loosen the fuel tank mounting nuts under the car; slide the tank downward a bit to give more clearance at the top.*

6. Reinstall the pump, making certain it is correctly seated and not wedged or jammed. Install the retaining nuts, tightening them evenly and alternately to 6 Nm (10 ft. lbs.) only.

7. Install the fuel lines. Make certain the clamps are secure; use new ones if necessary.

8. Connect the wiring.

9. Install the maintenance access cover and seal or gasket, if used.

10. Reposition the carpeting in the luggage compartment.

11. Start the engine; it may crank longer than normal until fuel pressure is established.

TESTING

NOTE: *Always check the fuel filter for clogging and/or the fuel lines for crimping or blockage before testing the fuel pump. A fuel pressure gauge and a 1 graduated quart container are required for these procedures.*

Externally Mounted Fuel Pumps

1. Turn the ignition OFF. Remove the screws holding the underdash fuse box to its mount. Remove the fuel cut-off relay from the back of the fuse block and turn the block so you can see the relay mount.

2. Use a jumper wire to connect the two left-most terminals of the relay mount. On Preludes, these terminals are for the Black/Yellow wires; on Accord, they are designated Terminals 1 and 2.

3. Disconnect the fuel line at the fuel filter in the engine compartment. Connect a pressure gauge to the fuel line.

4. Turn the ignition key ON until pressure on the gauge stabilizes, then turn the key OFF.

5. Pressure should be 2.4–3.1 psi for Accords and 2–3 psi for Preludes. If the pressure shown is below minimum, the pump must be replaced. If pressure is at least minimum, continue with the volume portion of the test.

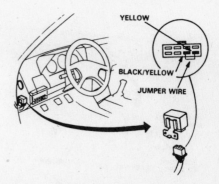

Accord fuel cut-off relay and fuse block

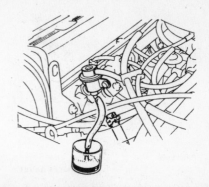

Checking Accord fuel volume

6. Remove the pressure gauge from the fuel line; hold the line in the quart container. Have an assistant turn the ignition switch ON for 60 seconds, then shut it OFF.

7. Fuel flow in 60 seconds must be at least 500 cc (17 oz.) for Accord or 680 cc (23 oz.) for Prelude

8. If fuel pump volume is below specification, the pump must be replaced.

9. Remove the jumper wire at the fuse block. Reinstall the fuel cut-off relay. Reinstall the fuse block on its mount.

In-Tank Fuel Pumps

ACCORD

1. Turn the ignition OFF. Remove the screws holding the underdash fuse box to its mount. Remove the fuel cut-off relay from the back of the fuse block and turn the block so you can see the relay mount.

2. Use a jumper wire to connect the two left-most terminals of the relay mount, terminal 1 to terminal 2.

3. Disconnect the fuel line at the fuel filter in the engine compartment. Connect a pressure gauge to the fuel line.

4. Turn the ignition key ON until pressure on the gauge stabilizes, then turn the key OFF.

5. Pressure should be 2.6–3.3 psi for Ac-

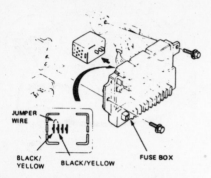

Prelude fuel cut-off relay and test connections

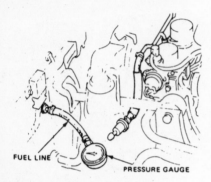

Testing carbureted Prelude fuel pressure

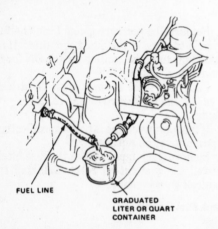

Testing fuel volume on Prelude

cords. If the pressure shown is below minimum, the pump must be replaced. If pressure is at least minimum, continue with the volume portion of the test.

6. Remove the pressure gauge from the fuel line; hold the line in the quart container. Have an assistant turn the ignition switch ON for 60 seconds, then shut it OFF.

7. Fuel flow in 60 seconds must be at least 760cc (25.7 oz).

8. If fuel pump volume is below specification, the pump must be replaced.

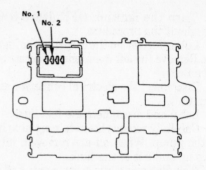

Connect terminals 1 and 2 to test the Accord fuel pump

9. Remove the jumper wire at the fuel block. Reinstall the fuel cut-off relay. Reinstall the fuse block on its mount.

PRELUDE

1. Remove the dashboard under cover; remove the fuel cut-off relay from the fuse block.

2. Use a jumper wire to connect the top 2 terminals (Terminals 1 and 2) of the relay mount.

3. Disconnect the fuel line at the fuel filter. Connect a pressure gauge to the line; plug the filter end of the line.

4. Turn the ignition key ON until pressure on the gauge stabilizes, then turn the key OFF.

5. Pressure should be 2.6–3.3 psi. If the pressure shown is below minimum, the pump must be replaced. If pressure is at least minimum, continue with the volume portion of the test.

6. Remove the pressure gauge from the fuel line; hold the line in the quart container. Have an assistant turn the ignition switch ON for 60 seconds, then shut it OFF.

7. Fuel flow in 60 seconds must be at least 760cc (25.7 oz).

8. If fuel pump volume is below specification, the pump must be replaced.

9. Remove the jumper wire at the fuse block. Reinstall the fuel cut-off relay.

Carburetor

ADJUSTMENTS

1984–85 Accord

THROTTLE CABLE

1. The throttle cable should operate smoothly with no binding. If the cable is kinked or binding, replace it.

2. Check the cable free play at the linkage. The cable should be loose enough to deflect $3/16$–$3/8$ in. (4.7–9.5mm) between the locknut and the bell crank.

3. If the deflection is not correct, loosen the locknut. Turn the adjusting nut to tighten or

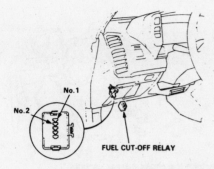

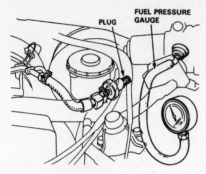

Testing the Prelude fuel pump

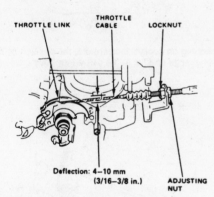

1984-85 Accord throttle cable adjustment

loosen the cable as necessary. Once properly set, tighten the locknut.

4. Check the throttle plate (valve) while an assistant holds the accelerator pedal to the floor. The throttle should be fully open; the throttle plate should be vertical. Check carefully to see that the throttle plate is opening fully but is not going "over center"; that is, passing the vertical position and sitting at an angle. Additionally, the throttle plate must close quickly and smoothly when the accelerator pedal is released.

CHOKE COIL TENSION AND LINKAGE

1. The engine must be cold before performing these tests.

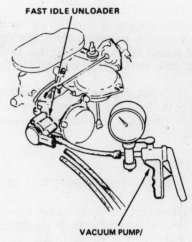

Testing the fast idle unloader

2. Remove the air cleaner.

3. Depress the accelerator to the floor and release it smoothly to set the choke plate. The plate should close completely. If engine temperature is above 82°F (28°C), the plate will not close totally but should close to within ⅛ in. (3mm) of total closure.

4. If the choke plate closes properly, continue with the fast idle unloader and choke opener tests.

5. If choke does not close completely, check carefully for signs of dirt or binding in the linkage. Spray the linkage with carburetor cleaner and retest.

6. If the choke still will not operate properly, remove the choke cover and inspect the linkage for freedom of motion. When reassembling, make certain the index marks align on the carburetor body and choke cover.

7. If the choke still will not operate correctly, replace the choke cover.

FAST IDLE UNLOADER

1. Engine coolant temperature must be below 86°F (30°C).

2. Disconnect the two hoses from the fast idle unloader.

3. Depress the accelerator to the floor and release it smoothly to set the choke plate (if not already set from previous test).

4. Start the engine; it should run at fast idle. If the engine is not on fast idle, shut the engine OFF and remove the choke cover. Inspect the operation of the fast idle cam.

5. Connect a vacuum pump to the inner fitting of the unloader and draw vacuum. The fast idle speed should drop. If the idle speed does not drop, check the unloader for leaks, damage or failed diaphragm. Replace the unloader if necessary.

6. Reconnect the hoses.

7. Allow the engine to warm up. As the engine comes up to temperature; the fast idle speed should drop below 1400 rpm as the unloader pulls the choke linkage off the fast idle cam.

8. If the fast idle does not drop, check for vacuum in the lines and freedom of motion in the linkage. Check for vacuum at thermovalves A and B.

CHOKE OPENER

1. This test must be performed on a cold engine.

2. Disconnect the choke heater wires.

3. Depress the accelerator to the floor and release it smoothly to set the choke.

4. Start the engine. The choke should open partially. If the choke does not open partially, inspect the linkage for freedom of motion, repairing as needed. If the choke still does not open, check the choke opener diaphragm.

   a. Remove the two screws.

   b. Attach a vacuum pump to the hose fitting.

   c. Hold a finger over the orifice in the opener while drawing enough vacuum to pull the opener rod all the way in.

   d. If the rod will not stay in, replace the opener.

   e. If the rod stays in, inspect the vacuum port in the carburetor. Clean it if necessary.

5. If the coolant temperature is below 52°F (11°C), tab A on the choke opener should not be seated against the carburetor. If it is touching, disconnect the choke opener hose. If the tab comes off its seat, check vacuum hose 18 for blockage and check that thermovalve B is operating properly. If the tab does not come off the seat, press down of the choke opener lever until it does; if it won't stay off, clean the choke opener vacuum port with a 0.5mm drill bit and retest.

6. If the coolant temperature is above approx. 66°F (19°C), tab A should be seated against the carburetor. If this is true, reconnect the choke heater wires; the test is concluded.

7. If the tab is not seated properly, check vacuum hose 18 for blockage and check that thermovalve B is closed.

FAST IDLE

NOTE: *This test may be performed on a warm engine.*

1. With the engine OFF, connect a tachometer.

2. Disconnect and plug the inner vacuum hose from the fast idle unloader.

3. Engage the fast idle cam by opening and

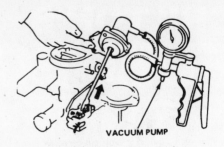

Checking the choke opener vacuum

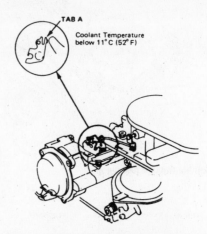

Depending on coolant temperature, the position of Tab A will change relative to the carburetor body

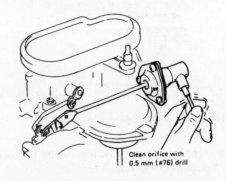

It may be necessary to clean the vacuum port

closing the throttle fully while holding the choke blade closed.

4. Restart the engine. Fast idle should be 2000–3000 rpm.

5. If necessary, adjust the fast idle speed by turning the fast idle adjusting screw.

CHOKE COVER REPLACEMENT

1. Remove the air cleaner assembly.

2. Cover the carburetor with a clean rag to

CHILTON'S
FUEL ECONOMY
& TUNE-UP TIPS

Tune-up • Spark Plug Diagnosis • Emission Controls

Fuel System • Cooling System • Tires and Wheels

General Maintenance

CHILTON'S FUEL ECONOMY & TUNE-UP TIPS

Fuel economy is important to everyone, no matter what kind of vehicle you drive. The maintenance-minded motorist can save both money and fuel using these tips and the periodic maintenance and tune-up procedures in this Repair and Tune-Up Guide.

There are more than 130,000,000 cars and trucks registered for private use in the United States. Each travels an average of 10-12,000 miles per year, and, and in total they consume close to 70 billion gallons of fuel each year. This represents nearly ⅔ of the oil imported by the United States each year. The Federal government's goal is to reduce consumption 10% by 1985. A variety of methods are either already in use or under serious consideration, and they all affect you driving and the cars you will drive. In addition to "down-sizing", the auto industry is using or investigating the use of electronic fuel delivery, electronic engine controls and alternative engines for use in smaller and lighter vehicles, among other alternatives to meet the federally mandated Corporate Average Fuel Economy (CAFE) of 27.5 mpg by 1985. The government, for its part, is considering rationing, mandatory driving curtailments and tax increases on motor vehicle fuel in an effort to reduce consumption. The government's goal of a 10% reduction could be realized — and further government regulation avoided — if every private vehicle could use just 1 less gallon of fuel per week.

How Much Can You Save?

Tests have proven that almost anyone can make at least a 10% reduction in fuel consumption through regular maintenance and tune-ups. When a major manufacturer of spark plugs sur-

TUNE-UP

1. Check the cylinder compression to be sure the engine will really benefit from a tune-up and that it is capable of producing good fuel economy. A tune-up will be wasted on an engine in poor mechanical condition.

2. Replace spark plugs regularly. New spark plugs alone can increase fuel economy 3%.

3. Be sure the spark plugs are the correct type (heat range) for your vehicle. See the Tune-Up Specifications.

Heat range refers to the spark plug's ability to conduct heat away from the firing end. It must conduct the heat away in an even pattern to avoid becoming a source of pre-ignition, yet it must also operate hot enough to burn off conductive deposits that could cause misfiring.

The heat range is usually indicated by a number on the spark plug, part of the manufacturer's designation for each individual spark plug. The numbers in bold-face indicate the heat range in each manufacturer's identification system.

Manufacturer	Typical Designation
AC	R **45** TS
Bosch (old)	WA **145** T30
Bosch (new)	HR **8** Y
Champion	RBL **15** Y
Fram/Autolite	**415**
Mopar	P-**62** PR
Motorcraft	BRF-**42**
NGK	BP **5** ES-15
Nippondenso	W **16** EP
Prestolite	14GR **5** 2A

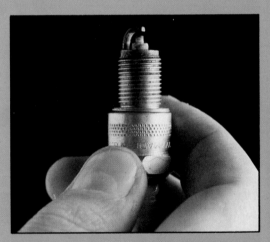

Periodically, check the spark plugs to be sure they are firing efficiently. They are excellent indicators of the internal condition of your engine.

On AC, Bosch (new), Champion, Fram/Autolite, Mopar, Motorcraft and Prestolite, a higher number indicates a hotter plug. On Bosch (old), NGK and Nippondenso, a higher number indicates a colder plug.

4. Make sure the spark plugs are properly gapped. See the Tune-Up Specifications in this book.

5. Be sure the spark plugs are firing efficiently. The illustrations on the next 2 pages show you how to "read" the firing end of the spark plug.

6. Check the ignition timing and set it to specifications. Tests show that almost all cars have incorrect ignition timing by more than 2°.

veyed over 6,000 cars nationwide, they found that a tune-up, on cars that needed one, increased fuel economy over 11%. Replacing worn plugs alone, accounted for a 3% increase. The same test also revealed that 8 out of every 10 vehicles will have some maintenance deficiency that will directly affect fuel economy, emissions or performance. Most of this mileage-robbing neglect could be prevented with regular maintenance.

Modern engines require that all of the functioning systems operate properly for maximum efficiency. A malfunction anywhere wastes fuel. You can keep your vehicle running as efficiently and economically as possible, by being aware of your vehicle's operating and performance characteristics. If your vehicle suddenly develops performance or fuel economy problems it could be due to one or more of the following:

PROBLEM	POSSIBLE CAUSE
Engine Idles Rough	Ignition timing, idle mixture, vacuum leak or something amiss in the emission control system.
Hesitates on Acceleration	Dirty carburetor or fuel filter, improper accelerator pump setting, ignition timing or fouled spark plugs.
Starts Hard or Fails to Start	Worn spark plugs, improperly set automatic choke, ice (or water) in fuel system.
Stalls Frequently	Automatic choke improperly adjusted and possible dirty air filter or fuel filter.
Performs Sluggishly	Worn spark plugs, dirty fuel or air filter, ignition timing or automatic choke out of adjustment.

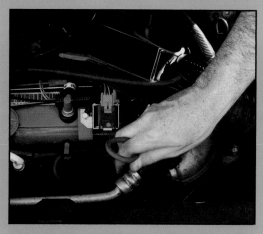
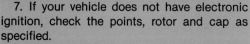

Check spark plug wires on conventional point type ignition for cracks by bending them in a loop around your finger.

Be sure that spark plug wires leading to adjacent cylinders do not run too close together. (Photo courtesy Champion Spark Plug Co.)

7. If your vehicle does not have electronic ignition, check the points, rotor and cap as specified.

8. Check the spark plug wires (used with conventional point-type ignitions) for cracks and burned or broken insulation by bending them in a loop around your finger. Cracked wires decrease fuel efficiency by failing to deliver full voltage to the spark plugs. One misfiring spark plug can cost you as much as 2 mpg.

9. Check the routing of the plug wires. Misfiring can be the result of spark plug leads to adjacent cylinders running parallel to each other and too close together. One wire tends to pick up voltage from the other causing it to fire "out of time".

10. Check all electrical and ignition circuits for voltage drop and resistance.

11. Check the distributor mechanical and/or vacuum advance mechanisms for proper functioning. The vacuum advance can be checked by twisting the distributor plate in the opposite direction of rotation. It should spring back when released.

12. Check and adjust the valve clearance on engines with mechanical lifters. The clearance should be slightly loose rather than too tight.

SPARK PLUG DIAGNOSIS

Normal

APPEARANCE: This plug is typical of one operating normally. The insulator nose varies from a light tan to grayish color with slight electrode wear. The presence of slight deposits is normal on used plugs and will have no adverse effect on engine performance. The spark plug heat range is correct for the engine and the engine is running normally.

CAUSE: Properly running engine.

RECOMMENDATION: Before reinstalling this plug, the electrodes should be cleaned and filed square. Set the gap to specifications. If the plug has been in service for more than 10-12,000 miles, the entire set should probably be replaced with a fresh set of the same heat range.

Oil Deposits

APPEARANCE: The firing end of the plug is covered with a wet, oily coating.

CAUSE: The problem is poor oil control. On high mileage engines, oil is leaking past the rings or valve guides into the combustion chamber. A common cause is also a plugged PCV valve, and a ruptured fuel pump diaphragm can also cause this condition. Oil fouled plugs such as these are often found in new or recently overhauled engines, before normal oil control is achieved, and can be cleaned and reinstalled.

RECOMMENDATION: A hotter spark plug may temporarily relieve the problem, but the engine is probably in need of work.

Incorrect Heat Range

APPEARANCE: The effects of high temperature on a spark plug are indicated by clean white, often blistered insulator. This can also be accompanied by excessive wear of the electrode, and the absence of deposits.

CAUSE: Check for the correct spark plug heat range. A plug which is too hot for the engine can result in overheating. A car operated mostly at high speeds can require a colder plug. Also check ignition timing, cooling system level, fuel mixture and leaking intake manifold.

RECOMMENDATION: If all ignition and engine adjustments are known to be correct, and no other malfunction exists, install spark plugs one heat range colder.

Photos Courtesy Fram Corporation

Carbon Deposits

APPEARANCE: Carbon fouling is easily identified by the presence of dry, soft, black, sooty deposits.

CAUSE: Changing the heat range can often lead to carbon fouling, as can prolonged slow, stop-and-start driving. If the heat range is correct, carbon fouling can be attributed to a rich fuel mixture, sticking choke, clogged air cleaner, worn breaker points, retarded timing or low compression. If only one or two plugs are carbon fouled, check for corroded or cracked wires on the affected plugs. Also look for cracks in the distributor cap between the towers of affected cylinders.

RECOMMENDATION: After the problem is corrected, these plugs can be cleaned and reinstalled if not worn severely.

MMT Fouled

APPEARANCE: Spark plugs fouled by MMT (Methycyclopentadienyl Maganese Tricarbonyl) have reddish, rusty appearance on the insulator and side electrode.

CAUSE: MMT is an anti-knock additive in gasoline used to replace lead. During the combustion process, the MMT leaves a reddish deposit on the insulator and side electrode.

RECOMMENDATION: No engine malfunction is indicated and the deposits will not affect plug performance any more than lead deposits (see Ash Deposits). MMT fouled plugs can be cleaned, regapped and reinstalled.

High Speed Glazing

APPEARANCE: Glazing appears as shiny coating on the plug, either yellow or tan in color.

CAUSE: During hard, fast acceleration, plug temperatures rise suddenly. Deposits from normal combustion have no chance to fluff-off; instead, they melt on the insulator forming an electrically conductive coating which causes misfiring.

RECOMMENDATION: Glazed plugs are not easily cleaned. They should be replaced with a fresh set of plugs of the correct heat range. If the condition recurs, using plugs with a heat range one step colder may cure the problem.

Ash (Lead) Deposits

APPEARANCE: Ash deposits are characterized by light brown or white colored deposits crusted on the side or center electrodes. In some cases it may give the plug a rusty appearance.

CAUSE: Ash deposits are normally derived from oil or fuel additives burned during normal combustion. Normally they are harmless, though excessive amounts can cause misfiring. If deposits are excessive in short mileage, the valve guides may be worn.

RECOMMENDATION: Ash-fouled plugs can be cleaned, gapped and reinstalled.

Detonation

APPEARANCE: Detonation is usually characterized by a broken plug insulator.

CAUSE: A portion of the fuel charge will begin to burn spontaneously, from the increased heat following ignition. The explosion that results applies extreme pressure to engine components, frequently damaging spark plugs and pistons.

Detonation can result by over-advanced ignition timing, inferior gasoline (low octane) lean air/fuel mixture, poor carburetion, engine lugging or an increase in compression ratio due to combustion chamber deposits or engine modification.

RECOMMENDATION: Replace the plugs after correcting the problem.

Photos Courtesy Champion Spark Plug Co.

EMISSION CONTROLS

13. Be aware of the general condition of the emission control system. It contributes to reduced pollution and should be serviced regularly to maintain efficient engine operation.

14. Check all vacuum lines for dried, cracked or brittle conditions. Something as simple as a leaking vacuum hose can cause poor performance and loss of economy.

15. Avoid tampering with the emission control system. Attempting to improve fuel econ-

FUEL SYSTEM

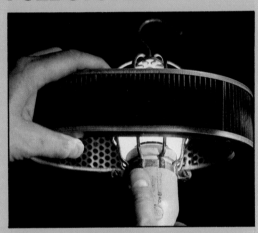

Check the air filter with a light behind it. If you can see light through the filter it can be reused.

Extremely clogged filters should be discarded and replaced with a new one.

18. Replace the air filter regularly. A dirty air filter richens the air/fuel mixture and can increase fuel consumption as much as 10%. Tests show that ⅓ of all vehicles have air filters in need of replacement.

19. Replace the fuel filter at least as often as recommended.

20. Set the idle speed and carburetor mixture to specifications.

21. Check the automatic choke. A sticking or malfunctioning choke wastes gas.

22. During the summer months, adjust the automatic choke for a leaner mixture which will produce faster engine warm-ups.

COOLING SYSTEM

29. Be sure all accessory drive belts are in good condition. Check for cracks or wear.

30. Adjust all accessory drive belts to proper tension.

31. Check all hoses for swollen areas, worn spots, or loose clamps.

32. Check coolant level in the radiator or expansion tank.

33. Be sure the thermostat is operating properly. A stuck thermostat delays engine warm-up and a cold engine uses nearly twice as much fuel as a warm engine.

34. Drain and replace the engine coolant at least as often as recommended. Rust and scale

TIRES & WHEELS

38. Check the tire pressure often with a pencil type gauge. Tests by a major tire manufacturer show that 90% of all vehicles have at least 1 tire improperly inflated. Better mileage can be achieved by over-inflating tires, but never exceed the maximum inflation pressure on the side of the tire.

39. If possible, install radial tires. Radial tires deliver as much as ½ mpg more than bias belted tires.

40. Avoid installing super-wide tires. They only create extra rolling resistance and decrease fuel mileage. Stick to the manufacturer's recommendations.

41. Have the wheels properly balanced.

omy by tampering with emission controls is more likely to worsen fuel economy than improve it. Emission control changes on modern engines are not readily reversible.

16. Clean (or replace) the EGR valve and lines as recommended.

17. Be sure that all vacuum lines and hoses are reconnected properly after working under the hood. An unconnected or misrouted vacuum line can wreak havoc with engine performance.

23. Check for fuel leaks at the carburetor, fuel pump, fuel lines and fuel tank. Be sure all lines and connections are tight.

24. Periodically check the tightness of the carburetor and intake manifold attaching nuts and bolts. These are a common place for vacuum leaks to occur.

25. Clean the carburetor periodically and lubricate the linkage.

26. The condition of the tailpipe can be an excellent indicator of proper engine combustion. After a long drive at highway speeds, the inside of the tailpipe should be a light grey in color. Black or soot on the insides indicates an overly rich mixture.

27. Check the fuel pump pressure. The fuel pump may be supplying more fuel than the engine needs.

28. Use the proper grade of gasoline for your engine. Don't try to compensate for knocking or "pinging" by advancing the ignition timing. This practice will only increase plug temperature and the chances of detonation or pre-ignition with relatively little performance gain.

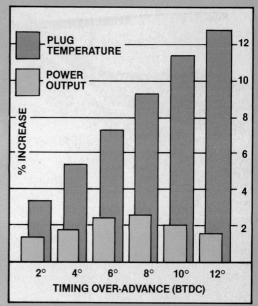

Increasing ignition timing past the specified setting results in a drastic increase in spark plug temperature with increased chance of detonation or preignition. Performance increase is considerably less. (Photo courtesy Champion Spark Plug Co.)

that form in the engine should be flushed out to allow the engine to operate at peak efficiency.

35. Clean the radiator of debris that can decrease cooling efficiency.

36. Install a flex-type or electric cooling fan, if you don't have a clutch type fan. Flex fans use curved plastic blades to push more air at low speeds when more cooling is needed; at high speeds the blades flatten out for less resistance. Electric fans only run when the engine temperature reaches a predetermined level.

37. Check the radiator cap for a worn or cracked gasket. If the cap does not seal properly, the cooling system will not function properly.

42. Be sure the front end is correctly aligned. A misaligned front end actually has wheels going in differed directions. The increased drag can reduce fuel economy by .3 mpg.

43. Correctly adjust the wheel bearings. Wheel bearings that are adjusted too tight increase rolling resistance.

Check tire pressures regularly with a reliable pocket type gauge. Be sure to check the pressure on a cold tire.

GENERAL MAINTENANCE

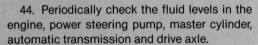

Check the fluid levels (particularly engine oil) on a regular basis. Be sure to check the oil for grit, water or other contamination.

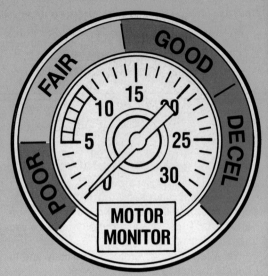

A vacuum gauge is another excellent indicator of internal engine condition and can also be installed in the dash as a mileage indicator.

44. Periodically check the fluid levels in the engine, power steering pump, master cylinder, automatic transmission and drive axle.

45. Change the oil at the recommended interval and change the filter at every oil change. Dirty oil is thick and causes extra friction between moving parts, cutting efficiency and increasing wear. A worn engine requires more frequent tune-ups and gets progressively worse fuel economy. In general, use the lightest viscosity oil for the driving conditions you will encounter.

46. Use the recommended viscosity fluids in the transmission and axle.

47. Be sure the battery is fully charged for fast starts. A slow starting engine wastes fuel.

48. Be sure battery terminals are clean and tight.

49. Check the battery electrolyte level and add distilled water if necessary.

50. Check the exhaust system for crushed pipes, blockages and leaks.

51. Adjust the brakes. Dragging brakes or brakes that are not releasing create increased drag on the engine.

52. Install a vacuum gauge or miles-per-gallon gauge. These gauges visually indicate engine vacuum in the intake manifold. High vacuum = good mileage and low vacuum = poorer mileage. The gauge can also be an excellent indicator of internal engine conditions.

53. Be sure the clutch is properly adjusted. A slipping clutch wastes fuel.

54. Check and periodically lubricate the heat control valve in the exhaust manifold. A sticking or inoperative valve prevents engine warm-up and wastes gas.

55. Keep accurate records to check fuel economy over a period of time. A sudden drop in fuel economy may signal a need for tune-up or other maintenance.

prevent metal chips from entering the carb throat. Use a $\frac{5}{32}$ in. (4mm) drill bit to drill out the retaining rivets holding the choke cover. Remove the retaining ring.

3. Remove the choke cover. Take care to retain the gears within the choke cover and case.

To install:

4. Reinstall the cover and adjust it so the index marks align.

5. Install gears A and B in the grooves in the choke cove and the case.

6. Reinstall the retainer ring and secure it with new rivets.

7. Reinstall the air cleaner.

FLOAT LEVEL ADJUSTMENT

With the vehicle on level ground and at normal operating temperature, check the primary and secondary fuel level inspection windows on the side of the carburetor. Snap the throttle from idle to 3000 rpm several times, then allow the engine to idle. If the fuel level is not touching the dot, adjust it by turning the adjusting screws which are located in recessed bosses above the inspection windows.

NOTE: *Do not turn the adjusting screws more than ⅛ turn every 15 seconds.*

When the correct fuel level is achieved in the window(s), paint the adjusting screws with a dot of white paint.

1984–87 Prelude

THROTTLE CABLE

1. The throttle cable should operate smoothly with no binding. If the cable is kinked or binding, replace it.

2. Check the cable free play at the linkage. The cable should be loose enough to deflect $\frac{3}{16}$–$\frac{3}{8}$ in. (4.7–9.5mm) between the locknut and the bell crank.

3. If the deflection is not correct, loosen the locknut. Turn the adjusting nut to tighten or loosen the cable as necessary. Once properly set, tighten the locknut.

4. Check the throttle plates (valves) while an assistant holds the accelerator pedal to the floor. The throttles should be fully open; the throttle plates should be horizontal in the bores. Check carefully to see that the throttle plate is opening fully but is not going "over center"; that is, passing the fully open position and sitting at an angle. Additionally, the throttle plates must close quickly and smoothly when the accelerator pedal is released.

5. If the vehicle is equipped with automatic transmission, adjust the transmission throttle control cable.

CHOKE COIL TENSION AND LINKAGE

1. The engine must be cold before performing these tests.

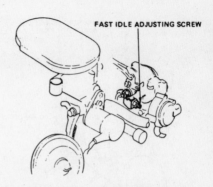

Loosen the locknut before adjusting the fast idle

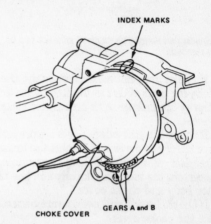

The index marks must be aligned when reinstalling the choke cover

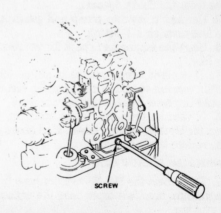

Remove the throttle controller bracket

2. Remove the air cleaner.

3. Depress the accelerator to the floor and release it smoothly to set the choke plate. The plate should close completely. If engine temperature is above 82°F (28°C), the plate will not close totally but should move to within ⅛ in. (3mm) of total closure.

4. If the choke plate closes properly, continue with the choke opener test.

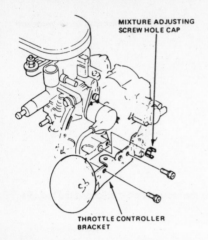

MIXTURE ADJUSTING SCREW HOLE CAP

THROTTLE CONTROLLER BRACKET

The adjusting screw may be reached after the cap or plug is removed

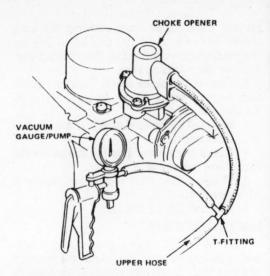

CHOKE OPENER

VACUUM GAUGE/PUMP

T-FITTING

UPPER HOSE

Testing the Prelude choke opener

5. If choke does not close completely, check carefully for signs of dirt or binding in the linkage. Spray the linkage with carburetor cleaner and retest.

6. If the choke still will not operate properly, remove the choke cover and inspect the linkage for freedom of motion. When reassembling, make certain the index marks align on the carburetor body and choke cover.

7. If the choke still will not operate correctly, replace the choke cover.

CHOKE OPENER

1. With the engine cold, disconnect the upper hose from the choke opener.

2. Connect a vacuum pump and gauge into the line through a T-fitting.

3. Start the engine and check for vacuum in the line.

4. If coolant temperature is above 59°F (15°C), vacuum should be available. No vacuum should be present below this temperature.

5. If vacuum tests are not as specified, inspect for blocked vacuum hoses. If all hoses are OK, replace thermovalve A.

CRANKING LEAK SOLENOID VALVE

1. Disconnect the No. 20 vacuum hose from the vacuum manifold pipes near the emission control box.

2. With the ignition OFF, apply vacuum to the hose; it should be possible to draw a vacuum. If vacuum is not held, replace the cranking leak solenoid.

3. With the vacuum pump still attached and showing vacuum, switch the ignition to START. The vacuum should be bled off. If it is not bled off, check that voltage is present at the cranking leak solenoid valve with the ignition in the START position. If voltage is present, replace the valve.

CHOKE COVER REPLACEMENT

1. Remove the air cleaner assembly.

2. Cover the carburetor with a clean rag to prevent metal chips from entering the carb throat. Use a $\frac{5}{32}$ in. or (4mm) drill bit to drill out the retaining rivets holding the choke cover. Remove the retaining ring.

3. Remove the choke cover.

To install:

4. Reinstall the cover and adjust it so the index marks align.

5. Reinstall the retainer ring and secure it with new rivets.

6. Reinstall the air cleaner.

FLOAT LEVEL

With the carburetors and float chambers removed, hold the assembly so that the float chamber surface is inclined about 30° from vertical. Use a float level gauge (Honda tool 07401–0010000 or equivalent) to measure the float level with the float tip lightly contacting the float valve. Correct measurement is 15–17mm (0.56–0.64 in). Adjust the floats as needed.

1986–89 Accord

CHOKE COIL TENSION AND LINKAGE

1. The engine must be cold before performing these tests.

2. Remove the air cleaner.

3. Depress the accelerator to the floor and release it smoothly to set the choke plate. The plate should close completely. If engine temperature is above 82°F (28°C), the plate will not close totally but should close to within ⅛ in. (3mm) of total closure.

4. If the choke plate closes properly, continue with the fast idle unloader test.

5. If choke does not close completely, check

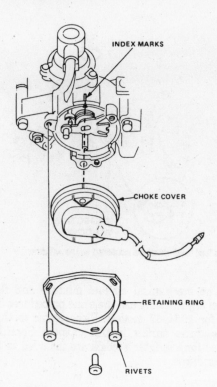

Prelude choke cover

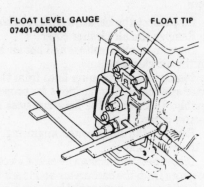

Setting Prelude float level requires removal of the carburetors and float chambers

carefully for signs of dirt or binding in the linkage. Spray the linkage with carburetor cleaner and retest.

6. If the choke still will not operate properly, remove the choke cover and inspect the linkage for freedom of motion. When reassembling, make certain the index marks align on the carburetor body and choke cover.

7. If the choke still will not operate correctly, replace the choke cover.

FAST IDLE UNLOADER

Cold Engine

1. Disconnect the two hoses from the fast idle unloader.

2. Depress the accelerator to the floor and release it smoothly to engage the fast idle cam.

3. Start the engine; it should run at fast idle. If it does not, remove the choke cover and check the operation of the fast idle cam.

4. Connect a vacuum pump to the inner fitting of the unloader and apply vacuum. The fast idle speed should drop with vacuum applied. If the idle speed drops, allow the engine to warm up fully and perform the hot engine tests.

5. If idle speed does not drop, check the unloader for leaks, blockage or damage. Remove the choke cover and check the unloader rod for freedom of movement. Repair as necessary.

Hot Engine

1. As the engine warms up, the idle speed should drop below 1400 rpm as the unloader pulls the choke linkage off the fast idle cam. If this is true, perform the fast idle check.

2. If the idle rpm does not drop below 1400 rpm, disconnect the tow unloader hoses. Check that vacuum is present.

3. If vacuum is present, check the unloader for leaks or blockage. If necessary, remove the choke cover and inspect the unloader rod for freedom of motion.

4. If there is no vacuum at the inner fitting, check for vacuum at the choke opener and thermovalve A.

5. If there is no vacuum at the outer fitting, check thermovalve A and replace it if necessary.

FAST IDLE

1. Start the engine and warm it up to normal temperature.

2. Switch the engine OFF; connect a tachometer.

3. Disconnect and plug the inner vacuum hose of the fast idle unloader.

4. Engage the fast idle cam by opening and closing the throttle fully while holding the choke closed.

5. Restart the engine. Fast idle should be 2000–3000 rpm.

6. If fast idle is not at specification, turn the fast idle adjusting screw.

FLOAT LEVEL ADJUSTMENT

With the vehicle on level ground and at normal operating temperature, check the primary and secondary fuel level inspection windows on the side of the carburetor. Snap the throttle from idle to 3000 rpm several times, then allow the engine to idle. If the fuel level is centered in the window, adjust it by turning the adjusting screws which are located in recessed bosses above the inspection windows.

NOTE: *Do not turn the adjusting screws more than ⅛ turn every 15 seconds.*

When the correct fuel level is achieved in the

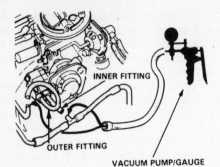

Testing the unloader on a cold engine

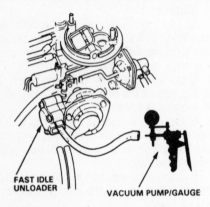

Fast idle unloader hot engine vacuum tests

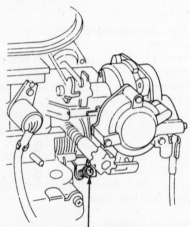

FAST IDLE ADJUSTING SCREW

The fast idle adjuster is located below the mechanical idle adjusting screw. It can be difficult to reach

window(s), paint the adjusting screws with a dot of white paint.

1988–90 Prelude

The carburetors on these vehicles are controlled by the PGM-CARB system. Please refer to the PGM-CARB troubleshooting charts in Chapter 4.

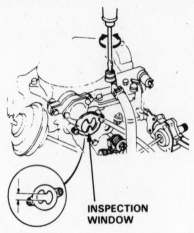

INSPECTION WINDOW

The fuel level must be centered in the window

The mechanical air/fuel mixture and float level adjustments use the same procedures listed for 1984–87 models. Please refer to those procedures earlier in this chapter. Specifications for the later models are included in the procedures.

REMOVAL AND INSTALLATION

Accord

1. Disconnect the negative battery cable.
2. Remove the air cleaner cover.
3. Disconnect the fresh air and hot air hoses from the air cleaner.
4. Disconnect the vacuum lines from the air cleaner and mark their positions for proper reassembly. Disconnect the breather hose from the valve cover.
5. Remove the air cleaner mounting nuts and the air cleaner.
6. Disconnect the vacuum lines and electrical connectors from the carburetor and mark their positions for proper reassembly.
7. Disconnect the throttle cable. Disconnect the throttle control cable and/or cruise control cables if so equipped.
8. Disconnect and plug the fuel lines.
9. Remove the carburetor mounting nuts. Lift the carburetor off the mounting studs.

NOTE: *On 1986–89, the carburetor base or insulator contains the Early Fuel Evaporator (EFE) screen. The grid is heated electrically and aids in vaporizing the fuel spray during cold operation. The screen must be protected from damage during disassembly.*

To install:

10. Reinstall the carburetor on the insulator. Take care to keep debris from falling onto the EFE screen. Tighten the carburetor mounting nuts to 24 Nm (17 ft. lbs).

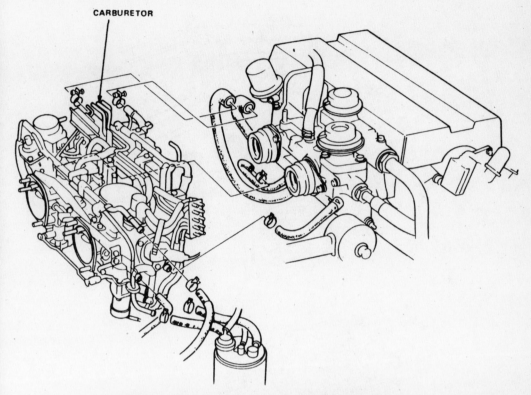

CARBURETOR

The Prelude carburetor assembly includes the left and right carburetor

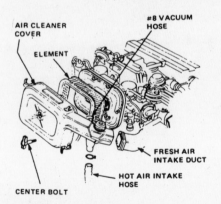

AIR CLEANER COVER

ELEMENT

#8 VACUUM HOSE

FRESH AIR INTAKE DUCT

HOT AIR INTAKE HOSE

CENTER BOLT

Prelude air cleaner components

11. Connect the fuel lines and secure the clamps.

12. Connect the cruise control and/or throttle control cables if they were removed. Connect and adjust the throttle cable.

13. Reinstall the vacuum lines to their correct ports. Double check the installation.

14. Connect the electrical connectors.

15. Install the air cleaner. Connect the fresh and hot air hoses. connect the breather hose(s) and vacuum lines to the air cleaner as necessary.

16. Connect the negative battery cable. Start the engine and adjust the engine as necessary.

Prelude

REMOVAL

1. Disconnect the fresh air intake duct and the hot air intake hose from the air cleaner.

2. Disconnect the vacuum hose to the hot air intake control diaphragm.

3. Remove the air cleaner cover and the filter element.

4. Disconnect the breather hose from the valve cover.

5. Carefully label and disconnect the vacuum hoses at the base of the air cleaner.

6. Disconnect the electrical connectors to the solenoid at the top of the air cleaner base.

7. Remove the 10mm nuts under the air cleaner base.

8. Remove the 4 nuts, air screens and their flanges.

9. Remove the air cleaner base.

10. Carefully label, then disconnect, the vacuum hose connections running to the carburetor assembly.

11. Disconnect the throttle cable.

12. Disconnect the vacuum hoses at the vacuum tube manifold.

13. Drain the coolant and remove the 3 coolant hoses at the thermowax valve.

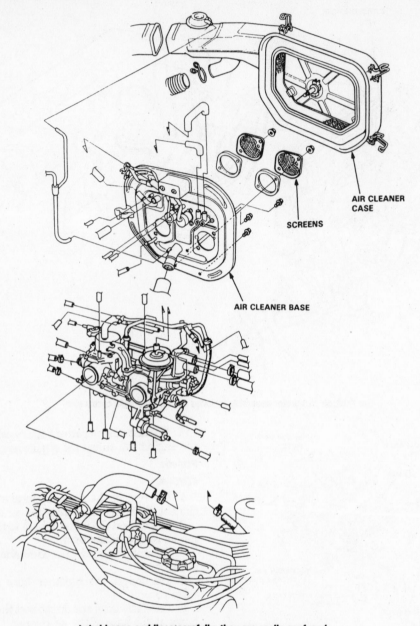

AIR CLEANER
CASE

SCREENS

AIR CLEANER BASE

Label hoses and lines carefully; they are easily confused

14. Disconnect the vent hose running from the canister to the air vent cut-off solenoid.

15. Disconnect the canister purge hose at the vacuum manifold.

16. Disconnect the carburetor wiring connector and the connector to the choke heater.

17. Remove the main fuel hose from the right side of the vacuum manifold.

18. Loosen the insulator bands and remove the carburetors as a unit with the vacuum manifold attached.

SEPARATION

1. Remove the four screws and disconnect the vacuum tubes from the carburetors; remove the upper manifold.

2. Disconnect the connectors for the fuel cut-off solenoid and air vent cut-off solenoid. Remove the vacuum hose from the carburetor. Remove the two screws and then remove the lower vacuum manifold.

3. Disconnect the fuel hoses from the carburetors and remove the two screws. Remove the fuel line.

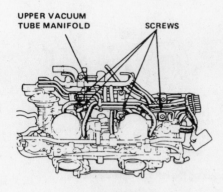

UPPER VACUUM
TUBE MANIFOLD

SCREWS

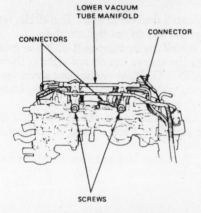

LOWER VACUUM
TUBE MANIFOLD

CONNECTOR

CONNECTORS

SCREWS

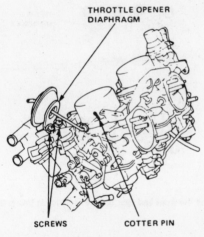

THROTTLE OPENER
DIAPHRAGM

SCREWS

COTTER PIN

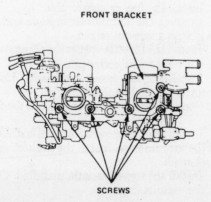

FRONT BRACKET

SCREWS

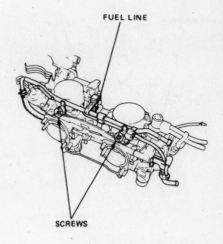

FUEL LINE

SCREWS

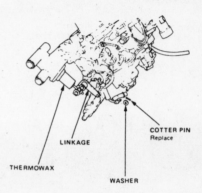

COTTER PIN
Replace

LINKAGE

THERMOWAX

WASHER

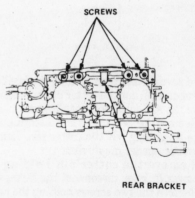

SCREWS

REAR BRACKET

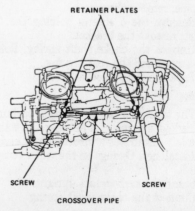

RETAINER PLATES

SCREW

SCREW

CROSSOVER PIPE

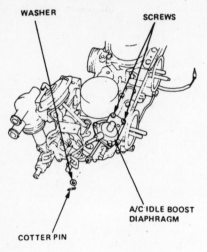

WASHER

SCREWS

A/C IDLE BOOST
DIAPHRAGM

COTTER PIN

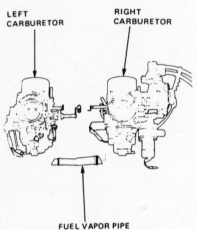

LEFT
CARBURETOR

RIGHT
CARBURETOR

FUEL VAPOR PIPE

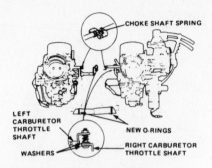

CHOKE SHAFT SPRING

LEFT
CARBURETOR
THROTTLE
SHAFT

NEW O-RINGS

RIGHT CARBURETOR
THROTTLE SHAFT

WASHERS

Connecting the left and right carburetor

5. Install the rear bracket. Install the retaining screws but do not tighten them.

6. Install the front bracket with new gaskets. Install the screws but do not tighten them.

WARNING: *Make certain the screw lengths are correct for the holes. Incorrect placement may cause carburetor damage.*

7. Check that the choke and throttle shafts move smoothly; there should be no binding or restriction.

8. Tighten the screws in the correct sequence.

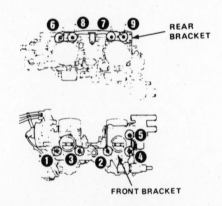

REAR
BRACKET

FRONT BRACKET

Tighten the front and rear bracket screws in this order

4. remove the 2 screws holding the idle boost diaphragm. Pull out the cotter pin and washer; remove the A/C idle boost diaphragm.

5. Remove the two screws and disconnect the linkage by pulling out the cotter pin. Remove the throttle opener diaphragm.

6. Remove the cotter pin holding the thermowax linkage; disconnect the linkage.

7. Remove the two screws holding the crossover pipe; remove the pipe.

8. Remove the 5 screws holding the front bracket; remove the bracket.

9. Unhook the choke shaft spring. Remove the 4 screws and the rear bracket.

10. Separate the two carburetors.

ASSEMBLY

1. The throttle shaft of the right carburetor has a forked end; insert it between the washers on the left carburetor's throttle shaft end.

2. Install new O-rings on the vapor tube and install it.

3. Stand the carburetors upright.

4. Connect the choke shaft spring.

9. Install the fuel crossover pipe.

10. Connect the thermowax linkage and secure it with a new cotter pin.

11. Install the throttle opener diaphragm and secure it with a new cotter pin.

12. Install the idle boost diaphragm. Use a new cotter pin and washer.

13. Connect the fuel hoses and secure the fuel line.

14. Install the lower vacuum manifold. Connect the vacuum hose. Install the connectors to the solenoids.

15. Install the upper vacuum manifold. Connect the vacuum lines.

INSTALLATION

1. Place the carburetors in position. Make certain they are fully seated and tight in the insulators. Install the retaining bands.

2. Install the main fuel hose to the right side of the vacuum manifold.

3. Connect the canister purge hose at the vacuum manifold.

4. Connect the canister vent hose.

5. Connect the 3 coolant hoses at the thermowax valve.

6. Connect the vacuum hoses to the vacuum manifold.

7. Install the throttle cable.

8. Connect the vacuum lines at the carburetor.

9. Install the air cleaner base.

10. Install the air screens and flanges.

11. Install the 2 10mm bolts under the air cleaner base.

12. Attach the connectors to the solenoid at the top of the air cleaner base.

13. Connect the vacuum hoses to the air cleaner base.

14. Connect the breather hose to the valve cover.

15. Install the air cleaner housing, filter element and cover. Connect the vacuum hoses and air ducting.

OVERHAUL

CAUTION: *Carburetor cleaner is a highly caustic liquid; wear eye protection whenever spray or liquid cleaner is in use or when compressed air is in use. Immediately remove cleaner from any painted surfaces on the car.*

Efficient carburetion depends greatly on careful cleaning and inspection during overhaul since dirt, gum, water or varnish in or on the carburetor parts are often responsible for poor performance.

Carefully disassemble the carburetor, referring often to the instructions and illustrations provided in the kit. Keep all similar and look-alike parts segregated during disassembly and cleaning to avoid accidental interchange during assembly.

When the carburetor is disassembled, wash all parts (except diaphragms, electric choke units, pump plunger and any other plastic, fiber or rubber parts) with carburetor solvent or spray. Do not leave parts in the solvent any longer than is necessary to sufficiently loosen the deposits. Excessive cleaning may remove the special finish from the float bowl and choke valve bodies, leaving these parts unfit for service. Blow them dry with compressed air or allow them to air dry.

Blow out all passages and jets with com-pressed air and be sure that there are no restrictions or blockages. Never use wire or similar tools to clean jets, fuel passages or air bleeds. Clean all jets and valves separately to avoid accidental interchange.

Check all parts for wear or damage. If wear or damage is found, replace the defective parts. Especially check the following:

1. Check the float needle and seat for wear. If wear is found, replace the complete assembly.

2. Check the float hinge pin for wear and the float(s) for dents or distortion. Replace the float if fuel has leaked into it.

3. Check the throttle and choke shaft bores for wear or an out-of-round condition. Damage or wear to the throttle arm, shaft or shaft bore will often require replacement of the throttle body. These parts require a close tolerance of fit; wear may allow air leakage, which could affect starting and idling.

NOTE: *Throttle shafts and bushings are not included in overhaul kits. If worn, the entire carburetor must be replaced.*

4. Inspect the idle mixture adjusting needles for burrs or grooves. Any such condition requires replacement of the needle, since you will not be able to obtain a satisfactory idle.

5. Test the accelerator pump check valves. Replace the valve if necessary.

6. Check the bowl cover for warped surfaces with a straightedge.

7. Closely inspect the valves and seats for wear and damage, replacing as necessary.

8. After the carburetor is assembled, check the choke valve for freedom of operation.

Carburetor kits are required for each overhaul. These kits contain all gaskets and new parts to replace those that deteriorate most rapidly. Failure to replace all parts supplied with the kit (especially gaskets) can result in poor performance later.

After cleaning and checking all components, reassemble the carburetor, using new parts and referring frequently to the instructions provided with the kit. When reassembling, make sure that all screws and jets are tight in their seats, but do not overtighten, as the tips will be distorted. Tighten all screws gradually, in rotation. Do not tighten needle valves into their seats; uneven jetting will result. Be sure to adjust the float level when reassembling.

Accord

Individual float and gasket kits for each specific Accord carburetor are available at Honda dealers. These kits contain detailed instructions for the individual carburetor. These procedures may generally be performed with the carburetor installed on the engine. This "on-car" repair is a great time saver and cures many problems.

Prelude

Prelude carburetor repair kits and replacement parts are available through your Honda dealer. The following procedure is used to disassemble each carburetor. When overhauling, inspect each component for wear. Clean each passage carefully and replace worn parts as necessary.

1. Remove and separate the carburetors.

2. Remove the vacuum chamber; remove the vacuum piston and spring.

3. Inspect the piston and needle for wear or damage, replacing parts as necessary.

4. Remove the seal ring and O-ring.

5. Remove the two screws, plate, jet covers, and gasket from the carburetor. This will expose the air passages.

6. Remove the primary and secondary main air jets and the slow air jet. Do NOT allow the jets to become confused; label and isolate each one as soon as it is removed.

7. Remove the accelerator pump cover, spring, and diaphragm from the left carburetor.

8. Inspect the diaphragm and spring for cracks or damage, replacing parts as necessary.

9. Remove the 3 screws, power valve cover, spring and the diaphragm. Inspect the diaphragm and spring for damage.

10. Remove the air vent cutoff solenoid valve at the right carburetor.

11. Remove the fuel cut-off solenoid valve.

12. Remove the float bowl.

13. Remove the float arm pin, float and float valve.

14. Remove the secondary main jet and needle jet holder.

15. Remove the primary main jet; it is press fit with an O-ring.

16. Remove the power valve jet.

17. Remove the needle jet, primary slow jet (located below the primary main jet) and the power valve nozzle, located under the power valve jet.

18. Clean all passages with spray carburetor cleaner; blow the passages clean with compressed air if possible.

To install:

19. Install each jet into its proper position. Use new O-rings and/or filter where necessary.

20. Install the float valve, float and arm pin. Set the float level.

21. Install the fuel cut-off solenoid valve.

22. Install the air vent cut-off solenoid valve on the right carburetor.

23. Install the power valve diaphragm, spring and cover.

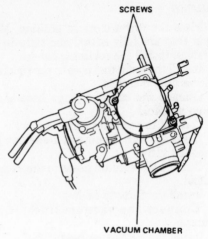

SCREWS

VACUUM CHAMBER

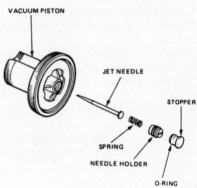

VACUUM PISTON

JET NEEDLE

STOPPER

SPRING

NEEDLE HOLDER

O-RING

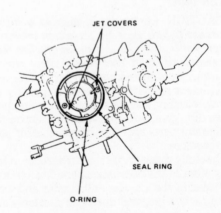

JET COVERS

SEAL RING

O-RING

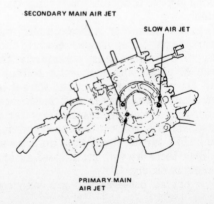

SECONDARY MAIN AIR JET

SLOW AIR JET

PRIMARY MAIN AIR JET

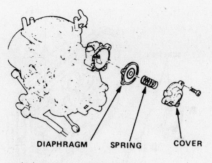

DIAPHRAGM   SPRING   COVER

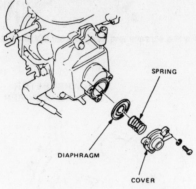

SPRING

DIAPHRAGM

COVER

SCREWS

AIR VENT CUT-OFF SOLENOID
VALVE

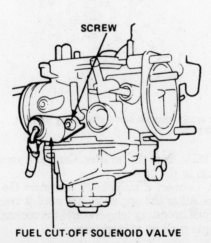

SCREW

FUEL CUT-OFF SOLENOID VALVE

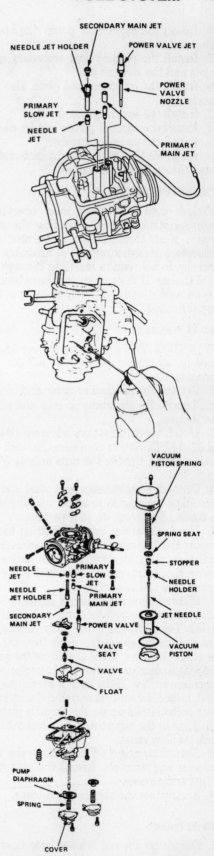

SECONDARY MAIN JET

NEEDLE JET HOLDER   POWER VALVE JET

POWER
VALVE
NOZZLE

PRIMARY
SLOW JET

NEEDLE
JET

PRIMARY
MAIN JET

VACUUM
PISTON SPRING

SPRING SEAT

STOPPER

NEEDLE
HOLDER

NEEDLE
JET

PRIMARY
SLOW
JET

NEEDLE
JET HOLDER

PRIMARY
MAIN JET

SECONDARY
MAIN JET

POWER VALVE

JET NEEDLE

VACUUM
PISTON

VALVE
SEAT

VALVE

FLOAT

PUMP
DIAPHRAGM

SPRING

COVER

24. Install the accelerator pump diaphragm, spring and cover.

25. Install the primary and secondary main air jets and the slow air jet.

26. Install the jet covers and plate. Use new gaskets.

27. Install the seal ring and O-ring.

28. Install the vacuum piston and jet needle.

29. Install the vacuum chamber.

30. Assemble the left and right carburetors. Install the carburetor assembly.

SYNCHRONIZATION

Prelude dual carburetors must operate in synchronization, that is, providing the same amount of air through each carburetor. The carburetors are synchronized at assembly and generally do not require resetting through the life of the car. If the carburetors have been removed and disassembled, they must be resynchronized.

1984–87 Prelude

WARNING: *The use of the correct special tool or equivalent is REQUIRED for this procedure.*

1. Remove the air cleaner cover and filter.

2. Remove the air intake screens and air intake flanges.

3. Install synchronization adapters (Honda tool 07504–SB00000 or equivalent) to each carburetor intake; tighten the nuts only to 5 Nm (3.5 ft. lbs).

4. Connect a tachometer and start the engine. Allow the engine to warm up fully until the cooling fans come on at least once.

5. Use a carburetor synchronization tool to measure the flow rate through both adapters. If the flow rates are identical, shut the engine off, remove the adapters and reassemble the air cleaner. The test is complete.

6. If the air flow rates are not identical, loosen the adjusting screw lock nut and adjust as needed. The adjusting screw only affects the right carburetor, so use the value from the left one as the baseline. Turn the adjusting screw clockwise to decrease airflow; counterclockwise to increase airflow. If the airflow cannot be balanced, inspect for air leaks around the carburetor or carbon build-up on the throttle plate.

7. Tighten the adjusting screw locknut. Recheck the flow rates.

8. Shut the engine OFF. Remove the synchronizer and adapters. Install the air intake flanges and screens.

9. Reassemble the air filter and cover.

1988–90 Prelude

1. Disconnect the red braided hose (marked

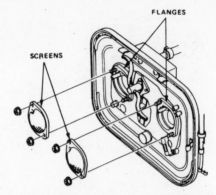

Remove the screens and flanges from the air cleaner base

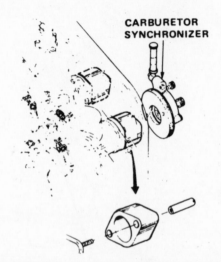

Use of the carburetor synchronizer requires installation of adaptors

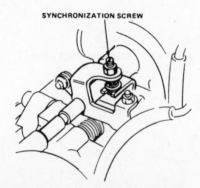

The synchronization screw affects only the right carburetor

PURGE) from the canister. Connect a vacuum gauge to the hose.

2. Connect a tachometer and start the engine. Allow the engine to run until it reaches normal operating temperature; the cooling fan should cycle on at least once.

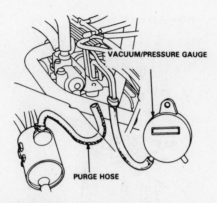

A vacuum gauge is required to synchronize late-model Prelude carburetors

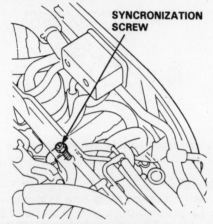

Turn the synchronization screw to adjust

3. Turn the idle speed adjusting screw until engine speed is 3000 rpm. Note the reading on the gauge.

4. While the engine speed is at 3000 rpm, pinch the smooth red vacuum hose under the choke housing and note the change, if any, in the gauge reading.

5. If there was no change on the gauge, the carburetors are properly synchronized.

6. If the reading changed when the hose was pinched, adjust the synchronization screw until the readings are the same.

7. Remove the vacuum gauge and connect the PURGE hose to the canister. Remove the tachometer.

8. Reset the idle speed.

PROGRAMMED FUEL INJECTION (PGM-FI)

The PGM-FI is a fully electronic fuel metering system. The control unit receives electric input signals from many sensors. Based on pre-pro-grammed values and computations, the output signals are controlled so as to deliver a precise amount of fuel into the engine for any combination of operating load, temperature or rpm. This precise control also allows excellent management of engine emissions and fuel economy.

SERVICE PRECAUTIONS

• Always safely relieve the fuel pressure before loosening or removing any fuel-bearing lines or components.

• Always replace washers at banjo-type fuel fittings any time they are loosened or removed.

• Always replace O-rings and seals associated with fuel lines and components any time they are removed or disassembled.

• Always double-check fuel fittings for leaks after re-assembly; attend to leaks immediately.

• Do not operate the fuel pump when the fuel lines are empty.

• Do not operate the fuel pump when removed from the fuel tank.

• Do not reuse fuel hose clamps.

• Make sure all ECU harness connectors are fastened securely. A poor connection can cause an extremely high surge voltage in the coil and condenser and result in damage to integrated circuits.

• Keep ECU all parts and harnesses dry during service.

• Before attempting to remove any parts, turn OFF the ignition switch and disconnect the battery ground cable.

• Always use a 12 volt battery as a power source.

• Do not attempt to disconnect the battery cables with the engine running.

• Do not disconnect any wiring connector with the engine running, unless specifically instructed to do so.

• Do not apply battery power directly to injectors.

Relieving Fuel Pressure

CAUTION: *Keep open flames or sparks away from the work area. Do not smoke while working on the fuel system. Be sure to relieve fuel pressure while engine is OFF. Have a Class B-C (dry powder) fire extinguisher within arm's reach at all times.*

1. Disconnect the negative battery cable.

2. Use a box end wrench on the 6mm service bolt at the top of the fuel filter, while counter-holding the banjo bolt with another wrench.

3. Place a rag or a shop towel over 6mm service bolt.

4. Slowly loosen the service bolt 1 complete turn. Pressurized fuel will be release from this connection.

5. Dispose of the fuel soaked rag safely, treating it as a flammable hazard.

NOTE: *A fuel pressure gauge can be attached at 6mm service bolt hole. Always replace the washer between the service bolt and the banjo bolt whenever service bolt is loosened to relieve fuel pressure. Replace all washers whenever bolts are removed to disassemble parts.*

Electric Fuel Pump

All Accords and Preludes covered by this book use an electric fuel pump located either near or inside the fuel tank. Accords through 1985 and Preludes through 1987 use an external fuel pump mounted under the car just forward of the left rear wheel. All other (later) vehicles use an electric fuel pump mounted inside the fuel tank. Note that on some vehicles, the fuel tank need not be removed to change the internal pump.

The fuel pump should be heard to run for just a few seconds when the ignition is turned ON without starting the engine. This builds pressure within the lines. In the event that a car with an external fuel pump is stranded, not starting, and the fuel pump is not heard, first check the applicable fuses. An emergency measure that sometimes works is to thump the fuel pump housing with a wooden hammer handle two or three times; occasionally the pump will come back to life. This is one of the few instances where a bit of controlled violence may get you home.

Fuel pumps mounted in the fuel tank are smaller, more efficient and quieter; they are also inaccessible in a hurry. Thankfully, they are protected from road hazards and rarely fail.

REMOVAL AND INSTALLATION
1985 Accord
1986–87 Prelude

1. With the engine OFF, safely relieve the fuel pressure.
2. Elevate the rear of the car, supporting it safely on stands.
3. Remove the left rear wheel.
4. Remove the fuel pump cover.
5. Remove the 3 bolts and remove the fuel pump with its mounts.
6. Label and disconnect the fuel lines and electrical connectors at the connectors.
7. Remove the clamp, then remove the fuel pump from its mount.
8. Disconnect the fuel line from the pump and remove the silencer chamber.

NOTE: *The fuel pump is not repairable and should not be disassembled.*

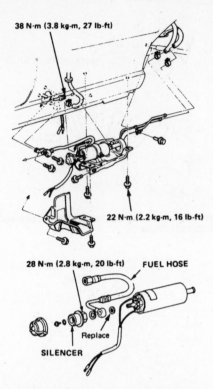

Fuel pump removal; Accord shown, Preludes similar

To install:

9. Install the fuel pump onto its mount.
10. Clean the sealing surface of the flared fuel line and install it onto the fuel pump. Tighten the flare nut to 28 Nm (20 ft. lbs).
11. Reconnect the wiring and install the pump. Tighten the mounting bolts to 22 Nm (16 ft. lbs.).
12. With the pump completely installed, have an assistant turn the ignition switch ON (without starting the engine); check the fuel line connections for any leakage. Cycle the ignition switch OFF and ON 2 or 3 times to build pressure. The fuel line joints must be totally dry — no leakage is permitted.

In-tank Fuel Pumps
1986–89 Accord
1988–91 Prelude

CAUTION: *Gasoline vapors are explosive. Remove components slowly and contain spillage. Observe no smoking/no open flame precautions. Have a Class B-C (dry powder) fire extinguisher within arm's reach at all times.*

1. Turn the ignition OFF; leave it OFF throughout the procedure.
2. Lift or reposition the carpet in the luggage area. Remove the left maintenance access cover in the floor.

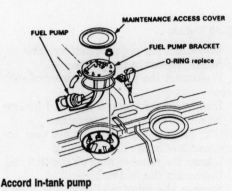

Accord in-tank pump

MAINTENANCE ACCESS COVER

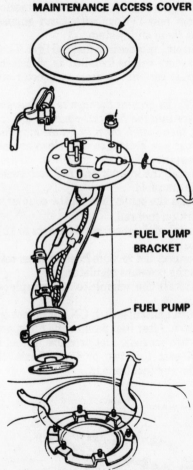

Prelude internal fuel pump

3. Disconnect the electrical connector at the pump unit.

4. Label and disconnect the fuel lines.

5. Carefully remove the retaining nuts holding the pump. When all are removed, lift the pump up and out of the tank.

NOTE: *The pump sits on an angle and may require some manipulation to remove. If the*

pump still won't come out, loosen the fuel tank mounting nuts under the car; slide the tank downward a bit to give more clearance at the top.

6. Reinstall the pump, making certain it is correctly seated and not wedged or jammed. Install the retaining nuts, tightening them evenly and alternately to 6 Nm (10 ft. lbs.) only.

7. Install the fuel lines. Make certain the clamps are secure; use new ones if necessary.

8. Connect the wiring.

9. Install the maintenance access cover and seal or gasket, if used.

10. Reposition the carpeting in the luggage compartment.

11. Start the engine; it may crank longer than normal until fuel pressure is established.

1990–91 Accord

CAUTION: *Gasoline vapors are explosive. Remove components slowly and contain spillage. Observe no smoking/no open flame precautions. Have a Class B-C (dry powder) fire extinguisher within arm's reach at all times.*

1. Relieve the fuel pressure using the correct procedure.

2. Remove the fuel tank after disconnecting all fuel lines and wiring running to the tank.

3. Remove the fuel pump mounting bolts and remove the fuel pump assembly.

4. Install the fuel pump; tighten the retaining nuts to 6 Nm (4 ft. lbs).

5. Reinstall the fuel tank.

Fuel Injectors

REMOVAL AND INSTALLATION

1985 Accord

1. Disconnect the negative battery cable.

2. Safely relieve the fuel pressure.

3. Remove air cleaner case.

4. Disconnect the electrical coupler of each injector.

5. Disconnect the vacuum hose and fuel return hose from the pressure regulator.

NOTE: *Place a rag or shop towel over hose and tube before disconnecting.*

6. Disconnect the two ground cables from intake manifold.

7. Disconnect the fuel lines.

8. Remove injector from intake manifold.

NOTE: *Use new O-rings, seal rings and cushion rings whenever disassembled. When installing the injector, check that the O-ring and seal ring are installed properly. Coat new O-rings and seal rings with clean engine oil before assembly. Install the injector with center line of the coupler aligned with index mark on intake manifold.*

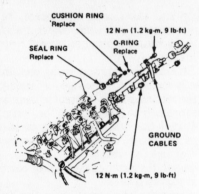

Fuel Injector and fuel rail assembly, 1985 Accord

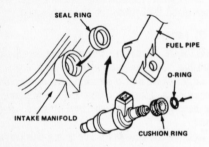

Always replace the seal, O-ring and cushion

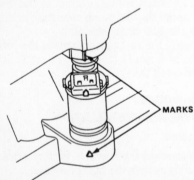

The mark on the Injector must align with the mark on the manifold

9. Slide a new cushion onto injector.

10. Put a new O-ring onto the injector.

11. Press the seal ring into the intake manifold and install the injector and fuel pipe assembly on manifold. Tighten the retainer nuts to 12 Nm (9 ft. lbs).

12. Connect the two ground cables.

13. Connect the vacuum hose and fuel return hose to the pressure regulator.

14. Install the couplers of injectors.

15. Turn the ignition switch ON but do not operate starter. After fuel pump runs for approximately two seconds, fuel pressure in fuel line will rise. Repeat this two or three times, then check for any fuel leakage.

1986–89 Accord
1986–88 Prelude

1. Disconnect the negative battery cable

2. Safely relieve the fuel pressure.

3. Disconnect the electrical coupler of each injector.

4. Disconnect the vacuum hose and fuel return hose from the pressure regulator.

NOTE: *Place a rag or shop towel over the hose and tube before disconnecting.*

5. Loosen the retainer nuts on the fuel rail.

6. Disconnect the fuel rail.

7. Remove the injector(s) from the intake manifold.

8. Slide a new cushion onto each injector.

9. Coat new O-rings with clean engine oil and put them on injectors.

10. Insert injectors into fuel rail first. The rail and injectors will be installed as an assembly. Take great care not to drop an injector out of the rail.

NOTE: *To prevent damage to O-ring, insert injector into the fuel rail squarely and carefully, then install them in intake manifold.*

11. Coat new seal rings with clean engine oil and press into the intake manifold.

12. Install the injector and fuel rail assembly into the manifold.

13. Align the center line on the coupler with the mark on fuel rail.

14. Install and tighten retainer nuts to 12 Nm (9 ft. lbs).

15. Connect the vacuum hose and fuel return hose to the pressure regulator.

16. Install the wiring to the couplers of injectors.

17. Turn ignition switch ON but do not operate starter. After fuel pump runs for approximately two seconds, fuel pressure in fuel line rises. Repeat this two or three times, then check for any fuel leakage.

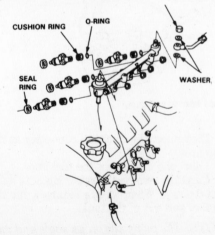

Prelude Injector and fuel rail assembly

FUEL PIPE

The Injectors and rail are installed as an assembly

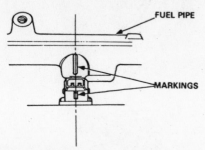

FUEL PIPE

MARKINGS

Align the marks on the injector and fuel rail; if properly installed, the injector should turn easily in its mount

1990–91 Accord
1989–91 Prelude

1. Relieve the fuel pressure.
2. Label and disconnect the electrical harnesses from the injectors.
3. Place a rag below the fuel pressure regulator. Disconnect the vacuum hose and disconnect the fuel line. Plug the fuel line to prevent spillage and the entry of dirt.
4. On Prelude, disconnect the fuel hose from the fuel rail.
5. On Prelude, remove the EACV from the intake manifold.
6. Remove the nuts holding the fuel pipe (rail) and the wiring harness.
7. Remove the fuel rail from the injectors, leaving the injectors in the manifold.
8. Remove each injector and remove the seal ring from each manifold port.
9. Remove the cushion ring and O-ring from each injector.

To install:

10. Install new cushion rings on each injector. Install new O-rings on each injector and coat the O-rings with a light coat of clean, thin oil.
11. Install the injectors into the fuel pipe. Make certain the O-rings seat properly and do not distort.
12. Coat new seal rings with a light coat of clean, thin oil and install the rings into the manifold.
13. Install the fuel rail and injectors to the in-

take manifold. Make certain the insulators are present on the mounting bolts before installing the fuel rail.

NOTE: *Assembling each injector into the rail off the engine prevents damage to the O-rings. Handle the rail and injector assembly carefully when reinstalling to the manifold. Don't drop an injector or bang the tips.*

14. With all injectors seated in the manifold, align the center mark on each injector electrical connector with the mark on the fuel rail.
15. Install the fuel rail retaining nuts and tighten them evenly. Make certain the wiring harness is retained in its clips.
16. Connect the vacuum hose and fuel hose to the regulator.
17. On Preludes, connect the fuel line to the fuel rail.
18. Install the connectors to the injectors.
19. Switch the ignition ON but do not engage the starter. The fuel pump should run for approximately 2 seconds, building pressure within the lines. Switch the ignition OFF, then ON, 2 or 3 more times to build full system pressure. Check the work area for fuel leaks.
20. On Prelude, reinstall the EACV to the manifold.

Throttle Body
REMOVAL AND INSTALLATION

1. Disconnect the air intake tube from the throttle body.
2. Drain the cooling system, at least to a level below the throttle body.
3. Disconnect the coolant hoses running to the throttle body.
4. Label and disconnect the vacuum hoses from the throttle body.
5. Disconnect the wiring connector(s) from the throttle body.
6. Label and disconnect the throttle control and/or accelerator cable. Do not kink the cable.
7. Remove the nuts holding the throttle body to the intake chamber or plenum. Loosen each nut 1–2 turns at a time to release the pressure evenly.
8. Remove the throttle body assembly. Remove and discard the gasket.

To install:

9. Install a new gasket on the plenum; install the throttle body onto the studs. Note that the gasket is usually not symmetric but has a either a tab or rounded corner; there is only one correct position for it.
10. Install the retaining nuts. Tighten them evenly and alternately to 16 ft. lbs. (22 Nm).
11. Install the throttle control and/or accelerator cables.

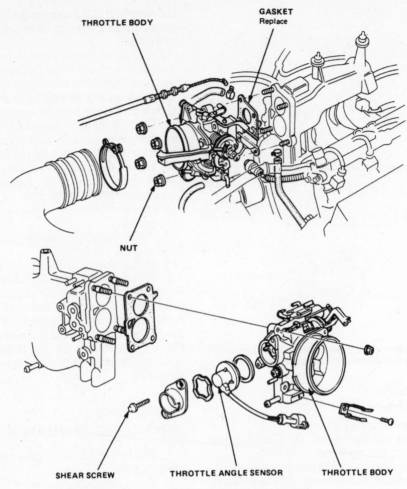

THROTTLE BODY

GASKET
Replace

NUT

SHEAR SCREW   THROTTLE ANGLE SENSOR   THROTTLE BODY

1985 Accord throttle body and external components

12. Connect the vacuum hoses.
13. Connect the coolant hoses.
14. Refill the cooling system.
15. Connect the air intake ducts.

Throttle Angle Sensor

REMOVAL AND INSTALLATION

The throttle angle sensor is located on the side of the throttle body and connected to the throttle axle or pivot. Once the throttle body is removed, the sensor may be removed by removing the retaining bolts. When reinstalling, make certain the sensor is correctly mated with the throttle body shaft. Install the bolts.

Fuel Pressure Regulator

REMOVAL AND INSTALLATION

1. Place a cloth or rag under the regulator. Be prepared to contain escaping fuel.

2. Relieve the fuel system pressure.
3. Disconnect the vacuum hose from the regulator.
4. Disconnect the fuel line from the regulator; plug the line to prevent spillage or the entry of dirt.
5. Remove the 2 retaining bolts and remove the regulator.
6. Remove the O-ring from the regulator and discard it.

To install:

7. Install a new O-ring on the regulator; coat the ring lightly with a thin coat of clean, fresh oil.
8. Install the regulator, making sure the O-ring is not distorted or damaged. Tighten the retaining bolts to 12 Nm (9 ft. lbs).
9. Connect the fuel line.
10. Install the vacuum line.

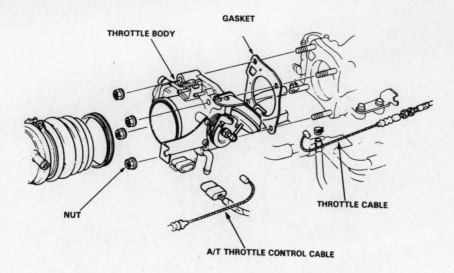

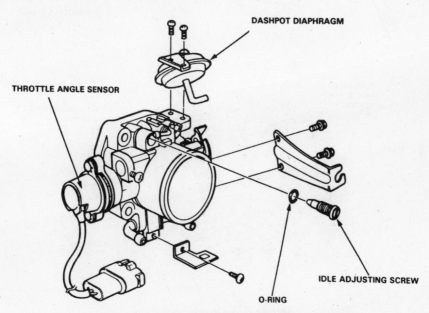

Throttle body assembly, 1986-89 Accord and 1986-87 Prelude

Injector Resistor

REMOVAL AND INSTALLATION

1. Switch the ignition OFF.
2. The resistor is located in the engine compartment on the left fender apron (inner surface) or on the shock tower. Disconnect the wiring connector to the resistor.
3. Remove or disconnect any wiring harness clamps or retainers holding the resistor harness.
4. Remove the retaining bolts holding the resistor; remove the resistor.
5. Reassemble in reverse order.

MAP Sensor

REMOVAL AND INSTALLATION

The MAP sensor is located within the emission control box on the firewall.

Remove the control box from its mounts and open the box. Disconnect the wire harness connector to the sensor, then disconnect the vacuum hose(s). Remove the sensor from its mount.

When reassembling, handle the unit carefully. Install it securely in the mounting and attach the vacuum line(s) and wiring connector. Reassemble and install the emissions box.

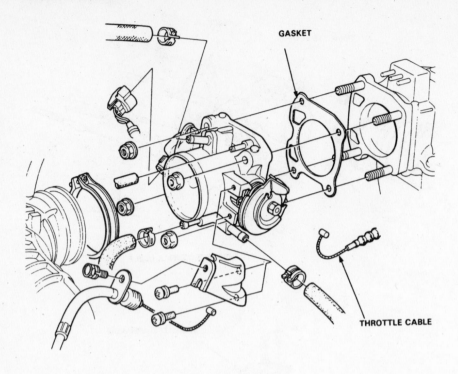

GASKET

THROTTLE CABLE

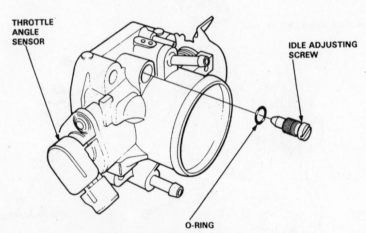

THROTTLE ANGLE SENSOR

IDLE ADJUSTING SCREW

O-RING

1990-91 Accord throttle body

Intake Air Temperature Sensor

REMOVAL AND INSTALLATION

The sensor is located on the intake manifold or air plenum. It is removed and installed in straightforward fashion; disconnect the wiring connector and remove the mounting screws. Remove the sensor.

EGR System Controls and Purge Control

REMOVAL AND INSTALLATION

The controls associated with control of the EGR and purge control system are located within the control box on the firewall. These components include the EGR control solenoid valve, the CVC valve and air chamber if used, as well as the purge cut-off solenoid valve.

Replacement of any of these items requires removing the control box from its mounts, disconnecting the external electrical connectors and opening the control box. Disconnect the vacuum hose(s) to the component and remove the component. Installation is in the reverse order of removal.

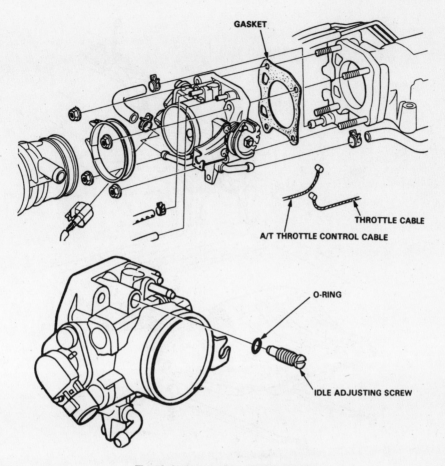

Throttle body assembly, 1988-91 Prelude

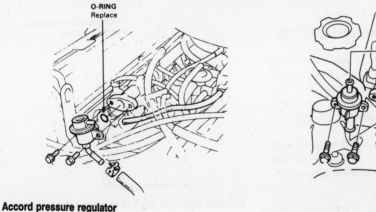

Accord pressure regulator

Prelude fuel pressure regulator

Electronic Air Control Valve (EACV) Fast Idle Valve

REMOVAL AND INSTALLATION

1. These air control valves are located at the side of the intake chamber or plenum downstream of the throttle body.

2. Disconnect the wiring connector at the valve.

3. Label and disconnect the vacuum hoses from the unit.

4. Remove the mounting bolts and remove the valve. Recover and discard the O-rings from the vacuum ports.

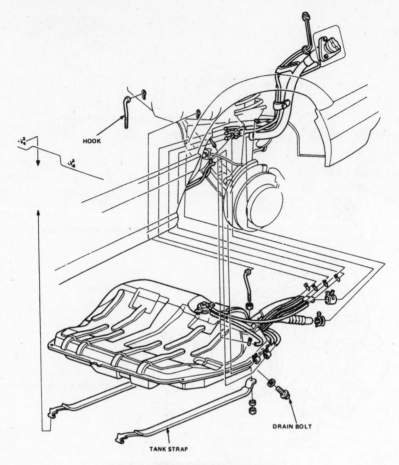

1984-85 Accord fuel tank

To install:

5. Replace the O-rings and make certain they are properly seated.

6. Install the valve and the retaining bolts. The pintle or control valve for the EACV must seat correctly in its port. For Accord and Prelude, tighten the EACV bolts to 22 Nm (16 ft. lbs) and the fast idle valve bolts to 12 Nm (9 ft. lbs).

7. Connect the vacuum hoses to the valve; make certain each hose is connected to the proper port. Connect the electrical connector.

Electric Load Detector

This sensor is used on 1990–91 Accord only and is located in the underhood fuse and relay box. The ELD unit is integral with the fuse box in which it is mounted; should the sensor fail, the fuse/relay box assembly must be replaced.

FUEL TANK

REMOVAL AND INSTALLATION

Although draining the tank is part of each

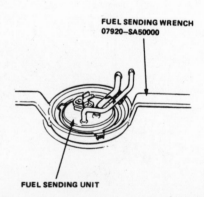

A special wrench is required to remove the fuel sender

procedure, it is unlikely that you can safely store large amounts of fuel during the repair. For this reason, the tank should be as empty as possible before removal is begun. The remaining few gallons must be drained and stored in approved fuel containers, never in gallon jugs or similar containers. The containers must be tightly capped.

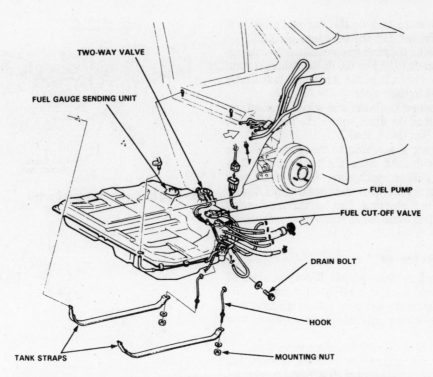

The fuel tank for 1986-89 Accords contains the fuel pump as well as the gauge sender

CAUTION: *Fuel and its vapors are extremely explosive. Take great care to eliminate all
sources of heat, flame and sparks from the
work area before beginning. This must include shutting off heaters or furnaces and
shutting off electric motors in machinery,
fans, etc. Keep a dry powder (Class B-C) fire
extinguisher within arm's reach at all times.*

1984–89 Accord
1984–85 Prelude

1. Block the front wheels. Elevate the rear of
the car and support it safely on stands.
2. Remove the drain bolt from the tank and
drain the remaining fuel into an approved fuel
container.
3. Disconnect the sending unit connectors.
4. Label and disconnect the hoses from the
pipes mounted to the body (over the suspension
control arm). Slide the hose clamps back on the
hose, then twist the hose while pulling it off the
fitting.
5. Use a floor jack and a broad piece of wood
under the tank. Adjust the position as necessary to allow the tank to be evenly supported.
6. Remove the nuts holding the tank straps;
let the straps fall free.
7. Lower the jack and remove the tank from
under the vehicle.
8. If the fuel gauge sending unit is to be removed, use Honda Tool 07920–
SA50000 or 07920–SA20000 to remove the re-

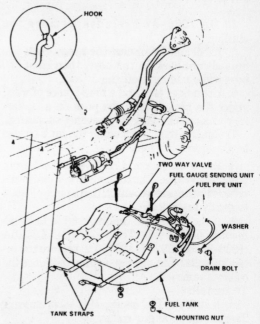

Prelude fuel tank, 1986-87

taining collar. Lift out the sending unit once the
collar is removed.
To install:
9. Install the fuel sender if it was removed.
Tighten the retaining collar.

10. Place the tank on the jack and position it under the car. Lift the tank into position.

11. Install the tank straps and tighten the retaining nuts to 22 Nm (16 ft. lbs). Make certain the opposite ends of the straps are still firmly mounted in their slots

12. Connect the hoses and wiring connectors.

13. Install the drain bolt in the tank; tighten it to 50 Nm (36 ft. lbs.)

14. Lower the vehicle to the ground. Reuse the fuel drained from the tank unless it is heavily polluted with rust, water, etc. Use a funnel at the fuel filler and pour the fuel slowly.

15. When starting, the engine may crank longer than usual due to lack of fuel in the lines.

1986–1991 Prelude

1. Block the front wheels. Elevate the rear of the car and support it safely on stands.

2. Remove the drain bolt from the tank and drain the remaining fuel into an approved fuel container.

3. On 1986–87 vehicles, disconnect the sending unit connectors. On 1988–91 vehicles, lift the carpet in the luggage area. Remove both access panels. Disconnect the wiring to the fuel pump and fuel sender. Remove the fuel feed line.

4. On 1986–87 Preludes, remove the muffler.

5. Label and disconnect the hoses. Slide the hose clamps back on the hose, then twist the hose while pulling it off the fitting.

6. Use a floor jack and a broad piece of wood under the tank. Adjust the position as necessary to allow the tank to be evenly supported.

7. Remove the nuts holding the tank straps; let the straps fall free.

8. Lower the jack and remove the tank from under the vehicle. The tank may be stuck to the vehicle by the undercoating. Use a piece of wood to gently pry it loose.

9. If the fuel gauge sending unit is to be removed, use Honda Tool 07GAC–SE0020A (1988–91) or 07920–SA20000 to remove the retaining collar. Lift out the sending unit once the collar is removed.

To install:

10. Install the fuel sender if it was removed. Tighten the retaining collar.

11. Place the tank on the jack and position it under the car. Lift the tank into position.

12. Install the tank straps and tighten the retaining nuts to 22 Nm (16 ft. lbs). Make certain the opposite ends of the straps are still firmly mounted in their slots.

13. Connect the hoses and wiring connectors. Reinstall the access covers if they were re-

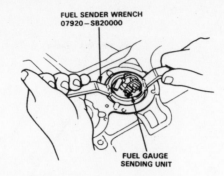

Removing the Prelude fuel gauge sender

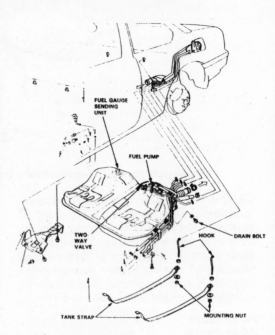

1988-91 Prelude fuel tank

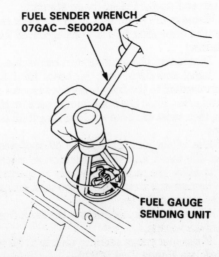

Removing the fuel gauge sender, 1988-91 Prelude

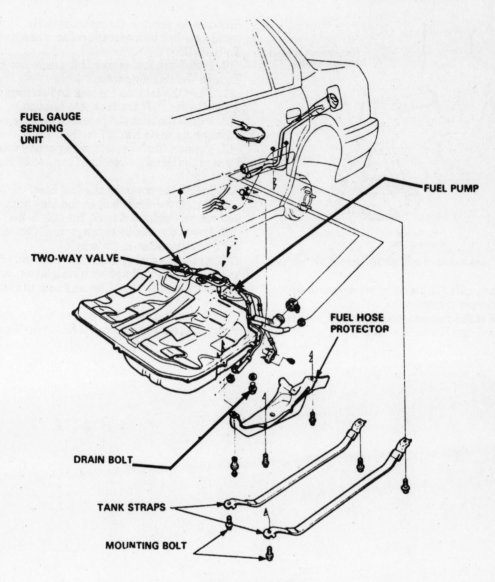

FUEL GAUGE
SENDING
UNIT

FUEL PUMP

TWO-WAY VALVE

FUEL HOSE
PROTECTOR

DRAIN BOLT

TANK STRAPS

MOUNTING BOLT

1990-91 Accord fuel tank

moved. Reposition the carpeting in the cargo area as needed.

14. Reinstall the muffler if it was removed. Use new nuts and gaskets.

15. Install the drain bolt in the tank; tighten it to 50 Nm (36 ft. lbs.)

16. Lower the vehicle to the ground. Reuse the fuel drained from the tank unless it is heavily polluted with rust, water, etc. Use a funnel at the fuel filler and pour the fuel slowly.

17. When starting, the engine may crank longer than usual due to lack of fuel in the lines.

1990–1991 Accord

1. Block the front wheels. Elevate the rear of the car and support it safely on stands.

2. Remove the drain bolt from the tank and drain the remaining fuel into an approved fuel container.

3. Disconnect the 3-pin connector in the trunk.

4. Remove the cover from the fuel hoses on the side of the tank.

5. Label and disconnect the hoses. Slide the hose clamps back on the hose, then twist the hose while pulling it off the fitting.

6. Use a floor jack and a broad piece of wood under the tank. Adjust the position as necessary to allow the tank to be evenly supported.

7. Remove the nuts holding the tank straps; let the straps fall free.

8. Lower the jack and remove the tank from under the vehicle. The tank may be stuck by the

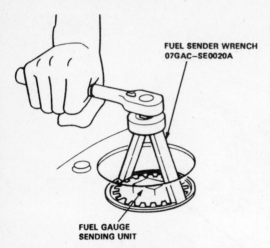

FUEL SENDER WRENCH
07GAC–SE0020A

FUEL GAUGE
SENDING UNIT

Fuel sender removal tool, 1990-91 Accord

undercoating on the body; use a piece of wood to gently pry it loose.

9. If the fuel gauge sending unit is to be removed, use Honda Tool 07GAC-

SE0020A to remove the retaining collar. Lift out the sending unit once the collar is removed.

To install:

10. Install the fuel sender if it was removed. Tighten the retaining collar.

11. Place the tank on the jack and position it under the car. Lift the tank into position.

12. Install the tank straps and tighten the retaining nuts to 38 Nm (27 ft. lbs).

13. Connect the hoses and wiring connectors. Tighten the threaded fuel line fitting to 37 Nm (26 ft. lbs).

14. Install the cover for the fuel lines.

15. Install the drain bolt in the tank with a new washer; tighten it to 50 Nm (36 ft. lbs.)

16. Lower the vehicle to the ground. Connect the 3-pin connector in the trunk.

17. Reuse the fuel drained from the tank unless it is heavily polluted with rust, water, etc. Use a funnel at the fuel filler and pour the fuel slowly.

18. When starting, the engine may crank longer than usual due to lack of fuel in the lines.

HEATING AND AIR CONDITIONING

Heater or Heater/AC Blower Motor

REMOVAL AND INSTALLATION

1984–89 Accord
1984–1987 Prelude

1. Remove the glove box.
2. Remove the blower duct between the blower and heater box.
3. Disconnect the wiring connector and the vacuum hose from the blower.
4. Remove the three mounting bolts and remove the blower assembly.
5. Install in reverse order, tightening the mounting bolts to 10 Nm (7 ft. lbs). Make certain the blower mating surfaces are tightly sealed. Install the blower duct; make certain there is no leakage at its joints.

1990–91 Accord

1. Remove the glove box.
2. Remove the glove box frame (lower support)
3. If not equipped with air conditioning, remove the three screws and remove the heater duct. Remove the blower mounting nuts. Disconnect the wiring from the blower motor, resistor and recirculation control motor, then remove the blower assembly.
4. If equipped with air conditioning, lift the carpet in the passenger compartment. Remove the side cover (kick panel). With the ignition OFF, remove the control unit bracket nuts; disconnect the five connectors (carefully!) and remove the control unit bracket.
5. If equipped with air conditioning, remove the band, then remove the blower lower covers. Do not break the tabs on the lower covers.
6. Remove the retaining nuts and remove the blower assembly.

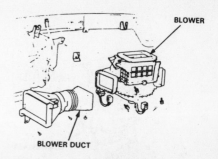

Blower motor removal, 1984-85 Accord

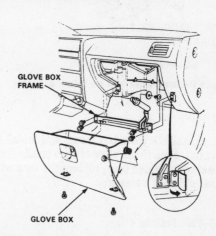

Remove the glove box and frame

7. Install the blower unit and tighten the retaining nuts.
8. On air conditioned vehicles, install the lower covers and the band.
9. Install the control unit bracket and carefully connect the wiring connectors to their proper location. Install the kick panel and reposition the carpet.
10. Connect the wiring to the blower assembly. For non-air conditioned vehicles, install the air duct and tighten the screws.

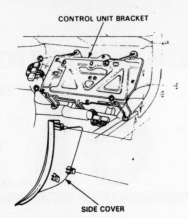

CONTROL UNIT BRACKET

SIDE COVER

Air conditioned cars require removal of the control unit; handle it carefully

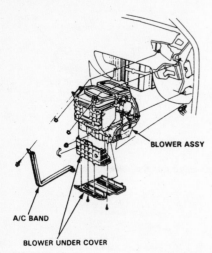

BLOWER ASSY

A/C BAND

BLOWER UNDER COVER

Remove the lower cover from the blower assembly

11. Install the glove box frame and install the glove box. Note that a piece of trim on the frame is held with 2-sided tape; replace the tape when reassembling if necessary.

1988–1991 Prelude

1. Disconnect the negative battery cable.
2. Remove the glove box and frame (lower support).
3. Remove the 4 screws and remove the heater duct.
4. Remove the 3 mounting bolts.
5. Disconnect the wiring connectors from the blower motor, resistor and recirculation controller. Remove the blower motor assembly.
6. Reinstall in reverse order. Make certain the blower mating surfaces are tightly sealed. Install the blower duct; make certain there is no leakage at its joints.

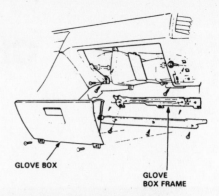

GLOVE BOX

GLOVE BOX FRAME

Remove the Prelude glove box and frame

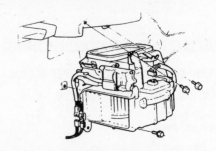

Prelude blower removal

Heater Core

REMOVAL AND INSTALLATION

CAUTION: *When draining the coolant, keep in mind that cats and dogs are attracted by the ethylene glycol antifreeze, and are quite likely to drink any that is left in an uncovered container or in puddles on the ground. This will prove fatal in sufficient quantity. Always drain the coolant into a sealable container. Coolant should be reused unless it is contaminated or several years old.*

1984–85 Accord

1. Drain the coolant from the bottom of the radiator and collect it for re-use. Put a drain pan underneath the hose connections at the firewall, carefully note hose locations, and then disconnect the two hoses.
2. Disconnect the heater valve cable from the heater water valve. Remove the heater lower mounting nut.
3. Remove the dashboard.
4. Remove the heater duct.
5. Disconnect the heater function cable and the air mix door cable at the heater unit.
6. Pry out retainer clips and remove the floor ducts from both sides of the vehicle. Disconnect the vacuum hose at the 5-way connector.
7. Remove the two heater mounting bolts (at top) and the heater from under the dash.

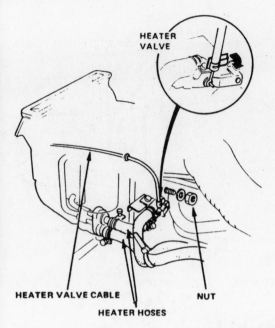
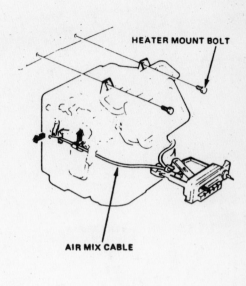

HEATER VALVE

HEATER MOUNT BOLT

AIR MIX CABLE

HEATER VALVE CABLE   NUT

HEATER HOSES

1985 Accord heater assembly

8. To install, reverse the removal procedures and note the following points:

a. Apply sealant to all grommets.

b. Check routing of inlet and outlet hoses to the heater core to make sure they are not reversed. Install clamps in proper positions and make sure they are securely tightened.

c. Refill and bleed the cooling system using the bleed bolt.

d. Make sure all door operating cables are securely connected and adjusted for proper door operation.

1986–89 Accord

1. Drain coolant from the bottom of the radiator and collect it for reuse. Put a drain pan underneath the hose connections at the firewall, carefully note hose locations and then disconnect the two connections.

2. Disconnect the heater valve cable from the heater valve. Remove the two lower heater mounting nuts.

3. On push button type heaters, disconnect the cool vent cable at the heater. On lever type heaters, disconnect the function cable and the air mix cable from the heater.

4. Remove the dashboard.

5. Remove the heater ducts.

6. On pushbutton type heaters, disconnect the air mix cable from the heater and the wiring harness from the connector.

7. Remove the heater bolts and pull the heater away from its mounts.

8. To install, reverse the reverse procedures, noting following points:

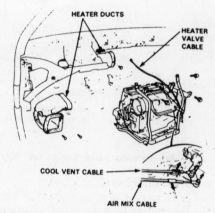

HEATER DUCTS

HEATER VALVE CABLE

COOL VENT CABLE

AIR MIX CABLE

1986-89 Accord with pushbutton controls

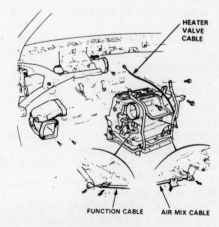

HEATER VALVE CABLE

FUNCTION CABLE   AIR MIX CABLE

1986-89 Accord with lever or slider controls

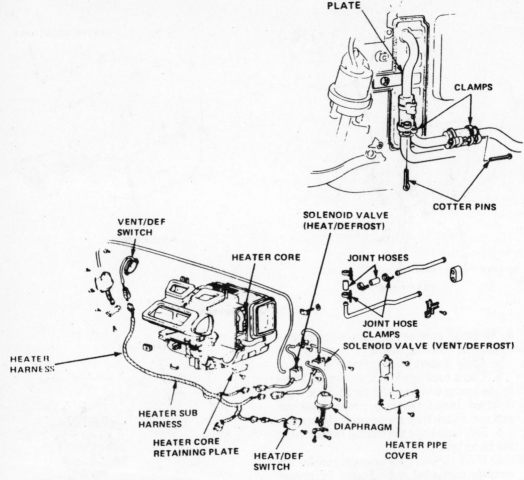

Prelude heater cores through 1987 may be removed with the heater assembly in the car

a. Apply sealant to all grommets.

b. Check routing of inlet and outlet hoses to the heater core to make sure they are not reversed. Install clamps in proper positions and make sure they are securely tightened.

c. Refill and bleed the cooling system with the bleed bolt.

d. Make sure all door operating cables are securely connected and adjusted for proper door operation.

1990–91 Accord

1. Drain the engine coolant.
2. Label and disconnect the heater hoses at the firewall. Be prepared to contain spilled coolant from the hoses and fittings.
3. Disconnect the heater valve control cable from the heater valve.
4. Remove the dashboard.
5. Remove the vertical support (sub-pipe).
6. Remove the 4 mounting bolts and remove the heater assembly.

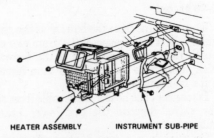

HEATER ASSEMBLY   INSTRUMENT SUB-PIPE

1990 Accord heater assembly

7. To install, reverse the reverse procedures, noting following points:

a. Apply sealant to all grommets.

b. Check routing of inlet and outlet hoses to the heater fittings to make sure they are not reversed. Install clamps in proper positions and make sure they are securely tightened.

c. Refill and bleed the cooling system with the bleed bolt.

d. Make sure all door operating cables are securely connected and adjusted for proper door operation.

1984–87 Prelude

NOTE: *Dashboard removal is NOT required.*

1. Drain the cooling system. Remove the heater pipe cover and heater pipe clamps.

2. Remove the heater hose cover (inside the car) and remove the heater hose clamps.

3. Remove the heater core retaining plate.

4. Pull the cotter pin out of the hose clamp joint and separate the heater pipes.

NOTE: *Engine coolant will drain from the heater pipes when they are disconnected. Place a drip pan under the pipes to catch the coolant.*

5. When all the coolant has drained from the heater core, remove it from the heater housing.

6. To install, reverse the removal procedures noting the following points:

a. Replace the hose clamps with new ones.

b. Turn the cotter pin in the hose clamps tightly to prevent leaking coolant.

c. Refill the cooling system with coolant and open the bleed bolt until coolant begins to flow from it. Tighten the bolt when all the air has escaped from the system.

1988–91 Prelude

1. Drain the engine coolant.

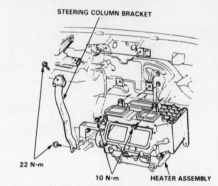

Removing the heater assembly from 1988–91 Prelude

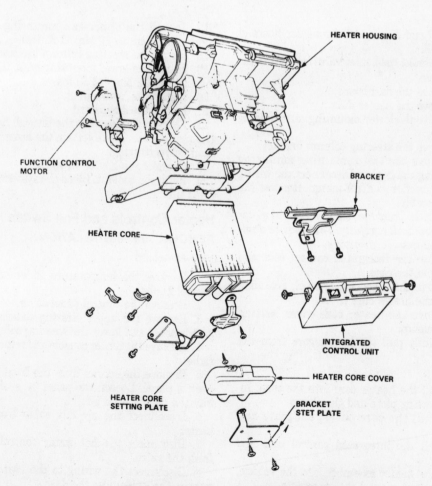

The Prelude heater core is within the heater case

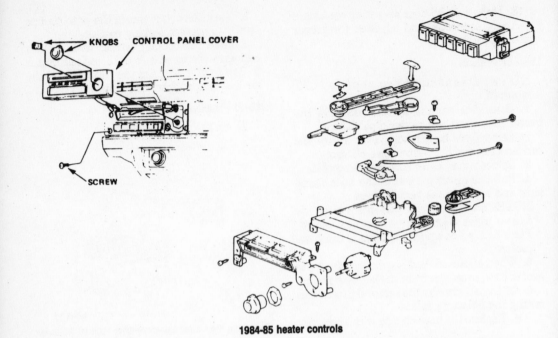

KNOBS CONTROL PANEL COVER

SCREW

1984–85 heater controls

2. Label and disconnect the heater hoses at the firewall.

3. Disconnect the heater valve cable from the heater valve.

4. Remove the dashboard.

5. Remove the heater duct.

6. Remove the lower mounting nuts holding the heater.

7. Remove the steering column bracket.

8. Remove the two remaining mounting bolts holding the heater. Disconnect the wiring from the function control motor. Remove the heater assembly.

WARNING: *Treat the function control motor and control unit carefully. They may be damaged by impact or dropping.*

9. Remove the integrated control unit and bracket from the case.

10. Remove the 2 screws, bracket, retaining plate and the heater core cover.

11. Remove the heater core cover, setting plate and clamp.

12. Carefully pull the heater core from the housing.

To install:

13. Install the heater core into the case. Install the setting plate and the clamp.

14. Install the core cover, set plate and bracket.

15. Install the integrated control unit and bracket.

16. Fit the heater assembly into the vehicle. Apply a sealant around the grommets.

17. Install the upper two mounting bolts, tightening them to 10 Nm (7 ft. lbs).

18. Install the steering column bracket.

19. Install the lower mounting nuts, tightening them to 22 Nm (16 ft. lbs.)

20. Install the heater duct.

21. Install the dashboard.

22. Connect the hoses at the firewall fittings. Use new clamps. Make certain the hoses are on their correct fittings.

23. Connect the heater valve cable.

24. Refill the coolant. Bleed the system at the bleed fitting.

Heater Controls and Fan Switch
REMOVAL AND INSTALLATION
1984–85 Accord

1. Remove the temperature slider and fan control knobs.

2. Remove the control panel cover.

3. Remove the upper steering column support bracket and lower the steering column.

4. Remove the center console and remove the radio.

5. Remove the screws from the front of the control panel. Loosen the panel by pushing it into the dash a little bit.

6. Disconnect the air mix cable from the heater.

7. Disconnect the hot water control cable from the valve.

8. Disconnect the wiring to the switch and remove the unit under the dash.

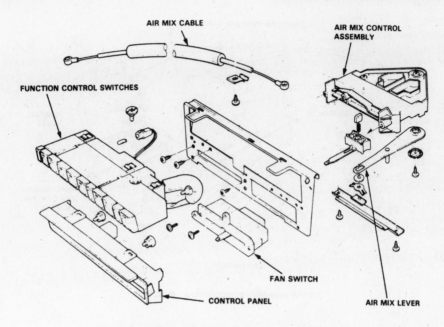

Control assembly components – pushbutton type

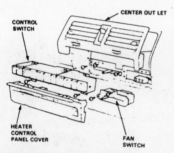

Removal of pushbutton control assembly

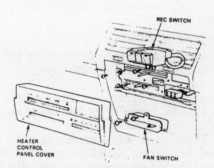

Removal of slider or lever control assembly

9. The control assembly may be disassembled into its component parts after removal.

To install:

10. Assemble the components if they were separated. Install the assembly from the back of the dash, sitting it loosely in place.

11. Connect the switch wiring. Make certain it is routed out of the way of the installation.

12. Connect and adjust the air and water control cables.

13. Install the front retaining screws.

14. Install the console and radio.

15. Reposition and secure the steering column.

16. Install the heater control cover panel; install the control knobs.

1986–89 Accord

PUSHBUTTON CONTROLS

1. Remove the knobs from the temperature and fan controls.

2. Remove the heater control panel cover.

3. Remove the instrument cluster visor.

4. Remove the center air outlet.

5. Remove the 4 screws holding the pushbutton unit and slide it outward gently. Disconnect the switch wires.

6. The blower fan switch may be removed individually if desired. Remove its mounting bolts and remove the switch.

7. If the temperature control lever is to be removed, remove the radio first. Disconnect the air mix cable at the heater box (not at the lever) and remove the assembly.

To install:

8. Assemble and install the individual components (fan switch or temperature control cable) if they were removed.

9. Connect the wiring harness and install the pushbutton controller. Install and tighten the retaining screws.

10. Install the center air outlet.

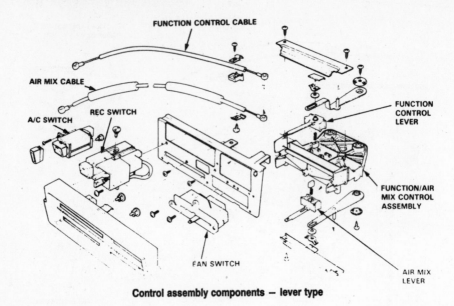

FUNCTION CONTROL CABLE

AIR MIX CABLE

A/C SWITCH   REC SWITCH

FUNCTION CONTROL LEVER

FUNCTION/AIR MIX CONTROL ASSEMBLY

FAN SWITCH

AIR MIX LEVER

Control assembly components — lever type

11. Install the instrument visor.

12. Install the control panel cover; install the control knobs.

LEVER OR SLIDER CONTROLS

1. Remove the knobs from the control levers.

2. Remove the control panel cover.

3. Remove the radio.

4. At this point, the temperature/function levers, the REC switch or the fan control switch may be removed individually.

5. If the main lever assembly is to be removed, remove the six retaining screws. Disconnect the temperature control cable and the function cable at the heater. Disconnect the wiring and remove the control unit.

6. If the fan switch or REC controller is to be removed, remove the retaining screws and disconnect the wiring connector.

To install:

7. Place the fan switch or REC connector in position, connect the wiring and secure the retaining screws.

8. Fit the heater controller into place and route the cables to the heater.

9. Connect the cables to their proper fittings at the heater.

10. Install the retaining screws holding the control panel.

11. Install the radio.

12. Install the control panel cover and install the knobs on the levers.

1990–91 Accord

1. Remove the ashtray. Remove the center console.

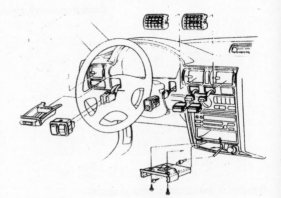

All the dash switches and air vents must be removed on 1990-91 Accord

2. Remove the coin box, air vents and ashtray lighting bracket.

3. Remover the dashboard switches on the left and right of the steering wheel.

4. Remove the radio/tape player. Note that there are concealed screws at the back or bottom of the radio unit.

5. Lower the steering wheel to its lowest position. Remove the dash visor. This is a large, one-piece assembly which includes the center dash trim. It's plastic; don't break it.

6. Disconnect the control cables at the heater assembly.

7. Remove the four screws and gently pull the control panel forward.

8. Disconnect the wiring connectors and remove the heater controller.

9. If the fan switch or other individual components are to be replaced, the appropriate con-

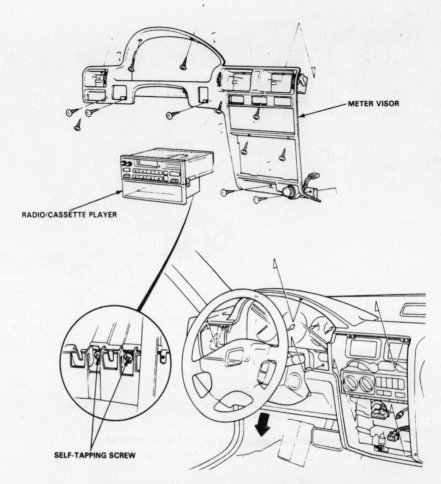

METER VISOR

RADIO/CASSETTE PLAYER

SELF-TAPPING SCREW

Use care in removing the instrument visor. The radio is mounted with concealed screws

trol knobs must be removed before disassembly.

To install:

10. Assemble the individual components if they were removed.

11. Insert the panel into the dash and route the cables to the heater box.

12. Connect the wiring connectors, making certain the harness is out of the way of the installation.

13. Connect the cables at the heater assembly. Install the 4 retaining screws holding the control panel.

14. Install the dash visor. Make sure it is square and that each retaining screw is in place.

15. Install the radio/tape player.

16. Install and connect the dash switches, air vents and ashtray bracket. Install the coin box.

17. Install the console; install the ashtray.

1984–87 Prelude

1. Disconnect the heater control harness.

2. Remove the temperature control assembly by removing the four screws. Remove the lower screws first.

3. Remove the outlet together with the control unit while removing the two screws from the bottom.

4. Remove the 4 screws and remove the control unit.

5. Reassemble in reverse order.

1988–91 Prelude

1. Remove the center console.

2. Remove the radio/tape player.

3. Remove the two screws at the bottom of the center air vent and remove the air vent assembly.

4. Disconnect the air mix cable at the heater assembly.

5. Remove the 4 screws holding the control assembly; pull the controller forward gently. Disconnect the wiring connectors and remove the heater control unit.

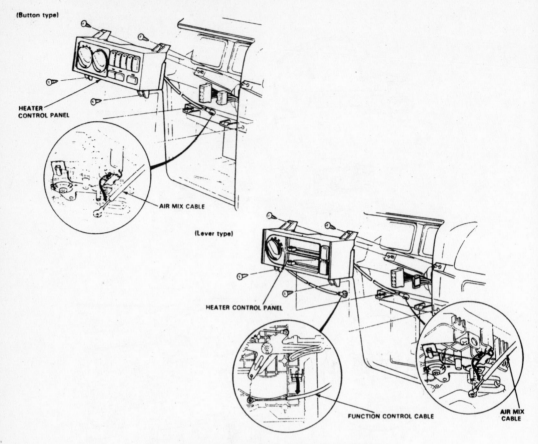

(Button type)

HEATER
CONTROL PANEL

AIR MIX CABLE

(Lever type)

HEATER CONTROL PANEL

FUNCTION CONTROL CABLE

AIR MIX
CABLE

The number of cables depends on the type of controller

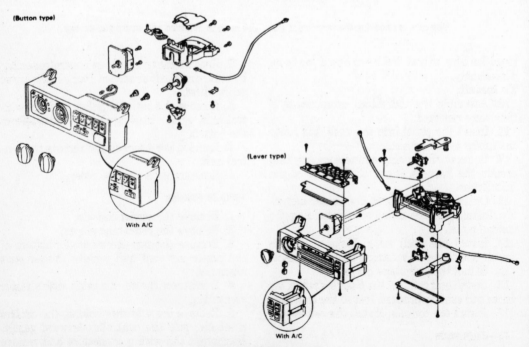

(Button type)

With A/C

(Lever type)

With A/C

Control assembly components

6. If the fan control switch is to be replaced, remove the control knob and remove the switch from the control assembly.

To install:

7. Reassembly any components removed from the control assembly.

8. Install the control assembly and tighten the retaining screws.

9. Connect the air-mix cable at the heater box.

10. Install the center air vent.

11. Install the radio/tape player.

12. Install the center console.

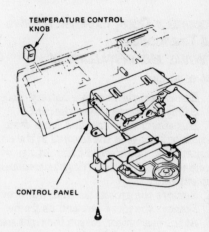

Removing 1984-87 Prelude heater controls

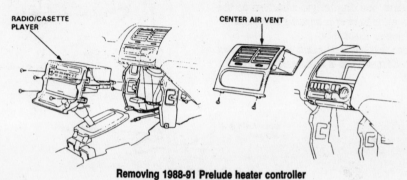

Removing 1988-91 Prelude heater controller

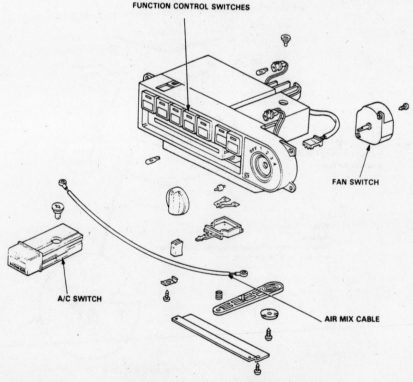

Detail of Prelude heater controller

Evaporator Core, Expansion Valve and Thermostat

REMOVAL AND INSTALLATION

1984–85 Accord

1. Disconnect the negative battery cable.
2. Safely discharge the refrigerant.
3. Disconnect the line and hose from the evaporator fittings at the firewall in the engine compartment. Counter-hold the fittings with a second wrench. Cap the fittings immediately to keep out dirt.
4. Remove the grommets from the firewall.
5. Remove the glove box and its frame.
6. At the evaporator, loosen the right sealing band; slide it to the left.
7. Remove the screw from the air door diaphragm. Leave the diaphragm attached to the arm. Remove the blower mounting bolts and remove the blower assembly.
8. Remove the left seal band and disconnect the wiring. Remove the 3 bolts and remove the evaporator.

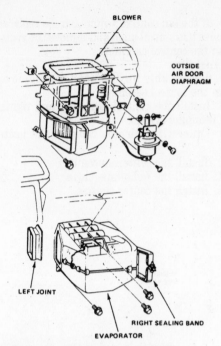

Removal of the 1984-85 Accord evaporator

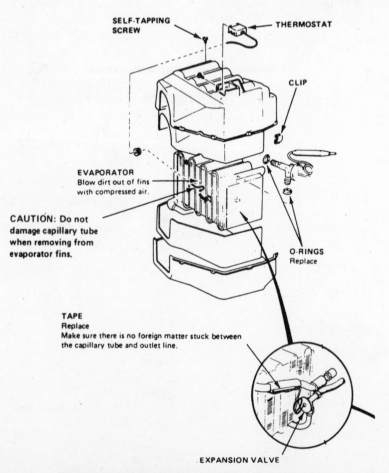

Evaporator case and components, early Accord and Prelude

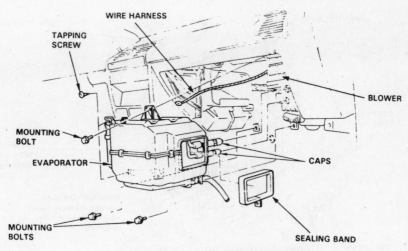

TAPPING SCREW

WIRE HARNESS

BLOWER

MOUNTING BOLT

EVAPORATOR

CAPS

MOUNTING BOLTS

SEALING BAND

Evaporator case removal, 1986-89 Accord

9. To disassemble the case, remove the screw and clips from the housing.

10. Carefully separate the halves of the case to gain access to the capillary tube. Remove the tube of the thermostat from the fins of the evaporator.

11. Separate the housing halves. Remove the cover.

12. Remove the expansion valve if necessary.

To install:

13. Reassemble the case components as necessary. Install the capillary tube in its original location. Reassemble the upper and lower case halves, making sure there are no gaps in the case.

14. Install the evaporator assembly and install the retaining bolts. Don't forget to attach the evaporator drain hose and route it out of the car.

15. Install the left sealing band. Connect the wiring.

16. Install the blower assembly.

17. Remount the air door diaphragm and tighten the screw.

18. Install the right seal band and tighten it. Double check each band; they should be square and tight.

19. Install the glove box and frame.

20. Install the grommets. Coat the contact surfaces with sealant before installation.

21. Connect the line and hose to the evaporator fittings. Replace the O-rings with new ones. Tighten the receiver line to 16 Nm (12 ft. lbs.) and the suction hose to 30 Nm (22 ft. lbs).

22. Evacuate and recharge the system. Operate the system and check for leaks.

1986-89 Accord

1. Disconnect the negative battery cable.

2. Safely discharge the refrigerant.

3. Disconnect the line and hose from the evaporator fittings at the firewall in the engine compartment. Counter-hold the fittings with a second wrench. Cap the fittings immediately to keep out dirt.

4. Remove the grommets from the firewall. Disconnect the drain hose from the evaporator case.

5. Remove the glove box and its frame.

6. At the evaporator, loosen the sealing band; slide it towards the blower.

7. Disconnect the thermostat wire; pull the wire out of the clamp at the top of the case.

8. Remove the three bolts and two screws; remove the evaporator case.

9. Remove the sealing band from the blower if necessary.

10. To disassemble the case, remove the screw and clips from the housing.

11. Carefully separate the halves of the case to gain access to the capillary tube. Remove the tube of the thermostat from the fins of the evaporator.

12. Separate the housing halves. Remove the cover.

13. Remove the expansion valve if necessary.

To install:

14. Reassemble the case components as necessary. Install the capillary tube in its original location. Reassemble the upper and lower case halves, making sure there are no gaps in the case.

15. Install the evaporator assembly and install the retaining bolts. Don't forget to attach the evaporator drain hose and route it out of the car.

16. Connect the thermostat wire and install it in the clip.

17. Install the seal band and tighten it. Check for correct positioning.

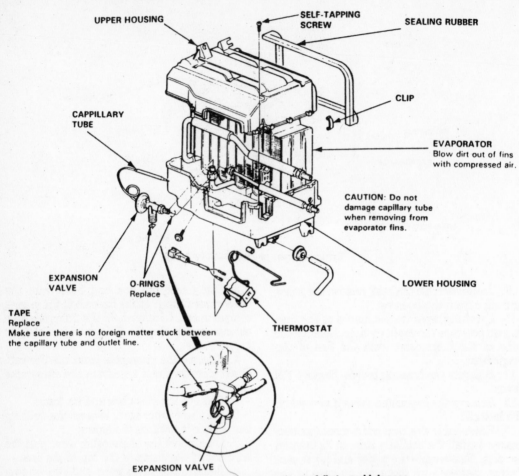

UPPER HOUSING

SELF-TAPPING SCREW

SEALING RUBBER

CLIP

CAPPILLARY TUBE

EVAPORATOR
Blow dirt out of fins
with compressed air.

CAUTION: Do not
damage capillary tube
when removing from
evaporator fins.

EXPANSION VALVE

O-RINGS
Replace

LOWER HOUSING

TAPE
Replace
Make sure there is no foreign matter stuck between
the capillary tube and outlet line.

THERMOSTAT

EXPANSION VALVE

Handle evaporator case and components carefully to avoid damage

18. Install the glove box and frame assembly.

19. Connect the line and hose to the evaporator fittings. Replace the O-rings with new ones. Tighten the receiver line to 16 Nm (12 ft. lbs.) and the suction hose to 32 Nm (23 ft. lbs).

20. Evacuate and recharge the system. Operate the system and check for leaks.

1990–91 Accord

1. Disconnect the negative battery cable.

2. Safely discharge the refrigerant.

3. Disconnect the line and hose from the evaporator fittings at the firewall in the engine compartment. Counter-hold the fittings with a second wrench. Cap the fittings immediately to keep out dirt.

4. Remove the glove box and its frame.

5. At the evaporator, loosen and remove the two bands.

6. Disconnect the thermostat wire.

7. Remove the drain hose. Remove the retaining nuts and remove the evaporator.

8. Pull the evaporator sensor from the fins.

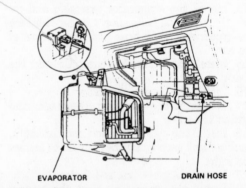

EVAPORATOR

DRAIN HOSE

The 1990 Accord evaporator is held by retaining nuts above and below

9. Remove the screws and clips holding the housing.

10. Carefully separate the housings and remove the covers.

11. Remove the expansion valve if necessary.

To install:

12. Reassemble the case components as necessary. Install the capillary tube in its original

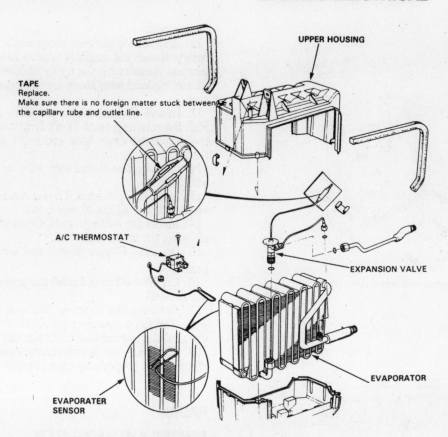

Detail of 1990-91 Accord evaporator

location. Reassemble the upper and lower case halves, making sure there are no gaps in the case.

13. Install the evaporator assembly and install the retaining nuts. Don't forget to attach the evaporator drain hose and route it out of the car.

14. Connect the thermostat wire.

15. Install the bands.

16. Install the glove box and frame.

17. Connect the receiver line and suction pipe. Use new O-rings before assembly. Tighten the receiver line to 17 Nm (12 ft. lbs.) and the suction line to 32 Nm (23 ft. lbs).

18. Evacuate and recharge the system. Operate the system and check for leaks.

Prelude

1. Disconnect the negative battery cable.

2. Safely discharge the refrigerant.

3. Disconnect the line and hose from the evaporator fittings at the firewall in the engine compartment. Counter-hold the fittings with a second wrench. Cap the fittings immediately to keep out dirt.

4. On 1984–87 cars, remove the hose grom-

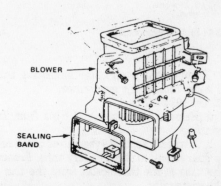

1987 Prelude blower assembly

mets from the firewall. Remove both lower dash panels.

5. On 1988–91 cars, remove the glove box.

6. Disconnect the wiring from the blower (1984–87) or the thermostat. Free the wiring from the clips.

7. On 1984–87 cars, remove the sealing band from between the blower and evaporator; remove the blower assembly.

8. On 1988–91 cars, remove the blower band if needed.

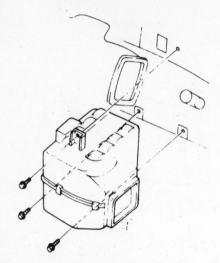

1987 Prelude evaporator assembly

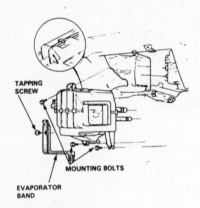

TAPPING
SCREW

MOUNTING BOLTS

EVAPORATOR
BAND

1988-91 Prelude evaporator

9. Remove the evaporator mounting nuts and bolts; remove the evaporator.

10. On 1984–87 cars:

a. Remove the screw and clips from the housing.

b. Carefully separate the halves of the case to gain access to the capillary tube. Remove the tube of the thermostat from the fins of the evaporator.

c. Separate the housing halves. Remove the cover.

d. Remove the expansion valve if necessary.

11. On 1988–91 Preludes:

a. Pull the evaporator sensor from the fins.

b. Remove the screws and clips holding the housing.

c. Carefully separate the housings and remove the covers.

d. Remove the expansion valve if necessary.

To install:

12. Reassemble the case components as necessary. Install the capillary tube in its original location. Reassemble the upper and lower case halves, making sure there are no gaps in the case.

13. Install the evaporator assembly and install the retaining nuts. Don't forget to attach the evaporator drain hose and route it out of the car.

14. Connect the thermostat wire or blower wire harness.

13. Install the glove box if it was removed. On early cars, install the blower motor.

14. Install the sealing bands. Check their positioning for an air-tight seal.

15. On 1984–87 cars, install the lower dash panels.

16. On 1984–87 cars, install the grommets at the firewall.

17. Connect the receiver line and suction hose. Tighten the receiver line to 17 Nm (12 ft. lbs) and the suction line to 32 Nm (23 ft. lbs).

18. Have the air conditioning system recharged at a properly equipped facility.

RADIO

REMOVAL AND INSTALLATION

NOTE: *Most Honda radio/tape players have a fuse mounted in the back of the unit. If the unit has stopped working, check the fuse before replacing the radio. Additionally, check the fuse in the regular fusebox.*

Accord

1. For cars before 1990, remove the floor console. On 1984–85 cars, if access to the back of the radio may be gained through other means, such as removing the "pocket" from the console, the console need not be removed.

2. Remove the ashtray and ashtray holder.

3. On 1986–89 cars:

a. Remove the coin box, air vents and ashtray lighting bracket.

b. Remove the dashboard switches on the left and right of the steering wheel.

c. Lower the steering wheel to its lowest position. Remove the dash visor. This is a large, one-piece assembly which includes the center dash trim. It's plastic; don't break it.

4. Remove the two screws holding the radio at the rear of the unit.

5. Carefully push the unit out the front of the dash. When access is gained, disconnect the multi-pin connector and the antenna cable from the unit. Remove the unit.

6. Reinstall in reverse order. Take great care

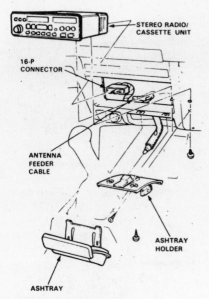

Stereo Installation, 1986-89 Accord

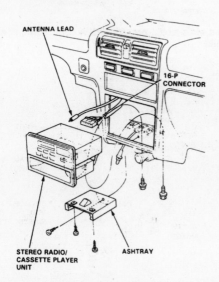

Radio/tape Installation, 1990-91 Accord

not to damage the dash trim and instrument visor. Make certain the connectors are firmly and squarely installed.

Prelude

1. Remove the console.
2. Remove the six screws holding the center instrument panel. Remove the panel with the switches and radio attached. Use care; the panel is easily damaged.
3. When access is gained, disconnect the multi-pin connector to the radio, the antenna connector (some Si models have two) and the cigar lighter connector.
4. With the dash panel and radio unit clear of

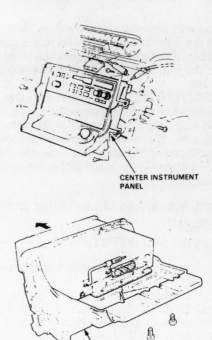

Prelude radio/tape unit removal

the dash, remove the two retaining screws holding the radio.
5. Reinstall the radio and secure the mounting bolts.
6. Connect the wiring, making sure connectors are firmly and squarely seated.
7. Fit the entire unit into the dash, taking care not to pinch or damage wiring.
8. Install the front console.

WINDSHIELD WASHERS AND WIPERS

Blade and Arm

REMOVAL AND INSTALLATION

NOTE: *Wiper blade element replacement is covered in Chapter 1.*

1. To remove the wiper blades, front or rear, lift up on the spring release tab on the wiper blade-to-wiper arm connector.
2. Pull the blade assembly off the wiper arm.
3. Press the old wiper blade insert down, away from the blade assembly, to free it from the retaining clips on the blade ends. Slide the insert out of the blade. Slide the new insert into the blade assembly and bend the insert upward slightly to engage the retaining clips.
4. To replace a wiper arm, unscrew the acorn nut which secures it to the pivot and carefully pull the arm upward and off the pivot. Install

the arm by reversing this procedure. Make certain the wiper arm is reinstalled in the correct position; if not correctly aligned, the blade will slap the bodywork at the top or bottom of its stroke.

CHILTON TIP: *If one wiper arm does not move when turned on or only moves a little bit, check the retaining nut at the bottom of the arm. The extra effort of moving snow or wet leaves off the glass can cause the nut to come loose − the pivot will move without moving the arm.*

Front Windshield Wiper Motor and Linkage

REMOVAL AND INSTALLATION

1. Remove the cap nuts and remove the wiper arms.
2. Remove the air grille or cowl. Use care not to mar the finish. The panels are held by plastic clips; the heads look like screws. Remove the plastic liner or seal below the cowl.
3. Pry the wiper linkage rod off the motor drive arm. The joint is a ball-and-socket type but can be very stiff to remove. On 1990–91 Accord, remove the center nut and washer to disconnect the motor shaft from the linkage.
4. If the motor has a protective cover, remove it.
5. Disconnect the wiring connector to the wiper motor.
6. Remove the mounting bolts and remove the motor.
7. If the linkage is to be removed, disconnect the rods from the wiper pivots. Joints are ball-and-socket and may be carefully pried apart.
8. The pivots are bolted to the firewall and may be unbolted for replacement.
9. Reassemble in reverse order. Make certain the linkage is firmly connected to the motor. Tighten the mounting bolts to 10 Nm (7 ft. lbs). When reinstalling the wiper arms, allow about 1 in. (25mm) of clearance between the base of the windshield and the blade. If the wipers are too far out of position − either high or low − they will slap either the bottom molding or pillar trim when operating on wet glass.

Rear Windshield Wiper Motor

REMOVAL AND INSTALLATION

1. Remove the tonneau (luggage cover) if equipped and remove the inner trim panel from the hatch lid.
2. Remove the wiper arm from the outside of the hatch lid. Remove the caps, washers and shaft nut from the wiper arm shaft.

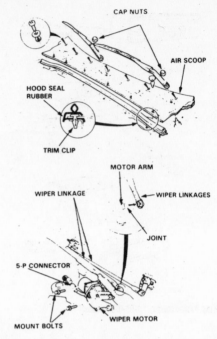

Front wiper motor removal; 1988 Accord shown, all are similar

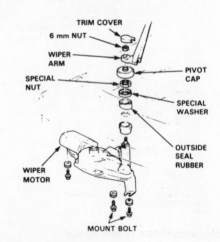

Accord rear wiper motor removal

3. Disconnect the wiring from the wiper motor.
4. Remove the mounting bolts and remove the motor.
5. Reassemble in reverse order. Make certain the linkage is firmly connected to the motor. Tighten the mounting bolts to 10 Nm (7 ft. lbs). When reinstalling the wiper arm, allow about 1 in. (25mm) of clearance between the base of the glass and the blade. If the wiper is too far out of position − either high or low − it will slap the bottom molding or pillar trim when operating on wet glass.

INSTRUMENTS AND SWITCHES

Instrument Cluster

REMOVAL AND INSTALLATION

1984–85 Accord

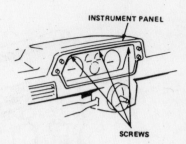

Remove the bezel screws first

1. Remove the steering wheel.
2. Remove the three screws at the top of the bezel (surround or trim piece). Using a spray lubricant such as silicone or vinyl protectant, lubricate the area between the bezel and the dashboard. The panel is a tight fit.
3. Remove the trim panel from the dash. A pulling tool may be used at the bottom, but great care must be taken not to crack the plastic.
4. When the panel is loose in the dash, remove the 4 screws holding the gauge assembly. Pull the gauge assembly forward just enough to allow access to the wires and speedometer cable.
5. Disconnect the speedometer cable and disconnect the electrical harnesses. Do not pull on the wires when disconnecting the harnesses. Remove the gauge assembly.

To install:

6. Individual instruments may be removed from the cluster after it is removed from the car. Avoid damage to any terminals or the printed circuit board.
7. Install the gauge cluster; connect the wiring and speedometer cable before it is fully in place. Install the retaining screws.
8. Re-lubricate the area contacted by the bezel. Install the bezel, making certain it is evenly placed with no gaps or bends.
9. Install the 3 retaining screws.
10. Install the steering wheel.

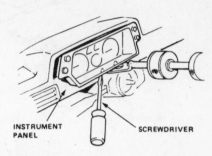

Use extreme caution if a puller is used — damage is easily caused

1986–89 Accord

1. Lower the steering wheel to its lowest position.
2. Remove each switch from the lower dashboard. The switches may be removed by gently prying up on the bottom edge to release them. Use a padded tool to avoid damage to the surrounding area. Once loose, pull the switch straight out and disconnect the wiring.
3. On the top of the instrument visor, remove the small access lid. Remove the two screws below the lid.
4. Remove the 4 lower screws (in the ports occupied by the switches). Remove the instrument panel.
5. Remove the four screws holding the gauge cluster. Pull it forward just enough to gain access to the wiring and speedometer cable.
6. Disconnect the wiring harness and the

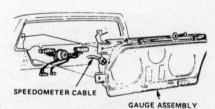

Disconnect the wiring and cable before removing the instrument cluster

speedometer cable. Remove the gauge assembly.

7. Individual instruments may be removed from the cluster after it is removed from the car. Avoid damage to any terminals or the printed circuit board.

To install:

8. Install the gauge cluster; connect the wiring and speedometer cable before it is fully in place. Install the retaining screws.
9. Install the panel, making sure it is squarely set and properly seated. Install the retaining screws at the top (2) and the bottom (4).
10. Install the upper lid.
11. Connect the wiring to each switch. Reinstall the switches, making sure they are firmly seated in place.

1990–91 Accord

1. Lower the steering column to its lowest position. The job will be easier if the wheel is removed.

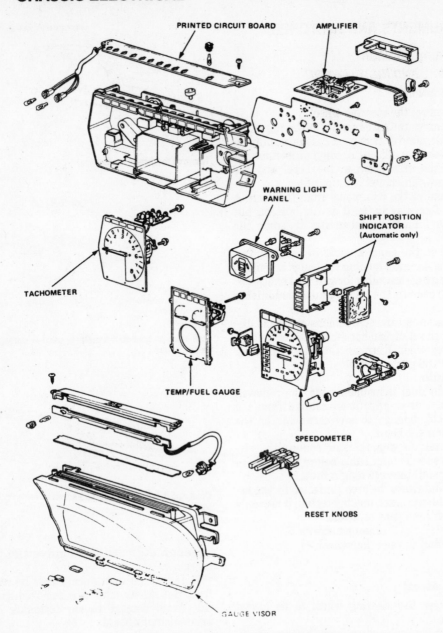

PRINTED CIRCUIT BOARD   AMPLIFIER

WARNING LIGHT
PANEL

SHIFT POSITION
INDICATOR
(Automatic only)

TACHOMETER

TEMP/FUEL GAUGE

SPEEDOMETER

RESET KNOBS

GAUGE VISOR

Instrument cluster components — Nippon Seiki

2. Remove the center console.

3. Remove the ashtray and ashtray holder.

4. Remove the radio/tape player.

5. Remove the coin box, switches and dash light controller from the instrument panel.

6. Remove the side and center air vents.

7. Remove the 12 mounting screws; remove the instrument panel. This is a large, formed piece of plastic — don't crack it.

8. Remove the four screws holding the instrument cluster. Pull the cluster forward enough to allow access to the wiring connectors.

9. Disconnect the wiring harnesses and remove the instrument cluster.

10. Individual instruments may be removed from the cluster after it is removed from the car. Avoid damage to any terminals or the printed circuit board.

To install:

11. Install the gauge cluster; connect the wiring before it is fully in place. Install the retaining screws.

12. Install the instrument panel. Make sure it is correctly placed. Install the 12 retaining screws.

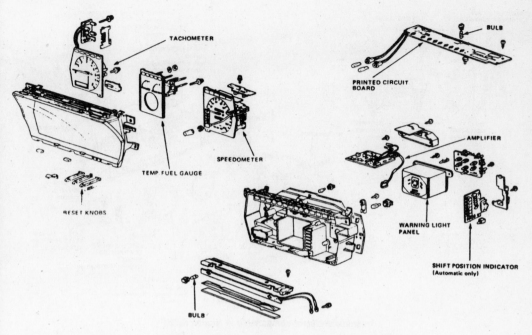

Instrument cluster components — Nippon Denso (ND)

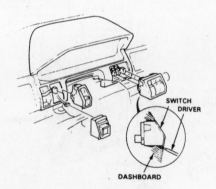

Use care when removing switch assemblies.

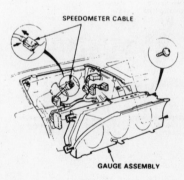

Removing the gauge assembly for 1986-89 Accord

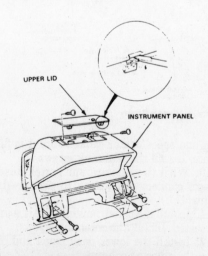

Don't break the tabs off the lid during removal

13. Install the air vents.

14. Install the coin box, switches and dash light controller.

15. Install the radio, ashtray holder and ashtray.

16. Install the console.

1984–87 Prelude

1. Lower the steering column.

2. Remove the lower dash panel.

3. Remove the four screws holding the instrument panel. Gently pull the panel away from the dash. Reach behind it and disconnect the wiring connectors to the switches.

4. Remove the panel.

5. Remove the two screws holding the gauge assembly. They are reached from under the dash and thread upwards.

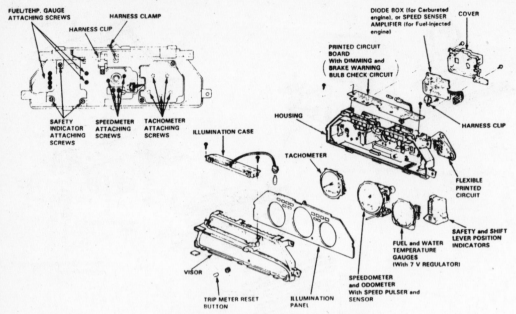

Instrument cluster components — Nippon Seiki

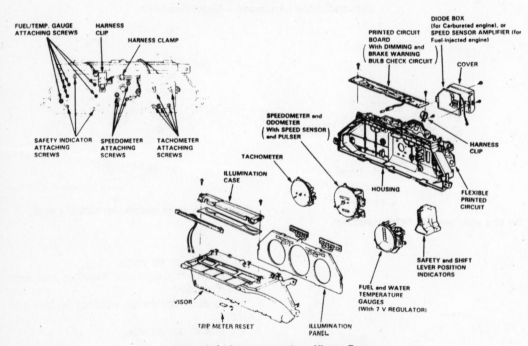

Instrument cluster components — Nippon Denso

6. Lift the gauge assembly; disconnect the wire connectors and the speedometer cable.

7. Remove the gauge assembly.

8. Individual instruments may be removed from the cluster after it is removed from the car. Avoid damage to any terminals or the printed circuit board.

To install:

9. Install the gauge cluster; connect the wir-ing and speedometer cable before it is fully in place. Install the retaining screws.

10. With the instrument panel loosely in place, connect the wiring to each switch or control.

11. Install the panel, making sure it is proper-ly seated. Install the retaining screws.

12. Install the lower dash panel and reposi-tion the steering column.

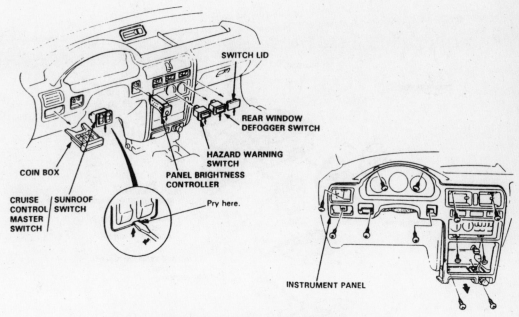

SWITCH LID

REAR WINDOW DEFOGGER SWITCH

HAZARD WARNING SWITCH

PANEL BRIGHTNESS CONTROLLER

COIN BOX

CRUISE CONTROL MASTER SWITCH

SUNROOF SWITCH

Pry here.

INSTRUMENT PANEL

Use great care in removing dash components on 1990- 91 Accord

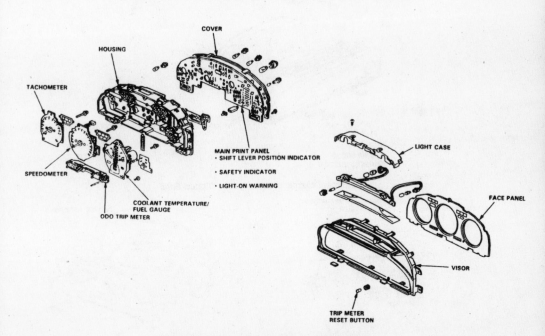

COVER

HOUSING

TACHOMETER

SPEEDOMETER

COOLANT TEMPERATURE/ FUEL GAUGE

ODO TRIP METER

MAIN PRINT PANEL
• SHIFT LEVER POSITION INDICATOR

• SAFETY INDICATOR

• LIGHT-ON WARNING

LIGHT CASE

FACE PANEL

VISOR

TRIP METER RESET BUTTON

Instrument cluster components — Nippon Denso

1988–91 Prelude

1. Lower the steering column to its lowest position.

2. Remove the dash light brightness controller and remove the headlight/foglight switch assembly.

3. Remove the five screws holding the instrument panel. Pull the panel away from the dash until the wires and connectors can be reached and disconnected.

4. Remove the four screws holding the gauge assembly and pull the assembly outward a bit. Disconnect the wiring connectors without pulling on the wiring.

5. Remove the gauge assembly.

6. Individual instruments may be removed from the cluster after it is removed from the car. Avoid damage to any terminals or the printed circuit board.

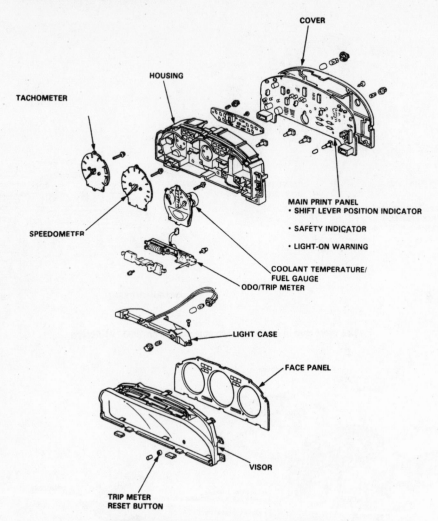

COVER

HOUSING

TACHOMETER

SPEEDOMETER

MAIN PRINT PANEL
- SHIFT LEVER POSITION INDICATOR
- SAFETY INDICATOR
- LIGHT-ON WARNING

COOLANT TEMPERATURE/
FUEL GAUGE

ODO/TRIP METER

LIGHT CASE

FACE PANEL

VISOR

TRIP METER
RESET BUTTON

Instrument cluster components – Nippon Selki

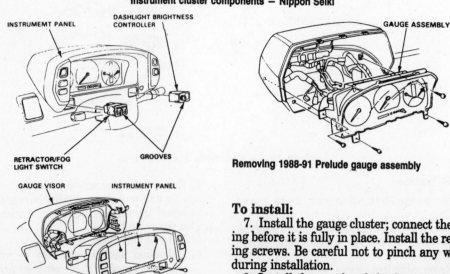

INSTRUMEMT PANEL

DASHLIGHT BRIGHTNESS
CONTROLLER

GAUGE ASSEMBLY

RETRACTOR/FOG
LIGHT SWITCH

GROOVES

Removing 1988-91 Prelude gauge assembly

GAUGE VISOR

INSTRUMENT PANEL

Removing 1988-91 Prelude Instrument panel

To install:
7. Install the gauge cluster; connect the wiring before it is fully in place. Install the retaining screws. Be careful not to pinch any wiring during installation.
8. Install the panel and the five screws.
9. Install the dash light controller and the lighting switches.

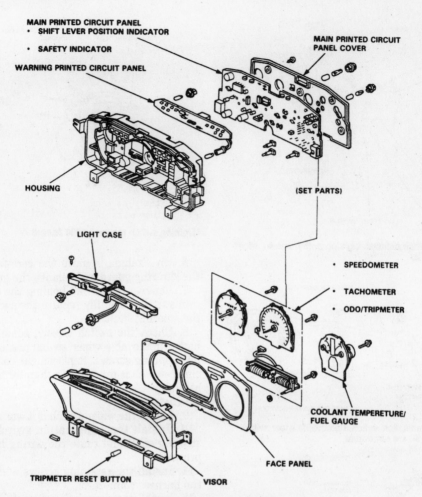

MAIN PRINTED CIRCUIT PANEL
• SHIFT LEVER POSITION INDICATOR
• SAFETY INDICATOR
WARNING PRINTED CIRCUIT PANEL
MAIN PRINTED CIRCUIT PANEL COVER
HOUSING
(SET PARTS)
LIGHT CASE
• SPEEDOMETER
• TACHOMETER
• ODO/TRIPMETER
COOLANT TEMPERETURE/ FUEL GAUGE
FACE PANEL
TRIPMETER RESET BUTTON
VISOR

1991 Prelude gauge assembly

Combination Switch
REMOVAL AND INSTALLATION
1988–91 Prelude

1. Remove the steering wheel.
2. Disconnect the wiring connector for the switch to be removed. The lighting switch involves a 14-pin connector at the main harness and an 8-pin connector at the fusebox. The wiper switch requires disconnecting the 10-pin connector at the fusebox.
3. Remove the lower dashboard panel.
4. Remove the upper and lower covers from the steering column.
5. Remove the two screws holding either the headlight or wiper switch to the housing and slide the switch outward. Be advised these mounting screws are tight — use a screwdriver of the correct size to avoid damaging the screw heads.
6. Installation is the reverse of removal. Make certain all wiring connections are tight and the harnesses are secured in place.

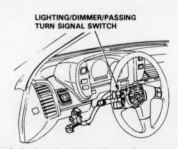

LIGHTING/DIMMER/PASSING TURN SIGNAL SWITCH

1988-91 Prelude turn signal/headlight switch wiring harnesses

1984–87 Prelude
1984–89 Accord

In some cases, the headlight/turn signal and wiper switches are not individually replaceable. If either switch fails (or the lever breaks off), the entire combination switch must be replaced. In general, later models may have replaceable switches.

1. Remove the steering wheel.

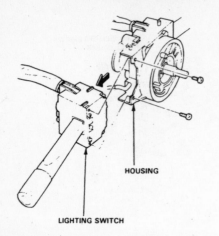

Detail of switch removal. Lighting switch shown, wiper switch similar

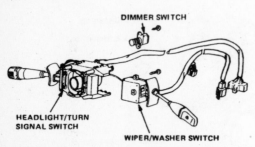

Prelude combination switch. Removable wiper switch shown; not all are removable

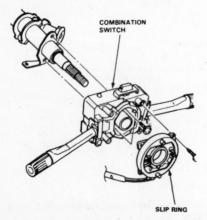

Accord and Prelude combination switch and slip ring

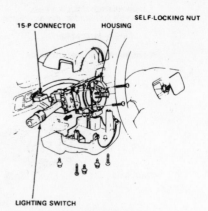

Lighting switch removal, 1990 Accord

6. On Prelude, remove the screws holding the slip ring guard and remove the guard.

7. Remove the screws holding the combination switch. Carefully remove the switch from the steering shaft.

8. Check the switch closely; some versions have a removable wiper switch assembly held by retaining screws. Replacement cost for the single switch is much lower than for the entire assembly.

To install:

9. Install the wiper switch if it was removed.

10. Install the combination switch on the steering shaft and route the wiring harnesses properly.

11. Install the retaining screws and connect the harness connectors.

12. Install the cancel sleeve; install the slip ring guard.

13. Install the upper and lower column covers.

14. Install the steering wheel.

1990–91 Accord

1. Remove the steering wheel.

2. Remove the upper and lower column covers.

3. Disconnect the wiring connector for the switch to be removed, either 15-pin for the lighting switch or 8-pin and 2-pin for the washer/wiper switch.

4. If equipped with cruise control, disconnect and remove the slip ring assembly.

5. Remove the two screws holding either the headlight or wiper switch to the housing and slide the switch outward. Be advised these mounting screws are tight – use a screwdriver of the correct size to avoid damaging the screw heads.

6. Installation is the reverse of removal. Make certain all wiring connections are tight and the harnesses are secured in place.

2. Remove the upper and lower column covers.

3. If equipped with cruise control, disconnect and remove the slip ring assembly.

4. Remove the turn signal canceling sleeve, a small fitting on the steering shaft inside the combination switch.

5. Disconnect the wiring harness connectors for the combination switch.

Speedometer Cable
REMOVAL AND INSTALLATION

1. Remove the instrument cluster and disconnect the cable at the speedometer. On some models it may be possible to disconnect the cable by reaching under the dash. Some connectors screw onto the back of the speedometer; others are held by plastic clips.

2. Disconnect the other end of the speedometer cable at the transaxle housing and pull the cable from its jacket at the transmission end. If you are replacing the cable because it is broken, don't forget to remove both pieces of broken cable.

3. Lubricate the new cable with graphite speedometer cable lubricant, and feed it into the cable jacket from the lower end.

4. Connect the cable to the transmission, then to the speedometer. Note that both ends of the cable are square; the ends must fit properly in the fittings.

5. Plug the electrical connector into the instrument cluster, and replace the cluster if it was removed..

LIGHTING

Headlights

REMOVAL AND INSTALLATION
Sealed Beams

CAUTION: *Most headlight retaining rings and trim bezels have very sharp edges. Wear gloves. Never pry or push on a headlamp; it can shatter suddenly.*

1. On cars with pop-up or retracting headlamps — 1986–89 Accords and all Preludes — turn the ignition switch OFF. Operate the retractor switch on the dash to bring the headlight doors UP. The headlights should be off when the doors are up.

2. Remove the headlight bezel (trim). On 1984–85 Accord, the trim involves the one piece lamp surround and corner molding.

3. The sealed beam is held in place by a retainer and either 2 or 4 small screws. Identify these screws before applying any tools.

DO NOT confuse the small retaining screws with the larger aiming screws. There will be two aiming screws or adjustors for each lamp. (One adjustor controls the up/down motion and the other controls the left/right motion.) Identify the adjustors and avoid them during removal. If they are not disturbed, the new headlamp will be in identical aim to the old one.

4. Using a small screwdriver (preferably magnetic) and a pair of taper-nose pliers if nec-

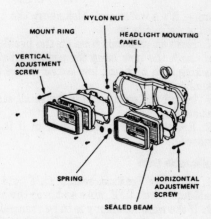

Headlamp replacement, — 1984-85 Accord

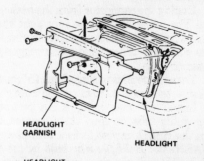

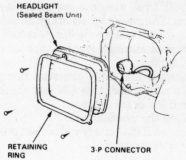

Headlamp replacement, — 1986-89 Accord and all Prelude

essary, remove the small screws in the headlamp retainer. DON'T drop the screws; they vanish into unknown locations.

CHILTON TIP: *A good kitchen or household magnet placed on the shank of the screwdriver will provide enough grip to hold the screw during removal.*

5. Remove the retainer and the headlamp may be gently pulled free from its mounts. Detach the connector from the back of the sealed beam unit and remove the unit from the car.

CAUTION: *The retainers can have very sharp edges! Wear gloves.*

6. Place the new headlamp in position and connect the wiring harness. Remember to install the rubber boot on the back of the new

lamp – it's a water seal. Make sure the head-light is right-side up.

7. Have an assistant turn on the headlights and check the new lamp for proper function, checking both high and low beams before final assembly.

8. Install the retainer and the small screws that hold it.

9. Reinstall the headlight trim if it was removed.

Replaceable Bulb

1. With the ignition switch OFF and the headlamp switch OFF, raise and prop the hood.

2. If the right headlamp is to be changed, lift out the coolant reservoir. Disconnect and re-move the battery.

3. Unplug the connector from the back of the lamp. The connector may be very tight and re-quire wiggling to loosen; support the lamp while with your other hand while wiggling the connector loose.

4. Turn the retaining ring about 45° counter-clockwise to loosen it. Remove the bulb.

5. Install the new bulb. Make certain all three guide tabs fit into their correct slots. Turn the ring clockwise to lock it in place.
WARNING: *Hold the new bulb by the base; do NOT touch the glass part with fingers or gloves. The grease left on the glass will form hot spots and shorten the life of the bulb. If the glass is accidentally touched, clean the glass with alcohol.*

6. Connect the wiring connector firmly.

7. Turn the headlights ON and check both high and low beam function.

8. Turn the headlights OFF.

9. Reinstall the battery and coolant reservoir if they were removed.

Signal, Marker and Interior Lamps
REMOVAL AND INSTALLATION

Newer cars use many sealed lamp units, the lens is not separately removable for bulb access. These sealed units are much more efficient at eliminating dust and water from the housing; bulb access is from the rear of the unit. In this case, the assembly must be removed from its mount. In some cases, the mounting screws are visible and in other situations, the lamp is on a bracket which attaches some distance from the lamp.

Whenever an assembly is to be removed, study the situation carefully; other trim pieces may need to be removed to expose retaining screws. Always beware of the hidden screw. Re-placement lens assemblies are not cheap.

For the rear lamps, front marker lamps and some front turn signals, the socket and bulb is

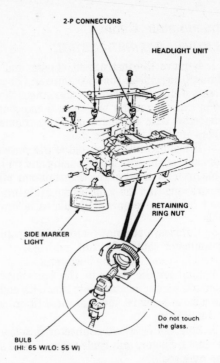

Accord replaceable bulb headlamp. Removal of the lens assembly is not required to change a bulb

removed from the lens with a counterclockwise turn. Once the socket is removed from the lens, the bulb is removed either with a half-twist mo-tion or, on smaller bulbs, by pulling straight out. Use care and wear gloves; bulbs break easily.

When installing new lamps, note that the socket for some turn signal bulbs have two dif-ferent length guide grooves; the lamp only fits correctly one way. (It is possible to do it wrong, but it requires a lot of force.) If you find that you're pushing on the bulb with no result dur-ing installation, you've got it backwards.

Smaller interior lenses usually fit in place with plastic clips and must be pried or popped out of place. A small, flat, plastic tool is ideal for this job; if other tools are used, care must be taken not to break the lens or the clip.

The lamps used on Honda vehicles are all US standard and may be purchased at any auto store or dealer. Because of the variety of lamps used on any vehicle, take the old one with you when shopping for the replacement.
WARNING: *Any light bulb gets hot when op-erating. If you're removing a good bulb to test or work on the circuit, either wear gloves or disconnect the circuit and allow the lamp to cool before removal. Many of the torpedo-shaped interior lamps can give a nasty burn when grabbed by the unsuspecting.*

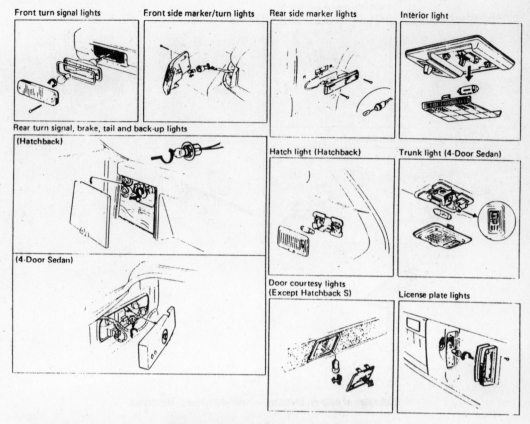

Front turn signal lights

Front side marker/turn lights

Rear side marker lights

Interior light

Rear turn signal, brake, tail and back-up lights

(Hatchback)

(4-Door Sedan)

Hatch light (Hatchback)

Trunk light (4-Door Sedan)

Door courtesy lights (Except Hatchback S)

License plate lights

Examples of bulb replacement — 1984-85 Accord

TRAILER WIRING

See Chapter 1 for information on which vehicles can be used for towing and review the restrictions.

CIRCUIT PROTECTION

Fusible Links

The fusible links serve as main circuit protection for certain high amperage circuits. The Honda fusible or main links are located at the in the under-hood fuse and relay box. On earlier models, these are large strips of conductive metal held by bolts between two terminals. The thickness and length of the material determines the amperage rating of the link. To replace one of these, turn the ignition switch OFF, unbolt the failed one and install the new one.

On later cars, the main links appear about the same size as the fuses; they are square cases with a small window on top. Close examination will reveal the amperage rating, usually 50 or 80 amps. Remove these links as you would a fuse.

If the link failed, it was due to a high amperage load passing through the circuit; find the cause or the new link will fail again.

Fuses

The fuse block is located below the left side of the instrument panel on all vehicles. Additional fuses are found on the underhood relay board. The radio or audio unit is protected by an additional fuse in the body of the unit. In the event that anything electrical isn't working, the fuse should be the first item checked. Generally, the in-car fusebox holds fuses for the cabin circuits such as wipers, cigarette lighter, rear defogger, etc. The underhood fusebox generally contains fuses and relays for engine and major electrical systems such as air conditioning, headlights (left and right separately), fuel injection components, etc.

It is in your best interest to read the owner's manual carefully and identify the location of certain fuses which could affect the safety and operation of the vehicle. You could drive home without the heater fan; could you make the same trip without headlights?

Each fuse location is labeled on the fuseblock, identifying its primary circuit, but designations

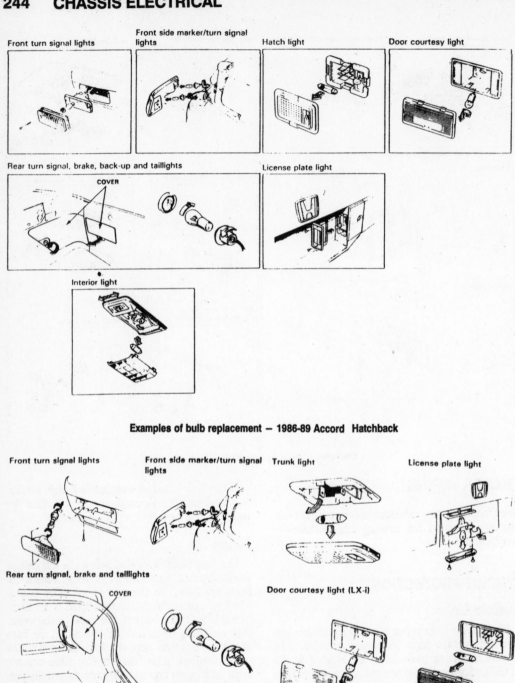

Front turn signal lights

Front side marker/turn signal lights

Hatch light

Door courtesy light

Rear turn signal, brake, back-up and taillights

COVER

License plate light

Interior light

Examples of bulb replacement — 1986-89 Accord Hatchback

Front turn signal lights

Front side marker/turn signal lights

Trunk light

License plate light

Rear turn signal, brake and taillights

COVER

Door courtesy light (LX-i)

Brake, Tail and back-up lights

Interior light

High mount brake light

Sunvisor light (LX-i)

Examples of bulb replacement — 1986-89 Accord Sedan and Coupe

Front turn signal lights

Front side marker and turn signal lights/position lights

Interior/cargo area light

Sunvisor light

Rear turn signal/brake and taillights/back-up lights

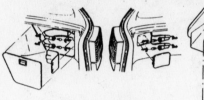

Door courtesy lights

(Front)

(Rear)

License plate lights

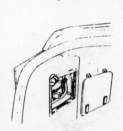

High-mount brake light

Bulb replacement — 1990-91 Accord Wagon

Front turn signal lights

Front side marker and turn signal lights/position lights

Interior light

Sunvisor light (LX/EX)

Rear turn signal/brake and taillights

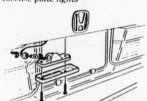

Door courtesy lights (LX/EX)

Trunk light

Brake and taillights/back-up lights

License plate lights

High mount brake light

Bulb replacement — 1990-91 Accord Coupe and Sedan

Rear side marker, turn signal, brake, taillights and back-up lights

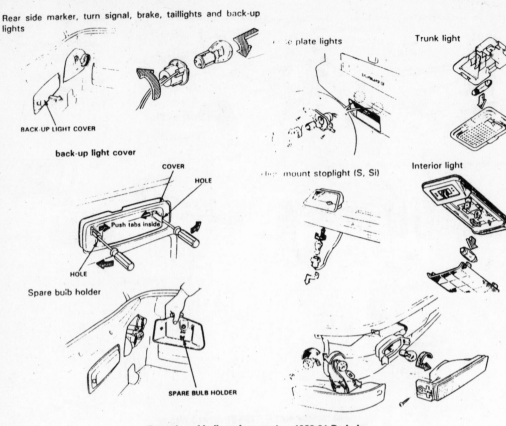

Examples of bulb replacement — 1988-91 Prelude

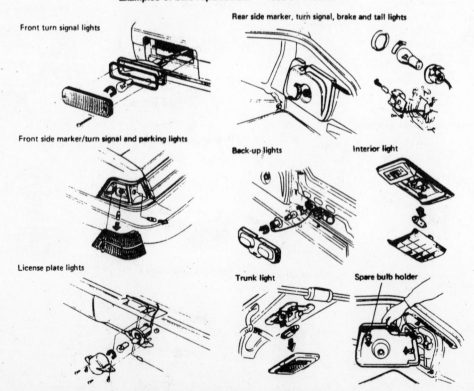

Examples of bulb replacement — 1984-87 Prelude

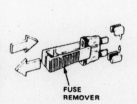

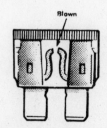

Blown

FUSE
REMOVER

The fuse puller makes removing a failed fuse much easier

such as BACKUP, CCON or IG 1 may not tell you what you need to know. A fuse can control more than one circuit, so check related circuits as well. This sharing of fuses is necessary to conserve space and wiring; if every circuit had its own fuse, the fuse box would be the size of the trunk lid.

The underdash or underhood fusebox contains a fuse puller which can be used to grip and remove the fuse. The fuse cannot be checked while in the fuseblock; it must be removed. View the fuse from the side, looking for a broken element in the center. Sometimes the break is hard to see; if you can't check the fuse with an ohmmeter for continuity, replace the fuse.

If a fuse should blow, turn off the ignition switch and also the circuit involved. Replace the fuse with one of the same amperage rating, and turn on the switches. If the new fuse immediately blows out, the circuit should be tested for shorts, broken insulation, or loose connections.

NOTE: *Do not use fuses of a higher amperage than recommended.*

Relays

As vehicles rely more and more on electronic systems and electrically operated options, the number of relays grows steadily. Many relays are located in logical positions on the relay and fuse board under the dash or in the engine compartment. However, many relays are located throughout the vehicle, often near the component they control. During diagnosis of a circuit, always suspect a failed relay until proven otherwise. Sometimes, a solid rap with the handle of a screwdriver will free an internally stuck relay and restore the system to operation. This isn't often the case, but when it works you'll brag about it for weeks.

Drive Train

7

MANUAL TRANSAXLE

Identification

A 5-speed synchronized manual transmission is available for all Accords or Preludes. Only one gearbox is offered for each family; there are no optional ratios or gear arrangements. The transaxle number, stamped on the case, indicates the family and running serial number for the transaxle. In general, transaxles are not interchangeable between model families.

If you're considering replacing the transaxle rather than repairing a failure, stick to the same transaxle group; i.e., if the old unit's trans number was A2Q5, then that is also what the replacement unit must be. Transaxle identification numbers begin with the following groups:

- 1984–85 Accord, California, 49 State and Hi Alt: GS
- 1984–85 Accord, Low Altitude (49 State only): GY
- 1984–85 Prelude, All: GM
- 1986–87 Accord, Fuel injected: A2Q5
- 1986–87 Accord, Carbureted: A2Q6
- 1986–87 Prelude, Fuel injected: A2K5
- 1986–87 Prelude, Carbureted: A1B5
- 1988 Accord, Fuel injected: E2Q5
- 1988 Accord, Carbureted: E2Q6
- 1988 Prelude, Fuel injected: D2J5
- 1988 Prelude, Carbureted: D2J4
- 1989 Accord, Fuel injected: E2R5
- 1989 Accord, Carbureted: E2R6
- 1989 Prelude, Fuel injected: D2J3
- 1989 Prelude, Carbureted: D2M4
- 1990–91 Accord, All: H2A5
- 1990–91 Prelude, All: D2A4

Adjustments

LINKAGE

On 1984–1989 Accords and 1984–1987 Preludes, the rods running between the shift lever and the transaxle are not adjustable. Trouble or stiffness in the mechanism is repaired by cleaning, lubrication or the replacement of worn bushings, seals, etc.

Later cars use a set of two cables rather than fixed-length rods to transfer the motion of the shifter. The cables are adjustable, but the need for adjustment is rare. The cables rarely go out of adjustment; altering their settings should only be considered in cases of collision repair or cable replacement. Even if the transaxle is removed, the cables may be disconnected without altering their settings.

1990–91 Accord

NOTE: *The select cable is on the driver's side of the shifter; the shift cable is on the right side of the shift lever.*

1. Firmly set the parking brake, block the wheels and place the shifter in neutral.
2. Remove the console.
3. At the select cable, measure the distance from the center of the mounting eye (at the shift lever) to the face just behind the locking clip (horseshoe clip). Correct distance should be 212.5–213.5mm (8.37–8.4 in.).
4. At the shift cable, measure the same interval. Correct distance is 174.3–175.3mm (6.86–6.90 in.).
5. If either cable is out of adjustment, remove the cotter pin holding the cable to the shifter, remove the plastic washer (take note of its correct position) and disconnect the cable from the shifter.
6. Loosen the locknut and turn the adjuster until the correct dimension is achieved. Measure the distance carefully each time and turn the adjuster in small increments.
7. Once the measurement is correct, tighten the locknut firmly.
8. Install the cable to the shift lever. Install the plastic washer and install a new cotter pin.

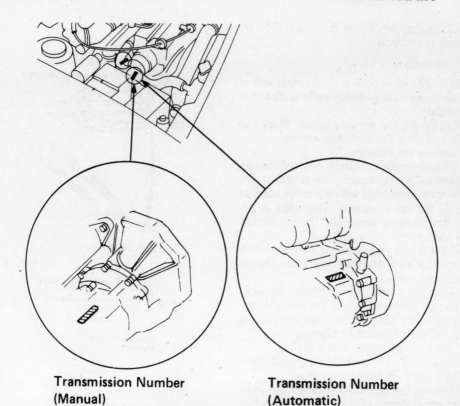

Transmission Number
(Manual)

Transmission Number
(Automatic)

Examples of transaxle number location

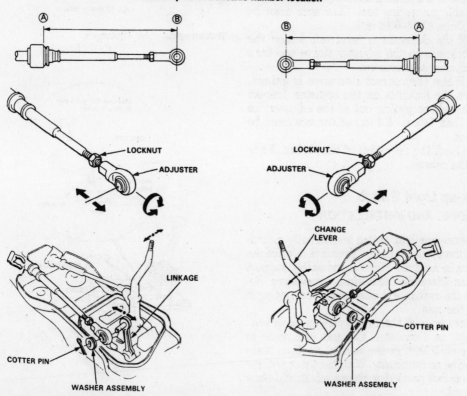

Adjusting the Accord select cable

Adjustment of the Accord shift cable

9. Check the operation of the gearshift lever. Reinstall the console.

1988–1991 Prelude

NOTE: *The select cable is on the right side of the shift lever; the gearshift cable is closest to the driver.*

1. Firmly set the parking brake, block the wheels and place the shifter in neutral.

2. Remove the console.

3. With the transmission in neutral, inspect the select cable adjustment. The groove in the lever bracket must align with the index mark or notch on the cable housing. The mark is between the adjusting sleeve and the connection to the shifter.

4. If the marks do not align, loosen the two locknuts on the adjuster sleeve and turn the adjuster as necessary.

5. When the marks align, tighten the locknuts on the adjuster. Inspect the threads projecting out of the adjuster; no more than 10mm (0.4 in.) of threads must be exposed.

6. Check the operation of the shifter.

7. Inspect the adjustment of the gearshift cable. Place the shift lever in 4th gear.

8. Measure the clearance between the lever bracket and the front edge of the stopper while pushing the lever forward. There is an inspection hole in the front of the bracket for using an insertable measuring tool. Clearance must be 6.0–7.0mm (0.24–0.28 in.).

9. If the clearance is incorrect, loosen the two locknuts on the adjuster sleeve and turn the adjuster as necessary.

10. When the correct clearance is gained, tighten the locknuts on the adjuster. Inspect the threads projecting out of the adjuster; no more than 10mm (0.4 in.) of threads must be exposed.

11. Check the operation of the shifter. Reinstall the console.

Back-up Light Switch

REMOVAL AND INSTALLATION

The reverse light switch is externally mounted on the transaxle case. To remove it, place the shifter in neutral. Elevate and safely support the car. Disconnect the wiring connectors. Remove the switch and washer by unscrewing it from the case.

Once removed, the switch may be easily tested with an ohmmeter. Connect one probe to each switch lead. In the normal position, there should be no continuity. With the tip or plunger of the switch pressed in, the switch should show continuity.

When installing, ALWAYS replace the wash-

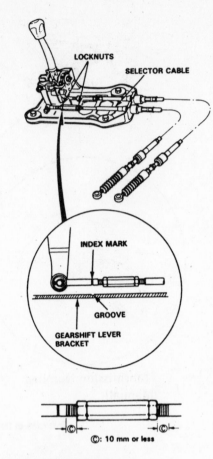

Prelude select cable adjustment

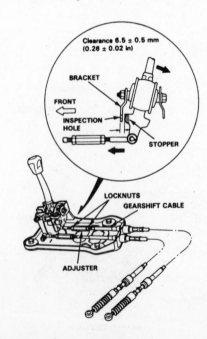

Adjusting the Prelude gearshift cable

er between the switch and the case. It not only guards against oil leaks but also sets the reach of the switch inside the transaxle. Install the switch and tighten it to 25 Nm (18 ft. lbs). Connect the wiring and lower the vehicle to the ground.

Halfshafts or Axles

REMOVAL AND INSTALLATION

1. Remove the wheel cover or hubcap from the front wheel and then remove the center cap.
2. Pull out the 4mm cotter pin and loosen but do not remove the spindle nut. Loosen the lugnuts.
3. Raise and safely support the front of the vehicle on jackstands. Double check the stand placement and the security of the support.
4. Remove the wheel lug nuts and the wheel.
5. Pry up the lock tabs and remove the large spindle nut.
6. Drain the transaxle.
7. Using a ball joint remover, remove the lower arm ball joints from the knuckle. Disconnect the tie rods from the steering

WARNING: *On models with a lower control arm, make sure that a floor jack is positioned securely under the lower control arm at the ball joint. Otherwise, the lower control arm may "jump" suddenly away from the steering knuckle as the ball joint is removed.*

8. On cars using a lower control arm, disconnect the stabilizer bar retaining bolts and free the bar.
9. On later cars with the "wishbone" suspension, remove the damper fork bolt and the damper pinch bolt.
10. To remove the driveshaft, hold the knuckle and pull it toward you. Then slide the driveshaft out of the knuckle.
11. At the inboard or transaxle end, pry the CV joint out about ½ in. (13mm). Prying the axle outward causes an internal lock ring to come out of its locking groove. Pry carefully to avoid damaging the oil seal.

WARNING: *Do not pull on the inboard CV joint; it may come apart.*

12. Pull the inboard side of the driveshaft out of the differential case.

To install:

13. Replace the spring clip on the inboard end of the axle.
14. Install the inner end of the axle to the transaxle. The splined fitting and clip must fit all the way into position; the clip will engage with a noticeable click. Double check it by prying lightly against it; don't pull on the CV joint to test it.
15. Pull the front hub outward and install the outer end of the halfshaft.

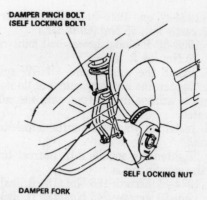

Wishbone suspension used on later Accords and Preludes

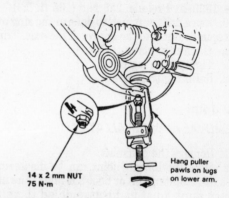

Removing the lower ball joint nut

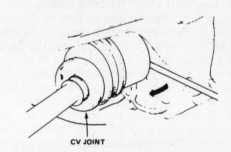

Pry carefully; the oil seal is easily damaged

16. Reassemble the suspension and steering ball joints. Use new cotter pins and new self-locking nuts for each fitting. Tighten the individual components as follows:
- 1984–85 Accord: Stabilizer bar bolts, 22 Nm (16 ft. lbs); lower ball joint 55 Nm (40 ft. lbs); tie rod castle nut, 44 Nm (32 ft. lbs).
- 1986–91 Accord: Damper pinch bolt, 44 Nm (32 ft. lbs.), damper fork or lower locknut, 65 Nm (47 ft. lbs.); lower ball joint castle nut, 55 Nm (40 ft. lbs).
- 1984–91 Prelude: Damper pinch bolt, 44 Nm (32 ft. lbs.), damper fork or lower locknut, 65 Nm (47 ft. lbs.)

• 1984–87 and 1990–91 Prelude: Lower ball joint castle nut, 55 Nm (40 ft. lbs.)

• 1988–89 Prelude: Lower ball joint castle nut, 75 Nm (54 ft. lbs.)

17. Install the washer and a NEW spindle nut. Tighten the nut very snug but do not attempt to achieve final torque with the vehicle elevated.

18. Install the wheel. Lower the vehicle to the ground.

19. Tighten the spindle nut. Correct torque for the spindle nut is:
• 1984–89 Accord: 185 Nm (134 ft. lbs)
• 1990–91 Accord: 245 Nm (180 ft. lbs)
• 1984–87 Prelude: 190 Nm (137 ft. lbs)
• 1988–89 Prelude: 185 Nm (134 ft. lbs)
• 1990–91 Prelude: 250 Nm (185 ft. lbs)

20. Use a drift or punch to deform the ring on the spindle nut into the groove in the axle. This locks the nut in place.

21. Tighten the lug nuts.

22. Refill the transaxle.

CV Joint

REMOVAL AND INSTALLATION

1. Remove the halfshaft.

2. Only the inboard joint can be disassembled. If the outer joint or boot has failed, the inboard joint must be disassembled to gain access.

3. Remove the large retaining band from the inboard boot. Remove the smaller band from the inboard boot and slide the boot off the joint.

NOTE: *The boot is filled with molybdenum disulfide ("moly") grease. This is an extremely slippery lubricant and very messy. Be prepared with plenty of rags. Wearing a shop apron or smock will protect your clothing.*

4. Carefully remove the stub-end of the inboard joint. Check the splines for cracks, wear or damage. Check the inside bore for any sign of wear.

5. Remove and discard the snap ring from the end of the halfshaft. This will allow removal of the spider assembly.

6. Mark the rollers, spider and the stub-end of the axle so that all parts may be reassembled in the same position. Remove the rollers from the spider.

7. Remove the second snap ring from the shaft. Remove the joint boot. On 1988–91 Prelude and 1990–91 Accord, remove the dynamic damper from the shaft.

8. If the boot for the outer joint is to be replaced, remove the boot clamps and slide the boot off the joint, then off the shaft. Hold the outer joint and swivel the end. Listen for any sound of failed bearings within. If the joint is

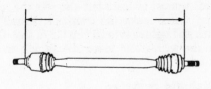

LEFT DRIVE SHAFT

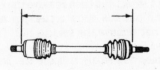

RIGHT DRIVESHAFT

Driveshaft length must be accurately set before installation

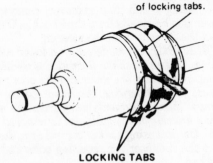

BOOT BANDS Bend both sets of locking tabs.

LOCKING TABS

Both sets of lock tabs must be engaged

noisy, it must be replaced. The replacement joint will come with a new shaft; the inner joint must be assembled onto the shaft.

9. Clean and inspect all disassembled parts. Any sign of wear requires replacement.

To install:

10. Thoroughly pack the inboard and outboard joints with moly grease. Use only moly grease; other lubricants will not last. Wrap the splines of the shaft in vinyl or electrical tape to protect the boots as they are installed.

11. Slide the boot for the outer joint over the shaft and onto the joint. Do not install the bands yet.

12. Slide the inner boot onto the shaft. Install the dynamic damper if it was removed.

13. Install the inboard snap ring on the shaft. Install the rollers and bearing races on the spider shafts. Hold the shaft upright, then slide the spider assembly into the inboard shaft joint. Install the outer snap ring.

14. Slide the boots over both joints. Position the small end of the boot the band will be cen-

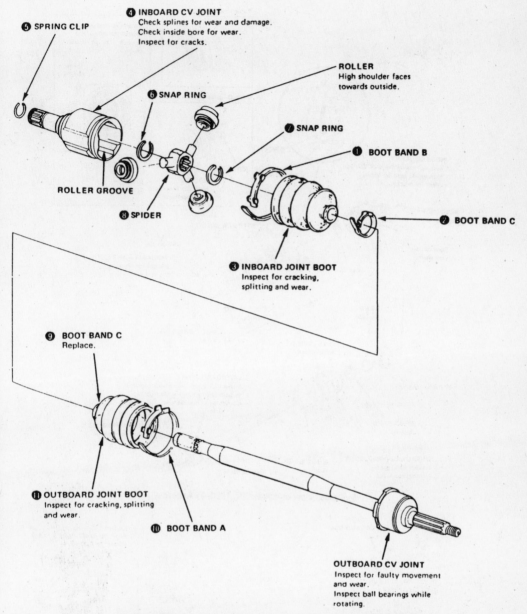

❺ SPRING CLIP

❹ INBOARD CV JOINT
Check splines for wear and damage.
Check inside bore for wear.
Inspect for cracks.

ROLLER
High shoulder faces
towards outside.

❻ SNAP RING

❼ SNAP RING

❶ BOOT BAND B

ROLLER GROOVE

❽ SPIDER

❷ BOOT BAND C

❸ INBOARD JOINT BOOT
Inspect for cracking,
splitting and wear.

❾ BOOT BAND C
Replace.

⓫ OUTBOARD JOINT BOOT
Inspect for cracking, splitting
and wear.

⓵ BOOT BAND A

OUTBOARD CV JOINT
Inspect for faulty movement
and wear.
Inspect ball bearings while
rotating.

Exploded view of driveshaft. Steps are numbered for disassembly

tered between the locating humps on the shaft. Install the band; bend both sets of locking tabs. Once the band is in place, expand and compress the boots once or twice; allow the boots to return to their normal size and length.

15. Adjust the length of the driveshaft to the specification given below. When the axle is at the correct length, adjust the boot to halfway between full extension and full compression. Correct shaft lengths are:

• 1884–85 Accord: Right, 496–500.5mm. Left, manual trans: 779–783.5mm. Left, automatic trans: 787–791.5mm.

• 1986–89 Accord: Right, 506–510.5mm. Left, manual trans: 805–809.5mm. Left, automatic trans: 812–816.5mm.

• 1984–87 Prelude, Carbureted: Right, 514–518.5mm. Left, manual trans: 800–804.5mm. Left, automatic trans: 809–813.5mm.

• 1984–87 Prelude, Fuel injected: Right, 506–510.5mm. Left, manual trans: 805–809.5 mm. Left, automatic trans: 812–816.5mm.

• 1988–91 Prelude: Left and right shafts, 496mm.

• 1990–91 Accord, manual trans: Left and right shafts, 478.7–483.7mm.

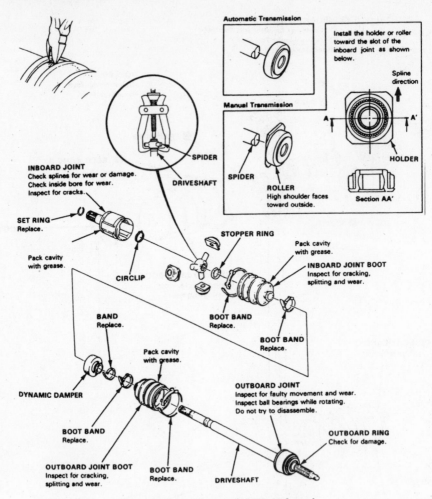

Install the holder or roller toward the slot of the inboard joint as shown below.

Automatic Transmission

Manual Transmission

SPIDER

ROLLER
High shoulder faces toward outside.

Spline direction

HOLDER

Section AA'

INBOARD JOINT
Check splines for wear or damage. Check inside bore for wear. Inspect for cracks.

SET RING
Replace.

Pack cavity with grease.

SPIDER

DRIVESHAFT

CIRCLIP

STOPPER RING

Pack cavity with grease.

INBOARD JOINT BOOT
Inspect for cracking, splitting and wear.

BAND
Replace.

BOOT BAND
Replace.

BOOT BAND
Replace.

Pack cavity with grease.

DYNAMIC DAMPER

BOOT BAND
Replace.

OUTBOARD JOINT
Inspect for faulty movement and wear. Inspect ball bearings while rotating. Do not try to disassemble.

OUTBOARD RING
Check for damage.

OUTBOARD JOINT BOOT
Inspect for cracking, splitting and wear.

BOOT BAND
Replace.

DRIVESHAFT

Exploded view of driveshaft, 1990–91 Accord

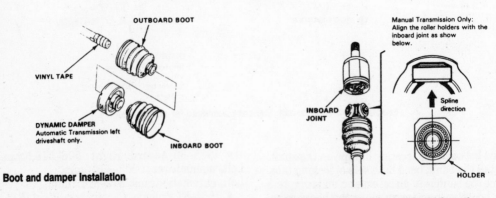

OUTBOARD BOOT

VINYL TAPE

DYNAMIC DAMPER
Automatic Transmission left driveshaft only.

INBOARD BOOT

Boot and damper Installation

Manual Transmission Only:
Align the roller holders with the inboard joint as show below.

INBOARD JOINT

Spline direction

HOLDER

Installing the spider and joint, 1990–91 Accord

• 1990–91 Accord, automatic trans: Left, 836.7–841.7mm. Right, 478.7–483.7mm.

16. Install new boot bands on the large ends of the boots. Be sure to bend both sets of locking tabs. Lightly tap the doubled-over portion of the band(s) to reduce the height. Do NOT hit the boot.

17. Position the dynamic damper so that it is 3–7mm from the CV boot. Install a new retaining band in the same fashion as the boot bands.

17. Install a NEW spring clip on the inboard end of the joint; install the driveshaft.

Transaxle

REMOVAL AND INSTALLATION

1984–89 Accord
1984–87 Prelude

NOTE: *All wires and hoses should be labeled at the time of removal. The amount of time saved during reassembly makes the extra effort well worthwhile.*

1. Disconnect the battery ground cable at the battery and the transmission case. Unlock the steering column; place the transmission in neutral.

2. Disconnect the following cables and wires:
   a. Clutch cable at the release arm.
   b. Back-up light switch wires.
   c. TCS (Transmission Controlled Spark) switch wires.
   d. Wire from the starter solenoid.

3. Release the engine sub-wiring harness from the clamp at the clutch housing. Remove the upper two transaxle mounting bolts.

4. Raise the front of the car and support it securely with safety stands. Double check the stand placement and security. Drain the transmission.

5. Remove the front wheels. Place a suitable transaxle jack into position under the transaxle.

6. Disconnect the speedometer cable.

NOTE: *When removing the speedometer cable from the transmission, it is not necessary to remove the entire cable holder. Remove the end boot (gear holder seal), the cable retaining clip and then pull the cable out of the holder. In no way should you disturb the holder, unless it is absolutely necessary.*

7. Disconnect the shift lever torque rod from the clutch housing. Remove the bolt from the shift rod clevis.

8. Disconnect the tie rod ball joints and remove them using a ball joint remover.

9. Remove the lower arm ball joint bolt from the right side lower control arm, then use a puller to disconnect the ball joint from the knuckle. Remove the damper fork bolt.

10. Disconnect the driveshafts from the transaxle. Move the axles out of the way but do not let them hang; support them with string or wire. Remove the right side radius rod.

11. Remove the damper bracket from the transaxle. Remove the clutch housing bolts from the front transaxle mount.

12. Remove the clutch housing bolts from the rear transaxle mounting bracket. Remove the clutch cover.

13. Remove the starter mounting bolts and remove the starter assembly through the chassis. Remove the transaxle mounting bolts.

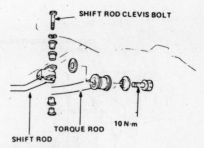

Shift linkage disassembly

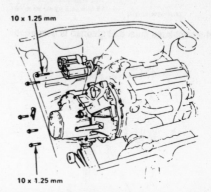

Transaxle and starter retaining bolts

14. Pull the transaxle away from the engine block to clear the two 14mm dowel pins and lower the transaxle jack.

WARNING: *Do not allow the transaxle to hang on the input shaft. Once removal begins, remove it completely from the engine.*

To install:

15. Place the transmission on the jack. Clean and grease the release bearing sliding surface.

16. Check that the two dowel pins are present in the bell housing.

17. Raise the unit enough to align the pins with the matching holes in the block.

18. Move the transaxle toward the engine and install the mainshaft into the clutch disc splines. If the left suspension was left in place, install new spring clips on both axles and carefully insert the left axle into the differential while installing the transaxle.

19. Push and wiggle the transaxle until it fits flush with the engine flange.

20. Tighten the bolts until the bell housing is seated against the engine block.

21. Loosely install the bolts for the front trans mount, then tighten them in sequence to 45 Nm (33 ft. lbs).

22. Install the rear transaxle mount, tightening the bolts to 45 Nm (33 ft. lbs).

23. Install the upper torque arm and its brackets. Tighten the bracket mounting bolts to 65 Nm (47 ft. Lbs) and the through-bolts to 75 Nm (54 ft lbs).

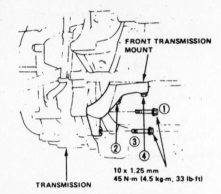

Front mount bolts must be tightened is sequence

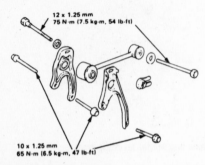

Upper torque arm and mount

24. Carefully remove the transmission jack.
25. Install the starter.
26. Install the driveshaft(s) if not previously done.
27. Install the lower arm ball joints, tie-rod ball joints and damper fork bolts.
28. Connect the shift rod linkage.
29. Connect the shift linkage.
30. connect the shift lever torque rod to the clutch housing. Tighten the 8mm bolt to 22 Nm (16 ft lbs).
31. Install the front wheels.
32. Double check that the transaxle drain plug is present and tightened.
33. The car may be lowered to the ground for the final steps.
34. Install the clutch cable at the release arm.
35. Coat a new O-ring with clean oil and install it on the speedometer gear holder. Install the holder in the transaxle and secure the hold-down tab and bolt.
36. Install the engine sub-wire harness in the clamp at the bell housing.
37. Connect the engine compartment wiring for the starter, starter solenoid and back-up light switch.
38. Fill the transaxle with the proper amount of lubricant.
39. Check the transaxle and clutch for smooth operation.

1988-91 Prelude

1. Disconnect the battery ground cable at the battery and the transmission case. Unlock the steering column; place the transmission in neutral.
2. Disconnect the following wires:
   a. Back-up light switch wires.
   b. Black/white wire from the starter solenoid.
3. On the fuel injected models, remove the air cleaner assembly.
4. Remove the power steering speed sensor from the transaxle without removing the power steering hose.
5. Remove the shift cable and the select cable from the top cover of the transaxle. Remove the mounting bolt from the cable stay. Be sure not to bend or kink the cable more than necessary. Remove both cables and the stay together.
6. Remove the upper transaxle mounting bracket. Remove the four transaxle-to-block attachment bolts that must be removed from the engine compartment.
7. Raise and support the vehicle safely. Remove both front wheels and remove the splash shield.
8. Drain the transmission oil into a drain pan. Remove the clutch slave cylinder. The cylinder may be moved out of the way without disconnecting the hose.
9. Remove the center beam. Remove the right radius rod completely. Remove the right and left drive shafts.
10. Remove the engine stiffener. Remove the clutch cover. Support the transaxle with a transmission jack.
11. Remove the three lower bolts from the rear engine mounting bracket. Loosen but do not remove the top bolt. This bolt will support the weight of the engine.
12. Remove the two remaining engine-to-transaxle mounting bolts.
13. With the transaxle on a transmission jack, disengage the input shaft from the clutch disc and lower the transaxle out of the vehicle.
WARNING: *Do not allow the transaxle to hang on the input shaft. Once removal begins, remove it completely from the engine.*

To install:

14. Place the transmission on the jack. Clean and grease the release bearing sliding surface.
15. Check that the two dowel pins are present in the bell housing.
16. Raise the unit enough to align the pins with the matching holes in the block.
17. Install and tighten the transaxle mount bolt on the engine side to 65 Nm (47 ft. Lbs.)
18. Install and tighten the transaxle bolts on the trans side to 65 Nm (47 ft lbs)

19. Install the transaxle mounting bracket; tighten the 3 bolts to 39 Nm (28 ft lbs). Tighten the horizontal bolt to 75 Nm (54 ft. Lbs).

20. Install the transaxle mounting bolts to the rear engine mounting bracket and tighten them to 75 Nm (54 ft lbs).

21. Install the engine stiffener. Tighten the bolts in sequence to 39 Nm (28 ft lbs).

22. Attach the intermediate shaft.

23. Install the driveshafts.

24. Install the center beam. Tighten the nuts to 51 Nm (37 ft lbs).

25. Attach the clutch slave cylinder; tighten the mounting bolts to 22 Nm (16 ft lbs).

26. Install the shift and select cables to the transaxle.

27. Connect the reverse lamp wiring.

28. Install the right and left front damper forks.

29. Install the speed sensor assembly.

30. Install the air cleaner case if it was removed.

31. Connect the starter ground and battery wires.

32. Connect the positive cable at the battery.

33. Install the front wheels.

34. Refill the transaxle with the proper amount of lubricant.

35. Check the shifter and clutch for smooth operation. Make adjustments as necessary.

1990–91 Accord

1. Disconnect the battery cables and remove the battery.

2. Raise and safely support the vehicle.

3. Remove the air intake hose and battery base.

4. Disconnect the starter wires and remove the starter.

5. Disconnect the transaxle ground cable and the back-up light switch wire.

6. Remove the cable support and then disconnect the cables from the top housing of the transaxle. Remove both cables and the support together. do not remove the clips holding the cables to the support.

7. Disconnect the connector and remove the speed sensor, but leave its hoses connected.

8. Remove the front wheels.

9. Remove the engine splash shield and drain the transaxle fluid.

10. Remove the mounting bolts and clutch slave cylinder with the clutch pipe and pushrod.

11. Remove the mounting bolt and clutch hose joint with the clutch pipe and clutch hose.

NOTE: *Do not operate the clutch pedal once the slave cylinder has been removed. Be careful not to bend the pipe.*

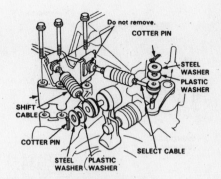

Disconnecting the transmission cables

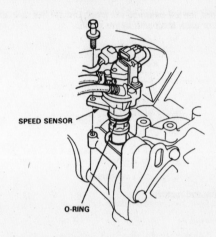

Use care when removing the speed sensor; always replace the O-ring

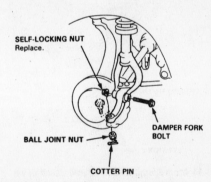

Disconnect the ball joint and damper fork bolt

12. Remove the center beam and the header pipe.

13. Remove the cotter pins and lower arm ball joint nuts. Separate the ball joints and lower arms using the correct tool.

14. Remove the damper fork bolt.

15. Pry the right and left halfshafts out of the differential and the intermediate shaft. Pull on the inboard joint and remove the right and left halfshafts.

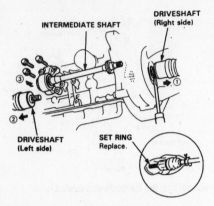

Remove the left intermediate shaft; protect the splined
ends of each shaft with heavy plastic

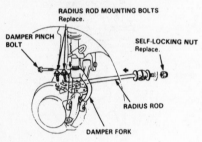

Radius rod removal

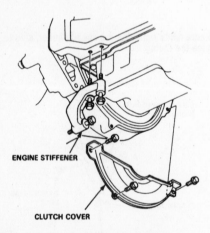

1990–91 Accord engine stiffener and clutch cover

16. Remove the 3 mounting bolts and lower
the bearing support.
17. Remove the intermediate shaft from the
differential.
18. Remove the right damper pinch bolt, then
separate the damper fork and damper. Remove
the bolts and nut, then remove the right radius
rod.
19. Remove the engine stiffener and the
clutch cover.
20. Remove the intake manifold bracket.

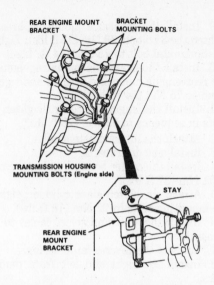

**Removing the rear engine support and transmission
bolts**

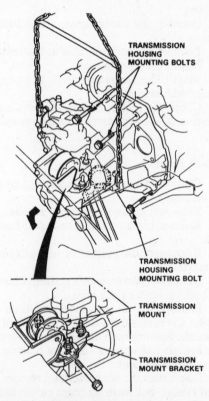

**Remove the weight from the transmission mounting
bolts before turning the bolts**

21. Remove the rear engine mount bracket
support and remove the 3 rear engine mount
bracket mounting bolts.
22. Remove the transaxle housing mounting
bolt on the engine side. Swing the right
halfshaft to the inner fender.

23. Place a suitable jack under the transaxle and raise the transaxle just enough to take the weight off the mounts.

24. Remove the transaxle mount bolt and loosen the mount bracket nuts.

25. Remove the 3 transaxle housing mounting bolts.

26. Remove the transaxle from the vehicle.

To install:

27. Make sure the 4 dowel pins are installed.

28. Raise the transaxle into position.

29. Install the 3 transaxle mounting bolts and tighten to 47 ft. lbs. (65 Nm).

30. Install the transaxle mount and mount bracket. Install the through bolt and tighten temporarily. Make sure the engine is level and tighten the 3 mount bracket nuts to 40 ft. lbs. (55 Nm). Tighten the through bolt to 47 ft. lbs. (65 Nm).

31. Install the transaxle housing mounting bolts on the engine side and tighten to 47 ft. lbs. (65 Nm).

32. Install the 3 rear engine bracket mounting bolts and tighten to 40 ft. lbs. (55 Nm).

33. Install the rear engine mount bracket stay. Tighten the mounting bolt to 39 Nm (28 ft. lbs.) and then tighten the mounting nut to 21 Nm (15 ft. lbs).

34. Install the intake manifold bracket and tighten the bolts to 16 ft. lbs. (22 Nm).

35. Install the clutch cover and tighten the bolts to 9 ft. lbs. (12 Nm).

36. Install the engine stiffener and loosely install the mounting bolts. Tighten the stiffener-to-transaxle case mounting bolt to 28 ft. lbs. (39 Nm), then tighten the 2 stiffener-to-cylinder block mounting bolts to 28 ft. lbs. (39 Nm) beginning with the bolt closest to the transaxle.

37. Install the radius rod. Tighten the radius rod mounting bolts to 76 ft. lbs. (105 Nm) and the radius rod nut to 32 ft. lbs. (44 Nm).

38. Install the damper fork. Tighten the damper pinch bolt to 32 ft. lbs. (44 Nm).

39. Install the intermediate shaft.

40. Install a NEW set ring on the end of each halfshaft. Install the right and left halfshafts. Turn the right and left steering knuckle fully outward and slide the axle into the differential until the spring clip is felt to engage in the differential side gear.

41. Install the damper fork bolt and ball joint nut to the lower arms. Tighten the nut while holding the damper fork bolt to 40 ft. lbs. (55 Nm). Tighten the ball joint nut to 40 ft. lbs. (55 Nm). Install a new cotter pin.

42. Install the header pipe and center beam. Tighten the center beam bolts to 28 ft. lbs. (39 Nm).

43. Install the clutch hose joint and clutch slave cylinder to the transaxle housing. Tighten the slave cylinder mounting bolts to 16 ft. lbs. (22 Nm).

44. Install the speed sensor. Tighten the mounting bolt to 13 ft. lbs. (18 Nm).

45. Install the shift cable and select cable to the shift arm lever and to the select lever respectively. Tighten the cable bracket mounting bolts to 16 ft. lbs. (22 Nm). Install new cotter pins.

46. Connect the back-up light switch coupler.

47. Install the starter. Tighten the 10 × 1.25mm bolt to 32 ft. lbs. (45 Nm) and the 12 × 1.25mm bolt to 54 ft. lbs. (75 Nm). Connect the starter wires.

48. Install the transaxle ground cable.

49. Install the front wheel and tire assemblies.

50. Fill the transaxle with the proper type and quantity of oil.

51. Lower the vehicle.

52. Install the battery and connect the battery cables.

53. Check the clutch pedal free-play.

54. Start the vehicle and check the transaxle for smooth operation.

CLUTCH

CAUTION: *The clutch driven disc contains asbestos, which has been determined to be a cancer causing agent. Never clean clutch surfaces with compressed air! Avoid inhaling any dust from any clutch surface! When cleaning clutch surfaces, use a commercially available brake cleaning fluid.*

Adjustments

PEDAL HEIGHT/FREE-PLAY

1984–89 Accord
1984–87 Prelude

1. Measure the clutch pedal disengagement height.

2. Measure the clutch pedal free play.

3. Adjust the clutch pedal free-play by turning the clutch cable adjusting nut, found at the end of the clutch cable housing near the release shaft.

4. Turn the adjusting nut until the clutch pedal free-play is 15–25mm (0.6–1.0 in).

5. After adjustment, make sure the free-play at the tip of the release arm is 5.2–6.4mm (0.12–0.16 in.).

NOTE: *Too little freeplay will lead to clutch slippage and premature wear; excessive play will lead to difficult shifting. Inspect the clutch freeplay frequently and adjust as necessary.*

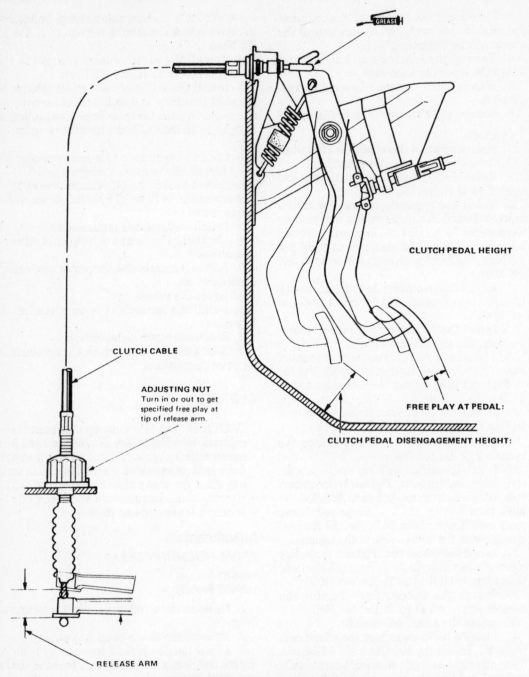

CLUTCH PEDAL HEIGHT

CLUTCH CABLE

ADJUSTING NUT
Turn in or out to get
specified free play at
tip of release arm.

FREE PLAY AT PEDAL:

CLUTCH PEDAL DISENGAGEMENT HEIGHT:

RELEASE ARM

Clutch cable and pedal adjustment dimensions

1990–91 Accord
1988–91 Prelude

NOTE: *The clutch is self-adjusting to compensate for wear. The total clutch pedal freeplay is 9–15mm (0.35–0.59 in). If there is no clearance between the master cylinder piston and pushrod, the release bearing is held against the diaphragm spring of the pressure plate, resulting in clutch slippage or other malfunction.*

1. Loosen the locknut on clutch pedal switch A; back off the pedal switch until it no longer touches the clutch pedal. Clutch pedal switch A is the switch that contacts the clutch pedal below the clutch pedal pivot.

2. Loosen the locknut on the clutch master cylinder pushrod and turn the pushrod in or

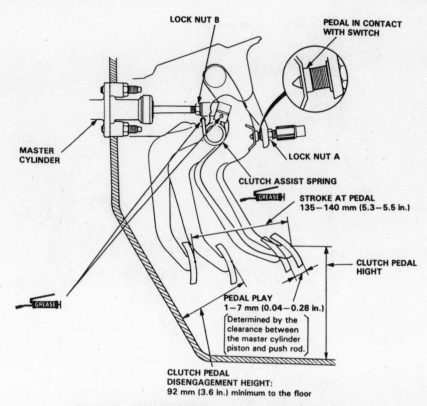

LOCK NUT B

PEDAL IN CONTACT
WITH SWITCH

MASTER
CYLINDER

LOCK NUT A

CLUTCH ASSIST SPRING

GREASE STROKE AT PEDAL
135—140 mm (5.3—5.5 in.)

CLUTCH PEDAL
HIGHT

GREASE

PEDAL PLAY
1—7 mm (0.04—0.28 in.)
Determined by the
clearance between
the master cylinder
piston and push rod.

CLUTCH PEDAL
DISENGAGEMENT HEIGHT:
92 mm (3.6 in.) minimum to the floor

Pedal height adjustment, 1988–91 Prelude and 1990–91 Accord

out to get the specified stroke and height at the clutch pedal. The pedal stroke should be 135–140mm (5.3–5.5 in.) on Prelude and 142mm (5.6 in.) on Accord. The pedal height should be 207mm (8.1 in.) on Prelude and 210mm (8.27 in.) on Accord.

3. Tighten the pushrod locknut.

4. Thread in clutch pedal switch A until it contacts the clutch pedal, then turn it in ¼–½ turn further.

5. Tighten the locknut on clutch pedal switch A.

Driven Disc and Pressure Plate
REMOVAL AND INSTALLATION

1. Disconnect the negative battery cable. Raise and safely support the vehicle. Remove the transaxle from the vehicle. Matchmark the flywheel and clutch for reassembly.

2. Hold the flywheel ring gear with a tool made for this purpose, remove the retaining bolts and remove the pressure plate and clutch disc. Remove the bolts 2 turns at a time working in a criss-cross pattern, to prevent warping the pressure plate.

3. At this time, inspect the flywheel for wear, cracks or scoring and replace, as necessary. Re-

surfacing the flywheel surface is not recommended.

4. If the clutch release bearing is to be replaced, perform the following procedure on all except Prelude and 1990–91 Accord:

a. Remove the 8mm bolt.

b. Remove the release shaft and the release bearing assembly.

c. Separate the release fork from the bearing by removing the release fork spring from the holes in the release bearing.

5. To remove the release bearing on Prelude and 1990–91 Accord, perform the following procedure:

a. Remove the boot from the clutch housing.

b. Remove the release fork from the clutch housing by squeezing the release fork set spring.

c. Remove the release bearing from the release fork.

6. Check the release bearing for excessive play by spinning it by hand. Replace if there is excessive play. The bearing is packed with grease; do NOT wash it in solvent.

To install:

7. If the flywheel was removed, make sure the flywheel and crankshaft mating surfaces

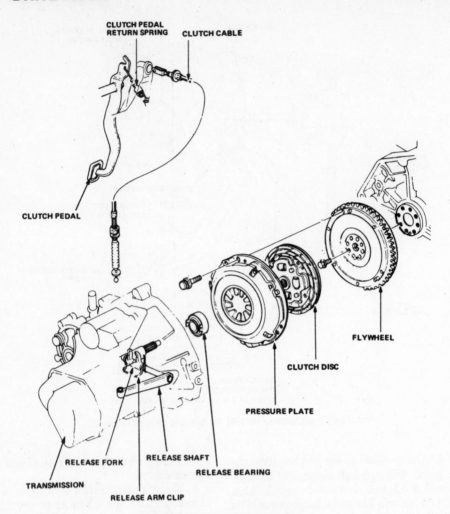

CLUTCH PEDAL RETURN SPRING

CLUTCH CABLE

CLUTCH PEDAL

FLYWHEEL

CLUTCH DISC

PRESSURE PLATE

RELEASE FORK

RELEASE SHAFT

RELEASE BEARING

TRANSMISSION

RELEASE ARM CLIP

Clutch components, 1984–89 Accord

are clean. Align the hole in the flywheel with the crankshaft dowel pin and install the flywheel bolts finger tight. Install the ring gear holder and tighten the flywheel bolts in a criss-cross pattern. Tighten the flywheel bolts to 76 ft. lbs. (105 Nm) on Prelude and Accord.

8. Install the clutch disc and pressure plate by aligning the dowels on the flywheel with the dowel holes in the pressure plate. If the same pressure plate is being installed that was removed, align the marks that were made during the removal procedure. Install the pressure plate bolts finger tight.

9. Insert a clutch disc alignment tool into the splined hole in the clutch disc. (These inexpensive tools are available at most auto supply or parts stores. Using the tool assures that the clutch disc and pressure plate are exactly centered.) Tighten the pressure plate bolts in a criss-cross pattern 2 turns at a time to prevent warping the pressure plate. The final torque should be 19 ft. lbs. (26 Nm).

10. Remove the alignment tool and ring gear holder.

11. If the release bearing was removed, replace it in the reverse order of the removal procedure. Place a light coat of molybdenum disulfide grease on the inside diameter of the bearing prior to installation.

12. Install the transaxle, making sure the mainshaft is properly aligned with the clutch disc splines and the transaxle case is properly aligned with the cylinder block, before tightening the transaxle case bolts.

13. Adjust the clutch pedal free-play and connect the negative battery cable.

Clutch Cable

REMOVAL AND INSTALLATION

1. Disconnect the negative battery cable.
2. Disconnect the cable end from the brake pedal.

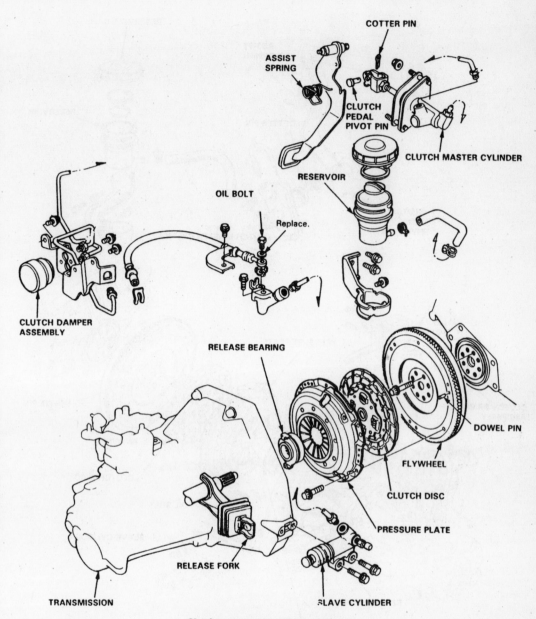

COTTER PIN

ASSIST SPRING

CLUTCH PEDAL PIVOT PIN

CLUTCH MASTER CYLINDER

RESERVOIR

OIL BOLT

Replace.

CLUTCH DAMPER ASSEMBLY

RELEASE BEARING

DOWEL PIN

FLYWHEEL

CLUTCH DISC

PRESSURE PLATE

RELEASE FORK

SLAVE CYLINDER

TRANSMISSION

Clutch components, 1990–91 Accord

3. Remove the adjuster nut assembly from its mounting.

4. Raise and safely support the vehicle.

5. Disconnect the cable end from the release arm. Remove the cable from the vehicle.

6. Installation is the reverse of the removal procedure. Adjust the cable to specification.

Master Cylinder

REMOVAL AND INSTALLATION

1. Disconnect the negative battery cable. At the top of the clutch pedal, remove the cotter pin and pull the pedal pin out of the yoke.

2. Remove the nuts and bolts holding the clutch master cylinder and remove the cylinder from the engine compartment.

3. Disconnect and plug the hydraulic lines from the master cylinder.

4. Installation is the reverse of the removal procedure. Bleed the clutch hydraulic system.

Slave Cylinder

REMOVAL AND INSTALLATION

1. Disconnect the negative battery cable.

2. Disconnect and plug the clutch hose from the slave cylinder.

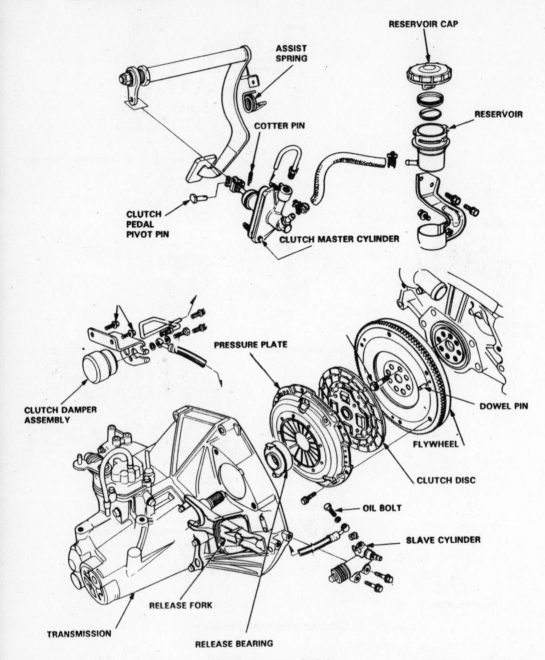

ASSIST SPRING

RESERVOIR CAP

RESERVOIR

COTTER PIN

CLUTCH MASTER CYLINDER

CLUTCH PEDAL PIVOT PIN

PRESSURE PLATE

DOWEL PIN

CLUTCH DAMPER ASSEMBLY

FLYWHEEL

CLUTCH DISC

OIL BOLT

SLAVE CYLINDER

RELEASE FORK

TRANSMISSION

RELEASE BEARING

Clutch components, Prelude

3. Remove the 2 retaining bolts and remove the slave cylinder.

4. Install in reverse order. Bleed the clutch hydraulic system.

Hydraulic Clutch System Bleeding

The hydraulic system must be bled whenever the system has been leaking or dismantled. The bleed screw is located on the slave cylinder.

1. Remove the bleed screw dust cap.

2. Attach a clear hose to the bleed screw. Immerse the other end of the hose in a clear jar, half filled with brake fluid.

3. Fill the clutch master cylinder with fresh brake fluid.

4. Open the bleed screw slightly and have an assistant slowly depress the clutch pedal. Close the bleed screw when the pedal reaches the end of its travel. Allow the clutch pedal to return slowly.

5. Repeat Steps 3–4 until all air bubbles are expelled from the system.

6. Discard the brake fluid in the jar. Replace the dust cap. Refill the master cylinder.

AUTOMATIC TRANSAXLE

NOTE: *For removal, overhaul and installation of the driveshafts, please refer to Halfshafts and Axles in the Manual Transaxle part of this chapter.*

Transaxle Assembly

REMOVAL AND INSTALLATION

1984–89 Accord
1984–87 Prelude

1. Disconnect the negative battery cable at the battery and the transaxle.
2. Unlock the steering and place the transaxle in N.
3. Disconnect the positive battery cable from the battery, then the starter and disconnect the wire from the starter solenoid.
4. Disconnect and plug the transaxle cooler hoses.
5. Remove the starter and the top transaxle mounting bolt.
6. Raise and safely support the vehicle. Double check the placement and security of the jackstands.
7. Remove the front wheels.
8. Drain the transaxle and reinstall the drain plug with a new washer.
9. Remove the throttle control cable by removing the cable end from the throttle lever, loosening the locknut on the cable-end side of the bracket and removing the cable from the bracket.
10. Remove the power steering speed sensor complete with speedometer cable and hoses.
11. Remove 2 upper transaxle mounting bolts.
12. Place a suitable transaxle jack securely beneath the transaxle. Attach a hoist to the engine and raise the engine just enough to take the weight of the engine off the mounts.
13. Remove the subframe center beam and splash pan.
14. Remove the ball joint pinch bolt from the right side lower control arm. Use a puller of the proper size to disconnect the ball joint from the knuckle. Remove the damper fork bolt.
15. Turn the right side steering knuckle to its most outboard position. Pry the CV-joint out approximately ½ in. (13mm), then pull the CV-joint out of the transaxle housing.

NOTE: *Do not pull on the halfshaft or knuckle since this may cause the inboard CV-joint to separate.*

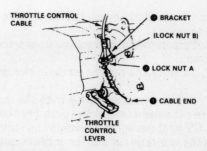

When disconnecting the throttle control cable, loosen only locknut A

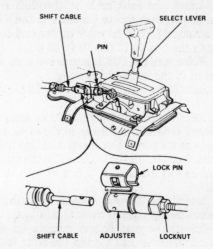

1984–89 Accord shifter assembly

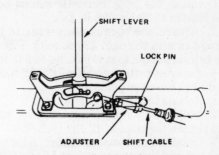

Shifter assembly and cable, 1984–87 Prelude

16. Remove the transaxle damper bracket located in front of the torque converter cover plate.
17. Remove the torque converter cover plate.
18. Inside the vehicle, remove the center console and shift indicator. Remember that the car is on stands.
19. Remove the lock pin from the adjuster and shift cable. Remove both bolts and pull the shift cable out of the housing.
20. Unbolt the torque converter assembly from the driveplate by removing the 8 bolts.
21. Remove the 3 rear engine mounting bolts

from the transaxle housing. Remove the rear engine mount.

22. Remove two bolts from the front transaxle mount.

23. Remove the lower transaxle mounting bolt.

24. Pull the transaxle away from the engine to clear the two 14mm dowel pins. Pry the left side CV-joint out approximately ½ in. (13mm). Pull the transaxle out and lower the transaxle.

To install:

25. Attach the shift cable to the shift arm with the pin, then secure the cable to the edge of the housing with the cable holder and bolt. Tighten the bolt to 12 Nm (9 ft. lbs).

26. Make sure the two 14mm dowel pins are installed in the transaxle housing.

27. Install new spring clips on the end of each axle.

28. Raise the transaxle into position, aligning the dowel pins with the holes in the block and the torque converter bolt heads with the holes in the driveplate. Fit the left axle into the differential as the transaxle is raised up to the engine.

29. Install the 2 lower transaxle mounting bolts but do not tighten them at this time.

30. Install the rear engine mounts on the transaxle housing and tighten the bolts to 39 Nm (28 ft. lbs).

31. Install the front transaxle mount bolts and tighten to 39 Nm (28 ft. lbs).

32. Attach the torque converter to the driveplate with the eight 12mm bolts. Tighten the bolts in 2 steps, first to 6 ft. lbs. (4.5 ft. lbs.) in a criss-cross pattern and finally to 12 Nm (9 ft. lbs.) in the same pattern.

33. Remove the transaxle jack.

34. Install the torque converter cover plate and tighten the bolts to 12 Nm (9 ft. lbs.).

35. Install the anti-windup rubber on the center beam and tighten the nuts to 55 Nm (40 ft. lbs). Install the anti-windup bracket on the transaxle housing and tighten the 3 bolts to 31 Nm (22 ft. lbs).

36. Remove the hoist equipment from the engine.

37. Install the starter.

38. Install the rear torque rod and brackets. Tighten the bracket mounting bolts to 65 Nm (46 ft. lbs.) and the torque rod bolts to 75 Nm (54 ft. lbs.)

39. Turn the right steering knuckle fully outward and slide the axle into the differential until the spring clip engages the differential side gear.

40. Reconnect the ball joint to the knuckle, then tighten the bolt to 55 Nm (40 ft. lbs.). Rein-

stall the damper fork and tighten the bolt to 44 Nm (32 ft. lbs).

41. Install the speedometer cable. Align the tab on the cable end with the slot in the holder. Install the clip so the bent leg is on the groove side.

NOTE: *After installing, pull gently on the speedometer cable to see that it is secure. It should be retained in place.*

42. Install the wheels and lower the vehicle.

43. Install the remaining transaxle mounting bolts. Tighten all the transaxle mounting bolts to 45 Nm (33 ft. lbs).

44. Connect the transaxle cooler hoses and tighten the banjo bolts to 29 Nm (21 ft. lbs).

45. Connect the positive battery cable to the starter, the solenoid wire to the solenoid, the wire to the water temperature sending unit and the wires to the ignition timing thermosensor.

46. Connect the negative battery cable to the transaxle.

47. Unscrew the dipstick from the top of the transaxle end cover and add 3.2 quarts (3 L) of Dexron®II ATF through the hole. Reinstall the dipstick.

NOTE: *If the transaxle and torque converter have been disassembled, add a total of 6.3 quarts (6 L).*

48. Install and reconnect the shift cable. Install the console.

49. Connect the negative battery cable, start the engine, set the parking brake and shift the transaxle through all gears 3 times. Allow each gear to engage momentarily before changing. Check for proper shift cable adjustment.

50. Let the engine reach operating temperature with the transaxle in N or P, then turn the engine off and check the fluid level.

51. Install the throttle control cable and adjust.

1990–91 Accord

1. Disconnect the battery cables and remove the battery.

2. Raise and safely support the vehicle.

3. Remove the air intake hose, air cleaner case and battery base.

4. Disconnect the throttle cable from the throttle control lever.

5. Disconnect the transaxle ground cable and the speed sensor connectors.

6. Disconnect the starter cables and remove the starter.

7. Remove the rear mount bracket stay nut first. Remove the bolt, then remove the rear mount bracket stay.

8. Remove the speed sensor but leave its hoses connected.

9. Disconnect the lock-up control solenoid

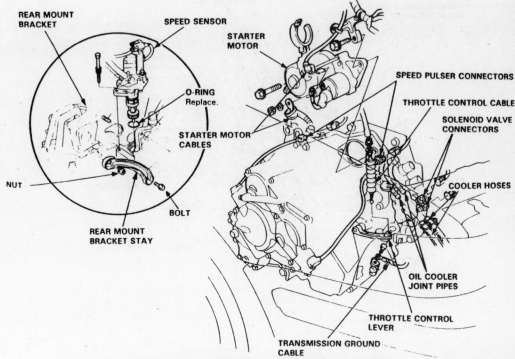

REAR MOUNT
BRACKET

SPEED SENSOR

STARTER
MOTOR

SPEED PULSER CONNECTORS

THROTTLE CONTROL CABLE

O-RING
Replace.

SOLENOID VALVE
CONNECTORS

STARTER MOTOR
CABLES

COOLER HOSES

NUT

BOLT

REAR MOUNT
BRACKET STAY

OIL COOLER
JOINT PIPES

THROTTLE CONTROL
LEVER

TRANSMISSION GROUND
CABLE

1990–91 Accord automatic transaxle external components

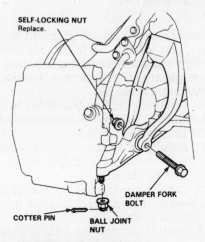

SELF-LOCKING NUT
Replace.

DAMPER FORK
BOLT

COTTER PIN

BALL JOINT
NUT

Ball joint and damper fork disassembly

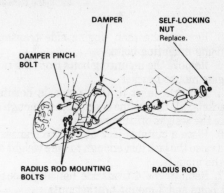

DAMPER

SELF-LOCKING
NUT
Replace.

DAMPER PINCH
BOLT

RADIUS ROD MOUNTING
BOLTS

RADIUS ROD

The right radius rod must be removed completely

valve and shift control solenoid valve
connectors.

10. Drain the transaxle fluid and reinstall the
drain plug with a new washer.

11. Disconnect the transaxle cooler hoses
from the joint pipes. Plug the hoses.

12. Remove the center beam.

13. Disconnect the oxygen sensor connector.

14. Remove the exhaust header pipe and the
splash shield.

15. Remove the cotter pins and lower arm ball
joint nuts, then separate the ball joints from
the lower arms using a ball joint tool.

16. Pry the right and left halfshafts out of the
differential. Pull on the inboard CV-joints and
remove the right and left halfshafts.

17. Remove the right damper pinch bolt, then
separate the damper fork and damper.

18. Remove the bolts and nut, then remove
the right radius rod.

19. Tie plastic bags over the halfshaft ends.

20. Remove the torque converter cover and
control cable holder.

21. Remove the shift control cable by removing the cotter pin, control pin and control lever
roller from the control lever.

22. Remove the plug, then remove the
driveplate bolts one at a time while rotating the
crankshaft pulley.

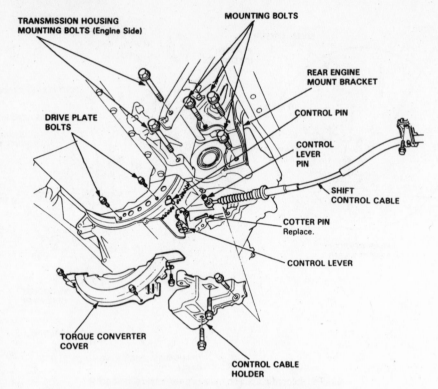

TRANSMISSION HOUSING
MOUNTING BOLTS (Engine Side)

MOUNTING BOLTS

REAR ENGINE
MOUNT BRACKET

DRIVE PLATE
BOLTS

CONTROL PIN

CONTROL
LEVER
PIN

SHIFT
CONTROL CABLE

COTTER PIN
Replace.

CONTROL LEVER

TORQUE CONVERTER
COVER

CONTROL CABLE
HOLDER

Automatic transaxle mounts and retaining bolts

23. Remove the rear, engine side transaxle housing mounting bolts.

24. Remove the mounting bolts from the rear engine mount bracket.

25. Attach a hoist to the transaxle hoisting brackets; lift the engine slightly, just enough to take the weight off the mounts.

26. Place a suitable jack under the transaxle and raise the jack just enough to take weight off of the mounts.

27. Remove the 4 transaxle housing mounting bolts and 3 mount bracket nuts.

28. Pull the transaxle away from the engine until it clears the 14mm dowel pins, then lower it on the transaxle jack.

To install:

29. Make sure the two 14mm dowel pins are installed in the torque converter housing.

30. Raise the transaxle into position and install the 4 transaxle housing mounting bolts. Tighten the bolts to 65 Nm (47 ft. lbs).

31. Install the transaxle-to-transaxle mount bracket and tighten the nuts to 39 Nm (28 ft. lbs).

32. Remove the transaxle jack.

33. Install the 2 engine side transaxle housing mounting bolts and tighten to 65 Nm (47 ft. lbs). Install the rear engine mount bracket bolts and tighten to 55 Nm (40 ft. lbs).

34. Attach the torque converter to the driveplate with 8 bolts. Tighten the bolts in 2 steps, first to 6 Nm (4.5 ft. lbs.) in a criss-cross pattern and finally to 12 Nm (9 ft. lbs.) in the same pattern. Check for free rotation after tightening the last bolt.

35. Install the shift control cable and control cable holder. Tighten the control cable holder bolts to 18 Nm (13 ft. lbs).

36. Install the torque converter cover and tighten the bolts to 12 Nm (9 ft. lbs).

37. Remove the hoist.

38. Install the radius rod. Tighten the mounting bolts to 105 Nm (76 ft. lbs.) and the nut to 44 Nm (32 ft. lbs).

39. Install the damper fork. Tighten the damper pinch bolt to 44 Nm (32 ft. lbs).

40. Install a new set ring on the end of each halfshaft.

41. Turn the right steering knuckle fully outward and slide the axle into the differential until the spring clip engages the differential side gear. Repeat the procedure on the left side.

42. Install the damper fork bolts and ball joint nuts to the lower arms. Tighten the nut to 55 Nm (40 ft. lbs.) while holding the damper fork bolt. Tighten the ball joint nut to 55 Nm (40 ft. lbs.) and install a new cotter pin.

43. Install the splash shield, the center beam and the exhaust header pipe. Tighten the center beam bolts to 39 Nm (28 ft. lbs).

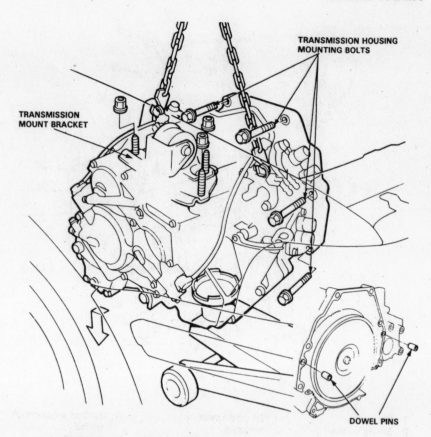

TRANSMISSION HOUSING
MOUNTING BOLTS

TRANSMISSION
MOUNT BRACKET

DOWEL PINS

Make certain the dowel pins are in place before reinstallation

44. Connect the oxygen sensor connector.

45. Install the speed sensor and tighten the bolt to 18 Nm (13 ft. lbs).

46. Install the rear mount bracket stay. Tighten the mounting bolt first, to 39 Nm (28 ft. lbs.) and then tighten the nut to 21 Nm (15 ft. lbs).

47. Install the starter. Connect the cables to the starter.

48. Connect the lock-up control solenoid valve and shift control solenoid valve connectors.

49. Connect the speed sensor connectors and the transaxle ground cable.

50. Connect the transaxle cooler hoses to the joint pipes.

51. Install the battery base, air cleaner case and air intake hose. Install the battery.

52. Install the wheels, lower the vehicle and connect the battery cables at the battery.

53. Fill the transaxle with the proper type and quantity of fluid.

54. Start the engine, set the parking brake and shift the transaxle through all gears 3 times, pausing momentarily in each gear. Check for proper control cable adjustment.

55. Let the engine reach operating tempera-
ture with the transaxle in N or P, then turn the engine off and check the fluid level.

1988–91 Prelude

1. Disconnect the negative battery cable at the battery and the transaxle.

2. Drain the transaxle fluid and replace the drain plug.

3. Disconnect the wiring for the starter, lock-up control solenoids, shift control solenoids and speed pulser.

4. On fuel injected vehicles, remove the air inlet hose and the air cleaner case.

5. Remove the speed sensor from the trans-axle without removing the hoses.

6. Disconnect the throttle control cable at the transaxle bracket.

7. Disconnect the transaxle cooler hoses at the joint pipes and cap the joint pipes.

8. Remove the upper transaxle mounting bracket.

9. Remove the transaxle-to-cylinder block attachment bolts that must be removed from the engine compartment.

10. Raise and safely support the vehicle. Dou-

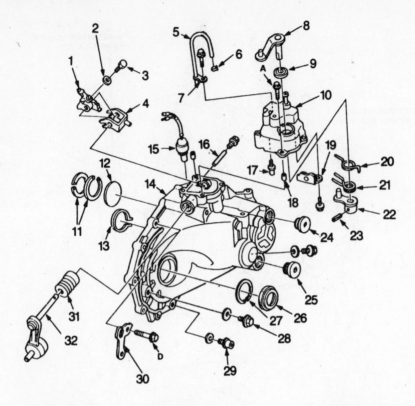

1. Shift arm
2. Spring washer
3. SWhift arm bolt
4. Interlock
5. Breather tube
6. Tube clamp
7. Breather clamp
8. Select lever
9. Oil seal
10. Shift arm cover
11. Thrust shim
12. Oil guide plate
13. Snapring
14. Transaxle housing
15. Reverse light switch
16. Stopper pin
17. Select return pn
18. Dowel pin
19. Reverse lock cam
20. 5th/reverse select return spring
21. 1st/2nd select return spring
22. select arm
23. roll pin
24. 28mm sealing bolt
25. 32mm sealing bolt
26. Oil seal
27. Thrust shim
28. Oil filler bolt
29. Oil drain plug
30. Transaxle hanger
31. Boot
32. Gear shift rod

Manual transaxle, 1991 Prelude

ble check placement and security of the jackstands.

11. Remove the front wheels.

12. Remove the splash shield and the center beam.

13. Remove the right radius rod completely.

14. Remove the right and left halfshafts and the intermediate shaft.

15. Remove the engine stiffener and the torque converter cover.

16. Remove the shift cable from the transaxle.

17. Remove the bolts from the driveplate.

18. Support the transaxle with a suitable jack.

19. Remove the lower bolt from the rear engine mounting bracket. Loosen, but do not remove, the top bolt. This bolt will support the weight of the engine.

20. Remove the remaining engine-to-transaxle mounting bolts.

21. Separate the transaxle from the engine block. Disengage the two 14mm dowel pins and lower the transaxle.

To install:

22. Raise the transaxle into position and install the mounting bolts. Tighten the bolts to 65 Nm (47 ft. lbs)

23. **Attach the torque converter to the** driveplate with the mounting bolts. Tighten the bolts in 2 steps, first to 6 Nm (4.5 ft. lbs.) in a criss-cross pattern and finally to 12 Nm (9 ft. lbs.) in the same pattern. Check for free rotation after tightening the last bolt.

24. Install the transaxle to the rear engine

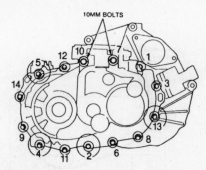

These retaining bolts must be removed from the engine side

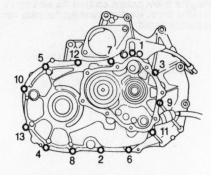

Prelude engine stiffener. The numbers show the tightening sequence when reinstalling

mount bracket with the mounting bolts. Tighten the bolts to 75 Nm (55 ft. lbs).

25. Install the shift cable with the control pin and a new cotter pin.

26. Install the torque converter cover and the cable holder.

27. Install the engine stiffener. The engine stiffener bolts must be tightened to 39 Nm (28 ft. lbs.) in their proper order. First, tighten the uppermost stiffener-to-transaxle housing bolt followed by the remaining stiffener-to-transaxle housing bolt. Next tighten the stiffener-to-cylinder block bolt closest to the transaxle followed by the remaining stiffener-to-cylinder block bolt.

28. Install the intermediate shaft and the halfshafts.

29. Install the center beam and the right and left front damper fork.

30. Install the radius rod on the transaxle side.

31. Install the transaxle mounting bracket and tighten the bolts to 39 Nm (28 ft. lbs).

32. Connect the lock-up control solenoid valve connector, the shift control solenoid valve coupler and the connector of the speed pulser.

33. Connect the throttle control cable to the throttle control lever.

34. Install the speed sensor assembly and the air cleaner case.

35. Connect the oil cooler hoses; connect the starter and ground cables.

36. Connect the battery cables to the battery.

37. Start the engine, set the parking brake and shift the transaxle through all gears 3 times, pausing in each to allow full engagement. Check for proper control cable adjustment.

38. Let the engine reach operating temperature with the transaxle in N or P, then turn the engine off and check the fluid level.

Adjustments

SHIFT CABLE

1. Start the engine. Shift the transaxle to R, checking that reverse gear engages.

2. Shut the engine off and disconnect the negative battery cable.

3. Remove the console.

4. On 1984–88 Accord, place the selector lever in D. On 1988 Prelude, place the selector lever in R. On 1989 Accord and Prelude, place the selector lever in N or R. On 1990–91 Accord and Prelude, place the selector lever in N. Remove the lock pin from the cable adjuster.

5. Check that the hole in the adjuster is perfectly aligned with the hole in the shift cable.

NOTE: *There are 2 holes in the end of the shift cable. They are positioned 90 degrees apart to allow cable adjustments in ¼ turn increments.*

6. If not perfectly aligned, loosen the locknut on the shift cable and adjust as required.

7. Tighten the locknut and install the lock pin on the adjuster. If the lock pin feels like it is binding when being installed, the cable is still out of adjustment and must be adjusted again.

8. Connect the negative battery cable, start the engine and check the shift lever in all gears. Install the console.

THROTTLE LINKAGE

Carbureted Engine

THROTTLE CONTROL CABLE BRACKET

1. Disconnect the negative battery cable.

2. Disconnect the throttle control cable from the throttle control lever.

3. Bend down the lock tabs of the lock plate and remove the two 6mm bolts to free the bracket.

4. Loosely install a new lock plate.

5. Adjust the position of the bracket by measuring the distance between the cable housing side of the bracket and the bracket side edge of the throttle control lever. Measure between the

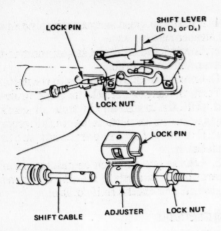

Shifter and lock pin

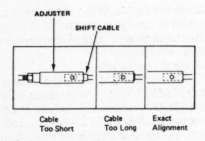

The cable must be perfectly aligned in the adjuster

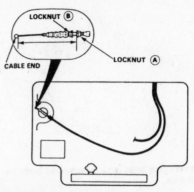

Adjusting the upper locknut controls the working length of the cable. Measure carefully; the cable must be precisely adjusted

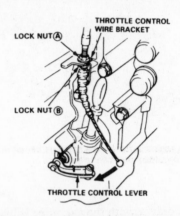

Reinstallation of the carbureted throttle control cable

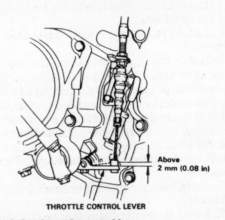

Check the play at the control lever

same points that the cable would pass through the bracket and lever.

6. Tighten the two 6mm bolts when the measurement is 3.287 in. (83.5mm) 1984–89 Accord. Tighten the two 6mm bolts when the measurement is 6.18 in. (157.0mm) on Prelude. The bolts should be tightened to 12 Nm (9 ft. lbs).

NOTE: *Make sure the control lever does not get pulled toward the bracket side as the bolts are tightened.*

7. Bend up the lock plate tabs against the bolt heads, connect the throttle control cable and connect the negative battery cable.

THROTTLE CONTROL CABLE
1984–88

1. Start the engine and warm it up to normal operating temperature. The cooling fan must come on at least once.

2. Make sure the throttle cable play, idle speed and automatic choke operation are correct.

3. Check the distance between the throttle control lever and the throttle control bracket and adjust as necessary.

4. Turn the engine off and disconnect the negative battery cable.

5. Disconnect the throttle control cable from the control lever.

6. If the vehicle is equipped with a dash pot, disconnect the vacuum hose from the dash pot, connect a vacuum pump and apply vacuum. This simulates a normal operating amount of pull by the dash pot, as if the engine were running.

7. Attach a weight of about 3 lbs. to the accel-

erator pedal. Raise the pedal, then release it. This will allow the weight to remove the normal free-play from the throttle cable.

8. Secure the throttle cable with clamps.

9. Place the end of the throttle cable on the shock tower.

10. Adjust the distance between the throttle control cable end and the locknut closest to the cable housing to 3.366 in. (85.5mm) on all except 1988 Prelude. The distance on 1988 Prelude should be 6.22 in. (158.0mm).

11. Insert the end of the throttle control cable in the groove of the throttle control lever. Insert the throttle control cable in the bracket and secure with the other locknut. Make sure the cable is not kinked or twisted.

12. Check that the cable moves freely by depressing the accelerator.

13. Remove the weight on the accelerator pedal and push the pedal to make sure there is at least 0.08 in. (2.0mm) play at the throttle control lever.

14. Connect the negative battery cable and the vacuum hose to the dash pot.

15. Start the engine and check the synchronization between the carburetor and the throttle control cable. The throttle control lever should start to move as the engine speed increases.

16. If the throttle control lever starts to move before the engine speed increases, turn the cable locknut closest to the cable housing counterclockwise and retighten the locknut closest to the cable end.

17. If the throttle control lever moves after the engine speed increases, turn the locknut closest to the cable housing clockwise and retighten the locknut closest to the cable end.

THROTTLE CONTROL CABLE
1989–91

1. Start the engine and bring it to normal operating temperature. The cooling fan must come on at least once.

2. Make sure the throttle cable free-play and idle speed are correct.

3. Check the distance between the throttle control lever and throttle control bracket and adjust, as necessary.

4. On 1990–91 Prelude, disconnect the vacuum hose from the throttle controller and connect a vacuum pump to the controller and apply vacuum.

5. Apply light thumb pressure to the throttle control lever. Have an assistant depress the accelerator. The lever should move just as the engine speed increases above idle. If not, proceed to Step 6.

6. Loosen the nuts on the control cable at the transaxle end and synchronize the control lever to the throttle.

NOTE: *The shift/lock-up characteristics can be tailored to the driver's expectations by adjusting the control cable up to 3mm shorter than the synchronized point.*

Fuel Injected Engine

THROTTLE CONTROL CABLE

1985–88

1. Loosen the locknuts on the throttle control cable.

2. Press down on the throttle control lever until it stops.

3. While pressing down on the throttle control lever, pull on the throttle linkage to check the amount of throttle control cable free-play.

4. Remove all throttle control cable free-play by gradually turning the locknut closest to the cable housing. Keep turning the locknut until no movement can be felt in the throttle link, while continuing to press down on the throttle control lever, pull open the throttle link. The control lever should begin to move at precisely the same time as the link.

NOTE: *The adjustment of the throttle control cable is critical for proper operation of the transaxle and lock-up torque converter.*

5. Have an assistant depress the accelerator to the floor. While depressed, check that there is at least 0.08 in. (2.0mm) play in the throttle control lever. Check that the cable moves freely by depressing the accelerator.

THROTTLE CONTROL CABLE
1989–91

1. Start the engine and bring it up to operating temperature. The cooling fan must come on at least once.

2. Make sure the throttle cable free-play and idle speed are correct.

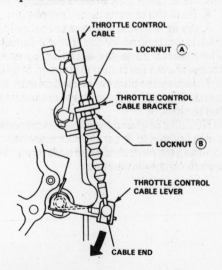

Throttle control cable for fuel injected engines

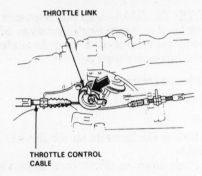

THROTTLE LINK

THROTTLE CONTROL CABLE

Check the amount of free play at the throttle link

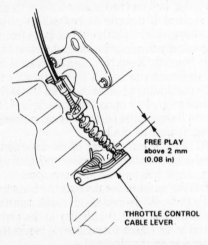

FREE PLAY above 2 mm (0.08 in)

THROTTLE CONTROL CABLE LEVER

Even with the accelerator pressed to the floor, there must be play in the control lever

3. On dashpot equipped vehicles, disconnect the vacuum hose from the dashpot, connect a vacuum pump and apply vacuum. This simulates a normal operating amount of pull by the dashpot as if the engine were running.

4. Remove the throttle cable free-play.

5. Apply light thumb pressure to the throttle control lever, then work the throttle linkage. The lever should move just as the engine speed increases above idle. If not, proceed to Step 6.

6. Loosen the nuts on the control cable at the transaxle end and synchronize the control lever to the throttle.

NOTE: *The shift and lock-up characteristics can be tailored to the driver's expectations by adjusting the control cable up to 3mm shorter than the synchronized point.*

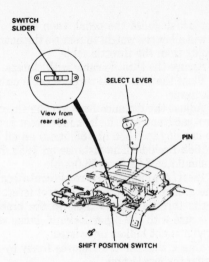

SWITCH SLIDER

SELECT LEVER

View from rear side

PIN

SHIFT POSITION SWITCH

Shift position switch. Accord shown, all are similar

7. Remove the vacuum pump and connect the vacuum hose to the dash pot.

Back-Up Light Switch
Neutral Safety Switch

On automatic vehicles, both the function of the reverse lamps and the neutral safety switch is controlled by the shift position switch at the base of the shift selector. This multi-circuit switch also sends signals to the various electronic control units (cruise control, automatic trans ECU, etc.) keeping them advised of the selected gear.

To replace the shift position switch, firmly set the parking brake and block the wheels. Place the shift selector in N. Remove the console. The shift switch is located on the side of the shift selector, held by 2 bolts or nuts. Disconnect the wiring connectors, then remove the switch.

When installing the switch, make sure the switch slider is positioned to align with the shifter arm or tab. Install the switch, tighten the retaining nuts or bolts and connect the wiring. Reinstall the console.

After installing the switch, check that the engine starts only in PARK or N; the starter should not engage with the shifter in any other position. Check also that the back-up lights come on when the selector is placed in Reverse.

FRONT SUSPENSION

CAUTION: *Exercise great caution when working with the front suspension. Coil springs and other suspension components are under extreme tension and result in severe injury if released improperly. Never remove the nut on the top of the shock absorber piston without using the proper spring compressor tool.*

The 1984–85 Accord uses a MacPherson strut type front suspension. In this type of front suspension, the struts used on either side are a combination spring and shock absorber with the outer casing of the shock actually supporting the bottom of the spring. This arrangement saves space, weight and allows the spring and shock absorber to work on the same axis of compression.

All Preludes covered by this book, and the 1986–91 Accord use a redesigned front suspension. Nicknamed the double wishbone system, the lower wishbone consists of a forged transverse link with a locating stabilizer bar. The lower end of the shock absorber mount has a fork shape to allow the driveshaft to pass through it. The wheel is kept in position by an upper arm as well as the lower arm and radius rod. The upper arm is located in the wheel well and is twist mounted; angled forward from its inner mount to clear the shock absorber.

Spring and Shock Absorbers MacPherson Strut

TESTING

Shock Absorbers

Contrary to popular rumor, the shocks do not affect the ride height of the car nor do they affect the ride quality except for limiting the pitch or bounce of the car. These factors are controlled by other suspension components such as springs and tires. Worn shock absorbers can affect handling; if the front of the car is rising or falling excessively, the "footprint" of the tires changes on the pavement and steering response is affected.

The simplest test of the shock absorbers is simply to push down on one corner of the unladen car and release it. Observe the motion of the body as it is released. In most cases, it will come up beyond its original rest position, dip back below it and settle quickly to rest. This shows that the damper is slowing and controlling the spring action. Any tendency to excessive pitch (up-and-down) motion or failure to return to rest within 2–3 cycles is a sign of poor function within the shock absorber. Obvious shock problems such as leakage or bending also indicate failure.

NOTE: *It is normal for any fluid damper to have a light film of oil around the top of the body due to normal air exchange. Don't mistake this for leakage. Under normal conditions, most original equipment shock absorbers used on Hondas last a very long time without replacement. The largest common cause of deteriorated ride quality is worn tires, not failed shock absorbers.*

REMOVAL, DISASSEMBLY AND INSTALLATION

WARNING: *The use of the correct special tools or their equivalent is REQUIRED for this procedure. A spring compressor must be used to retain the spring before removing it from the strut.*

1984–85 Accord

1. Raise and safely support the front of the vehicle. Make sure the stands are correctly placed.
2. Remove the front wheels.
3. Disconnect the brake hose clamp from the strut.

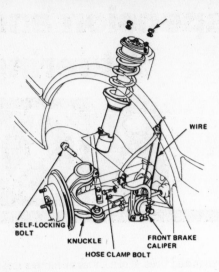

Front strut removal, 1984–85 Accord

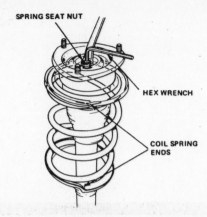

Keep the shaft from turning during reassembly. Note correct alignment of the spring ends in the seats

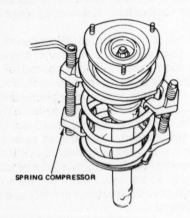

Make certain the spring compressor is properly installed but do not overtighten it

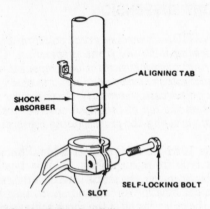

Align the strut before Installation

4. Remove the brake caliper mounting bolts and remove the caliper. Use string or stiff wire to hang the caliper out of the way. Do not disconnect the brake hose from the caliper.

5. Disconnect the stabilizer bar from the lower control arm.

6. Remove the self-locking pinchbolt at the bottom of the strut. Place a jack or other support under the control arm. Use a hammer to tap the knuckle downward and off the strut; do not allow the disc and knuckle assembly to fall when it comes loose.

7. In the engine compartment, remove the rubber cap and the 3 nuts from the upper shock mount.

CAUTION: *Do NOT remove the center or shaft nut from the top of the shock absorber.*

8. Remove the strut assembly from the vehicle.

Disassembly

9. Install a spring compressor on the spring. These tools are commonly available at auto parts suppliers. There are many different types; follow the manufacturer's instructions carefully. Tighten the compressor just enough to take the spring tension off the top spring seat.

10. With the spring compressed, remove the center or seat nut. Use a hex wrench of the correct size to keep the shaft from turning while the nut is removed.

11. Remove the upper mount. Carefully remove the seals, spacers and bearing at the top of the shock; keep them in order for proper reassembly. Remove the compressed spring.

12. If the spring is to be tested or replaced, release tension on the arms of the compressor slowly. Remove the tool when the spring is at normal length with no tension on the compressor.

13. By hand, check the shock absorber for smooth operation through the full range of travel. Check it also for smoothness during short strokes of 2–4 in. (51–102mm). Replace

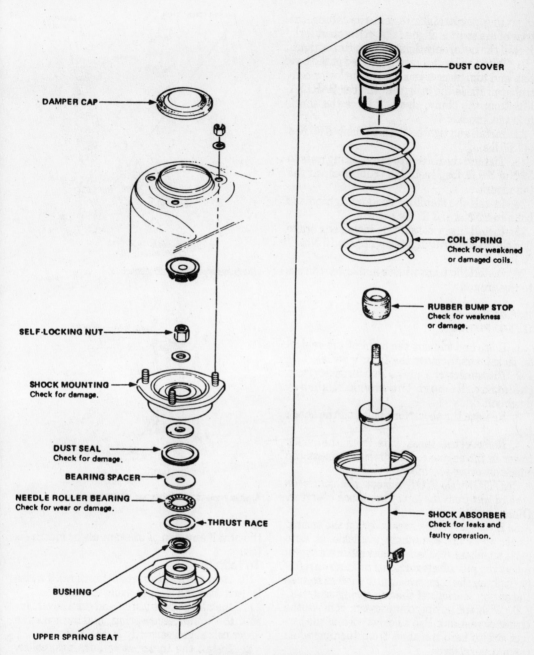

DAMPER CAP

DUST COVER

COIL SPRING
Check for weakened
or damaged coils.

SELF-LOCKING NUT

RUBBER BUMP STOP
Check for weakness
or damage.

SHOCK MOUNTING
Check for damage.

DUST SEAL
Check for damage.

BEARING SPACER

NEEDLE ROLLER BEARING
Check for wear or damage.

THRUST RACE

SHOCK ABSORBER
Check for leaks and
faulty operation.

BUSHING

UPPER SPRING SEAT

Strut and spring components

the unit if any sign of unevenness or binding is felt. The shock/strut assembly cannot be disassembled; there are no replaceable parts.

To install:

14. Hold the strut assembly upright. If a vise is used, pad the jaws to avoid damage.

15. Install the rubber bump stop on the shaft.

16. Compress the spring and install it onto the shock. Make certain the bottom coil is exactly aligned in the bottom seat. Install the shaft dust cover.

17. Install the upper spring seat, spacers, bearing, seal and mount. Coat both sides of the needle bearing with grease before installing it. Make certain the upper spring seat is aligned with upper coil of the spring.

18. Install a new upper shaft nut; tighten it to 45 Nm (33 ft. lbs.)

19. Slowly release the spring compressor, making sure the released spring fits into the upper mount correctly.

20. Place the strut into position at the top

mounting point. Make certain the tab on the base of the strut is aligned slot in the strut fork. Install the nuts; only tighten them finger tight.

21. With the strut correctly aligned at the bottom and top, place a jack under the lower control arm. Raise the jack until the car BARELY lifts from the stand; this will force the shock into the knuckle.

22. Install and tighten the pinchbolt to 65 Nm (47 ft. lbs).

23. Tighten the three upper mounting nuts to 39 Nm (28 ft. lbs). Install the rubber cap at the top mount.

24. Install the stabilizer rod and tighten the bolts to 22 Nm (16 ft. lbs.)

25. Install the brake caliper. Install the brake line clip to the strut; tighten it only to 10 Nm (7 ft. lbs).

26. Install the front wheels and lower the car to the ground.

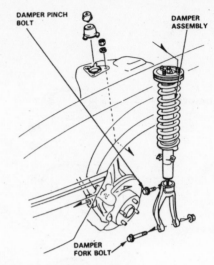

Wishbone-type shock absorber

1986–91 Accord
1983–91 Prelude

1. Raise and support the front of the vehicle on jackstands. Remove the front wheels.

2. Disconnect the brake line bracket from the strut. Remove the shock absorber pinchbolt.

3. Remove the shock fork bolt and the shock fork.

4. Remove the three nuts from the shock tower in the engine compartment. Remove the shock absorber assembly.

CAUTION: *Do NOT remove the center or shaft nut from the top of the shock absorber.*

Disassembly

5. Install a spring compressor on the spring. These tools are commonly available at auto parts suppliers. There are many different types; follow the manufacturer's instructions carefully. Tighten the compressor just enough to take the spring tension off the top spring seat.

6. With the spring compressed, remove the center or seat nut. Use a hex wrench of the correct size to keep the shaft from turning while the nut is removed.

7. Remove the upper mount. Carefully remove the seals, spacers and collar at the top of the shock; keep them in order for proper reassembly. Remove the compressed spring.

8. If the spring is to be tested or replaced, release tension on the arms of the compressor slowly. Remove the tool when the spring is at normal length with no tension on the compressor.

9. By hand, check the shock absorber for smooth operation through the full range of travel. Check it also for smoothness during short strokes of 2–4 in. (51–102mm). Replace

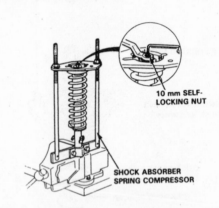

Always replace the upper nut with a new one

the unit if any sign of unevenness or binding is felt.

To install:

10. Hold the strut assembly upright. If a vise is used, pad the jaws to avoid damage.

11. Install the bump stop and dust cover. Install the compressed spring, making sure the lower coil aligns correctly in the seat.

12. Install the upper seat, bushings, collar, seals and mount base.

13. Install a new shaft nut and tighten it to 30 Nm (22 ft. lbs).

14. Install the damper fork over the driveshaft and lower arm. Install the shock absorber into the fork so that the strut tab matches the slot in the fork. Align the three upper bolts with the holes in the shock tower.

15. Install the bolts and nuts finger tight only, but make sure all are present and reasonably snug.

16. With the strut correctly aligned at the bottom and top, place a jack under the lower con-

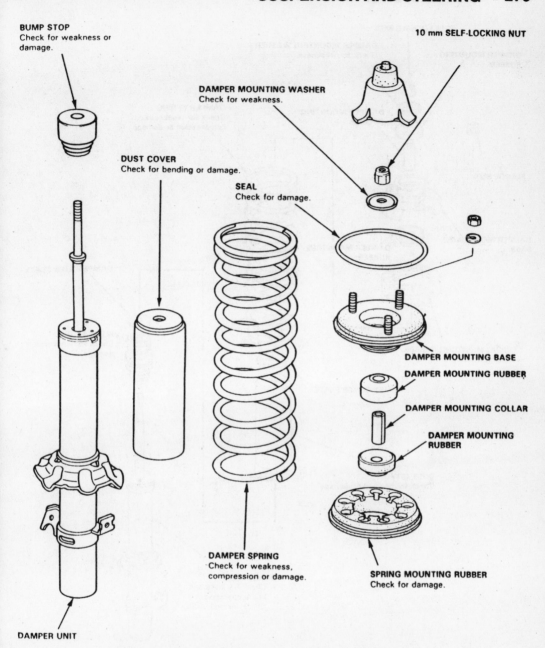

BUMP STOP
Check for weakness or
damage.

10 mm SELF-LOCKING NUT

DAMPER MOUNTING WASHER
Check for weakness.

DUST COVER
Check for bending or damage.

SEAL
Check for damage.

DAMPER MOUNTING BASE

DAMPER MOUNTING RUBBER

DAMPER MOUNTING COLLAR

**DAMPER MOUNTING
RUBBER**

DAMPER SPRING
Check for weakness,
compression or damage.

SPRING MOUNTING RUBBER
Check for damage.

DAMPER UNIT

1986–91 Prelude shock absorber assembly. 1986–89 Accord similar

trol arm. Raise the jack until the car BARELY lifts from the stand; this will force the shock into the fork.

17. Tighten the lower fork bolt to 65 Nm (47 ft. lbs).

18. Tighten the pinchbolt to 44 Nm (32 ft. lbs). Do not tighten the upper mount nuts now.

19. Install the brake hose clamp to the strut.

20. Install the front wheels. Lower the vehicle to the ground.

21. With the weight of the car on the suspen-

sion, tighten the upper mount nuts to 39 Nm (28 ft. lbs).

Upper Ball Joint

INSPECTION

1. Raise and safely support the vehicle.

2. Remove the front wheel.

3. Grasp the steering knuckle and move it back and forth.

4. Replace the upper control arm on all ex-

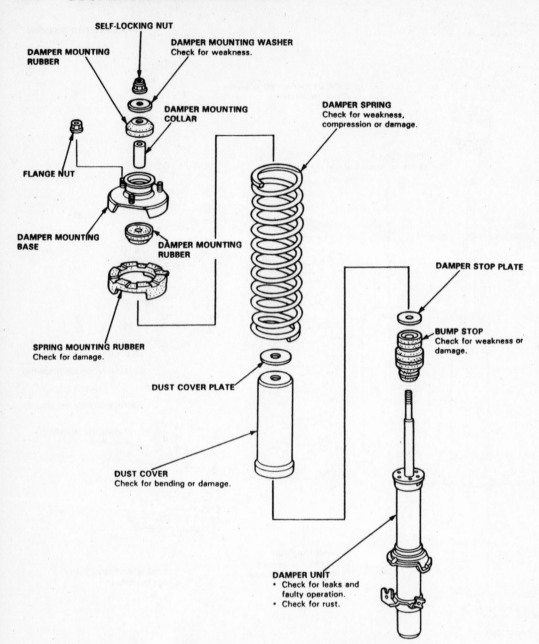

SELF-LOCKING NUT

DAMPER MOUNTING WASHER
Check for weakness.

DAMPER MOUNTING
RUBBER

DAMPER MOUNTING
COLLAR

DAMPER SPRING
Check for weakness,
compression or damage.

FLANGE NUT

DAMPER MOUNTING
BASE

DAMPER MOUNTING
RUBBER

DAMPER STOP PLATE

BUMP STOP
Check for weakness or
damage.

SPRING MOUNTING RUBBER
Check for damage.

DUST COVER PLATE

DUST COVER
Check for bending or damage.

DAMPER UNIT
• Check for leaks and
  faulty operation.
• Check for rust.

1990–91 Accord shock absorber components

cept Prelude if any play is detected. On Prelude, replace the upper ball joint.

REMOVAL AND INSTALLATION

Only the Prelude upper ball joints are replaceable. The 1984–85 Accord has no upper control arm and therefore, no joint. On 1986–91 Accords, the ball joint is permanently installed to the upper arm; it is not removable. If the joint fails or becomes loose, the upper arm assembly must be replaced.

To replace the Prelude upper ball joint:

1. Raise and safely support the vehicle.
2. Remove the front wheel.
3. Remove the cotter pin and castle nut from the upper ball joint.
4. Using a ball joint separator, separate the upper ball joint from the steering knuckle.
5. Remove the 2 retaining nuts holding the ball joint assembly to the upper control arm. Remove the ball joint.
6. Installation is the reverse of the removal procedure. Tighten the ball joint retaining nuts to 55 Nm (40 ft. lbs). Tighten the ball joint cas-

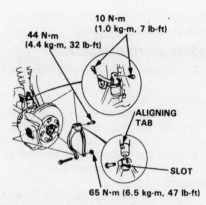

Reassembly detail. The tab must align with the slot before the strut is installed to the fork

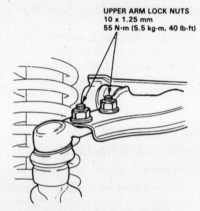

Prelude upper ball joint. Another benefit of the replaceable joint is adjustable camber during alignment

tle nut to 44 Nm (32 ft. lbs.) and install a new cotter pin.

7. Check the camber adjustment.

Lower Ball Joint

INSPECTION

Check ball joint play as follows:

1. Raise and support the front of the vehicle on jackstands.

2. Using a dial indicator clamp it onto the lower control arm and place the indicator tip on the steering knuckle, near the ball joint.

3. Using a pry bar, place it between the lower control arm and the steering knuckle.

4. Work the ball joint to check for looseness; if the play exceeds 0.5mm, replace the ball joint.

REMOVAL AND INSTALLATION

Lower ball joints on 19845–85 Accords are integral with the control arm; if the joint becomes loose, the arm, with a new ball joint, must be replaced.

1986–91 Accord
1983–88 Prelude

NOTE: *This procedure is performed after the removal of the steering knuckle and requires the use of the following special tools or their equivalent: Ball Joint Remover/Installation tool No. 07965–SB00100 or 07HAF-SF10110 (90–91 Accord) and Ball Joint Removal Base tool 07965–SB00200 (85–87 Prelude), 07965–SB00300 (86–89 Accord and 88–91 Prelude) or 07HAF–SF10130. Additionally, a large vise will be required. At installation, Clip Guide tool No. 07974-SA50700 or 07GAG–SD40700 will be required.*

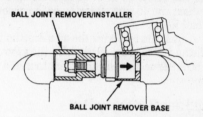

Using the special tools and vise to remove the ball joint

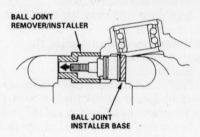

The installer base is used during installation of the new joint

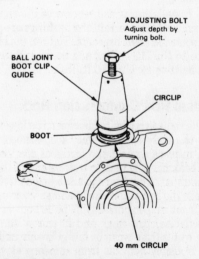

The boot clip guide must be used to seat the clip

1. After removing the knuckle with the joint attached, pry the snapring off and remove the boot.

2. Pry the snapring out of the groove in the ball joint.

3. Using the ball joint removal tool with the large end facing out, tighten the ball joint nut.

4. Position the removal base tool on the ball joint and set the assembly in a large vise. Press the ball joint out of the steering knuckle.

5. Position the new ball joint into the hole of the steering knuckle.

6. Install the ball joint installer tool with the small end facing out.

7. Position the installation base tool on the ball joint and set the assembly in a large vise. Press the ball joint into the steering knuckle.

8. Seat the 40 mm snapring in the groove of the ball joint.

9. Adjust the tool with the adjusting bolt until the end of the tool aligns with the groove on the boot. Slide the clip over the tool and into position.

Stabilizer Bar/Sway Bar

REMOVAL AND INSTALLATION

1. Raise and safely support the vehicle.

2. Remove the front wheels.

3. Disconnect the sway bar ends from both lower control arms.

4. Remove the bolts retaining the sway bar bushing brackets.

5. Remove the sway bar.

NOTE: *Examine the rubber bushings very carefully for any splits or deformation. Clean the inner and outer surfaces of the bushings before installation. Failed, dirty or compressed bushings can create a chorus of odd noises under the vehicle, particularly during cornering.*

6. Installation is the reverse of the removal procedure. Make certain the bushings are properly seated in their brackets. Tighten the brackets to 16 Nm (12 ft. lbs.) and the end mounts or link bolts to 22 Nm (16 ft. lbs).

Radius Rod/Compression Rod

The radius rod, bolted between the lower arm and the body or subframe, keeps the control arm in place against the forces of acceleration and braking. The rear or trailing end of the rod is mounted in bushings to allow just a bit of motion in the system. If the bushings wear or fail, the front suspension may be pulled out of position. Noise, tire wear and impaired handling may result from worn or faulty bushings. If the rod is visibly bent, as from someone elevating the car with a jack under the rod, the rod must be replaced. (The bend shortens the rod and pulls the wheel out of place.)

REMOVAL AND INSTALLATION

1. Elevate and safely support the front of the car.

2. Remove the wheel.

3. Loosen the nut at the rear of the radius rod. Remove the nut, washers, bushing, etc. Keep them in correct order for reinstallation.

4. Remove the bolts holding the rod to the control arm. Remove the rod.

To install:

5. Inspect the bushings carefully for wear or deformation. Replace them if any damage is found.

6. Fit the rod into place and install the bolts at the control arm. Tighten the bolts to 55 Nm (41 ft. lbs).

7. Install the bushings, washers and spacers at the rear of the rod in the correct order. Install a new locking nut. On all except 90–91 Accord, tighten the end nut to 44 Nm (33 ft. lbs.); for 90–91 Accord, tighten the nut to 105 Nm (76 ft. lbs).

Upper Control Arm

REMOVAL AND INSTALLATION

1990–91 Accord

1. Raise and support the vehicle safely.

2. Remove the front wheels. Support the lower control arm assembly with a jack.

3. Remove the self-locking nuts, upper control arm bolts and upper control anchor bolts. Separate the upper ball joint using a ball joint separator tool.

4. Place the upper control arm assembly into a holding fixture and Remove the though-bolts holding the upper arm anchor bolts.

To install:

5. Drive the new upper arm bushing into the upper arm anchor bolts. Drive in the bushing so the leading edges are flush with the anchor bolt.

6. Install the upper control arm assembly and install the upper arm bolts, then tighten the self locking nuts to 30 Nm (22 ft. lbs). Be sure to align the upper arm anchor bolt with the mark on the upper arm.

7. Install the upper arm, tightening the flange nuts to 65 Nm (47 ft. lbs.)

8. Connect the upper ball joint.

9. Install the wheel and lower the car.

Prelude and 1986–89 Accord

1. Raise and support the vehicle safely.

2. Remove the front wheels. Support the lower control arm assembly with a jack.

3. Remove the self locking nuts, upper control arm bolts and upper control anchor bolts. Separate the upper ball joint using a ball joint separator tool.

4. Place the upper control arm assembly into a vise; remove the self locking nut, upper arm bolt, upper arm anchor bolts and housing seals.

5. Remove the upper arm collar. Drive out the upper arm bushing using a drift.

6. Replace the upper control arm bushings, bushing seals and upper control arm collar with new ones. Be sure to coat the ends and the insides of the upper control arm bushings and the sealing lips of the upper control arm bushing with grease.

7. After Step 6 is completed, apply sealant to the threads and underside of the upper arm bolt heads and self locking nut. Install the upper arm bolt and tighten the self locking nut to 55 Nm (40 ft.lbs).

8. Install the upper arm, tightening the Accord flange bolts to 73 Nm (54 ft. lbs.) or the Prelude bolts to 83 Nm (61 ft. lbs.).

9. Connect the upper ball joint.

10. Install the wheel and lower the car.

Lower Control Arms

REMOVAL AND INSTALLATION

1. Raise the vehicle and support it safely. Remove the front wheels.

2. Properly support the hub and knuckle assembly with a jack. Use a ball joint separator to disconnect the lower arm ball joint. Be careful not to damage the seal.

3. Remove the stabilizer bar retaining bolts.

4. Remove the lower arm pivot bolt.

5. Remove the lower arm. Check the bushings carefully for wear or deterioration. Replace the bushings if any wear is found. Even if the bushings are not replaced, clean the centers and the bolt shafts; dirt and corrosion can cause binding.

6. Install in reverse order. Tighten the lower control arm to chassis bolt to 40 ft. lbs. (55 Nm).

Front Hub and Bearing

REMOVAL, REPACKING AND INSTALLATION

1984–85 Accord

(Honda tool numbers shown)

WARNING: *The use of the correct special tools or their equivalent is REQUIRED for this procedure. A hydraulic press and the correct diameter drivers and supports are required for disassembly of the hub and bearing. Do not attempt to substitute tools for the press. If necessary, take the knuckle assembly*

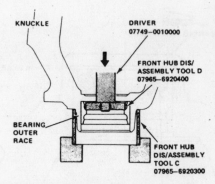

The outer race is removed with a hydraulic press

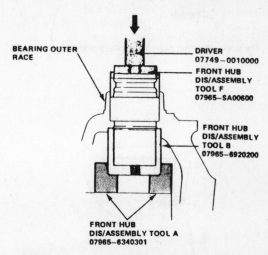

Use the correct tools to support the knuckle during reassembly

to a machine shop or dealership to have the bearings replaced.

1. Pry the lock tab away from the spindle, then loosen the nut. Slightly loosen the lug nuts.

2. Raise the front of the car and support it with safety stands. Remove the front wheel and spindle nut.

3. Remove the bolts retaining the brake caliper and remove the caliper from the knuckle. Do not let the caliper hang by the brake hose but support it with a length of wire.

4. Remove the disc brake rotor retaining screws (if so equipped). Screw two 8 x 1.25 x 12mm bolts into the disc brake removal holes, and turn the bolts to push the rotor away from the hub.

NOTE: *Turn each bolt only two turns at a time to prevent cocking the disc excessively.*

5. Remove the tie rod from the knuckle using a tie rod end removal tool. Use care not to damage the ball joint seals.

6. Remove the cotter pin from the lower arm ball joint and remove the castle nut.

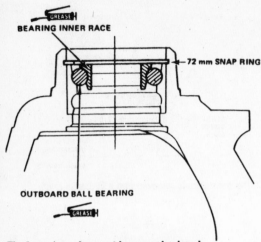

The large snap ring must be securely placed

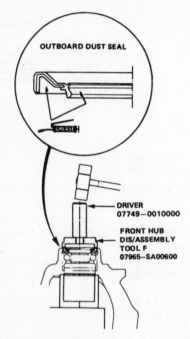

Installing the outboard dust seal

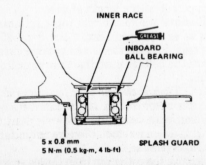

Install the inboard bearing with the knuckle inverted

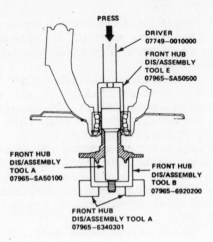

Installing the hub

7. Remove the lower arm from the knuckle using the ball joint remover.

8. Loosen the lockbolt which retains the strut in the knuckle. Tap the top of the knuckle with a hammer and slide it off the shock.

9. Remove the knuckle and hub, if still attached, by sliding the assembly off the driveshaft.

10. Remove the hub from the knuckle using correct drivers and a hydraulic press.

Bearing Removal

11. Remove the splash guard and the snapring, then remove the outer bearing.

12. Turn the knuckle over and remove the inboard dust seal, bearing and inner race.

13. Press the bearing outer race out of the knuckle using the correct tools and a hydraulic press.

14. Remove the outboard bearing inner race from the hub using a bearing puller.

15. Remove the outboard dust seal from the hub.

NOTE: *Whenever the wheel bearings are removed, they must be replaced with a new set of bearings and outer dust seal.*

16. Clean all old grease from the driveshafts and spindles on the car.

17. Remove all old grease from the hub and knuckle and thoroughly dry and wipe clean all components.

18. When fitting new bearings, you must pack them with wheel bearing grease. To do this, place a glob of grease in your left palm. Holding one of the bearings in your right hand, drag the face of the bearing heavily through the grease. This must be done to work as much grease as possible through the ball bearings and the cage. Turn the bearing and continue to pull it through the grease until the grease is thor-

oughly packed between the bearing balls and the cage, all around the bearing. You'll be able to see grease emerging from the clean side of the bearing if the lubricant is going all the way through. Repeat this operation until all of the bearings are completely packed with grease.

NOTE: *This messy job can be made much easier with the use of a bearing packer. This handy little item fits tightly over the bearing; grease is injected with a grease-gun. If this system is used, make very certain that the grease is evenly distributed and the bearing is completely packed. Although quicker and cleaner, the pressure packer is a bit less accurate — pay attention.*

19. Pack the inside of the rotor and knuckle hub with a moderate amount of grease. Do not overload the hub with grease.

20. Apply a small amount of grease to the spindle and to the lip of the inner seal before installing.

21. To install the bearings, press the bearing outer race into the knuckle using the tools used above, plus an installation base. Do not exceed 2.5 tons pressure with the press.

22. Install the outboard ball bearing and its inner race in the knuckle.

23. Install the snapring. Pack grease in the groove around the sealing lip of the outboard grease dust seal.

24. Drive the outboard grease seal into the knuckle, using a seal driver and mallet, until it is flush with the knuckle surface.

25. Install the splash guard, then turn the knuckle upside down and install the inboard ball bearing and its inner race.

26. Place the hub in the press holder; set the knuckle in position on the press and apply downward pressure. Do not exceed 2 tons of pressure during installation.

27. Pack grease in the groove around the sealing lip of the inboard dust seal.

28. Drive the dust seal into the knuckle using a seal driver.

29. Reinstall the knuckle. Always use a new spindle nut on the end of the driveshaft. Tighten the spindle nut snug. When the vehicle is on its wheels on the ground, tighten the spindle nut to 190 Nm (137 ft. lbs.) and stake the nut into the groove.

1986–89 Accord
1983–91 Prelude

WARNING: *The use of the correct special tools or their equivalent is REQUIRED for this procedure. A hydraulic press and the correct diameter drivers and supports are required for disassembly of the hub and bearing. Do not attempt to substitute tools for the*

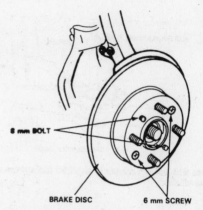

Remove the retaining screws, then use two 8 × 12mm bolts to remove the brake disc

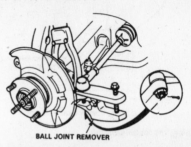

Use the correct tool to separate the tie-rod ball joint

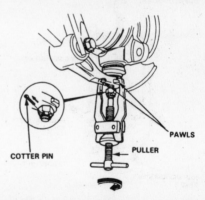

Use a puller on the lower joint. Leave the nut loose but in place until the joint is separated

press. If necessary, take the knuckle assembly to a machine shop or dealership to have the bearings replaced.

1. Pry the spindle nut stake away from the spindle and loosen the nut. Do not tighten or loosen a spindle nut unless the vehicle is sitting on all 4 wheels. The torque required is high enough to cause the vehicle to fall off the stands even when properly supported.

2. Raise and safely support the vehicle.

3. Remove the wheel and the spindle nut.

4. Remove the caliper mounting bolts and the caliper. Support the caliper out of the way

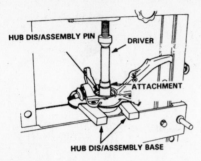

A press with correct drivers is required during removal and installation

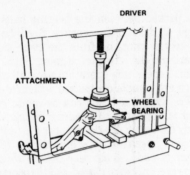

Pressing in the new bearing assembly

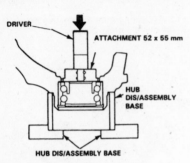

Removing the wheel bearing

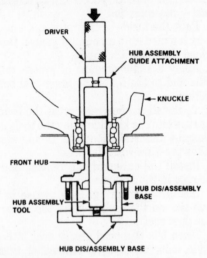

Installing the hub

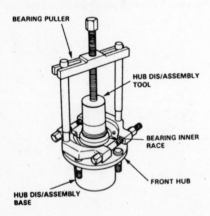

A puller is required to remove the outboard bearing inner race

with a length of wire. Do not let the caliper hang from the brake hose.

5. Remove the 6mm brake disc retaining screws. Screw two 8 × 1.25 × 12mm bolts into the disc to push it away from the hub.

NOTE: *Turn each bolt 2 turns at a time to prevent cocking the brake disc.*

6. Remove the cotter pin from the tie rod castle nut, then remove the nut. Separate the tie rod ball joint using a ball joint remover, then lift the tie rod out of the knuckle.

7. Remove the cotter pin and loosen the lower arm ball joint nut half the length of the joint

threads. The nut will retain the arm when the joint comes loose.

8. Separate the ball joint and lower arm using a puller with the pawls applied to the lower arm.

NOTE: *Avoid damaging the ball joint boot. If necessary, apply penetrating lubricant to loosen the ball joint.*

9. Remove the upper ball joint shield, if present.

10. Pry off the cotter pin and remove the upper ball joint nut.

11. Separate the upper ball joint and knuckle.

12. Remove the knuckle and hub by sliding them off the halfshaft.

13. Remove the splash guard screws from the knuckle.

14. Position the knuckle/hub assembly in a hydraulic press. Press the hub from the knuckle using a driver of the proper diameter while supporting the knuckle.

NOTE: *The bearing must be replaced with a new one after removal. It cannot be reused.*

15. Remove the splash guard and snapring from the knuckle.

16. Press the wheel bearing out of the knuckle while supporting the knuckle.

17. Remove the outboard bearing inner race from the hub using a bearing puller.

To install:

18. Clean the knuckle and hub thoroughly.

19. Press a new wheel bearing into the knuckle using a driver while supporting the knuckle.

20. Install the snapring.

21. Install the splash shield. don't overtighten the screws.

22. Press the knuckle onto the hub using a suitable fixture.

23. Install the front knuckle ring on the knuckle.

24. Install the knuckle/hub assembly on the vehicle. Tighten the upper ball joint nut and tie rod end nut to 44 Nm (32 ft. lbs). Install new cotter pins. Tighten the lower ball joint nut to 40 ft. lbs. (55 Nm) and install a new cotter pin.

25. With all 4 wheels resting on the ground, tighten the spindle nut to 185 Nm (134 ft. lbs.) except 1990–91 Prelude, where it is tightened to 250 Nm (180 ft. lbs).

1990–91 Accord

(Honda tool numbers shown)

WARNING: *The use of the correct special tools or their equivalent is REQUIRED for this procedure. A hydraulic press and the correct diameter drivers and supports are required for disassembly of the hub and bearing. Do not attempt to substitute tools for the press. If necessary, take the knuckle assembly to a machine shop or dealership to have the bearings replaced.*

1. Pry the spindle nut stake away from the spindle, then loosen the nut. Do not tighten or loosen a spindle nut unless the vehicle is sitting on all 4 wheels. The torque is high enough to cause the vehicle to fall even when properly supported.

2. Raise and safely support the vehicle.

3. Remove the wheel and the spindle nut.

4. Remove the caliper mounting bolts and the caliper. Support the caliper out of the way with a length of wire. Do not let the caliper hang from the brake hose.

5. Remove the cotter pin from the tie rod castle nut, then remove the nut. Separate the tie rod ball joint using a ball joint remover, then lift the tie rod out of the knuckle.

6. Remove the cotter pin and loosen the lower arm ball joint nut half the length of the joint threads. The nut will retain the arm when separated in the next Step.

7. Separate the ball joint and lower arm using a puller with the pawls applied to the lower arm.

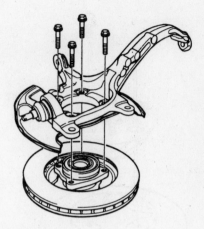

The knuckle is bolted to the hub on 1990–91 Accord

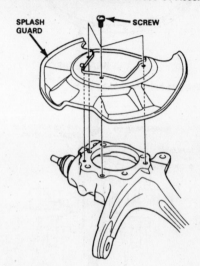

Splash shield removal

NOTE: *Avoid damaging the ball joint boot. If necessary, apply penetrating lubricant to loosen the ball joint.*

8. Pull the knuckle outward and remove the halfshaft outboard joint from the knuckle.

9. Remove the cotter pin and the upper ball joint nut. Separate the upper ball joint.

NOTE: *Avoid damaging the ball joint boot. If necessary, apply penetrating lubricant to loosen the ball joint.*

10. Remove the four bolts and remove the knuckle from the hub unit.

11. Remove the splash guard from the knuckle.

12. Remove the four bolts and separate the hub unit from the brake disc.

13. Position the hub in a hydraulic press. Press the wheel bearing from the hub while adequately supporting the hub.

14. Remove the outboard bearing inner race from the hub using a bearing puller.

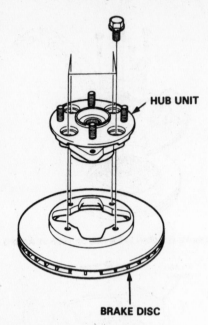

The disc and hub are held by bolts

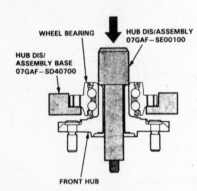

Press set-up for bearing removal

NOTE: *The wheel bearing must be replaced with a new one after removal.*

To install:

15. Clean the knuckle and hub thoroughly.

16. Position the hub in a hydraulic press. Press a new wheel bearing into the hub using a driver of the correct diameter.

17. Install the hub on the brake disc and tighten the bolts to 55 Nm (40 ft. lbs).

18. Install the splash shield.

19. Install the knuckle on the hub; tighten the bolts to 45 Nm (33 ft. lbs).

20. Install the knuckle/hub assembly on the vehicle. Tighten the upper ball joint nut and the tie rod nut to 44 Nm (32 ft. lbs.) and install new cotter pins. Tighten the lower ball joint nut to 55 Nm (40 ft. lbs.) and install a new cotter pin.

21. With all 4 wheels resting on the ground, install a new spindle nut and torque to 180 ft.

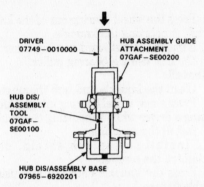

Guides and supports must fit exactly when installing the bearing

lbs. (245 Nm). After tightening, use a drift to stake the spindle nut shoulder against the spindle.

Front End Alignment

Alignment of the front wheels is essential if your car is to go, stop and turn as designed. Alignment can be altered by collision, overloading, poor repair or bent components.

If you are diagnosing bizarre handling and/or poor road manners, the first place to look is the tires. Although the tires may wear as a result of an alignment problem, worn or poorly inflated tires can make you chase alignment problems which don't exist.

Once you have eliminated all other causes, unload everything from the trunk except the spare tire, set the tire pressures to the correct level and take the car to a reputable alignment facility. Since the alignment settings are measured in very small increments, it is almost impossible for the home mechanic to accurately determine the settings. The explanations that follow will help you understand the three dimensions of alignment: caster, camber and toe.

CASTER

Caster is the tilting of the steering axis either forward or backward from the vertical, when viewed from the side of the vehicle. A backward tilt is said to be positive and a forward tilt is said to be negative. Changes in caster affect the straight line tendency of the vehicle and the "return to center" of the steering after a turn. If the camber is radically different between the left and right wheels (such as after hitting a major pothole), the car will exhibit a nasty pull to one side.

CAMBER

Camber is the tilting of the wheels from the

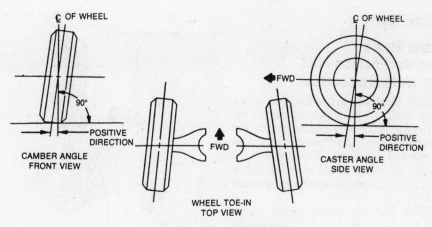

Camber, toe and caster angles

vertical (leaning in or out) when viewed from the front of the vehicle. When the wheels tilt outward at the top, the camber is said to be positive. When the wheels tilt inward at the top the camber is said to be negative. The amount of tilt is measured in degrees from the vertical. This measurement is called camber angle.

Camber affects the position of the tire on the road surface during vertical suspension movement and cornering. Changes in camber affect the handling and ride qualities of the car as well as tire wear. Many tire wear patterns indicate camber-related problems from misalignment, overloading or poor driving habits.

TOE

Toe is the turning in or out (parallelism) of the wheels. The actual amount of toe setting is normally only a fraction of an inch. The purpose of toe-in (or out) specification is to ensure parallel rolling of the wheels. Toe-in also serves to offset the small deflections of the steering support system which occur when the vehicle is rolling forward.

Changing the toe setting will radically affect the overall "feel" of the steering, the behavior of the car under braking, tire wear and even fuel economy. Excessive toe (in or out) causes excessive drag or scrubbing on the tires.

FRONT WHEEL ALIGNMENT

Year	Model	Caster Range (deg.)	Caster Preferred Setting (deg.)	Camber Range (deg.)	Camber Preferred Setting (deg.)	Toe-in (in.)	Steering Axis Inclination (deg.)
1984	Accord	7/16P–2 7/16P	1 7/16	1N–1P	0	0	12 1/2
	Prelude	1N–1P	0	1N–1P	0	0	6 13/16
1985	Accord	1/2P–2 1/2P	1 1/2P	1N–1P	0	0	12 1/2
	Prelude	1N–1P	0	1N–1P	0	0	6 13/16
1986	Accord	1/2N–1 1/2P	1/2P	1N–1P	0	0	6 13/16
	Prelude	1N–1P	0	1N–1P	0	0	6 13/16
1987	Accord	1/2N–1 1/2P	1/2P	1N–1P	0	0	6 13/16
	Prelude	1N–1P	0	1N–1P	0	0	6 13/16
1988	Accord	1/2N–1 1/2P	1/2P	1N–1P	0	0	6 13/16
	Prelude	1 13/16P–2 13/16P	2 3/8P	1N–1P	0	0	6 13/16
1989	Accord	1/2N–1 1/2P	1/2P	1N–1P	0	0	—
	Prelude	1 13/16P–2 13/16P	2 3/8P	1N–1P	0	0	—
1990	Accord	2P–4P	3P	1N–1P	0	0	—
	Prelude	1 13/16P–2 13/16P	2 3/8P	1N–1P	0	0	—
1991	Accord	2P–4P	3P	1N–1P	0	0	—
	Prelude	1 13/16P–2 13/16P	2 3/8P	1N–1P	0	0	—

P—Positive   N—Negative

REAR SUSPENSION

Spring and Shock Absorber/MacPherson strut

REMOVAL AND INSTALLATION

CAUTION: *Exercise great caution when working with the rear suspension. Coil springs and other suspension components are under extreme tension and result in severe injury if released improperly. Never remove the nut on the top of the shock absorber piston without using the proper spring compressor tool.*

WARNING: *The use of the correct special tools or their equivalent is REQUIRED for this procedure. A spring compressor must be used if the spring is to be removed from the strut.*

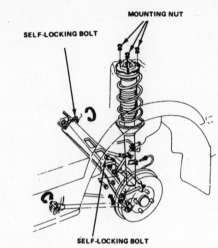

1985 Accord rear suspension

1984–85 Accord

1. Firmly block the front wheels. Elevate and safely support the rear of the car.
2. Remove the rear wheel.
3. Disconnect the brake line from the hose. Plug the line and hose immediately to prevent fluid leakage and entry of dirt.
4. Disconnect the stabilizer bar from the lower arm.
5. Remove the brake drum and disconnect the parking brake cable.
6. Remove the bolt holding the shock absorber to the hub carrier.
7. Remove the shock absorber mounting nuts.

CAUTION: *Do NOT remove the center or shaft nut from the top of the shock absorber.*

8. Remove the strut assembly from the vehicle.

Disassembly

9. Install a spring compressor on the spring. These tools are commonly available at auto parts suppliers. There are many different types; follow the manufacturer's instructions carefully. Tighten the compressor just enough to take the spring tension off the top spring seat.

10. With the spring compressed, remove the center or seat nut. Use a hex wrench of the correct size to keep the shaft from turning while the nut is removed.

11. Remove the upper mount. Carefully remove the seals, spacers and bearing at the top of the shock; keep them in order for proper reassembly. Remove the compressed spring.

12. If the spring is to be tested or replaced, release tension on the arms of the compressor slowly. Remove the tool when the spring is at normal length with no tension on the compressor.

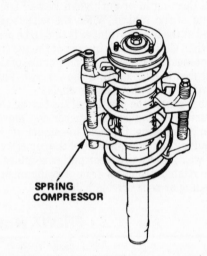

A spring compressor is required for rear spring removal

13. By hand, check the shock absorber for smooth operation through the full range of travel. Check it also for smoothness during short strokes of 2–4 in. (51–102mm). Replace the unit if any sign of unevenness or binding is felt. The shock/strut assembly cannot be disassembled; there are no replaceable parts.

To install:

14. Hold the strut assembly upright. If a vise is used, pad the jaws to avoid damage.

15. Install the rubber bump stop on the shaft.

16. Compress the spring and install it onto the shock. Make certain the bottom coil is exactly aligned in the bottom seat. Install the shaft dust cover.

17. Install the upper spring seat, spacers, bearing, seal and mount. Coat both sides of the needle bearing with grease before installing it. Make certain the upper spring seat is aligned with upper coil of the spring.

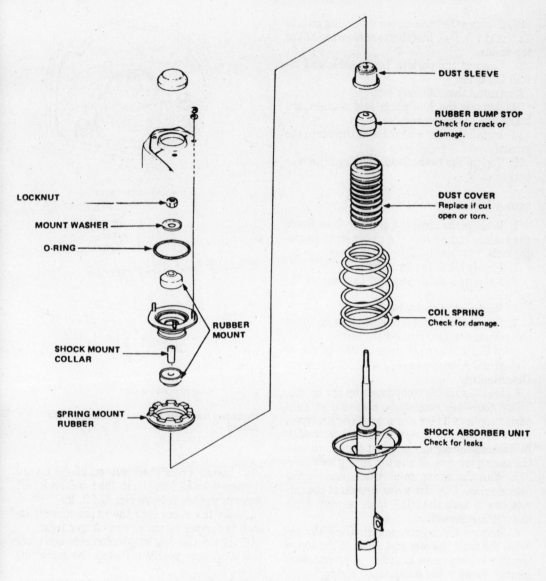

LOCKNUT

MOUNT WASHER

O-RING

RUBBER MOUNT

SHOCK MOUNT COLLAR

SPRING MOUNT RUBBER

DUST SLEEVE

RUBBER BUMP STOP
Check for crack or damage.

DUST COVER
Replace if cut open or torn.

COIL SPRING
Check for damage.

SHOCK ABSORBER UNIT
Check for leaks

Rear strut components, 1984–85 Accord

18. Install a new upper shaft nut; tighten it to 45 Nm (33 ft. lbs).

19. Slowly release the spring compressor, making sure the released spring fits into the upper mount correctly.

20. Place the strut into position at the top mounting point. Make certain the tab on the base of the strut is aligned slot in the strut fork. Install the nuts; only tighten them finger tight.

21. With the strut correctly aligned at the bottom and top, place a jack under the lower control arm. Raise the jack until the car BARELY lifts from the stand; this will force the shock into the knuckle.

22. Install and tighten the pinchbolt to 55 Nm (40 ft. lbs).

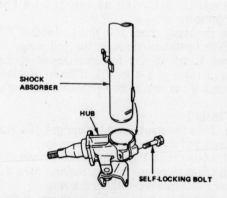

SHOCK ABSORBER

HUB

SELF-LOCKING BOLT

The tab must align with the hub before installation

23. Tighten the three upper mounting nuts to 22 Nm (16 ft. lbs). Install the rubber cap at the top mount.

24. Connect the parking brake cable and install the drum.

25. Install the stabilizer bar.

26. Remove the line plugs and connect the brake line to the brake hose.

27. Install the rear wheel; lower the car to the ground.

28. Top up the brake fluid and bleed the rear brakes.

1986–91 Accord

1. Remove the strut upper cover from inside the vehicle and remove the upper strut retaining nuts.

2. Firmly block the front wheels.

3. Raise and safely support the rear of the vehicle.

4. Remove the rear wheel.

5. Remove the strut mounting bolt, lower the suspension and remove the strut.

CAUTION: *Do NOT remove the center or shaft nut from the top of the shock absorber.*

Disassembly

6. Install a spring compressor on the spring. These tools are commonly available at auto parts suppliers. There are many different types; follow the manufacturer's instructions carefully. Tighten the compressor just enough to take the spring tension off the top spring seat.

7. With the spring compressed, remove the center or seat nut. Use a hex wrench of the correct size to keep the shaft from turning while the nut is removed.

8. Remove the upper mount. Carefully remove the seals, spacers and collar at the top of the shock; keep them in order for proper reassembly. Remove the compressed spring.

9. If the spring is to be tested or replaced, release tension on the arms of the compressor slowly. Remove the tool when the spring is at normal length with no tension on the compressor.

10. By hand, check the shock absorber for smooth operation through the full range of travel. Check it also for smoothness during short strokes of 2–4 in. (51–102mm). Replace the unit if any sign of unevenness or binding is felt.

To install:

11. Hold the strut assembly upright. If a vise is used, pad the jaws to avoid damage.

12. Install the bump stop and dust cover. Install the compressed spring, making sure the lower coil aligns correctly in the seat.

13. Install the upper seat, bushings, collar, seals and mount base.

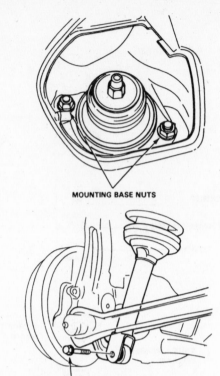

MOUNTING BASE NUTS

DAMPER MOUNTING BOLT

Upper and lower rear strut mounts for late-model Accord

14. Install a new shaft nut; on 86–89 Accord tighten it to 22 Nm (16 ft. lbs.) and on 90–91 Accord, tighten it to 30 Nm (22 ft. lbs).

15. Fit the shock into the upper mount; install the upper retaining nuts finger tight.

16. Lower the rear suspension arm and place the strut into position. Install the mounting bolt.

17. Place a jack under the lower strut mount. Raise the jack until the weight of the car is on the jack.

18. With the suspension under load, tighten the lower mount bolt to 55 Nm (40 ft. lbs). Tighten the upper nuts to 39 Nm (28 ft. lbs).

19. Install the rear wheel. Lower the vehicle to the ground.

1984–87 Prelude

1. Firmly block the front wheels.

2. Elevate and support the rear of the car.

3. Remove the rear wheel.

4. Remove the clamp holding the rear brake hose.

5. Remove the stabilizer from the lower arm.

6. Loosen the lower arm pivot (inboard) bolt.

7. Loosen the radius rod nut and the bolt holding the hub carrier to the lower arm.

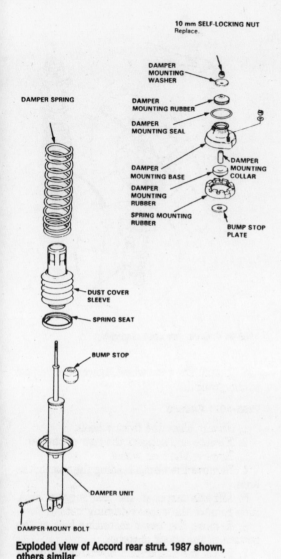

Exploded view of Accord rear strut. 1987 shown,
others similar

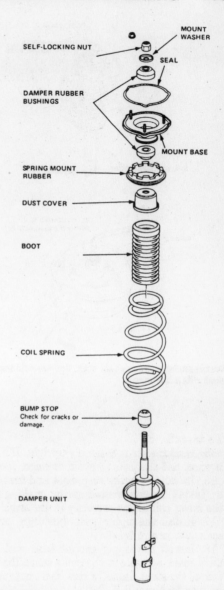

1984–87 Prelude rear spring and shock absorber
components

8. Remove the lock bolt holding the bottom of the strut.

9. Remove the three retaining nuts holding the top of the strut. Lower the suspension and remove the strut.

CAUTION: *Do NOT remove the center or shaft nut from the top of the shock absorber.*

Disassembly

10. Install a spring compressor on the spring. These tools are commonly available at auto parts suppliers. There are many different types; follow the manufacturer's instructions carefully. Tighten the compressor just enough to take the spring tension off the top spring seat.

11. With the spring compressed, remove the center or seat nut. Use a hex wrench of the correct size to keep the shaft from turning while the nut is removed.

12. Remove the upper mount. Carefully remove the seals, spacers, collar and other components at the top of the shock; keep them in order for proper reassembly. Remove the compressed spring.

13. If the spring is to be tested or replaced, release tension on the arms of the compressor slowly. Remove the tool when the spring is at normal length with no tension on the compressor.

14. By hand, check the shock absorber for smooth operation through the full range of travel. Check it also for smoothness during short strokes of 2–4 in. (51–102mm). Replace the unit if any sign of unevenness or binding is felt.

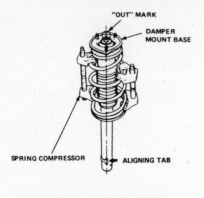

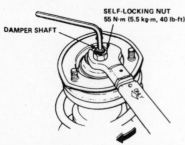

Reassembling a Prelude rear strut. Counter-hold the shaft with a hex-wrench

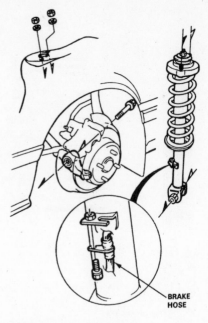

1988–91 Prelude rear strut assembly

To install:

15. Hold the strut assembly upright. If a vise is used, pad the jaws to avoid damage.

16. Install the bump stop, boot and dust cover. Install the compressed spring, making sure the lower coil aligns correctly in the seat.

17. Install the upper seat, bushings, collar, seals and mount base.

18. Install the upper mount base with the OUT mark opposite to the guide tab at the bottom of the strut. Install a new shaft nut; tighten it to 55 Nm (40 ft. lbs).

19. Fit the shock into the upper mount; install the upper retaining nuts finger tight.

20. Lower the rear suspension arm and place the strut into position. Install the mounting bolt. The tab on the strut must align with the groove in the hub carrier.

21. Place a jack under the lower strut mount. Raise the jack until the weight of the car is on the jack.

22. With the suspension under load, tighten the lower mount bolt to 55 Nm (40 ft. lbs). Tighten the upper nuts to 22 Nm (16 ft. lbs).

23. Tighten the radius rod nut to 65 Nm (47 ft. lbs.) and the lower arm pivot bolt to 55 Nm (40 ft. lbs).

24. Install the stabilizer bar.

25. Install the rear brake hose and secure the line clamp.

26. Install the rear wheel. Lower the vehicle to the ground.

1988–1991 Prelude

1. Firmly block the front wheels.

2. Elevate and support the rear of the car.

3. Remove the rear wheel.

4. Remove the clamp holding the rear brake hose.

5. Lift the carpet in the rear luggage area, then remove the upper retaining nuts.

6. Remove the lower mounting bolt at the bottom of the shock absorber.

7. Press the suspension downward; remove the strut from the car

CAUTION: *Do NOT remove the center or shaft nut from the top of the shock absorber.*

Disassembly

8. Install a spring compressor on the spring. These tools are commonly available at auto parts suppliers. There are many different types; follow the manufacturer's instructions carefully. Tighten the compressor just enough to take the spring tension off the top spring seat.

9. With the spring compressed, remove the center or seat nut. Use a hex wrench of the correct size to keep the shaft from turning while the nut is removed.

10. Remove the upper mount. Carefully remove the seals, spacers, collar and other components at the top of the shock; keep them in order for proper reassembly. Remove the compressed spring.

11. If the spring is to be tested or replaced, re-

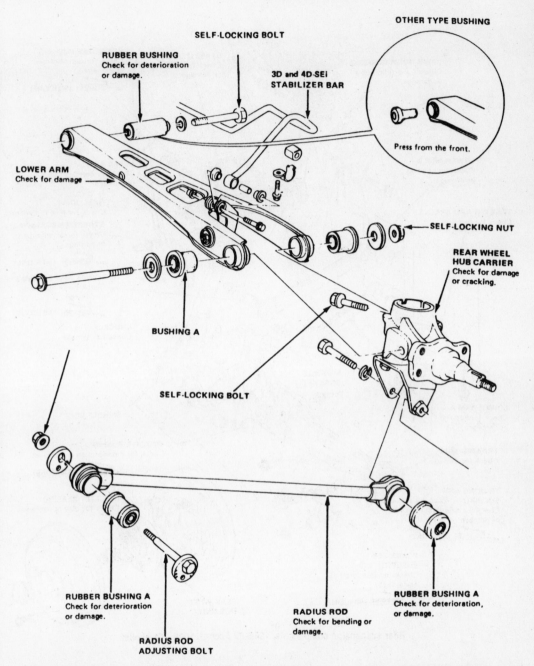

OTHER TYPE BUSHING

Press from the front.

SELF-LOCKING BOLT

RUBBER BUSHING
Check for deterioration
or damage.

3D and 4D-SEi
STABILIZER BAR

LOWER ARM
Check for damage

SELF-LOCKING NUT

REAR WHEEL
HUB CARRIER
Check for damage
or cracking.

BUSHING A

SELF-LOCKING BOLT

RUBBER BUSHING A
Check for deterioration
or damage.

RADIUS ROD
ADJUSTING BOLT

RADIUS ROD
Check for bending or
damage.

RUBBER BUSHING A
Check for deterioration,
or damage.

Rear suspension components, 1984–85 Accord and 1984–87 Prelude. Spring and shock absorber not shown

lease tension on the arms of the compressor slowly. Remove the tool when the spring is at normal length with no tension on the compressor.

12. By hand, check the shock absorber for smooth operation through the full range of travel. Check it also for smoothness during short strokes of 2–4 in. (51–102mm). Replace the unit if any sign of unevenness or binding is felt.

To install:

13. Hold the strut assembly upright. If a vise is used, pad the jaws to avoid damage.

14. Install the bump stop, boot and dust cover. Install the compressed spring, making sure the lower coil aligns correctly in the seat.

15. Install the upper seat, bushings, collar, seals and mount base.

16. Install the upper components and the up-

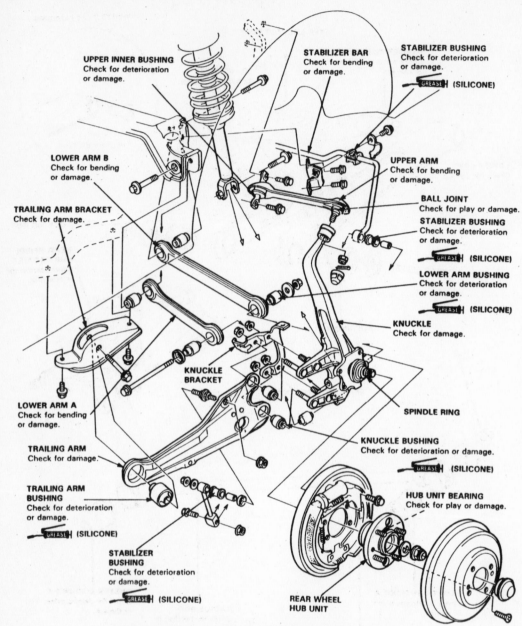

UPPER INNER BUSHING
Check for deterioration
or damage.

STABILIZER BAR
Check for bending
or damage.

STABILIZER BUSHING
Check for deterioration
or damage.

GREASE (SILICONE)

LOWER ARM B
Check for bending
or damage.

UPPER ARM
Check for bending
or damage.

BALL JOINT
Check for play or damage.

STABILIZER BUSHING
Check for deterioration
or damage.

GREASE (SILICONE)

TRAILING ARM BRACKET
Check for damage.

LOWER ARM BUSHING
Check for deterioration
or damage.

GREASE (SILICONE)

KNUCKLE
Check for damage.

LOWER ARM A
Check for bending
or damage.

**KNUCKLE
BRACKET**

SPINDLE RING

TRAILING ARM
Check for damage.

KNUCKLE BUSHING
Check for deterioration or damage.

GREASE (SILICONE)

**TRAILING ARM
BUSHING**
Check for deterioration
or damage.

GREASE (SILICONE)

HUB UNIT BEARING
Check for play or damage.

**STABILIZER
BUSHING**
Check for deterioration
or damage.

GREASE (SILICONE)

**REAR WHEEL
HUB UNIT**

Rear suspension components, 1986–89 Accord. 1990–91 similar

per mount. Install a new shaft nut; tighten it to
30 Nm (21 ft. lbs).

17. Lower the rear suspension arm and place
the strut into position. Install the mounting
bolt. The tab on the strut must align with the
groove in the hub carrier.

18. Fit the shock into the upper mount; install the upper retaining nuts finger tight.

19. Place a jack under the lower strut mount.
Raise the jack until the weight of the car is on
the jack.

20. With the suspension under load, tighten

the lower mount bolt to 65 Nm (47 ft. lbs).
Tighten the upper nuts to 39 Nm (28 ft. lbs).

21. Install the rear wheel and lower the car to
the ground.

Control Arms/Links

REMOVAL AND INSTALLATION
Trailing Arm
ACCORD

1. Raise and safely support the vehicle.

2. Remove the rear wheel.

3. Support the lower control arm using a jack.

4. Remove the bolt from the trailing arm bushing.

5. Remove the mounting nuts from the knuckle and remove the trailing arm.

6. Install in reverse order. When installing, make certain the passages in the bushings and the bolts are clean and lightly lubricated. Install the nuts and bolts finger tight, but do not apply final torque until the vehicle is on the ground. Tighten the four nuts to 55 Nm (40 ft. lbs.) and the pivot bolt to 65 Nm (47 ft. lbs.).

Upper Control Arm

1. Raise and safely support the vehicle.

2. Remove the rear wheel.

3. Support the lower control arm with a jack.

4. On Accord and Prelude, remove the cotter pin and castle nut from the upper ball joint. Use a ball joint separator to separate the ball joint from the knuckle.

5. Remove the upper control arm mounting bolts and the upper control arm. The Prelude upper ball joint is separately replaceable; the Accord ball joint is not.

6. If the Prelude ball joint is replaced, tighten the mounting nuts to 55 Nm (40 ft. lbs).

7. On Accord, install the upper arm mounts and tighten the bolts to 39 Nm (28 ft. lbs).

8. Connect the ball joint. Install the nut, tightening it to 44 Nm (32 ft. lbs) and install a new cotter pin.

9. Install the wheel; lower the car to the ground.

Lower Control Arm

1. Raise and safely support the vehicle.

2. Remove the rear wheel.

3. Remove the strut and/or radius rod mounting bolts from the lower control arm.

4. On Prelude, remove the cotter pin and castle nut from the ball joint and separate the ball joint from the knuckle using the proper tool.

5. Remove the lower arm mounting bolts and remove the lower control arm.

6. Install in reverse order.

Rear Wheel Bearings

REPLACEMENT

CAUTION: *Brake pads and shoes contain asbestos, which has been determined to be a cancer causing agent. Never clean the brake surfaces with compressed air. Avoid inhaling any dust from brake surfaces. When cleaning brakes, use commercially available brake cleaning fluids.*

1984–85 Accord

1. Slightly loosen the rear lug nuts. Raise the car and support safely on jackstands.

2. Release the parking brake. Remove the rear wheels.

3. Remove the rear bearing hub cap, cotter pin and pin holder.

4. Remove the spindle nut, then pull the hub and drum off the spindle.

5. Drive the outboard inboard bearing races out of the hub. Punch in a criss-cross pattern to avoid cocking the bearing race in the bore.

6. Clean the bearing seats thoroughly before going on to the next step.

7. Using a bearing driver, drive the inboard bearing race into the hub.

8. Turn the hub over and drive the outboard bearing race in the same way.

9. Check to see that the bearing races are seated properly.

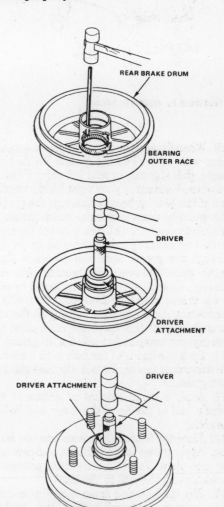

Removing and installing bearing races

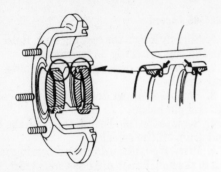

The races must seat squarely

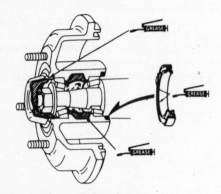

Grease must be applied as shown

10. When fitting new bearings, you must pack them with wheel bearing grease. To do this, place a glob of grease in your left palm. Holding one of the bearings in your right hand, drag the face of the bearing heavily through the grease. This must be done to work as much grease as possible through the ball bearings and the cage. Turn the bearing and continue to pull it through the grease until the grease is thoroughly packed between the bearing balls and the cage, all around the bearing. You'll be able to see grease emerging from the clean side of the bearing if the lubricant is going all the way through. Repeat this operation until all of the bearings are completely packed with grease.

11. Pack the inside of the hub with a moderate amount of grease. Do not overload the hub with grease.

12. Apply a small amount of grease to the spindle and to the lip of the inner seal before installing.

13. Place the inboard bearings into the hub.

14. Apply grease to the hub seal, and carefully tap into place. Tap in a criss-cross pattern to avoid cocking the seal in the bore.

15. Slip the hub and drum over the spindle, then insert the outboard bearing, hub, washer, and spindle nut.

16. Follow the Adjustment Procedure.

1986–91 Accord

NOTE: *Do not tighten or loosen a spindle nut unless the vehicle is sitting on all 4 wheels. The torque is high enough to cause the vehicle to fall even when properly supported.*

1. Loosen the rear lug nuts and the spindle nut. Raise the vehicle and support it safely.

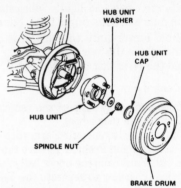

Bearing removal, 1986–91 Accord

2. Release the parking brake. Remove the rear wheel and the brake drum.

3. Remove the rear bearing hub cap and nut.

4. Pull the hub unit off of the spindle.

5. Install in reverse order of removal. With the vehicle on the ground, torque the new spindle nut to 185 Nm (137 ft. lbs.), then stake the nut.

Prelude

WARNING: *The use of the correct special tools or their equivalent is REQUIRED for this procedure. A hydraulic press and the correct diameter drivers and supports are required for disassembly of the hub and bearing. Do not attempt to substitute tools for the press. If necessary, take the knuckle assembly to a machine shop or dealership to have the bearings replaced.*

1. Slightly loosen the rear lug nuts. Raise the vehicle and support it safely.

2. Release the parking brake. Remove the rear wheel.

3. Remove the bolts retaining the brake caliper and remove the caliper from the knuckle. Do not let the caliper hang by the brake hose; support it with a length of wire.

4. Remove the two 6mm screws from the brake disc. Tighten two 8 x 12mm bolts into the holes of the brake disc, then remove the brake disc from the rear hub.

5. Remove the cotter pin of the lower arm B on 2-wheel steering vehicles or the tie rod on 4-

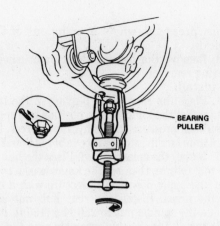

Disconnecting Prelude rear lower ball joint. Note that the nut is left loose but in place to retain the arm after separation

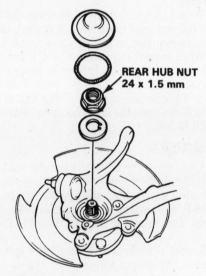

The rear hub nut must be removed

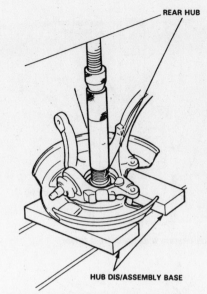

Use the press and driver to remove the hub

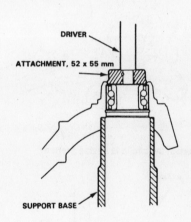

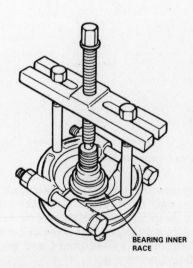

Removing the wheel bearing (above) and inner race

wheel steering vehicles and remove the castle nut.

6. Separate the tie rod ball joint using a ball joint removal tool.

7. Remove the cotter pin and loosen the lower arm ball joint nut half the length of the joint threads.

8. Separate the ball joint and lower arm using a puller.

9. Remove the cotter pin and castle nut. Separate the upper ball joint, using a ball joint removal tool. Remove the knuckle assembly from the vehicle.

10. Remove the rear hub spindle nut from the rear hub. Remove the splash guard mounting bolts. Using a hydraulic press, separate the hub from the knuckle.

NOTE: *Set the rear hub at the hub/disc as-*

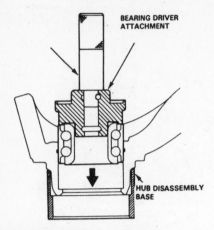

Install the bearing with the correct driver

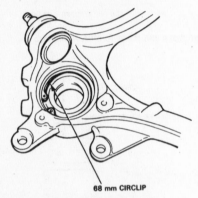

Make certain the circlip is seated properly

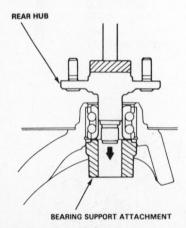

Installing the Prelude rear hub

sembly base firmly, so the knuckle will not tilt the assembly in the press. Take care not to distort the splash guard. Hold onto the hub to keep it from falling after it is pressed out.

11. Remove the splash guard and 68mm circlip from the knuckle.

12. Using a hydraulic press and proper press tools, press the wheel bearing out of the knuckle.

13. Remove the bearing inner race using a bearing remover.

To install:

14. Place the rear wheel bearing in the tool fixture. Set the knuckle into position and apply downward pressure with a hydraulic press. Fit the 68mm circlip into the groove of the knuckle.

15. Install the splash guard. Place the hub in the tool fixture, then set the knuckle into position and apply downward pressure with a hydraulic press. Install the rear hub nut and torque the spindle nut to 250 Nm (180 ft. lbs.

16. Install the knuckle assembly onto the vehicle and install all nuts and bolts loosely. Tighten the lower ball joint nut to 55 Nm (40 ft. lbs.), then tighten as required to install a new cotter pin.

17. On vehicles with 4-wheel steering, tighten the tie rod end joint to 44 Nm (32 ft. lbs.), then tighten as required to install a new cotter pin.

18. When everything is assembled, lower the vehicle and tighten the rubber bushing nuts and bolts with the weight of the vehicle on the wheels. Tighten the upper bushing nut to 44 Nm (32 ft. lbs.) and the lower bushing bolt to 55 Nm (40 ft. lbs).

ADJUSTMENT

1. Apply grease or oil on the spindle nut and spindle threads.

2. Install and tighten the spindle nut to 24 Nm (18 ft. lbs). Rotate the drum/disc 2–3 turns by hand, then retighten the spindle nut to 18 ft. lbs.

3. Repeat the above step until the spindle nut holds the proper torque after the disc or drum is rotated.

4. Loosen the spindle nut to 0 ft. lbs. This means loosen the nut until it just breaks free, but doesn't turn.

5. Retorque the spindle nut to 5.5 Nm (4 ft. lbs.)

6. Set the pin holder so the slots will be as close as possible to the hole in the spindle.

7. Tighten the spindle nut just enough to align the slot and hole, then secure it with a new cotter pin.

Rear Alignment

All the models covered by this guide have rear suspension systems on which bent or damaged components can cause unusual tire wear and/or handling problems. The alignment dimensions of caster, camber and toe are applicable to the rear wheels as well as the front. All Accords and

SUSPENSION AND STEERING 301

Preludes are adjustable for rear toe setting; some models are adjustable for camber.

Rear alignment should be checked periodically by a reputable alignment facility. Preludes with 4WS require rear alignment with every front wheel alignment.

NOTE: *When taking a 4WS Prelude to be aligned, make certain the shop can lock the rear steering mechanism in the centered position. The use of Honda lock pin 07HAJ–SF1020A or its equivalent is required.*

Checking the alignment of the rear wheels can be a quick, low-cost diagnostic tool when investigating rear tire wear. Discovering a bent component and replacing it can save the cost and aggravation of replacing two tires, only to have them wear out prematurely.

Additionally, check the alignment any time the rear wheels or suspension undergoes a heavy impact. Suspension components are reasonably strong in their normal working dimensions but a world-class pothole or off-road excursion can force them over the limit.

STEERING

1991 Airbag/SRS System

Certain 1991 Accord models are equipped with a Supplemental Restraint System (SRS), commonly referred to as an airbag. The bag itself is stored within the hub of the steering wheel; the sensors and control module are behind the dashboard. The airbag system is designed to aid in restraining the driver during a frontal collision; the system supplements (helps) the seat belt system. An airbag system is ineffective if seat belts are not worn.

The airbag is a fabric bag or balloon with an explosive inflator unit attached. The system employs two dash sensors and a cowl sensor as well as an inflator circuit and control module. A back-up power system is connected in parallel with the battery. No single sensor can trigger SRS deployment. The cowl sensor, centered under the dashboard, and at least one of the two dash sensors (positioned left and right in the front footwells) must engage together for at least 0.002 seconds. This "agreement" of the sensors is required to prevent deployment when not appropriate.

When the control unit receives these two signals, power is supplied to the inflator circuit, either from the battery or back-up system. A small heater causes a chemical reaction in the igniter; the non-toxic gas from the chemical mixture expands very rapidly (milliseconds), filling the bag and forcing it through the steering wheel pad. Since all this is happening very rapidly, the expanding bag should reach the driver before the driver reaches the steering wheel/column during a frontal collision. The chemical reaction is ended by the time the airbag is fully inflated; as the operator hits the bag, the gas is allowed to escape slowly through vents in the back of the bag.

The control unit contains a self-diagnostic circuit. When the ignition switch is turned ON, the SRS dash warning lamp should light for about 6 seconds, then go out. If the light does not come on, does not go out or comes on when driving, the system must be diagnosed and repaired by a Honda dealer. The system is NOT repairable at home.

CAUTIONS AND WARNINGS

While the SRS system is fully capable of operating trouble-free for years, its presence poses a great hazard during repair. Unintentional inflation can cause severe injury and/or property damage. For that reason ALL of the following items must be fully observed during any repair or procedure in or around the steering column or dashboard. Proper safety precautions MUST be observed at all times.

- Do not attempt to repair or alter any part of the SRS system. If the system needs repair or diagnosis, take the car to a Honda dealer.
- Before making repairs to the steering wheel or column, the system must be disarmed by installing the shorting connector.
- All SRS-related wiring and connectors are identified by yellow outer insulation. NEVER attempt to test these circuits with a volt-ohmmeter.
- Disconnect both battery cables when working on the vehicle.
- Once the steering wheel pad is removed, store it face UP in a clean area. If stored face down, accidental detonation could launch it.
- Keep the steering wheel pad in a clean, dry location. Contact with acid, water or heavy metals (copper, lead, mercury) can cause accidental discharge. Storage temperature must not exceed 200°F.
- Do not replace the original steering wheel with any other; do not interchange SRS parts between vehicles.

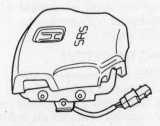

Always store the unit face-up

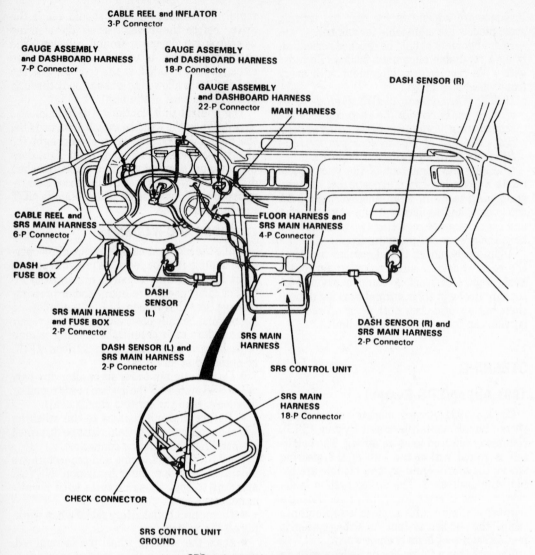

CABLE REEL and INFLATOR
3-P Connector

GAUGE ASSEMBLY
and DASHBOARD HARNESS
7-P Connector

GAUGE ASSEMBLY
and DASHBOARD HARNESS
18-P Connector

GAUGE ASSEMBLY
and DASHBOARD HARNESS
22-P Connector

MAIN HARNESS

DASH SENSOR (R)

CABLE REEL and
SRS MAIN HARNESS
6-P Connector

FLOOR HARNESS and
SRS MAIN HARNESS
4-P Connector

DASH
FUSE BOX

SRS MAIN HARNESS
and FUSE BOX
2-P Connector

DASH
SENSOR
(L)

DASH SENSOR (L) and
SRS MAIN HARNESS
2-P Connector

SRS MAIN
HARNESS

DASH SENSOR (R) and
SRS MAIN HARNESS
2-P Connector

SRS CONTROL UNIT

SRS MAIN
HARNESS
18-P Connector

CHECK CONNECTOR

SRS CONTROL UNIT
GROUND

SRS component location, 1991 Accord

- Never attempt to modify, splice or repair any SRS-related wire or cable. Do not disconnect SRS wiring during other repairs.
- The system must be inspected by a Honda dealer 10 years after the date of manufacture as shown on the certification plate. Note that this "build date" may be much earlier than your purchase date.
- The system must be checked after any frontal accident or body work, even if the system did NOT deploy.

DISARMING THE SYSTEM

CAUTION: *This procedure MUST be followed whenever the steering wheel or column is to be worked on. The shorting connector must be installed whenever the inflator connector is disconnected from the harness.*

1. Disconnect the negative battery cable, then the positive cable from the battery.
2. Remove maintenance lid A below the airbag, then remove the red shorting connector stored inside the lid.
3. Disconnect the connector between the airbag and the cable reel in the steering wheel. The connector can be reached through the opening made by removing the maintenance lid.
4. Install the shorting connector into the airbag side of the wiring connector.
5. DON'T forget to remove the connector when other repairs are finished.
6. Remove the shorting connector (replace it on the lid), attach the connectors in the steering wheel and reconnect the battery cables. Reinstall the maintenance lid.

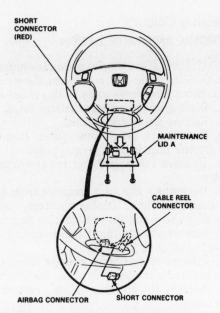

The shorting connector is contained inside the maintenance cover. Always install it to the airbag side of the junction

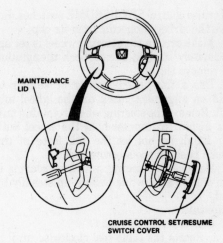

Removing the airbag assembly after disarming

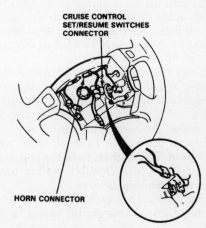

Steering wheel wiring connectors

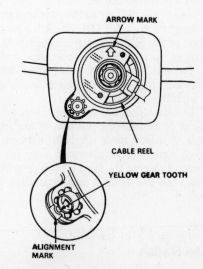

The cable reel must be properly aligned before the wheel is reinstalled

Steering Wheel

REMOVAL AND INSTALLATION

All Models without SRS

1. Disconnect the negative battery cable.
2. Remove the wheel pad. Disconnect the necessary electrical connections under the steering wheel pad.
3. Make certain the steering wheel is set approximately straight ahead. Lock the ignition and remove the key.
4. Use a fine-tipped marker or similar to make an alignment mark on the wheel and shaft. Remove the steering wheel retaining nut. It is helpful to counter-hold the wheel with your hand; do not let the full force of the wrench push on the steering lock.
5. Remove the steering wheel by rocking it from side to side, while pulling up steadily by hand.
6. Install in reverse order. Be sure to tighten the steering wheel nut to 50 Nm (36 ft. lbs).

1991 with SRS

1. If working on a vehicle equipped with SRS/airbag system, disarm the system following procedures given in this chapter.
2. Remove the left maintenance lid and remove the cover from the cruise control SET/RESUME switch.
3. Remove the two TORX® bolt using a T30 bit; remove the airbag assembly.
4. Disconnect the connectors from the horn

and cruise control SET/RESUME switches. Remove the airbag connector from its clip.

5. Make certain the steering wheel is set approximately straight ahead. Lock the ignition and remove the key.

6. Use a fine-tipped marker or similar to make an alignment mark on the wheel and shaft. Remove the steering wheel retaining nut. It is helpful to counter-hold the wheel with your hand; do not let the full force of the wrench push on the steering lock.

7. Remove the steering wheel by rocking it from side to side, while pulling up steadily by hand.

To install:

8. Center the cable reel:

a. Rotate the cable reel clockwise until it stops.

b. Rotate it counterclockwise approximately 2 turns until the yellow gear tooth aligns with the mark on the cover AND the arrow on the cable reel points straight up.

9. Install the steering wheel. Make certain the wheel shaft engages the cable reel. Tighten the nut to 50 Nm (36 ft. lbs).

10. Insert the cruise control SET/RESUME connector and the airbag connector into the steering wheel clips. Check that they are firmly seated.

11. Connect the horn connector.

12. Install the airbag assembly with new TORX® bolts. Tighten them to 10 Nm (7 ft. lbs.)

13. Install the SET/RESUME switch cover and the left maintenance cover.

14. Disconnect the shorting connector from the airbag harness. Connect the airbag to the cable reel.

15. Replace the connector on the maintenance lid and install the lid.

16. Connect the battery cables, positive first. Turn the ignition switch ON; check for proper operation of the SRS dash warning lamp. Confirm proper operation of the horn and cruise control buttons. Turn the steering wheel counterclockwise; check that the yellow tooth still aligns with the mark.

NOTE: *Check that the steering wheel spoke angle is correct for the position of the front wheels. If minor spoke angle adjustment is needed, have this adjustment done by an alignment shop at the front wheels (resetting the toe). Do not remove and reposition the wheel.*

Turn Signal/Wiper Switch
Ignition Switch

Please refer to Chapter 6, Chassis Electrical, for these procedures.

Steering Column
REMOVAL AND INSTALLATION

CAUTION: *If working on a vehicle equipped with SRS/airbag system, disarm the system following procedures given in this chapter.*

1. Disconnect the negative battery cable.

2. Remove the steering wheel.

3. Remove the lower cover panel. Remove the driver's knee bolster, if equipped.

4. Remove the upper and lower column covers.

5. Disconnect the wire couplers from the combination switch. Remove the turn signal canceling sleeve and the combination switch.

6. Remove the steering joint cover and remove the steering joint bolt(s).

7. Disconnect each wire coupler from the fuse box under the left side of the dashboard.

8. Remove the steering column retaining brackets.

9. Remove the nuts attaching the bending plate guide and bending plate (part of the tilt-wheel assembly) and remove the steering column assembly.

To install:

10. Fit the column into place and secure the bracket, bending plate and guide. Torque the nuts to 22 Nm (16 ft. lbs).

11. Install the steering joint bolts and torque to 22 Nm (16 ft. lbs).

12. Connect the wiring at the fuse box.

13. Install the switches and connect the wiring.

14. Install the knee bolster and steering wheel. Torque the wheel nut to 50 Nm (36 ft. lbs).

Steering Rack
Manual Rack and Pinion
REMOVAL AND INSTALLATION

1. Raise and safely support the front end of the car on jackstands. double check the placement and security of the stands.

2. Remove the cover panel and steering joint cover at the firewall. Unbolt and separate the steering shaft at the coupling.

3. Remove the front wheels.

4. Remove the cotter pins and unscrew halfway the castle nuts on the tie rod ends. Using a ball joint tool disconnect the tie rod ends. After the joints are separated, remove the castle nut and lift the tie rod ends out of the steering knuckles.

5. Remove the center beam.

6. On cars with manual transmissions, disconnect the shift rod and extension from the clutch housing.

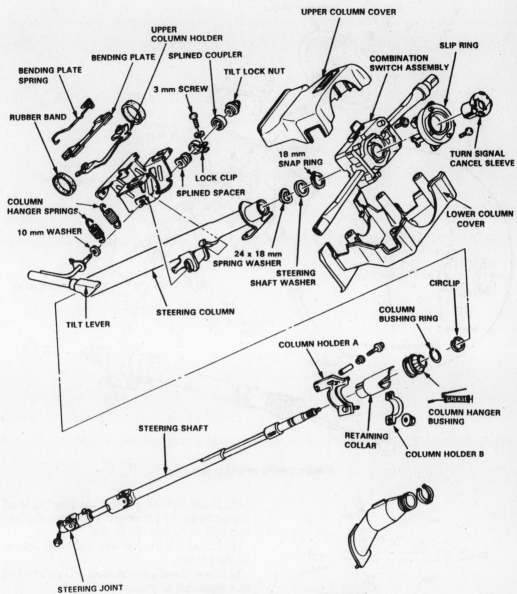

Steering column components, 1986–89 Accord

7. On cars with automatic transmissions, remove the shift cable guide from the floor and pull the shift cable down by hand.

8. Remove the nuts connecting the exhaust header pipe to the exhaust pipe and remove the exhaust pipe bracket. Move the exhaust pipe out of the way; support it with a piece of wire.

9. Push the rack all the way to the right (simulating a left turn) and remove the gearbox brackets. Slide the tie rod ends all the way to the right.

10. Drop the gearbox far enough to permit the end of the pinion shaft to come out of the hole in the frame channel, then rotate it forward until the shaft is pointing rearward.

11. Slide the gearbox to the right until the left tie rod clears the exhaust pipe, then drop it down and out of the car to the left.

To install:

12. Set the rack with the arms to the right (simulating a left turn). Install the rack by reversing the removal manipulation. Rotate the rack so that the pinion shaft fits into its hole in the frame channel.

13. Once in place and centered, install the mount brackets; tighten the bolts to 22 Nm (16 ft. lbs).

14. Reconnect the exhaust pipe and install the brackets. Tighten the pipe nuts to 55 Nm (40 ft. lbs) and the bracket nuts to 22 Nm (16 ft. lbs).

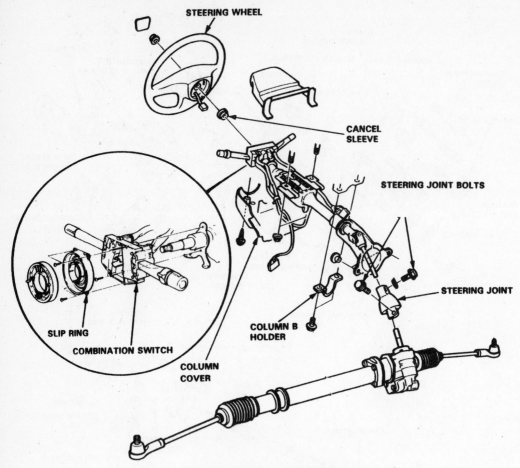

STEERING WHEEL

CANCEL SLEEVE

STEERING JOINT BOLTS

STEERING JOINT

SLIP RING

COMBINATION SWITCH

COLUMN COVER

COLUMN B HOLDER

Prelude steering column components

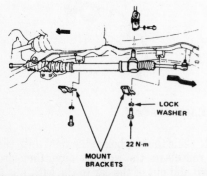

LOCK WASHER

22 N·m

MOUNT BRACKETS

Removing the manual steering rack

15. Reconnect the transmission controls, either the shift rod or shift cable guide.

16. Install the center beam. Make certain the insulator is centered with its mount on the transmission. It may be necessary to loosen the center beam bolt and insulator nuts to adjust the position. Tighten the center beam bolts to 50 Nm (36 ft. lbs.)

17. Connect the tie-rod ball joints, install the castle nut and fit a new cotter pin.

18. Inside the car, connect the steering shaft connector to the pinion shaft. Tighten the bottom bolt to 30 Nm (22 ft. lbs).

19. Install the front wheels and lower the car to the ground.

20. Have the alignment (toe) setting checked at a reputable alignment facility.

ADJUSTMENT

NOTE: *This procedure is to adjust steering effort only. Additionally, a steering gearbox locknut wrench such as Honda tool 07916–SA50001 or its equivalent, is required.*

1. Check the steering force by first raising the front wheels and placing them in a straight-ahead position. Using a spring scale, turn the steering wheel, check the steering force; it should be no more than 3.3 lbs.

2. Make sure that the rack is well lubricated.

3. Loosen the rack guide adjusting locknut.

4. Tighten the adjusting screw just to the point where the screw bottoms.

5. Back off the adjusting screw 45° and hold it in that position while tightening the locknut

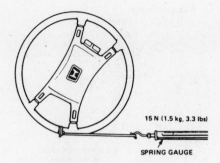

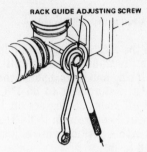

Always check the steering force before adjusting the steering rack

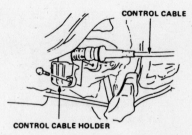

The control cable holder must be removed. Accord shown

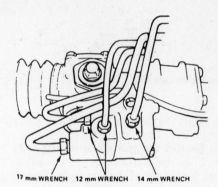

Use great care in disconnecting the 4 lines from the control unit

6. Recheck the play, then, move the wheels lock-to-lock, to make sure that the rack moves freely.

7. Check the steering force, repeating Step 1.

Power Steering Rack
REMOVAL AND INSTALLATION

Accord and Prelude

1. Disconnect the negative battery cable. Raise the vehicle and support it safely.

2. Remove the steering shaft joint cover and disconnect the steering shaft at the coupling.

3. Drain the power steering fluid by disconnecting the gearbox return hose at the reservoir. Plug the reservoir port and place the end of the hose in a container. Start the engine, running it while turning the steering wheel lock to lock. When the fluid stops draining, switch the engine off immediately. until fluid stops draining. Remove the plug and reinstall the hose.

4. Remove the gearbox shield.

5. Remove the front wheels.

6. Using a ball joint tool, disconnect the tie rods from the knuckles.

7. If equipped with manual transaxle, remove the shift extension from the transaxle case. Disconnect the gear shift rod from the transaxle case by removing the 8mm bolt.

8. If equipped with automatic transaxle, remove the control cable clamp.

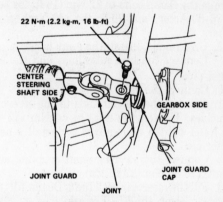

Disconnect the 4WS steering at the front joint

9. Remove the center beam.

10. On Preludes with 4 Wheel Steering, separate the joint guard cap and the joint guard. Remove the joint bolt from the driven pinion side. Remove the joint bolt from the center steering shaft side, then slide the joint back to disconnect it from the driven pinion.

11. Remove the exhaust header pipe.

12. Label and disconnect the hydraulic lines at the steering control unit. The 4 nuts are of three different sizes, 12 mm, 14mm and 17mm; use flare-nut wrenches which exactly fit the lines.

13. On Prelude, remove the mounting bolts and lower the front sway bar.

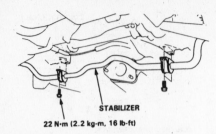

STABILIZER

22 N·m (2.2 kg-m, 16 lb-ft)

The Prelude stabilizer bar must be removed

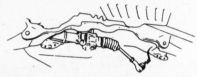

Removing the rack

14. Shift the tie rods all the way right, simulating a left turn.
15. Remove the gearbox mounting bolts.
16. Slide the gearbox right so the left tie rod clears the bottom of the rear beam. Remove the gearbox.

To install:

17. Position the gear box in the vehicle and torque the clamp bolts to 22 Nm (16 ft. lbs.) on 1986–89 Accord and 29 ft. lbs. (40 Nm) on all others.
18. On Prelude, install the sway bar.
19. Connect the hydraulic lines and the exhaust pipe.
20. Connect the shift linkage.
21. Connect the tie rod ends to the steering knuckles. Tighten the nuts to 44 Nm (32 ft. lbs.) and tighten as required to install a new cotter pin.
22. Connect the steering shaft coupling and tighten to 30 Nm (22 ft. lbs).
23. Fill the reservoir with fluid. Do not fill the reservoir above the FULL mark.

NOTE: *Remember that your Honda uses only Honda power steering fluid. Substitution of other fluids may damage the system*

24. Bleed the air from the system. After refilling the reservoir, start the engine and run it at fast idle while turning the steering wheel lock-to-lock several times. Check the fluid level and top it as necessary. Switch the engine OFF.

ADJUSTMENT

NOTE: *A steering gearbox locknut wrench such as Honda tool 07916-SA50001 or its equivalent, is required.*

Accord

1. Remove the steering gear splash shield, if equipped.

RACK GUIDE SCREW

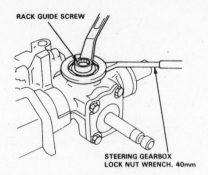

STEERING GEARBOX
LOCK NUT WRENCH, 40mm

Accord power steering rack adjustment

2. Loosen the rack guide adjusting locknut.
3. Tighten the adjusting screw until it compresses the spring and seats against the guide, then loosen it. Retorque it to 35 INCH lbs., then back it off about 25 degrees on 1986–89 Accord or about 35 degrees on 1990–91 Accord.
4. Hold it in that position while adjusting the locknut to 18 ft. lbs.
5. Recheck the play and move the wheels lock-to-lock to make sure the rack moves freely.

Prelude

1. Make sure the rack is well lubricated.
2. Loosen the rack guide adjusting locknut.
3. Tighten the adjusting screw until it compresses the spring and seats against the guide, then loosen it. Retorque it to 24 INCH lbs., then back it off 20–30 degrees or 15–25 degrees on 1990–91 vehicles. On 2 wheel steering vehicles, retighten the screw to 3 Nm (2 ft. lbs) and tighten the locknut to 25 Nm (18 ft. lbs.) On 4WS cars, back the adjuster off about 30–40 degrees, retighten it to 3 Nm (2 ft. lbs.) and secure the locknut.
4. Recheck the play and move the wheels lock-to-lock to make sure the rack moves freely.

4 Wheel Steering System

The 4WS Prelude adapts the front steering rack with the addition of an output pinion. The output pinion is connected to the rear steering box by a center shaft.

When the steering wheel is turned, the rack and pinion in the front steering gearbox moves the rack in desired direction. The rack steers the front wheels and also rotates the output pinion shaft. The center shaft is turned, transmitting the steering angle to the rear steering gearbox. A stroke rod at the rear is moved by this input. The stroke rod is connected to the rear tie-rods which move the rear wheels.

At the rear gearbox, the input or offset shaft turns a planetary offset pinion gear on a fixed internal gear. As the planetary gear turns, its vertical movement is absorbed by the slider and

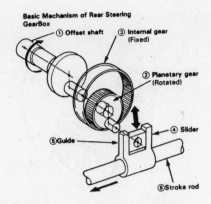

Basic Mechanism of Rear Steering GearBox

① Offset shaft
③ Internal gear (Fixed)
② Planetary gear (Rotated)
④ Slider
⑤ Guide
⑥ Stroke rod

Schematic of rear steering gearbox operation

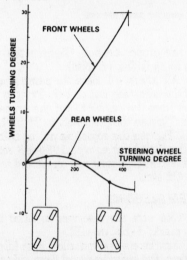

FRONT WHEELS

REAR WHEELS

STEERING WHEEL TURNING DEGREE

WHEELS TURNING DEGREE

Steering wheel angle vs. front and rear wheel steering angle

guide. Only the lateral or sideways force is transmitted to the stroke rod. The motion of the planetary gear pushes the stroke rod fully to one side, then pulls it back and pushes it fully to the opposite side.

Up to approximately 127 degrees of steering wheel motion, the rear wheels steer in the same direction as the front, i.e., both left or both right. If more steering lock is used, the rear wheels return to center and then track opposite to the fronts. This same-and-opposite arrangement allows agile handling at road speeds where steering angles are low (as in lane changing or cornering) and gives enhanced low-speed maneuvering where steering input angles are higher — parking, for example.

REMOVAL AND INSTALLATION
Precautions
Use of the rear steering Center Lock Pin, Honda tool 07HAJ–SF1020A, is REQUIRED

for this procedure. This is a special purpose tool, unlikely to be found in the aftermarket. It must be installed any time the rear steering gearbox or the center shaft is removed. It must also be used during rear wheel alignment.

• Once removed, handle the rear steering gearbox with extreme care.

• Do not twist or apply any torque to the off-set (input) shaft.

• Do not strike or apply force to the stroke rod.

• Do not attempt to disassemble or repair the gearbox. Do not loosen any of the external locknuts.

Procedure

1. Elevate and safely support the rear of the car. Double check the jackstands for correct placement and stability.

2. Remove the rear wheels.

3. Remove the cotter pins from the tie-rod joints. Loosen the castle nuts half-way. Separate the joint from the steering knuckle with the proper tool, then remove the nut and disconnect the tie-rod.

4. At the center shaft connection to the rear steering gearbox, slide the joint guard toward the front of the car. Remove the steering yoke bolt.

5. Remove the cap bolt from the gearbox. With the steering wheel centered, Install the center lock pin. If the steering is centered (and locked), no red will be visible around the shaft of the lock pin. If it is not correctly engaged, the red mark will be seen.

6. Remove the 4 gearbox retaining bolts. Note that the lower bolts are longer than the other two; they must be reinstalled correctly.

7. Remove the rear steering gearbox to the rear of the car, lifting it over the rear beam.
To install:

8. Place the gearbox in position.

9. Install the retaining bolts, making sure each is in its proper place. Tighten the bolts to 40 Nm (29 ft. lbs).

10. Connect the gearbox shaft to the center shaft. Tighten the yoke bolt to 22 Nm (16 lb. ft.) and install the joint guard.

11. Remove the center locking pin. Reinstall the cap bolt and washer.

12. Connect the tie-rods to the knuckles. Tighten the castle nuts to 44 Nm (32 ft. lbs) and install new cotter pins.

13. Install the rear wheels. Lower the car to the ground.

Power Steering Pump
REMOVAL AND INSTALLATION

1. Drain the fluid from the system as follows:

a. Disconnect the pump return hose from the reservoir and place the end in a large container. Plug the port in the reservoir.

b. Start the engine and allow it to run at fast idle. Turn the steering wheel from lock to lock several times, until fluid stops running from the hose. Shut off the engine immediately; don't run the pump without fluid.

c. Reattach the hose.

2. Disconnect the inlet and outlet hoses at the pump. Remove the drive belt.

3. Remove the bolts and remove the pump.

4. Install in reverse order. Adjust the belt tension, fill the reservoir and bleed the air from the system.

Reminder: Use only Honda power steering fluid. Installing any other fluid or ATF may damage the system.

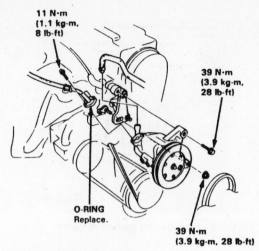

Power steering pump removal

BELT ADJUSTMENT

1. Push on the belt mid way between the pulleys with a force of about 22 lbs. The belt deflection should be as follows:
- 1984–89 Accord — 0.55–0.67 in. (14–17mm).
- 1984–87 Prelude — 0.55–0.67 in. (14–17mm).
- 1990–91 Accord — 0.50–0.62 in. (12.5–16mm).
- 1988–91 Prelude — 0.43–0.51 in. (11–13mm).

2. If belt deflection is not as specified, adjust as follows:

a. 1990–91 Accord – Loosen the pivot bolt and mounting nut. Turn the adjusting bolt to get the proper tension. Tighten the pivot bolt to 33 ft. lbs. (45 Nm) and the mounting nut to 16 ft. lbs. (22 Nm).

b. 1988–91 Prelude – Loosen the adjusting pulley bolt and turn the adjusting bolt to get the proper tension. Tighten the pulley bolt to 35 ft. lbs. (49 Nm).

c. All others — Loosen the pump pivot bolt and the adjusting nut or bolt. Pry the pump away from the engine to get the proper tension. Tighten the pivot bolt to 28 ft. lbs. (39 Nm). Tighten the adjusting nut or bolt to 28 ft. lbs. (39 Nm) except 1988–89 Accord. Tighten the adjusting nut on Accord to 16 ft. lbs. (22 Nm).

SYSTEM BLEEDING

1. Make sure the reservoir is filled to the FULL mark; do not overfill.

2. Start the engine and allow it to idle.

3. Turn the steering wheel from side to side several times, lightly contacting the stops.

4. Turn the engine off.

5. Check the fluid level in the reservoir and add if necessary.

BRAKE SYSTEM

CAUTION: *Brake pads and shoes contain asbestos, which has been determined to be a cancer causing agent. Never clean the brake surfaces with compressed air. Avoid inhaling any dust from brake surfaces. When cleaning brakes, use commercially available brake cleaning fluids.*

Adjustments

BRAKE PEDAL HEIGHT

1. Loosen the brake light switch locknut. Back off the switch until it no longer touches the pedal shaft.

2. Loosen the locknut on the pedal pushrod (at the top of the pedal); turn the pushrod in or out until the correct pedal height is achieved. When measuring the pedal height, do so with the carpets and formats removed. Correct pedal height is:

- 1984–85 Accord: 7.36 in. (187mm)
- 1986–89 Accord: 8.07 in. (205mm)
- 1990–91 Accord, manual trans: 7.48 in. (190mm)
- 1990–91 Accord, auto. trans: 7.68 in. (195mm)
- 1984–87 Prelude: 7.00 in. (176mm)
- 1988–91 Prelude, manual trans: 7.00 in. (176mm)
- 1988–91 Prelude, auto. trans: 7.20 in. (183mm)

3. Firmly tighten the locknut on the pushrod.

4. Screw in the brake light switch until the plunger is fully depressed. (The threaded end should be touching the pad on the pedal arm.) Back the switch off ½ turn and tighten the locknut.

5. Inspect the brake light function; the lights

Measure the pedal height from the contact surface to the bare floor

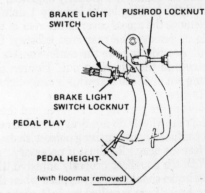

Loosen the locknut; move the shaft just enough to adjust the pedal

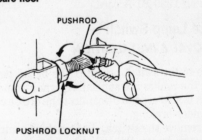

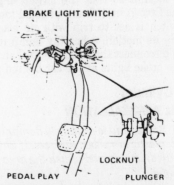

Make certain the switch is properly adjusted and the locknut retightened

should come on just after the pedal is pressed and go off when the pedal is released.

PARKING BRAKE

NOTE: *If the rear brakes have been serviced or replaced, start the engine and press the brake pedal several times to adjust the brakes before adjusting the parking brake cable. Incorrectly adjusted rear brakes (disc or drum) will affect the function of the parking brake mechanism.*

1. Raise and safely support the vehicle.

2. On rear disc brake equipped vehicles, make sure the lever of the rear brake caliper contacts the brake caliper pin.

3. On drum brake equipped vehicles, make sure the rear brakes are properly adjusted.

4. Pull the parking brake lever up 1 notch.

5. Remove the access cover at the rear of the console or remove the rear seat ashtray. On 1990–91 Accords, remove the center console to gain access to the adjusting nut. Tighten the adjusting nut until the rear wheels drag slightly when turned.

6. Release the parking brake lever and check that the rear wheels do not drag when turned. (Don't confuse a light brushing noise with drag; you'll feel the drag.) Readjust if necessary.

7. With the equalizer properly adjusted, the parking brake should be fully applied when the parking brake lever is pulled up 7–11 clicks on 1984–89 Accord and 1984–91 Prelude or 4–8 clicks on 1990–91 Accord.

Brake Lamp Switch
REMOVAL & INSTALLATION

The brake switch operates the brake lights when the brakes are applied. A signal from the switch is also used to disconnect the cruise control under braking.

To remove the switch, disconnect the wiring connector, loosen the locknut and remove the switch. When reinstalling, adjust the switch with the locknut so that the switch engages within the first ½ in. (13mm) of pedal motion. If the switch is set to trip with no slack or freeplay in its motion, a healthy bump in the road may disconnect the cruise control and&or flicker the brake lights at the car behind you.

Master Cylinder
REMOVAL & INSTALLATION

NOTE: *Brake fluid is extremely damaging to painted, plastic or rubber surfaces. If any fluid is spilled, immediately flush the area with clear water.*

Be prepared to plug brake lines and hoses during disassembly. Dirt and moisture

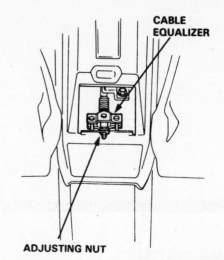

1987 Accord parking brake adjuster. Others similar

MUST be kept out of the system. Perform workbench operations in a clean, well-lit area.

1. Use a syringe or similar tool to remove as much fluid as possible from the fluid reservoir.

2. Label each brake line by its position on the master cylinder. Use flare-nut wrenches to loosen and disconnect the brake lines from the master cylinder. Contain spillage.

3. Remove the nuts holding the cylinder to the brake booster. Remove the master cylinder.
To install:

4. If the master cylinder has been disassembled or replaced, the pushrod clearance MUST be checked and adjusted before reinstallation. See separate procedure.

5. Install the master cylinder to the brake booster. Tighten the nuts to 15 Nm (11 ft. lbs)

6. Reconnect the brake lines. Hand thread the fittings to avoid stripping the threads; do not move or manipulate the lines to the point of bending or crimping them. Tighten the flare nuts to 15 Nm (11 ft. lbs).

7. Refill the reservoir with clean, fresh brake fluid. Do not reuse old fluid.

8. Bleed the brake system thoroughly.

PUSHROD CLEARANCE ADJUSTMENT

WARNING: *The use of the correct special tools or their equivalent is REQUIRED for this procedure. Rod bolt adjustment gauge, Honda tool 07975–SA50000 or –SE00100 must be used.*

1. Install the adjustment gauge tool on the end of the master cylinder. Adjust the bolt so the top of the gauge is flush with the end of the master cylinder piston.

2. Without disturbing the adjusting bolt's

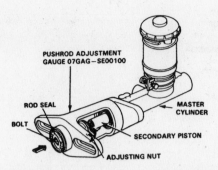

The special tool must be installed to measure pushrod clearance

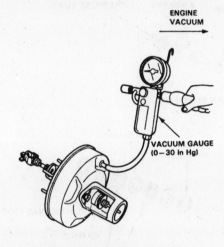

A vacuum gauge must be placed in the line

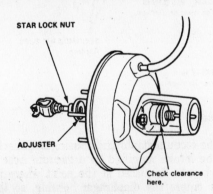

Measure clearance at the point shown; adjust the clearance at the rear of the booster

position, put the gauge upside down on the booster. Install the nuts and tighten them to 15 Nm (11 ft. lbs).

3. Install a vacuum gauge and T-fitting into the booster vacuum line. Start the engine; have an assistant maintain an engine speed yielding 500 mmHg (20 in. Hg) on the vacuum gauge.

4. Use a feeler gauge to measure the clearance between the gauge body and the adjusting nut. Correct clearance is 0–0.4mm or 0–0.016 in. If the clearance is incorrect, loosen the star locknut at the back of the booster; turn the adjuster to alter the position. Tighten the locknut securely.

5. Switch the ignition OFF.

6. Remove the vacuum gauge. Remove the adjusting gauge tool.

7. Install the master cylinder.

OVERHAUL

1984–89 Vehicles

1. With the master cylinder removed and the reservoir drained, remove the outer snapring.

2. remove the washer, secondary cup and secondary piston bushing from the shaft.

3. Remove the stop bolt. Push in on the secondary piston assembly (to take tension off the seal) and remove the snapring. Avoid scoring or damaging the inside wall.

4. Remove the secondary and primary piston assemblies.

5. Remove the screw from the secondary piston assembly; remove the spring.

6. Clean all parts thoroughly with clean brake fluid only. Any other cleaner will damage components.

To install:

7. Lubricate the new piston assemblies with clean, fresh brake fluid. Install them in the cylinder bore. Installation is easier if the pistons are rotated during insertion.

8. Stand the cylinder on the shaft and press downward on the cylinder; install the stop bolt with a new metal gasket.

9. Invert the cylinder so that the shaft is now up. Press down on the shaft and install the inner snapring.

10. Install the secondary cups, bushing and the outer snapring.

11. Install the seal on the master cylinder mounting flange.

1990–91 Accord and Prelude

Disassembly of the master cylinder is not recommended by the manufacturer. If an internal problem is suspected, the unit must be replaced.

Brake Booster

Virtually all cars today use a vacuum assisted power brake system to multiply the braking force and reduce pedal effort. Since vacuum is always available when the engine is operating, the system is simple and efficient. A vacuum diaphragm is located on the front of the master cylinder and assists the driver in applying the brakes, reducing both the effort and travel required to move the brake pedal.

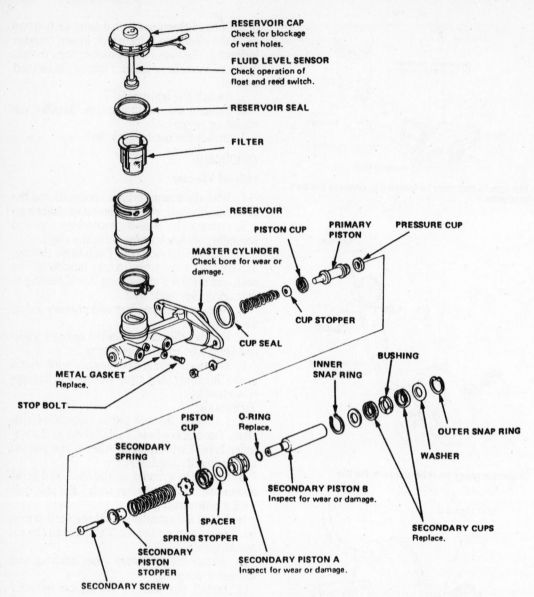

RESERVOIR CAP
Check for blockage
of vent holes.

FLUID LEVEL SENSOR
Check operation of
float and reed switch.

RESERVOIR SEAL

FILTER

RESERVOIR

PISTON CUP

PRIMARY PISTON

PRESSURE CUP

MASTER CYLINDER
Check bore for wear or
damage.

CUP STOPPER

CUP SEAL

METAL GASKET
Replace.

STOP BOLT

INNER SNAP RING

BUSHING

OUTER SNAP RING

WASHER

SECONDARY CUPS
Replace.

SECONDARY SPRING

PISTON CUP

O-RING
Replace.

SECONDARY PISTON B
Inspect for wear or damage.

SPACER

SPRING STOPPER

SECONDARY PISTON STOPPER

SECONDARY PISTON A
Inspect for wear or damage.

SECONDARY SCREW

Master cylinder components

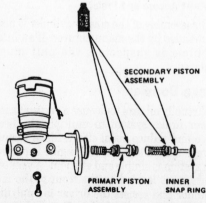

SECONDARY PISTON ASSEMBLY

PRIMARY PISTON ASSEMBLY

INNER SNAP RING

Piston assembly. Coat all components in clean brake fluid

The vacuum diaphragm housing is connected to the intake manifold by a vacuum hose. A check valve is placed at the point where the hose enters the diaphragm housing, so that during periods of low manifold vacuum brake assist will not be lost.

Depressing the brake pedal closes off the vacuum source and allows atmospheric pressure to enter on one side of the diaphragm. This causes the master cylinder pistons to move and apply the brakes. When the brake pedal is released, vacuum is applied to both sides of the diaphragm and springs return the diaphragm and master cylinder pistons to the released position.

If the vacuum supply fails, the brake pedal rod will contact the end of the master cylinder actuator rod and the operator can apply the brakes without any power assistance. The driver will notice that much higher pedal effort is needed to stop the car and that the pedal feels "harder" than usual.

REMOVAL & INSTALLATION

1. Disconnect the vacuum hose at the booster.

2. Remove the master cylinder. Plug the brake lines immediately. Place the master cyl-inder in a clean, protected location out of the work area.

3. Remove the brake pedal-to-booster link pin and the 4 nuts retaining the booster. The pushrod and nuts are located inside the vehicle under the instrument panel.

4. Remove the booster assembly from the vehicle.

5. To install, reverse the removal procedure. Tighten the 4 retaining bolts to 13 Nm (10 ft. lbs).

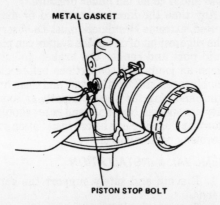

Install the stop bolt while the pistons are compressed

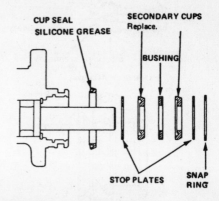

Install the cups and bushings correctly

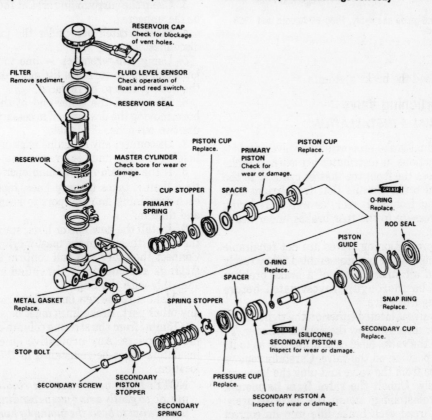

Master cylinder components, 1986–89 Accord and 1988–89 Prelude

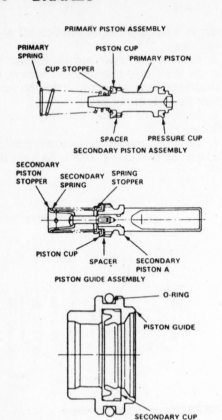

Piston and guide assembly, 1986–89 Accord and 1988–89 Prelude

6. Bleed the brake system.

Proportioning Valve

REMOVAL & INSTALLATION

The dual brake proportioning valve provides two functions. It distributes pressurized brake fluid from the from the master cylinder to the diagonal brake circuits (left front&right rear and right front&left rear) as well as reducing fluid pressure to the rear brakes under heavy braking.

The proportioning valves are not repairable and should never be disassembled. They rarely fail, and all other causes of a brake problem should be thoroughly investigated before changing this valve.

The valve is located either on the right fender apron or directly below the master cylinder. To remove the valve, label each brake line as to its correct position on the valve. Carefully remove the lines from the valve and plug the lines immediately. Unbolt the valve from its mount. When reinstalling, mount the valve securely. Hand thread each brake line into its correct port, then tighten the fittings to 15 Nm (10 ft. lbs) with a flare-nut wrench. Do not overtighten the line fittings.

Brake Lines and Hoses

Metal lines and rubber brake hoses should be checked frequently for leaks and external damage. Metal lines are particularly prone to crushing and kinking under the car. Any such deformation can restrict the proper flow of fluid and therefore impair braking at the wheels. Rubber hoses should be checked for cracking or scraping; such damage can create a weak spot in the hose and it could fail under pressure.

Any time the lines are removed or disconnected, extreme cleanliness must be observed. The slightest bit of dirt in the system can plug a fluid port and render the brakes defective. Clean all joints and connections before disassembly (use a stiff bristle brush and clean brake fluid) and plug the lines and ports as soon as they are opened. New lines and hoses should be blown or flushed clean before installation to remove any contamination.

REMOVAL & INSTALLATION

1. Elevate and safely support the car on stands.
2. Remove wheel(s) as necessary for access.
3. Clean the surrounding area at the joints to be disconnected.
4. Place a catch pan under the joint to be disconnected.
5. Using two wrenches – one to hold the joint and one to turn the fitting – disconnect the hose or line to be replaced.
6. Disconnect the other end of the line or hose, moving the drain pan if necessary. Always use two wrenches if possible.
7. Disconnect any retaining clips or brackets holding the line and remove the line.
8. If the system is to remain open for more time than it takes to swap lines, tape or plug each remaining line and port to keep dirt out and fluid in.
9. Install the new line or hose, starting with the end farthest from the master cylinder first. Connect the other end and confirm that both fittings are correctly threaded and turn smoothly with the fingers.

Make sure the new line will not rub against any other part. Brake lines must be at least ½ in. (13mm) from the steering column and other moving parts. Any protective shielding or insulators must be reinstalled in the original location.

NOTE: *If the new metal line requires bending, do so gently using a pipe bending tool. Do not attempt to bend the tubing by hand; it will kink the pipe and render it useless.*

FRONT   REAR

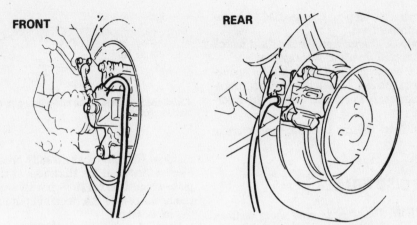

Examples of bleeding front and rear brakes. Prelude with rear disc brakes shown

10. Using two wrenches as before, tighten each fitting to 13–17 Nm or 9–12 ft. lbs. Brake hoses connecting to front or rear calipers should be tightened to 35 Nm (25 ft. lbs). Brake lines connecting to rear wheel cylinders (drum brakes) should be tightened to 19 Nm (14 ft. lbs).

11. Install any retaining clips or brackets on the lines.

12. Refill the brake reservoir with clean, fresh brake fluid.

13. Bleed the brake system.

14. Install the wheels and lower the car to the ground.

Bleeding

WARNING: *Cars equipped with Anti-lock Brake Systems (ABS) require separate bleeding procedures if any of the ABS components have been removed or the lines disconnected. Refer to the ABS part of this chapter. If non-ABS related repairs have been performed, such as replacing the master cylinder, brake linings or a brake hose at a wheel, the normal bleeding procedure may be used.*

It is necessary to bleed the hydraulic system any time system has been opened or has trapped air within the fluid lines. It may be necessary to bleed the system at all four brakes if air has been introduced through a low fluid level or by disconnecting brake pipes at the master cylinder.

If a line is disconnected at one wheel only, generally only that brake circuit needs bleeding although bleeding all four wheels is always recommended. If lines are disconnected at any fitting between the master cylinder and the brake, the system served by the disconnected pipe must be bled.

CHILTON TIP: *On cars with rear drum*

brakes, mis-adjusted brake shoes can cause a "long" pedal and reduced braking, giving the illusion of air in the lines. If you're trying to track down such a problem, adjust the rear brakes and test drive the car before bleeding the system.

1. Fill the master cylinder reservoir to the MAX or FULL line with brake fluid and keep it at least half full throughout the bleeding procedure.

2. It is strongly recommended that any time bleeding is to be performed all wheels be bled rather than just one or two. The correct order of bleeding is:

• Prelude: Left front, right rear, right front, left rear.

• 1984–89 Accord: Left front, right rear, right front, left rear.

• 1990–91 Accord: Right rear, left front, left rear, right front.

3. At the wheel to be bled, Place the correct size box-end or line wrench over the bleeder valve and attach a tight-fitting transparent hose over the bleeder. Allow the tube to hang submerged in a transparent container half full of clean brake fluid. The hose end must remain submerged in the fluid at all times.

4. Have an assistant pump the brake pedal several times slowly and hold it down.

5. Slowly unscrew the bleeder valve (¼–½ turn is usually enough). After the initial rush of air and fluid, tighten the bleeder and have the assistant slowly release the pedal.

6. Repeat Steps 4 and 5 until no air bubbles are seen in the hose or container. If air is constantly appearing after repeated bleedings, the system must be examined for the source of the leak or loose fitting. When finished with a wheel, the bleeder screw should be tightened to 7–9 Nm (5–7 ft. lbs).

7. Periodically check the reservoir on the

master cylinder, topping it as needed to maintain the proper level.

WARNING: *Do not reuse brake fluid which has been bled from the brake system.*

8. After bleeding, check the pedal for "sponginess" or vague feel. Repeat the bleeding procedure as necessary to correct. Top off the reservoir level.

9. Test drive the car to check proper brake function.

FRONT DISC BRAKES

CAUTION: *Brake pads and shoes contain asbestos, which has been determined to be a cancer causing agent. Never clean the brake surfaces with compressed air. Avoid inhaling any dust from brake surfaces. When cleaning brakes, use commercially available brake cleaning fluids.*

Disc Brake Pads

WEAR INDICATORS

The front disc brake pads are equipped with a metal tab which will come into contact with the disc after the friction surface material has worn near its usable minimum. The wear indicators make a constant, distinct metallic sound that should be easily heard. The sound has been described as similar to either fingernails on a blackboard or a field full of crickets. The key to recognizing that it is the wear indicators (not some other brake noise) is that the sound is heard when the vehicle is being driven WITHOUT the brakes applied. It may or may not be present under braking and is heard during normal driving.

It should also be noted that any disc brake system, by its design, cannot be made to work silently under all conditions. Each system includes various shims, plates, cushions and brackets to suppress brake noise, but no system can completely silence all noises. Some brake noise — either high or low frequency — can be controlled and perhaps lessened, but cannot be totally eliminated.

INSPECTION

The front brake pads may be inspected without removal. With the front end elevated and safely supported, remove the wheel(s). Unlock the steering column lock and turn the wheel so that the brake caliper is out from under the fender.

View the pads — inner and outer — through the cut-out in the center of the caliper. Remember to look at the thickness of the pad friction

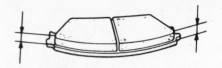

Check the thickness of the brake lining, not the backing plate

material (the part that actually presses on the disc) rather than the thickness of the backing plate which does not change with wear. Replace the brake pads if the remaining lining is below $3/32$ in. (2.4mm).

Remember that you are looking at the profile of the pad, not the whole thing. Brake pads can wear on a taper which may not be visible through the window. It is also not possible to check the contact surface for cracking or scoring from this position. This quick check can be helpful only as a reference; detailed inspection requires pad removal.

REMOVAL & INSTALLATION

NOTE: *If the car was recently driven, the brake components — particularly the rotor (disc) will be hot. Wear gloves.*

1. Raise and support the vehicle safely.

2. Remove the wheel.

3. As required, separate the brake hose clamp from the strut or knuckle by removing the retaining bolts.

4. Remove the lower caliper retaining bolt and pivot the caliper upward, off the pads.

5. Remove the pad shim and pad retainers. Remove the disc brake pads from the caliper.
To install:

6. Clean the caliper thoroughly; remove any rust from the lip of the disc or rotor. Check the brake rotor for grooves or cracks. If any heavy scoring is present, the rotor must be replaced.

7. Install the pad retainers. Apply a disc brake pad lubricant to both surfaces of the shims and the back of the disc brake pads. Do NOT get any lubricant on the braking surface of the pad.

8. Install the pads and shims. The pad with the wear indicator goes in the inboard position.

9. Push in the caliper piston so the caliper will fit over the pads. This is most easily accomplished with a large C-clamp. As the piston is forced back into the caliper, fluid will be forced back into the master cylinder reservoir. It may be necessary to siphon some fluid out to prevent overflowing.

10. Pivot the caliper down into position and tighten the mounting bolt to 45 Nm (33 ft. lbs).

11. Connect the brake hose to the strut or

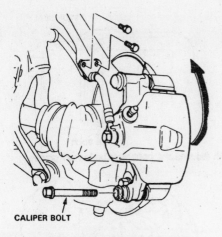

Remove the caliper bolts and the hose retaining bracket. Swing the caliper up and away from the pads.

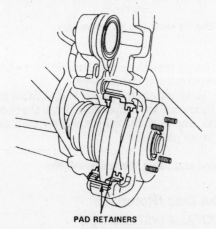

PAD RETAINERS

The pad retainers are important; don't forget them.

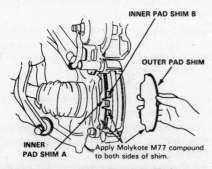

INNER PAD SHIM B

OUTER PAD SHIM

INNER PAD SHIM A   Apply Molykote M77 compound to both sides of shim.

Install the pads and shims. The pad with the wear indicator mounts in the inboard position

knuckle, if removed. Install the wheel and lower the vehicle to the ground.

12. Check the master cylinder and add fluid as required, then replace the master cylinder cover.

13. Depress the brake pedal several times and make sure that the movement feels normal.

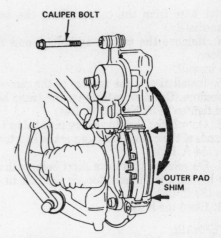

CALIPER BOLT

OUTER PAD SHIM

After compressing the piston, swing the caliper down and instal the bolt

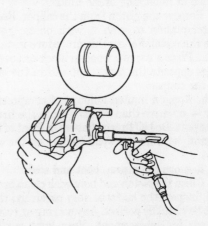

Keep your fingers clear of the emerging piston

The first brake pedal application may result in a very "long" pedal due to the pistons being retracted. Always make several brake applications before starting the vehicle. Bleeding is not usually necessary after pad replacement.

NOTE: *Braking should be moderate for the first 5 miles or so until the new pads seat correctly. The new pads will bed best if put through several moderate heating and cooling cycles. Avoid hard braking until the brakes have experienced several long, slow stops with time to cool in between. Taking the time to properly bed the brakes will yield quieter operation, more efficient stopping and contribute to extended brake life.*

Brake Caliper

REMOVAL & INSTALLATION

1. Raise and safely support the vehicle.
2. Remove the front wheel and tire assembly.
3. Remove the banjo bolt and disconnect the

brake hose from the caliper. Plug the hose immediately.

4. Remove the mounting bolt(s) and the caliper.

To install:

5. Installation is the reverse of the removal procedure. Use new gaskets on the banjo bolt and tighten to 35 Nm (25 ft. lbs).

6. On vehicles that have long pins below the threads of the caliper bolt, torque the bolt to 75 Nm (54 ft. lbs).

7. On vehicles that have short bolts with no pin beyond the threads, torque the bolt to 45 Nm (33 ft. lbs).

8. Bleed the brakes.

OVERHAUL

1. With the caliper removed from the car and drained of remaining brake fluid.

2. Remove the piston from the caliper. Resist the temptation to grab it with pliers; you'll score the metal. Follow this procedure instead:

   a. Place a narrow wooden block or several rags opposite the piston but within the jaws of the caliper.

   b. Apply a limited amount of compressed air – no more than 30 psi – into the brake line port. Do NOT place fingers in front of the piston; let it hit the wood stopper on the way out.

3. Remove the piston, boot and seal.

4. Clean the piston and bore with clean brake fluid. Inspect the surfaces very carefully; they must be virtually perfect. Any scoring or rust is grounds for replacement. Very light surface rust may be removed with fine crocus cloth wet with brake fluid, but any pitting requires replacement.

To install:

5. Apply brake cylinder grease to a new piston seal and install the seal into the groove of the cylinder.

6. Install the boot on the piston.

7. Lubricate the caliper bore and piston with clean brake fluid. Install the piston into the cylinder bore with the solid end in first. This installation can be maddening due to very close

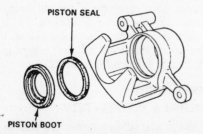

PISTON SEAL

PISTON BOOT

Piston seal and boot are included in the overhaul kit; pistons, if needed, may not be included

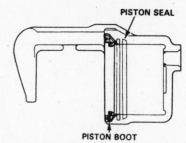

PISTON SEAL

PISTON BOOT

Both the seal and boot must be in their groove

PISTON

Installing the piston into the caliper bore

tolerances; keep the piston straight in the bore. Have patience; it can be done.

8. Make certain the piston boot is fitted into the lip around the caliper bore. Push the piston all the way in so the caliper will reinstall over the brake pads easily.

9. Reinstall the caliper. Fill the reservoir as needed and bleed the brake system.

Brake Disc (Rotor)

REMOVAL & INSTALLATION

Except 1990–91 Accord

1. Raise and safely support the vehicle.

2. Remove the wheel.

3. Disconnect the caliper from the caliper bracket. Support the caliper out of the way with a length of wire. Do not allow the caliper to hang from the brake hose.

4. Remove the caliper bracket.

5. Remove the two 6mm screws and the brake disc. If the brake disc is difficult to remove, install two 8mm bolts into the threaded holes and tighten them evenly and alternately to prevent cocking the rotor.

6. Installation is the reverse of the removal procedure.

1990–91 Accord

1. Pry the spindle nut stake away from the spindle nut, then loosen the nut.

2. Raise and safely support the vehicle.

3. Remove the wheel. Remove the spindle nut.

4. Remove the caliper and support it out of the way with a length of wire. Do not allow the

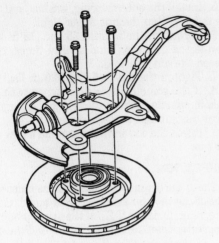

The hub and rotor unit is bolted to the knuckle

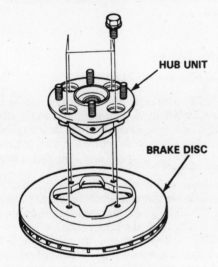

HUB UNIT

BRAKE DISC

Remove the brake disc from the hub unit

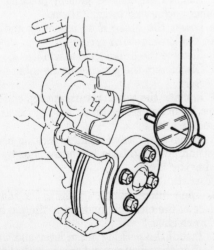

Measuring run-out. On the car, this measurement may only be taken on the outer face of the disc

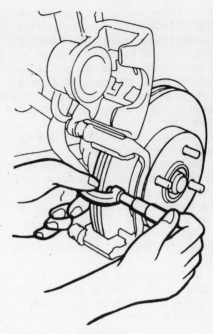

Thickness and parallelism check

caliper to hang from the brake hose. Remove the caliper bracket.

5. Remove the cotter pin and tie rod ball joint nut. Separate the tie rod from the steering knuckle using a ball joint separator tool.

6. Remove the cotter pin and loosen the lower arm ball joint nut half the length of the joint threads. Separate the ball joint and lower arm using the proper puller. Remove the lower ball joint nut.

7. Pull the steering knuckle outward and remove the halfshaft outboard CV-joint from the knuckle, using a plastic hammer.

8. Remove the 4 bolts retaining the hub unit to the steering knuckle and remove the hub unit.

9. Remove the 4 bolts, then separate the hub unit from the brake rotor.

To install:

10. Assemble the disc to the hub unit and tighten the bolts to 55 Nm (40 ft. lbs).

11. When installing the hub to the knuckle, use new self-locking bolts and tighten them to 45 Nm (33 ft. lbs).

12. When installing the steering knuckle, tighten the upper nut to 44 Nm (32 ft. lbs.) and the lower ball joint nut to 55 Nm (40 ft. lbs). Install a new cotter pin; if necessary, tighten the nut slightly to accommodate the pin.

INSPECTION

1. The brake disc develops circular scores during braking due to trapped dust and road

grit. Excessive scoring not only contributes to squealing brakes but also shortens the life of the brake pads. However, light scoring of the disc surface, not exceeding 0.38mm in depth, will result from normal use and is not detrimental to brake operation. In general, if the scoring is deep enough to catch a fingernail passing over it, it's too deep and requires corrective action.

NOTE: *Differences in the left and right disc surfaces can result in uneven braking.*

2. Disc runout is the movement of the disc from side-to-side; warpage or distortion. Excess run out causes wobble or pounding in the brake pedal. Position a dial indicator in the middle of the pad wear area and turn the disc, while checking the indicator. If disc runout exceeds 0.10mm or 0.004 in., replace or refinish the disc.

3. Disc parallelism is the measurement of variations in disc thickness at several locations on the disc circumference. It indicates whether or not the two faces of the disc are true and parallel. To measure parallelism, place a mark on the disc and measure the disc thickness with a micrometer. Repeat this measurement at eight (8) equal increments (about 45 degrees) on the circumference of the disc. If the measurements vary more than 0.015mm (0.0006), replace the disc.

REAR DRUM BRAKES

CAUTION: *Brake pads and shoes contain asbestos, which has been determined to be a cancer causing agent. Never clean the brake surfaces with compressed air. Avoid inhaling any dust from brake surfaces. When cleaning brakes, use commercially available brake cleaning fluids.*

Brake Drums
REMOVAL & INSTALLATION

1. Block the front wheels securely. Raise and support the rear of the vehicle on jackstands. Remove the rear wheels. Make sure that the parking brake is OFF.

2. Remove the bearing cap, cotter pin and the castle nut.

3. Pull off the rear brake drum. If the drum is difficult to remove, use a brake drum puller or tap it a few times with a rubber mallet. Make certain to remove it squarely; if cocked to one side, it will jam.

To install:

4. Make certain the brake shoes are adjusted to allow the drum clearance during installation. Fit the drum into position.

5. Install the outer bearing, washer, and castle nut. Tighten the nut finger tight.

6. Torque the hub nut to 25 Nm (18 ft. lbs). Rotate the drum by hand several times, then loosen the nut just to 0.

7. Tighten the nut to 5 Nm (3.6 ft. lbs.)

8. If the spindle nut is not aligned with the hole in spindle, tighten the nut just enough to align the nut and the hole.

9. Insert the cotter pin holder and a new cotter pin.

INSPECTION

Check the drum for cracks and the inner surface of the shoe for excessive wear and damage. The inner diameter (I.D.) of the drum should be no greater than 1mm (0.04 in) beyond the new or standard specification. Additionally, the drum should be no more than 0.10mm out-of-round.

Brake Shoes
REMOVAL & INSTALLATION

NOTE: *Although this procedure can be accomplished with common hand tools, there are a variety of specialty brake tools available in retail stores which make the job much easier. If you can only get one item, buy a brake spring tool.*

1. Raise and safely support the vehicle.

2. Remove the rear wheel and brake drum.

3. On 1990–91 Accord, remove the upper return spring from the brake shoe.

NOTE: *All springs and fittings should be labeled or diagrammed at the time of removal. The amount of time saved during reassembly makes the extra effort well worthwhile.*

4. Remove the tension pins by pushing the retainer spring and turning them.

5. Lower the brake shoe assembly and remove the lower return spring.

6. Remove the brake shoe assembly.

7. Disconnect the parking brake cable from the lever.

8. Remove the upper return spring, self-adjuster lever and self-adjuster spring. Separate the brake shoes.

9. Remove the wave washer, parking brake lever and pivot pin from the brake shoe by removing the U-clip.

To install:

10. Apply brake cylinder grease to the sliding surface of the pivot pin and insert the pin into the brake shoe.

11. Install the parking brake lever and wave washer on the pivot pin and secure with the U-clip.

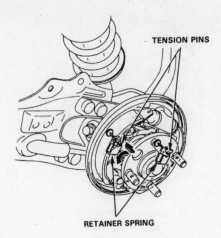

The tension pins must be pushed and turned to remove them

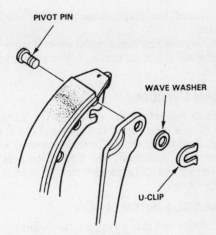

The U-clip must be spread before removal. Always replace it with a new one at reassembly

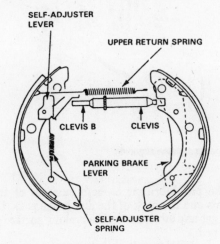

Drum brake components. Accord left side shown

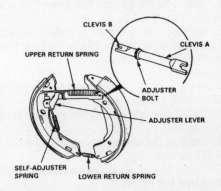

Make certain the adjusting lever is properly seated

NOTE: *Pinch the U-clip securely to prevent the pivot pin from coming out of the brake shoe.*

12. Connect the parking brake cable to the parking brake lever.

13. Apply grease on each sliding surface of the brake backing plate.

NOTE: *Do not allow grease to come in contact with the brake linings. Grease will contaminate the linings and reduce stopping power.*

14. Clean the threaded portions of the clevises of the adjuster bolt. Coat the threads with grease. Turn the adjuster bolt to shorten the clevises.

15. Hook the adjuster spring to the adjuster lever first, then to the brake shoe.

16. Install the adjuster bolt&clevis assembly and the upper return spring.

17. Install the brake shoes to the backing plate.

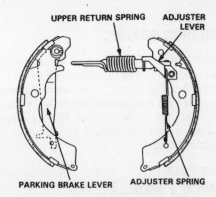

The 1990–91 Accord upper return spring installs around the adjuster

18. Install the lower return spring, the tension pins and retaining springs.

19. On 1990–91 Accord, connect the upper return spring.

20. Turn the adjuster bolt to force the brake shoes out until the brake drum will not easily go on. Back off the adjuster bolt just enough that the brake drum will go on and turn easily.

21. Install the wheel; lower the vehicle to the ground.

22. Depress the brake pedal several times to set the self adjusting brake. Adjust the parking brake.

Wheel Cylinder

When inspecting the cylinders for leakage, just lift the outer lip of the boot and check for fluid. A slight moistness, usually covered with brake dust, is normal. Any sign of wetness or running fluid is cause for immediate replacement.

REMOVAL & INSTALLATION

1. Raise and safely support the vehicle.
2. Remove the wheel.
3. Remove the brake drum and shoes.
4. Disconnect the brake line from the wheel cylinder. Plug the line.
5. Remove the 2 wheel cylinder retaining nuts on the inboard side of the backing plate; remove the wheel cylinder.

To install:

6. Apply a thin coat of grease to the grooves of the wheel cylinder piston.
7. Install the cylinder; tighten the nuts to 8 Nm (6 ft. lbs).
8. Connect the brake line and tighten the 15 Nm (11 ft. lbs).
9. Install the brake shoes and drum.
10. Bleed the brakes.
11. Install the wheel; lower the car to the ground.

REAR DISC BRAKES

CAUTION: *Brake pads and shoes contain asbestos, which has been determined to be a cancer causing agent. Never clean the brake surfaces with compressed air. Avoid inhaling any dust from brake surfaces. When cleaning brakes, use commercially available brake cleaning fluids.*

Brake Pads

REMOVAL & INSTALLATION

1. Raise and safely support the vehicle.
2. Remove the rear wheel.
3. Remove the 2 caliper mounting bolts and remove the caliper from the bracket.
4. Remove the pads, shims and pad retainers.

To install:

5. Clean the caliper thoroughly; remove any dirt or dust. Check the brake rotor for grooves or cracks and machine or replace, as necessary.
6. Install the pad retainers. Apply a disc

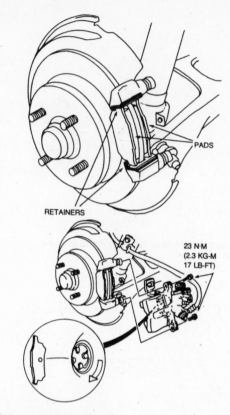

Caliper and piston alignment

brake pad lubricant to both surfaces of the shims and the back of the disc brake pads. Do not get any lubricant on the braking surface of the pad.

7. Install the pads and shims.
8. Use a suitable tool to rotate the caliper piston clockwise into the caliper bore, enough to fit over the brake pads. Lubricate the piston boot with silicone grease to avoid twisting the piston boot.
9. Install the brake caliper, aligning the cutout in the piston with the tab on the inner pad. Tighten the mounting bolts.
10. Install the wheel. Lower the vehicle.
11. Check the fluid in the master cylinder and add as required. Depress the brake pedal several times to seat the pads.

Brake Caliper

REMOVAL & INSTALLATION

1. Raise and safely support the vehicle.
2. Remove the rear wheel and tire assembly.
3. Remove the caliper shield.
4. Disconnect the parking brake cable from the lever on the caliper by removing the lock pin.
5. Remove the banjo bolt and disconnect the

brake hose from the caliper. Plug the hose immediately.

6. Remove the 2 caliper mounting bolts and the caliper from the bracket.

7. Installation is the reverse of the removal procedure. Use new gaskets on the banjo bolt and tighten it to 35 Nm (25 ft. lbs.).

8. Tighten the caliper bracket bolts to 39 Nm (28 ft. lbs.).

9. Bleed the brake system. Adjust the parking brake if necessary.

OVERHAUL

WARNING: *The use of the correct special tools or their equivalent is REQUIRED for this procedure.*

1. With the caliper removed from the car, remove the pad spring from the inside of the caliper housing.

2. Rotate the piston and remove the piston and boot. Take great care not to damage the components.

3. After removing the circlip, remove the washer, adjusting spring and the nut from the piston.

4. Carefully remove the piston seal.

5. Install Honda tool 07960–SA50002 or its equivalent between the caliper body and the spring guide.

6. Turn the shaft of the special tool to compress the adjusting spring; remove the circlip with snapring pliers.

7. Once released, remove the spring cover, adjusting spring spacer, bearing and adjusting bolt.

8. Remove the sleeve piston; remove the pin from the cam.

9. Disassemble the return spring, parking nut, spring washer, lever, cam and cam boot.

To install:

10. After cleaning and inspecting all parts for wear or deterioration, pack the needle bearing with rubber grease. Coat a new cam boot with the same grease and install it into the caliper.

11. Install the cam with the threaded end up.

12. Install the lever, spring washer and parking nut. Tighten the nut to 28 Nm (20 ft. lbs.).

13. Install the return spring.

14. Install the pin into the cam. Install a new O-ring onto the sleeve piston.

15. Install the sleeve piston. The hole in the bottom of the piston must align with the pin in the cam; the two pins on the piston must align with the holes in the caliper.

16. Install a new cup with its groove facing the bearing side of the adjusting bolt.

17. Install the bearing, spacer adjusting spring and spring cover onto the adjusting bolt. Install the bolt into the cylinder bore.

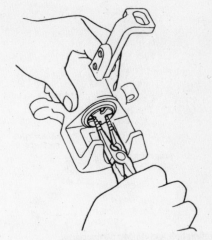

Rotate the piston during removal. Note the use of tape on the pliers to protect the piston

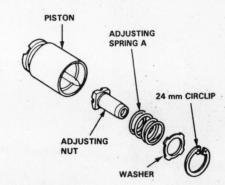

Piston components

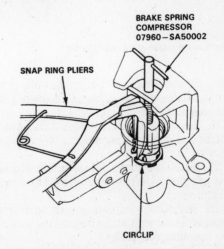

A special tool is required to compress the spring

18. Install rear caliper guide tool 07973–SA50000 or its equivalent into the cylinder. The cutout on the tool must align with the tab on the spring cover.

19. Install the spring compressor (used in

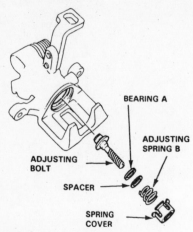

Adjusting bolt and related components

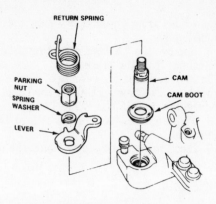

Parking brake actuating lever and related components

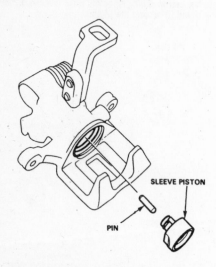

Remove the sleeve piston and the pin

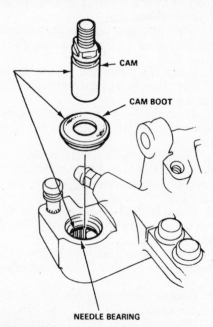

Apply rubber grease to the areas shown before reassembly

Step 5) and compress the spring until it bottoms. Make sure the caliper guide doesn't bind or hang-up while the spring is being

20. Remove the caliper guide. Make sure the flared end of the spring cover is below the clip groove.

21. Install the circlip. Make certain it is seated properly before removing the spring compressor.

22. Install the adjusting nut, spring and washer into the piston and secure the assembly by installing the circlip.

23. Coat a new piston seal and boot with silicone grease; install them into the caliper.

24. After coating the outside of the piston with silicone grease, install the piston on the adjusting bolt. Rotate the piston clockwise during installation. Take great care not to damage the piston boot.

25. Install the pad retainer.

Brake Disc (Rotor)
REMOVAL & INSTALLATION

1. Elevate and safely support the vehicle.
2. Remove the rear wheel.
3. Remove the rear brake caliper.
4. Remove the hub center cap.
5. Remove the cotter pin, holder and spindle nut.
6. Remove the brake disc. Remove the outer bearing and protect it from dirt, solvent, etc.
To install:
7. Install the disc to the spindle. Install the outer bearing.
8. Apply a light coat of grease or oil to the spindle nut and the spindle threads. Install the washer and spindle nut.

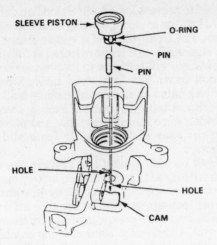

The sleeve piston and pin must be properly aligned at installation.

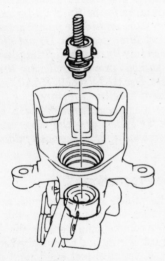

Installing the adjusting bolt

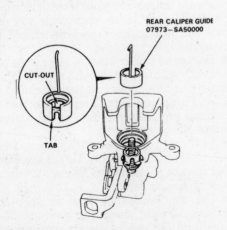

Installation of the rear caliper guide

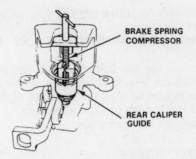

Keep the tools aligned during use.

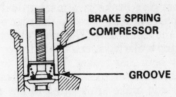

Profile view during spring compression; the spring cover must be below the circlip groove

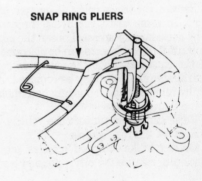

Installing the snapring or circlip

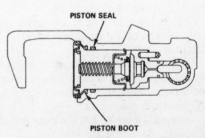

Cross section of piston seal and boot installation. Coat both with silicone grease before installation

9. Tighten the nut to 25 Nm (18 ft. lbs) and rotate the brake disc 2–3 turns. Retighten the nut to specification.

10. Repeat Step 9 until the nut holds its setting after the disc is turned through several rotations.

11. Loosen the nut until the nut just breaks

loose but does not turn freely and does not back off from the washer.

12. Retighten the spindle nut to 5.5 Nm (4 ft. lbs.)

13. Install the pin holder so that the slots align with the hole in the spindle. If the nut must be rotated to align the pin holes, tighten the nut just enough to allow alignment.

14. Install a new cotter pin.

PARKING BRAKE

Cables

The parking brake is a mechanical type which applies braking force to the rear wheels through the rear brakes. The cable, attached to the parking brake lever, extends to the equalizer and to both rear brakes. When the lever is pulled, the cable becomes taut, pulling both the both parking brake arms fitted to the brake shoes or rear calipers

REMOVAL & INSTALLATION

1. Remove the access cover at the rear of the console. In some cases, removing the console may be necessary for access. Loosen the adjusting nut until the cable ends can be disconnected from the equalizer. With the cables detached, the parking brake lever may be removed, if desired, by removing the mounting bolts holding it to the floor.

2. Raise and safely support the vehicle.

3. Remove the rear wheels.

4. On disc brake equipped vehicles, pull out the lock pin, remove the clevis pin and remove the clip.

5. On drum brake equipped vehicles, remove the brake drum and brake shoes. Disconnect the cable from the backing plate.

6. Detach the cables from the cable guides and remove the cables from the vehicle.

To install:

7. Fit the cable loosely into place. Begin reattachment at the rear brake shoes or calipers. Make certain the cable is routed correctly and firmly seated in it mounts.

8. Connect the cable(s) at the lever inside the car.

9. Install the cable bracket retaining bolts. Do not allow the cable to become kinked or bent. Make certain the rubber boots are in place where the cables pass into the cabin.

ANTI-LOCK BRAKE SYSTEM (ABS or ALB)

System Description

Anti-lock braking (ALB) systems are de-signed to prevent locked-wheel skidding during hard braking or during braking on slippery surfaces. The front wheels of a vehicle cannot apply steering force if they are locked and sliding; the vehicle will continue in its previous direction of travel. The four wheel anti-lock brake systems found on Honda automobiles hold the wheels just below the point of locking, thereby allowing some steering response and preventing the rear of the vehicle from sliding sideways.

Used on 1991 Accord and Prelude, the system is designed to prevent wheel lock-up during hard or emergency braking. By preventing wheel lock-up, maximum braking effort is maintained while preventing loss of directional control. Additionally, some steering capability is maintained during the stop. The ALB system will operate regardless of road surface conditions.

CAUTION: *The Honda anti-lock brake system contains brake fluid under extremely high pressure within the pump, accumulator and modulator assembly. Do not disconnect or loosen any lines, hoses, fittings or components without properly relieving the system pressure. Use ONLY tool 07HAA-SG00101 or equivalent to relieve pressure.*

Improper procedures or failure to discharge the system pressure may result in severe personal injury or property damage.

Service Precautions

● If the vehicle is equipped with an air bag (SRS) system, always properly disable the system before commencing work on the ALB system. Air bag wiring and connectors are yellow; do not use electrical test equipment on these circuits.

● Certain components within the ALB system are not intended to be serviced or repaired individually. Only those components with removal and installation procedures should be serviced.

● Do not use rubber hoses or other parts not specifically specified for the ALB system. When using repair kits, replace all parts included in the kit. Partial or incorrect repair may lead to functional problems and require the replacement of other components.

● Lubricate rubber parts with clean, fresh brake fluid to ease assembly. Do not use lubricated shop air to clean parts; damage to rubber components may result.

● Use only brake fluid from an unopened container. Use of suspect or contaminated brake fluid can reduce system performance and&or durability. Never reuse brake fluid recovered during bleeding or pressure release procedures.

• A clean repair area is essential. Perform repairs after components have been thoroughly cleaned; use only denatured alcohol to clean components. Do not allow ALB components to come into contact with any substance containing mineral oil or petroleum based products; this includes used shop rags.

• The control unit is a microprocessor similar to other computer units in the vehicle. Insure that the ignition switch is OFF before removing or installing controller harnesses. Avoid static electricity discharge at or near the controller.

• Never disconnect any electrical connection with the ignition switch ON unless instructed to do so in a test.

• Avoid touching connector pins with fingers.

• Leave new components and modules in the shipping package until ready to install them.

• To avoid static discharge, always touch a vehicle ground after sliding across a vehicle seat or walking across carpeted or vinyl floors.

• If any arc welding is to be done on the vehicle, the ALB control unit should be disconnected before welding operations begin.

• Never allow welding cables to lie on, near or across any vehicle electrical wiring.

• If the vehicle is to be baked after paint repairs, disconnect and remove the control unit from the vehicle.

Pressure Relief

CAUTION: *The Honda anti-lock brake system contains brake fluid under extremely high pressure within the pump, accumulator and modulator assembly. Do not disconnect or loosen any lines, hoses, fittings or components without properly relieving the system pressure. Use ONLY tool 07HAA–SG00101 or equivalent to relieve pressure.*

Improper procedures or failure to dis-

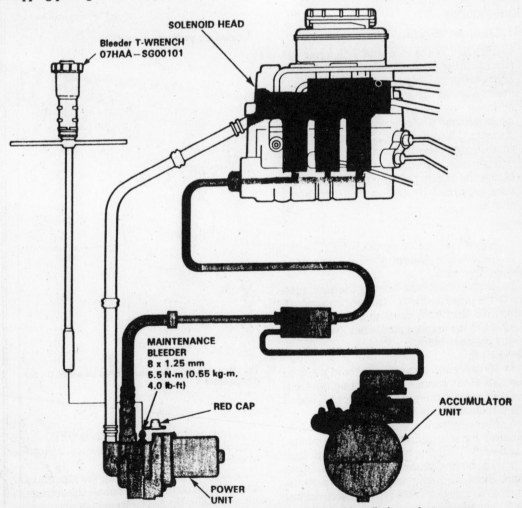

SOLENOID HEAD

Bleeder T-WRENCH
07HAA–SG00101

MAINTENANCE
BLEEDER
8 x 1.25 mm
5.5 N·m (0.55 kg-m,
4.0 lb-ft)

RED CAP

ACCUMULATOR
UNIT

POWER
UNIT

Shaded areas are under high pressure. Use only the correct tool for relieving system pressure

charge the system pressure may result in severe personal injury and&or property damage.

1. Insure the ignition switch is OFF.
2. Using a syringe or similar device, remove all the fluid from the master cylinder reservoir and the modulator reservoir.
3. Remove the red cover from the bleeder port on top of the pump assembly.
4. Install the bleeding tool onto the bleeder. Make certain the reservoir cap on the tool is secured.
5. Using the tool, turn the bleeder about 90 degrees to admit high pressure fluid into the reservoir. As the pressure drops, turn the bleeder open about 1 full turn to completely relieve the system.
6. Retighten the bleeder to 5.5 Nm (4 ft. lbs.) and remove the tool. Discard the captured brake fluid; do not reuse it. Install the red cap on the bleeder port.

Accumulator

REMOVAL & INSTALLATION

CAUTION: *The Honda anti-lock brake system contains brake fluid under extremely high pressure within the pump, accumulator and modulator assembly. Do not disconnect or loosen any lines, hoses, fittings or components without properly relieving the system pressure. Use only tool 07HAA–SG00101 or equivalent to relieve pressure.*

Improper procedures or failure to discharge the system pressure may result in severe personal injury and&or property damage.

ACCORD

1. Insure the ignition switch is OFF.
2. Relieve the system pressure using the bleeder T-wrench.
3. Remove the 3 bolts holding the accumulator to the pressure block. Remove the accumulator from the block; check that the O-ring on the neck of the accumulator is not lodged within the pressure block.

To install:
4. Make certain a new O-ring is in place on the neck of the accumulator. Position the accumulator against the pressure block and install the 3 retaining bolts finger tight.
5. Make certain the accumulator ball is squarely and securely placed against its mount. Tighten the retaining bolts to 9 Nm (7 ft. lbs).
6. Fill the modulator reservoir to the upper limit. Bleed the high pressure components using the ALB checker. Bleed the wheel circuits at each caliper.

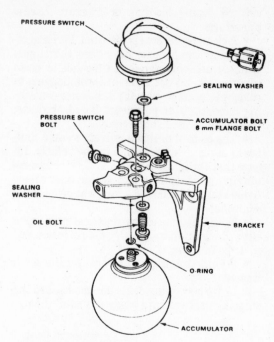

Accumulator assembly, Accord

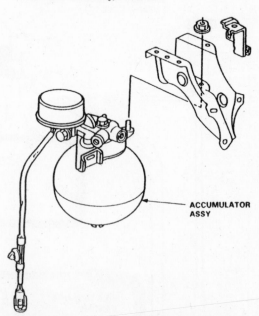

The Prelude accumulator is removed as a unit. Do not disassemble it

PRELUDE

1. Insure the ignition switch is OFF.
2. Relieve the system pressure using the bleeder T-wrench.
3. Remove the bolt holding the accumulator assembly to the bracket. Remove the accumulator assembly. Do NOT attempt to disassemble the unit.

Disposal

CAUTION: *The accumulator contains high-pressure nitrogen gas, even after fluid pressure is relieved. Do not puncture or expose to heat or flame. Do not attempt to disassemble the accumulator. Failure to follow correct safety precautions may cause the accumulator to explode, resulting in severe injury and&or property damage. The accumulator must be correctly relieved of internal pressure before disposal.*

1. After removal, secure the neck of the accumulator in a vise; the relief plug should point straight up.

2. Wear goggles or other face and eye protection. The escaping gas, although non-toxic, can carry dust and debris with it.

3. Slowly turn the relief plug 3½ turns; wait 3 minutes for all pressurized gas to escape.

NOTE: *Nitrogen is an inert, non-flammable, non-toxic gas. It is safe for release into the atmosphere.*

4. Slowly remove the relief plug completely. Dispose of the accumulator unit.

Electronic Control Unit
REMOVAL & INSTALLATION
PRELUDE

1. Make certain the ignition switch is OFF.
2. Remove the cover at the front of the console. The console need not be removed.
3. Remove the 4 mounting bolts holding the control unit.

NOTE: *When the mounting bolts are removed, any fault codes stored in the memory will be lost.*

4. Carefully disconnect the wiring harnesses.

To install:

5. Connect the wiring harnesses; fit the control unit into place.
6. Install the 4 retaining bolts; tighten them to 10 Nm (7 ft. lbs.)
7. Install the front cover on the console.
8. Turn the ignition switch ON and check for correct ALB system function.

ACCORD

1. Make certain the ignition switch is OFF. Remove the control unit attaching bolts. Don't lose the nuts behind the stay. Disconnect the bolt holding the ground lug.

NOTE: *Once the bolts are removed, any stored codes are lost.*

2. Remove the control unit and cover. Remove the cover.
3. Carefully disconnect the connectors from the control unit.

To install:

4. Install the connectors to the unit.

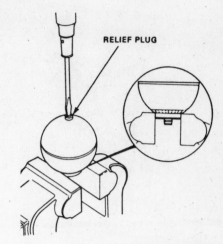

Relieve the accumulator pressure before disposal

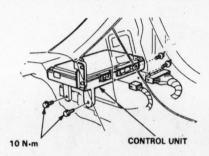

10 N·m   CONTROL UNIT

Prelude anti-lock control unit

5. Fit the cover into position; install the assembly and tighten the bolts snugly. Install the bolt holding the ground lug.
6. Turn the ignition switch ON and check for correct ALB system function.

Wheel Speed Sensor
REMOVAL & INSTALLATION

CAUTION: *Vehicles equipped with air bag systems (SRS) may have components and wiring in the same area as the front speed sensor wiring harnesses. The air bag system connectors are yellow. Do not use electrical test equipment on these circuits. Do not damage the SRS wiring while working on other wiring or components. Failure to observe correct procedures may cause the air bag system to inflate unexpectedly or render the system totally inoperative.*

1. Raise and safely support the vehicle as necessary for access.
2. Make certain the ignition switch is OFF.
3. Disconnect the sensor harness connector.
4. Beginning at the connector end, remove grommets, clips or retainers as necessary to free the harness. Take careful note of the placement and routing of the

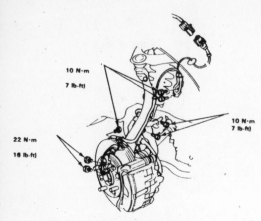

Accord front wheel speed sensor installation

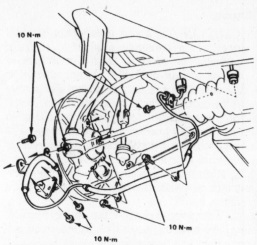

Rear wheel speed sensors, Prelude

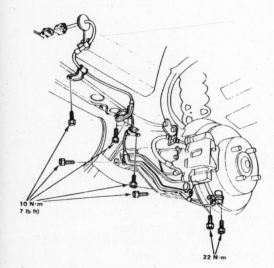

Rear wheel speed sensor installation – Accord

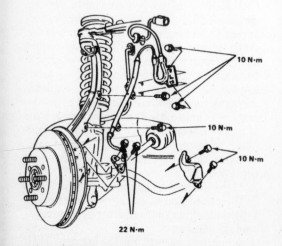

Prelude front wheel speed sensors

harness; it must be reinstalled in the exact original position.

5. Remove the bolts holding the speed sensor to its mounting; remove the sensor. If it is stuck in place, gently tap on the side of the mounting flange with a hammer and small punch; do not tap on the sensor.

To install:

6. Place the sensor in position; install the retaining bolts loosely. Route the harness correctly. Avoid twisting or crimping the harness; use the white line on the wires as a guide.

7. Once the harness and sensor are correctly but loosely placed, tighten the sensor mounting bolts. Accord front and rear sensor bolts should be tightened to 22 Nm (16 ft. lbs). Prelude front sensor retaining bolts should be tightened to 22 Nm (16 ft. lbs.); Prelude rear sensor bolts are tightened only to 10 Nm (7 ft. lbs).

8. Working from the sensor end to the connector, install each clip, retainer, bracket or grommet holding the sensor harness. The harness must not be twisted. Tighten any bolt holding brackets to 10 Nm (7 ft. lbs.). If the harness must pass through a body panel, make certain the rubber grommet is correctly and firmly seated.

9. Connect the wiring connector.

Pulsers (Toothed Wheels)

REMOVAL & INSTALLATION

The pulser wheels are integral with either the front constant velocity joints or the rear hub assembly. If a pulser is damaged or requires replacement, a new joint or hub must be installed. The toothed wheels may be visually inspected for chipped or damaged teeth without removal.

AIR GAP INSPECTION

The air gap between the tip of the sensor and the pulser is critical to the proper operation of the system. The gap is established by the correct installation of the wheel speed sensor; the gap may be measured for reference but is not adjustable.

Use a non-metallic feeler gauge to measure the gap. Rotate the hub or axle slowly by hand, taking measurements at several locations. The front or rear air gap must be 0.016–0.039 in. (0.4–1.0 mm) at every location. If the gap exceeds 0.039 in. (1.0mm) at any location, there is a high probability of a damaged or distorted suspension knuckle.

NOTE: *Access to the Prelude rear sensor and pulser requires removal of the wheel, caliper and brake disc.*

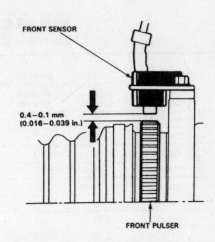

Example of measuring air gap at the wheel speed sensor; Prelude front sensor shown. All sensors are measured in similar fashion

Fluid and Bleeding

FILLING THE SYSTEM

The ALB brake system uses 2 brake fluid reservoirs, one on the master cylinder and one on the modulator. Each must be maintained at minimum fluid levels for the system to operate properly.

While relieving the system pressure is not required when adding fluid, the caps of the reservoirs and the surrounding area must be wiped clean of dirt before the cap is removed. The slightest amount of dirt or foreign matter in the fluid may impair the ALB function.

Use only DOT 3 or DOT 4 brake fluid from an unopened can. Do not use other grades or types of brake fluid; never reuse aerated brake fluid which has been bled or removed from the system. Bring the fluid level only to the word MAX or UPPER level on the reservoir. Overfilling the reservoir may cause overflowing during testing or system operation. After filling, install the reservoir cap tightly.

BLEEDING THE SYSTEM

Brake Lines and Calipers

The brake lines and calipers are bled in the usual fashion with no special procedures required. Make certain the master cylinder reservoir is filled before the bleeding is begun and check the level frequently. The system should be bled in the correct sequence; always bleed all 4 calipers. Each bleeder should be tightened to 9 Nm (7 ft. lbs.).

Bleeding sequence:
- Accord — Left rear, right front, right rear and left front
- Prelude — Right rear, left front, left rear and right front.

Bleeding High-Pressure Components

The modulator, accumulator and power unit must be bled if any of their lines are removed or loosened during repairs or if any component is replaced. Bleeding can ONLY be accomplished with Honda's ALB checker and the special bleeder T-wrench or their equivalents. Do NOT attempt to use any other procedures or tools to bleed the high pressure components.

BRAKE SPECIFICATIONS

All measurements in inches unless noted.

| Year | Model | Brake Disc | | | Brake Drum Diameter | | Minimum Lining Thickness | |
		Original Thickness	Minimum Thickness	Maximum Runout	Original Inside Diameter	Max. Wear Limit	Front	Rear
1984	Accord	0.75	0.67	0.006	7.87	7.91	0.059	0.080
	Prelude	0.75④	0.67①	0.004	—	—	0.120	0.060
1985	Accord	0.75	0.67	0.004	7.87	7.91	0.059	0.080
	Prelude	0.75④	0.67①	0.004	—	—	0.120	0.060

BRAKE SPECIFICATIONS

All measurements in inches unless noted.

Year	Model	Brake Disc			Brake Drum Diameter		Minimum Lining Thickness	
		Original Thickness	Minimum Thickness	Maximum Runout	Original Inside Diameter	Max. Wear Limit	Front	Rear
1986	Accord	0.75	0.67	0.004	7.87	7.91	0.120	0.080
	Prelude	0.75④	0.67①	0.004	—	—	0.120	0.060
1987	Accord	0.75	0.67	0.004	7.87	7.91	0.120	0.080
	Prelude	0.75④	0.67	0.004	—	—	0.120	0.060
1988	Accord	0.75⑥	0.67	0.006	7.87	7.91	③	0.080
	Prelude	0.83⑤	0.75①②	0.004	—	—	0.120	0.080
1989	Accord	0.75⑥	0.67	0.006	7.87	7.91	③	0.080
	Prelude	0.83⑤	0.75①②	0.004	—	—	0.120	0.080
1990	Accord	0.91	0.83	0.004	8.66	8.70	0.063	0.079
	Prelude	0.83⑤	0.75①②	0.004	—	—	0.060	0.060
1991	Accord	0.91④	0.83①	0.004	8.66	8.70	0.063	0.079
	Prelude	0.83④	0.75①	0.004	—	—	0.060	0.060

① Rear Disc: 0.31
② DX, LX and S: 0.67
   LX-i and Si: 0.75
③ DX and LX:0.120
   SEi and LX-i: 0.060
④ Rear Disc: 0.39
⑤ S: 0.75
⑥ SE-i: New 0.83; Limit 0.75

EXTERIOR

Doors

REMOVAL AND INSTALLATION

Front and Rear

1. Matchmark the hinge-to-body and hinge-to-door locations. Support the door either on a padded jack or have somebody hold it for you.

2. On models with a center door check bar, push in on the claw and pull out the stopper pin. Alternatively, unbolt the door check from the door.

NOTE: *Depending on equipment, it may be necessary to disconnect various wires running into the door. This will require removal of the door pad.*

3. Remove the lower hinge-to-door bolts.

4. Remove the upper hinge-to-door bolts and lift the door off the hinges.

NOTE: *The door will be heavier than it looks; be prepared*

5. If the hinges are being replaced, remove them from the door pillar.

6. Install the door and hinges with the bolts finger tight.

7. Adjust the door and tighten the hinge bolts.

ADJUSTMENT/ALIGNMENT

When checking door alignment, look carefully at each seam between the door and body. The gap should be constant and even all the way around the door. Pay particular attention to the door seams at the corners farthest from the hinges; this is the area where errors will be most evident. Additionally, the door should pull in against the weatherstrip when latched to seal out wind and water. The contact should be even all the way around and the stripping should be about half compressed.

The position of the door can be adjusted in

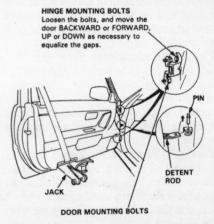

HINGE MOUNTING BOLTS
Loosen the bolts, and move the door BACKWARD or FORWARD, UP or DOWN as necessary to equalize the gaps.

PIN

DETENT ROD

JACK

DOOR MOUNTING BOLTS

The door-to-hinge bolts may be loosened to adjust the door. The detent or retainer should be disconnected during adjustment

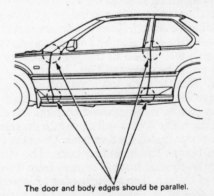

The door and body edges should be parallel.

Check the indicated areas for parallel edges with no gaps

three dimensions: fore and aft, up and down, in and out. The primary adjusting points are the hinge-to-body bolts. Apply tape to the fender and door edges to protect the paint. Two layers of common masking tape works well. Loosen the bolts just enough to allow the hinge to move

STRIKER

Adjust the striker as necessary to position the trailing edge of the door

in place. With the help of an assistant, position the door and retighten the bolts. Inspect the door seams carefully and repeat the adjustment until correctly aligned.

The in-out adjustment (how far the door "sticks out" from the body) is adjusted by loosening the hinge-to-door bolts. Again, move the door into place, then retighten the bolts. This dimension affects both the amount of crush on the weatherstrips and the amount of "bite" on the striker.

Further adjustment for closed position and smoothness of latching is made at the latch plate or striker. This piece is located at the rear edge of the door and is attached to the bodywork; it is the piece the latch engages when the door is closed.

Although the striker size and style may vary between models or from front to rear, the method of adjusting it is the same:

1. Loosen the large cross-point screw(s) holding the striker. Know in advance that these bolts will be very tight; an impact screwdriver is a handy tool to have for this job. Make sure you are using the proper size bit.

2. With the bolts just loose enough to allow the striker to move if necessary, hold the outer door handle in the released position and close the door. The striker will move into the correct location to match the door latch. Open the door and tighten the mounting bolts. The striker may be adjusted towards or away from the center of the car, thereby tightening or loosening the door fit.

The striker can be moved up and down to compensate for door position, but if the door is correctly mounted at the hinges this should not be necessary.

NOTE: *Do not attempt to correct height variations (sag) by adjusting the striker.*

3. Additionally, some models may use one or more spacers or shims behind the striker or at the hinges. These shims may be removed or

added in combination to adjust the reach of the striker or hinge.

4. After the striker bolts have been tightened, open and close the door several times. Observe the motion of the door as it engages the striker; it should continue its straight-in motion and not deflect up or down as it hits the striker.

5. Check the feel of the latch during opening and closing. It must be smooth and linear, without any trace of grinding or binding during engagement and release.

It may be necessary to repeat the striker adjustment several times (and possibly re-adjust the hinges) before the correct door to body match is produced. This can be a maddening process of loosen/tighten/check/readjust; have patience.

Hood

REMOVAL AND INSTALLATION

NOTE: *You'll need an assistant for this job.*

1. Open the hood and support it on the prop rod.

2. Disconnect the washer hose from the hood.

3. On 1984–85 Accord and 1984–87 Prelude, remove the grille.

4. Matchmark the hinge position on the hood (use a felt-tipped marker).

5. Remove the hood-to-hinge bolts and lift off the hood.

6. If the hinges are to be removed, matchmark their position and remove the mounting bolts.

7. Installation is the reverse of removal. Loosely install the hood and align the matchmarks. Adjust the position, then tighten all bolts.

8. Reinstall the grille if it was removed.

9. Connect the washer hose.

ADJUSTMENT

Once the hood is installed, tighten the hood-to-hinge bolts just snug. Close the hood and check for perfect seam alignment. The hood seams are one of the most visible on the car; the slightest error will be plainly obvious to an observer.

Loosen the bolts and position the hood as necessary, then snug the nuts and recheck. Continue the process until the hood latches smoothly and aligns evenly at all the seams.

NOTE: *Do not adjust hood position by moving the latch.*

The hood bolts and the hinge mount bolts may be loosened to adjust their positions. Shims may be used behind the hinge mounts if

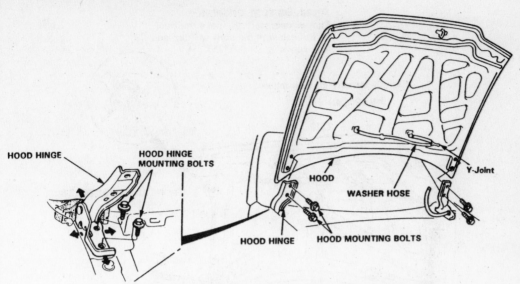

HOOD HINGE

HOOD HINGE
MOUNTING BOLTS

Y-Joint

HOOD

WASHER HOSE

HOOD HINGE   HOOD MOUNTING BOLTS

Hood removal. Don't forget to connect the washer hose after reassembly

necessary. When everything aligns correctly, final-tighten the bolts to 10 Nm (7 ft. lbs).

The elevation of the hood at the latch end may be adjusted by turning the rubber stops or cushions. These bumpers have threaded bottoms and move up or down when turned. An annoying hood rattle on bumps may be caused by these cushions being missing or out of adjustment.

Trunk Lid

REMOVAL AND INSTALLATION

1. Open the trunk lid; have an assistant support it.

2. On 1986–91 Accords, disconnect the wiring connectors from the latch and lighting units inside the trunk lid. Label or identify each connector to ease reassembly. Tie a long piece of string to the end of the wire harness. Slowly and carefully remove the harness from the trunk lid. Leave the string in place to reroute the harness at reassembly.

3. Support the trunk lid (so it doesn't fall and damage the paint). Remove the bolts holding the lid to the hinges. Lift the trunk lid clear of the vehicle.

4. Installation is the reverse of removal. Tighten the bolts just snug until the position is adjusted.

ADJUSTMENT

Once the trunk lid is installed, tighten the bolts just snug. Close the lid and check for perfect seam alignment.

Loosen the hinge bolts and position the trunk lid as necessary, then snug the nuts and re-

check. Continue the process until the lid latches smoothly and aligns evenly at all the seams.

The striker may be adjusted in fashion similar to adjusting a door striker. Shims may be added or removed as necessary. It should not be necessary to adjust the latch to align the trunk lid. Tighten the mounting bolts to 10 Nm (7 ft. lbs).

Accord Hatchback

REMOVAL AND INSTALLATION

1. Remove the tailgate trim panel; this is the small shelf on the inside of the lid.

2. Remove the plastic trim at the rear of the headliner.

3. Lower the rear of the headliner from the roof of the car.

4. On 1984–85 cars, remove the taillight cover(s). On 1986–91 cars, remove the hatch trim panel and side moldings.

5. Disconnect the wire harness in the hatch lid. Label or identify each connector to ease reassembly. Tie a long piece of string to the end of the wire harness. Slowly and carefully remove the harness from the lid. Leave the string in place to reroute the harness at reassembly.

6. Have an assistant hold the hatch up; disconnect the hatch support struts from the lid.

7. Disconnect the washer hose from the lid.

8. Pull the headliner down enough to allow access to the hinge mounting nuts. Make certain the lid is properly supported; remove the mounting nuts. Remove the hatch lid.

To install:

9. Position the lid (2 persons required) and

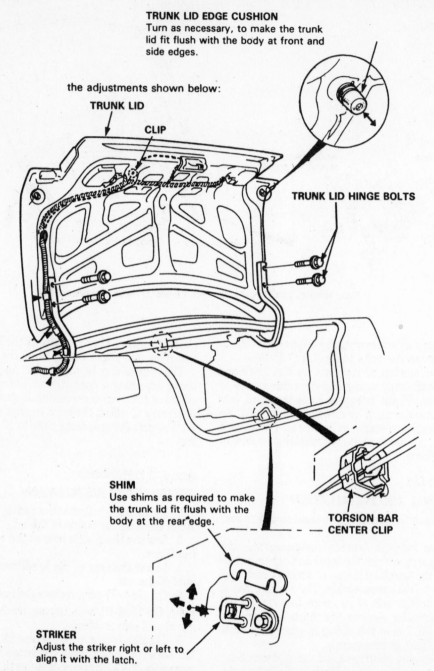

TRUNK LID EDGE CUSHION
Turn as necessary, to make the trunk lid fit flush with the body at front and side edges.

the adjustments shown below:

TRUNK LID

CLIP

TRUNK LID HINGE BOLTS

SHIM
Use shims as required to make the trunk lid fit flush with the body at the rear edge.

TORSION BAR CENTER CLIP

STRIKER
Adjust the striker right or left to align it with the latch.

Example of trunk lid removal. The wiring harness must be removed from the lid prior to removal

install the hinge mounting nuts just snug. Adjust the lid fore-and-aft or left-right at the hinges. Install shims as necessary. Check the latching ease and seam match all the way around. When everything is properly aligned, tighten the mounting nuts to 10 Nm (7 ft. lbs).

10. Install the hatch support struts.

11. Install the wiring harness and attach the connectors. Connect the washer hose.

12. Reinstall the trim panels.

13. Reposition the headliner and install the trim at the roof.

14. Install the rear trim panel.

Accord Wagon Tailgate
REMOVAL AND INSTALLATION

1. Remove the tailgate upper and lower trim

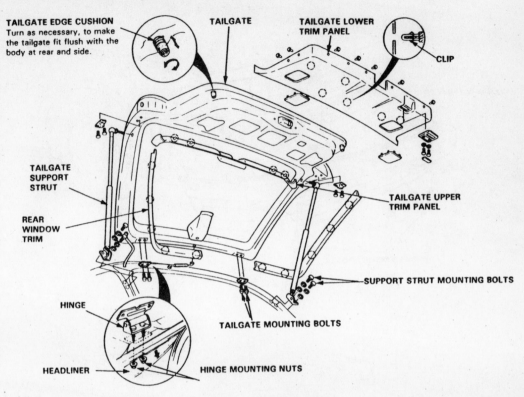

TAILGATE EDGE CUSHION
Turn as necessary, to make the tailgate fit flush with the body at rear and side.

TAILGATE

TAILGATE LOWER TRIM PANEL

CLIP

TAILGATE SUPPORT STRUT

REAR WINDOW TRIM

TAILGATE UPPER TRIM PANEL

SUPPORT STRUT MOUNTING BOLTS

HINGE

TAILGATE MOUNTING BOLTS

HEADLINER

HINGE MOUNTING NUTS

Accord wagon tailgate removal

panels. The panels are held by both clips and screws.

2. Disconnect the washer hose.

3. Disconnect the wire harness in the tailgate. Label or identify each connector to ease reassembly. Tie a long piece of string to the end of the wire harness. Slowly and carefully remove the harness from the tailgate. Leave the string in place to reroute the harness at reassembly.

4. Have an assistant hold the hatch up; disconnect the tailgate support struts from the tailgate.

5. Remove the bolts holding the tailgate to the hinge. Remove the tailgate. Use care not to damage the roof, headliner or tailgate.

NOTE: *The tailgate is heavy. Be prepared.*

6. If the hinge must be removed, lower the rear of the headliner enough to allow access to the hinge mounting bolts. Remove the bolts and remove the hinge.

To install:

7. Install the hinge if it was removed. Tighten the hinge mounting nuts to 22 Nm (16 ft. lbs.)

8. Position the tailgate and install the mounting bolts. Tighten them just snug.

9. Install the tailgate support struts.

10. Adjust the position of the hinges and striker as needed to provide matched seams and

ease of latching. When the lid is in its final position, tighten the bolts to 10 Nm (7 ft. lbs).

11. Install the wiring harness and attach the connectors. Connect the washer hose.

12. Install the upper and lower trim panels.

Bumpers

REMOVAL AND INSTALLATION

1984–85 Accord

FRONT

1. Remove the splash guard under the engine.

2. Remove the bumper mount bolts.

3. Slide the bumper forward off the clips holding the corners near the wheel well.

4. Reassemble in reverse order. The bumper must be slid over the end clips at the time of installation. Tighten the bumper bolts to 39 Nm (28 ft. lbs).

REAR

1. Remove the 3 screws or clips holding the bumper at each wheel well.

2. Remove the bumper mounting bolts and remove the bumper.

3. Reassemble in reverse order. Tighten the mounting bolts to 39 Nm (28 ft. lbs.).

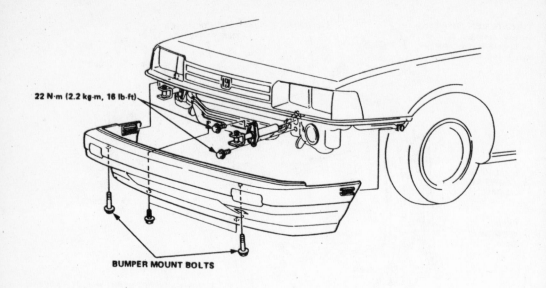

22 N·m (2.2 kg·m, 16 lb·ft)

BUMPER MOUNT BOLTS

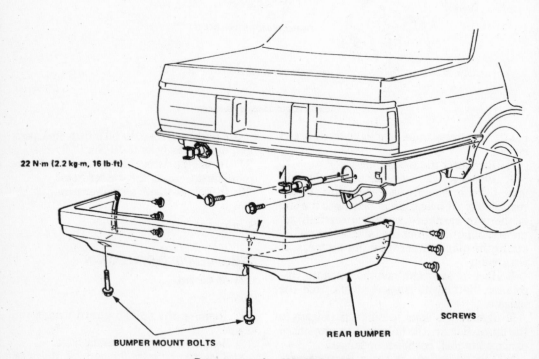

22 N·m (2.2 kg·m, 16 lb·ft)

SCREWS

REAR BUMPER

BUMPER MOUNT BOLTS

Bumper removal — 1984-85 Accord

1986–89 Accord

FRONT

1. Remove the front side and turn signal fixtures and disconnect the wiring.

2. Remove the two rear bumper mount screws at each wheel well.

3. Remove the two lower bumper mount bolts.

4. Remove the four bumper mount bolts; remove the bumper by sliding it forward.

5. Reinstall in reverse order. Tighten all bumper mounting bolts to 22 Nm (16 ft. lbs). Reinstall the signal lamp assemblies.

REAR

1. Remove the 3 screws or clips holding the bumper at each wheel well.

2. Remove the bumper mounting bolts and remove the bumper.

3. Reassemble in reverse order. Tighten the mounting bolts to 39 Nm (28 ft. lbs.)

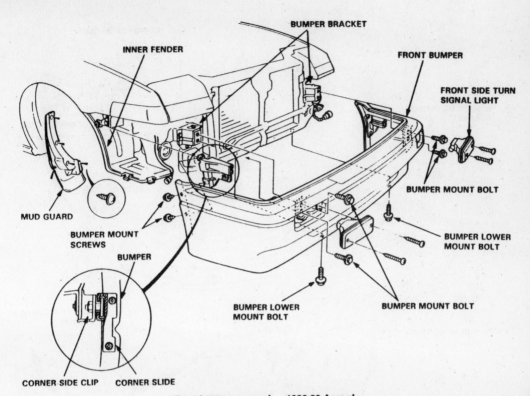

BUMPER BRACKET

INNER FENDER

FRONT BUMPER

FRONT SIDE TURN
SIGNAL LIGHT

MUD GUARD

BUMPER MOUNT BOLT

BUMPER MOUNT
SCREWS

BUMPER

BUMPER LOWER
MOUNT BOLT

BUMPER LOWER
MOUNT BOLT

BUMPER MOUNT BOLT

CORNER SIDE CLIP   CORNER SLIDE

Front bumper removal — 1986-89 Accord

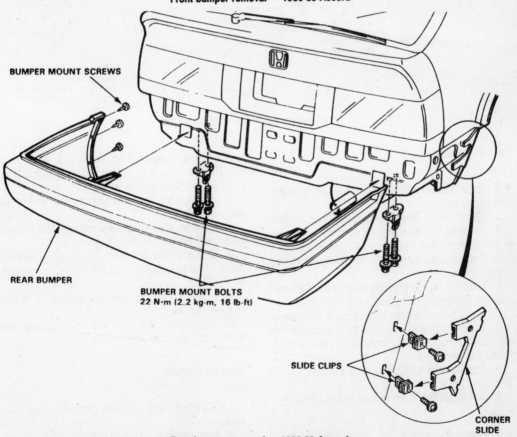

BUMPER MOUNT SCREWS

REAR BUMPER

BUMPER MOUNT BOLTS
22 N·m (2.2 kg-m, 16 lb-ft)

SLIDE CLIPS

CORNER
SLIDE

Rear bumper removal — 1986-89 Accord

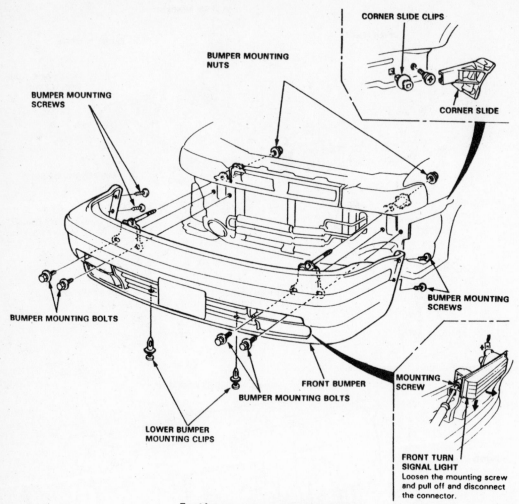

CORNER SLIDE CLIPS

BUMPER MOUNTING NUTS

BUMPER MOUNTING SCREWS

CORNER SLIDE

BUMPER MOUNTING SCREWS

BUMPER MOUNTING BOLTS

MOUNTING SCREW

FRONT BUMPER

BUMPER MOUNTING BOLTS

LOWER BUMPER MOUNTING CLIPS

FRONT TURN SIGNAL LIGHT
Loosen the mounting screw and pull off and disconnect the connector.

Front bumper removal — 1990-91 Accord

1990–91 Accord

FRONT

1. Open the hood and remove the bumper mounting nuts.

2. Remove the front turn signal assemblies.

3. Remove the two screws at each rear edge of the bumper (at the wheels)

4. Remove the two lower bumper mounting clips.

5. Remove the four mounting bolts. Lift and remove the bumper by sliding it forward.

6. Install the bumper by sliding it into place.

7. Loosely install all the mounting bolts; check the position of the bumper on the car, adjusting if necessary.

8. Tighten the mounting nuts and bolts to 25 Nm (18 ft. lbs.)

9. Reinstall the turn signal assemblies.

REAR

1. Open the trunk lid. Remove the small round access covers from the trunk liner panels. Remove the two upper bumper mounting nuts from the trunk side.

2. Remove the bumper mounting screws at each wheel well.

3. Remove the clips, then remove the protectors from below the trunk floor.

4. Remove the 2 lower bumper mounting nuts. Remove the center clip from under the trunk floor.

5. Remove the bumper by sliding it to the rear of the car.

6. Install in reverse order. Tighten the mounting bolts to 25 Nm (18 ft. lbs.)

1984–85 Prelude

FRONT

1. Remove the splash guard under the engine.

2. Remove the bumper mount bolts.

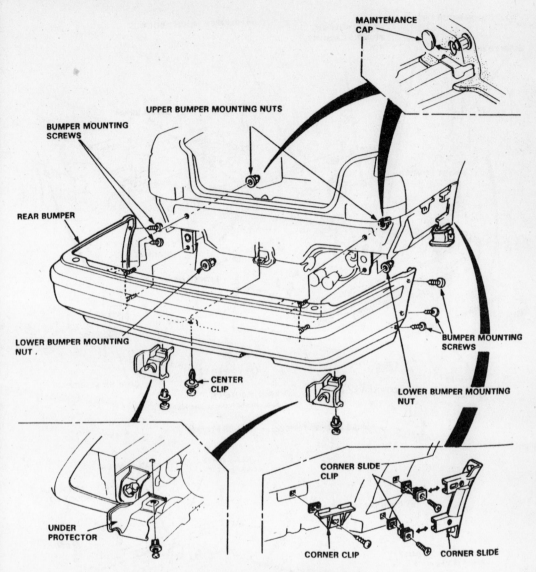

MAINTENANCE CAP

UPPER BUMPER MOUNTING NUTS

BUMPER MOUNTING SCREWS

REAR BUMPER

LOWER BUMPER MOUNTING NUT

CENTER CLIP

BUMPER MOUNTING SCREWS

LOWER BUMPER MOUNTING NUT

UNDER PROTECTOR

CORNER SLIDE CLIP

CORNER CLIP

CORNER SLIDE

Rear bumper removal — 1990-91 Accord

3. Slide the bumper forward off the clips holding the corners near the wheel well.

4. Reassemble in reverse order. The bumper must be slid over the end clips at the time of installation. Tighten the bumper bolts to 22 Nm (16 ft. lbs).

REAR

1. Remove the 3 screws or clips holding the bumper at each wheel well.

2. Remove the bumper mounting bolts and remove the bumper.

3. Reassemble in reverse order. Tighten the mounting bolts to 22 Nm (16 ft. lbs.).

1986–91 Prelude

FRONT

1. Remove the side marker and turn signal lamps if mounted in the bumper.

2. Remove the fog lamps or the lid if so equipped.

3. Remove the 2 bumper lower mount bolts and the 4 bumper mounting bolts.

4. Remove the bumper by sliding it forward.

5. Reinstall in reverse order. Tighten the mounting bolts to 22 Nm (16 ft. lbs).

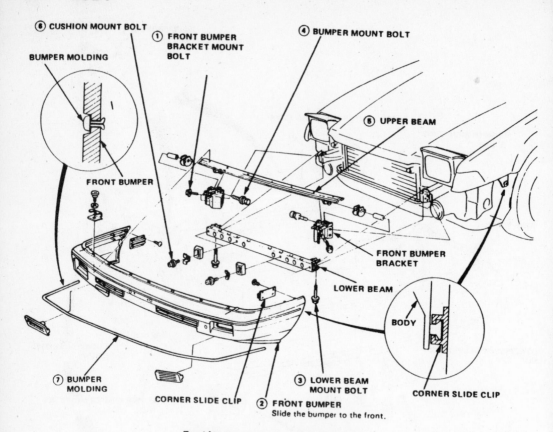

⑥ CUSHION MOUNT BOLT

① FRONT BUMPER BRACKET MOUNT BOLT

④ BUMPER MOUNT BOLT

BUMPER MOLDING

⑤ UPPER BEAM

FRONT BUMPER

FRONT BUMPER BRACKET

LOWER BEAM

BODY

⑦ BUMPER MOLDING

CORNER SLIDE CLIP

③ LOWER BEAM MOUNT BOLT

② FRONT BUMPER
Slide the bumper to the front.

CORNER SLIDE CLIP

Front bumper removal — 1984-85 Prelude

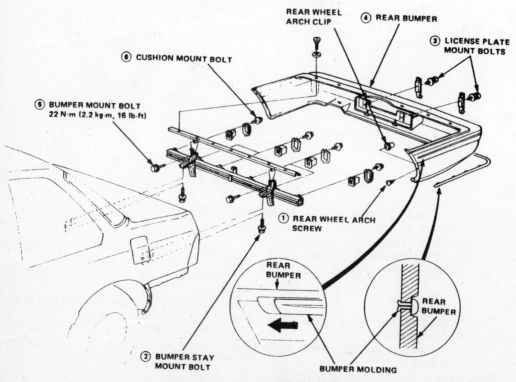

REAR WHEEL ARCH CLIP

④ REAR BUMPER

③ LICENSE PLATE MOUNT BOLTS

⑥ CUSHION MOUNT BOLT

⑤ BUMPER MOUNT BOLT
22 N·m (2.2 kg·m, 16 lb·ft)

① REAR WHEEL ARCH SCREW

REAR BUMPER

REAR BUMPER

② BUMPER STAY MOUNT BOLT

BUMPER MOLDING

Rear bumper removal — 1984-85 Prelude

Si:

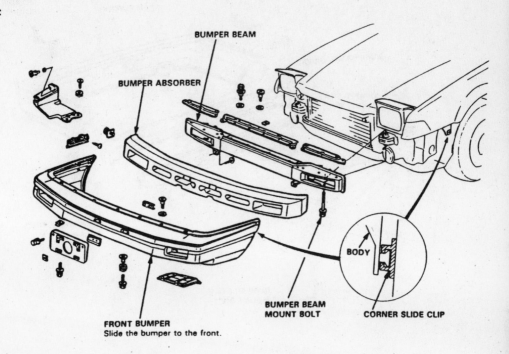

BUMPER BEAM

BUMPER ABSORBER

BODY

FRONT BUMPER
Slide the bumper to the front.

BUMPER BEAM
MOUNT BOLT

CORNER SLIDE CLIP

Dx:

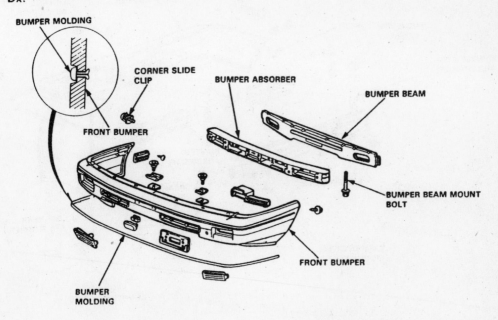

BUMPER MOLDING

CORNER SLIDE
CLIP

BUMPER ABSORBER

BUMPER BEAM

FRONT BUMPER

BUMPER BEAM MOUNT
BOLT

FRONT BUMPER

BUMPER
MOLDING

Front bumper removal — 1986-87 Prelude

Si:

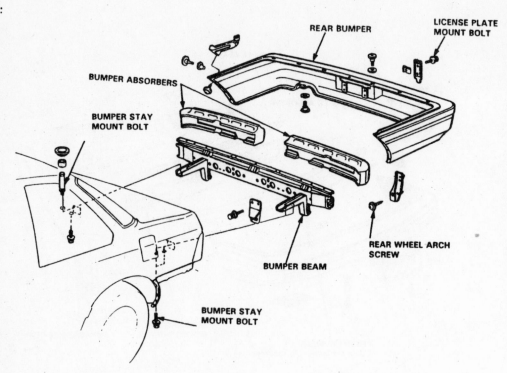

Dx:

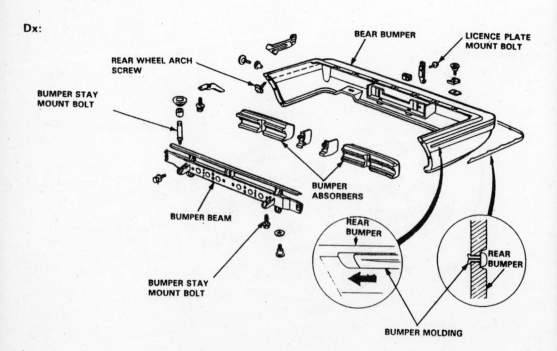

Rear bumper removal — 1986-87 Prelude

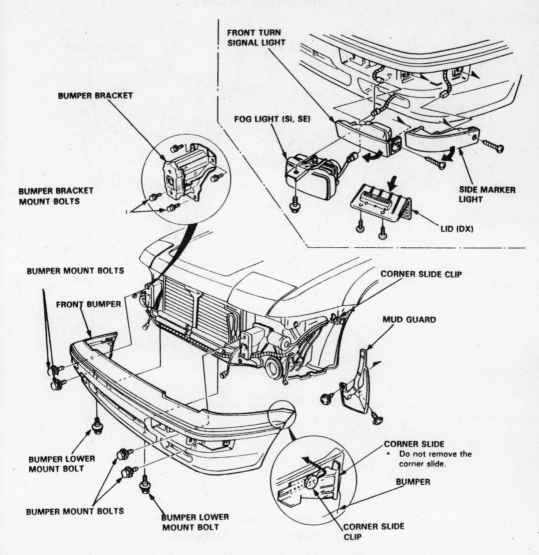

FRONT TURN
SIGNAL LIGHT

BUMPER BRACKET

FOG LIGHT (SI, SE)

BUMPER BRACKET
MOUNT BOLTS

SIDE MARKER
LIGHT

LID (DX)

BUMPER MOUNT BOLTS

FRONT BUMPER

CORNER SLIDE CLIP

MUD GUARD

BUMPER LOWER
MOUNT BOLT

CORNER SLIDE
• Do not remove the
corner slide.

BUMPER

BUMPER MOUNT BOLTS

BUMPER LOWER
MOUNT BOLT

CORNER SLIDE
CLIP

Front bumper removal – 1988-91 Prelude

Grille
REMOVAL AND INSTALLATION

1984–85 Accord

Remove the five mounting screws and re-move the grille.

1986–89 Accord

Remove the five screws and three nuts. Re-move the grille. The end caps are held by two separate bolts under each cap.

1990–91 Accord

1. Remove the five screws holding the top of the grille.

2. Use a thin flat tool to compress and re-lease the lower clips.

3. Remove the grille.

4. When installing, set the clips in place on the grille; install the grille and make certain each clip engages firmly.

1984–91 Prelude

1. Raise the headlights (use the UP/DOWN switch on the dash) and remove the two screws at the side of the grille.

2. Remove the three screws on the front of the grille.

3. Remove the grille.

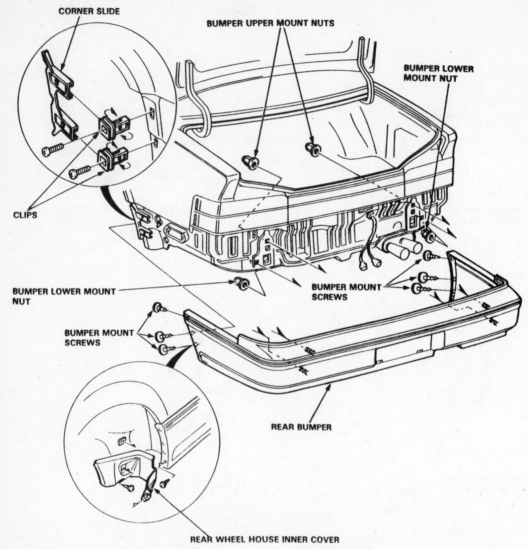

Rear bumper removal — 1988-91 Prelude

Outside Mirrors

REMOVAL AND INSTALLATION

Except for 1988–91 Prelude, the mirrors can be removed from the door without disassembling the door liner or other components. On late model Preludes, the door panel must be removed. Both left and right outside mirrors may be either manual remote (small lever on the inside to adjust the mirror) or electric remote. If the mirror glass is damaged, replacements may be available through your dealer or a reputable glass shop. If the plastic housing is cracked or damaged, the entire mirror unit must be replaced. To remove the mirror:

1. If the mirror is manual remote, check to see if the adjusting handle is retained by a hidden screw, usually under an end cap on the lever. If so, remove the screw and remove the adjusting knob.

2. Remove the delta cover. That's the triangular inner cover where the mirror mounts to the door. It can be removed with a blunt plastic or wooden tool. Don't use a screwdriver; the plastic will be marred.

3. Depending on the model and style of mirror, there may be concealment plugs or other minor parts under the delta cover. Remove them. If electric connectors are present, disconnect them.

4. Support the mirror housing from the outside and remove the three bolts or nuts holding the mirror to the door. Remove the mirror.

5. When installing, fit the mirror to the door and install the nuts and bolts to hold it. Con-

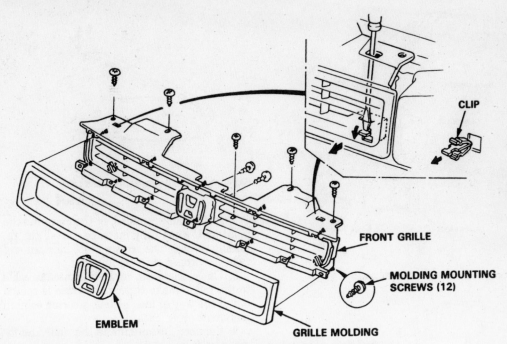

Grille, 1990-91 Accord. Others similar without lower clips

CLIP

FRONT GRILLE

MOLDING MOUNTING
SCREWS (12)

EMBLEM

GRILLE MOLDING

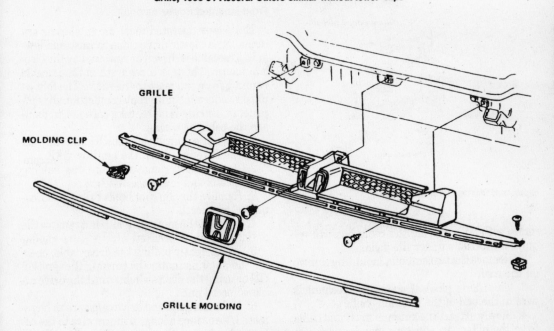

GRILLE

MOLDING CLIP

GRILLE MOLDING

Example of Prelude grille

nect any wiring. Pay particular attention to the placement and alignment of any gaskets or weatherstrips around the mirror; serious wind noises may result from careless work.

6. Install the delta cover, pressing it firmly into position. Install the control lever knob if it was removed.

Antenna

REMOVAL AND INSTALLATION
Front Mounted Manual Antenna

1. Remove or loosen the radio in the dash and disconnect the antenna cable. On some models it may be possible to disconnect the an-

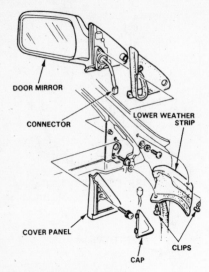

Example of power mirror Installation

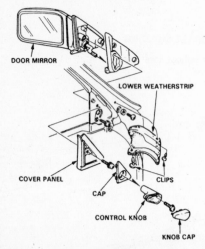

Example of manual mirror Installation

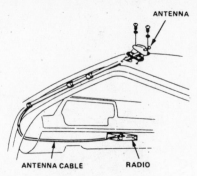

Replacing a manual antenna mast and cable

tenna without removing the radio but will require contortions under the dash.

2. Remove the two antenna mounting screws on the roof.

3. Tie a long piece of string or mechanic's wire to the end of the antenna cable.

4. Slowly extract the antenna mast and cable from the pillar. An assistant may be useful in directing the wire through the other harnesses under the dashboard.

5. Remove the antenna cable completely; when the connector is clear of the roof, untie the string or wire leaving it in the pillar.

To install:

6. Attach the pull string or wire to the connector on the antenna cable. Feed the cable down the roof pillar. Have an assistant pull gently on the string to guide it along.

7. As the cable is pulled, fit the mast into the pillar and, when fully installed, install the retaining screws. The screws must be clean and tight for proper antenna function.

8. Under the dash, route the antenna cable to the radio. Make certain the cable is routed out of the way of feet, pedals, steering column motion or other hazards.

9. Connect the antenna to the radio and install the radio.

Front Mounted Power Antenna

The power operated mast on an electric antenna has a plastic drive cable to raise and lower it. The cable is driven or rewound by the electric motor. There is a separate antenna cable running from the mast to the radio. The following procedure includes replacement for all components. During repairs, take care not to damage the cable or wiring.

1. Turn the ignition switch ON and fully extend the antenna. Turn the ignition OFF.

2. If necessary, remove the 2 bolts holding the fusebox and lower the fusebox.

3. Remove the clip that holds the antenna cable to the sheath.

4. Remove the mounting nut and remove the antenna from its bracket.

5. While lightly pulling the drive cable, operate the antenna motor (by turning the ignition ON or using the dash switch.) until the drive cable is forced out.

6. If the antenna and drive cable are to be replaced, tie or tape a long string or wire to the cable end before pulling it out of the pillar. Leave the feeder in the pillar when the mast is removed.

To install:

7. Extend the antenna and tape or tie the string to the cable end and sheath. Pull the feeder through the pillar until it can be reached at the bottom.

8. remove the string and slide the sheath up enough to expose several inches (centimeters) of the drive cable.

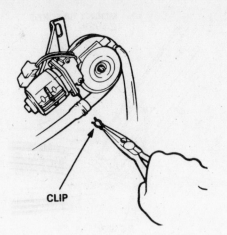

CLIP

Remove the clip holding the sheath to the motor. Don't lose the clip

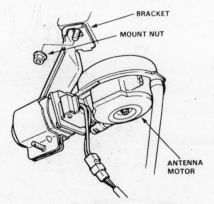

BRACKET

MOUNT NUT

ANTENNA MOTOR

Example of antenna motor mounting; mounts vary by model

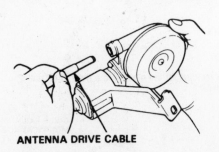

ANTENNA DRIVE CABLE

Insert the drive cable into the motor

9. Insert the drive cable into the motor. Operate the motor to pull the drive cable into the motor housing.

10. When the motor is stopped and the cable retracted, attach the cable sheath to the motor and install the clip.

11. Turn the ignition OFF. Install the motor on the bracket.

12. Install the motor drain hose and fit it into the drain hole.

Rear Mounted Power Antenna

MAST AND CABLE

1. The mast can be replaced without removing the motor. Remove the special antenna nut, spacer and bushing at the base of the mast. Use of tool 07JAA–001000A or equivalent is recommended for turning the special nut.

2. Turn the ignition switch ON and operate the antenna, either by the switch or by turning the radio on.

3. Allow the motor to expel the mast and cable from the bodywork. Pull up gently to assist the cable. Do not let the mast fall and damage the body or paint of the car.

To install:

4. Install the new drive cable into the housing; the teeth of the cable must face the rear of the car. When the cable is fed into the housing, check that the teeth are engaged on the motor gear by gently moving the cable up and down; you'll be able to feel the engagement.

5. Operate the antenna by using the switch or turning the radio OFF. The motor will rewind, drawing the cable and mast into the housing. If the motor runs but does not engage the cable, the teeth are not engaged. Reset the motor to the UP position. Twist the cable a small amount until the teeth are felt to engage, then use the motor to rewind the cable.

6. Install the bushing, spacer and tighten the antenna nut.

7. Operate the antenna several times, making sure the mast extends and retracts fully.

ELECTRIC ANTENNA MOTOR

1. Remove the trunk side panel.

2. Disconnect the wiring connector from the motor. Disconnect the antenna lead.

3. Remove the special nut, using tool 07JAA–001000A or equivalent if possible, then remove the two mounting nuts.

4. Reinstall in reverse order. Tighten the special nut before tightening the two mounting nuts. Connect the wiring harness and antenna lead.

Power Sunroof

REMOVAL AND INSTALLATION

NOTE: *Many vehicles have had aftermarket electric sunroofs installed by dealers or owners. These procedures are only for factory-installed Honda sunroof assemblies.*

1. Slide the sun shield all the way back.

2. Carefully pry out the plug from each bracket cover. Remove the screw and slide each cover off to the rear.

3. Close the glass roof completely.

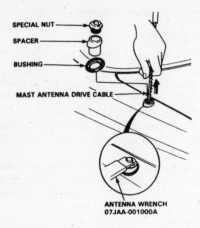

Removing the special nut is easier when the correct tool is used

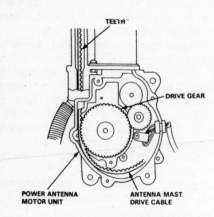

The cable teeth must engage the drive gear before retraction

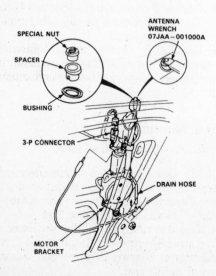

Motor replacement

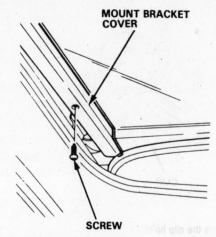

The screw is concealed by a plug

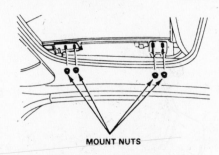

Glass retaining nuts

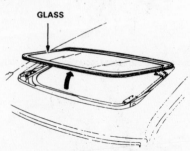

To remove, lift the glass at the front, then pull it forward

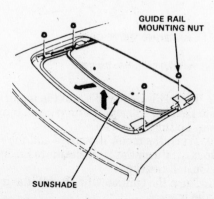

Removing the sunshade. Not all models use the guide rail mounting nuts

4. Remove the nuts from the front and rear mounts on both sides.

5. Lift the front of the glass upward, then pull forward to remove it.

6. Remove the sun shade from the tracks. On some models, remove the six guide rail mounting nuts, then spread the rails to remove the shade. The shade may be bent slightly to ease removal.

To install:

7. Reinstall the shade; position the tracks correctly and install the rail nuts if they were removed.

8. Install the glass. Place the rear edge in at an angle and lower the front edge into position.

9. Install the nuts

10. Install the covers, retaining screws and plugs.

INTERIOR

Dashboard

REMOVAL AND INSTALLATION

NOTE: *The dashboard removal procedures require removal of the steering wheel and/or instrument cluster before beginning these procedures. Please refer to Chapter 8: Steering Wheel Removal and Installation and Chapter 6: Instrument Cluster Removal and Installation.*

All wires and hoses should be labeled at the time of removal. The amount of time saved during reassembly makes the extra effort well worthwhile.

1984–85 Accord

1. Remove the left side lower dash panel and the fuse box cover. Take careful note of the screw installation positions; what appears to be a screw hole in the panel is the sound outlet for the seat belt buzzer.

2. Lower the steering column.

3. Disconnect the instrument panel wire harness from the fusebox, the side wiring harness, the interior lighting harness, brake light harness and the engine harness.

4. Remove the heater control panel.

5. Remove the heater control bracket.

6. Remove the dashboard center access panel.

7. Remove the ashtray.

8. Remove the nine dash mounting bolts. Don't forget the two bolts at the sides of the dash; they are concealed by plastic caps.

9. With an assistant, lift the dash to release the center guide pin; support the dash evenly and remove it from the car.

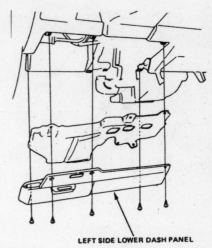

LEFT SIDE LOWER DASH PANEL

Lower left dash panel. When reinstalling, make sure the screws are in correct locations

To install:

10. Fit the dash into position, making sure the guide pin is engaged.

11. Install the nine bolts and tighten them just snug. Check the position of the dash in all dimensions and adjust as necessary. When in final location, tighten the mounting bolts.

12. Install the ash tray and center access panel.

13. Install the heater control bracket and the heater controls.

14. Connect the wiring connectors. Make certain all harnesses are routed and secured properly.

15. Install the steering column.

16. Install the fuse box cover and install the lower dash panel.

1986–89 Accord

1. Remove the lower dash panel.

2. Remove the steering column cover(s).

3. Remove the turn signal cancel sleeve and the combination switch.

4. Remove the ashtray holder.

5. Disconnect the wire harnesses at the fuse box area. Label everything for correct reassembly.

6. Remove the hood release but do NOT disconnect the cable.

7. Disconnect the cables at the center outlet of the heater duct. disconnect the antenna cable at the radio.

8. Remove the dash mounting bolts.

9. With an assistant, lift the dash to release the center guide pin; support the dash evenly and remove it from the car.

To install:

10. Fit the dash into position, making sure the guide pin is engaged.

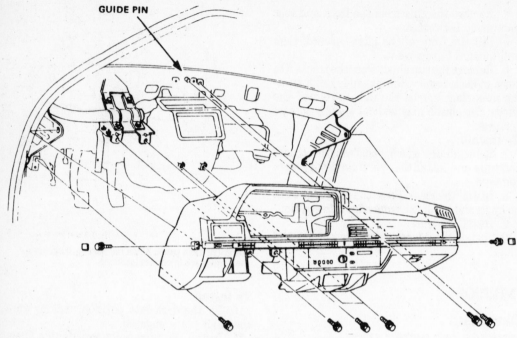

GUIDE PIN

Dash removal, 1984-85 Accord

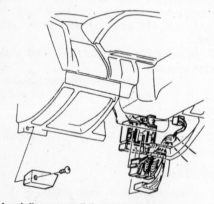

Label and disconnect all the wiring at the fusebox

11. Install the bolts and tighten them just snug. Check the position of the dash in all dimensions and adjust as necessary. When in final location, tighten the mounting bolts. Double check for pinched wires or interference with heater control cables.

12. Connect the antenna cable.

13. Connect the cables at the center heater outlet.

14. Install the hood release handle.

15. Connect the wiring connectors at the fusebox.

16. Install the ashtray holder.

17. Install the combination switch, cancel sleeve and the steering column cover(s).

18. Install the dash lower panel.

1990–91 Accord

1. Slide the seats back all the way.

2. Remove the console.

3. Remove the knee bolster and lower panel.

4. Remove the steering column. Refer to Chapter 8; observe all precautions for airbag (SRS) systems.

5. Disconnect the dash wiring harness from the individual connectors and the fusebox.

6. Unclip the carpet; disconnect the antenna lead.

7. Disconnect the heater control cable and function control cable.

8. Remove the caps on the side panels of the dashboard.

9. Remove the clock.

10. Remove the seven mounting bolts.

11. With an assistant, lift the dashboard and remove it from the vehicle.

To install:

12. Fit the dash into position, making sure the guide pin is engaged.

13. Install the bolts and tighten them just snug. Check the position of the dash in all dimensions and adjust as necessary. When in final location, tighten the mounting bolts. Double check for pinched wires or interference with heater control cables.

14. Install the clock. Install the caps on the side bolts.

15. Connect the heater control and function cables.

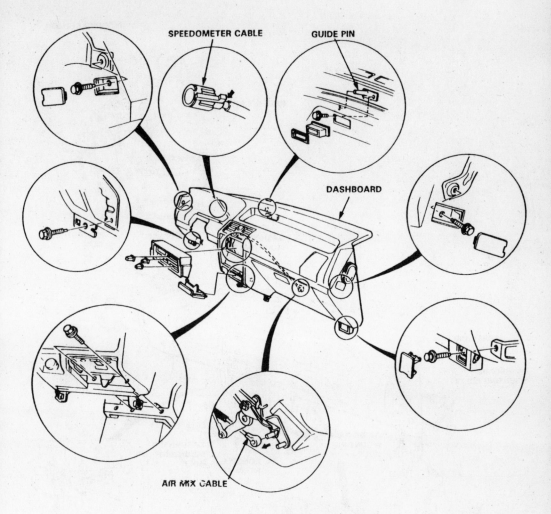

SPEEDOMETER CABLE

GUIDE PIN

DASHBOARD

AIR MIX CABLE

Dashboard retaining bolts, 1986-89 Accord

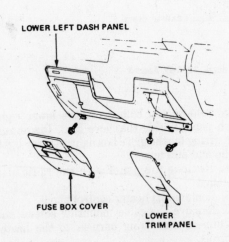

LOWER LEFT DASH PANEL

FUSE BOX COVER

LOWER TRIM PANEL

Don't damage plastic surfaces during removal

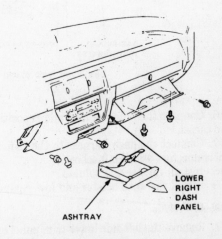

LOWER RIGHT DASH PANEL

ASHTRAY

Remove the lower right dash panel with the radio installed

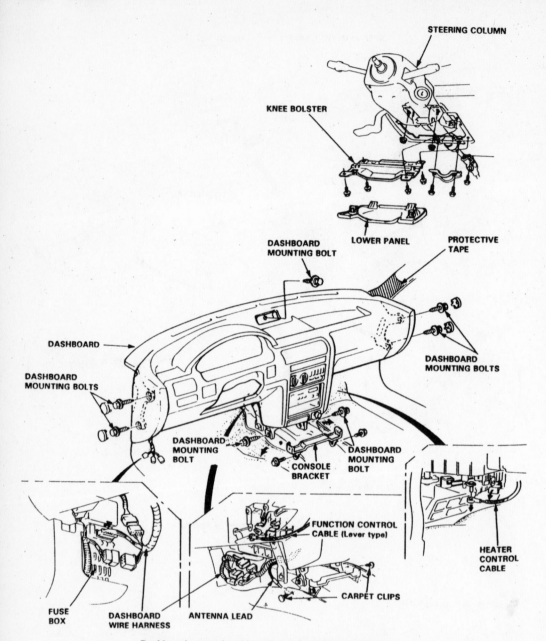

STEERING COLUMN

KNEE BOLSTER

LOWER PANEL

PROTECTIVE TAPE

DASHBOARD MOUNTING BOLT

DASHBOARD

DASHBOARD MOUNTING BOLTS

DASHBOARD MOUNTING BOLTS

DASHBOARD MOUNTING BOLT

DASHBOARD MOUNTING BOLT

CONSOLE BRACKET

FUNCTION CONTROL CABLE (Lever type)

HEATER CONTROL CABLE

FUSE BOX

DASHBOARD WIRE HARNESS

ANTENNA LEAD

CARPET CLIPS

Dashboard removal and installation detail, 1990-91 Accord

16. Connect the antenna lead and reposition the carpet.

17. Connect the dash harness to the individual connectors and the fusebox.

18. Install the steering column.

19. Install the knee bolster and lower panel.

1985-87 Prelude

1. Remove the left side lower trim panel and the fuse box cover. Remove the lower left dash panel by removing the four bolts.

2. Open the glove box. Remove the ashtray.

3. Remove the bolts from the lower right dash panel (inside the glove box). Disconnect the wiring for the glove box light, ashtray light, radio and antenna.

4. Remove the panel with the radio still installed.

5. Remove the heater control panel.

6. Remove the cable mounting screws and disconnect the wiring harness to the heater controls.

7. Remove the instrument cluster if not already done.

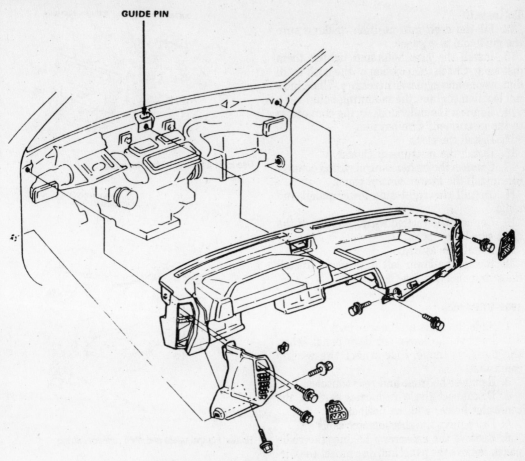

Dashboard mounting bolt locations, 1984-87 Prelude

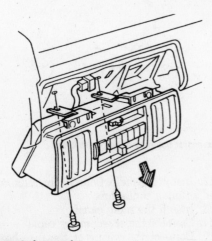

Heater control removal

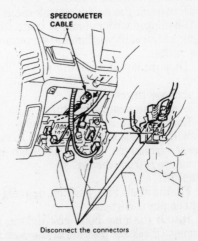

Label the wiring before disconnecting the leads

8. Remove the clock.
9. Label and disconnect the instrument harness from the fuse box, side harness, instrument sub-harness, heater, interior light timer and chime.
10. Remove the nine dash mounting bolts.

Don't forget the two bolts at the sides of the dash.
11. With an assistant, lift the dash to release the center guide pin; support the dash evenly and remove it from the car.

To install:

12. Fit the dash into position, making sure the guide pin is engaged.

13. Install the nine bolts and tighten them just snug. Check the position of the dash in all dimensions and adjust as necessary. When in final location, tighten the mounting bolts.

14. Connect the individual wiring connectors to the instrument wire harness.

15. Install the clock.

16. Install the instrument cluster.

17. Connect the heater control wiring connector; install the heater control panel.

18. Install the right side lower panel and radio.

19. Connect the related wiring circuits at the right side lower panel.

20. Install the ashtray.

21. Install the lower left dash panel. Install the trim panel and fuse box cover.

1988–91 Prelude

1. Slide the seats all the way back.

2. Remove the lower left dash panel; when the panel is loose, disconnect the wiring connector.

3. Remove the front and rear consoles.

4. Disconnect the wire harnesses from the connector holder and the fusebox.

5. Disconnect the speedometer cable.

6. Remove the six screws holding the radio panel, remove the panel and disconnect the wiring and antenna at the radio.

7. Remove the radio assembly.

8. Disconnect the heater control cable.

9. If equipped with automatic transmission, disconnect the shift position switch connectors at the shifter.

10. Disconnect the wiring at the heater control.

11. Remove the clock.

12. Lower the steering column.

13. Remove the dash mounting bolts

14. With an assistant, lift the dash to release the center guide pin; support the dash evenly and remove it from the car.

To install:

15. Fit the dash into position, making sure the guide pin is engaged.

16. Install the nine bolts and tighten them just snug. Check the position of the dash in all dimensions and adjust as necessary. When in final location, tighten the mounting bolts.

17. Raise and install the steering column.

18. Install the clock.

19. Connect the wiring to the heater controls.

20. Connect the wiring to the automatic shift selector.

21. Install the heater control cable.

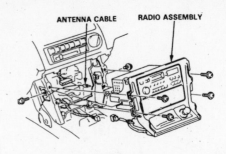

Use care when removing the radio

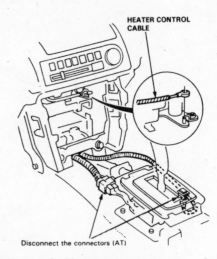

Disconnect the connectors (AT)

Heater control cable and shift position wiring

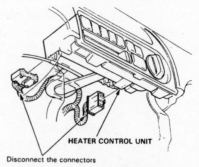

HEATER CONTROL UNIT

Disconnect the connectors

The heater control has two connectors

22. Install the radio. Connect the radio wiring and antenna connectors.

23. Install the radio panel.

24. Connect the speedometer cable.

25. Connect the wiring at the fuse box and connector holder.

26. Install the front and rear consoles.

27. Install the lower dash panel.

Consoles

REMOVAL AND INSTALLATION

WARNING: *Always firmly block the wheels*

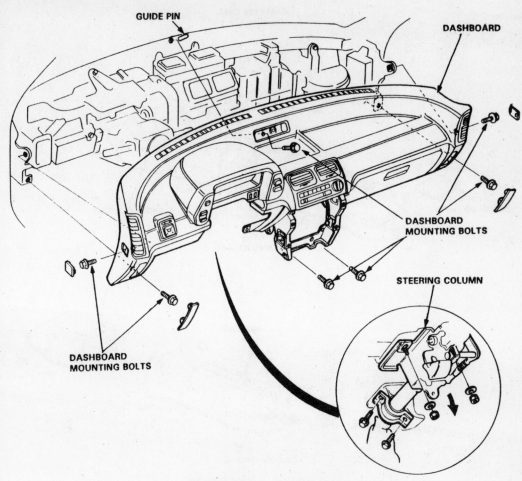

GUIDE PIN

DASHBOARD

DASHBOARD
MOUNTING BOLTS

STEERING COLUMN

DASHBOARD
MOUNTING BOLTS

Prelude dashboard mounting bolts

*front and rear before this procedure. During
removal, the parking brake lever and/or shifter may need to be released or moved to allow
the console to be manipulated.*

1. Remove the manual shift knob. For
1984–85 Accords and 84–87 Preludes, remove
the automatic shift selector handle.

2. Remove the rear ash tray, end cap or
lighter as required. Remove the mounting
screws for the console rear mount.

3. Remove the side retaining screws and
carefully remove the rear console. Disconnect
any wiring connectors as soon as access is
gained.

4. Remove the side retaining screws and remove the front console. Disconnect any wiring
connectors as soon as access is gained.

5. When installing, fit and secure the front
console first. Make certain the brackets did not
get bent or moved during other repairs. The
console must be in its final position so that all
bolt holes align before tightening the bolts. Install the rear console in the same fashion. Re-

member to connect the wiring during
reassembly.

Door Panels
(Door Pads or Liners)
REMOVAL AND INSTALLATION

NOTE: *This is a general procedure. Depending on vehicle and model, the order of steps
may need to be changed slightly.*

1. Remove the inner mirror control knob (if
manual remote) and remove the inner delta
cover from the mirror mount.

2. Remove the screws holding the armrest
and remove the armrest. The armrest screws
may be concealed behind plastic caps which
must be popped out with a non-marring tool.

3. Remove the surround or cover for the inside door handle. Again, seek the hidden screw;
remove it and slide the cover off over the
handle.

4. If not equipped with electric windows, re-

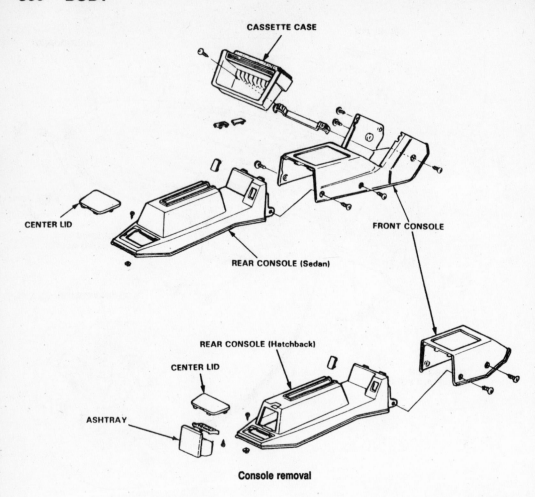

CASSETTE CASE

CENTER LID

REAR CONSOLE (Sedan)

FRONT CONSOLE

REAR CONSOLE (Hatchback)

CENTER LID

ASHTRAY

Console removal

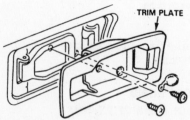

TRIM PLATE

The door handle trim must be removed

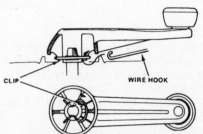

CLIP

WIRE HOOK

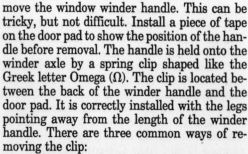

A homemade tool is handy for removing the window winder clip

move the window winder handle. This can be tricky, but not difficult. Install a piece of tape on the door pad to show the position of the handle before removal. The handle is held onto the winder axle by a spring clip shaped like the Greek letter Omega (Ω). The clip is located between the back of the winder handle and the door pad. It is correctly installed with the legs pointing away from the length of the winder handle. There are three common ways of removing the clip:

a. Use a door handle removal tool. This inexpensive slotted and toothed tool can be fitted between the winder and the panel and used to push the spring clip free.

b. Use a rag or piece of cloth and work it back and forth between the winder and door panel. If constant upward tension is kept, the clip will be forced free. Keep watch on the clip as it pops out; it may get lost.

c. Straighten a common paper clip and bend a very small J-hook at the end of it. Work the hook down from the top of the winder and engage the loop of the spring clip.

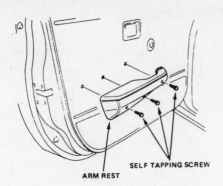

ARM REST

SELF TAPPING SCREW

The armrest screws may be concealed by plugs

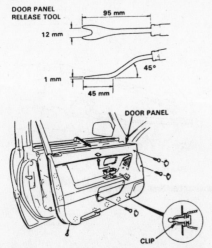

DOOR PANEL
RELEASE TOOL

95 mm

12 mm

1 mm

45°

45 mm

DOOR PANEL

CLIP

A door panel tool may be purchased in most supply shops. Loosen all the plastic clips, then lift the pad up and off the door

As you pull the clip free, keep your other hand over the area. If this is not done, the clip will vanish to an undisclosed location, never to be seen again.

5. In general, power door lock and window switches mounted on the door pad (not the armrest) may remain in place until the pad is removed. Some cannot be removed until the doorpad is off the door.

6. If the car has manual vertical door locks, remove the lock knob by unscrewing it. If this is impossible (because they're in square housings) wait until the pad is lifted free.

7. Using a broad, flat-bladed tool — not a screwdriver — begin gently prying the door pad away from the door. You are releasing plastic inserts from plastic seats. There will be 6 to 12 of them around the door. With care, the plastic inserts can be reused several times.

8. When all the clips are loose, lift up on the panel to release the lip at the top of the door. This may require a bit of jiggling to loosen the

panel; do so gently and don't damage the panel. The upper edge (at the window sill) is attached by a series of retaining clips.

9. Once the panel is free, keep it close to the door and check behind it. Disconnect any wiring for switches, lights or speakers which may be attached.

NOTE: *Behind the panel is a plastic sheet, taped or glued to the door. This is a water shield and must be intact to prevent water entry into the car. It must be securely attached at its edges and not be ripped or damaged. Small holes or tears can be patched with waterproof tape applied to both sides of the liner.*

10. When reinstalling, connect any wiring harnesses and align the upper edge of the panel along the top of the door first. Make sure the left-right alignment is correct; tap the top of the panel into place with the heel of your hand.

11. Make sure the plastic clips align with their holes; pop each retainer into place with gentle pressure.

12. Install the armrest and door handle bezel, remembering to install any caps or covers over the screws.

13. Install the window winder handle on vehicles with manual windows. Place the spring clip into the slot on the handle, remembering that the legs should point away from the long dimension of the handle. Align the handle with the tape mark made earlier and put the winder over the end of the axle. Use the heel of your hand to give the center of the winder a short, sharp blow. This will cause the winder to move inward and the spring will engage its locking groove. The secret to this trick is to push the winder straight on; if it's crooked, it won't engage and you may end up looking for the spring clip.

15. Install any remaining parts or trim pieces which may have been removed earlier. (Map pockets, speaker grilles, etc.)

16. Install the delta cover and the remote mirror handle if they were removed.

Door Locks

KEY LOCK IN DOOR HANDLE

1. Remove the door pad.

2. Carefully remove the inner door liner. Take great care not to rip or damage the plastic.

3. Disconnect or release the clips holding the link rods to both the lock cylinder and the door handle. Depending on the model, it may be easier to disconnect the other end of the rod (at the latch assembly) first.

4. Disconnect any wiring harnesses running to the lock or handle. Generally, these cables have connectors in the line; do not try to disconnect the wiring right at the lock.

5. Remove the retaining nuts or bolts holding the handle assembly to the door and remove the handle. The lock portion can be removed by a competent locksmith.

To install:

6. Before reinstalling, the lock assembly must be installed in the door handle and the small lever (arm) attached. Place the handle in the door and secure the mounting nuts and bolts.

7. Connect the wiring, if any, to the handle or lock.

8. Carefully connect the link rods to the handle and lock, using new clips as necessary. Reconnect the rods to the latch if any were removed.

9. Reinstall the moisture liner. Apply a bead of waterproof sealer to the outer edge if needed and align the sheet carefully.

KEY LOCK IN DOOR

1. Remove the door pad.

2. Carefully remove the inner door liner. Take great care not to rip or damage the plastic.

3. Disconnect or release the clips holding the link rods to both the lock cylinder and the door handle. Depending on the model, it may be easier to disconnect the other end of the rod (at the latch assembly) first.

4. Disconnect any wiring harnesses running to the lock or handle. Generally, these cables have connectors in the line; do not try to disconnect the wiring right at the lock.

5. The lock cylinder is held to the door by a horseshoe-shaped spring clip. Remove the clip and remove the lock cylinder. The cylinder may be repaired by a competent locksmith. Disassembly by the owner/mechanic is not recommended due to the number of small parts and springs within the lock.

6. Install the cylinder into the door and fit the horseshoe clip. Make sure the cylinder is firmly held in place.

7. Connect the link rod, using new clips if necessary.

8. Reinstall the moisture liner. Apply a bead of waterproof sealer to the outer edge if needed and align the sheet carefully.

9. Install the door liner and trim pieces.

Door Glass and Regulator

REMOVAL AND INSTALLATION

Front and Rear Doors

1. Remove the door pad and inner moisture barrier.

2. If working on the rear window of a sedan, remove the two upper screws holding the center channel. Remove the two lower bolts (in the door) holding the channel and remove it. On

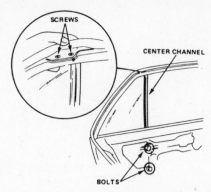

Remove the sedan rear door center channel if the door glass is to be removed

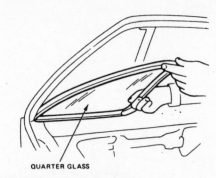

Removing the rear quarter glass

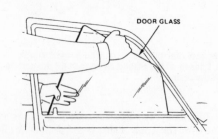

Remove the door glass carefully

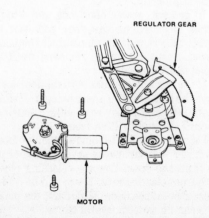

Use caution in removing the power window motor; the regulator gear will move suddenly and may cause injury

BREATHER PIPE

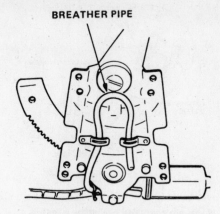

The breather pipe is important to motor operation; make certain it is installed properly

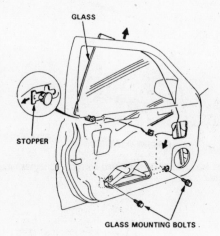

Window removal, 1990-91 Accord

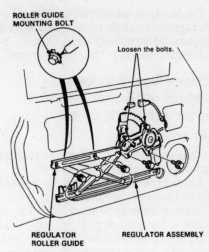

ROLLER GUIDE MOUNTING BOLT

Loosen the bolts.

REGULATOR ROLLER GUIDE

REGULATOR ASSEMBLY

1991-92 Accord front regulator

Place a mark on the roller guide mounting bolts to show the original position.

8. For power windows, remove the motor from the regulator if desired.

CAUTION: *The regulator gear will move suddenly when the motor is removed due to action of the large spring. Keep hands well clear.*

To install:

9. Inspect the regulator carefully for any sign of damage or binding. Grease all the sliding surfaces of the regulator before installation.

10. For power units, compress the regulator gear by hand. When in position, install the motor with the collar and mounting bolt.

11. On power window motors, check the position of the breather pipe; it must be correctly mounted to keep water out of the motor.

12. Install the regulator.

13. Install the front door run channel; just snug the bolts at this time.

14. Fit the glass into position inside the door. Set it loosely on the regulator.

15. Adjust the position of the regulator until the glass mounting bolts align with the access holes. On power windows, connect the wiring and operate the window switch briefly to move the regulator.

16. Install the glass holder bolts and tighten then just snug. Operate the window up and down, checking the placement of the glass and the front run channel. Make minor position adjustments as necessary; you rarely get it right the first time.

17. Tighten the front run channel bolts and tighten the glass holder bolts.

18. For sedan rear doors, install the quarter glass.

19. For sedan rear doors, install the center channel and tighten the mounting bolts.

some cars, the two screws are concealed below the weather strip.

3. For sedan rear doors, remove the quarter glass; the entire glass and rubber seal may be removed as an assembly from the door.

4. Lower the door glass until the glass holder mounting bolts are accessible. One will be easily seen in the large access hole in the door; the other must appear in the smaller, round access hole. Remove the bolts.

5. Stand next to the inside of the door. Tilt the door glass and remove it through the slot.

WARNING: *The glass is easily broken; don't force it while removing and handle it very gently. Store it out of the work area in a protected location.*

6. On front doors, remove the bolts holding the front run channel and remove the channel.

7. Remove the regulator mounting bolts and remove the regulator. On later models, there are additional roller guide bolts to be removed.

20. Double check the operation of the window in all regards. It should move smoothly and evenly, sealing completely when closed.

21. Reinstall the door liner and door pad.

Hatchback Vent Windows (Swing-out or Quarter Windows)

REMOVAL AND INSTALLATION

1984–85 Accord

1. Release the latch. Remove the latch mount cover and remove the screws.

2. Remove the upper and lower quarter trim panels and remove the quarter trim.

3. Remove the window hinge mounting nuts and remove the window glass.

4. On the window, remove the E-clip holding the latch assembly to the glass. Before removal, take careful note of the placement of the washers and pads; they must be reassembled in the correct sequence.

5. If the window is to be replaced with another piece, remove the nuts and remove the pillar trim.

6. Remove the clips from the pillar trim.

7. Remove the moldings and weatherstrip.

8. Transfer the pillar trim, molding and weatherstrip to the new glass.

To install:

9. Reassemble the latch onto the glass; make certain each washer and pad is in the correct location. Installing the E-clip is harder than it looks; don't damage the glass. If the clip is not firmly in place, the latch will loosen.

10. Install the assembled window glass to the pillar and tighten the mounting nuts.

11. Install the mounting bolts for the latch assembly.

12. Install the quarter trim along with the upper and lower trim panels.

13. Install the cover on the latch mount.

1986–89 Accord

1. Release the latch. Remove the latch mount cover and remove the screws.

2. Remove the screws and remove the outer quarter pillar molding.

3. Remove the window hinge mounting screws and remove the window glass.

4. On the window, remove the E-clip holding the latch assembly to the glass. Before removal, take careful note of the placement of the washers and pads; they must be reassembled in the correct sequence.

5. If the window is to be replaced with another piece, remove the weather strip and upper molding. Transfer them to the new glass.

To install:

6. Reassemble the latch onto the glass; make

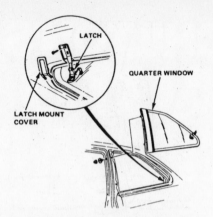

The hinges are concealed behind the pillar trim

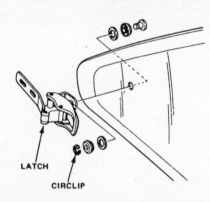

If the latch is not reassembled correctly, the glass may shatter

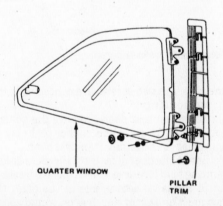

If the glass is to be replaced, transfer the outer trim to the new panel

certain each washer and pad is in the correct location. Installing the E-clip is harder than it looks; don't damage the glass. If the clip is not firmly in place, the latch will loosen.

7. Install the assembled window glass to the pillar and tighten the mounting bolts

8. Install the mounting bolts for the latch assembly.

CHILTON'S
AUTO BODY REPAIR TIPS

**Tools and Materials • Step-by-Step Illustrated Procedures
How To Repair Dents, Scratches and Rust Holes
Spray Painting and Refinishing Tips**

With a little practice, basic body repair procedures can be mastered by any do-it-yourself mechanic. The step-by-step repairs shown here can be applied to almost any type of auto body repair.

TOOLS & MATERIALS

You may already have basic tools, such as hammers and electric drills. Other tools unique to body repair — body hammers, grinding attachments, sanding blocks, dent puller, half-round plastic file and plastic spreaders — are relatively inexpensive and can be obtained wherever auto parts or auto body repair parts are sold. Portable air compressors and paint spray guns can be purchased or rented.

Auto Body Repair Kits

The best and most often used products are available to the do-it-yourselfer in kit form, from major manufacturers of auto body repair products. The same manufacturers also merchandise the individual products for use by pros.

Kits are available to make a wide variety of repairs, including holes, dents and scratches and fiberglass, and offer the advantage of buying the materials you'll need for the job. There is little waste or chance of materials going bad from not being used. Many kits may also contain basic body-working tools such as body files, sanding blocks and spreaders. Check the contents of the kit before buying your tools.

BODY REPAIR TIPS

Safety

Many of the products associated with auto body repair and refinishing contain toxic chemicals. Read all labels before opening containers and store them in a safe place and manner.

• Wear eye protection (safety goggles) when using power tools or when performing any operation that involves the removal of any type of material.

• Wear lung protection (disposable mask or respirator) when grinding, sanding or painting.

Sanding

1 Sand off paint before using a dent puller. When using a non-adhesive sanding disc, cover the back of the disc with an overlapping layer or two of masking tape and trim the edges. The disc will last considerably longer.

2 Use the circular motion of the sanding disc to grind *into* the edge of the repair. Grinding or sanding away from the jagged edge will only tear the sandpaper.

3 Use the palm of your hand flat on the panel to detect high and low spots. Do not use your fingertips. Slide your hand slowly back and forth.

WORKING WITH BODY FILLER

Mixing The Filler

Cleanliness and proper mixing and application are extremely important. Use a clean piece of plastic or glass or a disposable artist's palette to mix body filler.

1 Allow plenty of time and follow directions. No useful purpose will be served by adding more hardener to make it cure (set-up) faster. Less hardener means more curing time, but the mixture dries harder; more hardener means less curing time but a softer mixture.

2 Both the hardener and the filler should be thoroughly kneaded or stirred before mixing. Hardener should be a solid paste and dispense like thin toothpaste. Body filler should be smooth, and free of lumps or thick spots.

Getting the proper amount of hardener in the filler is the trickiest part of preparing the filler. Use the same amount of hardener in cold or warm weather. For contour filler (thick coats), a bead of hardener twice the diameter of the filler is about right. There's about a 15% margin on either side, but, if in doubt use less hardener.

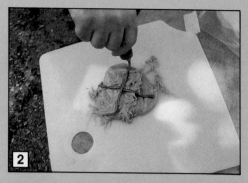

3 Mix the body filler and hardener by wiping across the mixing surface, picking the mixture up and wiping it again. Colder weather requires longer mixing times. Do not mix in a circular motion; this will trap air bubbles which will become holes in the cured filler.

Applying The Filler

1 For best results, filler should not be applied over 1/4″ thick.

Apply the filler in several coats. Build it up to above the level of the repair surface so that it can be sanded or grated down.

The first coat of filler must be pressed on with a firm wiping motion.

Apply the filler in one direction only. Working the filler back and forth will either pull it off the metal or trap air bubbles.

REPAIRING DENTS

Before you start, take a few minutes to study the damaged area. Try to visualize the shape of the panel before it was damaged. If the damage is on the left fender, look at the right fender and use it as a guide. If there is access to the panel from behind, you can reshape it with a body hammer. If not, you'll have to use a dent puller. Go slowly and work the metal a little at a time. Get the panel as straight as possible before applying filler.

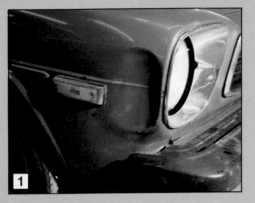

1 This dent is typical of one that can be pulled out or hammered out from behind. Remove the headlight cover, headlight assembly and turn signal housing.

2 Drill a series of holes ½ the size of the end of the dent puller along the stress line. Make some trial pulls and assess the results. If necessary, drill more holes and try again. Do not hurry.

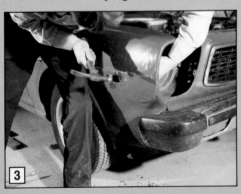

3 If possible, use a body hammer and block to shape the metal back to its original contours. Get the metal back as close to its original shape as possible. Don't depend on body filler to fill dents.

4 Using an 80-grit grinding disc on an electric drill, grind the paint from the surrounding area down to bare metal. Use a new grinding pad to prevent heat buildup that will warp metal.

5 The area should look like this when you're finished grinding. Knock the drill holes in and tape over small openings to keep plastic filler out.

6 Mix the body filler (see Body Repair Tips). Spread the body filler evenly over the entire area (see Body Repair Tips). Be sure to cover the area completely.

7 Let the body filler dry until the surface can just be scratched with your fingernail. Knock the high spots from the body filler with a body file ("Cheese-grater"). Check frequently with the palm of your hand for high and low spots.

8 Check to be sure that trim pieces that will be installed later will fit exactly. Sand the area with 40-grit paper.

9 If you wind up with low spots, you may have to apply another layer of filler.

10 Knock the high spots off with 40-grit paper. When you are satisfied with the contours of the repair, apply a thin coat of filler to cover pin holes and scratches.

11 Block sand the area with 40-grit paper to a smooth finish. Pay particular attention to body lines and ridges that must be well-defined.

12 Sand the area with 400 paper and then finish with a scuff pad. The finished repair is ready for priming and painting (see Painting Tips).

Materials and photos courtesy of Ritt Jones Auto Body, Prospect Park, PA.

REPAIRING RUST HOLES

There are many ways to repair rust holes. The fiberglass cloth kit shown here is one of the most cost efficient for the owner because it provides a strong repair that resists cracking and moisture and is relatively easy to use. It can be used on large and small holes (with or without backing) and can be applied over contoured areas. Remember, however, that short of replacing an entire panel, no repair is a guarantee that the rust will not return.

1 Remove any trim that will be in the way. Clean away all loose debris. Cut away all the rusted metal. But be sure to leave enough metal to retain the contour or body shape.

2 Grind away all traces of rust with a 24-grit grinding disc. Be sure to grind back 3-4 inches from the edge of the hole down to bare metal and be sure all traces of paint, primer and rust are removed.

3 Block sand the area with 80 or 100 grit sandpaper to get a clear, shiny surface and feathered paint edge. Tap the edges of the hole inward with a ball peen hammer.

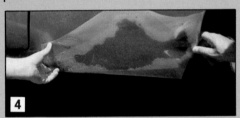

4 If you are going to use release film, cut a piece about 2-3″ larger than the area you have sanded. Place the film over the repair and mark the sanded area on the film. Avoid any unnecessary wrinkling of the film.

5 Cut 2 pieces of fiberglass matte to match the shape of the repair. One piece should be about 1″ smaller than the sanded area and the second piece should be 1″ smaller than the first. Mix enough filler and hardener to saturate the fiberglass material (see Body Repair Tips).

6 Lay the release sheet on a flat surface and spread an even layer of filler, large enough to cover the repair. Lay the smaller piece of fiberglass cloth in the center of the sheet and spread another layer of filler over the fiberglass cloth. Repeat the operation for the larger piece of cloth.

7 Place the repair material over the repair area, with the release film facing outward. Use a spreader and work from the center outward to smooth the material, following the body contours. Be sure to remove all air bubbles.

8 Wait until the repair has dried tack-free and peel off the release sheet. The ideal working temperature is 60°-90° F. Cooler or warmer temperatures or high humidity may require additional curing time. Wait longer, if in doubt.

9 Sand and feather-edge the entire area. The initial sanding can be done with a sanding disc on an electric drill if care is used. Finish the sanding with a block sander. Low spots can be filled with body filler; this may require several applications.

10 When the filler can just be scratched with a fingernail, knock the high spots down with a body file and smooth the entire area with 80-grit. Feather the filled areas into the surrounding areas.

11 When the area is sanded smooth, mix some topcoat and hardener and apply it directly with a spreader. This will give a smooth finish and prevent the glass matte from showing through the paint.

12 Block sand the topcoat smooth with finishing sandpaper (200 grit), and 400 grit. The repair is ready for masking, priming and painting (see Painting Tips).

Materials and photos courtesy Marson Corporation, Chelsea, Massachusetts

PAINTING TIPS

Preparation

1 SANDING — Use a 400 or 600 grit wet or dry sandpaper. Wet-sand the area with a 1/4 sheet of sandpaper soaked in clean water. Keep the paper wet while sanding. Sand the area until the repaired area tapers into the original finish.

2 CLEANING — Wash the area to be painted thoroughly with water and a clean rag. Rinse it thoroughly and wipe the surface dry until you're sure it's completely free of dirt, dust, fingerprints, wax, detergent or other foreign matter.

3 MASKING — Protect any areas you don't want to overspray by covering them with masking tape and newspaper. Be careful not get fingerprints on the area to be painted.

4 PRIMING — All exposed metal should be primed before painting. Primer protects the metal and provides an excellent surface for paint adhesion. When the primer is dry, wet-sand the area again with 600 grit wet-sandpaper. Clean the area again after sanding.

Painting Techniques

P aint applied from either a spray gun or a spray can (for small areas) will provide good results. Experiment on an old piece of metal to get the right combination before you begin painting.

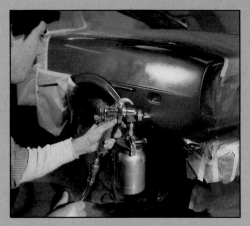

SPRAYING VISCOSITY (SPRAY GUN ONLY) — Paint should be thinned to spraying viscosity according to the directions on the can. Use only the recommended thinner or reducer and the same amount of reduction regardless of temperature.

AIR PRESSURE (SPRAY GUN ONLY) — This is extremely important. Be sure you are using the proper recommended pressure.

TEMPERATURE — The surface to be painted should be approximately the same temperature as the surrounding air. Applying warm paint to a cold surface, or vice versa, will completely upset the paint characteristics.

THICKNESS — Spray with smooth strokes. In general, the thicker the coat of paint, the longer the drying time. Apply several thin coats about 30 seconds apart. The paint should remain wet long enough to flow out and no longer; heavier coats will only produce sags or wrinkles. Spray a light (fog) coat, followed by heavier color coats.

DISTANCE — The ideal spraying distance is 8"-12" from the gun or can to the surface. Shorter distances will produce ripples, while greater distances will result in orange peel, dry film and poor color match and loss of material due to overspray.

OVERLAPPING — The gun or can should be kept at right angles to the surface at all times. Work to a wet edge at an even speed, using a 50% overlap and direct the center of the spray at the lower or nearest edge of the previous stroke.

RUBBING OUT (BLENDING) FRESH PAINT — Let the paint dry thoroughly. Runs or imperfections can be sanded out, primed and repainted.

Don't be in too big a hurry to remove the masking. This only produces paint ridges. When the finish has dried for at least a week, apply a small amount of fine grade rubbing compound with a clean, wet cloth. Use lots of water and blend the new paint with the surrounding area.

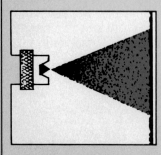

WRONG

Thin coat. Stroke too fast, not enough overlap, gun too far away.

CORRECT

Medium coat. Proper distance, good stroke, proper overlap.

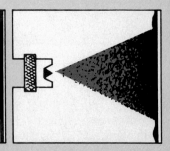

WRONG

Heavy coat. Stroke too slow, too much overlap, gun too close.

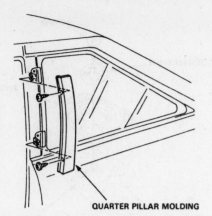

QUARTER PILLAR MOLDING

The outer pillar trim may be removed from the outside

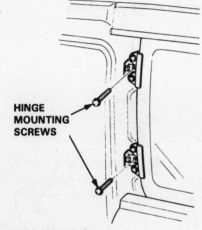

HINGE
MOUNTING
SCREWS

Removing the hinge bolts

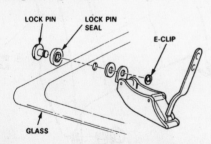

LOCK PIN   LOCK PIN
            SEAL

E-CLIP

GLASS

If the latch is not reassembled correctly, the glass may shatter

9. Install the quarter pillar trim panel.
10. Install the cover on the latch mount.

Inside Rear View Mirror

NOTE: *The inside mirrors on all Hondas are designed to break loose under impact. If your mirror has fallen or been knocked off the mount, it can usually be reinstalled without any new parts.*

REMOVAL AND INSTALLATION

1. Remove the rubber damper from the shaft of the mirror if one is present.
2. Carefully pry off the plastic cover. On 1988–91 Preludes, press in at the front of the cover to release the clips. Remove the cover.
3. Remove the retaining screws holding the base. On late model Preludes, the screws also hold the warning lamp assembly; be prepared to remove and disconnect it.
4. Remove the large cross-point screw holding the mirror to the base.
5. Reassemble in reverse order.

Seats

REMOVAL AND INSTALLATION

Front

WARNING: *Many electrical components are mounted on the floor under the seats. Do not damage the components during removal or installation of the seat.*

1. Slide the seat fully forward. In the rear passenger area, remove the covers from the two seat retaining bolts.
2. Remove the bolts.
3. Slide the seat fully to the rear. Remove the front mounting bolt covers and remove the bolts.
4. Remove the seat.
5. Reinstall in reverse order; tighten the seat rail mounting bolts to 32 Nm (23 ft. lbs).

Rear

1984–89 ACCORD

1. With your hands, press down on the seat cushion where it meets the seat back. Locate the retaining bolt(s). Some models hold the seat with one bolt in the center; others use two, evenly spaced left and right.
2. Remove the retaining bolts.
3. Lift the back of the seat upwards, rotating to the front of the car.
4. Disconnect the hooks at the front edge (during the rolling motion) of the seat and remove the seat bottom.
5. On hatchback Accords and all Preludes, disconnect or remove the carpeting from the back of the seat back.
6. Remove the bolts holding the bottom of the seat back.
7. On 1984–85 Accord Sedans, push against the middle of the seat back just below the top edge with one hand while pulling up firmly on the bottom edge with the other hand. This combined motion releases a J-shaped hook holding the seat back at each lower edge.
8. On 1986–89 Accord Sedans, wiggle and lift

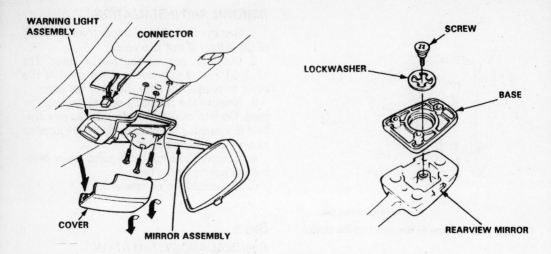

WARNING LIGHT ASSEMBLY
CONNECTOR
SCREW
LOCKWASHER
BASE
COVER
MIRROR ASSEMBLY
REARVIEW MIRROR

Inside mirror removal. Late model Prelude shown; others similar without the warning light assembly. Make certain the lock washer is correctly installed at reassembly

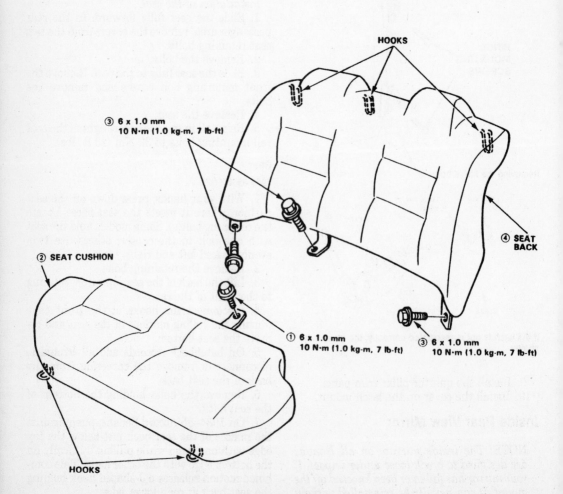

HOOKS

③ 6 x 1.0 mm
10 N·m (1.0 kg-m, 7 lb-ft)

② SEAT CUSHION

① 6 x 1.0 mm
10 N·m (1.0 kg-m, 7 lb-ft)

③ 6 x 1.0 mm
10 N·m (1.0 kg-m, 7 lb-ft)

④ SEAT BACK

HOOKS

1987 Accord rear seat

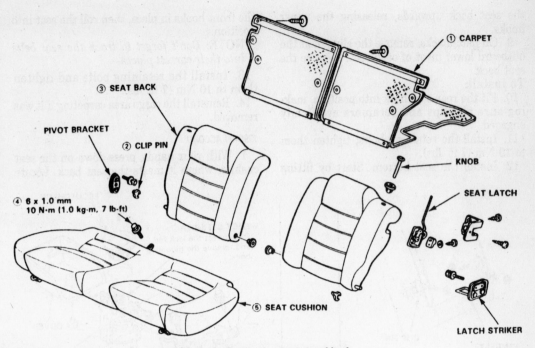

Example of Hatchback rear seat and back

Labels: ① CARPET, KNOB, SEAT LATCH, ③ SEAT BACK, PIVOT BRACKET, ② CLIP PIN, ④ 6 x 1.0 mm 10 N·m (1.0 kg·m, 7 lb-ft), ⑤ SEAT CUSHION, LATCH STRIKER

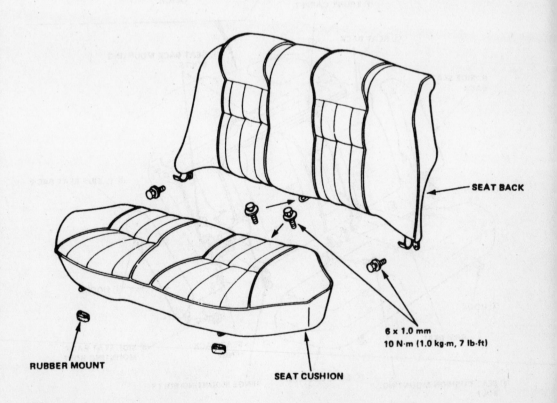

Labels: SEAT BACK, 6 x 1.0 mm 10 N·m (1.0 kg·m, 7 lb-ft), RUBBER MOUNT, SEAT CUSHION

1984-85 Accord rear seat. Note the J-hooks at the bottom of the seat back

the seat back upwards, releasing the upper hooks.

9. On hatchbacks, remove the clip pin at the outboard lower pivot of each seat. Remove the seat back

To install:

10. Fit the rear seat back into position, making sure all clips and retainers are firmly engaged.

11. Install the retaining bolts; tighten them to 10 Nm (7 ft. lbs).

12. Install the seat bottom. Start by fitting

the front hooks in place, then roll the seat into position.

NOTE: *Don't forget to track the seat belts into their correct places.*

13. Install the retaining bolts and tighten them to 10 Nm (7 ft. lbs).

14. Reinstall the cargo area carpeting if it was removed.

1990-91 ACCORD

1. With your hands, press down on the seat cushion where it meets the seat back. Locate

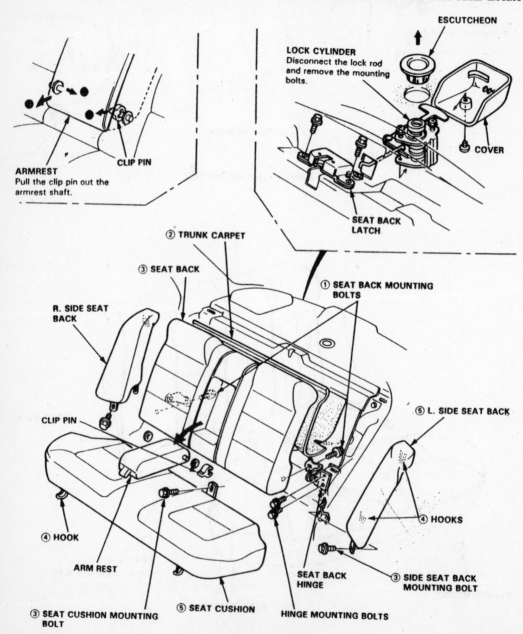

1990-91 Accord rear seat and back

the retaining bolt(s). Some models hold the seat with one bolt in the center; others use two, evenly spaced left and right.

2. Remove the retaining bolts.

3. Lift the back of the seat upwards, rotating to the front of the car.

4. Disconnect the hooks at the front edge (during the rolling motion) of the seat and remove the seat bottom.

5. Disconnect the carpet from the rear of the seat backs.

6. Remove the seat back mounting bolts from the luggage compartment side.

7. Lift out the seat back.

8. If the rear side bolsters or pads are to be removed, remove the lower mounting bolt, then push upward to free the hooks.

To install:

9. Install the side bolsters if they were removed.

10. Install the seat bottom, engaging the front hooks first. Tighten the bolts to 10 Nm (7 ft. lbs).

11. Install the seat back.

12. Install the seat back retaining bolts; when they are just snug, check the fit of the seat and its position in the upper latch. Adjust as necessary.

13. Tighten the bolts to 22 Nm (16 ft. lbs.)

14. Install the rear carpeting to the seat back.

PRELUDE

1. Pull the seat back all the way down. Re-

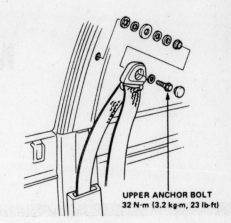

UPPER ANCHOR BOLT
32 N·m (3.2 kg·m, 23 lb-ft)

Prelude rear seat components

move the luggage area carpet from the back of the seat.

2. Remove the clip pin on the left side of the seat back. Slide the seat back to the left (removing it from the right mount) and remove the back.

3. Remove the bolt(s) holding the seat bottom

4. Move the rear of the seat upwards and towards the front; disengage the hooks from the floor holes.

5. Reassemble in reverse order. Tighten the seat mounting bolts to 10 Nm (7 ft. lbs). Don't forget to track the seat belts through the pockets in the seat bottom.

Mechanic's Data

11

1″:254mm
TAX
10.16mm Liter
Parts
Overhaul

General Conversion Table

Multiply By	To Convert	To	
LENGTH			
2.54	Inches	Centimeters	.3937
25.4	Inches	Millimeters	.03937
30.48	Feet	Centimeters	.0328
.304	Feet	Meters	3.28
.914	Yards	Meters	1.094
1.609	Miles	Kilometers	.621
VOLUME			
.473	Pints	Liters	2.11
.946	Quarts	Liters	1.06
3.785	Gallons	Liters	.264
.164	Cubic inches	Liters	61.02
16.39	Cubic inches	Cubic cms.	.061
28.32	Cubic feet	Liters	.0353
MASS (Weight)			
28.35	Ounces	Grams	.035
.4536	Pounds	Kilograms	2.20
—	**To obtain**	**From**	**Multiply by**

Multiply By	To Convert	To	
AREA			
6.45	Square inches	Square cms.	.155
.836	Square yds.	Square meters	1.196
FORCE			
4.448	Pounds	Newtons	.225
.138	Ft. lbs.	Kilogram/meters	7.23
1.356	Ft. lbs.	Newton-meters	.737
.113	In. lbs.	Newton-meters	8.844
PRESSURE			
.068	Psi	Atmospheres	14.7
6.89	Psi	Kilopascals	.145
OTHER			
1.104	Horsepower (DIN)	Horsepower (SAE)	.9861
.746	Horsepower (SAE)	Kilowatts (KW)	1.34
1.609	Mph	Km/h	.621
.425	Mpg	Km/L	2.35
—	**To obtain**	**From**	**Multiply by**

Tap Drill Sizes

National Coarse or U.S.S.

Screw & Tap Size	Threads Per Inch	Use Drill Number
No. 5	40	39
No. 6	32	36
No. 8	32	29
No. 10	24	25
No. 12	24	17
1/4	20	8
5/16	18	F
3/8	16	5/16
7/16	14	U
1/2	13	27/64
9/16	12	31/64
5/8	11	17/32
3/4	10	21/32
7/8	9	49/64

National Coarse or U.S.S.

Screw & Tap Size	Threads Per Inch	Use Drill Number
1	8	7/8
1 1/8	7	63/64
1 1/4	7	1 7/64
1 1/2	6	1 11/32

National Fine or S.A.E.

Screw & Tap Size	Threads Per Inch	Use Drill Number
No. 5	44	37
No. 6	40	33
No. 8	36	29
No. 10	32	21

National Fine or S.A.E.

Screw & Tap Size	Threads Per Inch	Use Drill Number
No. 12	28	15
1/4	28	3
6/16	24	1
3/8	28	Q
7/16	20	W
1/2	20	29/64
9/16	18	33/64
5/8	18	37/64
3/4	16	11/16
7/8	14	13/16
1 1/8	12	1 3/64
1 1/4	12	1 11/64
1 1/2	12	1 27/64

Drill Sizes In Decimal Equivalents

Inch	Decimal	Wire	mm
1/64	.0156		.39
	.0157		.4
	.0160	78	
	.0165		.42
	.0173		.44
	.0177		.45
	.0180	77	
	.0181		.46
	.0189		.48
	.0197		.5
	.0200	76	
	.0210	75	
	.0217		.55
	.0225	74	
	.0236		.6
	.0240	73	
	.0250	72	
	.0256		.65
	.0260	71	
	.0276		.7
	.0280	70	
	.0292	69	
	.0295		.75
	.0310	68	
1/32	.0312		.79
	.0315		.8
	.0320	67	
	.0330	66	
	.0335		.85
	.0350	65	
	.0354		.9
	.0360	64	
	.0370	63	
	.0374		.95
	.0380	62	
	.0390	61	
	.0394		1.0
	.0400	60	
	.0410	59	
	.0413		1.05
	.0420	58	
	.0430	57	
	.0433		1.1
	.0453		1.15
	.0465	56	
3/64	.0469		1.19
	.0472		1.2
	.0492		1.25
	.0512		1.3
	.0520	55	
	.0531		1.35
	.0550	54	
	.0551		1.4
	.0571		1.45
	.0591		1.5
	.0595	53	
	.0610		1.55
1/16	.0625		1.59
	.0630		1.6
	.0635	52	
	.0650		1.65
	.0669		1.7
	.0670	51	
	.0689		1.75
	.0700	50	
	.0709		1.8
	.0728		1.85

Inch	Decimal	Wire	mm
	.0730	49	
	.0748		1.9
	.0760	48	
	.0768		1.95
5/64	.0781		1.98
	.0785	47	
	.0787		2.0
	.0807		2.05
	.0810	46	
	.0820	45	
	.0827		2.1
	.0846		2.15
	.0860	44	
	.0866		2.2
	.0886		2.25
	.0890	43	
	.0906		2.3
	.0925		2.35
	.0935	42	
3/32	.0938		2.38
	.0945		2.4
	.0960	41	
	.0965		2.45
	.0980	40	
	.0981		2.5
	.0995	39	
	.1015	38	
	.1024		2.6
	.1040	37	
	.1063		2.7
	.1065	36	
	.1083		2.75
7/64	.1094		2.77
	.1100	35	
	.1102		2.8
	.1110	34	
	.1130	33	
	.1142		2.9
	.1160	32	
	.1181		3.0
	.1200	31	
	.1220		3.1
1/8	.1250		3.17
	.1260		3.2
	.1280		3.25
	.1285	30	
	.1299		3.3
	.1339		3.4
	.1360	29	
	.1378		3.5
	.1405	28	
9/64	.1406		3.57
	.1417		3.6
	.1440	27	
	.1457		3.7
	.1470	26	
	.1476		3.75
	.1495	25	
	.1496		3.8
	.1520	24	
	.1535		3.9
	.1540	23	
5/32	.1562		3.96
	.1570	22	
	.1575		4.0
	.1590	21	
	.1610	20	

Inch	Decimal	Wire & Letter	mm
	.1614		4.1
	.1654		4.2
	.1660	19	
	.1673		4.25
	.1693		4.3
	.1695	18	
11/64	.1719		4.36
	.1730	17	
	.1732		4.4
	.1770	16	
	.1772		4.5
	.1800	15	
	.1811		4.6
	.1820	14	
	.1850	13	
	.1850		4.7
	.1870		4.75
3/16	.1875		4.76
	.1890		4.8
	.1890	12	
	.1910	11	
	.1929		4.9
	.1935	10	
	.1960	9	
	.1969		5.0
	.1990	8	
	.2008		5.1
	.2010	7	
13/64	.2031		5.16
	.2040	6	
	.2047		5.2
	.2055	5	
	.2067		5.25
	.2087		5.3
	.2090	4	
	.2126		5.4
	.2130	3	
	.2165		5.5
7/32	.2188		5.55
	.2205		5.6
	.2210	2	
	.2244		5.7
	.2264		5.75
	.2280	1	
	.2283		5.8
	.2323		5.9
	.2340	A	
15/64	.2344		5.95
	.2362		6.0
	.2380	B	
	.2402		6.1
	.2420	C	
	.2441		6.2
	.2460	D	
	.2461		6.25
	.2480		6.3
1/4	.2500	E	6.35
	.2520		6.
	.2559		6.5
	.2570	F	
	.2598		6.6
	.2610	G	
	.2638		6.7
17/64	.2656		6.74
	.2657		6.75
	.2660	H	
	.2677		6.8

Inch	Decimal	Letter	mm
	.2717		6.9
	.2720	I	
	.2756		7.0
	.2770	J	
	.2795		7.1
	.2810	K	
9/32	.2812		7.14
	.2835		7.2
	.2854		7.25
	.2874		7.3
	.2900	L	
	.2913		7.4
	.2950	M	
	.2953		7.5
19/64	.2969		7.54
	.2992		7.6
	.3020	N	
	.3031		7.7
	.3051		7.75
	.3071		7.8
	.3110		7.9
5/16	.3125		7.93
	.3150		8.0
	.3160	O	
	.3189		8.1
	.3228		8.2
	.3230	P	
	.3248		8.25
	.3268		8.3
21/64	.3281		8.33
	.3307		8.4
	.3320	Q	
	.3346		8.5
	.3386		8.6
	.3390	R	
	.3425		8.7
11/32	.3438		8.73
	.3445		8.75
	.3465		8.8
	.3480	S	
	.3504		8.9
	.3543		9.0
	.3580	T	
	.3583		9.1
23/64	.3594		9.12
	.3622		9.2
	.3642		9.25
	.3661		9.3
	.3680	U	
	.3701		9.4
	.3740		9.5
3/8	.3750		9.52
	.3770	V	
	.3780		9.6
	.3819		9.7
	.3839		9.75
	.3858		9.8
	.3860	W	
	.3898		9.9
25/64	.3906		9.92
	.3937		10.0
	.3970	X	
	.4040	Y	
13/32	.4062		10.31
	.4130	Z	
	.4134		10.5
27/64	.4219		10.71

Inch	Decimal	mm
	.4331	11.0
7/16	.4375	11.11
	.4528	11.5
29/64	.4531	11.51
15/32	.4688	11.90
	.4724	12.0
31/64	.4844	12.30
	.4921	12.5
1/2	.5000	12.70
	.5118	13.0
33/64	.5156	13.09
17/32	.5312	13.49
	.5315	13.5
35/64	.5469	13.89
	.5512	14.0
9/16	.5625	14.28
	.5709	14.5
37/64	.5781	14.68
	.5906	15.0
19/32	.5938	15.08
39/64	.6094	15.47
	.6102	15.5
5/8	.6250	15.87
	.6299	16.0
41/64	.6406	16.27
	.6496	16.5
21/32	.6562	16.66
	.6693	17.0
43/64	.6719	17.06
11/16	.6875	17.46
	.6890	17.5
45/64	.7031	17.85
	.7087	18.0
23/32	.7188	18.25
	.7283	18.5
47/64	.7344	18.65
	.7480	19.0
3/4	.7500	19.05
49/64	.7656	19.44
	.7677	19.5
25/32	.7812	19.84
	.7874	20.0
51/64	.7969	20.24
	.8071	20.5
13/16	.8125	20.63
	.8268	21.0
53/64	.8281	21.03
27/32	.8438	21.43
	.8465	21.5
55/64	.8594	21.82
	.8661	22.0
7/8	.8750	22.22
	.8858	22.5
57/64	.8906	22.62
	.9055	23.0
29/32	.9062	23.01
59/64	.9219	23.41
	.9252	23.5
15/16	.9375	23.81
	.9449	24.0
61/64	.9531	24.2
	.9646	24.5
31/32	.9688	24.6
	.9843	25.0
63/64	.9844	25.0
1	1.0000	25.4

AIR/FUEL RATIO: The ratio of air to gasoline by weight in the fuel mixture drawn into the engine.

AIR INJECTION: One method of reducing harmful exhaust emissions by injecting air into each of the exhaust ports of an engine. The fresh air entering the hot exhaust manifold causes any remaining fuel to be burned before it can exit the tailpipe.

ALTERNATOR: A device used for converting mechanical energy into electrical energy.

AMMETER: An instrument, calibrated in amperes, used to measure the flow of an electrical current in a circuit. Ammeters are always connected in series with the circuit being tested.

AMPERE: The rate of flow of electrical current present when one volt of electrical pressure is applied against one ohm of electrical resistance.

ANALOG COMPUTER: Any microprocessor that uses similar (analogous) electrical signals to make its calculations.

ARMATURE: A laminated, soft iron core wrapped by a wire that converts electrical energy to mechanical energy as in a motor or relay. When rotated in a magnetic field, it changes mechanical energy into electrical energy as in a generator.

ATMOSPHERIC PRESSURE: The pressure on the Earth's surface caused by the weight of the air in the atmosphere. At sea level, this pressure is 14.7 psi at 32°F (101 kPa at 0°C).

ATOMIZATION: The breaking down of a liquid into a fine mist that can be suspended in air.

AXIAL PLAY: Movement parallel to a shaft or bearing bore.

BACKFIRE: The sudden combustion of gases in the intake or exhaust system that results in a loud explosion.

BACKLASH: The clearance or play between two parts, such as meshed gears.

BACKPRESSURE: Restrictions in the exhaust system that slow the exit of exhaust gases from the combustion chamber.

BAKELITE: A heat resistant, plastic insulator material commonly used in printed circuit boards and transistorized components.

BALL BEARING: A bearing made up of hardened inner and outer races between which hardened steel balls roll.

BALLAST RESISTOR: A resistor in the primary ignition circuit that lowers voltage after the engine is started to reduce wear on ignition components.

BEARING: A friction reducing, supportive device usually located between a stationary part and a moving part.

BIMETAL TEMPERATURE SENSOR: Any sensor or switch made of two dissimilar types of metal that bend when heated or cooled due to the different expansion rates of the alloys. These types of sensors usually function as an on/off switch.

BLOWBY: Combustion gases, composed of water vapor and unburned fuel, that leak past the piston rings into the crankcase during normal engine operation. These gases are removed by the PCV system to prevent the buildup of harmful acids in the crankcase.

BRAKE PAD: A brake shoe and lining assembly used with disc brakes.

BRAKE SHOE: The backing for the brake lining. The term is, however, usually applied to the assembly of the brake backing and lining.

BUSHING: A liner, usually removable, for a bearing; an anti-friction liner used in place of a bearing.

BYPASS: System used to bypass ballast resistor during engine cranking to increase voltage supplied to the coil.

CALIPER: A hydraulically activated device in a disc brake system, which is mounted straddling the brake rotor (disc). The caliper contains at least one piston and two brake pads. Hydraulic pressure on the piston(s) forces the pads against the rotor.

CAMSHAFT: A shaft in the engine on which are the lobes (cams) which operate the valves. The camshaft is driven by the crankshaft, via a belt, chain or gears, at one half the crankshaft speed.

CAPACITOR: A device which stores an electrical charge.

CARBON MONOXIDE (CO): a colorless, odorless gas given off as a normal byproduct of combustion. It is poisonous and extremely dangerous in confined areas, building up slowly to toxic levels without warning if adequate ventilation is not available.

CARBURETOR: A device, usually mounted on the intake manifold of an engine, which mixes the air and fuel in the proper proportion to allow even combustion.

CATALYTIC CONVERTER: A device installed in the exhaust system, like a muffler, that converts harmful byproducts of combustion into carbon dioxide and water vapor by means of a heat-producing chemical reaction.

CENTRIFUGAL ADVANCE: A mechanical method of advancing the spark timing by using flyweights in the distributor that react to centrifugal force generated by the distributor shaft rotation.

CHECK VALVE: Any one-way valve installed to permit the flow of air, fuel or vacuum in one direction only.

CHOKE: A device, usually a moveable valve, placed in the intake path of a carburetor to restrict the flow of air.

CIRCUIT: Any unbroken path through which an electrical current can flow. Also used to describe fuel flow in some instances.

CIRCUIT BREAKER: A switch which protects an electrical circuit from overload by opening the circuit when the current flow exceeds a predetermined level. Some circuit breakers must be reset manually, while other reset automatically

COIL (IGNITION): A transformer in the ignition circuit which steps of the voltage provided to the spark plugs.

COMBINATION MANIFOLD: An assembly which includes both the intake and exhaust manifolds in one casting.

COMBINATION VALVE: A device used in some fuel systems that routes fuel vapors to a charcoal storage canister instead of venting them into the atmosphere. The valve relieves fuel tank pressure and allows fresh air into the tank as fuel level drops to prevent a vapor lock situation.

COMPRESSION RATIO: The comparison of the total volume of the cylinder and combustion chamber with the piston at BDC and the piston at TDC.

CONDENSER: 1. An electrical device which acts to store an electrical charge, preventing voltage surges.
2. A radiator-like device in the air conditioning system in which refrigerant gas condenses into a liquid, giving off heat.

CONDUCTOR: Any material through which an electrical current can be transmitted easily.

CONTINUITY: Continuous or complete circuit. Can be checked with an ohmmeter.

COUNTERSHAFT: An intermediate shaft which is rotated by a mainshaft and transmits, in turn, that rotation to a working part.

CRANKCASE: The lower part of an engine in which the crankshaft and related parts operate.

CRANKSHAFT: The main driving shaft of an engine which receives reciprocating motion from the pistons and converts it to rotary motion.

CYLINDER: In an engine, the round hole in the engine block in which the piston(s) ride.

CYLINDER BLOCK: The main structural member of an engine in which is found the cylinders, crankshaft and other principal parts.

CYLINDER HEAD: The detachable portion of the engine, fastened, usually, to the top of the cylinder block, containing all or most of the combustion chambers. On overhead valve engines, it contains the valves and their operating parts. On overhead cam engines, it contains the camshaft as well.

DEAD CENTER: The extreme top or bottom of the piston stroke.

DETONATION: An unwanted explosion of the air fuel mixture in the combustion chamber caused by excess heat and compression, advanced timing, or an overly lean mixture. Also referred to as "ping".

DIAPHRAGM: A thin, flexible wall separating two cavities, such as in a vacuum advance unit.

DIESELING: A condition in which hot spots in the combustion chamber cause the engine to run on after the key is turned off.

DIFFERENTIAL: A geared assembly which allows the transmission of motion between drive axles, giving one axle the ability to turn faster than the other.

DIODE: An electrical device that will allow current to flow in one direction only.

DISC BRAKE: A hydraulic braking assembly consisting of a brake disc, or rotor, mounted on an axle, and a caliper assembly containing, usually two brake pads which are activated by hydraulic pressure. The pads are forced against the sides of the disc, creating friction which slows the vehicle.

DISTRIBUTOR: A mechanically driven device on an engine which is responsible for electrically firing the spark plug at a predetermined point of the piston stroke.

DOWEL PIN: A pin, inserted in mating holes in two different parts allowing those parts to maintain a fixed relationship.

DRUM BRAKE: A braking system which consists of two brake shoes and one or two wheel cylinders, mounted on a fixed backing plate, and a brake drum, mounted on an axle, which revolves around the assembly. Hydraulic action applied to the wheel cylinders forces the shoes outward against the drum, creating friction and slowing the vehicle.

DWELL: The rate, measured in degrees of shaft rotation, at which an electrical circuit cycles on and off.

ELECTRONIC CONTROL UNIT (ECU): Ignition module, module, amplifier or igniter. See Module for definition.

ELECTRONIC IGNITION: A system in which the timing and firing of the spark plugs is controlled by an electronic control unit, usually called a module. These systems have not points or condenser.

ENDPLAY: The measured amount of axial movement in a shaft.

ENGINE: A device that converts heat into mechanical energy.

EXHAUST MANIFOLD: A set of cast passages or pipes which conduct exhaust gases from the engine.

FEELER GAUGE: A blade, usually metal, of precisely predetermined thickness, used to measure the clearance between two parts. These blades usually are available in sets of assorted thicknesses.

F-Head: An engine configuration in which the intake valves are in the cylinder head, while the camshaft and exhaust valves are located in the cylinder block. The camshaft operates the intake valves via lifters and pushrods, while it operates the exhaust valves directly.

FIRING ORDER: The order in which combustion occurs in the cylinders of an engine. Also the order in which spark is distributed to the plugs by the distributor.

FLATHEAD: An engine configuration in which the camshaft and all the valves are located in the cylinder block.

FLOODING: The presence of too much fuel in the intake manifold and combustion chamber which prevents the air/fuel mixture from firing, thereby causing a no-start situation.

FLYWHEEL: A disc shaped part bolted to the rear end of the crankshaft. Around the outer perimeter is affixed the ring gear. The starter drive engages the ring gear, turning the flywheel, which rotates the crankshaft, imparting the initial starting motion to the engine.

FOOT POUND (ft.lb. or sometimes, ft. lbs.): The amount of energy or work needed to raise an item weighing one pound, a distance of one foot.

FUSE: A protective device in a circuit which prevents circuit overload by breaking the circuit when a specific amperage is present. The device is constructed around a strip or wire of a lower amperage rating than the circuit it is designed to protect. When an amperage higher than that stamped on the fuse is present in the circuit, the strip or wire melts, opening the circuit.

GEAR RATIO: The ratio between the number of teeth on meshing gears.

GENERATOR: A device which converts mechanical energy into electrical energy.

HEAT RANGE: The measure of a spark plug's ability to dissipate heat from its firing end. The higher the heat range, the hotter the plug fires.

HUB: The center part of a wheel or gear.

HYDROCARBON (HC): Any chemical compound made up of hydrogen and carbon. A major pollutant formed by the engine as a byproduct of combustion.

HYDROMETER: An instrument used to measure the specific gravity of a solution.

INCH POUND (in.lb. or sometimes, in. lbs.): One twelfth of a foot pound.

INDUCTION: A means of transferring electrical energy in the form of a magnetic field. Principle used in the ignition coil to increase voltage.

INJECTION PUMP: A device, usually mechanically operated, which meters and delivers fuel under pressure to the fuel injector.

INJECTOR: A device which receives metered fuel under relatively low pressure and is activated to inject the fuel into the engine under relatively high pressure at a predetermined time.

INPUT SHAFT: The shaft to which torque is applied, usually carrying the driving gear or gears.

INTAKE MANIFOLD: A casting of passages or pipes used to conduct air or a fuel/air mixture to the cylinders.

JOURNAL: The bearing surface within which a shaft operates.

KEY: A small block usually fitted in a notch between a shaft and a hub to prevent slippage of the two parts.

MANIFOLD: A casting of passages or set of pipes which connect the cylinders to an inlet or outlet source.

MANIFOLD VACUUM: Low pressure in an engine intake manifold formed just below the throttle plates. Manifold vacuum is highest at idle and drops under acceleration.

MASTER CYLINDER: The primary fluid pressurizing device in a hydraulic system. In automotive use, it is found in brake and hydraulic clutch systems and is pedal activated, either directly or, in a power brake system, through the power booster.

MODULE: Electronic control unit, amplifier or igniter of solid state or integrated design which controls the current flow in the ignition primary circuit based on input from the pickup coil. When the module opens the primary circuit, the high secondary voltage is induced in the coil.

NEEDLE BEARING: A bearing which consists of a number (usually a large number) of long, thin rollers.

OHM: (Ω) The unit used to measure the resistance of conductor to electrical flow. One ohm is the amount of resistance that limits current flow to one ampere in a circuit with one volt of pressure.

OHMMETER: An instrument used for measuring the resistance, in ohms, in an electrical circuit.

OUTPUT SHAFT: The shaft which transmits torque from a device, such as a transmission.

OVERDRIVE: A gear assembly which produces more shaft revolutions than that transmitted to it.

OVERHEAD CAMSHAFT (OHC): An engine configuration in which the camshaft is mounted on top of the cylinder head and operates the valve either directly or by means of rocker arms.

OVERHEAD VALVE (OHV): An engine configuration in which all of the valves are located in the cylinder head and the camshaft is located in the cylinder block. The camshaft operates the valves via lifters and pushrods.

OXIDES OF NITROGEN (NOx): Chemical compounds of nitrogen produced as a byproduct of combustion. They combine with hydrocarbons to produce smog.

OXYGEN SENSOR: Used with the feedback system to sense the presence of oxygen in the exhaust gas and signal the computer which can reference the voltage signal to an air/fuel ratio.

PINION: The smaller of two meshing gears.

PISTON RING: An open ended ring which fits into a groove on the outer diameter of the piston. Its chief function is to form a seal between the piston and cylinder wall. Most automotive pistons have three rings: two for compression sealing; one for oil sealing.

PRELOAD: A predetermined load placed on a bearing during assembly or by adjustment.

PRIMARY CIRCUIT: Is the low voltage side of the ignition system which consists of the ignition switch, ballast resistor or resistance wire, bypass, coil, electronic control unit and pick-up coil as well as the connecting wires and harnesses.

PRESS FIT: The mating of two parts under pressure, due to the inner diameter of one being smaller than the outer diameter of the other, or vice versa; an interference fit.

RACE: The surface on the inner or outer ring of a bearing on which the balls, needles or rollers move.

REGULATOR: A device which maintains the amperage and/or voltage levels of a circuit at predetermined values.

RELAY: A switch which automatically opens and/or closes a circuit.

RESISTANCE: The opposition to the flow of current through a circuit or electrical device, and is measured in ohms. Resistance is equal to the voltage divided by the amperage.

RESISTOR: A device, usually made of wire, which offers a preset amount of resistance in an electrical circuit.

RING GEAR: The name given to a ring-shaped gear attached to a differential case, or affixed to a flywheel or as part a planetary gear set.

ROLLER BEARING: A bearing made up of hardened inner and outer races between which hardened steel rollers move.

ROTOR: 1. The disc-shaped part of a disc brake assembly, upon which the brake pads bear; also called, brake disc.
2. The device mounted atop the distributor shaft, which passes current to the distributor cap tower contacts.

SECONDARY CIRCUIT: The high voltage side of the ignition system, usually above 20,000 volts. The secondary includes the ignition coil, coil wire, distributor cap and rotor, spark plug wires and spark plugs.

SENDING UNIT: A mechanical, electrical, hydraulic or electromagnetic device which transmits information to a gauge.

SENSOR: Any device designed to measure engine operating conditions or ambient pressures and temperatures. Usually electronic in nature and designed to send a voltage signal to an on-board computer, some sensors may operate as a simple on/off switch or they may provide a variable voltage signal (like a potentiometer) as conditions or measured parameters change.

SHIM: Spacers of precise, predetermined thickness used between parts to establish a proper working relationship.

SLAVE CYLINDER: In automotive use, a device in the hydraulic clutch system which is activated by hydraulic force, disengaging the clutch.

SOLENOID: A coil used to produce a magnetic field, the effect of which is produce work.

SPARK PLUG: A device screwed into the combustion chamber of a spark ignition engine. The basic construction is a conductive core inside of a ceramic insulator, mounted in an outer conductive base. An electrical charge from the spark plug wire travels along the conductive core and jumps a preset air gap to a grounding point or points at the end of the conductive base. The resultant spark ignites the fuel/air mixture in the combustion chamber.

SPLINES: Ridges machined or cast onto the outer diameter of a shaft or inner diameter of a bore to enable parts to mate without rotation.

TACHOMETER: A device used to measure the rotary speed of an engine, shaft, gear, etc., usually in rotations per minute.

THERMOSTAT: A valve, located in the cooling system of an engine, which is closed when cold and opens gradually in response to engine heating, controlling the temperature of the coolant and rate of coolant flow.

TOP DEAD CENTER (TDC): The point at which the piston reaches the top of its travel on the compression stroke.

TORQUE: The twisting force applied to an object.

TORQUE CONVERTER: A turbine used to transmit power from a driving member to a driven member via hydraulic action, providing changes in drive ratio and torque. In automotive use, it links the driveplate at the rear of the engine to the automatic transmission.

TRANSDUCER: A device used to change a force into an electrical signal.

TRANSISTOR: A semi-conductor component which can be actuated by a small voltage to perform an electrical switching function.

TUNE-UP: A regular maintenance function, usually associated with the replacement and adjustment of parts and components in the electrical and fuel systems of a vehicle for the purpose of attaining optimum performance.

TURBOCHARGER: An exhaust driven pump which compresses intake air and forces it into the combustion chambers at higher than atmospheric pressures. The increased air pressure allows more fuel to be burned and results in increased horsepower being produced.

VACUUM ADVANCE: A device which advances the ignition timing in response to increased engine vacuum.

VACUUM GAUGE: An instrument used to measure the presence of vacuum in a chamber.

VALVE: A device which control the pressure, direction of flow or rate of flow of a liquid or gas.

VALVE CLEARANCE: The measured gap between the end of the valve stem and the rocker arm, cam lobe or follower that activates the valve.

VISCOSITY: The rating of a liquid's internal resistance to flow.

VOLTMETER: An instrument used for measuring electrical force in units called volts. Voltmeters are always connected parallel with the circuit being tested.

WHEEL CYLINDER: Found in the automotive drum brake assembly, it is a device, actuated by hydraulic pressure, which, through internal pistons, pushes the brake shoes outward against the drums.

ABBREVIATIONS AND SYMBOLS

A: Ampere

AC: Alternating current

A/C: Air conditioning

A-h: Ampere hour

AT: Automatic transmission

ATDC: After top dead center

μA: Microampere

bbl: Barrel

BDC: Bottom dead center

bhp: Brake horsepower

BTDC: Before top dead center

BTU: British thermal unit

C: Celsius (Centigrade)

CCA: Cold cranking amps

cd: Candela

cm^2: Square centimeter

cm^3, cc: Cubic centimeter

CO: Carbon monoxide

CO_2: Carbon dioxide

cu.in., in^3: Cubic inch

CV: Constant velocity

Cyl.: Cylinder

DC: Direct current

ECM: Electronic control module

EFE: Early fuel evaporation

EFI: Electronic fuel injection

EGR: Exhaust gas recirculation

Exh.: Exhaust

F: Fahrenheit

F: Farad

pF: Picofarad

μF: Microfarad

FI: Fuel injection

ft.lb., ft. lb., ft. lbs.: foot pound(s)

gal: Gallon

g: Gram

HC: Hydrocarbon

HEI: High energy ignition

HO: High output

hp: Horsepower

Hyd.: Hydraulic

Hz: Hertz

ID: Inside diameter

in.lb.; in. lb.; in. lbs: inch pound(s)

Int.: Intake

K: Kelvin

kg: Kilogram

kHz: Kilohertz

km: Kilometer

km/h: Kilometers per hour

kΩ: Kilohm

kPa: Kilopascal

kV: Kilovolt

kW: Kilowatt

l: Liter

l/s: Liters per second

m: Meter

mA: Milliampere

mg: Milligram

mHz: Megahertz

mm: Millimeter

mm^2: Square millimeter

m^3: Cubic meter

MΩ: Megohm

m/s: Meters per second

MT: Manual transmission

mV: Millivolt

μm: Micrometer

N: Newton

N-m: Newton meter

NOx: Nitrous oxide

OD: Outside diameter

OHC: Over head camshaft

OHV: Over head valve

Ω: Ohm

PCV: Positive crankcase ventilation

psi: Pounds per square inch

pts: Pints

qts: Quarts

rpm: Rotations per minute

rps: Rotations per second

R-12: A refrigerant gas (Freon)

SAE: Society of Automotive Engineers

SO$_2$: Sulfur dioxide

T: Ton

t: Megagram

TBI: Throttle Body Injection

TPS: Throttle Position Sensor

V: 1. Volt; 2. Venturi

μV: Microvolt

W: Watt

∞: Infinity

<: Less than

>: Greater than